CN3 LT

WAR and WORDS

and WAR WORDS

The Northern Ireland Media Reader

Edited by
Bill Rolston
David Miller

First published in 1996
by
Beyond the Pale Publications
PO Box 337
Belfast BT9 7BT
Tel: +44 (0)1232 645930

British Library Cataloguing-in-Publication Data.
A catalogue record for this book is available from the British Library.

ISBN 1 900960 00 1

Printed by
Colour Books Ltd, Dublin

Cover photographs: Belfast Exposed

Contents

ACKNOWLEDGEMENTS

The editors and publishers wish to thank the following for permission to reproduce the chapters in this book, as follows:

chapter 1, the estate of Rex Cathcart; chapter 2, *Index*; chapter 3, Robert Fisk; chapter 4, BBC; chapter 5, *Index*; chapter 6, Pluto Press; chapter 7, Michael Leapman; chapter 8, Virgin Publishing; chapter 9, BBC; chapter 10, Simon Hoggart; chapter 11, Macmillan General Books and Paul Foot; chapter 12, Duncan Campbell; chapter 13, Pluto Press; chapter 14, Routledge; chapter 15, Brandon Book Publishers; chapter 16, *British Journalism Review*; chapter 17, Macmillan Press; chapter 18, Liz Curtis; chapter 19, Pluto Press; chapter 20, Leicester University Press; chapter 21, Philip Schlesinger, Graham Murdock and the estate of Philip Elliott; chapter 22, Poolbeg Press; chapter 23, *Race and Class*; chapter 24, David Miller and Greg McLaughlin.

David Miller is a Lecturer in Film and Media Studies at Stirling University and a member of the Stirling Media Research Institute.

Bill Rolston is a Senior Lecturer in Sociology at the University of Ulster at Jordanstown.

INTRODUCTION:
WAR, WORDS AND SILENCE

The origins of this book are in a telephone conversation between the editors about the desirability of republishing a book edited by one of us, but later withdrawn by the publishers (Rolston, *The Media and Northern Ireland*, 1991). The conclusion of this conversation was that, although there might be value in making that book available to a wider audience, a book which brought together some of the best writing on the media and Northern Ireland would be a more valuable resource.

Some of the literature we had in mind was out of print, and some in relatively inaccessible sources. But our over-riding rationale was that the literature on the media and Northern Ireland was widely scattered and furthermore, that there was in fact a surprisingly small amount of work in the area despite the length and intensity of the conflict and its centrality to the politics of both Britain and Ireland. Northern Ireland continues to be a subject around which both academics and journalists tend to tread gingerly. The cumulative testimony of the chapters in this book is more than enough evidence of the penalties for journalists of attempting to look into the dark corners of the conflict. As Rex Cathcart concluded: 'Northern Ireland has provided the means by which the professional broadcasters have steadily been brought to the government's heel' (*Fortnight*, November 1988). It could be argued that academics too have often shied away from researching or theorising Northern Ireland and its conflict, for broadly comparable reasons. Certainly, publishing books on Northern Ireland can ensure that one runs up against the same kind of nervousness from publishing houses which seems to afflict parts of broadcasting and the press.

To cite a case in point: *The Media and Northern Ireland* was withdrawn by the publisher following a request that a small error in the·chapter by Betty Purcell (reprinted here without the error) be corrected in any future edition. The complainant did not specifically ask for the book to be withdrawn, but the publisher, apparently overly anxious about the possibility of litigation, unilaterally decided to withdraw the book.

In another example, a proposal for a book on the media and Northern Ireland (eventually published as Miller 1994) was initially rejected by a number of major academic publishers, despite positive readers' reports, on the grounds that books on Northern Ireland do not sell well. However, an editor of one of the publishers later verbally reported that legal worries were also a factor. Although the debate about censoring the 'troubles' usually revolves around newspapers, broadcasting and film, there is at least some evidence that the climate of caution and self-censorship to which many authors refer in the pages which follow, affects other areas of the media, such as publishing, as well.

A key part of our reason for editing this book was to reintroduce some classic material on the media and censorship to a wider audience.

We have selected a total of 24 chapters from a much longer list of materials for possible inclusion. There is of course a sense in which any such collection is, if not arbitrary, at least informed by the interests and concerns of the editors. Certainly, different editors might have made different choices. What we have set out to do is to provide both a broad coverage of the period of the 'troubles' and to rescue material which is out of print or not easily accessible. We also wanted to provide a reasonably representative selection of material from the range of academics and journalists who have taken part in the debate. Other material on the media and Northern Ireland remains available, and it is to be hoped that readers of this volume will be encouraged to explore such material if they have not already done so. There are book length studies (cf. Butler 1995; Miller 1994) and chapters in books (cf. Schlesinger 1987), and there is a wide range of references to pursue cited in the chapters which follow.

One group of authors whose works are not represented here, although they have taken part in public debate on the topic, are the counterinsurgency theorists. Their work tends to lay claim to the mantle of political science, but it is equally concerned with developing the state's ability to manage and police the media. As a result, dispassionate analysis is not their forte. Many such authors are former or serving members of the British military (Clutterbuck 1981; Hooper 1982; Tugwell 1981 and 1986). In one case, that of Maurice Tugwell, his professional responsibility whilst in the military was to direct the disinformation activities of the Information Policy Unit at British army headquarters in Lisburn. As a result, we think that the accuracy and credibility of much of this material and work of a similar vein is fatally compromised. Furthermore, the voices of the counterinsurgency theorists have tended to dominate the political debate about the media and Northern Ireland to the detriment of other voices which we allow to speak here.

With one exception, all the pieces in this book have previously been printed elsewhere. We have made editorial interventions in most of the chapters, mainly for reasons of length, but also occasionally for reasons of style. We have tried to keep these interventions to a minimum, although there are one or two chapters where we thought that more substantial editing was necessary. All of our interventions, whether additions for clarity or the removal of text, are indicated by the use of square brackets.

The book is divided into five fairly self-explanatory sections. In addition, section one and two are arranged chronologically and together give an overview of the last thirty (and sometimes more) years of coverage of Northern Ireland and its conflict. Section one includes material on the developing relationship between broadcasters and the state. Section two includes work on propaganda and promotional strategies. Section three deals with direct censorship and the use of the law in policing the media. Section four features a range of analyses of factual and fictional coverage and of British and U.S. media. The last section contains one piece dealing with television coverage of the peace process.

We believe that this book will be of use to students of the media (in or out of formal education) and indeed students of the conflict in Ireland in general, and that it will help to remind us all of the dangers of silence.

Bill Rolston
David Miller
September 1996

References

Butler, David. *The Trouble with Reporting Northern Ireland*, Aldershot, Avebury, 1995.

Clutterbuck, Richard. *The Media and Political Violence*, Basingstoke, Macmillan, 1981.

Hooper, Alan. *The Military and the Media*, Aldershot, Avebury, 1982.

Miller, David. *Don't Mention the War: Northern Ireland, Propaganda and the Media*, London, Pluto, 1994.

Rolston, Bill (ed). *The Media and Northern Ireland: Covering the Troubles*, Basingstoke, Macmillan, 1991.

Schlesinger, Philip. *Putting 'Reality' Together: BBC News*, 2nd edition, London, Routledge, 1987.

Tugwell, Maurice. 'Politics and Propaganda of the Provisional IRA', *Terrorism*, 5(1-2), 1981: 13-40.

Tugwell, Maurice. 'Terrorism and Propaganda: Problem and Response', *Conflict Quarterly*, 6, 1986: 5-15

SECTION ONE INTRODUCTION:
BROADCASTING STRUGGLES

British broadcasting in Northern Ireland is almost as old as the state itself. Three years after partition (1921), with its attendant political violence, 2BE, the Belfast station of the BBC, was inaugurated. As **Rex Cathcart** reveals, under its first controller, Geoffrey Beadle, 2BE was incorporated into the unionist establishment and unionist culture. Forty years later, as **Anthony Smith** shows, the initial attempt by the BBC in Northern Ireland to avoid political debate altogether was replaced with a spurious philosophy of 'balance'; a remarkably similar pattern emerged in ITV which began broadcasting in the late 1950s.

The civil rights campaign and the re-emergence of political violence in the late 1960s set the stage for a series of running battles over questions such as 'balance' and 'objectivity' in broadcasting. While Smith chronicles the early clashes between the broadcasters and the state and the mounting pressures on television coverage of the conflict, **Robert Fisk** recounts (and criticises) the BBC's role in the Ulster Workers' Council (UWC) strike of 1974. A British-government sponsored attempt to solve the political violence led to a power-sharing government in Northern Ireland, with ministerial posts held by unionists and nationalists. Widespread opposition from loyalists followed, which included a fourteen-day long general strike led by the UWC. The BBC quickly succumbed to the influence of the UWC, often carrying their warnings and predictions of doom without criticism.

The serious questions raised about the BBC's lack of impartiality in this issue led the then Controller of BBC Northern Ireland, **Richard Francis**, to defend the Corporation's role. The problems of broadcasting to a society in conflict are itemised, as well as the oft-repeated claim that they must have the balance right if they are attacked by both sides. The Corporation, he argues, is performing impeccably in an almost impossible situation. The lecture by Francis also signals the evolution of an alternative approach to broadcasting to a 'community in conflict'. Francis sets out the key problem for a broadcaster claiming to be impartial, while at the same time excluding the political representatives of the republican movement. The reorientation,

1

which Butler describes as a shift from consensus to 'dissensus' broadcasting, led to a position in the 1980s where Sinn Féin representatives were regarded as having a legitimate voice in local broadcasting and appeared regularly (see Butler 1995: 71-74). However, they were not treated with the same degree of legitimacy as other so-called 'constitutional' parties.

ITV was not exempt from disputes over its coverage of the Northern Ireland 'troubles'. **Peter Taylor** recounts his own difficulties in producing three critical programmes in the 'This Week' series in 1977. The end result of his run-ins with the IBA over these programmes was that he was, in effect, told to lay off Northern Ireland. He locates his experience in the general analysis that reporting Northern Ireland has become the key instance of state-versus-broadcasting confrontation in Britain. Government pressure on broadcasters is constant because the government does not want the attention of independent investigative critical journalism. The state defines public interest and government interest as more or less identical, and to a great extent broadcasting authorities have gone along with this conclusion.

Liz Curtis considers another instance of confrontation, that over the filming by a 'Panorama' team of an IRA roadblock in Carrickmore, County Tyrone in 1979. Although the footage was not broadcast at the time, the British government's protests led the BBC to strengthen its internal controls over programmes on Northern Ireland. At the core of control, she argues, is the 'reference up' system, whereby decisions are taken out of the hands of programme maker's and put in the hands of a few top executives. A similar system exists in ITV. The end result is an effective filter, not only censoring programmes in advance but leading, because of the degree of difficulty involved for programme makers, to self-censorship.

The tightened reference-up system was again put to the test with the BBC's 1985 'Real Lives: on the Edge of the Union', considered in detail by **Michael Leapman**. The programme focused on two politicians from Derry, Martin McGuinness of Sinn Féin, and Gregory Campbell of the Democratic Unionist Party. Even before it was broadcast it met with government opposition, not least because of the exploits of the *Sunday Times*. Government attempts to have the programme scrapped and the ensuing conflict among top management and governors at the BBC is examined. The BBC decision to postpone the programme led to unprecedented industrial action from journalists. In the end, an altered version of the programme was broadcast, but the legitimacy of the BBC as an independent source of investigation and critical assessment was severely dented as a result of this confrontation.

The next major confrontation between government and broadcasters - over 'Death on the Rock' in 1988 - was focused on independent television rather than the BBC. The editor of the programme, **Roger Bolton**, recounts here the process of producing the documentary about the killing in Gibraltar by undercover British agents of three IRA members, Mairead Farrell, Seán Savage and Daniel McCann. British government claims about the incident were subjected to intense scrutiny with the help of eye-witnesses located by the programme makers and various legal and military experts. The Thatcher government attacked the programme as 'trial by television', even though Bolton was careful to avoid any conclusions about summary execution. The official assault on the programme, together with a sustained PR campaign around the shootings coordinated by a special cabinet sub-committee, helped to undermine the truth about the shootings and to secure a majority verdict of lawful killing from a Gibraltar jury (see Jack 1988 and 1995; Miller 1991). However, seven years after the shootings, the European Court of Human Rights found for the relatives of the three that 'excessive force' had been used. Nevertheless, the verdict did little to dispel the conclusion that making critical programmes on Northern Ireland was not the best route to promotion.

The combined wisdom of the broadcasters at BBC and ITV over twenty-five years of reporting the conflict in Northern Ireland is contained not merely in the folk memory of broadcasters such as Bolton, Taylor and others but also in specific written instructions. The final chapter in this section reproduces extracts from the BBC's **Producers' Guidelines** and from the BBC **Style Guide**. These provide BBC personnel with guidance on the reference-up system, on the language which can and cannot be used, and on pronunciation. Prior to its publication in 1989, the BBC's editorial wisdom was contained in successive editions of the BBC *News and Current Affairs Index* which had an odd, semi-secret status. According to Deputy Director General Alan Protheroe, the Index 'is not a "classified" document. Neither is it a document for distribution to the public' (BBC 1987: 7). We include extracts here for public scrutiny.

References

BBC, *BBC News and Current Affairs Index*, 3rd edition, London, BBC, March 1987
Butler, David. *The Trouble with Reporting Northern Ireland*, Aldershot, Avebury, 1995
Jack, Ian. 'Gibraltar', *Granta* 25, London, Penguin, 1988
Jack, Ian. 'A huge smoke-screen of humbug', *Independent on Sunday*, 1 October 1995: 23
Miller, David. 'The Media on the Rock: the Media and the Gibraltar Killings', in Bill Rolston (ed), *The Media and Northern Ireland: Covering the Troubles*, Basingstoke, Macmillan 1991

1.

Rex Cathcart

2BE Consolidates: the Early Years of the BBC in Northern Ireland

(From *The Most Contrary Region: the BBC in Northern Ireland, 1924-1984*, Blackstaff Press, 1984, pages 36-59)

The BBC's Managing Director, John Reith, looked to South Africa for his new Station Director in Belfast. Almost two years earlier he had sent a young Englishman to Durban in Natal to set up and run a broadcasting station for the municipality. Gerald Beadle had gone willingly, even though he had only one year's experience in the BBC. He coped successfully, and by the summer of 1926 his contract in South Africa was coming to an end, enabling Reith to write offering him the vacant post in Belfast. Beadle accepted without hesitation.

In later years Sir Gerald Beadle, who was to become Director of BBC Television Broadcasting, recalled the situation he encountered in Northern Ireland and its impact on him:

> [...] When I arrived in Northern Ireland I was made to feel for the first time in my life that I was a person of some public importance, and this was in spite of the fact that the BBC was less than four years old and its Northern Ireland operation was not much more than two. Obviously the BBC's prestige had grown out of all recognition during my two years' absence in South Africa, and I, as its chief local representative, shared the fruits of it. I was invited to become a member of the Ulster Club, where almost daily I met members of the Government; the Governor, the Duke of Abercorn, was immensely helpful and friendly, and Lord Craigavon, the Prime Minister was a keen supporter of our work. In effect I was made a member of the Establishment of a province which had most of the

paraphernalia of a sovereign state and a population no bigger than a moderate sized English county.[1]

Beadle was absorbed into the Unionist regime quite quickly, a process which other heads of the BBC in Northern Ireland were to experience in the future. It was a situation in which any sense of autonomy which the broadcaster might have could be lost. Beadle, being 'young and naïve' as he was to say later, succumbed at first.[2] He resolved within a few months to create 'a closer liaison between the Government and the BBC'. Before he could formally raise the matter with the Northern Ireland Prime Minister, Lord Craigavon, however, he needed advice on the legal position. He therefore wrote to Reith:

> I would like to make my mind clear as to the exact relationship between ourselves and the Northern Government. I understand that the Belfast Station, like all our other stations, is ultimately responsible to the British Government for its actions and that it has no actual responsibilities towards the Northern Irish Government. Nevertheless, I am sure that our position here will be strengthened immensely if we can persuade the Northern Government to look upon us as their mouthpiece.[3]

Beadle was not aware of how sensitive the issue of BBC-Government relations had become during his absence in South Africa. In May 1926 the BBC in London had been faced with a Government take-over during the General Strike. Only after heated debate in the Imperial Cabinet was it decided that Reith should be allowed to continue running the Company during the crisis. He acted on behalf of the Government but managed to ensure that the BBC's news bulletins retained a credibility with the general public which was denied to the partisan daily newspaper published by the Government during the Strike. The crisis confirmed Reith in his conviction that the BBC could best serve the national interest if it was allowed an autonomous role. Later in the year the Government accepted this principle when it provided the BBC with a charter converting it into a 'public utility' corporation.[4]

The General Strike proved a turning point in the early history of broadcasting. An editorial in the Dublin *Radio Journal* at the time indicated its significance:

> Most people have been looking at wireless and broadcasting as a delightful pastime. But all along while they were using it to listen to opera and jazz, to band and to chorus, they were really handling, in frivolous moments, an agency of national and international concern, a new medium and weapon of such possibilities that it became part of the battlefield the very instant this vast conflict began. The opening acts of hostilities included pressure brought to bear on the press with a view to influencing the nature of the news and comments issued. This was resented ... The government at once invoked broadcasting ... Here, at any rate, we have clearly defined

the high status of wireless broadcasting in the armoury of a modern nation.[5]

It was against the background of the General Strike and the new Charter that a reply to Beadle's inquiry was drawn up in Head Office. It restated Beadle's question and then provided an answer. 'Can you unreservedly place the Station at the service of that Government to be made use of at that Government's direction? No. Moreover, it will be injudicious even to assure the Prime Minister that in the event of a national emergency in Ireland the station would be entirely at his service; this would only be so to the extent which the British Government (by consent sought from Head Office) might approve.' Reith did not sign the draft. He pencilled in a comment instead: 'It might be better to talk over the matter and clear up doubtful points. It is rather involved. We cannot help the Government in a *party* question. We can help them in uncontroversial things. In an *emergency* - this is officially declared by the King in Parliament and if notice is given us (according to Charter) we're not responsible then - they take us over. This did not actually happen in the General Strike, but nearly did. We were allowed considerable discretion. J.C.W.R.'[6]

Head office refused to write to Craigavon directly as Beadle had requested but suggested that Beadle should simply discuss with the Prime Minister the limited range of ways in which the Belfast Station could help him. Later in 1927 Beadle outlined the position in the BBC's *Year Book*:

> The broadcasting Station, though in no sense under the control of the Northern government, does to a considerable degree co-operate with it. Announcements of public importance are frequently made at the request of one or other of the Ministries, and the elucidation of new Government regulations is broadcast by Northern Government officials.[7]

In the following year Beadle offered another formulation:

> The Government of Northern Ireland, although it exercises no direct control over the Irish Station, enjoys its co-operation in all matters outside party politics.

A notable field in which 2BE gave the Government assistance from the beginning was agriculture. Ministry of Agriculture officials had access to the microphone to speak to farmers, informing them of changes in regulations and in general advising them. Farm prices provided by the Ministry were regularly broadcast.

Beadle, however, remained determined to demonstrate to the Government and to the unionist majority of the population the more comprehensive value of the BBC to them. He propounded a view of the BBC's role in Northern Ireland:

> The Ulster Broadcasting Station, situated in Belfast, radiates to its listeners most of the important London programmes, and on occasions programmes are relayed from Scotland, Wales and the

North of England. Thus the broadcasting service reflects the sentiments of the people, who have thus retained a lively sympathy with, and an unswerving loyalty to, British ideals and British culture. The chimes of Big Ben are heard as clearly in County Tyrone as they are in the County of Middlesex, and the news of the day emanating from the London Studio is received simultaneously in Balham and Ballymacarett.[8]

Beadle even asserted that, before the BBC came to Belfast, 'The Government of Northern Ireland evidently believed that one of the most efficient ways of fostering the imperial link was through broadcasting.'[9] There is no evidence to substantiate this claim. On the contrary all the evidence suggests that broadcasting was initially viewed by Government officials as an unwelcome nuisance.[10]

Curiously, when Beadle propounded the idea that the BBC 'provides a living contact with the "hub of the Empire" and there are no more enthusiastic lovers of our Empire than the people of Ulster', he described it as the *second* most important function of the Belfast Station. He considered that 'first of all' the Belfast Station was 'an indispensable adjunct to Irish music, Irish drama and Irish life'.[11] Beadle took a broad view of Irish culture and saw no ideological contradiction in promoting it over the air alongside the relaying of programmes from the rest of the United Kingdom. These were the early years of partition and few people had drawn any cultural conclusions from the political division. Beadle was therefore very happy to develop close co-operation with the new Dublin station, 2RN, with a view to mounting Irish programmes of all kinds.

2RN had come on the air on 1 January 1926. It had been reluctantly established by the Irish Post Office as a branch of its own operations. This followed the recommendation of a parliamentary committee which rejected the Postmaster General's plan for an Irish company similar to the original British Broadcasting Company. A state service was preferred because the committee viewed the use of radio 'for entertainment, however desirable, as of vastly less importance than its use as ministering alike to commercial and cultural progress'.[12] In the event the service provided by 2RN in its first years was remarkably similar to that which emanated from the early 2BE.

Within four months of opening, on 20 April, 2RN and 2BE mounted an ambitious joint programme. Belfast led off with a half hour of Mozart; Dublin replied with a similar period of 'good' music. Then from 9.00 to 9.30 p.m. 'Mrs Rooney' of Belfast and others presented a variety of Ulster humour; from 9.30 until 10.00 p.m. 2RN offered light music and Dublin humour.

Co-operation built up steadily until Beadle could write in the BBC's 1931 *Year Book*:

> ... the most important feature of activities in the year under review (1930) has been the increasing co-operation between the BBC and the Irish Free State Post Office which directly administers the Free

State Broadcasting Stations. The result can he seen in the many interesting broadcasts which have passed between the centres. Seamus Clandillon the energetic Dublin Station Director, has given invaluable practical advice on all matters, especially as to artists resident in the South, with the happy result that many of them have found a place in the Belfast programmes.[13]

The British press reported these developments with approval. The *Daily Express,* for example, under the headline 'Broadcasting Partners', told of 'the steadily improving relationships between the British Broadcasting Corporation ... and the Irish Free State Post Office'. It went on: 'Probably at present the Free State has more to gain than has the British Broadcasting Corporation but Dublin has relayed recently over the border to Belfast some interesting broadcasts, and there are undoubtedly vast untapped sources of good programmes in the Free State'.[14]

[...] Actors and actresses from Dublin's Abbey Theatre Company were invited to play leading roles in 2BE drama productions. [...]

To judge by the voluminous correspondence in Belfast newspapers these drama productions provoked a mixed reception. There were those who were incensed that the BBC should give air time to such southern productions. [...]

[...] in 1931 [...] the special programme for St Patrick's Day stimulated a correspondence in the Belfast *News Letter* and the *Northern Whig* which went on for weeks. The sharpness of the controversy owed much to the awareness that an image was being projected to Great Britain. The programme, based entirely in Northern Ireland, consisted of Irish airs played by the Belfast City and Cathedral organist, Charles J. Brennan; his performance was followed by an Ulster sketch entitled, 'The Things that Happen', written by A. McClure Warnock, which involved a conversation between a practical Belfast woman and an impractical poetic countrywoman; the Derry Orpheus Male Voice Choir sang folksongs by Irish composers; Mat Mulcaghey recounted one of his tales of County Tyrone; the Irish pipers of the Royal Inniskilling Fusiliers and the Belfast Wireless Orchestra gave a selection of jigs and traditional airs; the seventy-minute programme concluded with the carillon from St Patrick's Cathedral, Armagh.

The programme received favourable reviews in a number of British national papers including the *Manchester Guardian* and the *Observer*.

In the popular imagination St Patrick (together with shamrock, shillelaghs, eternal twilights, keenings and the Abbey Theatre Players) is more closely associated with Southern Ireland than the North. But last night's broadcast of the St Patrick's Day programme from Belfast gave us quite a new set of associations to link with the Saint's name ...[15]

The *Guardian,* however, went on to suggest that, 'It would have been a more complete experience, though, if one could have heard part of Dublin's station's broadcast last night. We should then have had a more composite picture of Ireland, North and South, the green and the orange blending to make a harmonious whole'.

By contrast, a correspondent in the Belfast *News Letter* had no praise and no reservations: 'For sheer banality I commend the St Patrick's night broadcast for your readers' condemnation ... How can anyone say this was Ulster (much less Ireland) is beyond me'.[16] He was supported by another who bemoaned the fact that it was one of the few Belfast broadcasts relayed during the year throughout the United Kingdom: 'I would suggest that for the future when an Irish or Ulster night is being given, the programme should not be solely made up by Englishmen, who in the nature of things cannot have much Irish feeling and that pure "classical" musicians be asked to take a back seat.'[17]

A dozen or more correspondents took up the refrain in both the Belfast *News Letter* and the *Northern Whig*. The general tone was expressed by one who wrote, '... the organisation of this unfortunate 'concert' was another glaring injustice to my native land'. Correspondents began to exempt Mat Mulcaghey's performance from the general criticism. A couple quoted the enthusiastic reception accorded the programme by the critic of the *Observer* in its defence. Constructive suggestions were made by many indicating possible contents of future programmes but there was a return to the proposal that 'if the BBC staff have no appreciation of Irish sentiment, why not be modest enough to ask a small committee of Irish authors, playwrights, and composers to arrange, or suggest, a St Patrick's night programme'.[18]

The programme as transmitted had one determined defender who signed himself 'No Surrender':

> ... With no part of Ireland has St Patrick been as closely associated as Ulster. Slemish, Armagh, Downpatrick. It is fitting, therefore, that Ulster's capital should have the honour of sending out *to* the balance of these islands the annual programme. By implication, some of your correspondents would have us believe that Ulster is bankrupt in culture, and would have us borrow the culture of our neighbours on a night like St Patrick's.[19] [...]

The editors of the two morning papers eventually closed their columns to this particular spate of correspondence. In doing so they were only temporarily damming the flow which had begun earlier with the reactions to the performances of the Abbey Theatre players on 2BE. Thereafter programmes with an Irish dimension could usually be counted on to provoke listeners to write to the papers. The phenomenon suggests that a decade after partition people in Northern Ireland, especially in the Protestant community, were awaking to its cultural consequences. When Beadle arrived in 1926 there would appear to have been little sensitivity to the situation. His first essays in Irish programming had elicited no recorded reaction, and he had found that by avoiding the overtly controversial he could avoid controversy. Now he discovered that the cultural assumptions inherent in a programme could at one and the same time enthuse some listeners and enrage others. The divided communities were adopting their preferred cultural positions. Broadcasting was undoubtedly a catalyst in the process of cultural differentiation. [...]

From the correspondence it is clear that the Protestant community had problems in deciding on its cultural alignment. Some Protestants protested their Irishness by assertion or implication. Others affirmed their distinctive Ulsterness. Those who took the view that they were first and foremost British would in many cases have been quite happy simply to have had programmes relayed from Great Britain and to have done without locally produced programmes. The rejection of regional accents, of Ulster dialects and of portraits of rural life revealed in local drama indicated a disposition to deny an Ulster identity and a wish to be aligned with the cultural attitudes and values of the south east of England. 'Malone Road', as correspondents designated the more pretentious middle class, wished to be seen to be metropolitan, not provincial. The BBC in Linenhall Street could scarcely share this particular outlook, charged as it was with the production of local programmes. Nevertheless, reflecting the BBC's own middle-class stance at the time, the local BBC endeavoured to prevent most manifestations of Ulster Protestant working-class culture from appearing before the microphone. Orangeism in any form was denied access; pipe and flute bands appeared only rarely.

So long as there was local production, however, the BBC policy of staffing the station with English and Scottish personnel was bound to provoke criticism. 'Why should the Belfast Station announcers not be local people with Northern Ireland accents, and thus be characteristic of the people whom the station serves?'[20] '... the time has fully come when a representative committee ought to make suggestions to the Ulster Station - putting before them the local point of view ...'[21]

But press controversy about the BBC was by no means confined to issues involving distinctive local cultural sensitivities. Belfast made its contribution to the barrage of criticism of BBC programme policies which came from every part of the United Kingdom. A special correspondent in the *Northern Whig* reported on these wider complaints: 'The growlers want to be entertained through the medium of their wireless sets, and the BBC (so they say) will insist upon firing at them through the ether in the interests of culture ... matter that neither entertains nor instructs them.'[22] 'It is good to see that Belfast listeners are awakening to the fact that they are being slowly but surely chloroformed by heavy doses of the Belfast Wireless Orchestra.'[23] Suggestions flowed as to how the programmes might be made more popular: 'Cut out 75 per cent of the talks and substitute gramophone records (not of the pianoforte variety). Have more brass bands, light orchestral music and groups of songs (confined to two songs). Give vaudeville in plenty. If we must have a symphony concert let us have it on Sunday afternoons, 3.30 p.m. to 6.00 p.m...'[24]

In the autumn of 1931, the attack reached a crescendo - the *Northern Whig* referred to 'the enormous number of letters in our columns' – and the 'lowbrows' fought the 'highbrows' through hundreds of column inches. The Belfast Station Director, Gerald Beadle, found it necessary to defend BBC policy. 'I always welcome criticism from our listeners, because that is the best means by which we can estimate the public tastes, but listeners must remember that we have to cater for a large variety of tastes, and it is quite impossible to please everyone all the time. All tastes are catered for as far as is possible, and it is up to the listener to choose those programmes which he likes and to avoid those which he does not like.' Asked, 'Is there any foundation for the criticism made by some correspondents that there is too much orchestral music?', Beadle replied, 'That is an impossible question to answer because what is too much for one listener may not be enough for another.' 'On the subject of "highbrow" music, Mr Beadle said that the term "highbrow" was a very unfortunate one. It meant different things to different people. What was highbrow to one man was lowbrow to another.' On being asked how he gauged public taste, Beadle replied, 'By experience' and added, 'The secret is to acquire the art of suppressing one's own likes and dislikes. The critical listener can seldom do this. He nearly always falls into the trap of imagining that the majority share his own tastes.' Beadle concluded by saying that 'he would like to he able to give his listeners more humour and more Ulster dialect plays, because he knew there was a very big demand for both. Unfortunately good humourists were very rare indeed; there were not nearly enough of them. As to plays, a few of the good playwrights had shown signs of writing for the microphone, and he hoped many more would do so in the future.'[25]

A solution, at least in part, to these problems was being developed which, among other things, would save Beadle prevaricating. The provision of two contrasting programme schedules on different wavelengths throughout the United Kingdom would ensure that all listeners had a choice and therefore a greater chance of being satisfied. In 1926, before Beadle returned from South Africa, it had become apparent that technological advances had made this possible. The change was only one facet of a major transformation proposed for the BBC system. Much more powerful transmitters could now be built and the existing network of main and relay stations replaced. Fewer transmitters were necessary and these were to be sited at strategic points throughout the United Kingdom, away from the centres of population which had had to be favoured in the first instance; the signals would become much more readily available to country dwellers. This was the BBC's 'regional scheme'. Initially the planners thought that both schedules should be produced in London with programme production centralised and, as a consequence, standards raised. Subsequently it was decided that one schedule would be left to be filled by a reduced number of provincial production centres.

The first transmitter in the new 'regional scheme' was built at Daventry. It came on air in August 1927 and was soon offering trial alternative programmes on two wavelengths. The 'regional scheme' had to proceed very slowly, however, because of the disruption caused among the listening public, many of whom found that their receiving apparatus needed major adjustment or replacement. The immediate effect of Daventry on Belfast's 2BE was to provide another means by which simultaneous broadcasts could reach it. Instead of using land lines and the submarine cable it was now possible to take programmes off air and relay them. For some time this occurred mainly during the daytime; interference prevented its effective use at night.

The number of simultaneous broadcasts taken by 2BE by lines from London and from other stations had begun to rise some six months after the opening night in 1924 and, in consequence as time passed the proportion of locally produced programmes dropped. The demands on the Station Orchestra in particular were reduced and it became possible for it to give more public performances. Before that happened, however, it had to be improved. [...] The Orchestra got an additional two violins and a second trumpet as a consequence and within three years its complement rose from twenty-one to thirty musicians.

The Orchestra was not threatened by the 'regional scheme', as elsewhere other station orchestras were, sometimes being reduced to octets or nonets. The unreliable lines from Great Britain helped Beadle to argue that the Orchestra remained as an essential provider of programmes. Nonetheless the drive which Head Office was making at the time to raise programme standards by concentrating production increasingly in London did affect the Orchestra. Local station directors were required to 'take from London what you cannot do better yourself, and do yourself what London cannot give you'.[26] When Godfrey Brown began planning a production of the opera *Samson and Delilah*, he was stopped by the Music Director in London: 'Our policy is definitely to concentrate large musical works on London, where conditions are more favourable.' Beadle accepted London's diktat but remarked:

> I am afraid I have always acted on the assumption that Belfast was outside this policy, and that so far as possible we were expected to run our own programmes ... We are expected to do 4$^{1}/_{2}$ nights a week of local work, a difficult task if a high standard is to be maintained. During the last eighteen months we have done many large musical works in order to make up for those things we do not take from London. Of course, we take all the libretto operas from London and, therefore, a ban on opera pure and simple would not handicap us so badly, though it will mean that Belfast listeners will seldom hear an opera decently transmitted. A ban on all large musical works is a different matter and, I am afraid, will involve a considerable curtailment of local activities and a corresponding increase in S.B. work with its accompanying technical imperfections.[27]

Beadle asked for guidance on what programme policy was meant to be for Belfast. He was told he could go ahead safely on the following basis:

Music: Everything except opera and very ambitious symphonic work.

Productions: *Plays*. Only limited by studio and technical equipment necessary to give an adequate performance. *Vaudeville* entirely according to your own judgement, bearing in mind the quality of S.B. programmes as received by line, and the expense of local productions.[28]

Beadle had always regarded drama as the most rewarding field to promote. On arrival in 1926 he had endeavoured, without success, to persuade Tyrone Guthrie to return from Scotland to be his drama assistant. He was, however, lucky enough to get John Watt instead, for here was a talented man who was quickly to rise to be the BBC's Head of Variety Programmes. Watt stayed in Belfast from 1927 to 1930. On his departure a correspondent in the *Irish News* wrote to say how sorry he was to see him go.

I once saw him do an extraordinary thing: I saw him conducting a play, just as a conductor directs the orchestra and the singers in an opera. Wireless technique in plays is a comparatively new thing. When a play is being produced the actors sit round, scripts in hand. The producer gives the sign and conducts the small orchestra for the preliminary effects. Then, at the right moment, he points to the beginners to get ready, just as the conductor of an orchestra warns his violins. Then he points to the microphone, and off the play goes ... Then the producer scans his script, gets the next players ready, points to them at the critical time, and gets them speaking. It was an extraordinary sight to see a play being produced like this ... I am not surprised to see Mr Watt has gone to London.[29] [...]

Until the BBC became a corporation it was not allowed to cover public events and sporting occasions with outside broadcasts. The press had been determined to prevent any encroachment on what it regarded as its preserve. From January 1927, however, running commentaries and eyewitness accounts became possible. As a consequence, that summer the Ulster Grand Prix motorcycle races were relayed for the first time and in the following year, the International Tourist Trophy race on the Ards Circuit was covered. The first of many launchings of Belfast-built ships was described on 2BE in 1927: 'The cracking of timber and the rush of water as the ship took to her natural element were conveyed in a most realistic manner to those who were unable to witness the launch.'[30] Important rugby matches were relayed from Ravenhill Road and then from Lansdowne Road, Dublin. The Association Football authorities were not nearly so co-operative because they were convinced that broadcast commentaries affected 'the gates'. 2BE crossed the border for other commentaries besides those on the rugby internationals: the Irish Derby from the Curragh and similar events in the racing calendar were covered and relayed to Britain.

The activities of the devolved government and of the local houses of parliament provided the occasion for a variety of outside broadcasts. On 19 May 1928, for example, the laying of the foundation stone for the government buildings at Stormont took place and the microphone was there.

In the beginning special telephone links were laid to St James's Parish Church and to Fisherwick Church in Belfast so that Church of Ireland and Presbyterian services could be relayed from one or the other once a month on Sundays. To these were soon added lines to Belfast Cathedral, Carlisle Memorial Methodist Church, and the Church of Ireland Cathedrals in Derry and Armagh. No lines were laid to Catholic churches because no co-operation was forthcoming from the Catholic bishops ... at least until 1932, when Cardinal MacRory let it be known that he would welcome coverage of the Eucharistic Congress which was called to celebrate the 1,500th anniversary of St Patrick's landing in Ireland. Such was the national and international interest in the Congress that the Catholic hierarchy was keen to involve the broadcasters, north and south. In the Irish Free State pressure was put on the authorities to bring the powerful new transmitter at Athlone hurriedly into commission for the period of the Congress. The Belfast Station Director, Gerald Beadle, travelled to Armagh to discuss the arrangements in the north. He hoped he could persuade the Cardinal to co-operate with the BBC in return. Years later Beadle recalled their extraordinary conversation. 'I remember the Cardinal saying one thing to me that shocked me. "I wish you would yourself appear before the microphone," I said. He replied, "You wouldn't let me, you'd censor me. '"We would not but we would have to restrain you from being rude about Protestants." He said, "What do you think I'm here for? What do you think I'm employed for?"'[31] The Cardinal clearly shared with other Catholic churchmen a dislike of the 'common Christian platform' which the BBC required the churches to take. In fact, the fear that the Congress was intended to be 'a militant and controversial occasion' had caused the BBC to hesitate in offering its co-operation. In the event, a commemorative service of pontifical High Mass was relayed from St Patrick's Cathedral, Armagh.

The other outside institutions with which the BBC endeavoured to establish a sound relationship were the schools. The Education Advisory Committee which Beadle had inherited was very keen for him to organise, in contrast to previous experience, a successful demonstration of schools' broadcasting for teachers. This he did in the Ulster Minor Hall on 14 December 1926. There was a good attendance including some leading figures from Northern Ireland's educational world. The Minister of Education, Lord Charlemont, was one of those who addressed the meeting. 'Wireless,' he said, 'had done an enormous amount of good to heighten the cultural standards of the community' but as far as schools were concerned, while recognising the potential of broadcasting for them, he had to be conscious of the expense involved. '£50 is needed for a set and most regional committees would prefer to spend this amount on improving sanitary arrangements or accommodation.' The Minister praised the programmes he had heard, for he had taken the trouble to attend a conference and demonstration before this in Glasgow. He still ended on a warning note: 'When all is said and done, wireless could never be more than a supplementary aid in schools, and could not attempt to replace the teacher. Children must be coaxed and led in the direction of knowledge, and a teacher would teach more in an hour's personal teaching than could be done on wireless in the course of a year.'[32] Lord Charlemont was no help to the BBC in its educational mission. The reception of the London programmes for the demonstration had, in fact, been very good and the audience had been made fully aware of what was on offer.

Beadle was conscious of a challenge and was keen to press forward persuasively. So, in one of his quarterly broadcasts to listeners shortly after the demonstration, he devoted some time to the objections raised by teachers. The first was 'the loudspeaker is a dead thing and though it may be very wonderful, it cannot hold the attention in the same way as the presence of a living teacher'. Beadle quoted scientific experiments in a classroom in Scotland to show that this was not true. He turned to a second objection: 'What is the use of wireless, when we are here to teach the children? Wireless must be either superfluous or else we are superfluous.' Beadle said that 'wireless can no more take the place of the school teacher than books can'. He went on to quote teachers who came from the Ulster countryside and had spoken with him. 'They all tell me the same thing - that books are difficult to get; that sometimes it is difficult to keep in touch with the latest cultural developments, and that if wireless can do this for them, it will be bestowing an inestimable benefit upon them. I am sure that it can.' Beadle offered to provide individual schools with demonstrations.[33]

His efforts did not prove particularly fruitful and he was forced to declare that 'the BBC has gone as far as it can until some Authority takes it up seriously'.[34] He was about to lose the support of his Educational Advisory Committee too. It had been established to advise the Company on local production but when the BBC became a corporation in 1927 it was resolved to concentrate schools' production in London and to have a central advisory body, the Central Council for Schools' Broadcasting, which would meet there. This arrangement took a year or so to implement. The Advisory Committee in Belfast was wound up and local production of schools' programmes came to an end. Such production was not to be renewed for more than thirty years; in the meantime Northern Ireland was represented on the Central Council, at first by a lone inspector from the Ministry of Education.

The Belfast BBC's other provision for children, originally called *Children's Corner* and then *Children's Hour,* was very much more successful. The programme occupied a 45-minute slot which varied over the early years in its placing between 5 p.m. and 6.30 p.m. The tangible sign of its success was the membership figures in the Radio League, a charitable organisation run by the programme. After a little more than a year, in December 1925, over 3,000 children in the Belfast area were members. Again, the numbers of letters which arrived from the young listeners permitted the launching of a regular short programme, before the main programme, devoted to readings from them. [...]

All of the station's programme activity, rehearsals as well as productions, was for long confined to one studio, the one so vividly recalled by Tyrone Guthrie. When Beadle arrived he realised that this cramping of a heavy work schedule into such a limited space had a serious effect on standards of production. He was able to persuade London Head Office to expand BBC premises substantially in Linenhall Street and to reconstruct them along the latest lines. Two new studios were built to replace the old. 'No. 1' was a 'spacious, luxuriously carpeted hall, 29 by 53 feet ... decorated in the modernised Greek style, its slender grey pilasters rising to a height of 19 feet. Gone are the old days when the ambition of the BBC engineers was to damp out every trace of echo or resonance; the walls are innocent of draping and the panels between the woodwork are covered with wallpaper of a tasteful design, over a layer of specially prepared felt. This studio is used principally for Orchestral and Band Concerts, and there is no difficulty in accommodating a full orchestra, chorus and principals for operatic productions ... No. 2 studio is a very much smaller affair and resembles more a comfortable music lounge. The decorations are in dark oak with panelling of Japanese design in buff and gold. Here are performed plays and chamber music, and the studio is also used for talks and what is probably one of the most popular of all transmissions - the Children's Hour.'[35] The new extension also provided, for the first time, an effects room, an echo room and a control room.

On 20 March 1928, 'No. 1' was used for a major inaugural programme, a production of *Peer Gynt* given to mark the centenary of the birth of Ibsen. The lead parts were played by Irene Rooke, better known at the time as a film actress, and by the young Robert Speaight. It was a memorable occasion.[36]

In 1932 Beadle had the satisfaction of presiding over the opening of a third studio and a dramatic control room. In the course of his last two years he also added to his staff. Until 1930, outside broadcasts were handled chiefly by the Station Director himself. As Beadle wrote: 'Whenever possible I myself have attended any OBs of a specially important or difficult nature, and acted as the BBC representative. However, owing to other calls on my time, I have had to miss many such OBs and in practice the senior engineer present has had to carry out functions which are not normally his. Furthermore, I am often invited as a guest to functions which we are broadcasting, and it is difficult for me under these circumstances to attend to the OB.' Beadle added 'the amount of OB work is on the increase, partly because the province is going ahead rapidly and there are a larger number of broadcastable events than there used to be. Lately, moreover, we have done a few OBs from the Irish Free State and we now find that there are a number of valuable OB sources in the Irish Free State which we could with advantage make use of. But it will be difficult to extend activities in this field without more staff.'[37]

Beadle was also concerned about the nature of the local news bulletins. These were still supplied as ready-made bulletins by a local journalist from the *Belfast Telegraph,* nominated by the Central News Agency. Beadle thought that he was 'not fully conversant with the subtleties of the BBC's news policy. I doubt whether he could ever be made to appreciate the finer points, and, also, his literary style is poor'. Beadle reported that London news department itself had complained about the local news and he was of the opinion that the situation would only improve if they had a satisfactory news editor on the staff. 'At one time,' he continued, 'I thought we might be able to improve things by changing our news representative and getting a man on the staff of one of the two morning papers,[38] but I now find that the morning papers are rather annoyed with our news representative because he gives too much news. They say he frequently gives us items which are too late for inclusion in the evening paper and, therefore, ought to be held over for first publication in the morning papers.' Beadle thought a news editor on the BBC staff would be able to 'vet' and rewrite the bulletins which arrived from the *Belfast Telegraph.*[43] The outcome of Beadle's representations was that C.A. Roberts was appointed in December 1930 to be news editor, publicity man and to have responsibility for OB work. Roberts was joined by Henry McMullan at the beginning of 1931. Roberts resigned in June 1931, and his role was taken over by McMullan, who was to remain with the BBC Belfast for the next forty years.

Henry McMullan had been a journalist on the staff of the *News Letter* and in that capacity had discovered in London, on inquiry at the BBC's Head Office, what the fate of the Belfast Station under 'the regional scheme' was to be. It had been decided that a new high-powered transmitter would be established outside Belfast and that as a consequence the whole of Northern Ireland would be served for the first time. Beadle had subsequently confirmed that this was the proposed arrangement. At the time he denied the rumour that the new transmitter would simply be a relay station and that local production would stop in Belfast as a consequence.[40] The *News Letter* kept this rumour alive and three years later was suggesting that the Belfast Station would be closed down altogether because of the comparatively small number of licences taken out in Northern Ireland.[41] The BBC, however, not only accepted its obligation under the Charter to provide broadcasting services for Northern Ireland but also recognised that local programme production was necessary because 'of the bad SB lines, which tended to exclude Belfast from SB schemes in general and to make it an isolated unit, and the fact of its being a separate Governmental Centre'.[42]

In 1963, Sir Gerald Beadle recalled his time in Northern Ireland and the efforts to protect Belfast and other regional stations from centralisation.

> My six years there turned out to be a period of difficult relations between the BBC's regions and the Headquarters at Savoy Hill, because the new Director of Programmes in London, Roger Eckersley, had realised that the newly-perfected network made it possible to concentrate programme production on London and feed the rest of the country from there. This in turn would enable the BBC to concentrate more money and talent at the centre and thus raise programme standards for the whole country. The regional controllers opposed this form of centralization as damaging to the proper reflection of local life and talent, which was their special concern ... It was largely due to the inevitable clash of interests that regional controllers were encouraged to spend a lot of their time in London. I calculate that I crossed the Irish Sea, generally by night, about a hundred and fifty times in the six years between 1926 and 1932 - and that was long before the journey could be done by air. In a further attempt to maintain regional harmony Reith appointed a travelling liaison officer ...[43]

Modesty prevented Sir Gerald Beadle from stating that the appointment of this Director for Regional Relations had been suggested by him and that it had been the outcome of a crucial struggle in which the power of those station directors who survived as regional directors had been preserved from the pressures for programme centralisation. The intention had been to place whatever programme production continued in the new regional centres directly under the control of the heads of programme production departments in London and thus leave regional directors as mere BBC ambassadors in their regions. Beadle's resistance preserved the directors' power in the regions and ensured that the regions could preserve and develop their own distinctive regionalisms.[44]

Beadle's success in this respect was a fitting culmination to his work in Belfast. He had accomplished much in his six years. 2BE had been consolidated into a significant institution. His achievement had been recognised by his senior colleagues in London and elsewhere.[45] Above all he had been responsible for some notable programme productions. The Abbey Theatre Company of Dublin had made its first radio broadcast from Belfast and had gone on to give two distinguished seasons of plays from the Station. W.B. Yeats had also been enticed to the microphone for the first time.[46] George Shiels had been persuaded to write for radio and Ulster drama had made its own distinctive contribution over the air. The Wireless Orchestra had given many public performances and, to judge by its popularity at concerts, was revitalising musical life in Belfast.

Endnotes

1. G.C. Beadle, *Television: a critical review,* London, 1963, p. 23.
2. Sir Gerald Beadle in an interview with the author, 15 May 1974.
3. G.C. Beadle to Director General, 1 March 1927.
4. Asa Briggs, *The Birth of Broadcasting,* London, 1961, pp. 360-84.
5. *Irish Radio Journal,* 2, no. 46, 15 May 1926, pp. 1638-9.
6. Goldsmith's draft reply to G.C. Beadle with Reith's note, as filed 16 March 1927. File R13/366/1.
7. *BBC Year Book,* 1928, p. 181.
8. *BBC Year Book,* 1930, p. 111.
9. *BBC Year Book,* 1929, p. 91.
10. PRONI File Com. 21/12 PO 1846.
11. *BBC Year Book,* 1928, p. 181.
12. *First, second and third interim Reports and the final Report of the Special committee to consider the Wireless Broadcasting,* Stationery Office, Dublin, 1924, pp. ix-x.
13. *BBC Year Book,* 1931, p. 146.
14. *Daily Express,* 28 June 1930.
15. *Manchester Guardian,* 18 March 1931.
16. Belfast *News Letter,* 20 March 1931.
17. *Northern Whig,* 21 March 1931.
18. Belfast *News Letter,* 24 March 1931.
19. Belfast *News Letter, 27* March 1931.
20. *Northern Whig,* 31 October 1931.
21. Belfast *News Letter,* 3 January 1929.
22. *Northern Whig,* 23 January 1929.
23. *Northern Whig,* 3 November 1931.
24. *Northern Whig,* 31 October 1931.
25. *Northern Whig,* 23 November 1931.
26. Asa Briggs, *The Golden Age of Wireless,* London, 1965, p. 307.
27. Belfast Station Director to Director of Programmes, Head Office, 10 September 1929.
28. Assistant Director of Programmes to Belfast Station Director, 20 September 1929.
29. *Irish News,* 17 March 1930.
30. *BBC Year Book,* 1928, p. 181.
31. Extract from recorded interview played in 'Belfast Calling', a 50th anniversary programme, NI Radio 4, 18 September 1974.
32. Minutes of Educational Advisory Committee, Belfast, 1924-8, 14 December 1926.
33. *Irish News,* 2 April 1927.
34. Minutes of Educational Advisory Committee Belfast, 1924-8. Beadle's report on 22 March 1927.
35. 'Talking to the World: H.R.W. visits the Belfast Broadcasting Station', *Sunday Independent,* 10 January 1930; the same correspondent wrote a similar piece but with interesting additions in *Irish Motoring,* 22 December 1928, p. 449.
36. Belfast *News Letter,* 21 March 1928.

37. Belfast Station Director to Controller, Head Office, 5 May 1930.

38. A significant remark. There were three morning newspapers, the third being the Catholic *Irish News*. Beadle clearly did not contemplate employing a member of its staff.

39. Belfast Station Director to Controller, Head Office, 22 October 1930.

40. Belfast *News Letter,* 12 November 1927.

41. Belfast *News Letter,* 9 December 1930.

42. Minutes of Control Board Meeting, 8 May 1928.

43. G.C. Beadle, *Television: a critical review,* London, 1963, p. 24.

44. Asa Briggs, *The Golden Age of Broadcasting,* London, 1965, pp. 293-339. The story of the struggle to establish regional broadcasting deserves more extended treatment than Briggs could afford in his work. The Archives reveal the major role played by Beadle. A meeting held in Head Office on 11 July 1932, to discuss regionalism, under the chairmanship of the Director General, proved a turning point. File: Regional Broadcasting 460, 1923-39.

45. Northern Area Director to Director General, 4 May 1928: '... it is very gratifying to have in one's area a station which is so ably run ...'; entry on Beadle, G.C. in *Who's Who in Broadcasting,* London, 1933: ' ... he was recalled by the BBC to take over the very difficult job of directing the station at Belfast. This duty he carried out to such uniform efficiency that ...', etc.

46. Belfast *News Letter,* 9 September 1931.

2.

Anthony Smith

TELEVISION COVERAGE OF NORTHERN IRELAND

(From *Index on Censorship*, 1(1), 1972, pages 15-32; also reproduced in Anthony Smith, *The Politics of Information*, London, Macmillan, 1978, pages 106-128.)

Ever since the problems of the unhappy province of Northern Ireland returned to the front pages of British and foreign newspapers in the middle of 1969, they have presented a fascinating challenge to the prevailing notions of what constitutes a proper degree of control of the content of the broadcasting media. Broadcasting is the only instrument of social communication that is wedded inextricably to an *ideology* as well as a function of its own. That ideology is variously described as neutrality, objectivity, fairness [...] In Northern Ireland, however, we have a province in which a large section of the population has for many decades been deprived of various rights considered normal in the rest of Great Britain; and while the ideology of broadcasting operates in a manner designed to prevent the medium becoming a *maker* of events, as well as a reflector of them, it can only operate in that neutral way when the receiving society as a whole accepts a common set of standards. [...]

In Northern Ireland, to raise the question of equality of opportunity in jobs, education and council housing before the growth of the civil rights movement was to be inflammatory. [...] For radio and television to report on its internal affairs using the normal ethical and social terms of reference of the rest of Britain in the 1950s and 1960s was considered a breach of broadcasting's neutrality. A profound silence prevailed for several decades, until the processes of political change made Northern Ireland once more a centre of news. At that point, pressmen, reporters and producers from every part of the globe poured into the province, bringing their own assumptions and prejudices to bear upon the problems they saw there.

Spanish reporters came and saw the afflictions of fellow Catholics. Soviet reporters came and saw the final spasms of British military imperialism. French marxist pressmen saw a liberation movement enacted before their eyes. Maoists came and saw the birth of a European Cuba. But for British broadcasters and journalists the anguish of Ulster lay outside these categories: it lay in the revelation of the existence of inequities and oppression within these islands of a kind unthinkable in any other part of the country and sanctioned by a kind of helpless feeling of inevitability. The existence of those conditions, it was widely felt, was somehow partly the fault of a long period of cowardice by all the media towards Northern Ireland. [...]

The tensions between broadcasting and authority were thus to a great extent part of an argument about what kind of instrument broadcasting was and should become. [...] Should it always be a reflector and deliberately step back from being an influencer or causer of events? The answer of the broadcasting authorities was clear: radio and television were to reflect and not to provoke. The answer of (some of) the broadcasters was the reverse. The 'real' meaning of the censorship argument in regard to Northern Ireland was thus a struggle between old and new attitudes towards television journalism.

It is very difficult to discern in the discussion anything resembling a traditional argument about 'censorship' or even 'self-censorship' as those terms are usually understood. For one thing, it is difficult to decide which is the self that is conducting the censorship. Is it the reporter, or the producer, or the departmental head, or the Director General, or the Chairman of the Board of Governors of the BBC or of the Independent Television Authority? Where truly does the editorial centre of broadcasting lie? The BBC has a quick and easy answer: it lies with the institutional authorities who in the course of the weary months of crisis gradually asserted themselves in actual daily practice as well as in title as 'editors' of the programme content. But how far away from the straight reporting process can you get and yet remain truly an editor? In 1968 it was not felt that Broadcasting House could realistically keep hour to hour contact with and control over news. In 1972 that control is a reality. It is a reality thrust upon broadcasting by its political critics and by the fears of senior officials that without the show and then the reality of central control, power over broadcasting would be taken away and placed in the hands of a Broadcasting Council or some other instrument of political intrusion. Undoubtedly in the Northern Ireland crisis the whole independence of broadcasting was (and is still) at stake. At the same time I believe that the sequence of events leading to this profound change in the structure of British broadcasting was, however unfortunate, inevitable. The point is that beneath events perceived on the surface there lies a pattern. In the detail of all the public rows over specific programmes, a series of dilemmas repeatedly crops up. First, the question of whether the reporting of an event will cause a counter-event, whether by describing a gathering crowd of Catholics at a given street one is going to encourage a crowd of angry Protestants to gather as well; secondly, how to report the activities of illegal and ever more frequently armed organisations; thirdly, how to 'balance' discussions and reports in political terms in a society with so many political factions; and fourthly, to what extent to make programmes which seem in themselves to be usurping certain of the functions of government. To some extent all broadcasting is conducted against a backdrop of the anticipated reaction of the audience: the whole debate about violence in television programmes involves a steady consideration of the likely immediate effect of a given piece of programme content. In Northern Ireland the producer and the broadcasting manager are confronted with a mass audience whose characteristics of arousability and immediate involvement are known. He can quickly see the results of any judgement he has made in the reaction of members of the audience on the streets as well as by letter and telephone. There is probably no part of the world today where the audience is as much involved with the content of television programmes as in Northern Ireland, where the discussion about the effects of broadcasting is not at all an abstract matter. What is objective or impartial in British (that is, English, Scottish, Welsh) terms is not necessarily so in Irish terms; there is no shared frame of reference on the question of Ireland, no generally agreed centre of intellectual or political gravity. A glance at the history of broadcasting in Ireland will show how carefully over the years the problem was dealt with by avoidance and retreat.

Inevitably, broadcasting in Northern Ireland tended to be heavily influenced by the special political problems of the province. While the civil war within the Irish Free State in the early 1920S prevented Marconi (with the intended help of the *Daily Express)* from developing a radio station, developments were able to take place more easily in the North. The first station on Irish soil was called B.E.2, it first took the air from the converted linen warehouse in Belfast in September 1924. The Government of Northern Ireland possessed the right to stop transmissions if the public interest required it. Listeners south of the Border, at least those with the most advanced kinds of apparatus, were able to listen in. But all the news came from a locally owned news agency and the only political statements allowed were those delivered by major local politicians. All events south of the Border were studiously ignored; even the results of matches played by the Gaelic Athletic Association were refused air time. (As if replying in kind, Dublin radio in its early days refused to broadcast the results of Association Football matches.) In 1926 Gerald Beadle became station manager (later he became Director of BBC Television) and battled with the province's nerve-wracking sectarian problems. His drama department was attacked for its use of 'southern' accents in some of its plays; his decision to celebrate St Patrick's Day brought a storm of Unionist protest; his policy was to act as if the Border was an Atlantic Coast. None the less the BBC produced a flourishing musical culture and created a small school of Ulster dramatists .

It was the mid-1930s which produced the major crisis in broadcasting-governmental relationships. The riots of 1935 brought demands that the BBC be taken over completely by Stormont, so that it could be used to send out daily ripostes to the propaganda of Radio Eireann which broadcast from Dublin and was uninhibited about reporting Belfast events. Under G.L. Marshall the Director of BBC Northern Ireland (as it had become) there was a move towards a kind of liberalisation: a debate was broadcast between Queen's University Belfast and the two university colleges of Dublin. But northern Unionist opinion made itself vigorously felt to oppose any development of a normal friendly station-to-station relationship, just as opinion south of the Border similarly served to inhibit Radio Eireann. On the whole, however, the Unionist establishment felt content with the role of the BBC which steered clear of coverage of extremist Unionist sentiment as much as of opposition sentiment. No election broadcasts took place at all before the Second World War. The annual 12 July demonstrations of the Orange Order were not reported. Marshall's policy, continued until his retirement well after the war, was to keep an iron grip on all local news and allow nothing to go out which suggested that anything in Northern Ireland could or would ever change. The BBC, apart perhaps from its enterprising drama department, spoke in the tones of the Ulster establishment and worked in their interests. Also, foreshadowing the problems of a later day, Marshall demanded and was given the right to be consulted by all departments of the BBC on any matter relating to Ireland in any way. Thus, the chief in Belfast came to act as a kind of censor over the whole of the BBC's output from London both in its domestic and overseas services, and naturally this tended to give a Unionist tinge to everything that came out. Similarly, the Controller Northern Ireland was deemed to have the right to prevent any communication between the Overseas Service and Radio Eireann except through his office and with his knowledge. But this, as it turned out, was to prove self-defeating, for it was the Overseas Service which first rebelled against the system, because it obstructed easy contact with Dublin.

Meanwhile London occasionally tried to moderate Marshall's policies, especially during the Second World War when, with the Republic remaining neutral, the Ministry of Information was anxious for Irish listeners to hear the presentation of a British point of view. The Ministry wanted the BBC to build up its relationship with Eire, and the BBC responded by starting, with the approval of Radio Eireann, a regular 'Irish Half-Hour'. Simultaneously it started an 'Ulster Half Hour' which was soon dropped. It was a strange irony that dictated a wartime situation in which a London government wanted the BBC deliberately to foster a sense of Irish nationhood while the Belfast government continued to browbeat the BBC's local officials into maintaining the restrictions of the 1920s and 1930s.

After the war considerable measures of liberalisation appeared. The Roman Catholic Church sent a representative to the religious advisory committee. A regional advisory council was set up with fairly broad representation. Gaelic games were reported at last, and so were demonstrations on 12 July, live and on the spot. But events south of the Border were still ignored, and nothing was heard on Marshall's airwaves which hinted at discontent or injustice in Northern Irish society. But when he retired in the late 1940S political comment became slightly more realistic. There were talks on Ulster history and a Catholic nationalist was allowed to take part in weekly discussions on local affairs. Not until the 1960S, however, were programmes permitted which dealt with Irish history as a whole. Strangely enough, the new regional advisory council of the BBC was one of the extremely rare places where Catholic nationalist and Protestant unionist opinion were able to come together anywhere in the province.

Television came to Belfast in time for the Coronation to be seen throughout the province, and in the late 1950S a certain amount of locally produced programming began to appear. That was the time of an earlier bout of IRA activity; and the streets of Belfast gave BBC cameramen their first experience in covering street violence, that speciality of the Belfast news scene. Lord Brookeborough, Prime Minister at Stormont, who paid scrupulous and tireless attention to the work of BBC news, took part in a number of spectacular contests over various items of television content, in some of which he was successful. Amid a blaze of publicity the second of two programmes with Siobhan McKenna was dropped in which, unscripted, she declared to Ed Murrow that some of the IRA internees in the Republic, who had been released despite British opposition, were 'young idealists'. Lord Brookeborough intervened personally in this affair, as a result of which the BBC withdrew the programme and suffered an internal convulsion of protest for its pains. Later, Brookeborough intervened to cause the disappearance of an item about the Border, presented by Alan Whicker, from the schedules of 'Tonight'. He also protested at the showing of a film about rural electrification in the Republic on the grounds that viewers might be misled into thinking it referred to Northern Ireland. He did not shrink from the dramatic phone call to Broadcasting House - today a regular feature of our political life. And it was this backstairs obscurantism of Unionist politicians that tended to deflect criticism from the person of the BBC's senior official on the spot. In the late 1960S, however, the carpet under which so much dust had been shovelled was suddenly tugged away: attempted suppression ceased to be a valid technique for Unionists. Television news-collecting created new facts of life for the politicians of Belfast. Until 1965 it had been possible to prevent reporters from London from ever setting foot in the province at all. After 1968, such a course became totally unthinkable.

The basic problem for the broadcasting authorities, as we have seen, was to prevent the coverage on radio or television of political or social events from being itself the cause of further events. The BBC (together with broadcasting authorities the world over) has always been shy of committing any act that can be construed as outright interference in the world it is observing. But in a province as tightly controlled as Northern Ireland, living in a sense an artificial political life based on the suppression of a series of social forces by means of manipulated boundaries and police powers, it was difficult to provide any kind of broadcast coverage (in an organisation committed to objectivity) which failed to arouse tempers and invoke the ever-latent spirit of civil commotion. Broadcasting in such a context is inevitably an agent of political action; the very facts under observation could only continue in existence if they remained unreported. The very fact of the unity of Northern Ireland and Great Britain should have necessitated comparison in any reporting of the situation. The paradox of Northern Ireland's pretensions to be British while trying to live apart, however, made it impossible for any coverage to be done according to the usual BBC standards that would yet satisfy the needs of a Unionist society as interpreted through the local office of the BBC.

But perhaps the most important new fact of the late 1950s was the coming into existence of commercial television in Belfast. When, late in 1958, the ITA announced that bids for a Northern Ireland franchise were invited, two groups based in the province contended: the first was headed by the Duke of Abercorn and represented interests in local cinemas and *The Northern Whig* newspaper, the second was headed by the Earl of Antrim and involved the Belfast *Newsletter* as well as a wide spectrum of other local interests. The latter won the contest and became the basis of UTV, Ulster Television, under the management of Brum Henderson, whose brother runs the virulently Unionist *Newsletter,* as well as The Century Press, which prints a number of government papers including the Stormont *Hansard.* He is also chairman of the Ulster Unionist Party's publicity committee and is believed to be a great force in the counsels of his party.

Nevertheless, commercial television is a great equaliser of men: there is no point in setting out to sell goods if you cut yourself off editorially from a third of your potential public. Ulster Television accordingly earned itself, to the surprise of many pessimists, a good reputation for its fairness in coverage: it did, however, have to be nagged and cajoled at times into venturing into public affairs coverage on any important scale. UTV quickly gained 65 per cent of the audience, although it originates only six hours of material a week within the province. It fought to get all sections of the population to turn to its programmes. It started its own newsroom a decade ago and presented a local magazine which, true to the principles of the Television Act, provided impartial and balanced coverage of local affairs.

The BBC responded in kind. The political atmosphere of Northern Ireland television began to change substantially. Processes which were occurring throughout Britain as a result of the growth of commercial competition were inevitably felt in Northern Ireland in an accentuated form. When the civil rights movement began in 1968, broadcasting in Northern Ireland was already reformed. After Marshall the most prominent senior figure in Northern Ireland broadcasting was probably Henry MacMullan who built up the role of the Head of Programmes. He was, many thought, a liberalised version of Marshall. In 1966, however, a new professional newsman, Waldo Maguire, took over the Controller's chair at the height of the Greene era at Portland Place. Maguire was a native Ulsterman who, although he was to earn considerably greater opprobrium at home and derision abroad than the previous holders of his post, ill deserved such abuse. He set about the task of running his bureau in the manner to which he had become accustomed in the newsroom at Alexandra Palace: reporters from London were welcomed and helped to do their work; dissenters of all kinds were allowed to take part in programmes; local talent, Protestant and Catholic alike was encouraged.

But the Controller's power over content remained. Maguire was still expected to exercise the right of enforced consultation with all programme-makers from London. Technically he had the power to insist on being told the details of every programme project dealing with Ireland, north and south. Increasingly, as the political crisis deepened, reporters from news and current affairs, sound and vision, working out of London were expected to work from his office under a high degree of supervision. His seniority in the organisation of the BBC is extremely high: to appear over his head the reporter or producer must get the ear of the Director General or his constant aide, the Editor of News and Current Affairs (ENCA). Theoretically *editorial authority* does not reside with Controller Northern Ireland, but through the programme producer and his departmental head with Broadcasting House, although the Controller has the right for his views on every aspect of the programme content to be heard by the producer. But a further problem intruded: in the era of Greene it was decreed that as far as possible the content of the BBC's programmes should be identical in Britain and in Northern Ireland - the transmitters were not to divide their content as far as the province's crisis was concerned. If something was to be said about Northern Ireland in England then it could be said to the population of Northern Ireland to their faces. At the same time the Controller of BBC Northern Ireland did have editorial authority over anything that went out through his own local transmitter up on Divis Mountain. Thus Maguire, while he could not forbid a producer to put out a given interview, could insist on shutting off his transmitter and putting out a different programme if the producer continued with his plan. Meanwhile, the Director General had also instructed producers to do nothing that would provoke Maguire into the need, or supposed need, for such an action. It was a case of 'Catch 22'. On only one occasion was a decision made to allow BBC Northern Ireland to opt out of a major programme dealing with the crisis: that was when in 1970 'Panorama' presented a report which contained a widow crying for vengeance for her dead husband, shot by terrorists. It was decided that the report might provoke further bloodshed and Belfast 'opted out' of that one edition.

In UTV, meanwhile, the situation had developed differently and was far less interesting than during the early days. It was an independent company, which had to work in close consultation with the locally resident official of the ITA. With his approval, it could opt out of the regular current affairs programmes. It often urged him to do this and succeeded on six or seven occasions. It also presented far less coverage of the situation, *in toto,* than the BBC. Perhaps that was part of the reason why it was subject to so little local attack. At the same time *The Newsletter,* blood relation to the commercial television company, took to protesting against BBC coverage almost incessantly. Year after year it conducted a campaign of attack on the BBC and the wretched figure of Maguire, wanting to be liberal, highly excitable, warm, well-informed and, like the BBC as a whole, prone at times to retreat into extreme caution. He was similarly abused and condemned by extremists from all sides, especially the more militant Unionist elements and like other prominent figures in Northern Ireland who have tried to follow a policy of fairness within a polarised population, was vilified and intimidated beyond all endurance. The attack came from all sides, within the BBC and within the province and it was progressively extended to the senior staff to whom his powers were delegated within the office at Belfast.

By the end of 1971 the situation had become chaotic and on 31 December an anonymous BBC reporter [later revealed to be Jonathan Dimbleby] described it in the *New Statesman* as follows: 'Any current affairs editor who wants to do an item on Northern Ireland now has to submit the idea both to the News Editor in Belfast and the Editors of Current Affairs for television or radio in London. On approval, the items are recorded and then once again submitted for inspection to London and Belfast, and frequently as well to the Editor of News and Current Affairs for final approbation.' This complicated system began to operate in a way which many reporters and producers found humiliating (although others found it wise and unrestrictive in practice).

It was accused of leading to the BBC's failure to report allegations about the torture of internees (which ultimately led to the Widgery Tribunal) until after the *Sunday Times* had reported them. It was accused too of leading to various forms of bias within reported stories, such as the occasion when, in a report of a tarring and feathering incident in Londonderry, all reference was omitted to the fact that no woman could be found to condemn the incident. One programme was allegedly required to ignore a meeting of the Alternative Parliament after the opposition withdrawal from Stormont.

The anonymous reporter in the *New Statesman* argued that these and similar incidents constituted a degeneration of the BBC's refusal to allow IRA terrorism the right of outright advocacy on the air into informal support for the army against the whole Catholic minority. A more likely explanation, however, is that these decisions were the result of broadcasting's desire to be 'secondhand', to report nothing really big that had not already been reported elsewhere. One aspect of 'cautious' broadcasting is that news editors feel easier reporting a report, rather than taking the initiative in reporting a new phase or an incident of especially controversial significance. That really is the essence of the dilemma that gradually defined itself during the months of greatest tension when IRA violence really began to mount: should broadcasting go out on a limb and behave like an independent and self-confident reporting instrument or should it hang back and refrain from taking any significant initiative? This tension emerged as a dispute between two groups as to what manner of role radio and television should play within the media.

As the dispute increased in intensity, it was not merely the hapless Maguire who was under attack; the entire management of the BBC found itself ceaselessly and personally under fire from the beginning of the crisis in 1969, and especially after January 1971, when the Provisional Wing of the IRA took spectacular control of the situation at the Ballymurphy flats and found itself in direct conflict with the Army. Whenever an institution is being criticised from two sides it is always a simple matter to turn the argument to its own advantage. John Crawley, special assistant to the Director General, told a conference of Conservative women in December 1971 that 'some reporters and producers and junior editors in radio and television ... are apprehensive or uneasy about the strictness of the control we are applying'. In a letter to Mr Maudling on 19 November Lord Hill had defended the reporting staff against the allegation of pro-Catholic bias: 'The charges are that the BBC reporters and editors snipe at the Army, and are "soft" towards the IRA. The charges are untrue, and are deeply resented by our staff, many of whom do their work at great risk to themselves. The reality of the BBC's reporting of the Army's role is strikingly different from the picture painted by some of its critics.' But Desmond Taylor, the overall Editor of News and Current Affairs, justified the growing supervision of reporting work in Ireland on the grounds that it 'protected reporters and avoided mistakes of judgement'. 'I am just acting more like an editor and less like a bureaucrat', he said in the BBC's house magazine.

The rule that interviews with members of the IRA (north or south of the Border) had to be referred upwards through the ENCA to the Director General in every instance before being *sought*, let alone conducted or transmitted, was progressively enforced. At first it was part of an attempt to orchestrate the BBC's coverage in a manner that would not exacerbate the troubles of the province; it was presented as an act of 'self-restraint' on the part of the BBC. After January 1971 the system of reference upwards operated (more or less) as a means to ban interviews with the IRA altogether. Permission had always to be sought and therefore was requested less and less often - and when requested it was more and more frequently refused. At first the BBC was coy about the whole thing. One reporter said his boss treated the rule as a kind of guilty secret. But as events moved on and the pressure mounted, the rule was openly paraded as an act of statesmanship. Lord Hill wrote to Maudling, the Home Secretary: 'But, between the British Army and the gunmen, the BBC is not and cannot be impartial.' (It was not under the rubric of impartiality that access to the IRA was required by reporters, but rather out of the need to reach primary sources in the course of collecting information.) As the dual supervision between Belfast and Broadcasting House continued, power gradually moved away from the former towards the latter, and as it did so, and as editorial supervision therefore moved away from the eye of the storm, it liberalised. In respect to the coverage of Northern Ireland itself, the growth of the power of ENCA in Portland Place was editorially liberating. The trouble was that the process meant that ENCA, through the Irish crisis, had developed a controlling influence which would be used in future across the board in respect to a rapidly increasing area of subject matter.

It is important to emphasise that not all reporters felt the broadcasting authority's restrictions to be stifling. When a wave of indignation at 'covert censorship' spread through various sections of the public and commercial systems, the ordinary BBC newsmen were largely puzzled by it. In the reporting of straight news the restrictions were not troublesome; battles, shootings and burnings could all be frankly and factually described. Key figures in events could be interviewed. Public press conferences by IRA men, even self-confessed gunmen, could be filmed and transmitted. The apparatus of internal censorship did not interfere with the normal course of interviewing major political figures and 'Panorama' staff, for instance, did not to any great extent feel that their functions were becoming difficult to discharge. It was 'World at One', 'World in Action' and '24 Hours' which found the new situation cramping. As one of this group of reporters recently put it to me: 'There exists between us and BBC Belfast a fundamental difference about the nature, purpose and style of current affairs broadcasting which cannot be bridged by amendments to scripts, however much effort and goodwill is expended on such an exercise.'

One significant incident, which has frequently been referred to in the press since, arose from a '24 Hours' report on changing sentiment within the Ulster Unionist Party, shortly before the resignation of Mr Chichester-Clark as Prime Minister in Northern Ireland in February 1971. The report included film of a number of party meetings at which Chichester-Clark was roundly condemned, and in which Paisleyite sentiment within the party was shown to be widespread and unconcealed. The gist of the report was that Northern Ireland could well find itself in search of a new Prime Minister within a very short space of time. The report was not shown on the persistent advice of the Belfast Controller, pending a series of changes, including most importantly some indication of the feelings of 'moderate opinion' within the Ulster Unionist Party. The whole point of the report was that moderate opinion was evaporating, and the later addition of an interview with a 'moderate' saying precisely that did not reconcile Belfast to the notion of transmitting the report. As the days passed the event predicted actually occurred, and the report was rendered valueless.

BBC Belfast appeared to have begun, in its fear of the consequences of failure by the Ulster Unionist moderates to hold onto power, to slip into the shoes of moderate Ulster Unionism itself. Maguire and some of his staff seemed to fear that the BBC, by pointing to behind-the-scenes pressure on Chichester-Clark at that moment, would help to bring about the very collapse of his power it was predicting. But by neglecting to point out to a British audience the kind of pressures that existed within the province at the moment the BBC made it, if anything, harder for Chichester-Clark to bring home to Maudling why the processes of reform were proving so difficult. Once broadcasting tries, for reasons however liberal, to lighten the burdens of government, it steps upon a slippery slope that ends with fear and reality becoming progressively indistinguishable.

Within the world of independent television an astonishingly similar pattern of events was asserting itself. While the BBC had in its complex internal processes of consultation been trying to work out a way to serve the purposes of journalism without interfering in the active work of government, or, for that matter, in the active work of opposition, the ITA almost unconsciously was in the midst of a similar voyage.

The ITA has always felt that its distinctively loose structure, devoid of any outright editorial control at the centre, makes it less vulnerable to attack and more democratic at the same time. The role of the regional officer of the ITA, for instance, is a hazy one, varying from region to region, and in Northern Ireland the regional officer has been involved not merely in an exercise of restraint, but in encouraging the local company UTV to be, if anything, more daring. But in an initial panic reaction to the political crisis in the summer of 1969, UTV decided to limit its reporting of the situation to hard news and not to go out of its way to solicit comment. It decided also that its reporters and cameramen should, if they found themselves in danger, remove themselves immediately from the scene. Finally, it decided (in contrast to the BBC) not to allow any activists or extremists to take part in studio discussions in the studios of UTV for fear of provoking direct attacks on UTV buildings and property. The ITA was also involved in setting these conditions for the operation of UTV, but relaxed them in August 1969. At the same time the ITA cautioned Independent Television News that the dividing line between information and incitement was difficult to draw, but should at all times be a subject of concern. 'Balance' in reporting did not necessarily result in calming events and could in fact cause a double provocation.

Simultaneously the ITA began to scrutinise programmes, especially 'World in Action' and 'This Week', with a view to determining whether each edition should be shown in Northern Ireland. Community leaders joined a delegation to the ITA asking it to ensure that its programmes avoided anything likely to exacerbate the situation or lead to public disorder. The Television Act forbids any programme which 'incites to public disorder' and the ITA's interpretation of this in the context of the crisis then led to a series of decisions to allow UTV to opt out of programmes, sometimes without their being viewed at all [in] a finished state. Later, as the situation deteriorated, the rule of the ITA's consultations with the programme companies increased considerably: ITA officials, national and local, began to apply exactly the same criteria to the work of ITN and the programme companies as high officials at Broadcasting House. Although UTV could more easily than BBC Belfast choose not to show a given programme within the province, it became ITA policy not to encourage this. Programme-makers within the independent system were thus hoist with the same petard as those in the BBC: they had to make programmes that could be seen as though uncompromising reporting in England, Scotland and Wales while not provoking politically involved groups within the province itself. The story of the recent 'South of the Border' affair illustrates just how far the ITA has moved since 1969 in developing a central editorial policy strikingly parallel with that of the BBC.

There had been a history of mild conflict between Granada's 'World in Action' team and the ITA beforehand - in the BBC it would have been seen as 'creative conflict', but within the independent system it led to a slowly degenerating relationship based upon a series of minor cuts in programmes, delayed transmissions, accusations of bias, soured bouts of 'consultation'. In mid-September 1971 the ITA made its view known that the withholding of a network transmission of a programme dealing with Ulster 'was in some sense a public admission of failure'. Granada meanwhile indicated that it wanted to prepare a programme which would show the pressures present in the Republic of Ireland as a result of the crisis in the north. In consultation with the ITA's staff, Granada proceeded to shoot film for the programme using the October Sinn Féin convention in Dublin as its starting point. The programme was to examine the IRA in Ireland from a critical standpoint, and to include interviews with Dublin politicians hostile to the IRA. The Managing Director of Ulster Television informed the ITA that the showing of such a programme anywhere in the United Kingdom would be deplorable in that it would simply give publicity to IRA extremists. The ITA decided that the programme would be unacceptable for transmission and informed Granada accordingly. At that point the programme consisted only of uncompiled and unedited rushes. The Authority had held only a brief discussion on the matter lasting for a few minutes, before making its decision.

This unwonted quickness of decision gave rise to allegations that the ITA had been 'got at' by government ministers. Certainly no formal instruction in regard to the programme had been issued by Maudling (which of course he has the power to do), but equally certainly the government was anxious that the IRA should not be presented on any of the domestic media in a favourable light.

There followed an exchange of statements between Granada and the ITA on the issue of whether the ITA had given authority for the company to continue working on the programme. By early November, however, on its own initiative, Granada had in fact finished the programme and asked the ITA to view it. The ITA, through its Director General, had been at pains to point out that its objection was to the subject matter fundamentally and not to the treatment. Nevertheless, on 16 November members of the ITA watched the completed programme and decided that it was lacking in the necessary balance. Their reason was that none of the governments concerned in the Irish question, in Dublin, Belfast or London, was represented in the programme and that this gave the offensive impression that the IRA and the Provisionals were 'a properly established political party in a democratic community'. Simultaneously the ITA vigorously rejected allegations made in the press at the time that it was being subjected to political pressure and had decided to 'ban' any kind of coverage of the problems of Northern Irish affairs at all, while Granada proceeded to show the press 'South of the Border' and received comment that was generally favourable to itself and hostile to the ITA decision (although *The Guardian* expressed the view that the programme also suffered from a number of weaknesses). The whole affair brought to a head the deteriorating relationship between Granada and the ITA and led the latter to charge that Granada's 'World in Action' series showed a decided political bias and was guilty of partial reporting.

The rumpus that followed marked a turning point in the history of Independent Television with consequences that have not yet been fully digested. What is certain, however, is that when members of the ITA came to look back on the affair a month or two later, in early 1972, it was clear to all of them that the authority had travelled a good distance in the course of the Northern Ireland crisis. First there was the fact that the ITA was sharing editorial control with the companies, in a positive as well as a negative way, and was exercising power over the choice of subject matter as well as its treatment. Second, according to one member of the authority, it had made a decision in effect not 'to make the task of government more difficult' in any programme over which it exercised its new-found editorial control. Granada had offended by giving prominence to men who were public outlaws: it had confused 'balance' within the context of Republic politics with 'balance' within the only context that mattered, i.e. that of British politics. By now, moreover, the ITA had also made up its mind more clearly on the whole question of incitement to violence and 'opting out'. Although it had traditionally made a distinction between transmitting a programme within the area in which violence was potentially to be provoked, and its transmission elsewhere, now the need to show the same material throughout the country was conceived as so overwhelming that *all programmes* had to be fit to show in Northern Ireland. At the same time the Director General continued to emphasise that the ITA, despite the highly publicised visit of its Chairman to the Home Secretary, was in no way being subjected to governmental pressures.

There has not previously been so explicit a revelation of the relationship between the ITA and the programme-makers, or between a British broadcasting authority and the government, as occurred during those troubled days. The Irish question within commercial television, as within the BBC, had caused a solidification of relationships and the delineation of a set of tensions which are likely to develop in the next decade. No actual changes in power are involved; the BBC retains all editorial authority, in a legal sense, at its highest level, and so does the ITA. What has happened in the course of the Irish troubles is that the structures of control have digested the actual nature of the professional decisions that are made in the course of programme-making and have caught up with them. Broadcasting House and the staff of the Independent Television Authority have understood how programmes are made, and are confidently taking over various reins which they had previously left slack.

After the banning of the 'World in Action' film, 'South of the Border' by the ITA, a public meeting was hastily arranged to protest against the ban and the alleged growing 'censorship' in Ulster reporting. Although its organisation had been hasty, several hundred reporters and producers turned up at the ICA in London, some of them from very far afield. The gathering included representatives of all the media involved in reporting the Northern Ireland scene - with one exception: no broadcasting 'official' was there. Protests flowed freely. One radio reporter alleged that a free and accurate representation of events on radio was being prevented. Several television reporters described their daily frustrations. But no picture emerged of a phenomenon corresponding to a classic definition of 'censorship'. Rather what the television and radio reporters were saying was that they wished to operate the machinery of broadcasting as if it were the press, free of any special requirement of 'impartiality' or 'objectivity'. The tension emerging between the broadcasters and their employers was a tension between an old feeling about broadcasting and a new one, between the view that broadcasting should invariably create and transmit a simulated, balanced model of the prevailing political scene and the view that broadcasting should now exist as a reporting tool pure and simple. The doctrine of impartiality had forced on broadcasting organisations a social role that now made them extremely vulnerable. Since objectivity did not flow naturally out of the material being presented, it had to be imposed by hierarchy. [...]

The paradox in the British system of broadcasting is that the organisations are powerful in self-defence as well as irresistible in their periodic fits of caution. In the case of 'A Question of Ulster', the BBC programme in which three distinguished men sat on a kind of 'tribunal' and questioned a group of people representing the whole spectrum of Irish politics, the BBC was able to ignore a concerted attempt by Home Secretary Maudling and the Prime Minister of Ulster, Brian Faulkner, to get a perfectly straightforward, predictable and untroublesome programme off the air. The sheer power generated by the size of the BBC was sufficient to thwart government pressures of that kind, which in this case were aimed at persuading intending participants to withdraw. And as it came about, both Stormont and Downing Street were left without live representation in the discussion, which was marked by its atmosphere of all-round restraint. Of course the Home Secretary's fear was that the open and comprehensive nature of the programme would tend to usurp the function of government in bringing the various elements in Northern Ireland together: but ministers constantly fail to appreciate the difference between television and reality: a television programme is a representation, it is not the real thing.

But there is a further lesson to be absorbed from television's 'Irish crisis'. All programme formats are in essence formulae for handling events and explaining them. Once you define a programme format you create a tool which is likely to implant its own image on the events it is trying to represent. There are things which cannot be contained within 'Panorama', certain perspectives fail to become visible in that particular context among that particular group of reporters and presenters. Similarly 'World in Action' contains a different set of opportunities and concomitant limitations. News is itself a formula, a format, into which some phenomena fit and some don't, some expectations can be realised and others cannot. What has happened in some respects in Northern Ireland is that reporting on television quickly ran out of formulae; the 'Panorama' or '24 Hours' 'story' which depends on the depiction of events around a theme chosen by the reporter, around a personality or a paradox or an issue, was simply unable to contain the kind of material which the situation was accumulating in a way which could satisfy the BBC's own special needs. To explain the events of Ulster using anything more than the straight day-to-day techniques of news reporting, you have to go back to the beginning of the story each time, or you have to ensure that each partisan group involved in a particular situation was studiedly represented. The 'film story' as a formula simply cannot cope with the amount of detail involved.

On a number of occasions the major current affairs programmes went back to 'the beginning', to 1969, to 1916, to 1912, or to 1688, to explain fairly and accurately the origins of a particular issue. But to do that properly involves a colossal amount of intellectual and technical work, even to cram the material into a programme of an hour's or two hours' length. That work has been done, frequently and adequately. But it cannot be done every day and the issues and events week by week cannot always be placed in a vessel of that nature. The whole set of formulae by which current affairs programmes have lived in this country since the foundation in 1957 of 'Tonight' and the extension of daily and weekly journalism into television is under strain as a result of Northern Ireland's crisis.

No one could call the manifestations of this strain 'censorship', not when viewed from outside the broadcasting organisation as a whole. But inside, in a context in which the reporter sees his duty as coinciding with and competitive with that of the print journalist, and at a time when the techniques available actually enable him to provide a service of this kind, the impending and existing restraints *feel* like censorship, or a demand for self-censorship. The question therefore is how broadcast journalism is to be controlled in future. There is little likelihood that the authorities are going to relax their control soon, especially when it is being partially exercised to ward off worse threatened form of control from outside (a Broadcasting Council, the splitting of the BBC into separate groups, etc.), which are being pressed for in certain quarters.

In my view the only viable path ahead is another slow and irksome one, involving the growth of professional organisations among programme-makers and 'media workers' in general. These could create their own counter-pressures and their own counter-precedents. In Germany there has for two years now been a considerable growth in organisation among producers to combat the increasing interference of politicians directly in the internal affairs of the programme companies. In France too the trade unions within television have taken an increasing interest in questions involving programme content as well as pay and conditions. So many of the day-to-day problems are difficult to resolve by argument; they are questions of mood and emotion. But at some stage the increasing centralisation of power in our broadcasting organisations is bound to invoke countervailing force to balance it.

3.

Robert Fisk

THE BBC AND THE 1974 ULSTER WORKERS' COUNCIL STRIKE

(From *The Point of No Return: the Strike which Broke the British in Ulster*,
London, Andre Deutsch, 1975, pages 127-144 and 236-237)

'As an independent institution, we had a duty to reflect significant
bodies of opinion - however arrived at - as much as to support
institutions of democracy not widely accepted.'

Official BBC internal report on the UWC strike

'The miners taught us that the mass media could make or break us.
The BBC were marvellous - they were prepared to be fed any
information. They fell into their own trap that "the public must get
the news". Sometimes they were just a news service for us; we
found that if the media was on our side we didn't need a gun.'

Harry Murray, after the strike

Around lunch time on Tuesday, only four hours after the union marches
had failed, Dick Francis's secretary in the regional Belfast office of the
BBC received a phone call from a civil servant at Stormont Castle. As
controller of broadcasting in the province for the past eleven months
Francis, an energetic Yorkshireman of 40 who was one of the BBC's most
experienced documentary and current affairs producers, had already had
some contact with Stormont officials. On several occasions over the past
six days he had asked - indeed pleaded - with civil servants to make
spokesmen available for local news broadcasts in order to balance the
statements being put out by the UWC. This telephone call, however, was
of a more serious nature than the others, not only because it was initiated

at Stormont but because it contained a request for the BBC controller to go to see Rees[1] 'to discuss ways in which the situation can be covered'. Francis did not regard it as a summons when he travelled up to Stormont that afternoon, although he was already acutely aware of the displeasure felt by both British Government and executive at the coverage of the strike by the BBC.

That very morning the early Northern Ireland news bulletin had carried a report which cast more than a little doubt on the ability of the authorities to maintain any kind of order in the streets of Belfast. Only seconds after the news reader had repeated Stormont's promise to keep the roads open, Brian Walker, one of the BBC'S most able reporters in the city, was stating, 'We've just heard that new road-blocks are going up in Belfast.' He named the locations of eight new hijacking incidents, referred to 'gangs of men roaming around the Greenisland estate hijacking vehicles' and to barricades in Carrickfergus, Newtownards, Bangor and south Belfast. It was a style of reporting - fast, dramatic and in Walker's case completely accurate - that made Rees, Faulkner and their respective ministers look fools. How could people be expected to believe Stormont's earnest promises to maintain order if the BBC was saying that the facts did not accord with what the Government was promising?

Francis was shown into the Castle drawing room to find both Rees and Orme present, together with their civil servants. Rees did the talking and he was surprisingly mild. He asked how Francis thought the strike should be covered in future, and how the views of the Northern Ireland Office could be put on the air most effectively. How, he asked, could Government communiqués be relayed on the BBC to counteract statements put out by the UWC? Francis replied instantly, 'Put forward spokesmen who will talk.' There was a discussion about that morning's news broadcast (in which information given to the Government by the Army was once more at variance with information given by the police to the BBC) and Francis also tried to disabuse Rees of the idea, understandable in the circumstances, that to reply to the UWC statements in some way gave credibility to the strikers. By the end of the short interview the ball was back in Rees's court. But both Francis and the officials present gained the impression that while the Secretary of State may have understood the BBC's problems, he was also speaking on behalf of a far less sympathetic executive.[2] Rees was aware that news would be presented as quickly as possible and that Francis felt a duty to his listeners to report all events to them; the executive, particularly John Hume, felt itself being betrayed by the broadcasting authorities.

Francis was under no illusions about the traumas which faced the BBC from the situation in Northern Ireland. He had not only spent months in the United States helping to supervise coverage of Watergate and the American elections, but before being appointed to the province had presented two major and highly controversial programmes on *The Question of Ulster*. When the first of these was broadcast prior to direct rule, Reginald Maudling, who was then the Home Secretary, had pointedly refused to take part. So had Faulkner, who was then Prime Minister, although he appeared in the second programme a year later. Besides, the regional BBC, housed in a great concrete and brick office on the corner of Ormeau Avenue, had been the centre of countless arguments since the very start of the civil war in the north of Ireland. A reference by a news reader to a shooting incident would inevitably bring dozens of calls from outraged 'eye-witnesses' claiming that the BBC were taking an untruthful account of the violence from the security forces; an interview with an extremist leader would bring private but equally vehement protests from the authorities. There was often some basis of truth in both complaints; the BBC - which in its earlier days had been very much under the thumb of Unionist Governments - originally accepted at face value far too many highly suspect Army statements about events in Belfast while too many republicans (and later Protestant) extremists were interviewed simply to show that the BBC had managed to find them. In more serious vein and of even more relevance to the strike was a suggestion that by misreporting, or by reporting an incident so soon after it occurred, the BBC unintentionally helped to create more violence. Back in 1969, it was blamed for helping to foment a riot outside the Catholic Unity Flats at the bottom of the Shankill Road by broadcasting an account of stones being thrown at a Junior Orange procession there.[3] Several reporters have also felt concerned at the impact of the BBC news on events in the city.[4] One of Faulkner's party faithful, Lord Brookeborough, had long argued the case for self-imposed delay in news broadcasting.[5] In late 1974, the police were asking the BBC as well as other news media not to mention the religion of sectarian assassination victims because RUC detectives suspected that such reports were directly responsible for some revenge killings. Neither the BBC nor the press complied with the request.

But such intricate arguments were nothing to the crisis which enveloped the BBC during the May strike. The stoppage was to push the British broadcasting authorities into their severest test of impartiality since the invasion of Suez in 1956, and the bitterness which still lingers on in Ulster and the Irish Republic over the BBC'S role in the strike - its handling of the UWC leaders and of the steadily worsening deterioration in power, gas and all essential services - bears comparison with that which followed the BBC'S coverage of the 1926 General Strike in Britain. Although it was only one BBC region that was involved, it had its own reporters serving about a million and a half people and for them the issues were in many ways the same as those in 1926. At least one secret Government report has been compiled at Stormont and sent to Whitehall on the way in which the BBC coped, and at times lamentably failed to cope, with the constitutional problems presented by the UWC, by the emergence of an insurrection inside the United Kingdom.

Since 1969, the five- and ten-minute bulletins put out by the BBC in Northern Ireland had been treated by the people of Ulster much in the way that the British had regarded their wartime news broadcasts; the information may sometimes have been viewed with slight suspicion by one or other of the two communities but it was nevertheless obligatory listening for men and women who realized that their future welfare, their jobs and perhaps even their lives, depended on the events going on around them. 98 per cent of the province's population received BBC radio and BBC1 television.[6] In May of 1974 they were able to hear a minimum of six local news broadcasts each day. But the two television bulletins were effectively put off the air by power cuts after the first week of the strike and listeners had to rely on their transistors for information. During the course of the stoppage, these six radio summaries were extended and multiplied as the political situation in the province grew more serious but it was on the late night bulletin of 14 May that the BBC first ran into trouble. What they did was to broadcast Harry Murray calling for a strike. It was not a particularly rousing statement and like everyone else the BBC assumed that any strike which did materialize would collapse within hours. Francis was to point out afterwards that since thousands of workers turned up at the factories on the morning of the 15th, the broadcast could not have had much practical effect. Yet by the following Tuesday, when Francis was making his way back from the Castle, several executive ministers, indulging in the luxury of hindsight, were regarding that late-night news bulletin as a seminal moment. They felt that from that night the BBC forgot its responsibilities to the democratically elected administration and had given support - consciously or otherwise - to the strikers.

Francis had in fact given some thought to the recorded Murray interview before it was put on the air but concluded that even if the broadcast influenced people, it was not the BBC's job to be subjective, to report one strike because it appeared to be industrial but to suppress news of another because it was political or because it might prove successful. And when UWC spokesmen were brought to the studio to explain themselves over the next three days, they were subjected to some sharp and distinctly unsympathetic questioning. The UWC actually complained to the BBC at this time that they were not being treated fairly, alleging that radio news bulletins were deliberately playing down support for the strike but exaggerating isolated incidents of intimidation. The Workers Association strike bulletins turned against the BBC in the first week. 'Your reporting has acted as provocation,' one of their bulletins said. 'You have attempted to bring the Ulster Workers Council into disrepute and to represent the strikers as a rampaging mob. You are feeding British public opinion with false reporting which backs up the political bungling of Rees and Orme. You are bringing yourselves into contempt.'[7] Yet within a few days of that broadsheet's publication the BBC was being attacked in the Assembly, where Faulkner told his party men that the Northern Ireland Economic Council was of the opinion that 'radio reports had not been helpful to the situation'. Unionist Assemblyman Peter McLachlan said that the BBC had contributed to an escalation of the strike through the manner in which it was reporting the UWC's activities. To be criticized by two opposing sides in Northern Ireland has traditionally, if somewhat falsely, been equated by the press as a sign of its own impartiality, and so in the first week of the strike most of the BBC staff assumed there was little wrong with their coverage.

By and large, they were probably right. But by the Tuesday of Francis's visit to Rees, Radio Four Northern Ireland was still treating the strike as if it was just one more crisis in the province, more dramatic than earlier loyalist stoppages perhaps, but potentially no more serious in the long term. For this reason, UWC spokesmen were still being interviewed as if they were elected representatives - on the grounds that both sides in a dispute should be given time to put forward their views - and Jim Smyth was thus able to use the BBC on Tuesday evening to tell his supporters that they should resist the British Government:

> *Interviewer:* Do you agree that there has been a certain amount of intimidation this morning and that people couldn't get to work because of this?

> *Smyth:* I think myself that part of the policy of the BBC, the Northern Ireland Office and all other sorts of people has been to try and suggest that there is not widespread support for the stoppage. The Government is trying to deny democratic rights of the majority in this country and we will not be denied.[8]

Smyth was allowed to condemn the authorities, as well as the BBC, without challenge and, when faced later in the same programme with questions about the maintenance of essential services in Ulster, there was no attempt to prevent him stone-walling the points at issue.

The UWC were still being treated with the same indulgence three days later when the *Round-Up Reports* programme carried an extended interview with Harry Murray, Harry Patterson and Pagels. This time the questions were put by Malcolm McCallister, one of the BBC's local staff reporters. Murray said that the UWC was formed 'by grassroot Ulster trade unionists' (which of course was true) but then the broadcast continued:

> *McCallister:* How exactly were the officers of the (UWC) Council elected?

> *Murray:* Democratically - you know, people suggesting that Harry Murray becomes chairman and a vote was taken. So Harry Murray became chairman, and so right down the line.

The interview, in a fifth-floor BBC studio, touched on the UWC executive's system of voting, on Harry Patterson's daily routine as a strike leader - some people, he said, called them the 'Womble government'- and Pagels said that the agricultural industry was not in danger. Then Murray was asked if he was prepared to let people die in hospitals for lack of power. 'It's a very hard question,' he said, 'but I believe in what we are doing and what must be must be. The only thing I would add now is this: it's so critical that I would appeal to all Ulster men and women to lend their weight behind us. The more they do, the more we may force talks and get this over and bring normality back to this province.' Patterson was questioned again on intimidation. 'It was never true in the first place, we never attempted to intimidate anybody going into work - definitely not.' Murray was asked about the UDA's relationship with the UWC. 'The UDA has no connection whatsoever with our organization. These people are honest, industrious. They're workers the same as us but I would say the Ulster Defence Association - the word speaks for itself. They are defensive ... It's a constitutional stoppage and we have the backings *[sic]* of I would say 450,000 people who represent Craig, Paisley and West.'[9]

So once again the strikers were able to use the BBC to put over what was, in effect, a simple propaganda line: that they, and not the Government, represented the people and that almost any action was justified if it helped to bring down Faulkner's executive. Murray's declaration that the UWC council was elected democratically - by 'people suggesting that Harry Murray becomes chairman'[10] - was patently absurd and Patterson's denial of intimidation, which he later softened, was if anything more hollow.[11] Yet both men were allowed to get away with these statements and the only serious attempt to question Murray's conduct - over the issue of power supplies to hospitals - was turned effortlessly into an emotive appeal to Ulstermen 'to lend their weight behind us'. Murray's assertion that the UDA had no connection with the UWC was untrue, as everyone in Belfast knew, although the two organizations did remain technically autonomous; and his vague idea that almost half a million people supported the strike was at the least tendentious since the authorities later estimated that only around a fifth of this figure were actually absent from work at the height of the stoppage.

Not unnaturally, the executive ministers took such broadcasts as evidence that the BBC could not be trusted to support them, if in fact it was not actively engaged in helping the strikers. Their suspicions were not allayed by the few interviews conducted with Faulkner's men. When Paddy Devlin was questioned about a new emergency system of social services payments - which meant that a large number of strikers would not receive the full rate of unemployment benefit - the question was put in such a way that the audience listening must have felt the interviewer distrusted the executive. 'Politically,' the reporter began, 'you'll probably be accused as a member of the SDLP of taking away money from the Protestant working class. How do you feel about that?'[12] Devlin was forced to flounder on about how determined he was people should get 'money they're entitled to' and how 'I don't think there's anything involved in Catholics and Protestants at all'.

Up at Stormont, two ministers asked Rees whether the BBC should be prevented from broadcasting interviews with the UWC leaders, pointing out that the strike was clearly an attempt to overthrow the Government of the province and that it was the duty of the BBC as a state broadcasting organization to stand by the authorities. In times of national crisis, they reasoned, the BBC had always lent its support to the legal government. It did not broadcast Nazi propaganda during the Second World War, nor carry friendly interviews with anarchists threatening to overthrow the British Government; it was not in the habit of inviting the leaders of countries hostile to Britain to express their hostility on the air. So why should the BBC allow the Ulster strikers that right? It was a strong argument. Although the BBC had permitted Hugh Gaitskell, as the Westminster opposition leader, to fulminate against the 1956 invasion of Suez as British soldiers were waiting to disembark from troop ships in the Mediterranean, it had given no credit to the trade unions in the great strike of 1926. Under Reith's management, the BBC had given almost overt support to the Government at that time.[13]

In Ulster in 1974, however, the BBC was not only allowing the strikers air time; it was quoting the UWC's statements at great length, repeating the time when the UWC were to permit shops to open. The strike headquarters regularly issued badly typed sheets of paper listing various restrictions which they had decided to impose on the community and these were passed on to the BBC by the spokesmen on the telephone. Listeners to the twelve fifty-five local news on 21 May, for instance, heard the newsreader interrupt his bulletin to say, 'And we've just learnt that the Ulster Workers Council has agreed to the resumption of bulk supplies of animal feeding stuffs.' The six fifty a.m. bulletin on 24 May reported that 'the Ulster Workers Council has said that there are to be no road blocks but that only what they call "essential users" will get petrol'. At twelve thirty p.m. on 21 May a BBC reporter had begun part of his broadcast with the words; 'Well, at this moment the Ulster Workers Council is engaged in what they describe as "a very important meeting" - and we hope to bring you news of the outcome of that meeting immediately it's over.' It was as if the BBC hung upon the UWC's every word, as to some extent it did. A bulletin on 29 May, the day after the executive fell, announced: 'And now, here's a news flash. The Ulster Workers Council, in a statement just a few minutes ago, said it was now recommending a phased return to work.'

The BBC's constant desire to furnish its audience with news, sometimes of a slender nature, made it seem as though all initiatives in Northern Ireland were being taken by the strikers. And the UWC, sensing the power they had thus acquired, began to use the BBC shamelessly. Two days before the strike ended, I was talking to Harry Patterson outside the strike headquarters in Hawthornden Road when a worried shipyard worker interrupted us to tell the UWC leader that the Harland and Wolff dry-dock was in danger of flooding. What should he do, he asked. 'The Army will have to cope with it,' Patterson told him, 'but if you want instructions, just listen to our statements on the BBC.' Harry Murray, who by the end of the strike had become a proficient broadcaster, was probably the most forthcoming of the strikers when questioned about the BBC's role later in the year. He remembered the publicity that had been accorded to the miners in Britain when they started the national crisis in the winter of 1973 by striking for more pay and eventually brought about the February election which pushed the Tories from office. 'The miners taught us that the mass media could make or break us,' he said. 'The BBC were marvellous - they were prepared to be fed any information. They fell into their own trap that "the public must get the news". Sometimes they were just a news service for us; we found that if the media was on our side we didn't need a gun.'

What finally convinced the SDLP members of the executive that the BBC - or at least a section of its staff - openly sympathized with the aims of the Protestant strike (a conviction for which there was no real justification) was a remarkable broadcast in which a reporter actually gave out the telephone number of the UWC headquarters so that listeners could contact the self-elected loyalist leaders for passes and permission to obtain petrol. The number of the official Government information centre had been given over the air some days previously and by supplying the UWC's number as well, the BBC appeared to be acknowledging the authority of the strikers, perhaps even giving them a stamp of approval. Rees was furious when this was reported to him and Faulkner made strong representations to civil servants at Stormont about the incident. Even Francis, who listened to nearly every local broadcast in his first-floor office in Ormeau Avenue, had reservations about the decision, although he still felt that the BBC's duty to give information to its audience over-rode other considerations. He was to go on record later as saying:

> Perhaps we should have said: 'If you wish to contact the UWC, the number to ring is ...' We may have made a mistake in saying, merely, 'The number to ring is ...' But I think we were absolutely right to carry the UWC statements. Any statement liable to affect the welfare and daily life of people in the province deserves to be reported.'[14]

To some degree, this was a doctrine which was sternly if not always enthusiastically embraced by the BBC in 1926 when a national rather than a regional strike was threatening the Government. Regular news bulletins on the infant BBC included information about Government statements, Parliamentary reports and messages while special bulletins were prepared on rail and road transport during the General Strike. There were extra news flashes on BBC Northern Ireland in May 1974 to cope with the changing situation on the roads, the barricades put up by the UDA and bus services. The 1926 BBC also carried a regular feature analysing the news, an 'appreciation of the situation'[15] which may have borne a faint similarity to the reports in May 1974 of W. D. Flackes, the BBC Northern Ireland's very uncontroversial political correspondent. But there the parallel ends, for a directive to BBC station directors on 7 May 1926 said that 'nothing calculated to extend the area of the strike should be broadcast'.[16] In 1926 the BBC failed to put labour or trade unionist speakers on the air since the strike had been declared illegal. During the Ulster Workers Council strike, no such practice was adopted by the BBC in Northern Ireland. UWC statements, like those of the 1926 strikers, were included in regular news bulletins but the decision to allow the UWC men to continue to broadcast in Belfast long after Merlyn Rees had described the strike as 'political' - the nearest any minister came to the concept of illegality - was unprecedented. It was not surprising, therefore, that the Ulster executive began seriously to question the BBC's loyalty. The Unionists, including Faulkner, thought that the old Reithian traditions (impartiality combined with 'responsibility' to elected government) had been forgotten, while the SDLP, who had in the past regarded the BBC as a tool of the Unionist Government, felt doubly betrayed since it no longer seemed to be supporting the establishment once Catholics had a share of power.

They had other complaints. During the strike, the BBC could call on the resources of sixteen news reporters and nine copytakers and secretaries as well as six producers, nine freelance reporters and five secretaries in its current affairs department in Northern Ireland. But, with almost hourly bulletins and at one time five magazine programmes each day, this small staff could hardly keep pace with the amount of work that was required of them. One freelance made 72 broadcasts in just twelve days while another earned a total of £800 in the same period of time. Nearly all were Northern Ireland reporters, born and brought up in the province and - for this needs to be remembered - there is not a scrap of evidence to suggest that any deliberately tried to bias their reports in favour of one side or another. What did happen, however, was that the staff were forced by circumstances - principally the sheer amount of time devoted to live broadcasting - to abandon any attempt at examining the political and constitutional implications of the strike. They used up their talents in composing the unending stream of special news bulletins which detailed the location of road-blocks, the political statements, the problems of the social services, the availability of bread and transport; constantly trying to keep this information up to date and searching for a new angle to make their summaries more informative, they could do no more than scratch the surface when it came to analysing the causes of the strike and the intentions of the men behind it. It was not their fault nor McCallister's in that interview with the UWC - that no attempt was made to probe the background, both social and political, of such a serious situation.

But this failure created its own problems. The reporters, most of them not yet graduated to the national staff of the BBC, became at times almost infatuated with the drama which they were reporting and unintentionally, some of them began to inject a sensational note into their reports. This particularly applied to reports on the farming industry. Reporter Frank Hannah, for instance, began one item on the subject in this way: 'Disaster, chaos, the greatest crisis ever - some of the words used yesterday to describe the effects the strike was having on agriculture ...' No one troubled to explain who, if anyone, had used these clichés but the BBC's Ulster agriculture correspondent, John Johnston, added a few of his own. 'Many livestock farmers,' he began, 'must be afraid to wake up this morning. Where animal food is concerned, this is "D-Day" and the terrible possibility is that it could be "D for Disaster" ... our most important industry faces this morning the grim reality of being in unprecedented chaos.'[17] Only an hour later, the loquacious Johnston - himself an Antrim farmer - was to add: 'It's true to say that agriculture is virtually on its knees and the repercussions will take a long time to resolve - an industry in total disarray.' The prophecies about Ulster's farming industry grew gradually more frenetic as the strike continued, culminating in an extraordinary broadcast at eight thirty a.m. on 28 May by reporter Alan Giff who announced that 'in less than two weeks, a multi-million pound industry is facing a collapse never before witnessed in the western world.' He forgot, of course, two world wars, countless religious conflicts in Europe, the Hundred Years' War and the economic consequences of the fall of the Roman Empire. Reporters in Ulster occasionally suffered the sin of the ancient cartographers: of thinking Jerusalem was the centre of the world. Both Johnston and Giff had become caught up in the speed, the intense journalistic excitement, of reporting an important news story, but they allowed their own apocalyptic account of events to outdistance the seriousness of the deteriorating situation around them. They were not alone in this.

For the most memorable of all the broadcasters during the strike - a man who was to become a household name for thousands of people in Ulster but who was to infuriate executive ministers - was a cheerful, informed, hard-working, sincere middle-aged man called Hugo Patterson, the official spokesman for the Northern Ireland Electricity Service. He was also the BBC's regional cricket correspondent but during the stoppage he was employed solely by the NIES and took no remuneration from the BBC. Patterson, a rotund, homely figure who could be seen as an almost permanent fixture in the BBC offices during the strike, was constantly on the telephone to the electricity board for situation reports, walking between studios for interviews on local and national radio, sometimes even for the World Service of the BBC. His message was almost inevitably one of gravity and doom: that the electrical power in the province was being steadily reduced by the strikers towards a point at which it would be impossible - perhaps for several weeks - to return power to the province. A city without power - indeed a state without power creates food riots and looting and although Patterson did not use such a description it was the ultimate disaster which, he threatened, would engulf the province.

On 21 May Patterson told the population that so far as electricity was concerned there was 'no joy at all for anybody'. The system was 'teetering on the brink of collapse' with only half the province on power at any one time. That was at around seven thirty in the morning. An hour later, he was to say: 'If anything breaks, if anything goes down, we are really in trouble because the system ... will just die and the rest of the province will be without supply permanently.' At five thirty that evening, Patterson told his audience that 'the situation remains critical, balanced on a knife-edge'. Listeners who could neither cook nor travel nor work nor undertake any form of social activity save to sit at home in darkness at night understandably took the electricity spokesman seriously. Their sense of fear was further increased only 24 hours later when Patterson was explaining that there was a shortage of chemicals at Ballylumford power station. 'We're beginning to accept,' he said, '... that the whole system may have to close down in four days at the most ... so this must be the beginning of the end. There's no more tricks we can play. There's nothing else we can do to pull out of the bag ... It now looks a hopeless situation going steadily out of control ... a complete blackout is staring us in the face.' The UWC were to release some of those vital chemicals, but five days later Patterson was back at his work again, this time announcing that the electricity system was working 'on a wing and a prayer'.

John Hume wanted Patterson taken out of the BBC. In fact several of Faulkner's ministers asked Rees whether the Government could not censor the BBC and prevent the kind of broadcast - 'scaremongering' as they saw it - which was being made by Patterson. As Hume was Minister of Commerce, he had control over the management of the electricity industry but, such was the division of political power between sovereign and regional administrations in Ulster, it never occurred to the executive that they had the ability to silence Patterson without any recourse to censorship. So the indefatigable electricity spokesman was allowed to continue his almost hourly broadcasts and, notwithstanding evidence to the contrary (namely the obvious desire of the UWC not to break up the power system unless no other alternative was left to it), the population was warned again of the terminal experience that it was to undergo. By 27 May, the first of three generators had been shut down at Ballylumford and Patterson was saying that the system would now be unable to resume operations even if the machine was brought back to life. 'By midnight tomorrow,' he said, 'there'll be no power at all from the station.' Two hours later, just after nine thirty, Patterson was interviewed by freelance reporter Barry Cowan and, in view of later events and the considerable effect this particular broadcast had upon Faulkner and his ministers, it is worth recording:

Patterson: Let's be clear about this; this shutdown is on, it's complete, it's final, it's irrevocable. I don't think there's any going back on this one now.

Cowan: In other words, as of two minutes ago, nine-thirty, the complete shutdown of power in Northern Ireland has begun and cannot now be stopped.

Patterson: ... you're right.

Patterson had twice been telephoned by Stormont civil servants. On one occasion he had suggested on the BBC that power would be cut off if the Army entered the power stations and this drew an instant reproof from Rees's men. On the second, he implied that power would be cut off for good if the Army manned petrol stations in Belfast. This gained him his second call from Stormont. But his message remained the same and it was summed up in his own unforgettable but trite phrase: 'We are past the point of no return.' Neither the electricity service, nor the province which it supplied, was ever in that situation but it provided the most potent symbol of the strike: the inevitability of catastrophe if the executive remained in office. It was a message which the BBC, in its news broadcasts, its magazine programmes, its interviews and its on-the-spot reports, repeated again and again although this was neither a deliberate nor, in many cases, even a conscious act.

Indeed, the BBC jealously guarded its independence. It stood up to threats from the UWC and one member of the management refused to be intimidated when a loyalist politician told him that if all power was cut off as a result of a BBC broadcast - which had referred to a 'climb-down' by the strikers - then it would be the direct responsibility of the reporters concerned. The politician was told that his statement was no more than a trick. And Francis, aware that the BBC's generators could be affected by the UWC's petrol blockade, perfected and put into operation a dramatic plan to maintain fuel supplies at the BBC.

With the tacit permission of both Stormont and the Irish Government, he arranged for hundreds of gallons of fuel to be secretly transported overnight from the Irish Republic across the border into Ulster. Reporters travelling south of the frontier on business were urged to return with petrol cans filled with diesel fuel and on one occasion a BBC lorry was used to ferry petrol over the County Louth border at Killeen. Many of the staff did not know of the scheme until, late one night, a reporter saw a BBC truck being unloaded behind the radio offices in Ormeau Avenue. The fuel was bought mainly in Dublin but also in the Irish border town of Dundalk which, like nearly every other town in the Republic, was unaffected by the strike in the north. Vans containing engineering equipment and props also arrived in Belfast with jerry-cans stacked in their trailers. [...] In this way, Francis ensured that whatever happened to the Northern Ireland coalition, the BBC'S own stand-by generators could remain in operation. The BBC, in short, was to remain independent and no UWC strike was going to take that independence away.

But this brave gesture only served to emphasize the weakness of the BBC. By concentrating on hourly news reports, on instant journalism, it appeared characteristically and damagingly conformist, apparently prepared to respect whichever group possessed political power. While Patterson - who was quite genuinely broadcasting information gleaned from managerial colleagues in the electricity service and was not in a position to interpret events - was presented each day as a regular magician, so the bulletins sounded occasionally as if they were part of a schoolboy adventure. If an attempt had been made to explore the political and moral issues behind the strike, it is possible that the BBC could have aroused people's awareness to the lack of decisive government action, the failure of will in the police force, the right-wing, apparently fascist nature of the UWC and the fact that the future of Northern Ireland and not just the executive was at stake. In the event, the strike sometimes created an almost carnival atmosphere on the airwaves and the BBC, in its desire to be fair to both sides in the strike, fell between two stools; it could convince neither the Government nor the strikers of its impartiality.

But to throw blame for the BBC's political failure upon the BBC itself is unfair. Many people telephoned Francis and his colleagues after the stoppage to thank them for their work; a high proportion of these callers wanted to express their personal gratitude to Hugo Patterson who had told them details of every power cut during the strike. The BBC's young reporting staff in Belfast coped as best they could with a national news story of immense importance to their own lives. They were sometimes in physical danger as they went about their jobs and some of their reports - particularly during the days of barricade-building - were not only graphic but made Faulkner and his ministers embarrassed at the lack of action by the security forces. Barry Cowan in particular distinguished himself by annoying the UWC in a brutal interview towards the end of the stoppage in which he questioned their motives more sharply than most of his fellow press reporters had done. And if the clichés, the exaggeration and the artificial atmosphere of crisis engendered by the BBC can be criticized, they do not balance out the signal failure of the Government and executive to speak for themselves. Their own weakness and indecision was heightened by their refusal to take Francis's advice that Tuesday morning. Repeatedly - and this was an experience shared by Ulster Television - reporters would ask for official spokesmen to give a point of view on behalf of the administration, yet these spokesmen would never be forthcoming. If the BBC helped to create the atmosphere of crisis, so did the executive. Caught between a desire to emphasize the serious effects of the strike and a natural wish to demonstrate that the UWC could not overcome the Stormont ministers, officials vacillated between predictions of chaos and total silence. It was the executive which had suggested the social service system was on the verge of collapse. And it was John Hume who predicted on 27 May in a radio interview that 'there will be anarchy, there will be civil strife' if the UWC gained their objectives. It was the Ulster Farmers Union, stunned by the Government's impotence, that persuaded Johnston that their industry was facing financial disaster. The BBC, as an accurate mirror of society, only reflected these failings. To some extent, the BBC might have been compared to the innocent and ubiquitous medieval messenger who told the king that his army was losing a battle; unable to visit his wrath upon those responsible, the sovereign would traditionally assault the messenger instead.

Francis later wrote a report to the BBC board of governors on the strike and his views were also given to the BBC advisory council. It was the indecisive nature of Rees's and Faulkner's administration that was showed up by one of Francis's conclusions. 'As an independent institution,' his report said, 'we had a duty to reflect significant bodies of opinion - however arrived at - as much as to support institutions of democracy not widely accepted.'

It was not the fault of the BBC that the executive lacked acceptance although it might have unintentionally added support to the significant body of opinion. This was certainly the view south of the border where Dr Conor Cruise O'Brien, the Irish Minister for Posts and Telegraphs, rang the BBC in London from his office in the Dublin General Post Office to ask whether Sir Charles Curran, the Director General, was aware of the nature of the Northern Ireland broadcasts. He said - it was a typical 'Cruiser' phrase - that Ulster's programmes contained 'a sizeable pro-strike propaganda charge' and were 'on the wrong lines'. The Irish Government never revealed that one of their ministers had made such a complaint and neither did the BBC. John Crawley, Curran's chief assistant, replied to the Dublin minister in a confidential letter dated 28 May, saying that 'nobody echoed your own view that we were on the wrong lines', that some points of criticism had been passed on to Belfast but that regional broadcasts in Ulster had been 'unexceptionable and valuable' during the strike. Curran stood by these words when he said in the BBC's own staff magazine later in 1974 that he had been 'proud' when he listened to the tapes of the local Northern Ireland strike programmes. 'If ever,' he said, 'there was a public service - solid, reliable information, useful to those who were hearing it, and yet objective to a degree that was almost incredible - this was it.'[18]

Curran's praise was as far from reality as the Government's condemnation of the BBC - Radio 4 Northern Ireland could scarcely boast 'solid, reliable information' when Hugo Patterson was pushing out so many inaccurate predictions - but as usual it was the UWC which put such arguments into perspective. For whether the BBC had remained independent or not, the strikers had their own plans ready for broadcasting in the event of a full-scale revolt. They did not want to take over the BBC because they had their own radio station ready for action. Its existence, which was first revealed in a local Belfast Sunday newspaper in the spring of 1975,[19] was known only to a few UWC men. There were at least two transmitters, one of them operating in the Portadown area from a truck, and nearly all the material was to be taped before broadcasting, giving the Army no chance of discovering the names of the people behind the station should the electrical equipment fall into the hands of the military authorities. The UWC claim, quite wrongly, that a test broadcast was picked up in Scotland. But it was heard all over Belfast and Protestants would undoubtedly have tuned in to what was to have been called the Ulster Broadcasting Corporation. One news bulletin that actually went on the air would have been listened to by the British Government as well, had they known of the new radio station operating from County Armagh. 'This is the Ulster Broadcasting Corporation,' it began in the second week of the strike. 'Here is the news. The London Government has been sternly warned that if troops are used in any capacity, other than in security, work will cease immediately in all services throughout Ulster, including all essential services. The latter would include both power stations and oil and petroleum refining and distribution ...' [...]

The lessons of May 1974 were still being considered in Northern Ireland a year later when the loyalist politicians and private armies - in a rare moment of unanimity - were preparing to celebrate the first anniversary of their *coup d'état*. Debates were still going on, for instance, within the BBC and the Northern Ireland Office about the role of broadcasters when the existence of the state is in question. Should the BBC have undertaken a measure of self-censorship, refusing to allow the UWC air time and giving out less information about road-blocks, violence and intimidation? Or, conscious of its primary duty - to its listeners - should it have given time to every viewpoint, filling every available minute with news and political comment?

In the weeks after the strike, Wilson's officials at Downing Street, who were resentful and highly critical of Rees's own public relations men at Stormont for the way they had handled the crisis, decided that the Secretary of State should have a consultant on public relations attached to him at Stormont Castle. During the summer Michael Cudlipp, a highly reticent civil servant who had once been deputy editor of *The Times* and then gone on to be chief editor of a commercial broadcasting station (only to resign nine months later), arrived in Belfast. He never chose to reveal all his functions. (When I questioned him on the telephone about his job in the spring of 1975, he agreed that he chaired 'a committee' but would not disclose its purpose. He said this was 'a private matter', complained of feeling unwell and asked to terminate the conversation.) However, he made a considerable number of inquiries about the BBC and according to Army sources, he brought with him a number of 'psychological operations' officers from the Ministry of Defence. He even went so far as to question journalists about the loyalties of the BBC staff over a dinner at the Culloden Hotel at which both Merlyn Rees and one of his ministers, Don Concannon, were present. Cudlipp, whose appointment at Stormont ended in August 1975, is believed to have written a long report on the BBC in Northern Ireland, although its contents remain unknown. What is known is that very senior civil servants assisting Rees were still deeply dissatisfied at the BBC's coverage during the strike. When Francis's *modus vivendi* about the BBC having 'a duty to reflect significant bodies of opinion however arrived at as much as to support institutions of democracy not widely accepted' was read out to one of them, his only comment was, 'I suppose they had to say something.' Yet this avoids the issues with which the BBC had to grapple during the strike. The Northern Ireland service lacked analysis and it lacked perspective, but it could not act as a historical commentator when events were changing in rapid succession. There was a lack of depth in the questioning of all the leading participants of the strike yet the suppression of a section of these participants - in this case the UWC - would hardly have added perspective to anyone's understanding of the crisis. 80 per cent of the BBC's advisory council to whom Francis's report was sent were convinced that the BBC was bound to cover the strike in the way it did, and only three members thought that the UWC statements should not have been carried in full. Yet what is to happen in Britain if trade unions, political parties or other groups stage industrial unrest on such a scale as to endanger the Government? Could the BBC, in these circumstances, continue to broadcast the comments of the strike leaders as they did in Ulster when Jim Smyth was able to appeal to the population over the air to support the UWC? The Government may already have concluded that some form of statutory power will be needed, and must already be drawn up in rough draft, if civil unrest spreads on the mainland of Britain. The BBC's struggle in May 1974, against a Government that was both vacillating and at times more than incompetent, will have been the test case upon which such legislation is based. In the Republic of Ireland, the Dublin Government, under section 31 of an amended Broadcasting Act, could prohibit certain broadcasts which encourage crime. It is more than likely that a similar bill exists in London. [...]

Endnotes

1. Merlyn Rees, Secretary of State for Northern Ireland. One of his Northern Ireland Office ministers, mentioned later, was Stan Orme.
2. When Westminster MPS objected the following November to an interview with David O'Connell, the IRA chief of staff, on Thames Television, Rees saw no harm in the programme. He took the line that the public would now know the nature of the man who led the Provisionals.
3. Lord Scarman's report (p. 50) said that no such broadcast had in fact been made but his findings were important nonetheless. The two witnesses who

were 'adamant' they had heard the report must have concluded missiles were hurled at the Protestants because the BBC news referred to 'an incident in which bottles and stones were thrown'. But the BBC did not say who they were thrown at.

4. Simon Winchester in his book *In Holy Terror* (p. 142) refers to an incident in 1971 when he was watching angry Orangemen milling around Unity Flats. He was aware, as the crowd was not, that four Protestants had just been shot in east Belfast:

> Naturally enough I kept quiet. But what if I had been working for the BBC, and had reported the shooting; and what if one of the Loyalists in that crowd had had a transistor set? I began to have doubts, from that moment on, about the precise role the press - and particularly the broadcasters - were playing in Ireland. Would not this have been the ideal case for some kind of self-censorship, I wondered? Did we always have to report everything we saw, as we saw it, warts and all?

5. Brookeborough (then John Brooke) argued in 1971 for a form of BBC self-censorship, a one-hour delay in reporting incidents.

6. There are twelve transmitter stations in the province and the IRA had bombed them on a number of occasions. On 6 January 1971 the Brougher mountain relay station in County Tyrone was damaged by gelignite and just over a month later a BBC landrover was blown up by a mine a few yards from the transmitter with the loss of five lives. But during the strike no sabotage occurred to BBC property by either the IRA or Protestant extremists.

7. The Workers' Association also raised the question of interviews with extremist leaders and suggested that standards applied to the IRA were not adopted by the media when Protestants wished to make their case known. Their bulletin took a swipe at me as well: 'Many of you, in the name of impartial reporting, have spent much time talking to Provisionals, and reporting their version of events. Robert Fisk of *The Times,* to cite one example, justified this approach on Northern Ireland radio recently. He justified impartial reporting of the "enemy" case because he regarded the Northern Ireland conflict as a civil disturbance within the state rather than as a conflict between the state and its enemies. But when it comes to the Ulster Workers Council and an industrial strike ... Mr Fisk's journalistic impartiality evaporates, and he reports the strike as if he were a paid propagandist of Merlyn Rees' Ministry.' The Workers Association, of course, made no mention of intimidation.

8. Broadcast, Radio 4 Northern Ireland, 5.40 p.m., 21 May.

9. Broadcast, Radio 4 Northern Ireland, 8.10 a.m., 24 May.

10. It was, of course, Hugh Petrie who first suggested Murray as chairman of the UWC.

11. 'Naturally,' he said, 'in a situation like this you will get people exploiting the situation such as certain rabble.'

12. Broadcast, Radio 4 Northern Ireland, 8.10 a.m., 24 May.

13. Asa Briggs noted that 'even in the General Strike the BBC had been "used" to back the government of the day'; *The History of Broadcasting in the United Kingdom,* Vol. II, *The Golden Age of Wireless,* Oxford University Press, 1965, p. 503.

14. Quoted in *Radio Times*, 12 September 1974, p. 14.
15. See Briggs, Vol. 1, *The Birth of Broadcasting*, Oxford University Press, 1961, p. 369.
16. *Ibid.*, p. 373.
17. Broadcast, Radio 4 Northern Ireland, 7.10 a.m., 21 May.
18. *Ariel*, BBC Staff Journal 18 September 1974, p. 1.
19. *Sunday News*, 30 March 1975, p. 8.

4.

Richard Francis

BROADCASTING TO A COMMUNITY IN CONFLICT - THE EXPERIENCE IN NORTHERN IRELAND

(A lecture given at the Royal Institute of International Affairs, Chatham House, 22 February 1977; published as a BBC pamphlet)

[...] 'Broadcasting to a Community in Conflict - the Experience in Northern Ireland': the very title might suggest a fallacy. Certainly we have conflict in Northern Ireland, but it would be unwise to consider it is contained within a single community! Indeed, our task is not only to broadcast to two distinct communities and to reflect two cultures within the province, but also in network programmes to broadcast to people throughout the United Kingdom, and incidentally to half the population in the Republic of Ireland who can also see and hear our programmes. All this makes the job for the broadcaster in Northern Ireland both more difficult and more telling.

Broadcasting of its very nature transcends borders; in a fractured society, propagation of a singular point of view or an objective version of events is significant in itself. Thus, our programmes on Irish history for all schools in the province are of rare value in a divided education system. Our Neighbourhood programmes, produced in the heart of sectarian ghettos but heard across the divide, demonstrate the other man's problems are no different ... significant in a province where de facto segregation is becoming ever more marked.

Conflict of course doesn't necessarily mean violence. Between and within the communities of Northern Ireland there is conflict because the normal reconciliation mechanisms have not worked. Often, as at the moment, when there is a political vacuum in the province, the broadcaster finds himself providing a unique forum for the exchange of conflicting views. But because there is notoriously no consensus in Northern Ireland, what many people want from the broadcaster is not so much reason or impartiality but the reinforcement of their prejudices.

For the first three or four years of the present troubles, whenever we broadcast an objective version of events, there would be loud protests from one side or other of the divide. The chorus has diminished over the years. It seems now that, apart from wearying of the problems, Ulster people have come to recognise that the broadcasters are going to tell them how it is and that some of the things they hear they will not like. Nowadays it is more often the moderates who object to the views of extremists being aired.

One thing everyone in Northern Ireland still wants is news of the situation. Whenever there is trouble in the streets or the sound of an explosion rocks the town, people turn to the radio to find out what is happening. [...] If we fail to report incidents of violence invariably we will attract criticism from people in the vicinity.

The BBC in Northern Ireland is no different in essence from Ulster Television or any of the media. The several members of staff who have joined the BBC from UTV or the press all agree they find no real difference in policy or practice. But we do have a problem in being the British Broadcasting Corporation. The very title creates an expectation on the part of some people on the loyalist side that we should overtly support British institutions. When we allow people to attack these institutions on the air we are accused of undermining authority. On the other hand, the 'British' in our title creates an air of suspicion among republicans. Nevertheless, it has been important to our broadcasters in Northern Ireland that we are part of a national institution such as the BBC. It is important in resisting pressures that we are answerable to the Director General and to the BBC's Board of Governors in London. The various BBC advisory bodies in the province, such as the Northern Ireland Advisory Council, do provide guidance for the professionals and a local sounding board for the products of our policies and judgements. But, ultimately, it is the BBC's editorial unity which provides the essential stability in an often unstable environment.

Perhaps there are lessons to be learnt from Northern Ireland simply because the experience there, of sharp conflict between and within deeply divided communities, throws into relief some of the fundamental issues for the broadcaster in any democratic society today. At least I believe it illustrates the need to enlarge public understanding of the most uncomfortable problems in their midst. I believe it illustrates the need to minimize public concern when actions, often inexplicable and horrific, threaten everyday life. I believe it throws light on the problems of impartially reflecting significant forces in society, of whatever origin, as much as supporting democratic institutions not wholly accepted. Above all, I think it illustrates the need for the broadcaster jealously to guard his independence and his credibility.

In taking an independent and impartial position, we are sometimes asked whose side is the BBC on? The implication is that we should take sides, that in a situation lacking consensus the BBC should stand by the government 'in the national interest'. But which government? Which national interest? Often the government at Westminster has been at odds with Stormont. Often the Westminster government's point of view has been opposed, not only by undemocratic and violent organisations, but also by a majority of elected politicians in the province. Surely, the national interest must lie in solving the problem, and the public's interest in being given reliable information about the problem in their midst?

The experience in Northern Ireland, where communities and governments are in conflict but not in a state of emergency or a state of war, suggests a greater need than ever for the media to function as the 'fourth estate,' distinct from the executive, the legislature and the judiciary. But if the functions are to remain separate, it must be left to the media themselves to take the decisions (within the limits of responsibility) as to what to publish, as to when, and as to how. That puts a lot of responsibility on all of us to answer these questions wisely, not, I submit, by adopting special criteria for Northern Ireland, but by deploying the best available professional skills and by scrupulously fair dealing.

There is a commonly held belief that, if only the media would cease or tone down their reporting, the problem would go away. It has been suggested that Northern Ireland is an example of a region where violence is often reported but not the determination of the great majority of people to preserve the real values in society. Certainly these feelings are apparent in Westminster. But the perception of the BBC in Northern Ireland is very different to people living in the province than it is to those living this side of the water. In Britain the dominant image is that of the front page pictures of destruction on television news and the ritual recital of overnight violence on the Radio 4 morning bulletins. Whereas the 40-second film clip of an explosion is explicit, a 60-minute Ulster play on Radio 4 or a 30-minute concert by the BBC Northern Ireland Orchestra on Radio 3 are only implicit in demonstrating normal life in the province. Yet there can be no question of managing news for the national networks in order to restore some sort of balance between 'good' and 'bad'.

In Northern Ireland, our extensive coverage of sport, our sponsorship of musicians, writers and actors, the daily advertising of events and discussion of household matters in regional programmes such as *Good Morning Ulster, Taste of Hunni,* and our access and community programmes are all apparent. More than 80 per cent of Radio Ulster's output is concerned with normality. The BBC is committed to supporting such important ventures as the Queen's Festival, the Belfast City Festival, the Derry Feis, and so on. But I would argue that our coverage of bad news also contributes to maintaining real values in society. A thorough and reliable knowledge of society's ills and of the other man's unpalatable views are essential for any realistic evaluation. The Peace Movement stemmed from popular revulsion amongst the working class ghettos at the endless violence in their midst. The media's relentless chronicling of every bomb and bullet cannot fail to have spread the ugly message into less affected homes - remember Vietnam?

Arguably, where the network news can go wrong over Northern Ireland is by doing too little; news values are relative, and disruption in the province (two bombs and one killing a day on average last year) is no longer exceptional. But when shootings and explosions destroying whole businesses in the UK'S eighth largest city go unreported on the network news and in the national dailies - as happens more and more frequently - when a small incendiary in Liverpool rates a headline before the assassination of a prominent Ulster industrialist; when a bomb in a north-west London pillar-box rates the same amount of film as the destruction of Belfast's central parcels sorting office ... then perhaps we are no longer concerned for the real values in our society! If the violent activities of terrorists go unreported, there must be a danger that they may escalate their actions to make their point. And, if we don't seek, with suitable safeguards, to report and to expose the words of terrorist front organisations, we may well be encouraging them to speak more and more with violence.

Does the BBC as a whole pay too little attention to the underlying problems of Northern Ireland? I don't think so. Despite the diminished news interest, the flow of analytical programmes has been fairly constant. Over the last six years, on the BBC television networks alone, there have been 349 current affairs features about Northern Ireland (anything from 5 to 50 minutes) - that's rather more than one a week. Over the last fortnight there have been two complete editions of *The Money Programme* on BBC 2 looking into the province's economic difficulties. Since 1971 there have been three major studio enquiries into the political options for Ulster, 24 documentary films, ten 25-minute programmes (twice repeated) and an accompanying book on the historical background - coverage far in excess of any other regional problem in the UK, including devolution!

Do we give the violence too much prominence on regional programmes? Do radio and television concentrate on violence because of its immediacy or its visual impact? I doubt it. The people in the worst affected areas invariably accuse us of underplaying their plight. To give you one example: between 13 and 16 February last year, Northern Ireland had one of its worst weekends of violence. There were eight deaths, 87 shootings, 56 hijackings, 17 bombs and 126 arrests. The regional television news programmes over that weekend totalled exactly one hour. The reporting of all this violence amounted to no more than 15 minutes (25 per cent), politics amounted to 20 minutes (one-third), and the rest of the time, 25 minutes or just under half the total, was devoted to news of other peaceful matters - plans for a new power station; cheaper petrol; the Arts Council annual report; cheap bus fares to London; a fashion-show; sport and weather, etc.

One reason the BBC has found itself under pressure in Northern Ireland stems from its historical position. Regional radio started from Belfast in 1924, less than three years after partition. Originally, for understandable reasons, it was felt that broadcasting like other institutions in Northern Ireland, should not question the fundamental premise on which the new State was built. [...]

Even when the BBC Northern Ireland Advisory Council was introduced in 1947, at the very first meeting the Chairman ruled that the question of Partition and the Border was out of order. A solemn directive was issued by the Regional Director at that time stating that BBC policy was 'not to admit any attack on the constitutional position of Northern Ireland'. That was in 1947. During the 50's and 60's things began to change, and efforts were made to emphasise not only what was common between the different communities. Programmes were introduced in which consistently, but in controlled circumstances, essential differences could be aired. But the fact is that up to 1968 the accent on the positive, coupled with the periodic denial of air time to people outspoken in their criticism of the status quo, failed to convince the public of the troubles which were just over the horizon. By accentuating the middle ground, the BBC unwittingly may have lulled people into a sense of security which subsequent events were so rudely to shatter.

By 1968-69 the BBC, in common with the rest of the media, was faced with the physical manifestations of conflict and had to hold up a mirror to the reality. There was no way in which the facts of unrest within the country could go uncovered. The question then became not whether it should be covered, but how? And for the first time the BBC was faced within the United Kingdom with having to consider not merely the right of people to know what was happening in their midst, but also what effect the broadcasts might have on public behaviour.

Over the last eight years the greatest consideration has been given within the Corporation to the consequences of what is to be broadcast. It's one thing to broadcast about Northern Ireland for the people of Britain - that is perhaps parallel to the American experience in learning about Vietnam - it is quite another when those same broadcasts are heard and seen day and daily by the people caught up in the events themselves. Nevertheless, we learned early on that all programmes made in Britain about Northern Ireland should be suitable for transmission in the province. Only on one occasion, and to my mind it proved the rule, was a network programme not shown in Ulster because it was considered too inflammatory. [...]

There have been very real questions to answer about how to deal with the often unprecedented circumstances. Invariably, the question that I come back to is not what happens if we do broadcast such and such, but what happens if we don't? The key problem is how to exercise control of a free, pluralistic system when editorial decisions could put lives and livelihoods at risk. The BBC's system of delegating responsibility to the lowest practical level is essentially no different to that of any broadcaster - the reason is inherent in the medium. Managers and editors have to rely heavily upon the judgement of the man on the spot. Commensurate with this principle is the system of referring up, by exception, matters of doubt and difficulty. Normally, the onus to identify these matters is with the individual producer or editor - in the case of BBC programmes about Northern Ireland it is mandatory to consult with me or my deputies before proceeding and during their preparation. Early warning, briefing and consultation is essential if the Controller in Northern Ireland or the Editor of News and Current Affairs in London is not to be caught between last-minute 'censorship' or disregard. [...]

Delegation of responsibility puts a great deal of onus on selecting the right persons for the job, on training them, and on ensuring the growth of their experience over the years. We do have written editorial guidelines, but inevitably these are somewhat didactic and limited to anticipated situations. More importantly, we have a system of regular conferences between senior editors who study difficult and unprecedented cases, generally retrospectively. Through the minutes of these meetings, circulated amongst all the journalistic areas of the BBC, we build up precedents and case histories so that the lessons learnt on one occasion may be applied or considered for application to similar cases in the future. The strength of our news and current affairs programmes in and about Northern Ireland lies in their being considered in a continuous climate by a large number of professionals forming a view of the situation, each required to consult and to liaise. The calibre and credibility of the output depends mainly on the informed judgement of individuals rather than on rigid central control.

A prime example of the BBC having to proceed in Northern Ireland without benefit of carefully written guidelines was, of course, the UWC strike in May 1974. We were not alone in being affected by something unprecedented and unexpected. Coverage of the strike made for exceptional difficulties, both logistic and editorial. For supplies and transport, the BBC had to remain and to be seen to remain independent of both the UWC and the Army.

In seeking to report objectively, our task was not made easier by the fact that, throughout, the self-appointed UWC called the political tune and that, for long periods, the Northern Ireland Office and the Executive seemed to be powerless and speechless. News is abnormality, and with the situation liable to change by the hour there was a great deal of it to report; but most of it stemmed from the actions of the UWC. When we did take reports from around the province which indicated normality, owners of concerns still running implored us not to mention them lest they became targets. Similarly, for obvious reasons, very few of the people who told us they had been intimidated were prepared to come forward with chapter and verse. Inevitably, we were criticized for underplaying normality!

Clearly, the BBC's task was to report the situation as it presented itself as impartially as possible. But that in itself presented difficulties. The UWC strike was unique in that, on day one we were dealing with the equivalent of an unofficial industrial stoppage, by day fifteen we were dealing with a self-appointed body who had brought down a government by undemocratic means. To have changed our editorial posture during the strike - unless, for instance, the strike had been declared illegal - would have been unthinkable. Similarly, to have refused to carry UWC statements unless or until government retorts were forthcoming would have implied a power of veto. The UWC initiatives affected the daily lives of everyone in the province and the public had a right to know what was happening. In the face of Government inactivity and official silence, our coverage was inevitably somewhat unbalanced. Experience of the UWC strike suggests that the BBC's credibility depends more on impartiality than balance, and our responsibility lies as much in reflecting the significant voices of the people, including subversives, as in sustaining institutions of democracy not wholly accepted.

It must be stressed that we are not impartial as between democratic and undemocratic means. We do not give equal time to right and wrong, there never has been any question of that, though we have been accused of being prepared to give equal time to Satan and to Jesus Christ! The concept of impartiality is queried because, as I said earlier, some people believe we should be taking sides, that we should be positively on the side of authority and against the subversives. Often we have been accused of undermining the Army's credibility by introducing their statements with the phrase 'the Army say'; but the experience of all the media in Northern Ireland has led them to treat with circumspection statements, from whatever source, until the facts are established. Generally, therefore, we will report that 'the Army say', whereas the paramilitaries 'claim' or 'allege'. Wording is crucial. Similarly, we were heavily criticised during the UWC strike for giving status to the UWC by reporting the address and telephone number of their headquarters. I am sure we were right to give such information - many responsible people like doctors, nurses, teachers felt it their duty to get to work, even if it meant going to the UWC for petrol and passes. Where we did err was in the manner of giving it - some bulletins missed out the all-important words 'if you want to contact the UWC' and just said 'the number to ring is ...'.

We work in an environment in which propaganda plays a large part, but propaganda doesn't stem only from paramilitaries and illegal organisations - neither are they always wrong. It stems too from government, political parties and the security forces, and it is up to all journalists to weigh propaganda as an inescapable ingredient of the situation which they have to describe. Of course, propaganda itself is not an evil; it's the cause for which it speaks which has to be evaluated. Sometimes, not often, as in the cases of Majella O'Hare and the burning of a GAA Club, the Army's initial version of events turns out to be further away from the truth than that of the Provos. From time to time in this propaganda war, the Army have put themselves at a disadvantage. Invariably, if there is an incident during an Army patrol or search of a hard-line republican area, reporters following up the story will be met with a barrage of opinions from the locals. If the Army fails to put up a spokesman to give their version of events, wishing perhaps to avoid according status to their accusers, their case is liable to go by default. Newsmen cannot balance their accounts artificially, by inventing what the Army might have said.

The BBC is often accused of not 'getting the balance right', in the mathematical sense of over-representing 'minorities of minorities' as people like to regard the extremists. In the Northern Ireland situation, with a plethora of political parties, splinter groups and other pressure groups, the concept of balance is often an over-simplification. What matters more is relevance. It's important here to distinguish what happens in a news context - where we will seek the opinion of those most closely involved in a situation, whatever their background or persuasion - and current affairs - where we would frequently solicit a spectrum of opinion, including, when appropriate, the views of known extremists. In neither case are we considering a weighted average, such that the number of appearances or invitations is proportionate to the representation of the different elements in population or voting terms.

What is unquestionable is that we operate within the law, and I would say well within the law. Not by any means do we transmit everything that we might without being prosecuted, allowing the extent of law to be the ultimate determination of what is broadcastable. To do that would be highly irresponsible in many instances, because the law is neither equipped nor intended to consider all the consequences of broadcasting. Nor is it for us to pre-judge a person's legality. It has sometimes been suggested that we ought to treat some of the paramilitaries 'for what they are - thugs, murderers and bombers by any other name'.

If we were to ascribe that sort of label, or even make that presumption, we would very soon find ourselves in court. What we have to be concerned with is the legality of the subject matter. That is much more crucial than the legality of the organisations to which the authors may, or may purport, to belong. Many of the most bloodcurdling things have been said on the air by elected representatives, even MP's; and the more able spokesmen for the paramilitary organisations are also the most adept in avoiding infringements of the law.

Thus we must start by treating those paramilitary organisations, which the executive and the judiciary has seen fit to regard as legal, like any other body in the country. So long as Provisional Sinn Féin is encouraged by the government to play a political role, is accepted as a legal organisation, mounting rallies and making speeches without fear of prosecution under the law, we are bound to treat them accordingly. We have a clear duty to tell the public what they are doing and saying. It is often suggested that we should not interview the paramilitaries because they are the avowed mouthpieces of terrorists. But where does one draw the line, when some of their community and welfare activities are encouraged and when officials of Her Majesty's Government meet them for political talks? It would be illogical and impractical for the media not to cover their activities and, to do that responsibly, we believe it is necessary to interview and to investigate the unpalatable side when the information to be gained outweighs the possible propaganda effect.

Some of our more significant programmes have demonstrated to the public the terrorist potential of paramilitary yet legal organisations. *Panorama* filmed such a sequence with the UVF shortly before that organisation was re-proscribed in 1975. Last week the regional programme *Spotlight* interviewed a man who purported to speak for a new organisation, the Irish National Liberation Army, whose avowed aim is to get Britain out by attacking Ulstermen in the security forces and to establish a republican socialist State. Predictably, this caused offence in some quarters - 'such programmes do nothing but encourage violence' - the charge ran. But I am sure that it was our duty to demonstrate the very ugliness of the threat, and I am confident that the demeanour of our reporter left no doubt as to where we stood. [...]

Such interviews always demand forthright handling by experienced interviewers - invariably, paramilitary interviewees are treated as hostile witnesses. But there is considerable misconception as to how often we feature the paramilitaries and illegal organisations on BBC television and radio. There have been only two interviews with David O'Connell of the Provisional IRA in the last six years, the last being in June 1974. Each occasion requires the specific permission of the Director-General before proceeding. There is no 'ban' in the BBC of interviews with the IRA - there may be a justifiable editorial need to demonstrate what is in these people's minds. [...]

In the 12-month period from October 1975 to 1976 there were six interviews on BBC Northern Ireland Television with Provisional Sinn Féin and 12 with spokesmen for the Loyalists paramilitaries, six of them being elected representatives. These figures compare with a total of 307 interviews with elected representatives of all other parties, including 56 with UK ministers. In the same period there were 41 interviews with official Trades Union leaders and four with UWC spokesmen. All of these were on the basis of relevance, not according to a representational formula. So, over the year, the proportion of paramilitary interviews (18 out of 325) was extremely low, and incidentally contrasts with 18 interviews for the leaders of the Peace Movement in the first three months of its existence. Maybe we have been guilty of under-representing the forces which have had the most profound effect on everyday life in the province?

IRA or Sinn Féin statements, like all statements, are reported solely on their newsworthiness, neither automatically nor according to a quota. We do not give them wide propagation simply because they are issued. What is important is the news criterion, the amount of the statement which is relevant, and the context in which it is set. The frequency is bound to vary according to the level of paramilitary activity, but even in a busy month the average number of statements carried from Provo Sinn Féin and Provo IRA is unlikely to exceed one every other day. Loyalist paramilitaries and illegal organisations issue rather fewer warnings, claims and allegations. In considering threats for publication, whilst we make every effort to substantiate the source and to establish the bona fides (if I can use the phrase) of the organisation involved, the principal consideration must be the public's right to know those matters which constitute a threat to life or property.

Decisions on treatment are all-important. For example, just over a year ago, when the IRA threatened to extend its actions to the cities of England, it was important that the full impact of that threat was understood by the British public. One of the most threatening speeches, made in Derry, included the line 'let me warn (them) in Britain that they haven't seen anything yet compared to what they'll get in the not-too distant future'. The duty editor decided to show a filmed excerpt of the speech, because the threat lay less in the words than in the manner of their delivery. On the other hand, some of the most blood-curdling statements made in print have turned out to be less worrying when examined in interview, less liable to incite hatred than on mere reading. [...]

So, finally, I come to the sensitive issue of sectarian labels. It has been suggested by some people, including those in positions of high authority, that we exacerbate sectarian tension by reporting the religion of innocent victims. If we didn't announce their religion the chances of retaliation would be diminished, the argument runs. None of the media accept the proposition as being either practicable or desirable. In the first place, like the description of a man's colour, the label is only attached when it is relevant - successive Secretaries of State acknowledge that people are being killed for no apparent reason other than that they are Catholic or Protestant. Secondly, a sectarian label is a piece of shorthand; it's no different in essence from the description of a person's background, his name, where he went to school, the street where he lived and inevitably where he is to be buried, all facts which in Northern Ireland are liable to indicate a person's religion.

It doesn't need broadcasting to convey this sort of information in small communities. The danger is that, without accurate information, people may get it wrong. If you hear of a man with a Gaelic-sounding name, you may assume him to be a Catholic when he is not. If you hear a man has been shot dead in Andersonstown, you may assume he is a Catholic even though one or two per cent living there are Protestants. If two men are shot dead in a well-known Catholic pub, then who are they, who shot them, and why? The possibilities and the anxieties are endless if no details are given. So, in seeking to describe such stories, the victim's background must be given and, in Northern Ireland, invariably this involves his religion. What the reporter does need from the security forces, if he is to be sure the label is relevant, is an indication of the likely motive in each case. Again, it comes down to the public's right to know the truth, however worrying that may be.

There has been no more awful piece of news to convey recently than that of the cold-blooded murder of 10 Protestants in South Armagh on their way home in a mini-bus in January last year. That evening the MP for the area was in my office in Broadcasting House, Belfast, when the telephone rang. People in the constituency, knowing him to be there, rang him with the news, even before our newsroom received it. There was much rumour in the area, and according to local information the number dead varied considerably. But there was no doubt from their place of work or their destination that they were all Protestants. That news was put out as soon as the information could be verified with the police, and like few events in the province stunned the public. Despite fears that there would be retaliation, there were no serious incidents in South Armagh for the next 10 days. Perhaps this suggests that such traumatic news can have a cauterizing effect. But it is also worth noting that, three days later, it was announced officially that the SAS were to operate in the area. Local politicians reckon that this knowledge may have quenched the determination of some Loyalist paramilitaries to take the law into their own hands to exact revenge. On that occasion public knowledge almost certainly saved lives.

So the experience of broadcasting in Northern Ireland, for all the threats to society and to human life, suggests that the practice of free speech within a well-tested framework of responsibility is the best, if not the easiest, way to cover extraordinary circumstances. I believe we have a contribution to make to the maintenance of democracy, both by providing a forum where harsh differences of opinion can be aired and by reporting and courageously investigating the unpalatable truths which underlie the problems in our midst. I am sure that if and when the communities of Northern Ireland reconcile their conflicts it will be by understanding them rather than by ignoring them, and I would like to think that amongst those who will have contributed most to that understanding the broadcasters, and the BBC in particular, will have played their part.

5.

Peter Taylor

REPORTING NORTHERN IRELAND

(From *Index on Censorship*, 7(6), 1978, pages 3-11)

Writing in this journal six years ago, Anthony Smith[1] warned that the solidification of relationships and the delineation of tensions which the Irish question had imposed on the institutions of broadcasting were likely to develop in the next decade. His words were prophetic. Whereas few can have been surprised at the gradual unfolding of these relationships as the Irish conflict steadfastly defied solution and journalists persisted in asking nagging questions - albeit too few and too seldom - the sudden acceleration of the process in the past year has alarmed all parties, not least the journalists whose work is under attack.

Nowhere, in the British context, has the relationship between state, broadcasting institutions and programme makers been more sensitive and uneasy than in matters concerning Northern Ireland. Conflict arises whenever broadcast journalism challenged the prevalent ideology embodied in government policy and reflected in the broadcasting institutions it has established. In principle, the broadcasting authorities should stand between the media and the state as benevolent umpires, charged with the task of defending each against the excesses of the other, guardians of the public interest, upholders of a broadcasting service alleged to be the finest in the world. In practice, where Northern Ireland is concerned, they have become committed to a perspective of the conflict which identifies the public interest increasingly with the government interest. To question the government's ideology is to court trouble. The deeper the crisis and the more controversial the methods used to meet it, the greater the strain on the institutions of broadcasting forced to choose between the journalist's insistence on the public's right to know everything and the government's preference for it not to know too much.

The Irish question hangs over British politics like an angry and stubborn cloud that refuses to go away, despite the insistence of successive generations of British politicians that the cloud is just passing. The cloud has been there for 400 years. The words of British politicians from Robert Earl of Essex, servant of Elizabeth the First, to Roy Mason, servant of Elizabeth the Second, echo down the centuries voicing frustration with and issuing warnings to the Irish that have changed little over four centuries. The shadow of the current ten-year cloud under which we stand is no longer and darker than its predecessors. Northern Ireland is different, not because there is no consensus but because the nature of the consensus that exists makes any informed discussion of the problem difficult, if not increasingly impossible.

The official consensus runs something like this: Northern Ireland is a state in conflict because Catholics and Protestants refuse to live together despite the efforts of successive British governments to encourage them to do so: we (the British), at considerable cost to the Exchequer and our soldiers, have done all that is humanly possible to find a political solution within the existing structures of the Northern Irish state: now the two communities must come up with a political solution they are prepared to work and accept themselves: the terrorists, in particular the Provisional IRA, are gangsters and thugs: they are the cause, not the symptom of the problem.

This is, of course, a British mainland perspective. Others see it differently. When Jack Lynch, the Irish Prime Minister, suggested that Britain should withdraw from the North and encourage the reunification of the country. Westminster - and much of Fleet Street - was outraged at his impertinence in suggesting such a solution to a 'British domestic problem'.

To challenge these cosy assumptions about the conflict - deliberately fostered by those in high places either because they are convenient or because they believe them - is to run the risk of being branded at best a terrorist dupe, at worst a terrorist sympathiser. Journalists and politicians rash enough to dissent have felt the lash of tongues from both sides of the House of Commons and been called 'unreliable'. Yet some of us working there as journalists have come to believe that the conflict is political and not religious: that its origins lie in the conquest of Ireland by England and the subsequent establishment of a Protestant colony in Ulster to keep the province secure for the Crown; that the immediate conflict stems from the partition of the country 50 years ago, an artificial division designed to be only temporary, engineered by the British to guarantee Protestant supremacy in the remaining six counties of Ulster; that the Provisional IRA may lay claim to the mantle of the 'terrorists' who drove the British out of the 26 counties in 1919-20 in a campaign every bit as bloody and unpleasant as the IRA's current offensive to drive the British from the remaining six counties; and lastly (and currently most sensitive of all) that not all the RUC's policemen are wonderful.

The second battle of Culloden

Why has the issue come to a head over the past twelve months? The last great battle was fought by the BBC in late 1971 over *A Question of Ulster*, which the Corporation succeeded in transmitting despite enormous pressure from the Unionist government at Stormont and the Tory government at Westminster. The marathon programme was notable more for the fact of its transmission than its content. It was hailed as a victory for the Corporation's independence, but as Philip Schlesinger[2] has pointed out, it was a success story amidst general defeat, for had the BBC not resisted the political pressures, it would have undermined its own legitimacy and public confidence in the institution. In the years that followed, Northern Ireland was gradually relegated to the second halves of the news bulletins and the inside columns of the newspapers. Ulster ceased to be a story. When the media did return to the subject, coverage continued to be guided by the numbing principles outlined by Philip Elliott in his UNESCO report,[3] that the story should be simple, involving 'both lack of explanation and historical perspective'; of human interest, involving 'a concentration on the particular detail of incidents and the personal characteristics of those involved which results in a continual procession of unique, inexplicable events'; and lastly, a reflection of the official version of events to consolidate the 'production of a common image'.

But there were occasional squalls in spite of the media's generally low profile. In 1976 the IBA banned a *This Week* investigation into IRA fund raising in America before a foot of film had been shot, not because the subject matter was particularly contentious but because the 'timing' was felt to be wrong. The film was transmitted a week later, but it was a warning shot.

Meanwhile, Merlyn Rees, Secretary of State for Northern Ireland until the summer of 1976, negotiated the ending of internment and a cease-fire, his patience and persistence winning the respect of the public - even some Provos with whom he was brave enough to negotiate - and the goodwill of journalists. We felt that he was trying. His successor, however, Roy Mason, was a man hewn from rougher rock. His acquaintance with Ireland had begun as Minister of Defence (a position unlikely to encourage perspective when the Army was faced with its closest and most pressing security problem since the war). For him the problem was one of security and the present, not politics and the past: results were what he wanted, not history lessons or the niceties of media philosophy as expressed by the BBC's then Controller of Northern Ireland Dick Francis:

The experience in Northern Ireland where communities and governments are in conflict, but not in a state of emergency or a state of war, suggests a greater need than ever for the media to function as the Fourth Estate, distinct from the Executive, the Legislature and the Judiciary. But if the functions are to remain separate, it must be left to the media themselves to take the decisions, within the limits of responsibility, as to what to publish, when and how.

Under Mason, journalists were more than ever courted as allies in the war, not recorders of it. After only a few months in office the new Secretary of State is reported to have made his position brutally clear to Sir Michael Swann, Chairman of the BBC, at a private dinner at Belfast's Culloden Hotel, where he accused the BBC of showing disloyalty, supporting the rebels and purveying enemy propaganda. He is also said to have remarked that if the Northern Ireland Office had been in control of BBC policy, the IRA would have been defeated. Sir Michael later referred to this encounter as 'the second battle of Culloden', Mr Mason shared the text-book view expressed by the Army's senior counter-insurgency expert, Brigadier Frank Kitson:

> The countering of the enemy's propaganda and putting across of the government's point of view, can be achieved either by direct action, as for example the provision of leaflets, or the setting up of an official wireless or television network, or *by trying to inform and influence the existing news media* (my emphasis).[5]

But Kitson adds a warning: 'The real difficulty lies in the political price which a democratic country pays in order to influence the ways in which its people think.'

The BBC was first in the firing line. Despite pressure from the RUC and the government, in March 1977 the BBC's *Tonight* programme transmitted Keith Kyle's interview with Bernard O'Connor, an Enniskillen schoolmaster who alleged ill-treatment by the RUC's plainclothes interrogators at Castlereagh detention centre. If Northern Ireland is the most sensitive issue in British broadcasting, interrogation techniques are its most sensitive spot. Although under severe attack from Roy Mason and his unnatural but strongest ally in the House of Commons, the Conservative spokesman on Northern Ireland, Airey Neave, who accused the BBC of assisting terrorist recruitment and undermining the police, the BBC stood firm. In a letter to the *Times,* the Chairman, Sir Michael Swann (no doubt with Culloden in mind) wrote:

> The BBC has a responsibility to make available to the whole UK audience as truthful a picture as it can of the state of affairs in Northern Ireland.[6]

Whilst the BBC was having its showdown with Roy Mason, at the beginning of 1977, ITV's *This Week* was having the odd desultory clash with the IBA and the Northern Ireland Office: the IBA did not like a Provisional Sinn Féin spokesman calling for 'one last push' to get the British out, delivered at the end of a film about the fifth anniversary of Bloody Sunday. The sound was subsequently taken down and the 'offensive' sentiments lost in crowd noises and commentary.

Intolerable restrictions

Because the structures of ITV are vaguer and less rigid than the BBC's hierarchical pyramid, where decisions are constantly referred upwards, its programme makers have traditionally been more protected against political interference from above. Until recent years and the growing political imperatives that the Northern Irish conflict has placed upon it, the IBA was cautious in wielding its power over news and current affairs. But the Authority, now more powerful and confident with every decision it takes, increasingly tends to arrogate to itself the functions of judge, jury and executioner. If the programme companies, powerful and influential bodies in their own right, disagree with the Authority's decision, there is no redress. Television journalism is increasingly hampered by restrictions that Fleet Street does not have and would never tolerate. *The Sunday Times* may decide to publish and be damned - Thames Television cannot. It is the IBA that takes that decision for it. The Authority has always had an impressive panoply of weapons to hand in the form of wide-ranging statutes which give it the power to stop programmes that offend 'good taste and decency', are likely to 'incite to crime and disorder' or are 'offensive to public feeling'. But most awesome of all is Section 4 I (f) of the 1973 Broadcasting Act, which makes it incumbent on the Authority to see that 'due impartiality is preserved in matters of political controversy or *matters relating to current public policy*' (my emphasis).

As always, the interpretation and use of these statutes is a personal matter that depends on the predilections of the person at the top. In recent years the tone and style of the Authority has been set by its Chairman, Lady Plowden, who is believed not to favour or encourage investigative television reporting. Add to this a general public antipathy towards Northern Ireland and it is not surprising that the Authority tends to err on the side of caution when faced with controversy. Nor is the Authority, despite its protestations, immune from political pressure. In the end, when the interests of state and the interests of journalism conflict, the odds are that the former will triumph, particularly when the latter may be challenging the ideology which the Authority itself, by its structure, is bound to reflect. There is no statute in the Broadcasting Act that says that the interests of the state must be paramount. There is no need for one. Nor are the pressures from government on the Authority - or from the Authority on its contracting companies - overt: there are no official memoranda saying

'Thou shalt not ... ', rather letters 'regretting that ... ' and suggesting 'wouldn't it be better if ...'

When it comes to Northern Ireland the pressure is constant. It consists of not just the standard letters of protest from government and opposition to the IBA and the offending contracting company, but personal meetings between the Chairman of the Authority and the Secretary of State and Chief Constable of the RUC. These discussions are confidential, but their results gradually filter down through the broadcasting structures suggesting that more 'responsible' coverage would be welcome (there is little talk of censorship. Government and broadcasting authorities are usually far too adept and experienced to fall into that trap); that *This Week* might 'lay off' Northern Ireland for a while, or that 'another reporter' might cover it. And the pressures on the contracting companies are also formidable: in a couple of years' time the IBA has the power to renew or withdraw their lucrative licences; the second channel, much desired and lobbied for by ITV, is a gift for government to grant or withhold. ITV is in the end beholden to both institutions; it takes courage to challenge them. Small wonder then that controversial coverage of Northern Ireland is tolerated rather than encouraged.

Propaganda exercise

The problems that *This Week* has faced in the past year illustrate the difficulties confronting journalists attempting to report Northern Ireland as fully and freely as they would a conflict less close to home. The trouble started with 'In Friendship and Forgiveness' (August 1977), an alternative diary of the Queen's visit to Northern Ireland, her last engagement in Jubilee year. The world's press flocked to Belfast as never before even at the height of the 'war' in 1972, admittedly more as prospective vultures at the feast, awaiting the Provisionals' much-vaunted promise to 'make it a visit to remember', than as recorders of Her Majesty's progress through carefully chosen parts of her troublesome province. ITV's cameras covered the events live. ITN's senior newscaster declared from the Belfast rooftops that he could almost feel 'the peace in the air'. For Roy Mason the Royal visit represented a proconsular triumph which the world was there to record. The Provisionals' threats proved empty: they were humiliated, if not defeated. Television brilliantly orchestrated the Royal progress as it had throughout Jubilee year, but nowhere had its orchestration carried such political overtones which, however lost they might have been on its audience, were certainly not overlooked by the government officials who encouraged it. As a propaganda exercise its success was complete: it presented a picture of a province almost pacified, with grateful and loyal subjects from both sections of the community taking the Queen and her message to their hearts.

The reality was different. More than anything, the Royal visit highlighted the political divisions of the province: to Protestants it represented a victory for their tradition which they felt had been under attack for so long, whilst for many Catholics Her Majesty came as the head of a state they refused to recognise. Such was the context in which *This Week* placed its report, filming events that went largely unnoticed and unreported by the army of visiting pressmen - the funerals of a young IRA volunteer shot dead by the army whilst allegedly throwing a petrol bomb and a young soldier shot dead by the Provisionals in retaliation; a Provisional IRA road block in Ballymurphy; a Republican rally in the Falls Road; the Apprentice Boys parade in Derry and an earlier sectarian sing-song; Loyalist street celebrations in the Shankhill; and a four-hour riot - which was widely reported. This potent mixture was intercut with scenes of the Royal progress and interviews with proponents of the two conflicting traditions, John Hume and John Taylor, who placed the visit in its current and historical perspective.

The programme, scheduled for transmission a week after the visit, was banned by the IBA. (All *This Week* programmes on Ireland have to be submitted for the Authority's approval prior to transmission, which is rarely the case with other sensitive issues that *This Week* covers.) The IBA took exception to a section at the beginning of the film in which Andreas O'Callaghan, a Sinn Féinner from Dublin, stirred the crowd at the Falls Road rally with these words:

> While there is a British Army of occupation on our streets, any Irishman who has it within his means, meaning any Irishman who can get his hands on a gun or weapon; he has the duty not to keep that gun in cold storage or even less to use that gun against the people who are fighting the British Army, let them get out and fight the British Army themselves ... As long as there's one British soldier in any part of Ireland, there will always be people who will struggle, there will always be people who will resist.

These words could have been reported by any newspaper journalist but not, apparently, on television. Seeking refuge in Statute 4 (1) of the 1973 Broadcasting Act, the IBA deemed it likely that these words might constitute 'an incitement to crime' or 'lead to disorder'. Thames were advised to seek legal advice. Thames' counsel concluded:

> In the context of the programme and having regard to the careful way in which it is presented, I think it is unlikely that the excerpt could have any such effect. Having expressed my own opinion I do recognise that in a matter of judgement of this sort, it might be legitimately felt that the film with O'Callaghan's voice reproduced could have such an effect.

Significantly he added:

All things are *possible,* but the section requires the Authority to consider what is *likely.*

He also pointed out that Section 4 (I)b of the Act requires a news feature to be 'presented with due accuracy and impartiality'.

Accordingly, to play safe and to get the programme on the air, we decided to drop O'Callaghan's words and replace them with my neutered paraphrase in reported speech:

> Andreas O'Callaghan went on to urge Irishmen to carry on the fight against British soldiers in Northern Ireland using whatever weapons they could lay their hands on. It was an open call to arms.

Counsel felt that we were now in the clear. The IBA decided that we were not. Two minutes before transmission a phone call came from the Authority ordering Thames not to show the programme. A previous film I had made on 'Drinking and Driving' was put out in its place.

But the O'Callaghan speech was not the only section of the programme that worried the IBA. They were anxious about the Provisional IRA road block in Ballymurphy, which they suspected we had set up. We had not. My commentary made the position clear:

> Whilst the Queen was being welcomed at Hillsborough, the Provisional IRA mounted a road block in the Ballymurphy estate a few miles away. We were told earlier in the day that a snub to the Queen was planned. This was it - more propaganda than military exercise. Perhaps for our benefit, perhaps as a morale booster for their supporters. The checkpoint lasted five brief minutes. But it happened within half a mile of an army post round the corner, out of sight.

Nevertheless the Authority remained worried that we might be in breach of the Northern Ireland Emergency Provisions (Amendment) Act 1975 by 'aiding and abetting the offence of wearing a mask or hood in a public place'. Thames' counsel implied that this was nonsense.

Finally, the IBA expressed concern over my final lines of commentary delivered over film of the soldier's funeral in his Yorkshire mining village:

> The events of that week drew to a close not on the streets of Belfast, but in the lanes of a Yorkshire mining village. There the Army buried Private Lewis Harrison, the two-hundred-and-seventieth British soldier to die in Northern Ireland. For his family, the funeral was a bitter end to the Queen's Jubilee visit. It marked for them as only such grief can, the historical truth that lies behind the bewildering complexities of Ulster. Private Harrison died not because the Queen visited Ulster, but because the power she represents remains in that part of Ireland.

It was the last sentence that caused the agony. The IBA argued that it presented an 'incomplete' picture of the problem, there being no mention of religion, of Catholics and Protestants and the Army keeping them from each other. I argued that to amend the sentence as the Authority requested was a distortion of the essence of my report. After much discussion, my words were allowed to stand.

Dictating 'the issues'

'In Friendship and Forgiveness' was finally transmitted two weeks after the visit, trickling out over the ITV network in slots that ranged from Friday teatime and Sunday lunchtime to nearly midnight on Ulster Television. By then the visit was history, the impact and topicality of the film lost. Significantly, the film finally shown was not materially different from the version banned two minutes before transmission. Was there collusion with government to prevent a mass audience seeing a different version of 'reality' presented at peak time, whilst memories of the event were still fresh? What damage would this perspective have done to the cosmetic presentation so carefully served up by the media? One can only guess. One Northern Ireland Office official I spoke to afterwards said he thought the film 'stank'.

We had not planned 'In Friendship and Forgiveness' in advance. We had gone to Belfast to prepare a programme that examined conditions in the prisons and the issue of Special Category Status. When we saw the unreported impact of the Royal visit, we changed tack. We then returned to complete the prisons film we had started, 'Life Behind the Wire'. The programme, which included film secretly shot by the UDA inside the compounds of the Maze prison, showing prisoners parading openly in paramilitary uniform unchallenged by prison officers, highlighted the conflict between the government's insistence that the prisoners were common criminals lacking political motivation, and the inmates' view of themselves as political prisoners. Again, the programme was designed to examine the political nature of the conflict in Northern Ireland. The politicians did not like it. (During the research period, the Northern Ireland Office suggested I make a profile of Roy Mason's first year in office. The prisons, they repeated, were not an issue. They prefer to dictate the 'issues' themselves. Airey Neave called for 'the most immediate action to stop the flow of Irish terror propaganda through the British news media'. He protested to the IBA about the 'myth that the terrorists in Northern Ireland are heroic and honourable soldiers'. Interestingly, Unionist politicians attacked not *This Week*, but the government for tolerating such a situation in a British gaol. For their own political reasons, they welcomed our taking the lid off Long Kesh which Harry West, their leader, referred to a 'terrorist Sandhurst'. The government preferred the lid to be kept on. No one questioned the accuracy of the picture we presented.

We submitted the film to the IBA. They had no objections, although one of their officials remarked that the political perspective of the film disturbed him. The real outcry came over two weeks after the programme had been transmitted when the Provisional IRA shot dead Desmond Irvine, the Secretary of the Northern Ireland Prison Officers' Association, whose remarkable interview was the backbone of the film. Prison Officer Irvine agreed to the interview after long discussions with his colleagues, and decided to do it openly, fully aware of the risks he was taking. The Northern Ireland Office did not wish him to be interviewed. Political critics of the programme and of *This Week's* previous coverage, did not hesitate to lay responsibility for his death at our door, despite the public declaration by the Association that they did not blame the programme for P.O. Irvine's death. Nor was Desmond Irvine displeased with the film or his own contribution to it. A few days before his death, he wrote to me saying:

> I found the programme to be an accurate description of life at the Maze. Congratulations have poured in from many sources, including many messages from Great Britain. Your superb handling of a very delicate topic and the manner in which it was presented resulted in praise from staff and prisoners. Thank you for all your help.

His death, however unconnected it may have been with the programme, placed another weapon in the hands of *This Week* critics and those who wished to curb or prevent coverage of sensitive corners of Northern Ireland policy and practice. Moral pressure could now be applied even more forcefully not only to the programme makers, but to those to whom they were answerable. 'Putting lives at risk' and 'responsible reporting' took on a new dimension.

These arguments were widely used to try and stop *This Week* from making and transmitting its next film, 'Inhuman and Degrading Treatment', an investigation into allegations of ill-treatment by the RUC at Castlereagh interrogation centre. It proved to be the most delicate issue that *This Week* has tackled in Northern Ireland, highly sensitive because it questioned the interrogation techniques that were the cornerstone of the government's security policy. The undoubted successes that Roy Mason claimed in putting the 'terrorists behind bars' were in 80 per cent of cases the direct result of statements elicited - in theory voluntarily - in police custody, on which a suspect could be convicted in the absence of further evidence. For several months in 1977 there had been growing disquiet, initially amongst Catholics, eventually amongst Protestants too, concerning the manner in which these statements were being obtained. The allegations of ill-treatment were persistently dismissed by government and RUC as terrorist propaganda, the last cries of defeated and discredited organisations. During our numerous visits to Belfast the allegations grew stronger and more widespread. We had off-the-record discussions with senior figures in the legal field, who expressed growing anxiety at the way in which they believed some confessions were being obtained. They felt that our investigating the issue, within the context of the crisis and the special legal framework designed to cope with it, would be neither irresponsible nor untimely.

'Lay off Northern Ireland'

We examined 10 cases of alleged ill-treatment in the programme. Each case had strong corroborative medical evidence. We asked the RUC for a background briefing and assistance, acutely aware of the dangers of being taken for a ride by the paramilitary organisations whose causes were undoubtedly helped by the propaganda generated by the issue. After lengthy discussions, the RUC refused all cooperation. There were to be no facilities nor, more significantly, any interview with the Chief Constable. The Northern Ireland Office, washing their hands of the problem by saying it was 'one for the RUC', were quick to remind me of the death of Desmond Irvine.

We pressed ahead. Six days before transmission, we sent a detailed telex to the RUC - without whom the IBA thought the programme incomplete - listing the cases and medical evidence and outlining a script of the programme. Three days later, word came back that there was still to be no interview. No doubt the various hot lines buzzed. The day before transmission, the Chief Constable offered not an interview but an RUC editorial statement to camera. This compromise was unwelcome to the programme makers, but in the end we were forced to accept it. No statement - no programme. The institutions had triumphed again. A few hours before the programme was due to go out, the chief constable put his men on 'red alert', publicly declaring that his policemen were being put at risk by a television programme. Nothing happened. The Chief Constable, who invited Lady Plowden to lunch at his Belfast Headquarters, complained to the IBA that the programme was 'seriously lacking in balance'. (Whose fault was that?) The Northern Ireland Office issued an unprecedented personal attack on the reporter who had 'produced three programmes in quick succession which have concentrated on presenting the blackest possible picture of events in Northern Ireland', pointing out that 'after the last programme a prison officer was murdered'. Roy Mason accused the programme of being 'riddled with unsubstantiated conclusions' and being 'irresponsible and insensitive'. (Privately, senior legal figures welcomed the programme. They believed it to be accurate and welcome.) Letters of 'stern and strict' complaint were dispatched to the IBA and Thames Television, accusing *This Week* of 'consistently knocking the security forces in Northern Ireland'. A showdown was in the air. It came eight months later - a period in which 'This Week's' producer David Elstein was told to 'lay off Northern Ireland' - in the form of the Amnesty Report.

Amnesty International had sent a mission to Belfast to examine the allegations of ill-treatment a week after *This Week's* Castlereagh investigation. The government and RUC announced their intention to give the delegates every assistance, whilst refusing to discuss individual cases. Amnesty was given the facilities *This Week* was denied. Few could argue that their report would be unbalanced or one-sided. In the event, the Amnesty Report was a devastating document. 'Maltreatment,' it concluded, 'has taken place with sufficient frequency to warrant a public enquiry to investigate it.[7]

The Report was widely leaked ten days before publication. National newspapers reported its contents and the BBC's *Tonight* programme quoted extensively from it. In the light of the leaks, *This Week* planned a programme to discuss the Report through interviews with the usual Northern Ireland cross-section of people - mainly politicians - each of whom had read a copy of the report with which we had provided them. Over half the interviewees were well known for their staunch support of the RUC. The IBA banned the programme. There was no appeal. The decision was clear-cut. By chance, the 11 members who constituted the Authority had met that morning and reached a decision, it was argued, which it was impossible to countermand. On what legal grounds the decision was made was not, and still has not been, made clear. The Authority declared that it would be premature to discuss a report 'until it is public, thereby giving those involved and the general public a chance to study it in detail'. As Enoch Powell commented when told on his arrival at the studio that the programme had been banned: 'If we did not talk about what was premature, we would not talk about very much!'

There was no invocation of sections of the Broadcasting Act, as in the case of 'In Friendship and Forgiveness'; no discussion of amendments or compromises that might make it more acceptable as in 'Inhuman and Degrading Treatment'. The fact that the government had issued a ten-page reply to an unpublished report a matter of hours before the planned transmission of the programme, cut no ice with the Authority. The ban was an act of political censorship pure and simple: the pressures which had mounted over the past year at last had the desired effect. The IBA proved unable, perhaps unwilling, to resist them.

Menace to free communication

Not surprisingly, government and the Authority denied political interference. Few believed them. Anthony Smith's prophesy had been fulfilled four years ahead of its time: the institutional relationships between the broadcasting authorities and the state were now firmly cemented. ITV technicians blacked the screen in protest, a screen that was nevertheless loyally watched by 20 per cent of the London audience! Thames Television publicly attacked the IBA's decision, and Jeremy Isaacs, the Programme Controller, granted BBC *Nationwide's* request to transmit sections of the banned programme. Fleet Street rushed to Thames' defence. The *Sunday Times* described the IBA as 'one of the biggest menaces to free communication now at work in this country' and stated: 'Over Northern Ireland a new wave of political pressure is making itself felt.'[8] *The Economist* accused the IBA of 'an act of violence on free speech'.[9] *The*

Listener said the Authority should treat the programme companies and the viewers 'as adults'.[10] Even the *Sunday Telegraph* admitted that '"This Week's" record in Northern Ireland is pretty deplorable, so is the IBA's recourse to banning the other night's edition'.[11]

In an apologia in the *Sunday Times* a week later, Sir Brian Young, Director General of the IBA, limped to the defence of his Authority.[12] He wrote:

> Journalists have some clear imperatives. Their profession drives them to be first with the story or the perceptive comment; to expose what someone wants to conceal; to gain the reader's attention often by describing feet of clay rather than hearts of oak; and to influence the world, they hope, by campaigning for what they believe in. Fair enough ... But they are not absolute virtues, as journalists sometimes seem to claim. They may conflict with fairness, with an individual's rights, even with truth and the public good ... I would ask viewers to respect what real players do; but to respect also the men and women who blow the whistle.

What could have been more concerned with individual rights, the truth and the public good than the programme that *This Week* had planned? When the Authority blew the whistle on the Amnesty Report, they were clearly using a set of unwritten rules one side did not recognise.

The post mortem continues. The repercussions for the broadcasters have yet to be felt. The years ahead may be even more difficult. No British government is likely to be more tolerant of open reporting of Northern Ireland or less concerned about the politics of information. Events of the past year have made it clearer than ever that in reporting Northern Ireland the independence of broadcasting, as well as lives, is at stake.

Endnotes

1. *Index* 1/1972. Also reprinted in *The Politics of Information*, Macmillan, August 1978.
2. Philip Schlesinger: *Putting 'Reality' Together,* Constable 1978 (chapter eight 'The reporting of Northern Ireland').
3. Philip Elliott: *Ethnicity and the media*, Essay on Reporting Northern Ireland, UNESCO, 1978.
4. Richard Francis: lecture at the Royal Institute of International Affairs, February 1977.
5. Frank Kitson: *Bunch of Five* (Chapter 23 'Framework'), Faber, 1977.
6. The Times, 22 March 1977.
7. Amnesty Report, p. 68, 'Conclusions': Amnesty International, 1978.
8. *Sunday Times* editorial, 'The redundant censors', 11 June 1978.
9. *The Economist*, 'Light on Ulster' 17 June 1978.
10. *The Listener*, 'Why the IBA Ban?, 15 June 1978.
11. Philip Purser: 'The front end of the censors', *Sunday Telegraph*, 11 June 1978.
12. Sir Brian Young: 'Publish or be slammed', *Sunday Times*, 18 June 1978.

6.

Liz Curtis

THE REFERENCE UPWARDS SYSTEM

(From *Ireland: the Propaganda War*, London, Pluto Press, 1984, pages 173-189)

Development of the rules

The Carrickmore affair prompted the BBC into a rapid revision of its guidelines for programme makers working on Ireland. New instructions were issued on 27 November 1979, less than three weeks after the row had broken out.[1]

The BBC's rules were first worked out in 1971, the year which saw the IRA go on the offensive - on 6 February Gunner Robert Curtis became the first British soldier to die at their hands in the current 'troubles', and soon afterwards they began a commercial bombing campaign - and a year which brought, too, escalating troop brutality and, in August, internment and torture.

Television coverage of the North came under a barrage of attack from politicians and the press. Political scientist Jay G. Blumler summed up:

> For supposedly allowing instant interviews after controversial incidents, hectoring official spokesmen, giving a platform to IRA sympathisers, and publicising complaints about the security forces, television (mainly the BBC) is accused of harassing and disheartening the army and giving aid and comfort to the enemy.[2]

In response, the BBC drew up rules which were designed to minimise the number of items which might attract political flak. This was done by giving BBC management an unprecedented degree of control over programming decisions. On virtually every other topic, programme editors, producers and journalists are trusted to make appropriate decisions about what subjects to select and how to present them. They are expected to 'refer up' to their superiors for guidance only in cases of real doubt or difficulty. On Ireland, however, no one was to be trusted. The rules made it compulsory for programme-makers to consult management about all programmes on Ireland, so that the power to decide what would be made and broadcast was centralised in the hands of a few top executives. Desmond Taylor, who, as Editor of News and Current Affairs was a key figure in the control of Irish coverage, justified the growing supervision by saying it 'protected reporters and avoided mistakes of judgement', and commented that, 'I am just acting more like an editor and less like a bureaucrat'.[3] Reporter Jeremy Paxman, looking at the procedure from a different viewpoint, wrote that 'judgements about how to proceed can be made not by the journalists involved, but by their bosses.'[4]

Also in 1971, a similar system evolved in ITV. The Independent Television Authority, forerunner of the IBA, exercised increasingly tight control over programmes on the North made by Independent Television News and the programme companies.[5]

The rules have two basic components. Firstly, programme-makers have to consult top management, including the Northern Ireland Controller, and obtain their approval for all programmes on Ireland. This consultation has to take place at all stages of production, from the ideas stage onwards. All programmes that might be in the least bit controversial have to be viewed and approved by top management before transmission. Secondly, there are special restrictions governing interviews with members of banned organisations.

Worked out and put into operation in 1971, the new regulations were spelled out in the May 1972 edition of the BBC's *News Guide*, a handbook for journalists. The previous edition, produced in 1967, had said nothing about Ireland. The 1972 edition specified:

> 1. News staff sent to Northern Ireland work through Controller Northern Ireland and News Editor Northern Ireland, they must be consulted.

> 2. No news agency report from Northern Ireland should be used without checking with Belfast newsroom first.

> 3. The IRA must not be interviewed without prior authority from ENCA [Editor of News and Current Affairs]. There can be no question of doing the interview first and seeking permission for broadcast afterwards.[6]

The *News Guide* also forbade the use of broadcasts by illegal radios without reference to ENCA, and the reporting of bomb scares concerning BBC buildings: these strictures did not apply only to the North of Ireland.

The role of the Northern Ireland Controller

In the BBC'S reference upwards system, the role of the Northern Ireland Controller is crucial. *The Sunday Times* noted at the start of 1972,

> In practice, every item on Ulster has to be cleared in advance with Waldo Maguire, the BBC's regional controller in Belfast. Mr Maguire is a man of extreme caution, prone to a fast veto on 'controversial' topics. Appeals against his decisions can be made to Desmond Taylor, the BBC's Editor of News and Current Affairs, but it requires politicking at a high level.[7]

The power of the Northern Ireland Controller was in part a legacy of the 1930s, when G.L. Marshall, Director of BBC Northern Ireland, had been given the right to be consulted on all matters relating to Ireland.[8] When Waldo Maguire became Northern Ireland Controller in 1966, he inherited this power.

Theoretically Maguire had only the right to be consulted, not the right to make final decisions about programmes: editorial authority resided in London, not Belfast. But the BBC had earlier made a rule that the content of programmes transmitted in Britain and in the North of Ireland should be identical: nothing could be shown in Britain which could not also be shown in the North. So, as Maguire had authority over what was transmitted in the North, he could effectively veto programmes by threatening not to show them in his territory. Further, the Director General had also told producers not to do anything which would provoke Maguire into such an action. BBC Northern Ireland was allowed to opt out of only one major programme, a *Panorama* report made in 1970 which, according to Anthony Smith, included 'a widow crying for vengeance for her dead husband, shot by terrorists.' It was decided that this might provoke further bloodshed if it were shown in the North.[9]

Ulster Television, by contrast, was at first allowed to opt out of programmes shown on the ITV network provided that the ITA official in Belfast gave permission, and UTV did in fact opt out of six or seven programmes.[10] But during 1971 it became ITA policy not to encourage UTV to opt out. In mid-September that year the ITA said that the withholding of a network transmission of a programme on the North 'was in some sense a public admission of failure'.[11] So the Managing Director of UTV came to exercise a strong influence over programmes on Ireland. But his role was not as powerful nor as formalised as that of the BBC's Northern Ireland Controller. UTV was again to opt out of a networked programme - this time drama rather than current affairs - in August 1978, when the company refused to show the fourth episode in Southern Television's serial *Spearhead*, about a group of British soldiers. Set in the North, the episode was due for transmission on 8 August, the anniversary of internment.

During the Carrickmore affair, BBC Northern Ireland Controller James Hawthorne had, to his embarrassment, learned about *Panorama's* filming of an IRA roadblock not from within the BBC, but from a Northern Ireland Office official. As a result, shortly afterwards, according to *The Guardian*, BBC staff were instructed to inform Hawthorne personally when they planned to mention the North.[12] Then new guidelines were issued which dealt with the consultation process, and particularly the Northern Ireland Controller's role, in great detail.

The new rules were first released as an appendix to the minutes of the News and Current Affairs meeting held on 27 November 1979. It is at these top level meetings that BBC policy evolves and decisions are taken that become precedents for the future.[13] Then in 1980 the rules were incorporated in the new edition of the BBC'S *News and Current Affairs Index*, a slim yellow handbook which is issued to journalistic staff in both television and radio. The 'Standing Instructions and Guidance' on 'Coverage of Matters Affecting Northern Ireland' occupy just over four pages of the *Index*.[14] [...]

The scope of the rules

The reference upwards system acts firstly as a filter, removing 'undesirable' programmes or items at an early stage and, in theory, eliminating the need for embarrassing acts of censorship. Secondly, it is an early warning system, so that if a 'sensitive' programme is allowed through, such as Keith Kyle's 1977 *Tonight* film in which Bernard O'Connor alleged he had been tortured, not only can it be checked and double-checked, but also the upper echelons can prepare themselves for the inevitable onslaught from the right. Justifying the system, which he admitted was a departure from the normal procedure because it transferred responsibility from the individual producer or editor to top management, Richard Francis said, 'Early warning, briefing and consultation is essential if the Controller in Northern Ireland or the Editor of News and Current Affairs in London is not to be caught between last-minute "censorship" or disregard.'[15]

No item on Northern Ireland, however minor, escapes scrutiny. In early 1987, even a ten-minute summary of the Northern situation made for *See Hear*, a BBC programme for the deaf and the blind, had to be referred up prior to transmission. Nor does the procedure apply just to news and current affairs, but to every area of programming. In a talk on *The TV Play and Northern Ireland*, Richard Hoggart described how drama is affected:

> anything on the troubles is very sensitive and involves reference upward, discussion, sometimes stalling: and so quite a number of plays have been delayed, denied repeats or relegated to late-night slots. Unless a writer has a very strong sense that this is his [sic] topic he is not likely to expose himself to that sort of delay and fine-tooth combing over his work... imaginative insights into the complexity of the situation are largely denied us... A play which viewed the struggles from the angle of the terrorists, no matter how

full of insight it might be, would probably ... have a pretty rough ride.[16]

In ITV, programmes on Ireland have to be referred to the management of the television company concerned, and then to the IBA. Paul Fox, Managing Director of Yorkshire Television and previously Controller of BBC1, told in late 1981 how he was agonising over whether a three-part drama serial on Ireland should be made:

> It's an extremely difficult decision, and very delicate ... I'm concerned that when that play is made, and a transmission date happens, and the transmission date coincides with an attack or a bombing attack in London, what do you do? Do you show that play? Or do you pull the play out? ... It's written by a newspaperman, it's an exceptionally good script, it's been read by people in Northern Ireland who approve it, and yet I have enormous doubts about it.[17]

The play in question was *Harry's Game*, based on Gerald Seymour's best-selling thriller of the same name.[18] In the event Yorkshire Television went ahead with it and it was transmitted on the network in October 1982.[19] A somewhat unlikely tale of a British agent who operates undercover in West Belfast in pursuit of an IRA killer, the play did not seriously challenge conventional British ideas about the conflict: instead, it was marked by a dearth of politics and an emphasis on IRA cruelty.

Even songs come under the microscope. In 1972 the BBC banned Paul McCartney's song, 'Give Ireland Back to the Irish'. At that time, before the advent of commercial radio, the BBC had a monopoly challenged only by the pirate stations. The chorus of the song went:

> *Give Ireland back to the Irish,*
> *Don't make them have to take it away.*
> *Give Ireland back to the Irish,*
> *Make Ireland Irish today.*[20]

In September 1981 the BBC, apparently following in the footsteps of ITV,[21] banned a video made by the rock group Police to accompany their single, *Invisible Sun*. The video was described by *Times* correspondent Richard Williams as 'A collage of Ulster street scenes, incorporating urchins, graffiti, Saracens and soldiers.'[22] The BBC's justification for the ban was enigmatic. A spokesperson said, 'The theme of the single is anti-violence, but the presentation film could be said to convey meanings which are not present in the single.'[23] The group refused to change their film, and refused to perform the song live on *Top of the Pops*.[24]

The reference upwards rules even extend to the BBC'S internal 'central news traffic' system. Central traffic, located at Broadcasting House in central London, is the means by which sound items are transferred from their place of origin, for example a regional studio, to the programmes for which they are intended. When an item is coming through, it is announced on a tannoy and can be listened to in any news or current affairs office in the main BBC buildings. It is forbidden to send 'sensitive' items on Ireland through central traffic.

Rules on republican interviews

In both the BBC and ITV there are special rules governing interviews with members of banned groups. In practice, these rules almost exclusively affect republicans.

Though the loyalist Ulster Volunteer Force began killing Catholics in 1966, and started bombing in 1969, the BBC's rules drawn up in 1971 referred only to interviews with the IRA. In 1971 the BBC considered totally banning interviews with 'Republican extremists', but instead decided that 'such interviews should only be filmed and transmitted after the most serious consideration, and that the BBC should be seen to be clearly opposed to the indiscriminate methods of the extremists.'[25]

The rule adopted was that permission had to be obtained in advance from the Director-General, then Charles Curran, before the IRA could be interviewed. The rule amounted to a ban: Curran later said that he had only given prior permission for two IRA interviews, one in 1972 and another in 1974.[26] The BBC was apparently not anxious to publicise the restrictions. They did not admit to them openly until late November 1971, after a BBC radio *World at One* journalist had told a meeting of journalists protesting against censorship of news from the North that 'BBC staff were now forbidden to interview any member of the IRA except with the direct permission of the Director-General.'[27] Next day a BBC spokesperson confirmed that, 'In general we do have a ban. There can only be interviews with members of illegal organisations in exceptional circumstances and that would involve consultation at a high editorial level.'[28]

As a result of the regulations, journalists wishing to interview members of republican paramilitary groups faced a daunting rigmarole. Roger Bolton, who was editor of *Tonight* when, in its last edition in July 1979, it showed an interview with an INLA spokesperson, described the procedure that led up to it:

> We argued amongst ourselves so that we were convinced that such an interview was the proper thing to do; I then went through the BBC machinery which leads ultimately to the Director-General first to get authority to research the story, secondly on a separate occasion to get authority to see whether such an interview would be possible and thirdly the authority to do such an interview, and finally the interview was seen before transmission by the Director General's appointed deputy.[29]

When the BBC'S rules were redrafted at the end of 1979, they referred not just to the IRA but to 'terrorist organisations'. In practice this meant illegal groups, so, since the largest loyalist paramilitary organisation, the UDA, remained legal, republicans were still the main target of the rules. The loyalist groups banned in the North - though not in Britain - are the Ulster Volunteer Force, the tiny Red Hand Commandos, and, ironically, the Ulster Freedom Fighters - a cover name used by the UDA.

The BBC's 1980 *Index* instructs journalists to refer up for permission to interview not only 'members of terrorist organisations' but also 'those who are or may be associated with such organisations'. It says,

> In these cases the producer or editor making the proposal will make it first to his Head of Department who will refer to DNCA [Director of News and Current Affairs] and notify the Network Controller and CNI [Controller Northern Ireland]. **Interviews with individuals who are deemed by DNCA to be closely associated with a terrorist organisation may not be sought or transmitted - two separate stages - without the prior permission of the Director-General.**[30]

The restrictions no longer applied solely to members of paramilitary groups, but also to representatives of republican political organisations. In 1981, for example, it was necessary to obtain the Director-General's permission before interviewing Sinn Féin Vice-President Gerry Adams. Richard Francis, then Director of News and Current Affairs, said of the new guidelines, 'The decision about who is or is not associated with a terrorist organisation - the question of classification - now rests with me.'[31]

The IBA's regulations on Irish coverage appear in its *Guidelines* handbook under the heading 'Crime, anti-social behaviour, etc.'[32] Somewhat ironically, the section includes the statement that 'Political dissidents from foreign countries who are guilty of offences under the laws of their own countries may be interviewed, subject to the normal requirements of impartiality.' Immediately below this, under the heading 'Interviews with people who use or advocate violence or other criminal measures', the *Guidelines* specify:

> Any plans for a programme item which explores and exposes the views of people who within the British Isles use or advocate violence or other criminal measures for the achievement of political ends must be referred to the Authority before any arrangements for filming or videotaping are made. A producer should therefore not plan to interview members of proscribed organisations, for example members of the Provisional IRA or other para-military organisations, without previous discussion with his [sic] company's top management. The management, if they think the item may be justified, will then consult the Authority.

> In exceptional and unforeseen circumstances, it may be impossible for a news reporting team to consult before recording such an item. Consultation with the Authority is still essential to determine whether the item can be transmitted.[33]

The Guidelines add a further restriction:

> An interview conducted in Northern Ireland with a hooded person
> or the contriving by a production team of an incident involving
> hooded persons could be in breach of the Northern Ireland
> (Emergency Provisions) (Amendment) Act 1975. It is not an offence
> to show film or pictures of persons wearing hoods so long as it is
> clear that the incident was not 'set up' in collusion with those
> wearing hoods.[34]

Both the BBC and IBA handbooks detail the legal hazards facing journalists
working in the North, including the onus on them, under Section 5 of the
Criminal Law Act (Northern Ireland) 1967, to supply the police with any
information relating to criminal activities. The BBC's *Index*, collated after
the Carrickmore affair, also drew attention to the similar section in the
Prevention of Terrorism Act.

Balance

Two further requirements circumscribe the way television portrays the
nationalist case. Firstly, programmes which include republican views or
allegations against the British army or RUC have to be 'internally balanced',
with the opposite view put within the same programme. Secondly, all
republican interviewees or people making allegations against Britain have
to be treated in a hostile manner.

The minutes of the BBC's top-level News and Current Affairs meeting on
13 August 1971, four days after the start of internment, record Waldo
Maguire, then Northern Ireland Controller asking that 'the controversial
broadcasting rule (believed to be in force at Suez) - that each item or
programme should be self-balancing - should be reintroduced. The meeting
couldn't remember such a rule ever being enforced.'[35] Within less than
three months, the 'self-balancing' requirement had become policy.

At the ENCA meeting on 10 September 1971, *24 Hours* was criticised for
interviewing Jack Lynch, Prime Minister of the South of Ireland, without
'balancing' the interview with someone from the Unionist government in
the North.[36] On 17 September, *24 Hours* was again criticised for interviewing
Lynch without a 'balancing' Unionist interview. By 22 October, such
reproaches were no longer necessary. The meeting that day saw Editor of
News and Current Affairs Desmond Taylor congratulating everyone on the
BBC's performance and saying he

> had been glad to see that editors and producers had observed the
> policy of providing immediate balance in all current affairs items
> when contentious material had been sought out by the BBC, just as
> Controller, Northern Ireland, had recommended in the previous
> spate of allegations.[37]

The rule was a retreat from the position of former Director General Sir Hugh Carleton Greene, who maintained that 'balance' could be spread over a number of items.[35] It also conflicted with normal journalistic practice. Desmond Taylor, who became Editor of News and Current Affairs in 1971, wrote later, 'In our efforts to be fair, and fairness came to replace balance in our minds, we got to the point where each programme had to include both sides, even where normal editorial considerations did not call for it.'[39]

'Fairness' or 'balance' became an excuse for the suppression of nationalist views. Thus BBC film of the 'Alternative Parliament' set up by the Social Democratic and Labour Party was never shown because, according to *The Sunday Times*, 'it was deemed unbalanced'.[40]

As Jonathan Dimbleby, then a *World at One* reporter, pointed out, the 'balance' rule is applied in a strictly one-sided way:

> The damage caused by an absurd rule is compounded when that rule is broken consistently and discriminately. Thus Brian Faulkner and John Taylor (the junior Home Affairs Minister at Stormont), British army spokesmen, members of the British government, and (less easily) their Labour Shadows, can air their opinions in an 'unbalanced' way with impunity. But in the case of members of the SDLP, the government and the Opposition of the Irish Republic, all critics of the British army, the government, or of Stormont policy, the rule is strictly applied.[41]

Hostile interviews

Television and radio reporters interviewing republicans are required to deal with them in a 'tough' or hostile manner. This applies not only to interviews with members of illegal groups, but also to interviews with Sinn Féin representatives. Richard Francis, then Controller of BBC Northern Ireland, was including Sinn Féin in the 'paramilitary' category when he said, 'Such interviews always demand forthright handling by experienced interviewers - invariably, paramilitary interviewees are treated as hostile witnesses.'[42]

This means that the interviewee is questioned aggressively, usually with frequent interruptions. The interviewer repeatedly challenges or even flatly contradicts statements made by the interviewee. It also means, particularly where the interview is part of a film rather than a studio discussion, that the interviewee is presented in a very critical or unsympathetic context.

The reporter introduced *Tonight*'s July 1979 INLA interview, for example, by emphasising what Richard Francis later called 'the seedy perquisites of anonymity'.[43] Reporter David Lomax explained how

> In Dublin a man calling himself Mr Gray gave us telephone instructions to go to a series of different hotels. The trail led

eventually to a room which we found had been booked in my name in a hotel on the outskirts of the city. There we met two men wearing wigs, dark glasses and false moustaches. They also wore surgical rubber gloves and had strange bulges in the pockets of their anoraks.[44]

Interestingly, as Richard Francis confirmed two years later, the BBC had first approached the IRA for an interview and had been turned down. 'Mr Dick Francis, BBC director of news and current affairs, said that an approach was made to the INLA after the IRA rejected the opportunity,' reported *The Irish Times* on 17 July 1981. According to Sinn Féin spokesperson Richard McAuley, the IRA refused to do a back-to-camera interview because of the negative impression that would be given. Instead, the Republican Press Centre offered to provide a spokesperson who would answer any questions *Tonight* wanted to ask about the IRA, on condition that it was made clear at the start of the programme that the interviewee was not a member of the IRA.[45]

That *Tonight* approached the IRA first casts some doubt on a BBC spokesperson's claim that the INLA had been interviewed to add to public knowledge about 'a new force in terrorism'.[46] The interview was intended for, and transmitted in, *Tonight's* last edition, and the BBC team's rejection of the Republican Press Centre's offer suggests that they were less interested in illuminating the thinking behind the violence than in providing their programme with a sensational exit.

In November 1982, BBC'S *Panorama* showed a film entitled 'Gerry Adams: the Provos' Politician' which was a classic example of the hostile technique.[47] The film was prompted by the previous month's Assembly election, but reporter Fred Emery showed little interest in exploring why Adams had topped the poll in West Belfast. Instead, his overriding concern was to undermine Adams' new status and to establish that Adams was a member of the IRA. This approach was, except in propaganda terms, fruitless, since the courts had failed to prove the accusation, and since Adams was hardly likely to admit it. A more enlightening approach would have been to ask why a man who was associated - wrongly or rightly - in the public mind with the IRA, had won such widespread support among nationalist electors.

Emery set the scene by painting Adams as a sinister, conspiratorial figure, who 'assumes a spurious legitimacy', was 'the manipulator' of the hunger strike, and now works 'in the guise of community politician'. A succession of interviewees were wheeled out to testify against him, among them hardline Unionist Harold McCusker - 'I think he has been drenched in bloodshed for the best part of 10 or 12 years' - as well as Ian Paisley, former Northern Ireland Secretary Merlyn Rees and even Andy Tyrie of the loyalist paramilitary UDA - 'I am absolutely convinced ... that Gerry Adams is Chief of Staff of the IRA.'

The interview with Adams lasted no more than 15 of the programme's 50 minutes, and was like a cross between an inquisition and a battle, with Adams fighting to establish his analysis against Emery's completely opposing version of events:

> *Emery (interrupts):* And it's not on your conscience then that the sort of things you've advocated have helped fill up -
>
> *Adams (interrupts):* Well, what have I advocated?
>
> *Emery:* Well, in advocating the support of the armed struggle, you've helped fill the prisons with young men, you've helped fill the cemeteries with young men -
>
> *Adams (interrupts):* I mean the situation very, very simply -
>
> *Emery (interrupts):* Young Catholic men.
>
> *Adams:* The situation very, very simply is that for - there have been hundreds of thousands of young men and young women who have been through prison, right, and the responsibility for that, I mean before my time, lay with the British government. The responsibility for that during my time - I haven't anyone in prison, the British government has people in prison.

The interview in the end elicited little about Adams save his determination to stand his ground, and the programme as a whole threw no light on why nearly 10,000 people had just voted for him; Emery's approach ruled out the possibility of a sympathetic examination of nationalist attitudes.

Emery's treatment of Gerry Adams was very different from his approach to the other interviewees, including UDA leader Andy Tyrie. It was also in sharp contrast to the treatment given by television to another prominent nationalist, Gerry Fitt. In addition to his many other television appearances, Fitt had at the start of 1982 featured on BBC2's *The Light of Experience*, a quasi-religious programme in which the subject speaks directly, and at length, to the camera about his or her experiences.[48] On 17 October the same year Fitt was given a long and gentle interview on BBC1's *Out on a Limb*.

The media's hostility to Gerry Adams and sympathy for Gerry Fitt do not reflect their standing in the nationalist community, but rather attitudes held in London. The disintegration of Fitt's support in Belfast was made plain in May 1981 when, because of his hostility to the hunger strikers, he was humiliatingly defeated by an anti-H Block candidate in the local elections, losing his seat on Belfast City Council which he had held for 23 years. At Westminster, however, he continued to be almost universally admired. That he lost his parliamentary seat to Gerry Adams in June 1983 made little impact on British establishment attitudes towards him. Politicians and media alike eulogised him in his defeat, and his elevation to the peerage meant that he could continue to be treated as a 'spokesperson' on matters Irish even though he had been rejected at the ballot box.[49]

Censorship

The known instances of censorship have occurred at various points in the reference upwards procedure. Some programmes have been quashed while still at the planning stage, some when filming was in progress, and others have been banned, cut or altered at the final stage, when they were viewed by the IBA or top BBC executives.

The programmes or items that have been censored fall basically into two categories. Either they were critical of British policy, especially of the activities of the army or the police, or - and this is the bigger group - they illustrated republican activities or views. Not surprisingly, no item sympathetic to British government policy has ever been banned. Only one programme dealing with unionism has been censored. This was a BBC *24 Hours* film made in 1971. Implicitly challenging British strategy, the film showed the growing opposition inside the Official Unionist Party to 'moderate' Stormont Prime Minister Major James Chichester-Clark and the extent of sympathy with Ian Paisley. The film predicted Chichester-Clark's resignation, and was suppressed because Northern Ireland Controller Waldo Maguire thought it would help the campaign against him.[50] Chichester-Clark resigned soon afterwards, so the film became redundant.

While most of the decisions to censor programmes appear to have been taken autonomously by the broadcasting bodies, some have been made as a direct result of political pressures. Thus *Panorama's* 1979 project on the IRA met its end largely because of the uproar surrounding the Carrickmore incident. But political influence can also be more subtly exerted.

In 1973, BBC producer Michael Blakstad made a film called *Children in Crossfire*, based on a book by Morris Fraser about the psychological impact of the troubles on the children of the North. Northern Ireland Controller Richard Francis saw it in December and was said to have been 'content' with it.[51] In January 1974, however, the political situation altered when the power-sharing executive took office, and in February Francis expressed concern about the film to Blakstad. Blakstad had gained the support of the British army's eccentric public relations officer, Colin Wallace, but this did not impress Francis. The army, he told BBC Head of Science Features Phillip Daly in a cable, 'are no judges of political consequences and poor judges of social context.' Francis's cable continued: 'After the inauspicious start to the script, given the concern about this film expressed to me at the highest political level, I need to be satisfied that the final version can be made acceptable.' The 'highest political level' was believed to be Francis Pym, who was briefly Northern Ireland Secretary in January and February 1974. Francis went on to complain that the film made no reference to the 'progress' represented by declining violence in Derry and by job creation, and it contained 'not a single reference to the new executive and the remarkable effects of having Catholic Ministers of Housing, Community Relations, etc.'[52]

The film went out in March with a preface, written by Francis, appended to it. This, according to the magazine *Time Out*, said that 'power sharing was in the process of transforming the Northern Ireland political scene' and implied that the rioting shown in the film was a thing of the past.[53] Two months later, in May, the power-sharing executive collapsed and direct rule was reintroduced.[54]

The manner in which approaches are made to broadcasters by 'the highest political level' was illustrated in a Granada TV programme in their series titled, *The State of the Nation: the bounds of freedom.*[55] In this series, influential people were brought together and asked how they would react to hypothetical situations. The sixth programme dealt with the question of televising interviews with 'terrorists'.

Former Northern Ireland Secretary Merlyn Rees was asked if, in order to try to stop such an interview being shown, he would phone the Managing Director of the broadcasting company. Rees replied that he would tell a member of his staff to 'pop round and have a word with him': 'Tell him that I am concerned but I haven't got the full facts. And then perhaps if he wants to have a word about it, perhaps he'd pop over to the House [of Commons] this evening. We could have a drink, talk about it.'

Richard Francis was asked if he thought it right for a minister to invite him to dinner to convey such a request. Francis replied that he thought it 'would be a very suitable way to do it, because ... it recognises the proper distinction between the roles which the broadcasters have to play and those of the ministers responsible for the situation.' Agreeing that at the end of the day he would take his own decision, he said, 'the business of having dinner together is precisely designed to make it quite plain that it isn't a ministerial order and it isn't constraining us to take decisions for which we're not taking full responsibility.'[56]

Self-censorship

The ramifications of the system of internal controls go far beyond the known cases of censorship. The introduction of 'reference upwards' in 1971 led rapidly to the most insidious form of censorship: broadcasters began to censor themselves. As the secretary of the Federation of Broadcasting Unions protested to BBC Chairman Lord Hill, they were demoralised by the need to argue at length over programme suggestions, and feared that their careers were suffering because they had 'disagreed with others' over Irish stories.[57] Jonathan Dimbleby wrote at the end of 1971 that, 'They ignore a story here, resist an idea there, look for a safe angle, or seek out events which are not contentious and of marginal significance.'[58]

As the years passed, and Ireland remained the most politically sensitive topic for television, self-censorship continued. 'For every programme that gets banned, there are about twenty that don't get made,' remarked Mary Holland in 1981.[59] Reporters were inhibited by the procedure for obtaining clearance for stories. Editors dreaded what reporter Jeremy Paxman described as 'heavy duty negotiations with senior management',[60] and broadcasters at all levels feared the political fuss that questioning programmes inevitably provoked. They developed an instinct for how far they could safely go. BBC reporter Nick Ross observed, 'I think much more pernicious than any external authority which tells you, you must do this, you mustn't do that, is the sense of you ought to keep your copy book clean and that you shouldn't do anything which is going to rock the boat.'[61]

Unsurprisingly, only a few questioning reporters and filmmakers stayed the course. Some well-known 'crusading' reporters avoided the topic altogether. Some gave up trying after negative experiences. A handful battled on. As Mary Holland, one of the survivors, put it, to resist the pressures that are brought to bear on anyone trying to report against the political consensus 'takes cunning, it takes patience, and more than anything else it takes boundless energy. As you get older, the energy tends to flag, but it's the duty of journalists I think to try and keep it up.'[62]

A BBC radio editor once likened the situation in the BBC to 'dealing with ectoplasm': 'Nobody is entirely to blame, but the end result of all the "balancing" acts and concerned editing is effectively censorship.'[63] The system ensured that censorship was not only hard to pinpoint, but was also almost invisible to the general public. Precisely because of its subtlety, this 'British way of censorship', as Mary Holland dubbed it, has won the admiration of the international fraternity of 'anti-terrorism' experts, who have recommended it as an example worth following.[64]

Endnotes

1. Appendix to the NCA minutes of 27 November 1979.
2. Jay G. Blumler, 'Ulster on the small screen', *New Society*, 23 December 1971.
3. Quoted in Anthony Smith, 'Television Coverage of Northern Ireland', *Index on Censorship*, vol. 1, no. 2, 1972.
4. Jeremy Paxman. 'Reporting Failure in Ulster', *The Listener*, 5 October 1978.
5. See Anthony Smith, *op. cit.*
6. *News Guide*, 1972, quoted in Philip Schlesinger, *Putting 'Reality' Together: BBC News*, London, Constable, 1978, p. 214.
7. *The Sunday Times*, 2 January 1972.
8. Anthony Smith, *op. cit.*
9. *Ibid.*
10. *Ibid.*
11. *Ibid.*
12. *The Guardian*, 20 November 1979.

13. See Philip Schlesinger, 1978, *op. cit.*, chapter 6.
14. *News and Current Affairs Index*, BBC, October 1980.
15. Richard Francis, 'Broadcasting to a community in conflict - the experience in Northern Ireland', lecture given at the Royal Institute of International Affairs, Chatham House, London, 22 February 1977, London, BBC.
16. *The Listener*, 28 February 1980.
17. Interview with Paul Fox, BBC Radio 3, 18 November 1981.
18. Glasgow, Fontana 1975.
19. Transmitted on 25, 26, 27 October 1982.
20. See ed. Campaign for Free Speech on Ireland, *The British Media and Ireland: Truth the First Casualty*, London, Information on Ireland 1979, p. 34.
21. *The Irish Post*, 26 September 1981.
22. *The Times*, 16 December 1981.
23. *Daily Mirror*, 23 September 1981.
24. *Ibid.*
25. *Principles and Practice in News and Current Affairs*, BBC 1971, quoted in Philip Schlesinger, 1978, *op. cit.*
26. *The Listener*, 20 June 1974.
27. *The Guardian*, 23 November 1971.
28. *Financial Times*, 24 November 1971.
29. *Pandora's Box*, BBC Radio 4, 6 October 1982; see also ed. Brian Lapping, *The State of the Nation: the bounds of freedom*, London: Constable in association with Granada Television 1980, chapter 6.
30. *News and Current Affairs Index*, BBC, October 1980. The position of Director of News and Current Affairs was abolished with Richard Francis's departure to Managing Director of Radio; DNCA'S main functions passed to the Assistant Director-General.
31. *Broadcast*, 25 August 1980.
32. *Television Programme Guidelines*, IBA, revised edition, June 1979.
33. *Ibid*, p. 11.
34. *Ibid.*
35. Quoted in *Private Eye*, 15 November 1971.
36. Ibid.
37. *Ibid.*
38. *The Sunday Times*, 2 January 1972.
39. Desmond Taylor, 'Editorial Responsibilities', BBC Lunch-time Lectures, series 10, 13 November 1975.
40. *The Sunday Times*, 2 January 1972.
41. Unsigned article, *New Statesman*, 31 December 1971.
42. Richard Francis, 'Broadcasting to a community in conflict', *op. cit.*
43. *The Listener*, 27 March 1980.
44. *Tonight*, BBC1, 5 July 1979; for further discussion of the INLA interview, see Philip Schlesinger, Graham Murdock, Philip Elliott, *Televising 'Terrorism'*, London, Comedia, 1983, pp. 50-52.
45. Interview with Richard McAuley by the author.
46. *The Sun*, 7 July 1979.
47. BBC1, 22 November 1982.
48. BBC2, 16 January 1982.

49. The *Panorama* programme on Gerry Adams was discussed by Liz Curtis in *City Limits*, 10-16 December 1982, p. 65, and in Philip Schlesinger et al., 1983, *op. cit.*, pp. 55-56.

50. *The Observer*, 21 November 1971; see also Paul Madden in *The British Media and Ireland: Truth the First Casualty, op. cit.*

51. *Time Out*, 26 July - 1 August 1974.

52. *Ibid.*; see also *The Leveller*, 22 January - 4 February 1982.

53. *Time Out*, 26 July - 1 August 1974.

54. *Children in Crossfire* was repeated on BBC1 on 3 January 1982, and a follow-up film, *A Bright Brand New Day ...?*, produced by Jonathan Crane, was shown the next evening, 4 January 1982.

55. Transmitted on six consecutive Sundays from 17 June to 22 July 1979.

56. Granada TV, *The State of the Nation: The bounds of freedom*, programme 6, 'Terrorism', transmitted on ITV on 22 July 1979; see also the book of the same title, ed. Brian Lapping, London, Constable, in association with Granada Television, 1980.

57. *The Times*, 3 February 1972.

58. Unsigned article in *New Statesman*, 31 December 1971.

59. Speaking at NUJ/ACTT Conference on Media Censorship of Northern Ireland, Birmingham, 28 February 1981.

60. *Ibid.*

61. London Weekend Television, *Look Here*, transmitted on ITV on 8 July 1978; see also *Film and Television Technician*, August/September 1978.

62. NUJ/ACTT conference, 28 February 1981, *op. cit.*

63. *The Sunday Times*, 2 January 1972.

64. See Philip Schlesinger et al., 1983, *op. cit.*

7.

Michael Leapman

THE 'REAL LIVES' CONTROVERSY

(From *The Last Days of the Beeb*, London, Allen and Unwin, 1986, pages 290-331)

[...]

As a topic, the future of British broadcasting had to share the limelight at the 1985 television festival with a sensational incident that had occurred two weeks earlier. Like so many of the programme disputes of the last two decades, it concerned Northern Ireland. The BBC was about to screen a documentary in the *Real Lives* series that included an interview with a man reported as being the chief of staff of the Provisional IRA. Hearing of this the Home Secretary, Leon Brittan, wrote to the chairman of the governors, Stuart Young, asking for the programme to be withdrawn. The governors held an emergency meeting and took the unusual step of viewing the programme in advance. Having done so, they rejected the unanimous advice of the board of management and banned the film, provoking a ferocious dispute and a rash of front-page headlines that lasted for days.

Throughout the spring of 1985, there had been a feeling on the board of management that the governors were working up to some kind of a showdown. It was reinforced by a cluster of incidents in April where the governors made statements critical of decisions by Milne[1] and his staff. They appeared to have abandoned the notion that public solidarity with management was paramount. [...]

The spring sequence of misfortunes - the dropped balls and missed catches, in the sporting parlance popular at the Beeb - persuaded Young[2] and his colleagues that there was something essentially at fault with the corporation's senior direction. Looking at the composition of the board of management, they found it top-heavy with programme people, arts graduates and former producers, lacking the streak of worldly realism that Young, as

96

an accountant, detected and admired amongst the business executives he was used to dealing with.

At their May meetings the governors discussed changes at the highest level. At one point the position of the director-general himself was called into question, although there was never a serious move to replace him. At the beginning of June, press speculation about changes mentioned the possibility of Milne being replaced by Jeremy Isaacs, the head of Channel 4. [...]

When the anticipated reshuffle was announced after the board meeting in Plymouth on 6 June, [...] Michael Checkland was made deputy director-general. He had been director of resources for television and was a money man like Young, more familiar with cash flow than camera angles. It was a clear sign that the governors wanted commercial criteria to play a stronger role in management decisions. Somebody must rein in the programme people. The corporation had to operate in a more businesslike fashion.

In a perfect application of Sod's Law, the first time Checkland had to stand in for Milne was in a dispute over programming rather than management. Despite the high regard in which he was held by the board, he was unable to head off a graver public relations disaster than any that had occurred that spring, or for years previously. The governors' long period of muscle-flexing culminated in the delivery of a damaging punch to the Beeb's vital organs.

Real Lives was a BBC1 series produced by Will Wyatt's documentary features department at Kensington House. The linking theme was implied in the title. The programmes focused on people, often in stressful situations, and in the case of known figures it sought to penetrate their public image to explore the reality beneath. Its summer season in 1985 was expected to be its last, because Michael Grade was averse to providing too many fixed spots for documentaries in his schedules at prime time.

In 1984 Paul Hamann, a producer with fourteen years experience in the BBC and something of a specialist on Northern Ireland, made a film called *A Company*, about four disgruntled soldiers who had been in the army when troops were sent there in 1969. One of them had been responsible for the army's first killing. Hamann took them back to the province and they gave their views on the rights and wrongs of the dispute. Some Protestant partisans had objected to the film and Lucy Faulkner, the BBC's governor for Northern Ireland, expressed their and her concern to the board. But Hamann had earlier made a film that angered the Republicans. It was called *Fighting for Life* and concerned two British soldiers horribly injured by an IRA bomb, and the efforts of neuro-surgeons at Belfast's Royal Victoria Hospital to secure their recovery. When that was screened he received a telephoned threat from the IRA; so he felt justified in regarding himself as an impartial chronicler of the affairs of the province.

Hamann wanted to make another Northern Ireland film for *Real Lives* in 1985. Sir John Hermon, chief constable of the Royal Ulster Constabulary, tipped him off that during that summer's marching season, when Protestants stage provocatively triumphant marches through the towns and cities, more trouble than usual was anticipated. The police planned to stop or divert some marches and there would be confrontations. Hermon initially offered Hamann generous access to film the RUC as they implemented this policy, but in early April he changed his mind and withdrew the offer.

Hamann now had a camera crew at his disposal in Northern Ireland but no film to make, so he discussed alternatives with the producer of the *Real Lives* series, Eddie Mirzoeff [...] They agreed that he should try to get the agreement of two leading and opposing politicians in Derry (Londonderry), Ulster's second city, to make a film about the conflict as seen through their eyes. They decided upon Gregory Campbell, leader on the city council of Ian Paisley's Democratic Unionist Party, and Martin McGuinness of Provisional Sinn Féin, alleged in a *Sunday Times* report to be the chief of staff of the IRA (which he denied). Both are elected members of the Northern Ireland Assembly and both advocate violence, although neither has been convicted of carrying out violent acts. Hamann's first thought was to call the film *Elected Representatives*. At a later stage that was changed to *At the Edge of the Union*.

Campbell, who had received comparatively little national media exposure at that point, was keen on the idea from the start, but McGuinness took some persuading. He did not want to be accused by his Sinn Féin colleagues of seeking personal publicity. His wife Bernie was also opposed to the project and remained reluctant to participate even after McGuinness eventually agreed.

After Carrickmore, the BBC had strengthened its rules about interviews with people believed to be involved in terrorism. On page 52 of the *News and Current Affairs Index*, the following sentence appears in bold type:

> Interviews with individuals who are deemed by ADG (assistant director-general) to be closely associated with a terrorist organisation may not be sought or transmitted - two separate stages - without the prior permission of DG.

In addition, the rules demand that the controller in Northern Ireland should be consulted about any programmes concerning the province. Since those rules were framed, however, the position in Northern Ireland had changed. The Republican movement had begun to operate in the political arena, as well as espousing violence. The previous May, Sinn Féin had fifty-nine representatives elected to local councils. Despite the fact that most, including McGuinness, had links with the IRA, they were often interviewed on television in the province. There was no question of referring such interviews to the director-general.

When Wyatt learned that Hamann's revised contribution to the *Real Lives* series involved interviewing McGuinness, he told Mirzoeff to assure himself that this did not place the programme in the category that had to be referred to Milne. Mirzoeff consulted Cecil Taylor, acting controller for Northern Ireland in the absence of James Hawthorne, who was away sick. Taylor advised him that as an elected politician McGuinness was not in that category. Wyatt also confirmed that Taylor had told Protheroe[3] about the programme. He was convinced he had done enough to comply with the reference procedures, and so it would doubtless have proved were it not for an unfortunate and unforeseeable combination of circumstances.

Hamann had the film in the cutting room when, in June, Arab hijackers took over a TWA aircraft and held it at Beirut airport for several days. The American television networks gave the event extensive publicity, including interviews with the hijackers, who went so far as to organise a press conference. There was much criticism of the extent of the coverage and in July the Prime Minister added her voice at the American Bar Association's convention in London. 'We must try to find ways to starve the terrorists of the oxygen of publicity on which they depend,' she declared, to rousing applause.

Hamann feared the effect this statement might have on the reaction of his superiors to the programme. His distinctive style of film-making involves letting the characters speak for themselves, with no commentary and no challenging questions from an interviewer. So when McGuinness and Campbell spoke of violence and its inevitability, there was nobody to ask a question to weaken the impact of their advocacy. The film also showed them at home with their families, pointing up the contrast between their violent words and their peaceful domestic lives. Hamann foresaw that all this could be construed as offering a platform for terrorism and lending it a human face. He was additionally worried by a scene in which Campbell was shown loading a gun.

He was much relieved, therefore, when neither Wyatt or Hawthorne, when they saw it, suggested major changes. 'Difficult subject, well handled,' was the verdict of Hawthorne, who asked Hamann only to shorten a section where old news film showed the brutality of the RUC against Catholic civil rights marchers. Hamann did so. Wyatt had no changes to suggest. The programme was scheduled for 7 August and a three-page feature, with large colour pictures of the two men and extensive quotations from both, appeared in *Radio Times*.

But if Wyatt and Hawthorne had not recognised the new climate created by Thatcher's comments on publicising terrorists, the sharp journalists at the *Sunday Times* had. The first hint of the paper's interest came on Tuesday, 23 July, when Hamann received an apparently innocent call from Barrie Penrose, a reporter specialising in major investigations. Penrose wanted to confirm that the programme included an interview with

McGuinness. Hamann saw nothing sinister in the approach and was glad to help him. Producers naturally welcome advance publicity for their programmes and there was to be a screening for the press on the Friday.

Hamann did not bother to tell anyone else about Penrose's call until two days later, when he heard from Gregory Campbell that the *Sunday Times* had been in touch with him as well. 'I think they're trying to dig up a story,' said the Loyalist leader. The reporter had asked him whether he knew that McGuinness was going to be in the film when he agreed to take part in it. Campbell had responded scathingly that yes, of course he had known. The reporter seemed disappointed.

Hamann thought it sensible at this point to alert the BBC press officers about the newspaper's interest, and they in turn phoned Wyatt, who was not unduly alarmed. He advised them to respond that both McGuinness and Campbell were entitled to a salary from the British government as elected representatives in Ulster and were therefore legitimate interview subjects.

On Friday Penrose began seeking official reaction to the proposed film. He sent hand-delivered letters to Leon Brittan and Bernard Ingham, the Prime Minister's press secretary, inviting their comments. He spoke to Douglas Hurd, Secretary of State for Northern Ireland, who said he was 'alarmed' to hear of the interview. 'Giving space to terrorists has a very powerful effect and it is up to the broadcasting authorities to understand this,' he added.

What Penrose needed to make his story work was a comment from the Prime Minister herself. Not only had she made the 'oxygen of publicity' remarks but she had also been the intended victim of an IRA bomb in Brighton ten months earlier. She was now visiting Washington where Mark Hosenball, one of the paper's correspondents, was instructed to ask a question about the programme. The only chance he had was at a briefing for British reporters on Friday evening. Anxious not to alert rival papers to the story, Hosenball asked a general, hypothetical question without going into the details of the *Real Lives* documentary. How would the Prime Minister react if she learned that a British TV company was going to interview the IRA chief of staff? She replied that she would 'condemn them utterly', adding: 'The IRA is proscribed in Britain and in the Republic of Ireland. We have lost between 2,000 and 2,500 people in the past 16 years. I feel very strongly about it and so would many other people.' Next morning, the day before the *Sunday Times* appeared, a Downing Street spokesman phoned the paper to stress that Thatcher had been speaking hypothetically, not about any particular intended programme. Penrose did not make that clear in his report.

Alan Protheroe told Penrose that the film was 'responsible and balanced'. But a fatal weakness in the BBC's position was that the person ultimately responsible for it, as for all programmes, was still serenely unaware of its existence. A week earlier Alasdair Milne had set off for Scandinavia with his wife Sheila for a fishing holiday. It had begun in Norway and continued in Finland, where he was being looked after by Finnish Television. On Monday, 29 July, he was due to move on to Sweden.

There were two routes by which he should have heard of the *Real Lives* programme before he left London. By a strict interpretation of the News and Current Affairs Index, Wyatt ought to have told him. The second way was through the minutes of the fortnightly target meetings. These were convened by Brian Wenham for the specific purpose of pinpointing possible areas of controversy in forthcoming programmes, especially on Northern Ireland. Milne did not attend the meetings but received the minutes. Since the beginning of the year, though, the meetings had ceased through what Milne later described as administrative inertia. Wenham thought there was a good deal too much unproductive chat in the BBC and this was one meeting he could dispense with. Milne did not seek to dissuade him.

Had he been made aware of Hamann's film through either of these channels, Milne might have asked to view it for himself. At the very least, he would have mentioned it to Stuart Young. It is his habit to alert the chairman to any potentially troublesome programmes and to assure him that he is satisfied they can be defended in the event of criticism - which, in the majority of cases, does not materialise.

With the benefit of an advance warning signal, Young would not have been taken by surprise when, at his North London home in the late afternoon of Saturday, 27 July, he received a call from Lady Faulkner, telling him that she had just been telephoned by the *Sunday Times* seeking her comments on a programme of which she had not hitherto been aware. In her case, too, the usual referral procedures had failed to operate. Hawthorne's normal practice was to warn the Northern Ireland governor of any network programme concerning the province, in much the same way as Milne kept Young informed. But at the end of July Lady Faulkner would end her seven-year stint as governor. By the time the programme was due to be aired she would be replaced by Dr James Kincade, a Belfast headmaster. She had already attended what everyone believed would be her last board meeting, where formal farewells had been bidden. Hawthorne thought it inappropriate to discuss with her a programme that would be shown outside her term of office.

In her phone call, Lady Faulkner warned Young to expect an approach from the *Sunday Times*. It came almost immediately, in the form of a letter pushed under his door by a messenger who did not even wait long enough to ring the bell. The letter outlined the nature of the programme and asked for an interview with Young about it that very day. Young phoned the duty press officer who rang back to confirm that there was such a programme and that the *Sunday Times* was next day running a story saying that the government were critical of it.

Young was surprised that he had not previously heard about the film but believed that the row would be containable. He would assure himself that the correct consultation procedures had been followed. (The *Sunday Times* reported, falsely as it turned out, that Milne had given his permission for it to be broadcast.) Then he and the governors would defend the programme, at least until after it had been shown and they were able to appraise it critically. On Sunday he telephoned Sir William Rees-Mogg, his deputy, and Michael Checkland, doing his first stint as acting director-general since his appointment as Milne's number two. He also contacted David Holmes, the secretary, arranging to talk to him in the office first thing on Monday.

Checkland summoned the board of management to Broadcasting House early on Monday to see the film. Milne was the only one absent. It had not seemed to Checkland that the issue was important enough to warrant trying to reach him in Finland by telephone. The board decided to a man that *Real Lives: At the Edge of the Union* should be shown as scheduled, though most thought it would benefit from an introductory statement about its aim and a round table discussion on terrorism afterwards, probably on Newsnight. There was talk of a possible change to one of the captions. At 10.30 Checkland and Protheroe went to Young's fourth-floor office to report in those terms to the chairman and David Holmes.

Their meeting had been under way for about half an hour when Holmes was called away to take a phone call from Wilfred Hyde, a senior Home Office official. Hyde said that the Home Secretary had asked him to read over the phone a message that he was releasing to the press about the *Real Lives* programme. Holmes, a former reporter, took it all down in shorthand and rushed back to the chairman's office to read it aloud. It amounted to a public request to the governors not to show the film because of its security implications. It appeared to be 'giving succour' to terrorist organisations. 'It gave them the opportunity for public advocacy of terrorist methods by a prominent member of the IRA. This gave spurious legitimacy to the use of violence for political ends. It would be contrary to the national interest that a programme of the kind apparently envisaged should be broadcast.' If it was to be shown as scheduled, Brittan would like the chance to view it in advance. The Home Secretary insisted that he respected the BBC's independence and invited Young to telephone him whenever he wished.

Brittan did not see his move as unorthodox or as an attempt to exert improper pressure. As minister responsible for law and order he felt he had a right to express his opinion on the question. The fact that he was also minister responsible for broadcasting was not, in his view, a reason for staying his hand. Among the many criticisms made of him in the wake of the affair, it was pointed out that most of his predecessors would have sought to deal with the matter confidentially, without involving the press. Brittan, a lawyer by training, prefers to operate above board, not by off-the-record winks and nudges. A precise man, he appears, at least in public, to lack warmth and good fellowship. He had been made Home Secretary - an important promotion from his former post as Chief Secretary to the Treasury - because he shares Thatcher's brand of strict conservatism on financial and social issues. But he is not an instinctive politician: he is insufficiently calculating when it comes to assessing the consequences of what he does and the manner in which he does it. He was dismayed by the proposed interview with McGuinness and saw no reason not to make the point publicly.

Young was surprised and angry at what he saw as a blatant attempt by the government to lean so heavily on the BBC as to make nonsense of the independence that Brittan claimed he recognised. He told Holmes to phone the Home Office back and urge them to retract the message. He was certain the BBC was the victim of a *Sunday Times* set-up and that Brittan's intervention would compound it. But Hyde told Holmes it was too late. The text of Brittan's statement had already been released to the press.

Within half an hour the first edition of the *Standard,* London's evening paper, was delivered to Young. The main front-page story was headed BBC TOLD: BAN IRA FILM and it contained long quotations from Brittan's statement. As soon as he saw it Young telephoned Brittan, incensed at having read his comments in the newspaper before they had been conveyed to the BBC in writing.

'Do you really want a letter?' asked Brittan, who, having made his point publicly and forcefully, but informally, would have preferred to avoid committing it to paper. Young insisted. He was, he said, planning to summon an emergency governors' meeting the following day and needed a record of the precise terms of the Home Secretary's request. Without waiting for it to arrive, Holmes rang round the governors and to his surprise, seeing that it was August, he received promises from all but one of them to report to Broadcasting House on the following morning, Tuesday 30 July.

Brittan's long letter was not delivered at Broadcasting House until ten past seven on Monday evening. It began by insisting that the decision whether to broadcast the programme lay with the corporation alone.

> It is no part of my task as the minister with responsibility for broadcasting policy generally to attempt to impose an act of censorship on what should be broadcast in particular programmes. To do so would be inconsistent with the constitutional independence of the BBC, which is a crucial part of our broadcasting arrangements. I do, on the other hand, also have a ministerial responsibility for the fight against the ever present threat of terrorism ... The BBC would be giving an immensely valuable platform to those who have evinced an ability, readiness and intention to murder indiscriminately its own viewers. Quite apart from the deep offence that this would give to the overwhelming majority of the population and the profound distress that it would cause to families of the victims of

terrorism, it would also in my considered judgment materially assist the terrorist cause. Recent events elsewhere in the world have confirmed only too clearly what has long been understood in this country: that terrorism thrives on the oxygen of publicity ... Even if the programme and any surrounding material were, as a whole, to present terrorist organisations in a wholly unfavourable light, I would still ask you not to permit it to be broadcast.

The deliberate echoing of Thatcher's phrase about 'the oxygen of publicity' was a less than subtle hint by Brittan that his initiative represented the collective position of the Cabinet. In fact he had not discussed the issue with Thatcher. Several other ministers while approving the sentiment behind the letter, later questioned his confrontatory tactics. But at that stage only one of the principals, Stuart Young, seemed aware of the gravity of the position that had been created by Brittan's *démarche*. The other man most intimately concerned with this government assault on the corporation, the director-general, had, astonishingly enough, been informed for the first time about the dispute scarcely an hour before Brittan's letter arrived.

Alasdair Milne had fished in Norway and Finland and was about to fish in Sweden. His Swedish friends told him that quite the most delightful way of travelling from Helsinki to Stockholm was on the boat that left the Finnish capital at 6 p.m. every night, steamed through the Gulf of Finland and across the Baltic Sea to arrive in Sweden at 9 a.m. next day. Soon after 5 on 29 July he and Sheila boarded the boat and were making themselves comfortable in their cabin when he was summoned to the purser's office by loudspeaker. It was a message from his hosts, Finnish Television. There had been a call from London. Would he telephone Checkland as soon as he could?

By now the ship was less than half an hour from sailing time. There were three phone booths on board but they needed Finnish coins and he had changed all his into Swedish. Even had he been able to borrow some, all the booths were occupied until just before the boat sailed. Only when it left port was he able to use the ship-to-shore radio link to contact his deputy in London.

Checkland gave a rundown of the events of the weekend and told him the governors would meet next morning. It was the first Milne had heard of the contentious *Real Lives* programme. Checkland's main concern was to have his chief's advice on what to do if the governors insisted on viewing the film in advance of transmission. Milne equivocated. He told Checkland to argue with conviction that they should not go against precedent; but if they felt they could not answer Brittan's letter sensibly without seeing the programme, that was their right. Then he asked if there was any chance of the meeting being postponed to allow him to attend it. Had he been contacted earlier on the Monday he would have been able to get back by Tuesday morning. Now that the boat had left port it would be Tuesday before he reached dry land again, so there was no chance of getting back to London for the meeting unless it could be postponed. Checkland replied that he thought a postponement out of the question, since the governors had already been summoned.

That casual exchange was to become a critical moment in the drama. Checkland had not raised the possibility of postponement with anyone on the governors' side. It had not occurred to him. He had every confidence in his own ability to act properly in Milne's place, and after the events of recent months the director-general certainly needed his holiday. So did his wife Sheila, who had not been at all well.

Milne had not specified whether he was talking about putting the meeting off until Wednesday, when he could be there if he was willing to break his holiday, or until the following week, when he was due back in the office anyway. While Young would not have delayed the meeting for a week, he maintained later that he would, if asked, have postponed it for a day. But he was not asked. Some suspected that Checkland did not encourage Milne's return because he was keen to flex his muscles as acting DG for the first time. This is an unlikely explanation, for Checkland himself went on holiday shortly after the governors' meeting: had he been motivated by self-aggrandisement he would no doubt have altered his own arrangements. The likeliest reason is that he saw no point in Milne disrupting his private plans for what he thought was only the slimmest chance of altering the situation. It was an unfortunate decision, though, for in the event Milne's absence proved a key factor in persuading the governors first to view the film and then to ban it.

The morning of Tuesday, 30 July, was showery and miserable, an apology for high summer. Nor were the BBC governors in a sunny mood as they ran the gauntlet of photographers and reporters outside Broadcasting House. Some had been dragged up from holiday homes in the country: but they managed to look reasonably businesslike for the cameras as they walked into the newly refurbished art deco lobby and took the lift to the third floor board room.

The governors are an assorted bunch, but nowadays not assorted enough to satisfy those critics who, in the wake of this dispute, charged them with leaning too heavily towards the philosophy of the government - or, more bluntly, of being political placemen. As she showed when declining to appoint Mark Bonham-Carter as chairman, Thatcher has no time for consensus politics or its practitioners. When a vacancy occurred at the end of 1984 for a governor connected with the arts, the management were asked for suggestions. They proposed John Mortimer, the popular playwright and author who, as a lawyer, defended several cases involving human rights and freedom of expression. That made him too libertarian for the government, who instead appointed the Earl of Harewood, 62, a cousin of the Queen and former managing director of the English National Opera. Even under Labour and less ideological Conservative Prime Ministers, the board has tended to settle to the right of centre, simply because that is the natural political alignment of those from whose ranks the governors are mostly drawn.

Apart from Young and Harewood, the members of the board who met that day to discuss *Real Lives: At the Edge of the Union*, were:

Sir William Rees-Mogg, 57, vice-chairman, chairman of the Arts Council and former editor of *The Times*.

Lady Faulkner, 60, Northern Ireland governor, due to retire the following day. (Her successor, **James Kincade,** headmaster of the Methodist College in Belfast, also sat in.)

Watson Peat, 62, Scottish governor, in farming and meat production.

Alwyn Roberts, 51, Welsh governor, director of extramural studies at the University College of North Wales.

Sir John Johnston, 67, former diplomat and also on the point of stepping down.

Daphne Park, 63, another former diplomat and principal of Somerville College, Oxford.

Lady Parkes, 59, educationist, chairman of the College Advisory Committee.

Jocelyn Barrow, 56, born in Trinidad, former vice-chairman of the Campaign Against Racial Discrimination.

Malcolm McAlpine, 68, an executive of the building and property company that bears his family name.

(Sir John Boyd, 57, former president of the Confederation of Shipbuilding and Engineering Unions, was the only governor who could not attend the meeting on 30 July.)

A worthy bunch, but it is easy to understand the prevailing view at the Beeb that, with one or two exceptions, they are not of outstanding calibre. Most members of the board of management were there, and so was James Hawthorne, invited because of his special interest in the programme. Proceedings began at 10.30 a.m. with Young extending an especially warm welcome to Lady Faulkner, saying how much the other governors appreciated her attendance on her last day in office, after the formal farewells had been endured. Some felt that by paying that tribute Young, probably inadvertently, was placing Faulkner in an unusually strong position, increasing the chance that her view of the proper course of action would prevail.

When Young had explained the position he invited discussion on whether the governors should view the film and asked members of the board of management to speak first. Checkland admitted that there had been what he called a 'technical foul' in the matter of procedures. The programme should have been referred to the director-general, but was not. However, the rest of the management board had seen it and were confident that they could speak for Milne in their decision to show it under the conditions they had agreed the previous day. For this reason he felt the governors should not see it but, echoing the director-general's guidance of the evening before, he conveyed that he would not be fervently opposed if they decided on a viewing.

Bill Cotton, on the other hand, was adamant that the governors should not break with precedent by seeing the film, and he argued his case with passion. The last time the entire board had viewed a programme in advance was in 1967, the subject being bull-fighting. As for *Yesterday's Men* in 1971, only about half the board were present when Lord Hill decided on a screening. Alan Protheroe warned the governors to be careful about their reaction to something that had begun as a newspaper stunt. 'This mischievous action by the *Sunday Times* has taken the BBC and its procedures by surprise,' he declared - a characteristically neat turn of phrase, though its meaning was far from clear. Brian Wenham then argued for the specific format that had been agreed by management the day before, in which the programme would be followed by a discussion. He pointed out that, whatever happened, the film when shown would receive more than usual attention because of the dispute that had grown up around it.

When the governors began to speak it was clear that they resented having been put in a virtually impossible situation by a combination of the failure of management's reference procedures and the improper pressure being applied by the Home Secretary. It was true that the BBC had to be seen to be independent of government influence. It was also true that as governors they had the obligation to consider representations from all responsible sources. They were not at liberty to refuse to recognise complaints because they did not like the form in which they had been made.

At this point it became apparent that Milne's absence would have a crucial bearing on the outcome. If the director-general, the editor-in-chief they had appointed, had seen the film and passed it, the governors would in all probability have accepted his judgement, reasoning that not to do so would be to imply a lack of confidence in Milne personally. But Checkland's endorsement could not be regarded as of equal weight. He was, after all, a man whose experience was in administration rather than programmes. How could he judge the fine line between what was acceptable on the screen and what was provocative? In Milne's absence it was up to the governors to exercise final editorial control. They could not simply tell the Home Secretary that no, they had not seen fit to view the film, and neither had the director-general, but yes, they were all satisfied that the BBC ought to show it.

Nor could the governors fail to take into account previous occasions in recent months when they had been told that the director-general had been unaware of a set of circumstances that developed into a crisis. [...] The BBC was a large organisation and nobody could know everything that was going on inside it, but there did seem to be something wrong with Milne's intelligence system. Michael Swann had been convinced that the position of editor-in-chief was too onerous to be combined with all the administrative duties of a director-general, and he had insisted on the appointment of a director of news and current affairs to perform exactly that function. Richard Francis was the first to hold the position - and the last, for it lapsed when Milne became director-general and made him managing director, radio. The appointment of a DNCA had not prevented the Carrickmore uproar; but were it still in existence it would have provided a safety net for an accident-prone board of management.

The argument in favour of the governors viewing the *Real Lives* film was put most forcefully by the vice-chairman, Sir William Rees-Mogg. He exerted a powerful influence on the board because, amongst a group just below the first rank in British public life, he stood out as the best known, a man who moved easily in politics and journalism, who had Cabinet ministers to dinner at his house in Westminster. He was known to have favoured Young's appointment as chairman. Moreover, the vice-chairman had firm views on most issues and the ability to express them vividly - a gift developed while writing leaders for *The Times,* and one that Young lacked.

Rees-Mogg's view of the *Real Lives* programme was coloured by his suspicion of a deliberate bid by Hawthorne - despite the Ulsterman's denials - to keep it from Lady Faulkner. He did not accept that her impending departure from the board was an excuse for not keeping her informed. Earlier, Lucy Faulkner herself had surprisingly opposed viewing the programme, partly because, some years earlier, she had been outvoted by the other governors when she wanted to preview a programme about Ireland that discussed the role of her late husband. She pointed out that Brittan's chief fear seemed to be security and the board had no qualification to pronounce on that. That was why some governors felt the right action would be not to rule on the programme at all, but to invite the Home Secretary to ban it, using his reserve powers under the BBC licence agreement, if he thought it a security threat. But the majority felt that, in the light of Brittan's letter, to take that course would be to dodge the issue.

The arguments swung from one view to the opposite. Young, although he preferred as chairman to play a neutral role, thought on balance that they should watch it. He believed it would put them in a stronger position vis a vis Brittan when they decided as he was convinced they would - to broadcast the programme as scheduled. All the same, the decision to view the film in advance was a narrow one.

The governors moved to the adjoining dining room for lunch, a cold buffet with BBC house wine. As the coffee was being served the film began to run on the five screens scattered round the room. It was clear almost from the start that the group, staring in almost total silence, did not like it. A sullen, disapproving mood prevailed, like an impossibly extended catching of the breath. Afterwards Rees-Mogg and about half the governors went into a conclave near one of the screens. The management people thought that ominous. There were suggestions that someone should go and break up the circle. Nobody did.

After the viewing the governors returned to the board room to reconvene in formal session. Rees-Mogg was invited by Young to speak first and did so in immoderate terms, striking a keynote for the other governors. The programme was 'totally unacceptable' and ought not to be shown. It was not a technical foul, as Checkland had argued, but a major failure to apply safeguards that had been devised by the management and approved by the governors. The reference system existed so that programmes such as this could be considered at an early stage at the highest level.

Rees-Mogg is a strong believer in rigid lines of authority. Looking hard at Hawthorne, he said there had been no convincing explanation of why Lady Faulkner had not been consulted at an early stage. While there was no formal obligation on the controller's part to refer such matters to her, he had until now customarily done so and it was proper that he should. Both the usual procedures and standing instructions had been breached. If the rules were wrong or impossible to apply, they should be changed. If they were simply ignored the editing system broke down and decisions like these became purely arbitrary.

Turning to specific criticism of the programme, Rees-Mogg said it had given McGuinness the opportunity to make propaganda on behalf of the IRA, not countered by any effectively stringent questioning. This derived from Hamann's technique of letting the characters speak for themselves, rather than in an argumentative interview that would allow the flaws in extremist arguments to be pointed out instantly. He referred the board to another part of the News and Current Affairs Index. Dealing with the coverage of violence, page 79, paragraph 14 states: 'Great skill is required to tread the thin line between explanation of the role of these elements in the conflict and providing a platform for propaganda. Political rhetoric may be illustrated in a programme, but it should not be allowed to pass unchallenged.' In this case, it had been.

Rees-Mogg accepted Young's caution that if the governors banned the programme they would be attacked for caving in to the government, but they were not entitled to take that into account. Their responsibility was to decide the issue on the merits of the film they had just seen. Brittan had behaved improperly, he was sure of that. But, if the Home Secretary's view of the programme was right, to find against him because it would be embarrassing to find for him would be a betrayal of the board's function as a last court of appeal in BBC matters. *Real Lives: At the Edge of the Union* would offend many people and should not be shown.

Lady Faulkner spoke next, beginning in a combative manner. 'I can see, Jimmy,' she said, turning to Hawthorne, 'why you didn't tell me about this' - a sally Hawthorne found hurtful because he believed from earlier conversations that she had accepted his explanation of why he had not done so. She continued in the same vein, clearly feeling that Rees-Mogg's powerful opening speech gave her a licence to criticise the programme with a level of passion that she was normally chary of deploying. She said she was 'utterly horrified' by the film, which was inflammatory and would almost certainly lead to inter-communal violence in Northern Ireland. She especially disliked the file footage of the police in action against civil rights marchers - the segment that had been shortened at Hawthorne's request - pointing out that it was not balanced by any portrayal of violence by the IRA.

Stuart Young was by now seriously alarmed at the drift of the meeting. His hopes that the viewing would lead to approval of the broadcast - albeit with amendments - were clearly not going to be fulfilled. He pointed out to the governors the gravity of banning a programme at the government's behest. However genuine their reservations about the film, if they did not allow it to be shown they would certainly be accused of bowing cravenly to official pressure. The consequences, he warned, could be 'immeasurable'.

But he was powerless to alter the direction the meeting was taking. Johnston, Peat and Lady Parkes, while they did not match the extreme views of the first two speakers, all articulated worry about the film. McAlpine gave his verdict in two words: 'No show.' Harewood began his contribution by declaring: 'I hate it, I hate it, I hate it,' going on to describe the programme as 'smooth, odious and hateful'. Park was equally opposed to it. She said the scenes showing McGuinness with his family had the effect of domesticating the IRA. Barrow called it sinister, and made one point that had a powerful effect on some of her colleagues. She said that many young, disadvantaged black people believed violence was the only way to improve their condition. They would welcome this film because it lent legitimacy to that view. In a later contribution she objected to the fact that the army patrol in the film had been led by a black soldier, who had been made to look silly.

Kincade, although he had no formal vote, was asked for his view and showed solidarity with Lady Faulkner. He said he would have to consider his position as a governor if the film were broadcast. Young quipped that he could scarcely resign before taking office but in reality the chairman was in anything but a flippant mood. He could see now that the board were almost unanimous for banning the programme. He repeated his earlier warning, with scarcely any hope that it would be heeded. When he went round the table for a second time to confirm the governors' view, Roberts was the only one who voted against a ban.

Now the problem was how to announce the decision in a way that would limit the damage. A small group was set up to draft Young's reply to Brittan's letter. They felt it important to stress that they thought the Home Secretary had behaved badly.

> We would now wish to discuss with you the profound issues raised in your letter to me. We are anxious that those discussions be conducted in a neutral and dispassionate climate. Having seen the programme, the board of governors believes it would be unwise for this programme in the series *Real Lives* to be transmitted in its present form: the programme's intention would continue to be misread and misinterpreted.

The letter represented a subtle modification of what the governors had actually decided. The majority of them had assumed during their debate that they were talking definitively about whether to show the film or censor it. The phrase 'in its present form', leaving open the possibility of a later transmission after amendments, was inserted only in the drafting stage and formed the basis of the eventual compromise.

With the letter agreed, Young summoned the board of management back into the meeting room. It had, he said, been a tiring day, a momentous day. What he was now asking was that the management should show solidarity with the decision that had been taken by the governors. He knew they would be disappointed by it, but he felt that as loyal corporation men they had a responsibility to rally round at a time when the BBC would certainly come under heavy attack from the outside. He wanted them to defend the decision in front of their subordinates. If Young really believed he could coax support from the professionals, he was quickly disabused of the notion. 'We can't be solid on this one,' Cotton told him. That made Young and the other governors angry. They dispersed on a sour note.

The BBC management had believed that the governors would conform with precedent and decide not to view the film; that they would accept the judgement of the professionals that it should be broadcast. It was expected that the meeting would be over by lunch time. Will Wyatt sat in his office at Kensington House awaiting a call from Bill Cotton. When it did not come he phoned the press office, who told him the meeting was still going on and it could last a while yet. Even when he heard that the governors had decided to look at the film, Wyatt was not unduly worried. He thought the decision misguided but did not expect it to affect the eventual outcome.

The first indication that things had gone seriously wrong came at about 5 in the evening, when Wyatt was asked to join Michael Grade in Cotton's office at Television Centre to await the managing director's return from

Broadcasting House. As the two men sat there expectantly, Cotton phoned his secretary with the message that the film had been censored. So when he arrived with Brian Wenham, in the middle of the *Six O'Clock News*, they already knew the worst. The four were joined in Cotton's office by Graeme McDonald, controller of BBC2. Over drinks, they discussed how they could limit the effect of what they all agreed was a profound crisis for the BBC. The staff, they knew, would react badly. The quintet stayed to watch the extensive coverage of the governors' decision on the *Nine O'Clock News*, then Cotton, Grade and Wyatt went out for a Chinese meal, returning to Cotton's office to watch further criticism of the decision on *Newsnight*. They went home shortly before midnight, knowing that a grave event had occurred, wondering how serious the consequences would be.

It did not take them long to find out. All next morning's newspapers carried front-page headlines about the governors' decision and comments were sought from relevant bodies and personalities. In general, Conservative MPs and the right-wing press supported the ban, while organisations concerned with civil liberties and press freedom denounced it. On Channel 4 news, Sir Hugh Greene said it was 'one of the most fateful days in the corporation's history'. He went on: 'To put it mildly, I find this decision deeply disturbing because however it may be wrapped up in talk of further consultation with the Home Secretary, it is a case of giving way to government pressure. I cannot imagine BBC boards of the past giving way to such pressure.'

The Times and the *Telegraph* both made the point that the government's position was inconsistent. If Brittan thought the programme a threat to national security he had the power to forbid its broadcast on his own responsibility. 'Both the Prime Minister and the Home Secretary have emphasized the absence of censorship, though Mr. Brittan's quasi-diktat is scarcely distinguishable from it,' *The Times* wrote. Brittan contested that energetically. He was against censorship. He had been surprised first by Young's decision to call a meeting and secondly by the governors' reaction to the programme. He was glad they had banned it but he had not expected them to do so. He had assumed when he made his protest that they would go ahead with the programme regardless of it. In that case he would have made his point without creating such a fuss. He certainly had no intention of using his powers to enforce a ban.

The *Financial Times* commented: 'Independence is what the BBC is all about. It is what its reputation rests on at home and abroad. Where is that reputation now? Ultimately, one must ask: without independence, what is the point of the BBC?' While the *Guardian* said of the governors: 'They copped out; they caved in.'

Of all the senior BBC executives, James Hawthorne was the man wounded most by the fracas, and in a profoundly personal way. It was he, after all, who had cleared Hamann's film for transmission, and it was he who had been assailed by the redoubtable Rees-Mogg for failing to disclose its existence to the Northern Ireland governor. By an embarrassing coincidence, on that very Tuesday evening Hawthorne was due to host a cocktail party and dinner for Lady Faulkner at BBC headquarters in Belfast, a tribute to her on her retirement from the board.

As the meeting in London dragged on, it became clear that neither of them would be able to make the cocktail party in time, so that was cancelled, but they rushed together from Broadcasting House to Heathrow airport, on to the shuttle, and arrived only a little late for the dinner. Both were asked excitedly to report on the day's events and they did, though they managed to conceal in public the gravity of the differences between them. Both made friendly and mutually flattering speeches. In particular, Hawthorne gave no hint to Lady Faulkner or anyone else that he had as good as made up his mind to resign.

The decision had been taking shape since the governors agreed the terms of their letter to Brittan. Part of the reason for his disillusion was what he saw as the shabby hypocrisy of indicating in the letter that the programme might be shown in an amended form later, whereas he had been at the meetings where the governors had expressed their total rejection of it: 'No show, no show ... I hate it.' He felt it important that someone should be seen to behave honourably. He wanted to tell people what had really happened, and he could not so long as he remained with the corporation. It would, he knew, only be a gesture, but maybe at that stage a gesture was needed to prevent the BBC losing all the credibility it had accrued in its sixty-year existence. When he went home from the dinner he discussed his position with his wife and family. Tears flowed and the talk continued next morning at breakfast. By the time he left home to drive to the office, he had decided what to do.

At half past nine he telephoned Johnny Wilkinson, the director of public affairs in London. He told him he was going to quit, and would hold a press conference in Belfast to explain the reasons. Wilkinson urged him to postpone a final decision for twenty-four hours, and when Protheroe came on the line later to reinforce the appeal, Hawthorne agreed. There was another farewell party for Lady Faulkner at lunch time, this time for the Belfast staff. Hawthorne considered whether he ought to attend, and decided he should. In London, Richard Francis (his predecessor as controller in Northern Ireland) jumped on a plane for Belfast and Hawthorne invited him for dinner. Young had promised to issue a statement expressing full confidence in the management in general and the controller in Northern Ireland in particular, but that by itself would not have been enough to change Hawthorne's mind. He was more influenced by Francis's point that if anything was to be salvaged out of the rubble it was essential that the management should avoid dramatic gestures of this kind; although that did not mean they should refrain from expressing their dismay at the governors' decision.

By the time Francis left after dinner, Hawthorne was all but persuaded to withdraw his resignation. Next morning, Thursday, not long before lunch, Young telephoned him. With the BBC under pressure, said the chairman, it more than ever needed people like Hawthorne. 'I beg you, I beg you, I beg you to remain,' he pleaded. Hawthorne had already decided to hold a press conference for 4 p.m., where he was going to announce that he was not quitting after all, but he thought it appropriate to keep the chairman in suspense, promising only to think about it. He told the press conference that he would stay on, saying he had received assurances that the BBC's integrity would be maintained. When, three days later, Hawthorne appeared on ITV's *The World This Weekend* and made remarks criticising both the governors and the government, the chairman may have wondered whether he should have let him go after all.

Young had managed to keep the management intact, but stood no chance of mollifying the staff at lower levels. As current affairs and features producers wrote letters of protest to the press, members of the National Union of Journalists at the BBC decided to strike for twenty-four hours on Wednesday, 7 August - the day the programme was originally supposed to have been screened. They were supported by other unions as well as by journalists at Independent Television News. Staff of the external services at Bush House had never struck before, but because they perceived the issue as being of such extreme gravity for the corporation they came out with their colleagues on the home side. In doing so, by an odd irony, they helped to restore their service's reputation. It had looked as though the international good name of Bush House might become an incidental victim of the dispute. Although the overseas services are funded by the Foreign Office, they are proud of their comparative freedom from direct political interference. In the wake of the *Real Lives* affair other overseas broadcasting services, particularly those of Iron Curtain countries, were able to score propaganda points, maintaining that the incident proved all British broadcasting to be subject to government censorship. By striking for a day and forcing the world service to broadcast nothing but music, the staff demonstrated a degree of independence unthinkable for those who worked for the broadcasting services that criticised them.

Both for this reason, and because of their hostility to the governors' decision, senior management had sympathy with the strike, although they were naturally inhibited from saying so too openly. Alasdair Milne was kept in touch with events by Michael Checkland. Now on dry land in Sweden, the director-general could have returned whenever he liked, and he considered doing so early in the week. After the Tuesday meeting was over he asked Young, Checkland and Protheroe whether he should return the following day. They all advised against it, even though Checkland himself was starting his holiday the following day. Milne calculated that he would stand more chance of rescuing something from the ashes of the relationship between the two boards if he kept to his timetable and delayed his return until the weekend, when passions might have cooled a little.

When he arrived home on Saturday, 3 August, a cassette of the programme was waiting for him, and he viewed it that evening. He decided right away that the board of management were right, and that it could be shown with only a couple of minor amendments. On Sunday he telephoned some of his management colleagues to discuss how to proceed. They agreed to come to a decision at the regular weekly board meeting the next day. He telephoned Young and arranged to talk to him on Monday, too. Although his favoured solution would have been for the programme to be shown as scheduled, he recognised that there was no chance of the governors agreeing to lose face to that extent. What he hoped was that, without meeting again, they would authorise him to announce a firm date for the showing of the film, with the minor changes he thought necessary, no later than the autumn. This, he believed, might be enough to persuade the unions to call off the strike.

When Milne put that plan to him on Monday, Young said he would go along with it if Milne could persuade the other governors. That afternoon the director-general telephoned as many of them as he could find. Five agreed to his plan, but Daphne Park and Sir William Rees-Mogg did not. Young decided he would have to call another meeting the following day. It was nearly 7 p.m. before he made that decision, and he was again surprised next morning that they all turned up - even Sir John Boyd, who had not been there the previous week. Boyd indicated his position at the beginning, when he advised the other governors to stick to their guns and not be swayed by pressure from the press.

The hard-liners were one below strength because Lady Faulkner had now ended her term of office and her successor Kincade, freed from her influence, was more inclined towards compromise than he had been the previous week. Relieved of the cares of office, Lady Faulkner was now not inhibited from expressing her views in public. In a powerful article in the *Listener* that week, she was scathing about the film: 'The shots of McGuinness - who says he would be proud to be the chief of staff of the IRA - were like those foxes produced years ago for the anti-blood sports campaigners, pretty animals, like collie dogs. What one didn't see were the fowl in the hen-run with their heads pulled off.' And she placed the dispute in an interesting broader perspective: 'The BBC must get its act together. This is not the swinging sixties, when the winds of change were heady with promise and in-fighting was permissible.'

At the meeting on 6 August, Rees-Mogg was still proving the chief obstacle to a settlement. He did not want *Real Lives* shown at any time, however amended. He hoped - although he recognised it was unlikely - that Milne would take against the film and ban it on his own account. In the political context created by the governors' action that would have been virtually impossible for the director-general, even if privately he had disliked the work; which as it happened he had not.

Despite the support Milne had assumed from his Monday telephone calls, the governors would not name a date for the screening at their Tuesday meeting. Instead, they issued a long statement that began: 'The board of governors are the BBC and are therefore responsible for the editorial policy of the corporation. They devolve the day-to-day management to a director-general, whom they appoint, who is the editor-in-chief.' The statement concluded that the main issue was one of censorship by the government, which the board would not accept. They were disturbed at being accused - wrongly, they felt - of yielding to official pressure. The journalists had charged the governors with censorship and now the governors were appearing to try to off-load the responsibility by accusing the government of the same thing.

The journalists were not won over and Wednesday's strike was now inevitable. Milne admitted later that at this point he had considered resignation but decided, along with the other members of the board of management, that he should stay to steer the Beeb back to calmer waters. Alwyn Roberts, the single governor who had opposed the ban, also revealed that he had contemplated resigning.

The one-day strike crippled all the news programmes of the BBC and Independent Television News. The NUJ sponsored a screening of the banned film at the Institute of Contemporary Arts. During the discussion afterwards Gerald Kaufman, the shadow Home Secretary, pledged that a future Labour administration would free the media from controls. Lord Annan, chairman of the commission that produced the 1977 report, came up with the most memorable quotation of the entire affair when he described Brittan as 'a demented poodle who has been knocking over the china in his excitement'.

Young, Milne and Protheroe went to see the demented poodle that afternoon. It was not a cordial meeting. Brittan said he had the same rights as anyone else to comment on BBC programmes, and that he had not forced the BBC to accept his advice. It was a curious position to adopt. If he truly believed it - and there is nothing to suggest that he did not - then it was evidence of a political naïvety rare in a senior Cabinet minister. It was left to Milne to point out to him that being secretary of state responsible for broadcasting did place Brittan in a more sensitive position than other citizens.

Although no agreed statement emerged from the meeting, Young left convinced that it would be a long time before any future Home Secretary took an initiative (or a liberty, as he was more inclined to regard it) comparable with what Brittan had done. Milne issued a stirring and defiant message afterwards, criticising Brittan's comments on a programme he had not seen.

When such comment is further accompanied by a direct request to remove the programme no matter what its actual content and context - in this case by a minister of the crown - it will be assumed that the government is seeking to dictate programme policy. The BBC will firmly resist such pressure.

He added that he had considered resigning. 'I consulted my colleagues but in the end there is a job of work to be done here, so there will be no resignation.' With the rousing declaration: 'I am the editor in chief. I am in charge,' he gave an assurance that, after emendation, *Real Lives: At the Edge of the Union*, would be transmitted. He said the same in a longer statement the following day, although he was still not able to give a firm date: 'The governors feel they need time to allow the dust to settle.' So he was not *absolutely* in charge after all. [...]

Not until September [...] did things begin to look up. At the first governors' meeting of the month, when Milne asked for permission to show *Real Lives: At the Edge of the Union* in October, the board agreed. Rees-Mogg was still in favour of suppressing it but most governors, badly shaken by the events of August, took Milne's point that it could not be business as usual at the Beeb until the ban was lifted. It was screened on 16 October and watched by 4.8 million people - respectable enough for a documentary but less than a quarter of the figure for the soap opera *EastEnders*, the BBC's most popular show. It attracted sixty calls from viewers, no more than the average for a programme of that nature. About half the callers complained, while the remainder could not see what the fuss had been about. [...]

Endnotes

1. Alasdair Milne, Director General of the BBC.
2. Stuart Young, Chair of the Governors of the BBC.
3. Alan Protheroe, Deputy Director General of the BBC.

8.

Roger Bolton

DEATH ON THE ROCK

(From *Death on the Rock and Other Stories*, London, W.H. Allen, 1990, pages 189-248)

6.30 a.m. Monday, 7 March 1988. I switched on Radio 4 and listened eagerly to the BBC's *Today* programme for the latest details of the shootings that had taken place the previous afternoon in Gibraltar. The information Sunday night had been confused and I thought that by this morning there would be a much clearer picture. Peter Donaldson was reading the news in his usual calm professional way.

> It's now known that the three people shot and killed by Security Forces in Gibraltar yesterday were members of the Provisional IRA. It's thought they were challenged while trying to leave Gibraltar after planting a huge bomb in the centre of the colony.

After the news the presenter Peter Hobday talked to Joe Paley the BBC's correspondent in Gibraltar. He had been briefed by the authorities in there.

> HOBDAY: Tell me about the bomb which was finally defused. What sort of damage would it have done, had it gone off during the parade on Tuesday?
>
> PALEY: It would have done an enormous amount of damage. It was something like five hundred pounds of explosives, packed with bits of metal, shrapnel and so on.

After a few more questions Hobday turned to the BBC's Irish Affairs correspondent, David Capper, in Belfast. The IRA had issued a statement admitting that three of its members had been killed 'on active service', and naming them as Sean Savage, Daniel McCann and Mairead Farrell. Capper had further information.

HOBDAY: Do we know where they got the material for the bomb, or anything about that?

CAPPER: Well I've been told that the explosive found in the car is called Goma 2 ... everything points to ETA (the Basque terrorist organisation) as being the people that supplied them with the explosive.

That all seemed pretty definite and later on the Minister for the Armed Forces, Ian Stewart, stepped into the BBC's radio car to talk to the *Today* programme. He congratulated the Gibraltar Government and went on, 'Military personnel were involved. There was a car bomb found, which has been defused.'

All the daily newspapers had basically the same story. Some mentioned a shoot-out, all confirmed that a bomb had been found, and that the IRA members were armed. ITN said that 'A fierce gun battle broke out' and that 'Army explosives experts used a robot to defuse the bomb.' The *Daily Mail* agreed about the bomb saying 'RAF disposal men defused it later,' although the *Daily Mirror* reported that 'A controlled explosion failed to set off the bomb.'

It didn't seem to me that there was much in it for us. The news organisations would mop it all up, and there wasn't much fuss from either side when such shoot-outs occurred. The British military and the IRA regarded themselves as soldiers at war with each other. Most people would think the terrorists deserved what they got. I didn't disagree.

I shrugged, more wasted lives, pushed the papers away and went down to the cutting rooms to sort out that week's film [...]. As usual it took a few hours to sort out the structure and get an opening to the programme which would arrest people's attention. So I had a late lunch and when I came back to the office sat down with Julian Manyon and Chris Oxley [...]. They thought me somewhat preoccupied with Ireland so, rather playfully, asked me if I was going to do anything about the shootings. 'No, there's nothing left to say.'

Almost at that moment Oracle updated its report on Gibraltar quoting the Foreign Secretary's statement to the House of Commons.

Sir Geoffrey Howe described the deaths of the IRA members:

On their way to the Border, they were challenged by the Security Forces. When challenged, they made movements which led the military personnel, operating in support of the Gibraltar police, to conclude that their own lives and the lives of others were under threat. In the light of this response, they were shot. Those killed were subsequently found not to have been carrying arms.

Sir Geoffrey then revealed there was no bomb in the car, or anywhere else. I drew in my breath. Well, that put a very different perspective on the whole matter.

It seemed to me that this incident was now certain to become extremely controversial and be used by all sides in the Irish Question to their own advantage. It would clearly be seen by many people as an example of the alleged 'shoot to kill policy' operated by the British Government, and it took no great insight to realise that within a few days a madonna-like painting of Mairead Farrell would adorn the sides of houses in West Belfast, or that a Roman Catholic priest would refer to her as a martyr. The incident also appeared to indicate, despite the absence of a bomb, that the IRA had conveniently forgotten about what its political arm, Sinn Féin, had called 'the disaster' of Enniskillen.

I had to make a quick decision, should I pursue the story and if so who should I send to do it? Julian Manyon and Chris Oxley were not filming yet, but were due to set off on [a] Japanese project in forty-eight hours. Pulling them off one certain story for another speculative one that might come to nothing was risky.

As Editor of *This Week* I had six producers, five reporters, and five researchers at my disposal. All were occupied with other stories or were on leave. For this sort of project Julian and Chris were probably the best team available. [...] I decided to switch them to the Gibraltar story. I didn't give a lot of thought to the political repercussions. I knew it would be difficult and possibly controversial but I had decided long ago that I had to judge a story by its importance, not by the political fall-out one might face. [...]

The journalists were not very enthusiastic. Chris in particular was sceptical about our ability to find something fresh, but of course they would go and have a look.

The following day Chris flew to Gibraltar to check out matters there, and Julian flew to Spain to see what information he could discover about the joint Spanish/British surveillance operation that had so successfully identified and followed the three IRA members. I also sent a young Irish researcher [...] Eamon Hardy, to Belfast to see what he could discover there.

As the team set off I went to see Barrie Sales, my immediate boss, and Deputy Director of Programmes, to discuss the project with him. We both thought that the basic unresolved question at the heart of Sir Geoffrey Howe's statement was why three unarmed terrorists, when challenged by armed security personnel, should make suspicious movements, which gave the impression they were a threat? (At this stage one assumed the implication was that the soldiers thought the terrorists were going for their guns.) It did not make sense; there was no logic to it.

Within a week, official sources, presumably the MoD, had leaked to the *Sunday Telegraph* and the *Sunday Times* an apparently more convincing account. This was the 'button job' or remote-controlled bomb theory. According to this version of events the soldiers thought the terrorists were about to detonate a remote-controlled bomb, which they had been led to believe had been planted in the white Renault. In its essentials that was the explanation soldiers A, B, C and D were to subsequently give at the Inquest.

However, the 'button-job' explanation did not resolve the problem; the basic puzzle still remained. First why try to detonate a non-existent bomb? Secondly, why should the terrorists give the impression (Farrell going for her handbag, McCann going for his pocket) they were about to activate a remote-control device they did not possess? Again none of it quite added up.

Barrie was to tell the subsequent Windlesham/Rampton Inquiry,

> There was a further puzzle in my mind and that was why the Security Services should have been so convinced they were dealing with a remote-controlled bomb. On the balance of probabilities it seemed an odd conclusion to reach. Although I am not particularly knowledgeable about such matters, I was aware that remote-controlled bombs are usually detonated by line of sight and also over relatively short distances. A built-up area like Gibraltar did not seem the most obvious place for such a bomb.

> There was also the problem of the getaway. If you detonate a remote-controlled bomb inside Gibraltar how do you escape? With only one road in or out it would have been exceedingly risky. In all these circumstances a remote-controlled bomb did not seem an obvious choice; a timer would have been more logical. It was surprising therefore that the Security Services should have apparently reached such a firm conclusion.

Something else nagged at the back of my mind. I knew that in Northern Ireland when the Security Forces thought there was a bomb in a car they evacuated the area immediately. This had not been done in Gibraltar and indeed there seemed to have been a wait of around at least twenty minutes after the shootings before the car was searched. Still, would we be in danger of helping the IRA gain a propaganda victory? [...]

When Chris arrived in Gibraltar he made repeated visits to the Glacis and Laguna Estates, which surround and overlook the petrol station where McCann and Farrell died. He spoke to around fifty people who live in the area. Chris made contact with Josie Celecia and Stephen Bullock, who later appeared in the film. He also met two further people who said they were eyewitnesses to the shootings at the petrol station, Derek Luise and another man who would not give his name. [...]

While Chris Oxley was searching for witnesses Julian Manyon was trying to find out more about the surveillance of the terrorists before they reached the Rock. [...] The Spanish believed the British knew there was no bomb in the car and that the British knew exactly when the terrorists were coming. No one was caught offguard. So there were a number of questions demanding to be answered. If the British knew there was no bomb in the car why did they shoot the terrorists? And if the British also knew exactly when and where the terrorists were arriving why didn't they simply arrest them at the border? If, however, the British thought there was a bomb on board, why on earth let it be taken into a highly built-up and populated area, where it was many more times as dangerous? There was only one way into Gibraltar. Everyone had to come through a narrow isthmus, and across the Gibraltar airfield before entering the town. There was one road for cars and one entry for people on foot. Everyone had to stop to be checked.

So when Julian and Chris came back to the office on 15 March we had no real doubts about the nature of the surveillance operation, but reservations about the effectiveness of the Gibraltar Police investigative abilities in this case. [...]

Chris and Julian flew straight to the Rock with Alison and on 19 March interviewed two key witnesses, Stephen Bullock a barrister, and Josie Celecia, and her husband. Both Bullock and Celecia had already given detailed accounts of what they had seen to the police, the Gibraltar Broadcasting Corporation, and English newspapers. [...]

Following the leads which Chris Oxley had established, Alison [Cahn, researcher] contacted Derek Luise and wrote down his story in her notes. He said that following the sound of a police siren, he saw two gunmen fire on the terrorists on the petrol station side of the road. He said he saw a police car do a U-turn around the metal barrier in the middle of Winston Churchill Avenue and head toward the petrol station. Luise was visited several times and became increasingly reluctant to talk about what he had seen. When asked if he would give a television interview, he declined, and subsequently did not appear at the Inquest. [...]

At the end of March, Alison heard of a young woman who had apparently seen something of the shooting of Savage. After several days investigation Alison traced her, resulting in the interview with Dianne Treacey. The team had to talk through the door to her for ten to fifteen minutes before they were let in. Her father, who was there, was a former policeman and he was very disturbed by his daughter's account. The story she told, in quiet hushed tones, was dramatic. A man had rushed towards and past her, followed by another with a gun. She turned and saw the first man, Sean Savage, shot in the back.

In summary, we spoke to ten of the sixteen independent eye witnesses to the shootings who later appeared at the Inquest. [...]

On the afternoon of 6 March Major Bob Randall was at home in Nelson House on the Laguna estate. One of his sons told him what had happened and he went out to see for himself, then returned to pick up his video-camera to record the scene. Later that day he was told that the GBC, Gibraltar Broadcasting Corporation, had not managed to get any film of the aftermath of the shootings so he gave them his tape. Extracts from it were subsequently shown by the BBC, ITN, and many other world TV organisations. *This Week* wanted to obtain a copy of the original tape so on the evening of Tuesday, 22 March, Alison Cahn went to Major Randall's home. She asked him, as she was asking everyone she met, if he knew of anyone who had witnessed the shootings. [...] Major Randall then proceeded to tell Alison the account he had heard from a young man who he said was in a car nearby the shooting. He mentioned this young man had seen a gunman fire into Savage's body, then put a foot on Savage as he lay on the ground and put another shot in his head to finish him off. The soldier had then put on his black beret and shown his identity card. [...]

Alison asked Major Randall to contact the young man for her and to see if he would do an interview or at least meet her to discuss what he had seen. The following day [...] Randall said the boy was scared and did not want to get involved but had told Randall what he had seen, with the message that Randall was to pass this account on to Alison. Alison explained to Major Randall that we needed the young man's account in his own words. [...]

The young man was of course Kenneth Asquez who worked in the Algemene Bank as a clerk. [...] He gave Major Randall a hand-written statement the next day. There was no great significance attached to the fact that Asquez had not signed the hand-written statement, as the team knew Asquez did not want to reveal his identity. [...]

On Wednesday, 30 March, [...] Alison visited Christopher Finch, a lawyer who we had retained to advise the production team on matters of Gibraltar law and the collection of evidence, and to take statements from witnesses. [...] Alison told him she was trying to contact Kenneth Asquez [...]. Finch knew the Asquez family and phoned the young man's home to discover which bank he worked in. Finch told Asquez that he was working for Thames Television and that he wished to discuss that Asquez had seen. He suggested Asquez come to see him in the lunch hour. Asquez agreed. [...]

[Finch] told us that Asquez had given a detailed account of what he saw but had absolutely refused to do an interview. Finch told us that Asquez was frightened and had refused to sign anything for fear of being identified and perhaps called as a witness. Again we were told that Asquez was happy for us to use his account as long as we did not identify him. [...]

Meanwhile another very important witness had surfaced almost by accident. [...] It was while the team were filming at the petrol station where the shootings occurred that an elderly woman came up to Alison Cahn and spoke to her. 'I didn't actually understand what the woman was saying,' says Alison. 'I just felt I had to follow and try and find out. She was speaking Spanish, and my Spanish isn't any good. I followed the woman over to Rodney House and she called up at the window. Carmen Proetta put her head out.' The elderly woman had been her mother. 'I spent about five or ten minutes with Carmen up there at the window and me on the ground, and finally she agreed to let me in. She was fairly reluctant at first. So I went up and chatted to her. It was the first time I'd talked to someone who said they'd seen the start of the shooting.' She was a new witness and no one else had approached her, perhaps because she was only in Gibraltar at weekends. [...] 'She was reluctant,' said Alison, 'and I talked briefly I think about the possibility of doing it back to camera, but when she decided she would do it, she said she'd do it full face.' [...]

[On *Death on the Rock*, Proetta said:

> I looked out of the window ... and all of a sudden I saw a car - police car. It stops all of a sudden, and the doors were open, all of them, the four of them, and three men came out dressed in jeans and jackets, jumped over the intersection barrier in the road, guns in hand ... and they just went and shot these people. That's all. They did not say anything, they didn't scream, they didn't shout, they didn't do anything. These people were turning their heads back to see what was happening, and when they saw these men had the guns in their hands they just put their hands up... there was no interchange of words, there was just shots. And once they dropped down, one of the men - this man who still had the gun in his hand - carried on shooting. He bent down and carried on shooting at their heads.]

The team had brought with them our consultant Lt-Col. George Styles, and he listened to the interview as it was recorded and afterwards examined the view from Carmen's flat and talked to her about what she had seen. George Styles was particularly struck by Carmen Proetta's description of the SAS men getting out of a police car, jumping over the metal railings in the middle of Winston Churchill Avenue and opening fire. Indeed when the filmed interview was over George turned to Julian and Chris with a triumphant expression and said, 'QED.'

The reason for this was that when Lt-Col. Styles had earlier examined the bullet marks in two petrol pumps in the Shell station, he had declared unequivocally that the shots in question had been fired from a position slightly ahead of the two terrorists next to the metal railings in the middle of the road. At the time we put it to George that this was, on the face of it, an unusual scenario. Lt-Col. Styles replied, 'Facts are facts, and you can't argue with them.' He regarded Carmen Proetta's account as vindication of his point of view. [...]

On 29 March Alison Cahn drove Mr. Christopher Finch, the lawyer we had retained, to Spain where Mr. Finch took notes of a lengthy conversation with Mrs. Proetta. In the course of that conversation, Alison raised, at Julian Manyon's request, Lt-Col. Styles's theory that Carmen's perception of the hands being in the air, had been caused by bullets striking the two deceased in the chest. In spite of the factor of distance mentioned by George Styles, Carmen Proetta emphatically rejected this explanation. She said that the terrorists had their hands in the air for the 'couple of seconds or so' it took for the soldiers to take up their positions. She appeared to be describing a sequence of events, not a reaction. [...]

It was immediately clear to Julian and Chris that the contents of the interview with Carmen Proetta were highly controversial, and the decision as to how much weight to put on them must depend, in part, on an assessment of her character. On the day following the interview Julian Manyon discussed this question with Alison Cahn and Chris Oxley. He expressed the view that Carmen Proetta's background must be investigated, first to see if it could have influenced her account and then to see if anything in her past could be used in a smear campaign against her which would be a likely result of her appearance on television. Alison and Chris agreed. [...] It emerged at once that her husband was facing drug-related charges in Spain, a fact which Carmen herself volunteered [...]. After some consideration of this we came to the opinion that we had interviewed Carmen Proetta, not her husband, and that Mr. Proetta's legal difficulties in Spain did not appear to constitute a motive for his wife inventing or exaggerating a story about the British security forces. [...]

[...] the *Death on the Rock* team had established that the IRA were planning to bomb Gibraltar even before the atrocity at Enniskillen, where on Remembrance Day, 8 November 1987, the Provisional IRA had planted a bomb as a parade was due to take place. Eleven people were killed and sixty-three injured. It struck me that it was particularly hypocritical of Sinn Féin to deplore what Gerry Adams called 'the disaster of Enniskillen', while its military wing was planning what was intended to be another similar disaster.

It would be important to demonstrate in our film just what the IRA had intended to do. I had no doubt about their intention. [...]I conceived the idea of blowing up a car with the same amount of explosive the terrorists had intended to use. It would be expensive, but we'd use a clapped out vehicle. The resulting explosion, prefaced by scenes of a crowded Gibraltar, would bring home more vividly than anything else what was intended to happen. I rang the MoD and asked for help and advice. They would see. A short time later they rang back and said sorry they could not help in any way. 'This one is being run from No. 10,' they said, 'and we are not allowed to co-operate in any way.' [...]

We had never attempted to disguise what we were doing from the Government. Far from it. As soon as Chris Oxley had first arrived in Gibraltar he pursued the official sources trying to get their version of events.

In the first few days Chris spoke to both the Governor's assistant, Mr. R. Sindon, and the Gibraltar police spokesman, Inspector Glen Viagas in an attempt to clarify what had happened. They declined to provide any information relevant to the shootings, either on or off the record. They would not even answer the simplest question such as: what time did the incident happen? This apparently could prejudice the Inquest. At least it disproved the old saying, 'If you want to know the time ask a policeman'.

Chris also had the first of two background conversations with the coroner, Mr. Felix Pizzarello, who expressed his reservations over the Government's announcement that the Inquest would be the only inquiry into the shootings. The coroner indicated that journalistic investigation might play a helpful role.

After she arrived, Alison once again contacted both Mr. Sindon and Inspector Viagas. Neither would help with any details concerning the shootings. Alison later wrote directly to both the Governor and Commissioner of police requesting interviews. Both requests were declined.

On 8 April, Alison Cahn managed to see the Attorney-General of Gibraltar, Mr. Eric Thistlethwaite. He said that he had appealed for witnesses and was anxious for people to come forward. Later he agreed to meet Julian Manyon for an unattributable background conversation which took place on Monday, 18 April. Also present were DCI Emmanuel Correa and Alison Cahn. Waiting in an outer office was a Thames TV film crew in case the Attorney-General should agree to give an interview.

In this conversation Mr. Thistlethwaite and DCI Correa declined to provide concrete details about the shootings. All Thistlethwaite seemed interested in was pumping the *This Week* team for information about what they were going to report and trying to get them to name names. Julian promised all help - after the programme went out. The Attorney-General turned down an invitation to do a television interview or make an on the record statement.

While the team were in Gibraltar and Spain, I was repeatedly in contact with Martin Sands at the Ministry of Defence in London. I asked for an on-camera interview with a Government spokesman, or failing that, help with finding someone who could unofficially put forward the Government's point of view. I also asked for a briefing, either on or off the record, and requested permission to use a Ministry firing range in connection with our filming. All these requests were denied.

We kept up our requests to the bitter end. A week before transmission on 21 April, Julian Manyon had an off the record meeting with two senior officials at the Ministry of Defence. In the course of this conversation, Julian asked the two officials to amplify what the Foreign Secretary, Sir Geoffrey Howe, had told the House of Commons about the shootings. The two Ministry officials declined to supply a detailed account on the grounds of the forthcoming Inquest.

On the same day, Julian Manyon had written to Mr. Martin Sands at the MoD asking for guidance on a series of points. The Ministry replied in writing that they were unable to comment because of the forthcoming Inquest. (Despite the reluctance of the MoD to brief us on the shootings, a lengthy story detailing their version of events and quoting 'military sources', appeared in the *Sunday Times* newspaper on 8 May shortly after the transmission of *Death on the Rock.*)

I learned from my own sources at Westminster that a special Cabinet sub-committee had supervised the Gibraltar operation and, supplemented, had overseen the handling of the fall-out and propaganda offensive up to and during the Inquest. Our activities had been reported to them at regular intervals. For the first time ever in my experience of programmes covering an issue which involved Government we had no cooperation from them at all. It was most peculiar.

Frustrated in my attempt to have a car exploded I decided that we needed to begin the programme with a sequence about Enniskillen and the appalling casualties that had resulted. I sent Eamon Hardy off to fix that. He arranged for us to film a sequence with Ronnie Hill who, until he was incapacitated by the bombing, had been the much-loved Headmaster of the local high school. As Julian Manyon wrote in his commentary:

> Some wounds heal. Others last long after the memory of the atrocity has begun to fade... Today his [Ronnie Hill's] wife, Noreen, keeps watch as he lives on in a deep coma that, sadly, may prove irreversible. The coma began during emergency surgery to save Mr. Hill's life, after the blast had badly damaged his lungs.

As Julian pointed out, the Enniskillen atrocity was caused by a much smaller bomb than the one intended for Gibraltar.

Internal Politics

After three weeks of research and filming it was clear to me that we were not going to be able to encompass our findings in a standard length *This Week*, which is around twenty-six minutes. So on 31 March I went to see Thames's Director of Programmes. I told David Elstein we now had the makings of an important film but that it was clearly going to be controversial and that it was essential that we put the investigation in context. David, as an ex-Editor of *This Week*, quickly took the point and agreed to try and get us a longer slot. At the Network Programme Controllers' meeting it was agreed that the programme should run for forty-four minutes and transmission should move from 8.30 p.m. to 9 p.m. There was a catch, however. The film had to make that transmission slot because it was the only one with an extended duration. Had the programme remained at a standard length it could have been put back or brought forward almost at will.

While continuing to update Barrie Sales regularly on what was happening I decided we should give the IBA early warning. They are the 'publishers' of *This Week* and would clearly need to see it before transmission.

Two days before I talked to David Elstein I had been at an IBA dinner for Arab ambassadors. I took the opportunity to tell my regular contact at the Authority, Peter Ashforth, about the project and that I thought it would be a 'sensitive one'. I confirmed that there were no plans for secret filming, or for interviews with members of proscribed organisations. I would have needed the Authority's prior permission for that. When I had a definite transmission date and a better idea of how the programme would turn out I would get back to them. Peter said that the IBA would definitely want to preview the programme. At the Network Controllers Group on 11 April a senior member of the IBA was present when David Elstein outlined the programme and a transmission date was fixed, so they knew it was coming. To all of us concerned at Thames and the IBA it seemed a perfectly proper thing to be doing.

Hoping that I was playing the internal politics correctly, and in between editing the other editions of the programme and commissioning future work, I turned back to the film. I now knew how we would start the film (with Enniskillen) but how were we going to end it? The normal way would have been to put the evidence we had accumulated to a Government minister, but that didn't look as if it was going to happen.

[...] we approached George Carman, QC, who agreed to address some of the legal issues in an interview. Aware that we had collected eye witness statements that were in apparent conflict with the account given by Sir Geoffrey Howe in the House of Commons, George Carman said on film:

> What is important on the one hand is that Her Majesty's Government take all proper effective steps to stamp out the scourge of terrorism, and I imagine that's beyond dispute. Equally, on the other hand, it is important that the measures that are taken, however extreme and necessary they are, fall within the rule of law, which governs us all. Because even the activities of soldiers or police officers who have to face the awful problem of terrorism, have to be conducted within the framework of the rule of law. So of course it is desirable that there should be a full examination of what actually occurred.

George Carman, QC, went on to make a statement which we regarded as the most important in the film and which we deliberately placed at the end. He said that it seemed to him desirable that some senior judicial power, such as a High Court judge, be appointed to preside over an Inquiry of the kind taking place in Gibraltar.

> Clearly from everything you say, the programme indicates that there are serious important public issues involved, and speaking as a lawyer, one is always anxious that where there is contest on the facts in such important areas, they should be properly and efficiently investigated.

Thus, the last words of our report made no judgement on any of the statements reported earlier but referred instead to 'contest on the facts' and the need for an efficient investigation.

We now had nearly all the elements of the film and Chris Oxley started to put it together in the cutting rooms. Julian and I still carried on trying to get some reaction from the Government, with no luck. We had to discard some material due to the usual time constraints, i.e. whatever the length of the programme it is never long enough. [...]

I first saw the rough cut of the film about a week before transmission. [...] I didn't have many reservations [...] but argued that we needed to summarise, towards the end, the evidence we had gathered. That probably added to the furore because when the evidence was put together in that way it did make the Government's official version of events look very questionable. Julian wondered if we were overdoing it. Shouldn't we let the audience do its own summary? I disagreed.

I was sure that the programme was not trial by television. We had raised troubling questions and suggested that the inquest was unlikely to get to the bottom of things, but we had held back on giving a verdict ourselves because we didn't think we had the evidence to give one. Any number of things could have happened at Gibraltar, but we were pretty sure that much of the official version was questionable.

On Monday, three days before transmission I showed the film with a completed picture and an outline commentary to Barrie Sales and the Thames Legal Adviser, Louise Hayman. They made a few constructive remarks but left it largely untouched. Now for the IBA.

I had offered them a preview later that Monday at Thames but when the day came I was informed that the IBA staff preferred to see the programme complete at its own headquarters at Brompton Road, the usual practice. It wasn't the policy of the IBA to preview partly-completed programmes. The Authority seeks to avoid getting drawn into the editorial process, its responsibility being 'to see whether a programme as offered for transmission meets the requirements both of the IBA and of the Statutes'.

At about 6.00 p.m. on Tuesday, two days before transmission, a copy of the script was dispatched, with a cassette of the undubbed programme later in the evening. The dubbing of the commentary did not begin until the Wednesday and was completed on the morning of transmission, the normal practice. The IBA staff saw the film on Wednesday, 27 April and Peter Ashforth rang me back shortly afterwards, complimenting me on the programme, but asking for three changes to be made in the commentary. Senior staff in the Programme Division, together with the IBA's officer for Northern Ireland, felt that the programme's summing up suggested too strongly that the coroner's Inquest would be unable to establish the truth, and that the Gibraltar police evidence would be unreliable. I accepted these two points but the IBA accepted my arguments on the third point which concerned the Prime Minister's prior knowledge of the detection of an IRA unit in Spain. I had that myself from unimpeachable sources.

At the same time IBA staff also spoke to a Thames lawyer to check the legal position, particularly in relation to the question of possible contempt of court. They received satisfactory assurances. David Elstein, en route to a sales conference, watched the programme on Wednesday night and he was happy with it as well.

Everything seemed to be coming together. Now all that remained to be done was to get the introduction to the programme right. Here Jonathan Dimbleby was a great asset. He had covered Northern Ireland frequently himself and since taking over the BBC's *Any Questions* as well as presenting *This Week*, had developed into a fine all-round broadcaster. He watched the film, liked it and we discussed together what needed to be said.

He then typed out his introduction:

> The killing by the SAS of three IRA terrorists in Gibraltar has provoked intense debate not only in Britain but throughout the world - and especially in the Republic of Ireland and the United States.

> There are perhaps those who wonder what the fuss is about, who ask 'Does it really matter when or how they were killed?', who say 'They were terrorists, there's a war on, and we got to them before they got to us.'

> However in the eyes of the law and of the State it is not so simple. The question, which goes to the heart of the issue, is this: did the SAS men have the law on their side when they shot dead Danny McCann, Sean Savage and Mairead Farrell who were unarmed at the time?

> Were the soldiers acting in self-defence or were they operating what has become known as a 'shoot-to-kill policy' - simply eliminating a group of known terrorists outside the due process of law, without arrest, trial or verdict?

> There have been many calls for a public Inquiry to establish the facts, though the Government has insisted that the coroner's Inquiry in Gibraltar is an adequate forum at which to discover the truth.

> In either case, we believe that the evidence which *This Week* has uncovered for tonight's special programme is of critical importance for those who wish to find out what really happened in Gibraltar last month. Julian Manyon reports.

I thought that would do admirably and for the first time in many days began to relax. It was almost finished. I might even have lunch. The phone rang. It was the IBA again - just checking once more on our legal advice. I thought that was a bit peculiar. We'd been all through the legal position already to their satisfaction. What was up? 'Oh it's alright,' said Peter Ashforth, 'I'll tell you later.'

What I didn't know was that at that very moment Sir Geoffrey Howe, the Foreign Secretary, was trying to persuade Lord Thomson, the Chairman of the IBA, not to let the programme go ahead. We were on the verge of the biggest row between Government and broadcasters since *Real Lives*. In many ways it was to be an even greater crisis. I was in the kitchen again and it was hotting up.

The Government sub-committee responsible for the post-Gibraltar propaganda knew well in advance of the date of transmission of *Death on the Rock,* and at our last attempt to get information out of the Ministry of Defence on 21 April we had indicated the likely shape of the programme.

Sir Geoffrey Howe made his move with two days to go. On the evening of Tuesday, 26 April, he phoned the Chairman of the IBA, Lord Thomson, and asked that the showing of the programme should be postponed until after the Inquest. The Foreign Secretary gave as the principal reason for his request the fear that the broadcast might prejudice the Inquest. Lord Thomson said he would look into it and the IBA consulted the leading Counsel. At Thames we had done the same independently and both Thames and the IBA received the unequivocal opinion that the Inquest would not be prejudiced. (Just to be on the safe side we had withdrawn the sale of the programme to Spain and Gibraltar and advised Visnews and WTN, who had 'news access' to our material, that they should take their own legal advice, but that it would be safer to withhold it from Gibraltar.)

Lord Thomson and the IBA did not tell us at Thames what was going on but kept it to themselves. During Wednesday, 27 April, the film was seen by IBA officials who were satisfied with the final content of the script and who reported to an escalating hierarchy of the Director of Television, Director General, and finally the Chairman, each of whom viewed the programme. Lord Thomson was to write later:

> Paradoxically, in the light of the controversy it has aroused, the decision to allow the transmission of Thames Television's programme 'Death on the Rock', ... was not a difficult one. My colleagues and I saw no reason why the IBA should prevent Thames's journalists interviewing those who claimed to be eyewitnesses and investigating the affair exactly as numerous other journalists have done ever since the shootings, provided the criminal record of the terrorists and the enormity of the outrage they planned was made clear and the legal position had been established to our satisfaction.

Lord Thomson added robustly, 'Sir Geoffrey Howe did his duty and I did mine, and if you do not like that sort of conflict of duty between Government and broadcaster, then you should not be Chairman of an Independent Broadcasting Authority.' We were indeed fortunate to have such a man in charge of the Authority. [...]

On Thursday, 28 April, it was decided that the transmission of the programme should go ahead and the Director of Television, David Glencross, was instructed to telephone Sir Geoffrey Howe's Private Secretary to notify him of the Authority's decision, saying that it had been taken at the highest level and after taking legal advice. Sir Geoffrey was soon back on the phone. At about noon he personally telephoned the IBA, and in the absence of the Chairman, spoke to David Glencross. This time, Sir

Geoffrey, a former Solicitor-General, raised the issue of contamination and referred to the Salmon Report. The IBA immediately scrutinised the relevant parts of the Salmon Report and again consulted their advisers.

While they were doing so Sir Geoffrey raised the stakes again. The Foreign and Commonwealth Office held a press conference at which the Foreign Secretary's conversations were made public. It was later put about by Government circles that Thames had leaked the story. This was a straight lie. We didn't have the story to leak. [...]

Meanwhile the IBA had taken the same view of the dangers of contamination as our lawyer had. The subsequent Windlesham/ Rampton Report said that the reasons why the IBA felt Sir Geoffrey's arguments ought not to prevail were:

i) The programme had produced new witnesses for the Inquest who might not otherwise have been available.

ii) The programme did not set itself up as an alternative Inquest or Inquiry. It had volunteered all its information to the Gibraltar coroner.

iii) At the time of the programme, no date for the Inquest had been set.

iv) It was clear that the broadcast of the programme in the United Kingdom would not constitute a contempt under the existing law.

v) The effect of the Salmon Committee's recommendations was that any extension of the law of contempt should be limited to interviews or other material obtained or published with the deliberate intent or obvious likelihood of causing any relevant evidence to be altered, distorted, destroyed or withheld. The IBA's considered view was that the interviews with witnesses in *Death on the Rock* did not fall into that category.

vi) The Salmon Committee's recommendation was made in 1969. Under the Contempt of Court Act 1981, a publication can only incur liability for contempt if it creates 'a substantial risk that the course of justice ... will be seriously impeded or prejudiced.' In the IBA's opinion, the programme did not fall within that definition.

vii) Because Gibraltar is a small community, the shootings were already likely to have been the subject of much public comment and discussion, even without the benefit of press and broadcasting coverage. There had been a great deal of local coverage in the Gibraltar Press and on the shootings and the Thames programme. The Gibraltar authorities made no move to prevent this. There had also been extensive coverage in the UK Press, without comment from Government or the law officers.

viii) The programme was a legitimate piece of journalistic activity. It was not designed to usurp the function of the Inquest, nor was it trying to set itself up as a quasi-legal process.

Following the Foreign Office briefing about Sir Geoffrey's intervention, the news wires started humming and the matter was raised in the House of Commons. On these occasions there is always a backbencher who is willing to serve his Government's interests. In this instance it was Jerry Hayes, Conservative MP for Harlow. He had not, of course, seen the programme as it had not yet been transmitted. That was no restraint. He rose to the occasion, and put a question to the Minister present in the Commons Chamber, Tom King, then Secretary of State for Ireland.

He enquired if Mr. King would ask the Irish Foreign Minister whether he was as fed up as Conservative MPs with television companies 'Raking through the gutters of Gibraltar, finding people to rubbish the Security Services. Will he ask him if he is as fed up as we are with people who are weeping tears for an active IRA unit which would have been responsible for a major massacre in Gibraltar?' Mr. King replied 'I share his concern about the proposal for a television broadcast.' He told Parliament that the programme amounted to 'trial by television'. Mrs. Thatcher can always be relied upon to go one better. 'Trial by television or guilt by accusation is the day that freedom dies,' she told a group of Japanese journalists. Asked if she was furious about the programme she replied that her reaction went 'deeper than that'. She too had not seen the programme when she made that remark.

While all this was going on I was worried that the programme might not go out in the end because we couldn't get the transmission tape completed. We had to add graphics, maps, names and dates and replace cutting copies of library film with fine prints. With ten minutes to go we edited on Jonathan Dimbleby's closing link.

> That report [he said] was made, as you may have detected, without the co-operation of the British Government which says that it will make no comment until after the Inquest. As our film contained much new evidence hitherto unavailable to the coroner, we are sending the transcripts to his court in Gibraltar, where it's been made clear to us that all such evidence is welcomed. [...]

Surely the next morning's newspapers would have to pick up the evidence we had discovered and reopen their investigations into Gibraltar? How naïve we were: most of the papers were going to go after us.

We should have remembered the words of Colin Wallace, a former Captain in the British Army who worked in Psychological Operations in Northern Ireland in the seventies. He described the potential of misinformation to influence public opinion. 'The important thing is to get saturation coverage for your story as soon after the controversial event as possible. Even when the facts come out the original image is the one that sticks.' We were about to be saturated.

The Gentlemen of the Press

The television reviews of the programme in the serious papers were excellent. William Holmes in *The Times* wrote:

> From where I sit, out of the political firing line, the report seemed a significant, thoroughly responsible and serious examination of a most disturbing case ... Julian Manyon's script jumped to no conclusions and argued no extreme case with 'partial witnesses', nor could it remotely be described as 'trial by television' - Tom King's phrases in the House of Commons. It simply raised serious questions and suggested they required deep examination.

Editorials in the *Independent,* the *Guardian,* the *Daily Telegraph* and, later in the day, the London *Evening Standard,* supported the IBA's decision to authorise transmission.

The tabloids were a different story. The *Sun's* editorial was headed 'Blood on Screen - Thames' cheap telly scoop is just IRA propaganda,' and it began 'Does Thames Television want more innocent men, women and children to be killed by Irish Terrorists?' It argued that our report should have been held back until after the Inquest but did not explain why it had not done the same with its reporting. It attacked the IBA in its usual fair and understated way.

> Under the quivering geriatric chairmanship of ex-*Dandy* Editor Lord Thomson, it does not merely lack teeth. It has not a fibre of strength or guts in its entire being. [The editorial went on] But in *[sic]* this truly black day for television, the overwhelming guilt belongs to the Thames company. They are supposed to be a British concern and they derive their income from British advertisers.

> Their audience is made up of British men and women. *If that audience is diminished in the next few months by bullets or bombs in Ulster or in the rest of Britain, some of the blood will belong on their hands.*

Once more the *Sun* had represented the authentic voice of ignorance and prejudice. [...]

I turned to the *Daily Mail:* it usually had something special on such occasions. The headline read 'Fury over SAS "Trial by TV"' with a large picture of Carmen Proetta. Most of the papers had photos of Carmen prominently displayed. Inside the *Mail,* Geoffrey Levy's review of the programme was headed 'A woefully one-sided look at the killings.' I was about to read on when I noticed a photo of myself looking rather worried (where did they get that?) above a column by Garry Jenkins entitled 'Two men trailed by trouble.' It was an attack on Julian Manyon and myself. Carrickmore had reared its head again. Jenkins wrote, 'As the then Editor of *Panorama* he let a film crew co-operate with an IRA squad who tipped them off they were setting up a roadblock.' I made a mental note to sue (I did so successfully) and then got on with the business of trying to brief journalists.

Julian, Chris and Thames's Press Office were working flat out. The details were so complicated that it was difficult to get our story across. I asked *The Times* whether they would like an article from me explaining what we had been trying to do. The features editor said yes, if he could have it in two hours. I locked the door and wrote a thousand words. The sub put a headline on it 'Rock: facts we need to know', and the paper put it on the centre page. I was very grateful.

My 'flu was getting worse and I was getting ready to go home when Channel 4's *Right to Reply* programme came on the phone. Would I appear on that week's programme, to be recorded at 6 p.m? I said I'd ring them back and discussed it with Barrie Sales and Thames's Managing Director Richard Dunn, who had been like a rock himself over the last forty-eight hours. Richard's view was that I shouldn't appear.

He felt we were getting our case across - so why risk being stitched up? I disagreed. No one enjoyed going on a programme to be criticised but I didn't see how we could make tough critical programmes about others and yet refuse to be answerable to the viewer ourselves. *Right to Reply's* format was to invite ordinary viewers to put their criticism to the programme maker. We had to be accountable. Richard still didn't like it but let me make my own mind up. 'Be careful', he said. I thought he was being far too pessimistic.

[...] I was taken down a corridor into the hospitality area. Linda Agran, the presenter, was already recording other parts of the programme. I was shivering and kept my coat on. I didn't feel like talking any more. I was exhausted and would have loved a glass of whisky, but not before a recording.

After a couple of minutes I was taken into the studio and met the two 'ordinary viewers' who would question me. One was a retired naval commander and the other a young man called Christopher Monckton. He had dark hair and looked as though he had just come in from the City via the Guards. I seemed to have heard the name somewhere before, but couldn't place it, yet it troubled me. The recording began and the former naval officer politely put a number of questions and criticisms to me that I felt I answered adequately. We had so much more information than we could put on the screen that I was able to fill in the background to some of our statements. Monckton was different altogether. He avoided the facts and attacked my motives. He sounded like a *Daily Mail* editorial and I half waited to be called a Communist. I replied rather wearily. If I hadn't been so tired I would have lost my temper. I didn't mind people saying I was wrong but I couldn't stand being accused of being unpatriotic. Who was he to define patriotism? I let it go and tried to get back to the basic points. *Death on the Rock* had not been trial by television, we had not brought in a verdict.

The discussion was coming to an end. Linda gave the two 'ordinary viewers' the last word. The former serviceman remained critical but friendly. Then it was Monckton's turn. With the seconds ticking away he seemed to look down at a piece of paper and proceeded to slander me, accusing me of being associated with terrorists again. I tried to come back but the recording was over. It seemed to me a straightforward bit of character assassination.

I was furious and told Monckton and Channel 4 that if that recording went out I would sue. The producers were in a quandary because as a matter of principle they never edited such discussions. 'Well,' I said, 'you had better edit this one.' I was not at my most reasonable. Then I suddenly remembered the context in which I had met Christopher Monckton before. It had been at a Conservative Central Office cocktail party, yet he had rung up *Right to Reply* as an 'ordinary viewer' and said he was a journalist. I challenged him about his background. It transpired that not long before he had been a member of Mrs. Thatcher's private office at No. 10 Downing Street. I suggested to the producer that was a relevant piece of information to give the viewer and he agreed.

We were left with the slander. Liz Forgan, the Director of Programmes and Michael Grade, Chief Executive of Channel 4, had been watching the recording on closed circuit. They quickly came down to the studio and we all adjourned to Michael's office where the in-house lawyer joined us.

After protracted haggling in which I changed my mind more than once and Liz Forgan's considerable powers of common sense and diplomacy were fully deployed, I accepted that the discussion should be faded out just before the slanderous remarks and that the audience would be told why this had been done.

Smearing Carmen

I had hoped things would have quietened down a little by the Saturday following the programme. The serious newspapers reported continuing attacks upon us by Sir Geoffrey Howe and the Prime Minister but I regarded these as inevitable. The reporting was fair and balanced.

The tabloids, however, were something else. A smear campaign had been launched against our most prominent eyewitness, Carmen Proetta.

Nigel Bowden, a freelance journalist who supplied copy to the London dailies, was the original source of the stories. He had discovered that Mrs. Proetta was a director of a company called Eve International. He made some assumptions about this and the tabloids made rather more.

Their Saturday headlines included 'Shame of the SAS smear girl' (the *Star*), 'Trial by TV Carmen is Escort Girl boss' *(Daily Express)* and the appalling 'The Tart of Gib' in the *Sun*. Mr. Murdoch's finest alleged that Carmen used to be a prostitute. It also claimed that Mrs. Proetta had a criminal record in Gibraltar. The *Daily Express*, the *Daily Mail*, and the *Sun* alleged that she and her husband were anti-British. The *Star* went so far as to claim that Carmen Proetta 'campaigns for Spanish rule in Gibraltar.'

All these charges were rubbish and Mrs. Proetta has successfully sued a number of the papers. The *Sun* apologised to Carmen Proetta on 17 December 1988, sadly long after the Inquest had taken place and the damage had been done. The *Sun's* solicitor told the court the newspaper 'regretted that these untrue allegations about the Plaintiff had been published and apologised for them.' The paper accepted that 'Mrs. Proetta had given an honest account of what she remembers seeing and that she neither hated the British nor was she guilty or involved in the other misconduct described.' Carmen was paid very substantial damages.

Mrs. Proetta is in fact a court interpreter in Spain and she used her qualifications as a Spanish resident to help two non-Spaniards set up a firm called Eve International, whose purpose is stated on company documents to be 'providing escorts and tourist promotion services.' Shortly afterwards she renounced her shares and involvement in a legal document dated 14 March 1985, three years before the shootings.

She had no criminal record in Spain or Gibraltar and the 'senior police officer' named in the *Sun* story as having confirmed that Mrs. Proetta had a criminal record in Gibraltar denied he said any such thing to the *Sun*.

She has never been a prostitute and she does not have anti-British views. The latter is still the case which is rather surprising considering how the dogs of Fleet Street treated her. We all felt terrible that someone who hadn't wanted to be interviewed in the first place, whom we had persuaded to tell what she had seen, should have been pilloried in this way. My respect for those politicians who attacked us would have been greatly increased if one, just one, had raised a voice against this obscene press behaviour. There was of course silence. To some in Fleet Street it is treason to question the Government about a matter of public importance but perfectly all right to smear someone whose only mistake was to have looked out of her window one day in March 1988 and had the courage to tell what she had seen. The message to other potential witnesses was clear.

Nothing could get worse we thought, but we had not allowed for the *Sun's* stablemate in the Murdoch Empire, the *Sunday Times*.

Insight?

Mr. Murdoch had no love of the existing television order as the success of his extremely expensive Sky Television service depended in large part on breaking it up. The Editor of the *Sunday Times* [Andrew Neil] doubled as the Chief Executive of Sky TV and devoted his enormous energies to getting it launched. [...] Doubtless by coincidence Mr. Murdoch's newspapers, the *Sun, Today, News of the World, The Times,* and the *Sunday Times* all argued for the deregulation of television and the freeing of the skies for satellites. [...]

Mr. Neil had called his team together when the *Death on the Rock* row began and told them to take the programme apart and examine every bit of it. The zealous young Features Editor, Robin Morgan, was put in charge of the project. Reporters were dispatched to Gibraltar, to Ireland and throughout the United Kingdom. Their copy was sent back to the Wapping offices of the paper and edited by Robin Morgan.

When I opened the paper on Sunday morning I was devastated. Despite the changes of the last few years the paper was still largely respected and the massive centre spread feature that faced me was a scathing denunciation of *Death on the Rock*.

It was headlined *Inadmissible Evidence?* and claimed '"Insight" has investigated the documentary's evidence and reports that the picture which emerges actually contradicts many of the programme's claims. Indeed, vital witnesses are now complaining their views were not accurately reported.'

There was plenty of unsubstantiated Government public relations in the article such as the following statement, '"Insight" understands that the Government's lawyers at the Inquest will have evidence that is expected to silence the critics and undermine *This Week's* evidence. Whitehall sources with access to the official evidence are relishing the prospect. "Insight" has learnt that the Ministry of Defence believes that it can contradict Carmen Proetta's testimony with incontrovertible evidence ...' The article concluded 'What started as a "trial by television" may yet become a trial of television.'

Well we could take a lot of this huffing and puffing, but what were really damaging were the quotes attributed to two of our witnesses, Stephen Bullock and Josie Celecia, and to Lt-Col. George Styles. They all appeared to be claiming they were misrepresented. [...] In fact when we contacted Stephen Bullock and Josie Celecia they were outraged at the way their comments had been misused by the paper. Mrs. Celecia was quoted by 'Insight' as saying that Carmen Proetta's account was ridiculous, and accused *This Week* of missing out this inconvenient testimony. In fact Mrs. Celecia told the *Sunday Tribune* that she was 'quite distressed' by the *Sunday Times* report. 'I totally reject suggestions ... that I described the evidence of Carmen Proetta as ridiculous.'

The *Sunday Times* reported a 'crucial statement' made by the lawyer Stephen Bullock. He had told them 'categorically' that the police car he saw had 'Five uniformed officers in it', not plain clothes SAS men. It had pulled up alongside him, perhaps a hundred yards away from the garage, as two SAS men travelling on foot had raced along the pavement to the garage. The volley of shots, he said, rang out as the police car turned on its siren and raced towards the petrol station.

'So Proetta's evidence that the SAS men got out of the car outside the garage and shot the terrorists is contradicted by Bullock.' In fact Stephen

Bullock and Carmen Proetta were talking about two different cars in two different streets. Carmen said she had seen men in civilian cloths jump out of a car in front of the petrol station and open fire. Bullock had passed a police car with uniformed policemen in it in a different, but adjoining, street. Next to the car were two men in civilian clothes who then ran after Sean Savage. As they did so shots rang out and Bullock turned to see the same shootings as those witnessed by Carmen. He too saw McCann's hands in the air, but did not know whether they were in surrender or not. It was the *Sunday Times* not the witnesses who were confused. Stephen Bullock told the *Sunday Tribune* 'I emphatically deny that's what I said [to the *Sunday Times*].'

'Insight' gave what they said was Bullock's account about the terrorists raising their hands, saying that McCann's arms were 'Outstretched trying to shield himself,' and not, as Proetta claimed, in surrender. However, Bullock wrote to me to say what a good programme he thought *Death on the Rock* was and how disgraceful he considered the *Sunday Times* article. He rang up the paper to complain and was told there would be an inquiry. He heard nothing back.

The other participant in our programme who was supposed to be complaining was George Styles. He had clearly been told by a number of his friends that the programme was unpatriotic, and was under some pressure. However, he did not withdraw anything he said in the programme and indeed he had more space than anyone else to give his views. The *Sunday Times* said he was an 'angry' man who was writing 'a letter of complaint to Thames Television' with 'a copy ... to the Prime Minister.' In fact he did no such thing. He wrote to my researcher and did not copy it to anyone.

The newspaper alleged that two of his key views were missing from the programme. Firstly, his disagreement with Carmen Proetta over whether Farrell and McCann had raised their hands in surrender or had done so because of the impact of the bullets. The Colonel thought the latter.

This was a bizarre complaint because as anyone who watched the programme could see the Colonel's opinion on this *was* quoted in the programme. However, we did not include the second 'key view'.

George Styles was clear that a radio controlled device would not have been practicable in the Square in Gibraltar. That we had reported. However, he had gone on to say that perhaps there could have been a bomb in the car that the terrorists had left over the border in Spain to use for the getaway. Neither Sir Geoffrey Howe's statement in the House of Commons nor any on or off the record statement from the Government, or defence sources or the Spanish police ever referred to this possibility. Accordingly we did not include this section of Styles' interview. Why should the terrorists wish to explode a bomb in a car parked by a Spanish roadside?

The irony of this situation was that George Styles thought the Gibraltar shootings had been a straightforward 'taking out' operation by the Security

Forces - something he supported. As he wrote to us, 'My reading of the Gibraltar incident was that it was a carefully planned operation to prevent a disaster taking place rather than to catch terrorists after the event.'

When Chris Oxley rang up Lt-Col. Styles and said he was sorry if George felt badly about it all, he replied, 'You don't have to apologise to me.' He went on, 'The thing which makes me most cross is the way the Press has gone for Carmen Proetta because, you know, what she said was true.'

When Chris told me this I was very much relieved, but also well aware of the long uphill struggle we faced to persuade even our friends that we had got it right. The natural reaction to such disputed evidence is to think it's about fifty/fifty with both sides right and wrong.

With impeccable timing the IRA made our situation even worse. On Sunday, 1 May, the day of the 'Insight' attack, the organisation carried out the brutal and callous murder of three off duty British servicemen in Holland. They were returning after a Saturday night out when they were blown up and shot. You can imagine what the tabloids made of that. *Today* had a cartoon of a blown-up car and a *This Week* crew interviewing a bystander. The caption read, 'No sign of surrender - seems like the IRA were perfectly within their rights then?'

The *Sun*'s editorial screamed abuse at the Chairman of the IBA. It was headlined, 'For God's sake go, Thomson.' It attacked our programme again saying it was 'a piece of IRA propaganda. Its only purpose to discredit our Security Services. Its effect was to spur the IRA into fresh atrocities.'

We spent the next week trying to row back the tide, briefing every journalist we could. Bernard Ingham, the Prime Minister's Press Secretary, continued to damn the programme, and Carmen Proetta's life was made hell as the pack descended on her, offering money up and down the Costa Del Sol to anyone who would say something derogatory about her.

The *Sun's* front page 'The Tart of Gib' was plastered on lamp-posts where Carmen lived and at the border with Spain. Carmen was frequently in tears and almost snapped completely when she discovered that her young daughter was being chased to and from school for some quotes.

If ever there was a danger of 'contaminating' witnesses surely this was it. The tabloids ignored the fact that Mrs. Proetta would be giving evidence to the coroner's Inquiry, whose purity Sir Geoffrey Howe was so worried about. They harassed a witness. The Government spoke not a word. [...]

Relief came from an unexpected quarter. The BBC Northern Ireland current affairs programme *Spotlight* had done its own investigation into the events in Gibraltar, and intended to transmit it a week after our programme. Sir Geoffrey Howe tried to stop that one too. The new regime in the BBC were in a tight corner. They decided to let the programme go ahead but restricted its transmission to the audience in Northern Ireland, for which it was intended. Usually in such a case the programme, or significant chunks of it, would be repeated on the network. When Alex Thomson, the reporter, pointed out that the issues were clearly of national interest and therefore that the programme should get a network transmission he was told, 'Look, you've won one battle, don't push your luck.' The preservation of the Institution came before its journalistic duty. [...]

Sir Geoffrey Howe called the BBC's decision a tragedy which went against twenty years of high standards. We saw it rather differently. The *Spotlight* film fully confirmed what we had reported and went rather further, if anything. A number of journalists, notably Heather Mills in the *Independent,* began to pursue the unanswered questions about Gibraltar with great tenacity, and were to be followed by the *Observer,* the *Daily Telegraph* and the *Guardian* who all focused on the events rather than programmes which reported on them.

The Government responded by stepping up its campaign against the 'irresponsibility' of the British media. The Prime Minister's Press Secretary, Mr. Bernard Ingham, took the unusual step of speaking out on the record. He told the *Observer* that the standards of the media had declined 'to the point of institutionalised hysteria.' He was not referring to the *Sun.* The Prime Minister was said to be determined to 'remind the media of their responsibilities.' Broadcasters were to be told that they operated within society and were obliged to uphold its institutions, notably legal proceedings. The *Observer* reported that 'According to Home Office sources ... the Home Secretary is expected to seek an early meeting with the Chairman of both the BBC and the IBA.' By Sunday, 8 May, ten days after *Death on the Rock,* I began to think the tide was turning. The *Observer's* Ian Jack wrote an extremely shrewd and well informed analysis of the controversy and the paper pointed out that Carmen Proetta was 'the victim of a British newspaper campaign to discredit her as a witness'.

The paper even quoted Sir Joshua Hassan, Gibraltar's most eminent personage and its former Chief Minister, as describing Mrs. Proetta as 'A very intelligent woman,' and an old family client of his law firm.

Thames management had stood rock solid behind us with both the Chairman, Sir Ian Trethowan, and the Managing Director, Richard Dunn, going out of their way to be supportive. David Elstein, the Director of Programmes, wrote robust replies to the articles in the *Sunday Telegraph* and the *Sunday Times* which they, to their credit, printed.

The *Sunday Times* however published another detailed 'Insight' article on 8 May which was just as critical of us as the first, and repeated some of the same errors. The paper quoted 'military sources', something they were to do a great deal of over the next few months. They seemed to have a direct line to the Ministry of Defence. The paper managed to have its cake and eat it however. Having criticised us, its 'Comment' column argued that the Government was wrong to have tried to stop the programme going out, using 'bogus' legal arguments.

Well that was something but it was clear that the battles were going to continue right up and through the Inquest. [...]

9A.

BBC, *STYLE GUIDE*, 1993, SECTION 15

Northern Ireland has presented a unique editorial problem to the BBC. Never before have we had to face the immense difficulties of reporting large-scale and continuing violence and political upheaval within the United Kingdom. The following is a brief guide to help avoid some of the more common pitfalls in writing stories about Northern Ireland.

The first thing to remember is that the Belfast Newsroom is only an internal phone call away. Don't hesitate to ring them.

NORTHERN IRELAND is the only correct name for the north-eastern part of Ireland. Together with Great Britain it forms the United Kingdom. It is acceptable to call it 'Ulster' (though not in the first instance), but never 'the Six Counties'. (Some people call it that to emphasise that six counties were hived off from the nine-county Ulster - the usual implication being that it is a temporary arrangement.) Northern Ireland is a province of the United Kingdom, so secondary references to 'the Province' are also acceptable.

Although Northern Ireland is strictly not part of Great Britain, people born there are entitled to regard themselves as British, even if some of them choose not to. The people of Northern Ireland pay British taxes. So when we talk about the cost of the troubles to the British taxpayer, we mean to the people of the province, as well as to the people of Great Britain.

THE REPUBLIC OF IRELAND is the proper name for the southern part of Ireland, though 'The Irish Republic' is perfectly acceptable - it is in widespread use and does not cause offence. Unless we are broadcasting in Gaelic we should not call it by its Gaelic name 'Eire'.

ARMY. We call it 'the Army' and its personnel 'soldiers'. NOT 'the British Army' or 'British soldiers' when they are in Northern Ireland, unless to distinguish them from Irish Army soldiers (from the Irish Republic) in one and the same story.

UDR. The Ulster Defence Regiment was a regiment of the (British) Army. Some UDR soldiers were full-time, others part-time. In 1992 the UDR amalgamated with the Royal Irish Rangers to form The Royal Irish Regiment, a regiment of the army which recruits from Northern Ireland and the Irish Republic.

IRA. The Irish Republican Army. It's illegal north and south of the border (in GB too). Called 'Provisional IRA' to distinguish it from the Official IRA (now defunct), it is acceptable to call them 'The Provisionals' - but never 'The Provos' nor 'PIRA' (which is what the Army calls them).

UDA. The Ulster Defence Association. It too is illegal in Northern Ireland (but not elsewhere in the UK). The UDA is the main Loyalist paramilitary organisation, with some of its members also carrying out terrorist acts under the name of the Ulster Freedom Fighters (UFF).

SDLP is the main Nationalist Party in Northern Ireland. The initials stand for 'Social Democratic and Labour Party', NOT 'Social and Democratic...' We should not keep calling it 'the mainly-Catholic SDLP': we don't call the Unionist Parties 'the mainly-Protestant'.

STORMONT is a place. It's where Parliament Buildings are, where the Northern Ireland House of Commons sat when there was one. There, too, is Stormont Castle from which the Secretary of State for Northern Ireland and his Ministers run the Province. Stormont is therefore a synonym for 'government' in Northern Ireland, just as 'Westminster' is in the UK as a whole.

NATIONALISTS v REPUBLICANS: The difference between the two is more a matter of custom than of definition. North of the border, people who call themselves nationalists want to see a united Ireland, while republicans not only want to see a united Ireland but also support to a degree the right to use violence to achieve it.

These are not precise definitions, and the meaning of both terms has changed even during the present troubles. The correct use is best illustrated by examples and precedent:

• you would call West Belfast a largely nationalist area.

• you would call Crossmaglen a republican stronghold.

• you would describe the SDLP as a nationalist party, and Sinn Féin as republican.

• you would talk about republican prisoners.

Don't be tempted to take your cue from how one interested party describes another. 'Republican' is applied sometimes by Loyalists to Nationalists as a form of abuse.

TERRORISTS: Members of illegal organisations who bomb and shoot civilians are unquestionably terrorists - they use terror to achieve their objectives. If there are occasions when the term is not appropriate there are always other words available - IRA men, UVF men, killers, murderers, bombers, gunmen...

Paramilitary groups often adopt military structures and titles, but we must not give them spurious respectability by using their terminology unquestioned. So we don't speak of 'IRA volunteers' and we don't call groups of bombers 'Active Service Units' - if we are quoting someone, we should attribute it.

RESPONSIBILITY: Do terrorists 'claim', 'admit' or 'accept' responsibility? There are arguments for and against all three terms. So the best and simplest solution is to say 'The UVF say they did it' or 'The IRA say they carried out the bombing'. In the event of no claim/admission of responsibility, we can always say 'it's not clear yet who killed...'

INNOCENT VICTIMS: All people who are killed or injured while they are not committing a crime are innocent victims, so if we describe some of them that way we imply that others are somehow guilty. The circumstances will always make it clear whether a victim was 'innocent' or not.

EXECUTIONS: We do not call killing or murder 'execution' - a word that means capital punishment after judicial trial.

LONDONDERRY/DERRY: The name was changed to Londonderry centuries ago, but most nationalists and many local people whatever their politics still call it Derry. The best answer is to call it by its official name at first, but subsequent references MAY use the more colloquial 'Derry'.

In judging this, remember that it will usually be right when talking about Protestants to use 'Londonderry', and when talking about Catholics to use 'Derry'. It would be absurd to talk about the 'Londonderry brigade of the IRA'.

BISHOPS: There is no Bishop of Londonderry. The Roman Catholic bishop is, as you'd expect, 'The Bishop of Derry'; but the Church of Ireland bishop is 'The Bishop of Derry and Raphoe'. To call either of them the Bishop of Londonderry is wrong: to do so in the case of the former is also likely to be interpreted as a deliberate political insult.

PRONUNCIATION: Londonderry is pronounced 'London-Derry', not 'Londondree'.

Bangor is 'Bang-gor', not 'Banger'.

Omagh in County Tyrone is '**Oh**-mer', not 'Oh-**ma**' .

The 'y' in (County) Tyrone is pronounced like the 'i' in 'tip', not like the 'y' in 'type'.

THE GOLDEN RULE: If in doubt call the Belfast Newsroom. They live with these problems every day - and they live with the repercussions of any mistakes we might make.

It is essential that NCA staff assigned to Belfast should liaise and co-operate with the regional staff and, in particular, through Head of News and Current Affairs, Northern Ireland.

9B.

BBC, *GUIDELINES FOR FACTUAL PROGRAMMES*, 1989, SECTIONS 38, 40, 41, 79-83

38. NORTHERN IRELAND: GENERAL

1. The special circumstances of Northern Ireland require special guidelines. The consequences of bad judgements can be grave and motives are likely to be scrutinised very closely

The advice in this section also reflects the determination of the BBC to do all it can to protect the people who work for it in the dangerous conditions of Northern Ireland.

- Staff outside Northern Ireland must without fail seek advice from and discuss with local staff their programme plans affecting Northern Ireland, **at all stages**.

- This does not mean that responsibility for the programme is passed to Northern Ireland, nor even shared – it continues to rest with the originating department.

- The need for referral and special consideration was increased by the Notice served on broadcasting organisations by the Home Secretary in October 1988. This imposes legally enforceable restrictions relating to Northern Ireland (which are explained in detail later).

Programme makers should always remember that life in Northern Ireland contains much more than violence and political strife. Factual programmes should reflect all aspects of life and society.

2. On-the-Day Journalism

The first contact point for all matters arising on the day in both news and current affairs programmes is the Head of News and Current Affairs, Northern Ireland (HNCANI) or, in his absence, his nominated deputy. In cases of particular urgency or importance, HNCANI, with Editor, News and Current Affairs, Radio or Editor, News and Current Affairs, Television, as appropriate, will refer to Director, News and Current Affairs and will inform Controller, Editorial Policy.

3. Longer Term Proposals

All proposals for programmes or programme ideas touching on Irish issues in general or on Northern Ireland in particular, must be referred to Controller, Northern Ireland who will liaise with CEP as necessary. In the absence of CNI consult Head of Radio (NI) or Head of Television (NI).

• This referral includes proposals by daily current affairs programmes for longer term items, remembering that with these ENCAT or ENCAR must also be involved.

• If the agreement of Controller NI is not secured, CEP should be informed and the matter referred to the Deputy Director-General.

• Programme making contacts with BBC Northern Ireland at other levels, for instance when booking technical facilities, does not constitute a referral.

• **It is very important that the BBC in Belfast is kept aware of the evolution of projects, including the inevitable changes which take place as ideas are developed.**

• Sensitivities exist far beyond actual programmes, so consultation must extend to production and transmission dates, which can have a significance in Northern Ireland they do not have elsewhere.

It is the responsibility of the Editors of *Radio Times*, *The Listener* and *London Calling* to ensure that material appearing in their publications conforms to understandings reached with Controller, Northern Ireland, and others. In addition, Heads of Presentation and Heads of Publicity, are responsible for ensuring that publicity, promotion and presentation are in the forms agreed.

40. NORTHERN IRELAND: HOME SECRETARY'S ORDER, OCTOBER '88

A wide range of programmes is affected.

The Notice aims to prevent Northern Ireland terrorists and people anywhere in the world speaking for or in support of them being heard in BBC and Independent programmes. It bans direct expressions of support for a number of specified paramilitary and politically associated organisations. They are the Provisional and Official IRA, INLA, UVF, Sinn Féin, Republican Sinn Féin, the UDA, Cumann na mBan (the Women's Movement), Fianna Éireann (the Youth Movement), Saor Éire (Free Ireland), Ulster Freedom Fighters (UFF), and the Red Hand Commando.

The Notice works against two categories of people

• those who represent or purport to represent the Northern Ireland organisations named, and

• those who speak words of support for any of the organisations.

Any person who represents one of the organisations cannot be heard in a programme in that capacity. This is so even if they would have talked on a non-violent topic.

• People who in some situations represent one of the organisations may appear in other capacities: a local government councillor could, for instance, represent the council or one of its committees.

• Anyone at all who expresses support for one of the organisations is not allowed to be heard in a programme expressing that support unless the comments are made in Parliament at Westminster or by a person involved in an election campaign in the United Kingdom.

• If, for example, a United States Senator spoke in the Senate or any other American context in support of Sinn Féin a voice recording of his comments could not be used in our programmes.

• The same applies to an MP speaking outside the House of Commons.

• It applies to ordinary members of the public.

Anyone, including representatives of the organisations, can be quoted in reported speech.

• Pictures of them speaking can be shown but the words must be spoken in voice-over by reporter or presenter, or shown in caption.

• Television could show pictures of say UDA demonstrators waving banners of support for the UDA.

• The sound would have to be cut if they chanted support for the UDA. Other aspects:

• Programme makers should remember that actuality from the European Parliament is not exempt from the restrictions, nor is actuality from courts. As in other cases though, proceedings in the European Parliament and in courts can be fully covered in reported speech.

•Library material is also restricted.

• Reconstructions using actors and works of fiction are exempt, as are Irish rebel songs in genuine performances.

• Live programmes, especially phone-ins and those with studio audiences, must always be ready to stop anyone who starts to speak in support of any of the organisations.

• Generalised comments about or even in favour of terrorism in Ireland or about Irish republicanism are not prevented.

When a programme or programme item is materially changed in accordance with the Notice it is right to alert the audience to the fact. The form of words used should be clear and as **specific as possible about the nature of the change.**

When something is not in conflict with the Home Secretary's Notice the normal process of referral must still be followed.

41. NORTHERN IRELAND: SPECIAL LEGAL CONSIDERATIONS

The provisions of the Criminal Law Act (Northern Ireland) 1967 and the Prevention of Terrorism Act, greatly extend the obligations of all citizens to provide information about, and to refrain from dealing with, criminals or terrorists in Northern Ireland.

• There is no exemption for journalists from these obligations.

• The Northern Ireland (Emergency Provisions) Acts could also have an important bearing on programme makers.

• Editors of programmes dealing with Northern Ireland matters should take advice from The Solicitor's Department before attempting to pass through what is a legal minefield.

79. TERRORISM: INTERVIEWS

The BBC's approach to any dealings with terrorists is dictated by the nature of the particular terrorist group and the context of its activity.

• No approach to record an interview with a terrorist, in a British or a foreign context, may be made without reference through senior line management and CEP.

• **For interviews intended to be incorporated indirectly in copy or in reporter and correspondent voice pieces, approval should be sought in advance from the news editor or Head of Department.**

• A BBC journalist genuinely unable to refer a proposed interview, of either the above kind must take a responsible decision in line with BBC policy, and **report as soon as possible to the appropriate News Editor or Head of Department, who will in turn refer as necessary to CEP.**

• **IRA and other Irish terrorists are interviewed very rarely by the BBC.** It is always a matter for consideration at the highest level and permission will not be given unless there is very strong and clear editorial justification which serves public understanding. This applies even though what can be broadcast of such interviews is heavily restricted by the Notice served on the BBC by the Home Secretary in October 1988.

• **Interviews with people who are associated with Irish terrorist organisations** are not so rare because the people interviewed are active in the daily politics of Northern Ireland, nearly always in publicly elected positions. These interviews are also significantly affected by the Home Secretary's Notice.

Generally whenever interviews are allowed they should be used sparingly, short clips often being more appropriate than long extracts. Challenging questions should be used to get valid contributions to the examination of issues.

80. TERRORISM: LANGUAGE

Broadcasters are often accused of aiding terrorists by publicising what they do. Although news inevitably involves publicity this has to be set against the consideration that silence encourages rumour and may incite further and worse outrages. The careful use of language can minimise any risk of publicity furthering the cause of the terrorist.

• Avoid anything which would glamorise the terrorist, or give an impression of legitimacy. In particular, try not to use terms by which terrorist groups try to portray themselves as legitimate – terms like 'execute', 'court martial', 'brigade', 'active service unit'.

• If used, paramilitary terms should normally be attributed.

• Take care not to show terrorists or people closely associated with them in an approving light. This is largely a matter of detailed consideration, case by case.

When dealing with statements from terrorists in Northern Ireland or the Irish Republic, authentication and guidance should be obtained from Head of News and Current Affairs, Northern Ireland or BBC specialists.

• Such statements may contain important information but we should not take them at face value.

• They can be paraphrased to avoid the military titles and pomp.

• Avoid references to terrorist 'successes'; to most people they spell horror

81. TERRORISM: PARAMILITARY DISPLAYS

Publicly evident events like gunshots at gravesides and other demonstrations at funerals are common in Northern Ireland. As part of the political scene they should be reported when relevant.

There are other managed events of a surreptitious kind over which special care must be taken: restricted news conferences, demonstrations of manpower such as road blocks, or training sessions.

Sometimes reporters will be invited to such events, perhaps at instant notice. Sometimes the BBC will be supplied with material, maybe a video. **Referral is always necessary in these cases although occasionally it will be after the event because of pressure of circumstances.**

• If experienced judgement decides that a managed event is not a fake and it discloses information that the public ought to have, the BBC should report it.

• Its nature should be made clear and if the information was gained by unusual means we will need to say so.

• The material from others will usually need to be included in a larger piece of balanced journalism, not used in isolation.

82. TERRORISM: PEOPLE AT RISK

The BBC should do nothing which would increase the vulnerability of anyone to terrorist attack. Do not give information that would help in planning an attack.

Public Figures

When individuals are threatened they will often not be identified so as not to expose them further. This normally applies to public figures: the general threat is known; specific threats tend not to be. Care must be taken when giving information about the homes of prominent people which is not already widely known.

- Programmes should not give in speech or pictures details which would identify such private homes.
- Do not give addresses or precise locations.
- Locations should be mentioned only in the broadest terms. General descriptions such as 'near ...' can be given but do not name the village or other immediate locality.
- Do not show detailed maps, plans or aerial pictures.
- Pictures should not show security devices at the homes of public figures and reports should not normally speculate about them.
- Pictures of the home of a prominent person can be shown, provided they are neither close-ups which might reveal, say, window locks, nor very long shots which would show the layout of buildings.

It may be irrelevant that some undesirable facts have already been published: programmes should not repeat them.

Important individuals are at risk when they visit public places.

When, for instance, a government minister is to visit a new shopping area details of place or time should not normally be disclosed in advance.

Suppliers to the security forces are vulnerable to threats and, like exposed individuals, they are not usually identified.

Unmarked police cars may be shown, as in the aftermath of an incident, but try not to show registration numbers.

When **injured members of the security forces** are taken to hospital, the hospital should not normally be named.

SECTION TWO INTRODUCTION:
PROPAGANDA WARS

In the early years of the 'troubles' the British army was the leading official source for journalists. Following the emergence of the Provisional IRA and the introduction of internment (1971), the British army opted for disinformation as a key weapon against the IRA. The three pieces on this period collected here each deal with British army and official public relations from slightly different perspectives.

Simon Hoggart, in a classic article written in 1973, details the activities of the British army press office. Critical as the chapter is, its conclusions on disinformation are now known to be wholly false. This illustrates one of the key problems for journalists in telling truth from fiction when reporting a contemporary conflict.

Writing about the same period more than ten years later, **Paul Foot** and **Duncan Campbell** each reveal key details of the British army's secret 'black propaganda' unit known as Information Policy and the central role of Colin Wallace. The full extent and scope of Wallace's activities have yet to be fully aired, but the trajectory of Information Policy - from targeting the IRA, via smearing Northern Ireland politicians, to undermining their own superiors in an elected government - are clear enough. Foot and Campbell take slightly different positions on the Wallace saga and their accounts are included here partly for comparative purposes.

Since these accounts were published, Sir David Calcutt reported in September 1990 that Wallace's appeal against dismissal had been interfered with by MoD officials who 'were in private communication with the chairman of the hearing ... such communications should not have happened; and I believe that what occurred affected the outcome of the appeal', he wrote. Wallace received £30,000 in compensation. Later the Commons Defence Committee attempted to find out who had interfered with the committee and why the government had misled parliament over the affair. However, they were unable to find out because the MoD refused to divulge answers to their questions (see Foot 1996).

The next chapter is one of the few informed accounts of the development of the republican publicity operation. **Liz Curtis** examines both the development of republican newspapers such as *An Phoblacht/Republican News* and the emergence of the Republican Press Centre in Belfast. Although some other material in this area has been published, such as counterinsurgency theorist Wright's (1991) *Terrorist Propaganda*, Picard's work on *An Phoblacht/Republican News* (1991), and both Picard (1989)and Irvin's (1992) work on 'terrorist' PR, there remains a real dearth of material on the promotional activities of the republican movement. Material on unionist public relations is even more scarce and we have, unfortunately, not found a suitable piece for inclusion here.

Finally, **David Miller** updates the story on official PR by concentrating on the promotional activities of the Northern Ireland Office (NIO) which became the lead department in PR matters following the controversy over disinformation in the mid-1970s. Nevertheless the promotional activities of the RUC have remained important and under-researched.

References

Foot, Paul. 'MI5 Mischief', *The Guardian*, 22 July 1996

Irvin, Cynthia. 'Terrorists' Perspectives: Interviews', in D. Paletz and A. Schmid (eds), *Terrorism and the Media*, London, Sage, 1992

Picard, Robert, 'Press Relations of Terrorist Organisations', *Public Relations Review*, 15, winter 1989: 12-23

Picard, Robert. 'How Violence is Justified: Sinn Féin's *An Phoblacht*', *Journal of Communication* 41(4), 1991: 90-103

Wright, Joanne. *Terrorist Propaganda*, Basingstoke, Macmillan, 1991

10.

Simon Hoggart

THE ARMY PR MEN OF NORTHERN IRELAND

(*New Society*, 11 October 1973, pages 79-80)

The British army has learnt a lot in Northern Ireland, not least in press and public relations. For the first time this century, its members have felt the need to justify their actions, and sometimes their very presence, day by day in front of the entire British public, almost like any large industrial corporation, political party or pressure group.

The lessons have been swiftly learnt. For example, if the army now finds itself in any other major operation, here or abroad, it will send teams of specially trained public relations men with the soldiers, to set up emergency bases and feed the press with a rapid and up-to-date stream of information and opinion. Officers, many of whom once ignored, despised or feared the press, have now learnt that they must talk politely, even informatively, to inquiring newsmen. Four years of participation in Britain's most complex political problem have taught the army that it can no longer regard itself as the loyal and unthinking tool of government; it actually has to justify itself. From a military point of view, this part of the Ulster operation has been a considerable success.

By American standards, the manpower required is minute. No more than 24 people, including clerks, work in PR at the army's Lisburn headquarters. With the 25 or so public relations officers drawn from each regiment and brigade stationed in Ulster, the sum total of people whose first duty is public relations is scarcely over 50 - which most of the time is one third of 1 per cent of the garrison in Ulster.

Describing their job, most army PROs frequently use the word 'truth,' which tends to be identified with the military view of affairs. 'Our job is to tell the truth at all times,' a fairly senior officer in PR has said, 'and to

153

correct the deliberate misinformation put out by the other side. Occasionally we make mistakes, but we always correct them wherever possible. I have no objection to newspapers printing what the other side says, but I do get angry when they suggest that they are right.'

The 'truth' is passed on in two main ways. First, there is the straightforward information service, whose centre is the press desk at Lisburn. Here seven men and a coordinator, working on a rota system, read out a log of the day's activities to any journalist who cares to ring and ask. Mostly this is rather skeletal description of day-to-day incidents – a bombing, a riot, a few shots fired, a death. If an IRA rocket narrowly misses a school or hospital, this will usually be tacked on, since it is a fair bet for the first paragraph of a radio bulletin or newspaper report.

For extra details, the journalist can go to the spot, which he probably won't do if he is busy, or if the incident is too far away or not important enough. He can ring the local battalion PRO, who may be helpful, articulate and frank, or suspicious and monosyllabic. Some have a surprisingly intimate and sympathetic knowledge of their area; others are completely at sea, like the man who frantically rang round on a busy day trying to 'sell' a story about his men rescuing a wounded gull from some boys. Most are in-between.

Most journalists working in Northern Ireland are almost completely dependent on this information service (and the smaller one run by the police), simply because there is no other source for news of day-to-day violence. This means that the army has the immense advantage of getting in the first word, and it is left up to the integrity of the journalist to check that word out. Some do, some don't. Most only check when there is time or the incident looks like becoming controversial, and a few hardly bother at all. When the British press prints an account of an incident as if it were established fact, and it is clear that the reporter himself was not on the spot, it is a 99 per cent certainty that it is the army's version which is being given. (Irish newspapers, apart from the *Irish Times,* do much the same – but they use the accounts given by local residents in Catholic areas.)

Another part of the public relations job is the passing on of basically non-attributable information, which newspaper readers can recognise by the warning signal 'army sources believe' or 'senior officers in HQ allege.' This is information which no individual wants to be accountable for, and so inevitably must be treated with more caution. Again, it is entirely up to the judgment of the reporter whom he chooses to believe. Reporters who have worked in Belfast for some time tend to have their own blacklists of 'unreliable sources' – people who follow the army line too uncritically or whose information is bits of hearsay and wishful thinking. But people who tell it like it is do exist, and it doesn't take long to find them.

One myth the army and the IRA share is that the other side is engaged in a massive and highly skilled 'black propaganda' campaign, by which detailed lies are turned out and supported by forged evidence. Almost any allegation of brutality by soldiers is termed 'IRA propaganda' by the army, as if IRA men toured areas forcing residents to memorise detailed false evidence for journalists. Last year the *Guardian* said that the first battalion of the Parachute Regiment had become so unpopular that at least two units in Belfast had asked not to work with them. According to the *Daily Telegraph,* this was thought to be IRA propaganda, even though every scrap of evidence had been gathered entirely from army officers. Likewise, the IRA believe that the army invents elaborate stories against them. A recent example was a story about Long Kesh detainees, who wanted to leave the IRA, being beaten up by other Provisionals. This was dismissed as army black propaganda, even though the story had been initiated by a shocked Catholic politician, with an impeccable record of anti-army statements and allegations.

I cannot find any evidence of a black propaganda machine, and I do not believe it exists. However, there are other aspects of army PR work which, taken in sum, must look very much like it to someone with anti-army views:

1. Information about incidents has to be passed on to the press as soon as possible – often within 20 minutes of its happening. This means that the first account is always the unchecked word of the soldier on the spot. He may be mistaken, or he may be lying in order to avoid a possible charge (army discipline is so draconian – up to a year for a soldier who loses a rifle, for example – that men must inevitably present their side of the case as forcefully as possible). When, days later, the army investigation reveals something nearer the truth, it is too late for the papers.

2. Once the army version has been established, virtually every officer believes it implicitly. If a man is shot for carrying a gun, and locals say he was not, the army itself has no doubts at all. I believe that the army has been mistaken on several occasions, and its genuine belief that it is right must look exactly like deliberate lying to people who were on the spot. This is a highly dangerous state of affairs, accounting for much of the mistrust felt for the army by Catholics (and now Protestants) in troubled districts, and for the army's failure to understand that mistrust.

3. The army does feed anti-IRA stories to journalists, sometimes selected because their paper is favourable to the army, or even for the opposite reason. Any journalist who accepts and prints these stories without checking is being stupid or incompetent. A good example is the recent story about IRA funds being embezzled. This was started by a senior officer at Lisburn who came across a letter from Long Kesh (now called the Maze) written by an IRA man. It appeared only after long and meticulous checking by the *Sunday Times,* a paper which many army officers regard as virtually a news bulletin for the IRA. Like almost all other similar stories 'planted' by the army, this was true, partly because all PROs have a genuine horror of

the credibility gap the United States army managed to build up in Vietnam. They are terrified of being caught out in a deliberate lie, and avoid it by not lying. But, naturally enough, they do not plant stories which work against them, and so the net impression is one of bias.

An indication of how the PR operation has now become more sophisticated is the way that the army treats unsympathetic reporters. I can show this best from my own experience. Last year my predecessor, Simon Winchester, and I printed a run of three anti-army pieces in one week, ending with Winchester narrating how soldiers had shot at him during Bloody Sunday. The three articles came together quite by chance but, not surprisingly, were seen as deliberate aggression by the army. For about a fortnight we were given 'minimal cooperation' by Lisburn – curt, unwilling accounts of violence, and no background or extra information at all. It was an inconvenience, but no more, since we got the information from helpful colleagues, and it ended after a fortnight, following discussions at the Ministry of Defence.

A few months later I published another, fairly similar story, saying that soldiers had been unnecessarily brutal in putting down a Protestant riot. This time the treatment was quite different. I was invited to Lisburn for lunch and drinks, and shown papers which suggested that the soldiers might, to some extent, have been justified. I am sure the lunch and drinks had nothing to do with it, but, if I am completely honest, I think the approach might have made me a little more cautious, when writing about the army. This may or may not be a good thing, but I am quite certain that the opposite would have happened after another spell of 'minimal cooperation.'

Finally, this year, we said that the army had blackmailed an innocent young man into spying on his neighbours. The story, as Lord Carrington admitted, was true, and I would have expected some military hostility. In the event, a week later, I was given an excellent exclusive story by an army major, which also turned out to be true. This is the smartest approach of all, for in spite of journalists' reputations, any reporter would prefer a good story to a free drink. Drinks with informants, after all, come on expenses.

I don't relate these incidents to suggest that the army regards *Guardian* reporters as especially important, merely as illustrations. I know most reporters from other papers could tell stories similar to this.

Recently, policy seems to have switched again, with a series of melodramatic ructions involving Robert Fisk, the able and hard-working *Times* correspondent. In August, Fisk refused to accept the army's interpretation of a confidential document he had got his hands on. In the row that followed, the civilian head of army PR, Peter Broderick, described Fisk as 'a hostile reporter' in a message sent to the *Times* office. Fisk may or may not have been mistaken, but he is not 'hostile,' and the implication behind the use of the word is serious. It suggests that since everything the army says is true, anyone who doesn't happen to accept it is a conscious enemy.

This attitude reaches its height with army officers who believe that reporters should never say 'the army states' or 'troops claim' since this implies that they might be mistaken. Others even believe it implies that 'the other side' should not be given their say, since this would imply that they had a case. It is not a view shared by people working in PR, but ideas in the army have a habit of seeping downwards at a fairly rapid speed.

The firm belief that the army is always right seems to me more dangerous than deliberate lying, since lying can always be discovered. It makes it far more difficult for journalists to get at the real truth, and it makes it harder for the army itself to come to terms with the situation it finds itself in. For example, the overwhelming majority of officers genuinely and sincerely believe that the paratroopers were justified on Bloody Sunday. Until they can comprehend the opposite, their understanding of the whole situation must be suspect, and so must a lot of what they say about other issues, however honestly it is spoken.

On balance, however, the PR operation remains a considerable success. Hardly a word is breathed against the army in the popular papers or on radio and television in Britain. If criticism is made, it is invariably in the mouths of others, and always hedged with a full account of the army's position – however sceptical the reporter himself might be. Most of this must stem from Britain's traditional respect for its army and the genuine fact that it is much more gentle than other countries' armies or police (one wonders how the Falls or Shankill roads would react to the arrival of the French CRS). However, this goodwill would be quickly dissipated by an incompetent or else a deliberately misleading PR operation.

11.

Paul Foot

COLIN WALLACE AND THE PROPAGANDA WAR

(From *Who Framed Colin Wallace?*, London, Macmillan Books, 1990, pages 1-79)

Colin Wallace was born in June 1943 in Randalstown, a small town between Antrim and Ballymena in the Orange heartland of Northern Ireland.

[...] Most of his family were paid-up members (and sometimes senior officials) of the Orange Order or the Royal Black Institution. All the talk at his grandparents' house was of the history of the fight of Protestant people in Ireland to keep Republicans at bay. History started when King William won the Battle of the Boyne in 1690. Most of his uncles and great-uncles had been active in the B Specials, the heavily armed special Protestant-only police.

[...] As for the Catholic population of the same island, Colin doesn't remember having contact with any of them during the whole of his childhood. Everybody was Protestant. The 'enemy' lurked like weasels in the woods, unseen and undiscovered except perhaps to be shot at by a B Special patrol. He could see the hamlets where they lived from the high ground above Toomebridge and Moneyglass, but he never went near them. 'I grew up to believe above all else in the importance of loyalty to the Crown and service to my country,' Colin recalls. 'The attitude of complete, unswerving loyalty to the British sovereign state shaped the whole way I thought and behaved.' [...]

He went into Lisburn barracks as Assistant Command, Public Relations Officer for the Army in Northern Ireland on I May 1968. He was a civil servant, with an equivalent Army rank of major; and of course he kept his commission in the TAVR, where he was now training Irish Guards cadets. He was also commissioned as a captain in the Ulster Defence Regiment.

Proud as Colin felt on the first morning he walked into the Army headquarters, even he would not have argued that the job he had just won would test him too severely. Lisburn barracks, Northern Ireland, was known in the British Army at that time as Happy Valley. It was a pasture for old warhorses who had not quite reached retiring age. The much feared IRA campaign had fizzled out, after almost total failure, in 1962. The IRA itself seemed to exist only in name, a pathetic organisation which sang songs to itself about its brave and bloody past. What was left of Republican activism could be left to the B Specials and the Royal Ulster Constabulary, who knew how to sniff out recalcitrant Republicans and deal with them. The underlying causes of the violence which had wracked the north-east of Ireland over the centuries were still there, but at the beginning of 1968, the effects seemed to have disappeared. [...]

The role of the public relations officers was perhaps more important than that of anyone else at 'Happy Valley'. They at least had something to do: athletic achievements of soldiers in Northern Ireland needed to be reported in English local newspapers. Jovial Father Christmases had to be found for children's functions; voluntary activities 'showing the flag' were in high demand. They were Colin Wallace's speciality. He started to organise a free-fall parachute display team. He threw himself into all sorts of games, stunts and sports to promote the Army. One day he would be writing a bromide speech for the General; the next he would be falling out of an aeroplane; the next he would be assisting a repertory company with a production of *Oh What a Lovely War.* He was the happiest man in Happy Valley and his colleagues noticed at once that he was always the first to volunteer to do anything, however unpleasant. [...]

Then suddenly that October, when Colin had been at Lisburn less than six months, the whole atmosphere changed. A demonstration demanding civil rights for the Catholic minority in Northern Ireland was broken up with savage force by the Royal Ulster Constabulary. Suddenly, Northern Ireland was in the news. Journalists flooded in from all over the world to re-open the age-old controversies. Colin Wallace at first thought nothing of it. All his adult life there had been scares about a reawakening of old hostilities, but they had always proved illusory. The B Specials had gone in, a shot or two was fired, an angry word or two printed in the Catholic press and then comfortable complacency returned. [...]

It didn't take Colin long to change his mind. It was not merely that the civil rights movement grew in influence, nor that their marches continued to be insulted and physically attacked by the very forces of law and order in which Colin himself had served. It was the effrontery of the new movement which shook him into the realisation that something momentous was happening.

He was sitting in his office on 14 August 1969 when Tony Staughton [chief public relations officer at Lisburn] came in with astonishing news. 'The government's sending troops into Derry,' he said. 'You'd better go with them.' Riots in Derry had unleashed a violent backlash by B Specials and RUC, which threatened an outbreak of civil war. The Army went in to 'keep the peace'. Colin travelled to Derry in a four-ton truck which was full of barbed wire. He went straight with the first troops to be deployed to the Bogside, which was cordoned off by barricades. There he remembers a discussion between the officer commanding the Derry forces and a Queen's University student, Bernadette Devlin. He remembers a telephone call from Ulsterbus demanding the return of a bus which had been used for barricades. He negotiated with the demonstrators who said he could have the bus back if the Army would rebuild their barricade. 'We did just that,' he says. 'We built their barricade.' No wonder, on that first day, that the British troops were so popular with the Bogsiders.

The following day, he was whisked down by helicopter to Belfast, the scene of some of the worst rioting in the history of that city. As he tried to organise a press visit into the gutted Catholic areas in the Lower Falls, he remembers an object flying through the air at him. It was a medal case enclosing an MBE - a protest from an old warrior [...] outraged that the British Army should be seen to be helping Catholics. 'My memory of the Falls that day is very clear,' says Colin. 'There were whole streets gutted, empty buildings everywhere, a huge linen factory burnt to the ground. I just couldn't believe the scale of the devastation. The normal cheerful atmosphere of the place had been replaced by a sullen resentment. It was quite obvious that something very serious was happening, something quite different from anything that had ever happened while I'd been alive.' [...]

By 1971, however, there were two developments which made quite clear what was really happening. On 6 February, the first British soldier was shot in Northern Ireland - the first such life to be lost since the 1920s. Secondly, on 9 August, the British Conservative government sanctioned the right of the police and military authorities to intern dissidents without trial. Those interned included not just IRA suspects but many political dissidents as well, including Michael Farrell, the influential, non-sectarian leader of People's Democracy. Many of those arrested were tortured - as was later proved before, and denounced by, the European Court of Human Rights.

[...] Internment itself was hopelessly bungled. But the dictatorial methods used, and the 'inhuman and degrading treatment', as the European Court of Human Rights put it, helped to persuade large numbers of the more beleaguered of the Catholic population that the British authorities were propping up the Orange supremacy; and that the only effective protection for them was the armed militia - the Provisional IRA. Thus the two chief events of 1971 - the killing of the first British soldier and internment - led to a rapid growth in the influence and military effectiveness of the Provisional IRA; and in turn convinced the British and Northern Irish authorities that they were in for a long period of civil war.

Suddenly, the garrison at Lisburn was transformed from being the least important and most neglected of all the British Army headquarters to the most important and the best supplied. Happy Valley became Siege City. Every branch of activity there had to change, none more drastically than information and public relations.

In the lull immediately after the summer of 1969, the changes were minimal. Tony Staughton stayed in control, with Colin Wallace as his assistant. In 1969, on the very day of the Bogside riots, they were joined by Major Tony Yarnold, a military public relations man of enormous experience. He had served in Egypt, Cyprus, Malaya and Hong Kong where he had run the Press Office during the communist insurgency.

Tony Yarnold immediately overhauled the system of collecting information. He called in more clerks and secretaries. He supervised a round-the-clock, three-shift system for the Press Office. By 1971, there was a new dark room, a new printing press and a staff of at least forty. Staff officers were brought in from other regiments to sit in at the press desk and answer questions from journalists.

The new order was slowly, though reluctantly, recognised in Whitehall. In 1970, on the orders of the Ministry of Defence, the information department of the Army in Northern Ireland was reorganised. Tony Staughton remained in charge of public relations, with Colin and Colonel Yarnold in support. Side by side, a new unit was set up, entitled Information Liaison - later Information Policy - commanded by a military officer with the rank of lieutenant colonel. The first of these was Lieutenant Colonel Johnny Johnston. He was swiftly replaced by a hard-line paratroop officer, Colonel Maurice Tugwell. Information Policy was a separate unit working for the intelligence services but expected to operate under the cover of public relations. Its function was psychological warfare. The best definition of that comes from a Ministry of Defence document 'An Introduction to Psychological Operations' which was published in 1974.

> Psychological Operations (Psyops) is an all-embracing term defined by NATO as 'planned psychological activities in peace and war directed towards enemy, friendly and neutral audiences, in order to create attitudes and behaviour favourable to the achievement of political and military objectives' ...
>
> Strategic psywar pursues long-term and mainly political objectives. It is designed to undermine an enemy or hostile group to fight and to reduce the capacity to wage war.
>
> It can be directed against the dominating political party, the Government and/or against the population as a whole, or particular elements of it. It is planned and controlled by the highest political authority.

The references to 'the Government' and the 'dominating political party' were directed of course to the country in which the psychological warfare was being waged, and not to the British government or the ruling party in Westminster. This 'psyops' was not something new to the 1970s. It had been a routine feature in the British military response throughout the empire in the years after the Second World War. As the 1974 document made clear, psyops had become part of the military strategy of NATO countries, especially the United States of America where the techniques of psyops were developed throughout the Vietnam war.

In Northern Ireland, the normal activities of Army PR officers were left to the public relations department under Tony Staughton. Information Policy had a rather different function, namely to use information and disinformation from Intelligence as one of the many weapons in the war with the IRA. Tony Staughton describes the process. 'To start with, in the early part of the troubles, 1968, 1969 and 1970, I had a clear run in my department, as we did well against the IRA. I think we won the propaganda battle in those years. The IRA used to complain bitterly about us, but we had a really excellent record of getting stuff in the papers which did them down. I had a fundamental rule which I never broke in all my years of service - and I know that Tony Yarnold thought the same way: never lie to the Press. We didn't lie, we just carried out normal public relations from the Army side, and we had the better of the other side.'

'All this changed with internment. Immediately after internment, the IRA started to get the upper hand. And from that time on, the Foreign Office and the Intelligence people insisted on much more say in public relations. They sent a man over called Hugh Mooney - he was from a department of the Foreign Office called the Information Research Department (IRD). None of us ever knew what Mooney was about: who he reported to or what he was entitled to. All we knew was that they gave him a big house to live in and freedom to move at will throughout the barracks and Stormont. There was another man called Clifford Hill - I always imagined that he had something to do with Intelligence. None of us knew precisely what he was up to either.

'It was the same with Information Policy. I don't remember them being at all important until after internment. Then, after Maurice Tugwell took over, they became more important than we were. I remember some furious rows about who was responsible for what. It was always agreed that although Maurice Tugwell and I were of the same rank, I was in charge of public relations. Yet I remember at least one meeting at Stormont when it was clear that the Ministry and the Army were seeing Maurice for a job which was plainly part of my responsibilities.'

'The ordinary chain of command seemed again and again to be broken. People seemed to be doing what they wanted to do in information - often very puerile things which in my view gravely set us back.'

'The main cause of disagreement was my principle that you don't deceive people in the press - you tell them your side of the story, but if they ask for facts which you have at your disposal, you give them to them. If you want to tell them something else which you can't verify but which you're certain is true, you give it to the press 'off the record'. But the one thing you can't do is invent facts and stories, and pass them over as truth. If that's what they meant by 'psychological operations', as they always called it, I didn't see it as part of public relations: and I was always fighting them - more and more furiously until I finally dropped out with a coronary in 1973.' (Interview with the author, 10 October 1987.)

One of the jobs of the new unit was constantly to 'brief' visiting journalists. The journalists who were by now arriving in Northern Ireland in droves were not all hacks who could be persuaded to publish favourable propaganda because some PR man was being polite to them. The best journalists in Britain (and many from every other part of the world) were spending long periods in Northern Ireland. The roll call of British journalists who covered Northern Ireland at the time reads like a citation at a British Press Awards ceremony: Robert Fisk of *The Times;* Simon Winchester of the *Sunday Times*; Simon Hoggart of the *Observer*, Mary Holland of the *Observer* - these and other journalists of the highest flight were increasingly asking awkward questions. Why internment? Why torture? Does the Army assassinate people? What kind of war is being fought here and why is the Army fighting it?

British journalism was not mealy-mouthed and sycophantic as it became ten or twenty years later. Investigative journalism was the fashion and journalists had a nasty habit of refusing to accept the official version. Even editors could not always be relied on to co-operate with the Army. Ancestral calls on the solidarity of hierarchy were not necessarily answered. Sometimes they stung editors into insubordination. Harry Evans, then editor of the *Sunday Times*, gave full rein to the Insight team, whose investigative journalists swarmed throughout Northern Ireland, and who, Colin Wallace remembers, 'were always really hard to persuade'. [...]

Very quickly everyone who worked with Colin Wallace - his bosses, Tony Staughton and Tony Yarnold, his colleague Mike Taylor - everyone realised that they had in their barracks even before the troubles broke out a political and public relations operator of considerable skill and dedication.

One immediate result was that Colin was, in effect, though not in name, transferred out of public relations to Information Policy. Peter Broderick, who took over as head of the whole of Northern Ireland Army Information in 1973, explained this well:

> [...] Though on the staff of public relations, he [Wallace] was used by Information Policy as their outlet to the press. He also had a knowledge of the Irish situation which was totally unique in the headquarters and surpassed that even of most of the Intelligence Branch. As time progressed, he was not only the main briefer for the press, but also the adviser on Irish matters to the whole Headquarters and - because of his personal talents - contributed much creative thought to the Information Policy Unit. In order to

do his job, he had constant and free access to information of the highest classification and extreme sensitivity. (Peter Broderick's statement to Civil Service Appeal Board, October 1975.) [...]

Indeed, Colin Wallace was wanted far and wide throughout the Army in Northern Ireland. When top politicians came to Northern Ireland, the Army insisted that Colin was on hand to answer questions and help with briefings. When Edward Heath, the Prime Minister, visited Derry in 1972, Wallace was seldom more than a few yards away from him. When the Under-Secretary of State for the Army, Geoffrey Johnson Smith, called on an extended visit in 1973, Colin was permanently in attendance. When Harold Wilson made his first visit to the Province, Colin Wallace briefed him and arranged his press conference at RAF Aldergrove.

He was often seen on television. When James Burke, a popular presenter at the time, put on an hour-long programme about the arms trade, the man he quizzed about the arms (indeed the man who arranged for the arms to be shipped from Northern Ireland to the BBC headquarters) was Colin Wallace.

An indication of the importance attached to Colin by the Army authorities was his attendance at the tribunal, under Lord Chief Justice Widgery, into the killing of thirteen people by the Army after a civil rights' demonstration in Derry on 30 January 1972 - 'Bloody Sunday'. The outcry after the killings echoed all over the world. Critical journalists had a field day. The Army, and especially the Parachute Regiment (whose officers included Maurice Tugwell, then head of Information Policy) was at a low ebb. Enormous efforts were made by Information Policy to prove to the sceptics that the IRA had started the bloodbath. An impressive legal team was put together to represent the Army at the tribunal. It included Mr Brian Gibbens QC (later a judge), Michael Underhill QC (later a judge), Lieutenant Colonel Colin Overbury from the Army Legal Service and Major Henry Hugh-Smith, a staff officer in the Life Guards, sent over from Ministry of Defence headquarters to act as secretary to the legal team. Attached to this illustrious band, with full accreditation as though he himself were a barrister, was Colin Wallace. He attended every day at the inquiry, sat with the Army barristers and assisted them with the many inquiries which they put to him. [...]

Before he finally left his post after his stroke in the spring of 1973, Tony Staughton twice recommended Colin Wallace, who was not yet thirty years old, for the MBE, and to this day cannot understand how and why the recommendations were turned down. 'I've never known such a deserving case,' he says. 'I had the champagne on ice.' He concludes that an MBE for a twenty-nine-year-old is so exceptional that even in this exceptional case the authorities could not stomach it. Another reason, perhaps closer to the mark, is suggested by a sentence in Peter Broderick's official report: 'Wallace's dual role was particularly resented in Whitehall, while highly valued by the operational commander in Northern Ireland.' (Broderick's statement to Civil Service Appeal Board, October 1975.)

The dual role was soon made official. Peter Broderick took up the post of Head of Army Information Services in July 1973. [...] In order to comply with the strict rules in the Civil Service about advertising for jobs, and in order to ensure that Colin stayed ostensibly in a civilian role (and was therefore much more acceptable to journalists), Broderick, with the full agreement of his superiors, invented a job description which could be advertised without mentioning psychological warfare. You cannot advertise a post for a 'black propagandist', yet 'black propaganda' was what Colin was going to put out. He formally applied for the falsely-described post of Head of Production Services. In September 1974, he got the job, and was promoted to the rank of Senior Information Officer, a post which carried an equivalent rank of lieutenant colonel. Colin was just twenty-nine; the youngest man in the British Armed Services to hold such a senior rank. [...]

> Wallace's primary job was to win friends among the press and to gain their total confidence as a reliable source of information. By agreement with Intelligence in each case, he was supplied with selected information about terrorists, their activities, their sources of money and arms at home and overseas, of the allegiances of so-called innocents and such matters. This - together with his long-term and intimate knowledge of the Irish scene - made him an invaluable contact for the press. Almost all his background briefings he gave non-attributably and it is a measure of his skill and the regard for him by the press that I cannot recall a single occasion when any reporter, even from the hostile papers, disclosed the source of the briefings. (Broderick's statement to Civil Service Appeal Board, October 1975.)

For any journalist arriving to report on the 'troubles' in Northern Ireland after July 1973, the straightest and easiest road led to Colin Wallace's office. There you were met by a man with an easy-going, cheerful manner and a high regard for good journalism. Colin flattered the journalists every bit as much as he used them. He knew they were after information and he knew that most of them were too good to be satisfied with silly public relations or blatantly false stories.

His skill in dealing with journalists was recognised by the best of them. In his book *In Holy Terror*, Simon Winchester who reported on the 'troubles' for the *Sunday Times*, wrote:

> The Army have been of unique assistance. Not all who offered their help and advice would wish to be identified, but of those who allow their names to be published, Lieutenant Colonel Tony Yarnold and Colin Wallace must head the list. (S. Winchester, *In Holy Terror: Reporting the Ulster Troubles*, London, Faber and Faber, 1974, p. 9.)

Most of the information which Colin provided was true - but occasionally it was untrue. In this respect, he was breaching the rules set out by Tony Staughton who insisted that no press or information officer should ever divulge information which was false. Deceit of the type in which Colin was engaged for the British Army from 1970 to at least the end of 1973 was something he regarded as wholly justified. This was because the deceit was aimed at what he regarded as the most deadly enemy of his country: terrorism. The powerful patriotism of his youth was by far the strongest of the forces which inspired him.

Peter Broderick's official report has a revealing sentence: 'He [Colin] acted resolutely and to effect against anyone - Republican or Loyalist who was destroying his country.' (Broderick's statement to Civil Service Appeal Board, October 1975.)

This even-handedness was perhaps a little disingenuous. The real enemies for Colin at that time were the same weasels in the woods of his youth, the inhabitants of that undiscovered country down in the valley near Toomebridge, the ancestral foe: the IRA. It was not until 1974 that the menace of orange terrorism fully engaged him.

The purpose of the black propaganda which Colin Wallace put out was to disorientate and discomfort the terrorists: chiefly the IRA, but also Protestant terrorists. That, in his view, entirely justified the murky waters in which he was paddling.

'Only ill-informed people believe there can be a total military victory in Northern Ireland,' he says. 'All we could do was deal with terrorism: wean the terrorists away from the population, set them against one another, disorientate them and make their leaders unpopular both with their supporters and the population at large. That way, I believed we could isolate them, break them and return to peace, however uneasy that peace was - the peace I'd been used to in the past.'

'Black propaganda' or 'psychological operations' carries with it the suggestion that the information put out is necessarily false. But a lot of the work of Information Policy, and of Colin Wallace, was normal public relations. Campaigns, for instance, were run to stop people giving guns to their children for Christmas, for fear that the children might be shot by the Army if they went into the streets with their toy guns. There were also campaigns to stop people accepting gifts from strangers, since these 'gifts' might turn out to be terrorist bombs, handled by an innocent party. Such campaigns stemmed from genuine information and genuine fear, and were plainly unexceptionable. There were also 'deception operations' to which Colin contributed. A British Army 'laundry' was set up in the heart of the most militant Catholic area in Belfast. Clothes taken there were rushed back to Lisburn and tested for explosives, before being laundered elsewhere. Massage parlours were set up in which British Army and intelligence 'masseuses' picked up information from their clients. [...]

Many of the stories which Colin planted in reputable newspapers did indeed help to disorientate and confuse the IRA. He had information from the most secret sources that IRA bombs were exploding early killing the IRA men who were carrying them or planting them. The reason for this was their ultra-sensitive but unreliable timing devices. The Army was anxious that the IRA should not trace this source of the trouble so Information Policy leaked a series of stories that the reason the bombs were exploding early was that the IRA were using impure sodium chlorate for their bombs - imported from France.

Selected journalists, told of this 'unstable' source of IRA bombs, hurried into print. The *Guardian's* report on 23 August 1972 was followed the next day by one in the *Daily Telegraph* which promoted the story to a page 2 lead under the headline FAULTY BOMB CHEMICALS USED BY THE IRA GANGS. Six weeks later the story ran in the *Observer*, headlined IRA USING FRENCH CHEMICALS. Colin was amused to find himself described in the second paragraph as 'an army chemical expert'. His time at Woodside's, the chemists, had served him well. The completely bogus story, he is certain, had its effect. The IRA *were* more careful about the use of chlorate of soda, especially if it was imported from France. And Colin heard in the ensuing weeks of their continuing difficulties in finding a substitute anywhere else. He was also delighted that the real cause of the premature explosions was not discovered for many months after his expert story appeared in the newspapers.

Another story with a similar thrust was what Colin wryly describes now as the 'big cancer scare'. This was floated in the same month (August 1972) as the 'sodium chlorate' spoof. The paper chosen for launch was the one which sold more copies in Northern Ireland than any other: the *Sunday Mirror*. On 13th August 1972, the *Sunday Mirror* lead front page story declared: POISON IN THE STREETS.

This referred to another ingredient of IRA bombs - nitrobenzene. It was poisonous, not just to the IRA but to everyone else. The story quoted an Army spokesman (Colin Wallace) saying: 'Symptoms of nitro-poisoning are difficult to spot. By the time they are visible it is too late to treat the victim. Vomiting and a coma follow and later the glands and liver break down.'

The same point was made in an enormous article the next day in the *Guardian*, entitled: WORRY OVER POISON IN IRA BOMBS, by Peter Chippindale and Derek Brown. This article quoted 'informed sources in Belfast' (Colin Wallace) highlighting the poisonous qualities of nitrobenzene. 'Children finding it stored in a derelict house or people forced to store it by the Provisionals could suffer from the poisoning.'

Colin Wallace watched in delighted amazement as the 'cancer scare' took off in press and television. Learned scientists were interviewed on television late into the night about the possibility that thousands of Belfast people might catch leukaemia or other cancers from the storing of nitrobenzene. Colin himself had none of the scientific knowledge which was now being daily made available to the public in support of the wild theory he had floated - with the single intention of making IRA men and women feel uneasy about their explosive materials. The story ran and ran. In September 1973, more than a year after Colin first floated his cancer scare, he was earnestly telling one of his most frequent visitors, Gerald Bartlett of the *Daily Telegraph,* of the threat of cancer from nitrobenzene. Bartlett duly obliged: LEUKAEMIA THREAT TO PROVOS.

> Dozens of Provisional IRA members in Northern Ireland are believed to have contracted blood disorders caused by fumes from their home-made bombs. Medical experts say the disorders could lead in some cases to leukaemia and aplastic anaemia. One senior Belfast provisional who recently died of leukaemia may have contracted it in this way. (*Sunday Telegraph,* 9 September 1973.)

The article went on to say that several Provisionals may have died in this way, and quoted medical experts linking leukaemia deaths to nitrobenzene. The article ended: 'A leading leukaemia consultant said: "Certainly nitrobenzene poisoning can cause leukaemia. But I am not aware of any cases."'

Late in 1972, the Army heard of a new consignment of Russian rocket launchers which had been supplied to the IRA. The rocket launchers themselves presented a serious threat, since the screens necessary to protect armoured cars and police stations from such rocket launchers had not yet been installed. The Army needed time to install the screens and Information Policy was asked to help. From what he could find about the rocket attacks, Colin discovered that the IRA had been mishandling their weapons. The instructions were in Russian and the IRA did not fully understand them. Several rockets had been fired with the safety pins still in; others, which had been sent by the Russians to be used for training purposes only, had been used in action, and had not functioned properly. There was considerable disarray in the IRA about their much-vaunted new weapons and Colin Wallace set out to make it worse.

He chose perhaps the best journalist on station in Northern Ireland: Robert Fisk of *The Times*. Fisk, who later won many awards all over the world (especially the Middle East), was no push-over. The piece he wrote after the conversation with Colin Wallace was cautious and named the source: IRA ROCKETS MADE IN RUSSIA ARE IN DANGEROUS CONDITION, ARMY BALLISTICS EXPERTS SAY. 'Army ballistics engineers at the Ministry of Defence,' wrote Fisk, 'believe that most of the Soviet-manufactured rockets held by the Provisional IRA are in a dangerous condition because the explosive charge inside the warheads has deteriorated through age.' (*The Times,* 29 December 1972.)

The article then referred to 'Cyrillic markings' on the rocket launchers which showed that they should have been used 'more than a year ago'. It was this, Fisk reported, which accounted for the 'remarkably low rate of success' of the IRA rocket launchers.

By focusing on the wrong reasons for that low rate of success, Information Policy hoped to distract the IRA from the real reasons they were failing with their rocket launchers and at the same time, strain their relations with their Soviet suppliers. To make sure, Colin also had a conversation with Derek Brown of the *Guardian*, which resulted in a substantial story on the same day (29 December 1972) under a headline: IRA ROCKETS 'ARE TOO OLD TO EXPLODE'. In this article the multi-talented source was described as 'Army munitions experts'.

In August 1973, Information Policy was presented with another problem. The IRA was using women to plant their bombs. This had led to a number of fruitless and quite roughly handled searches of innocent women in the streets of Belfast and Derry - which had got the Army a bad name. Was there anything which could be done to try to stop the use of women as bomb-carriers?

One faintly ridiculous answer appeared in the *Sunday Mirror* on 19 August 1973 - again after a discussion between its author, Kevin Dowling, and Colin Wallace.

DANGER IN THOSE FRILLY PANTIES was the catching headline. The story underneath it started with the bizarre proposition: 'Frilly nylon undies worn by IRA bomb girls may have helped to kill three of them.' That, disclosed the report, was the verdict of Army experts', one of whom was quoted directly as saying: 'It is probable that static electricity generated by the bombers' clothes is responsible for at least some of the deaths.'

Colin Wallace enjoyed that one, though he was sceptical enough even then to doubt how sensitive the hardened cadre of the IRA were to that kind of propaganda. Certainly, there was no appreciable decline in the use of the women bomb-handlers by the Provisionals.

As the IRA established itself in 1972, so the British Army became concerned to shut off its arms supply. Early intelligence reports suggested that the main source of arms for the IRA was the United States of America where the IRA still enjoyed support in the large American Irish community.

In October 1972, Colin Wallace built up a stack of captured weapons and paraded it for the press as though it were a secret hoard of weapons supplied by IRA supporters in the United States. It featured dramatically in the *Daily Mirror* of 11 October 1972, under the headline THE CLUES OF HARDWARE HILL. 'The location of the hill,' warned the *Daily Mirror's* Joe Gorrod mysteriously, 'must remain secret.' The *Daily Express* followed with an enormous 'special investigation' headlined: WHERE THE IRA KILLERS GET THEIR GUNS. The information about the American sources of the weapons was exactly the same as in the *Daily Mirror*, and other papers, and was supplied to the newspaper, via British Intelligence, by Colin Wallace.

The point of these articles was to whip up hostility in the United States to the 'men of violence' who were being assisted by otherwise unexceptionable American arms traders. This effort was reinforced by an Information Policy campaign to link the IRA to American peaceniks and crypto-communists who had learnt how to fight in Vietnam and were using their skills to help the IRA.

There was very little evidence of any substance that there were any such Vietnam veterans in Northern Ireland and it therefore required considerable creativity on the part of Information Policy to 'interest' distinguished British journalists in this idea. Colin was specially delighted with an early success in this area, an article in the *Daily Express* on 30 March 1972 by 'Chapman Pincher, the man who gives you tomorrow's news today'.

'Tomorrow's news' on this occasion warned of the 'serious threat' from American ex-Vietnam soldiers being recruited to fight with the IRA 'as paid gunmen and saboteurs'. Pincher reported: 'There is no shortage of ex-Vietnam veterans - many of them Catholics of Irish origin prepared to hire out their services.'

He could not, however, provide evidence of any one such veteran, nor even an incident in which any such gunmen had been involved. But he speculated: 'The move to employ them actively as gunmen seems to he linked with a drive by pro-Irish muggers in New York to steal the passports of British visitors.'

The notion of a combined campaign by former Vietnam war veterans and street muggers (all of them Irish and probably Catholic) let off a smell which delighted the boys at Information Policy. They felt with some reason that this story could run and run. And so it did. As late as February 1973, Gerald Bartlett of the *Daily Telegraph*, a regular visitor to Colin's office, was reporting in the *Sunday Telegraph*: US VIETNAM VETERANS TRAIN IRA TERRORISTS.

The story was very much the same as Pincher's the previous year, except that Gerald Bartlett was able to report: 'One of the first American instructors to be recruited by the Provisionals lost a leg when a bomb he was constructing exploded prematurely. He was, it is understood, given forged papers and flown to the Chelsea Naval Hospital, Boston, as a Vietnam casualty.'

How did Gerald Bartlett come across this bizarre incident, and how was he unable to name the soldier, or even to check the matter with the hospital in Boston? One answer is that the source for his story was Colin Wallace who never went too far into details.

As the months wore on and the battle with the IRA turned into a war which the British Army seemed to have little hope of winning, the emphasis switched from the Americans to the Russians. In December 1972, for instance, the *News of the World* had an 'exclusive' on what it called the 'Emerald Isle Red Plot'. This was a remarkable story about 'three young intellectuals' - Trotskyists, apparently - who, in spite of the unpopularity which most Trotskyists encountered in Brezhnev's Russia, were lucky enough to have been smuggled into Ireland in a Russian submarine. All three, the story reported, died 'mysteriously'. Well, one of them, a young woman, died of cancer, but that could be put down to another of the stories manufactured by Information Policy - that IRA explosives can lead to cancer.

Colin chuckles today as he looks back on this 'exclusive', which was circulated to the *News of the World's* sixteen million readers. He specially likes the pictures of the Soviet submarine with 'Russian markings' on its conning tower 'off the coast of Donegal'. 'It was probably off the coast of Finland,' says Colin drily. The story was bunkum from start to finish, but its purpose - to demonstrate that the IRA were a sinister bunch of communists with close links to the Russians and the KGB - was triumphantly achieved.

Colin recalls being a little bit concerned that the fantasy might have been carried too far. There was, after all, nothing directly true about any of this story, and it seemed to stretch the connection with the Russians almost beyond belief. But the enemy was the enemy whether in Belfast or in Moscow, and it seemed to everyone in Information Policy at the time that this was fair game.

This is a small sample of the press work in which Colin and his associates in Information Policy were engaged both before and after he was officially assigned to the group when Peter Broderick took charge of Army Public Relations in the summer of 1973. That summer and autumn seem to Colin, in retrospect, as the high point of his life. He was just thirty, yet he was one of the most important and sought-after people in the whole vast effort of the British Army and the British government. [...]

He was in his element, rushing from place to place, anxious to keep up his military training and expertise at the same time as he perfected his new skills in public relations. He felt himself the most fortunate man in all the British Army. He wanted nothing more than to 'carry on' as a good and loyal servant of the British Crown.

When the change came, it came quietly. [...]

After the palpable failure of internment in 1971, the Heath government sought for a solution which would allow the Catholics some say in the government. They came up with a form of 'power-sharing' whereby certain offices in the government would be allotted to representatives of the Catholics. The proposal was, in effect, for a permanent coalition government which would always include several senior members who represented Catholics. The proposal split the Ulster Unionists. Protestant fundamentalists opposed it as the thin edge of the Papist wedge.

But the Unionist Prime Minister, Brian Faulkner, and other members of his Cabinet and of his party, were persuaded to attempt the experiment. At a conference at Sunningdale, Berkshire, in December 1973, the details were finally thrashed out. Without any elections being held, a power-sharing executive consisting mainly of ministers from the Official Unionists and the predominantly Catholic SDLP was established.

The solution did not commend itself to the ultras in Intelligence. They agreed with the Rev. Ian Paisley that it smacked of compromise and eventually of British troop withdrawal. Their fears had been stoked up by meetings between the Secretary of State for Northern Ireland, William Whitelaw, and the leaders of the Provisional IRA. These were followed [...] by meetings between Harold Wilson, leader of the British Labour Party, and the IRA.

Despite the grumbling on the right, however, the power-sharing executive took office. For a very short time, despite a horrific increase in assassinations, it looked as though it might succeed. What wrecked it was the February 1974 election, which gave the Northern Ireland people a chance to vote on the new experiment. The result was decisive: 422,000 people voted for candidates who opposed power-sharing; 246,000 for those who favoured it. The majority was bigger even than the majority of Protestants over Catholics.

The dam of resentment which had been building up in the Protestant populations, in the Army and in Intelligence over the Sunningdale Agreement broke over the heads of the minority Labour administration which took office on 1 March. Any suggestion of retreat in Ireland served merely to confirm the worst fears of the ultras: that the Labour government was being controlled from Moscow by the IRA. Thus when the new Secretary of State for Northern Ireland, Merlyn Rees, announced that he was legalising the political arm of the IRA, Sinn Féin (as had been planned by the Tory Government), or when a Catholic was appointed commander of the forces in the Derry area (as had been planned by the Tory government), this was all proof that the government was 'selling out' its armed forces and preparing to 'scuttle'. Conservative newspapers, which previously had held their fire against the initiatives of the Heath government, now fulminated against those same initiatives as they were carried out by Labour.

During the extraordinary period of the 'interregnum' of 1974 - the period between the two elections of that year, in February and October - Colin Wallace and his colleagues in Information Policy were involved in a series of 'information offensives' which were designed to disorientate and disrupt the new Labour administration at Stormont and in London.

The issue which made the running in the early weeks was the release of internees. Internment without trial had been a disaster. It had fanned the fury of Irish people in the United States of America. It had even been denounced in the European Court of Human Rights. When they were converted to power-sharing, the Conservative government stopped internment and ordered the steady release of internees. Internees were released all through 1973 without anyone noticing. As soon as the Labour government was elected, however, a press campaign started about the release of internees. As early as 31 March, almost before the new ministers had got their feet under their tables, an article appeared in the *Sunday Times* (regarded at that time by the Army as a 'hostile' newspaper) about the number of released internees who had been 'drawn back into violent courses'.

This theme persisted all through the months of April, May, June and July. Colin Wallace recalls: 'Almost every briefing we put out about assassinations or bombings was accompanied by some reference to the release of internees. We would say something like: "This was carried out by such-and-such a unit. The unit has been able to rebuild its strength since the release of its former leaders X and Y" - and then we would give the date of the release.'

This sort of propaganda infuriated Ministers. There was no clear evidence to refute it. No one save the intelligence services had the figures for the reinvolvement of internees in violence and even the intelligence figures were based on approximations and guesses. A classic example of the way the propaganda worked was in the Army's response to the release, early in July, of sixty-five internees, almost all of them on the Republican side. Rees himself had made it clear that he wanted the release to be 'discreet' and that there should be little or no publicity for it. But on 9 July, a select group of correspondents were personally invited to Lisburn for a press briefing. The journalists were told that the recent upsurge of violence could very largely be blamed on the rise in confidence in the IRA now that their ranks had been joined by a flow of internees, especially from the sixty-five just released. The following day the papers unanimously publicised 'Army Intelligence reports' that 'well over half' the released internees became reinvolved in violence almost at once.

This figure was also given to the politicians. Joe Haines, Press Secretary to the Prime Minister, was quoted in the *Sunday Times* three years later (3 March 1977) saying that 'figures given to the Cabinet' showed that 40 per cent of those released went back to violent activity. 'We felt that elements in the Army were working against us,' he said.

The *Sunday Times* article, written by David Blundy, concluded that the 'half' and '40 per cent' figures were pure fiction; and that the Army intelligence reports at the time deliberately inflated figures of reinvolvement. Blundy asked the Ministry of Defence for the real figures and was told that it all depended on what was meant by 'reinvolvement'. 'If you mean the number that went back to shooting and bombing, the percentage might be quite low,' a spokesman admitted. Yet that was exactly what Colin Wallace and his colleagues did mean in 1974 when they confidently told journalists of the reinvolvement of 'well over half'.

This repetition of completely false figures had a profound effect on the ministers' own confidence in their policies towards the Republican community. An interesting admission of this comes from the Secretary of State at the time, Merlyn Rees. Rees describes in his book, *Northern Ireland: A Personal Perspective*, the first Parliamentary debate on Northern Ireland after Labour took office. The debate was on 4 April and came at the climax of long and terrible weeks of assassinations and bombings, most of it inspired by the Protestant extremists, and responded to in kind by the IRA.

Rees confesses that he 'left it to Stan Orme', his beleaguered Minister of State, who wound up the debate, to outline yet another government scheme about the internees. It was a scheme which specially commended itself to Stan Orme since it fused his socialist instincts with practical policy. Orme and Rees reckoned that one of the main reasons why so many released internees went back to violence was, as Rees put it, 'the lack of job opportunities'. They therefore decided to appeal to decent citizens in Northern Ireland to provide work for former internees. (M. Rees, *Northern Ireland, A Personal Perspective*, London, Methuen, 1985, p. 56.) [...]

Merlyn Rees reckoned that Stan Orme's appeal went down pretty well in the House of Commons, but it was ridiculed in almost all the press. Information Policy in Belfast was quick to capitalise on the fundamental absurdity of asking for special jobs for suspected terrorists, and the newspapers responded with satirical headlines such as RENT A TERRORIST. Rees wrote:

> We had slipped up in other ways too, for no sooner was the announcement made than it was leaked from Army headquarters in Lisburn that the staff there preferred a variant of the idea by which detainees would go through the resettlement scheme before being released. (Rees, *op. cit.*, p. 56.)

This 'alternative' was nothing of the kind. Rees pointed out: 'Once detainees knew they were going to be released they would not co-operate.' Indeed, the idea was preferred by the Army precisely because it was a non-starter. But at any rate the information offensive from Lisburn had the desired effect long before it was necessary to consider an alternative. As Merlyn Rees rather pathetically admitted:

> The plan had all gone too wrong, however, for us to proceed and as early as April 24 Stan reported that the proposal was 'unacceptable and unworkable'. Later in the year he tried again with a variant of the scheme but that too had to be abandoned because of practical difficulties. (Rees, *op. cit.*, p. 57.)

As so often in his memoirs of these months, the former Secretary of State was very ready to ascribe the collapse of his initiatives and his policies to their intrinsic weakness and not so ready to place the blame where it most fitted the facts: on the Army Information officers who were meant to be publicising the government's plans.

Another curious 'leak' which caused all kinds of difficulties to ministers was the strange story of SAS troops in Northern Ireland. On 19 March 1974, less than three weeks after Labour took office, Colin Wallace leaked a report to the highly-respected *Times* correspondent in Northern Ireland, Robert Fisk. Fisk checked the facts as far as he was able and *The Times*' front page of 19 March reported: SAS MEN SERVE IN ULSTER AS UNDERCOVER AGENTS.

Fisk reported that members of the SAS had been sent to Northern Ireland 'to serve as military undercover intelligence agents in Belfast and Londonderry'. He went on:

> In spite of the obvious political implications of the move, the decision to involve the SAS in the Ulster war was prepared at the highest ministerial level in London, although its presence here had been revealed only to a few selected senior officers.

The announcement caused a bit of a storm not least among the new government's own backbenchers who wanted to know whether it was true that the SAS were operating in Northern Ireland. The minister in charge, Secretary of Defence Roy Mason, was not able immediately to help. For although Robert Fisk had reported that the decision to send in the SAS had been taken 'at the highest ministerial level', the Minister of Defence knew nothing about it.

Mason made what inquiries he could. On 9 April 1974 three weeks after Robert Fisk's exclusive report in *The Times*, he told the House of Commons that there was absolutely no truth in the story. There were, he said, 'no SAS in Northern Ireland'.

The doubts persisted, however, well stoked by Information Policy. On 14 August, Robert Fisk returned to the subject with a report entitled: SAS TRAIN TROOPS FOR ULSTER. He reported that 'about 43' members of the SAS had been withdrawn from Northern Ireland after eight months' training there in surveillance, photography and patrolling. The decision to send them in had been taken, he said, by the Tory Cabinet the previous January, but the government had always been 'unwilling' to discuss their role. 'Even when the *Times* published details of their activities on March 19, the Army scarcely acknowledged them.'

Robert Fisk did not refer to Mason's categorical denial the previous April that the SAS were in Northern Ireland. No one asked how it was that SAS troops, sent in by a Tory Cabinet in January, were not known to a Labour Secretary of State in April. If they had asked the question, they might have considered another one: why did Army Information officers leak the presence of SAS troops in Northern Ireland in the first place? One answer might be that they knew perfectly well that Mason did not know the SAS were there; that he would publicly deny it and that he would look an incompetent fool when it was eventually revealed that the SAS, whose presence in Northern Ireland he had so vociferously denied, had been there all along.

Roy Mason, never the most radical or sensitive of the new Labour ministers, was at the centre of another early controversy in which Colin Wallace and his colleagues were involved.

On 24 April, Mason spoke to Staffordshire miners at Newcastle-under-Lyme. Most of the speech was standard Ministry of Defence rhetoric about the dangers of defence cuts. It sounded like a Ministry of Defence brief.

Towards the end, the Secretary of State moved to Northern Ireland and made the not very controversial point that the people of that area should do more themselves to end the terror and rely less on British troops. To emphasise this argument, Mr Mason went on:

> Pressure is mounting on the mainland to pull out the troops. Equally, demands are being made to set a date for the withdrawal, thereby forcing the warring factions to get together and hammer out a solution.

There was nothing in the original draft of this speech which suggested that the minister had a view about these 'pressures'. He simply advanced the fact of the 'pressures' as an argument for the urgency of solving the Northern Ireland problem quickly, with more help from the people who lived there. The context in which the argument was put made it quite clear that he regarded the withdrawal of British troops with distaste.

Certainly there was nothing in Mr Mason's past to suggest that he had the slightest sympathy for the 'Troops Out' lobby. He was firmly placed on the traditional right wing of the Labour Party. He was not a Roman Catholic. He supported Labour Party policy one hundred per cent, and Labour Party policy was firmly *against* withdrawing British troops from Northern Ireland. Withdrawal had been proposed at the Labour Party conferences of 1971 and 1973 and heavily defeated. Merlyn Rees himself had made it plain in the House of Commons in the 4 April debate that the government's policy was to keep troops in Northern Ireland as long as they were needed.

Mr Mason was absolutely right to say that there were 'pressures' for withdrawal. In 1971, for instance, the *New Statesman*, then an influential journal of the Left, whose editor, Richard Crossman, was a former Labour Cabinet minister, had argued that a date should be set for withdrawing British troops from Northern Ireland. The argument had caught on in some sections of the left, though there were no more than a handful of Labour MPs who dared publicly to raise the issue. On the other hand, the (very rare) public opinion polls on the matter suggested a growing disillusionment about British involvement in Ireland.

Mason's speech was circulated in the ministry several hours before it was made and was quickly the subject of outrage among the 'ultras' in Intelligence and Information Policy, including Colin Wallace. Mild as Mason's words were, they seemed to provide the proof for all the wildest fears that the new Labour government, in due deference to their masters in the Kremlin or the Falls Road, were planning to 'scuttle'. To the intelligence services in Northern Ireland the speech proved that the traitors Mason, Wilson, Rees and Orme were preparing to lead the British Army into the worst (and far less glorious) defeat since Dunkirk.

They set to work among the more intelligent correspondents to 'draw their attention' to the apparently innocuous words in Mason's speech. One result on the day after Mason's speech was a huge headline in the

Guardian by Simon Hoggart, one of the most perceptive journalists on that paper's political staff, who had first-hand experience in Northern Ireland. MASON LIGHTS A FUSE ON TROOP PULL-OUT was the headline. The article started: 'The Minister for Defence Mr Roy Mason hurled into Westminster the ticking time-bomb of a possible pull-out of British troops from Ulster.' Some effort was made to sustain this rather extravagant interpretation of the minister's words, which Simon Hoggart conceded were 'mild enough'. He highlighted the 'implication' which he suggested was 'quite clear' - 'if the Ulster people did not do more to help themselves, the pressure to pull the troops out could become overwhelming'.

That no such implication was ever intended was rapidly made clear by the ministry.

The ministry Press Office had been under siege all the previous afternoon as correspondents from all kinds of papers were referred to the dangerous passage in Mr Mason's speech by Colin Wallace in Belfast and associates of Information Policy in Britain. The ministry press officers appeared to be surprised and shocked by the reaction, which they regarded as quite unjustified. When they found that their assurances were not enough, they resorted to the unusual device of putting out a statement to 'clarify' what the minister had said. On the first clarification, just an hour after he had made his speech, Mr Mason 'made it clear that he was merely reflecting the pressure on him for withdrawal, and registering a view which was presented to him'. He went on to make his own view clear: the troops must stay. 'As long as there is a job for the troops to do, then they must stay there.'

That sounded clear enough, but it did not satisfy the increasingly hysterical questioners. Half an hour after his first clarification, Mr Mason was panicked into another one.

> The Secretary of State wishes to make it clear that the forces will stay in Northern Ireland as long as it is necessary. It is not, and will not be Her Majesty's Government's policy to set a date for withdrawing troops there, and there is no chance whatsoever that anyone would bomb the Army out of Northern Ireland, or their way to the conference table. The Government's policy is unchanged.

The Secretary of State had been bounced into line by his own information officers. It mattered not that the 'line' was one he had consistently held anyway. Nor did it matter particularly that his two 'clarifications' did not dissuade editors from headlining the non-existent change of line. What mattered was that the minister had been exposed, in the eyes of the people running his intelligence services and psychological warfare officers, as a potential traitor, and had been brought to heel for it.

The unfortunate Mason was never allowed to forget his 'withdrawal' speech. He never referred again to the pressures for withdrawal, though they continued to mount. He proved himself so loyal to his military officers that they eventually successfully backed him as Merlyn Rees's successor as

Secretary of State for Northern Ireland. But he remained for ever, in their eyes, a closet withdrawer.

The same was true of the Secretary of State for Northern Ireland, Merlyn Rees. On taking office, Rees reiterated his faith in a British Northern Ireland and refused even to countenance whatever pressures there might be for British withdrawal from the Six Counties.

On 10 May, however, in conditions of great unrest in Northern Ireland, a letter was leaked to the press. Once more *The Times* was singled out for special favours. The letter had been written by Merlyn Rees on 19 March 1973, when he was Shadow Secretary of State for Northern Ireland. A woman had written to him from the Republic of Ireland saying she wanted the British out of the North. He replied patiently setting out his view that the British Army was not in occupation in Northern Ireland, that there was no economic or military advantage in its presence there and that the British Army's role in Ireland was not simply to satisfy the will of the British people. 'Frankly,' his letter ended, 'we have not the faintest desire to stay in Ireland and the quicker we are out the better.' If the sentence is quoted in isolation, away from paragraphs of earnest insistence that the troops must stay because it was their duty to prevent lawlessness and violence, it reads as though Merlyn Rees was for withdrawal of the troops. That interpretation, needless to say, was triumphantly paraded by the papers which used the letter, though none of them asked where it had come from.

The notion that the Labour leaders were secret supporters of a 'pull-out' from Northern Ireland was also used to split the consensus between the two major parties. On 2 June 1974, the day before a major debate on Northern Ireland, the *Observer* carried an article from the Parliamentary lobby which was headlined: TORIES FEAR THAT WILSON IS HEADING FOR A PULL-OUT. It predicted that 'Harold Wilson's alleged personal inclination for pull-out would be the dominant preoccupation of Tory leaders in the two-day debate'.

Nothing in Harold Wilson's career had suggested a personal inclination for pull-out from Northern Ireland. Since taking office in 1974, he had on several occasions made clear that he stood unreservedly by his party's policy of keeping troops in Northern Ireland (a policy, which, incidentally, had been constitutionally laid down by the Government of Ireland Act, 1948, when a Labour government was in office and when Harold Wilson, then twenty-eight, was President of the Board of Trade). Yet the 'prediction' in the *Observer* article became true. Francis Pym, the opposition spokesman on Northern Ireland, devoted a lot of his speech in the debate to rumours of a possible withdrawal. In the Labour Party, said Pym, there was an 'orchestration of the demand to bring our soldiers home'. The orchestration of the demand, however, came not from inside the Labour Party, where the Troops Out movement had negligible support, but in the Army and in Intelligence, especially in Lisburn.

Harold Wilson unwittingly played a major role in the next big offensive against his government by the information services of his own government in Northern Ireland. All through April, the violence in Northern Ireland, most of it started on the Protestant side, swelled. A grave constitutional crisis was not far away and it broke on the government in an unusual and unexpected form: a strike. The strike was called not to improve anyone's wages or conditions (such strikes are rarer in Northern Ireland than in Britain or in the Irish Republic) but in order to bring down the government. The Ulster Workers Council, a self-appointed group of shop stewards, Orange fanatics and extremist Unionist politicians, never for a moment disguised their political intentions. They intended to smash power-sharing, which was the official policy of the Conservative Party, the Labour Party, the Liberal Party, the Scottish and Welsh Nationalist Parties, and even of the Communist Party. Outside the ranks of Ian Paisley's Democratic Unionist Party there was hardly a political voice in all Europe which disapproved of the principle of power-sharing between Protestant and Catholic representatives in Northern Ireland. The Ulster Workers Council, however, believed (rightly) that they represented the majority of people in Northern Ireland; and they declared that they intended to stop all work in Northern Ireland until the power-sharing executive was dismantled.

This was a direct challenge to the British constitution and democratic government, upon which subjects Harold Wilson had so often intoned in the past, and which had brought him to high office. If the UWC strike even partially succeeded, the credibility of his administration and all other elected administrations would be called into question. If he could not defeat a gang of isolated sectarians in Northern Ireland, whom could he defeat?

The strike was called for Wednesday, 15 May. On Monday, 13 May, the Prime Minister rose in the House of Commons to make a statement about Northern Ireland. He did not mention the Protestant workers' strike. His statement was about something completely different.

The origin of his statement went back to 1969, when in the Divis Flats riot Protestant mobs in Belfast had attacked Catholic homes with familiar savagery. The police had joined in the fray with machine-guns on the side of the Protestants. Only the intervention of British troops prevented a pogrom which could well have ended in the enforced migration of a quarter of a million people.

One effect of 1969 was a rebirth of the comatose and almost entirely ineffective IRA, whose 'Provisional' section took up arms to defend the Catholic areas. Through the next three years, the leadership of the Provisionals reacted sharply to the criticism that they were not around to defend the Divis Flats when they were attacked in 1969. They felt it necessary to make plans in the event of any such attack in the future. Certainly they were convinced there was no point in relying on British troops as they had done in 1969. The troops considered themselves at war with the Provisional IRA and would, it was felt, be no more use in the event of a Protestant uprising than would the RUC or the (now disbanded) B Specials.

Accordingly, plans were made for resistance. In the event of a 1969-style attack from the Protestants, all armed Republicans would come together. Under cover of a 'scorched earth' campaign (burning cars, bombing lorries and so on) they would engineer the evacuation of the entire area under attack - perhaps 100,000 people - to the South. Part of this plan was first discussed in Long Kesh internment camp by the interned IRA leaders in 1971 and 1972.

Those plans were discovered by Intelligence officers and leaked to the press by Colin Wallace. The result was not dramatic, since a scheme to evacuate a population under attack was not specially unsympathetic. The *Daily Mirror's* Malcolm Nichol gave the plan rather short shrift in a report entitled: IRA RIVALS JOIN IN A 'DOOMSDAY' PLOT. The report made it clear that the 'Doomsday' plan was, crucially, a proposed *reaction* to a Protestant attack.

The same report appeared in other newspapers, without any sensational treatment. The word 'Doomsday', however, was universally used.

Two years later, in the week before the Ulster Workers Council strike was due to begin, the Army raided the homes of suspected IRA leaders. In one of them, documents and maps were found which referred, in rather more detail than previously, to the Doomsday plan. They were brought to Information Policy officers at Lisburn. Colin Wallace recalls it well.

> I remember being rather irritated because normally when something like this was found, we were asked for our opinion about what it meant. On this occasion, we were simply given the documents and told to prepare them for a press conference which would announce to the world that an IRA plan had been uncovered to blow up half of Belfast, including large areas occupied by ordinary people.

> I looked at the stuff and immediately recognised the doomsday plan we had exposed two years earlier. I remember making it clear to our intelligence people that this was all old hat and that if we tried to turn what had been a *defensive* into an *offensive* plan, we could be made to look a bit foolish. The IRA had pretty good propaganda outlets too, and they were not amateurs. I warned about coming off second best in a rather silly propaganda offensive.

> I was told not to bother. It was made clear that this was not going to be an ordinary leak, or even an ordinary press conference. This wasn't going to be something which was presented to the world by the Army. I myself, for instance, wasn't going to be involved at all. A big press conference was going to be organised from Stormont. It would be a government initiative. And anyway the whole thing was going to be a back-up operation. The new Doomsday plot would be announced first in the British Parliament - by the Prime Minister.

Colin also recalls that it was made clear that if the whole plan did backfire, it wouldn't matter too much since the man who would take the flak would be the Prime Minister. So Colin set to work to prepare those parts of the maps and documents which would reveal the IRA plan - and to take out anything in them which gave a clue to their defensive strategy.

On 13 May, Harold Wilson stunned the House of Commons with a 'dramatic revelation'.

> In the last few days the Security Forces in Northern Ireland have come into possession of a number of documents. These documents reveal a specific and calculated plan by the IRA by means of ruthless and indiscriminate violence to foment inter-sectarian hatred and a degree of chaos with the object of enabling the IRA to achieve a position in which it could proceed to occupy and control certain pre-designated and densely populated areas in the city of Belfast and its suburbs. The plan shows a deliberate intention to manipulate the emotions of large sections of the people by inflicting violence and hardship on them in the hope of creating a situation in which the IRA could present itself as the protector of the Catholic population. (*House of Commons Official Report*, 13 May 1974.)

The IRA's intention, Wilson went on, 'would have been to carry out a scorched earth policy of burning the houses of ordinary people as it was compelled to withdraw ... An apparent IRA operation,' the Prime Minister concluded, 'of potentially great danger has been brought to light.'

The documents proving all this would be published, he said, though only selectively.

The statement was greeted with a chorus of 'Hear Hears' around the House, especially from the Conservatives, who were delighted with the Prime Minister and said so. Edward Heath, leader of the Tory Party, and Captain Orr, spokesman for the Ulster Unionists, went out of their way to congratulate Wilson on his statement. In reply to Heath, Harold Wilson anticipated a possible objection:

> There will be an attempt to misrepresent this information - which is a genuine find by the security authorities - but I can assure the House that these documents are genuine and not even put forward by the IRA themselves for any other purpose except that which it had in mind to pursue. (*ibid.*)

That afternoon, at Stormont Castle, senior officers provided a press conference with the documents which had indeed come from a 'genuine find' by the security services. The documents were, however, as Wilson himself had warned, selective. They showed areas which would be occupied, buildings which would be burned and so on. They did not disclose the circumstances in which these plans would be put into effect.

The documents were confirmed the following day by an impeccable source - the Provisional IRA. They agreed at once that the documents were genuine; but said they were part of the plan drawn up in 1972 in the event of a Protestant attack on the Catholic areas such as the attempted pogrom in 1969. The IRA tried to persuade the more serious journalists in Belfast that the plan was old, the documents irrelevant and the importance given to it by the Prime Minister ridiculous.

They had some success at least with Robert Fisk of *The Times*. After reporting the statement of the IRA, Fisk added his own interpretation. 'There seems to be some evidence,' he wrote, 'that the plans were drawn up at least a year ago.' Fisk came at once to the crucial point:

> If, as Mr Wilson has said, they represented a campaign that was about to be put into action, then the Provisionals, who have always claimed to be non-sectarian, emerge as an organisation of awe-inspiring cynicism.
>
> If the idea was to put such a campaign into action only in circumstances where an Armageddon situation already existed, then the IRA has only acted as many other extremist organisations have done in Northern Ireland. Loyalist groups have boasted in the past that they too have 'Doomsday' plans to be used if they thought Ulster was being pushed into a United Ireland. (14 May 1974.)

The line between a 'scorched earth campaign' *in defence* against sectarian attack and a similar plan as an *offensive* was absolutely crucial. But it was easily glossed over by withholding some documents and altering others. Even in the documents released, however, there is a clue which points to the defensive nature of the plans. The IRA's declaration accompanying the plans included the statement: 'In the emergency which has been forced upon us, the IRA has had no alternative but to employ its full resources to the defence of its people, in the face of the armed offensive against the Catholic working class.' (IRA declaration, *The Times*, 14 May 1974.)

If there had been no 'armed offensive against the Catholic working class', how could such a statement have been issued? And did not the sentence suggest that the plan and the declaration had been drawn up specifically to reply to such an armed offensive? If such was the case, as Colin Wallace insists it was, then the new documents had no significance whatever. They were merely proof that the Doomsday plan discovered in 1972 had been genuine (and had almost certainly been scrapped when the Official IRA, which was then still influential, had refused either to approve it or to pledge to take part in it).

Most journalists, however, were only too happy to take the Doomsday plot at face value, especially when it was so forcefully exposed in Parliament by the Prime Minister. If the documents had been tampered with, if the disclosures were not complete - why should anyone worry when they had so comprehensively convinced the Prime Minister? [...]

The effect of the unanimous shock/horror approach to the plot was not only to antagonise the British public to the IRA. The IRA was already unimaginably unpopular - almost as unpopular as an enemy in time of war. The chief effect of the doomsday plan publicity was to fix the minds of the public on planned atrocities by the IRA at just the time when Loyalist extremists were embarking on an act of sectarian rebellion against the British government. The day after Wilson's House of Commons statement, when the papers and television were full of the Doomsday plot, the newly-constituted Ulster Workers Council called its general strike throughout the Six Counties.

The strike was perhaps the most successful major industrial action in the history of the British Isles. It lasted barely two weeks. The one and only demand of the strikers, the end of power-sharing, was unconditionally conceded. By the time the House of Commons debated the new situation in Northern Ireland on 3 June (two and a half weeks after the strike began), the power-sharing Executive had collapsed. The Prime Minister of Northern Ireland, Brian Faulkner, had resigned and all his ministers with him. The entire constitutional reform, established with so much hope and effort at Sunningdale the previous autumn, had disintegrated. The British government remained in 'direct rule' over Northern Ireland, but the undisputed victor was the Orange supremacy.

The official view of this extraordinary episode was recounted some years later by the Secretary of State at the time, Merlyn Rees, in his book *Northern Ireland: A Personal Perspective*. 'We were in fact,' he wrote, 'beaten technically on all aspects of the strike.' *(op. cit.,* p. 69.)

It was claimed by Rees, echoed by the Prime Minister and endorsed by the Conservative opposition and the Ulster Unionists that the strike in Northern Ireland had been so unanimous and so successful that no government could have withstood it. In particular, it was said, the problems of the supply of power became insurmountable. The Army could guarantee internal security, but they could not maintain the power supply. For that technical reason alone, the strike was bound to triumph.

There was, however, substantial evidence to suggest otherwise. The power stations - and there were not many of them - could easily have been kept running by a combination of Army technicians and, if necessary, technicians from the British CEGB flown in and protected by the Army. Even a moderate military campaign would have ensured that the power stations stayed open through the summer (and the summer was just starting: the UWC strike took place at the worst time of year for the strikers). There is also some evidence that at the start of the strike the Protestant people of Northern Ireland were split.

A vote in the Harland and Wolff shipyard, for instance, then as now entirely dominated by Protestants, turned (narrowly) against a general strike. The evidence was that if the government and the Army had set themselves, from the outset, resolutely to break the strike, they could have done so; and the Executive would have remained in office.

The Army was equivocal from the start. In his excellent account of the strike (which was detested by the government and the Army), *Point of No*

Return (London, Andre Deutsch, 1975), Robert Fisk again and again drew attention to the Army's lack of purpose in breaking the strike.

> Military advisers at Lisburn had told some of the more senior Press Officers at Thiepval Barracks, Lisburn, that the Army was unhappy about the adoption of a strike-breaking role, and this view was passed on, in confidential conversations, to newspapermen covering the strike. (p. 87.)

The 'unhappiness' spilled over into the Ministry of Defence. Fisk quoted the government's own Civil Service record for Saturday, 18 May:

> During the late evening, strong pressure had to be brought to bear on Ministry of Defence officials to hasten the arrangements for lifting troops to Northern Ireland. *(ibid.,* pp. 87-8.)

As he drove around strike-bound Belfast, Fisk noticed again and again how the Protestant barricades were tolerated by the Army; and how troops refused to intervene to free the streets of the strikers' influence. 'When confrontations seemed almost inevitable, it was the Army who withdrew,' he concluded. *(ibid.,* p. 93)

Later he noticed a soldier and a member of the UVF (Ulster Volunteer Force - the most violently sectarian of all the Protestant extremist groups) side by side, pointing down the street with their rifles, 'UVF and Army together'.

> The loss of public confidence in the authorities during the second week of the strike had much to do with scenes such as this. It was the logical and inevitable result of a military and police policy that took no account of the political aims of the strike and which opted for expediency rather than confrontation on the streets ... Would the UWC have sanctioned a war with the Army? It seems doubtful. (*ibid*, p. 156.)

Fisk records how the Prime Minister himself was shaken by this approach and changed his attitude to the strike. On the evening of Saturday, 25 May, he had made arrangements to broadcast to the nation on the serious emergency caused by the UWC strike. His mood, as he wrote the speech with the help of his adviser, Bernard Donoughue, was still defiant. He had a deep hatred of extreme Orangemen and was furious that the decisions of elected governments should be flouted. In the first draft of his speech, he referred to a 'rebellion against the Crown'; a rebellion, he went on to imply, which would be met with the firmest possible resolve by the government and its troops. This was the mood he had shown at a meeting at Chequers a day or two previously, in which he had reassured Brian Faulkner, the beleaguered Northern Ireland Prime Minister, that troops would be used on the ground and in the power stations to help break the strike. Fisk's account continues:

> But between twelve and two o'clock Wilson changed his mind about the statement. In those two hours, he took a sudden and final

decision, sharply reversing the mood and content of his speech and abandoning the Executive to their fate. (*ibid.*, p. 197.)

All references to 'rebellion' were cut out. Robert Fisk had no doubt as to the cause of this volte-face:

> It was the Army's influence, the military expression of military influence, that caused Wilson to place a new interpretation upon his promise to the Executive of action against the UWC... (*ibid.*, p. 198.)

That conclusion was inescapable. If the Army and their ministry were reluctant to intervene against the strike, what hope had the government, armed with mere words, of victory! [...]

The Ulster Workers Council triumph, however, was not entirely due to the British Army. The Army's attitude was one of hesitant abstention rather than open defiance. Organised defiance indeed came not so much from the Army, but from the increasingly powerful political forces inside MI5 and their colleagues in Army Intelligence and Information Policy.

Thirteen years after the strike, on 22 March 1987, the *Sunday Times* published a story on its front page entitled: 'MI5 "plotted" Ulster strikes'. Its author, Barrie Penrose, had been working for some weeks with Colin Wallace, and an article about Wallace and his background had led to a phone call from a James Miller, who described himself as a former MI5 agent.

Miller was an Englishman, born in 1932, who had married an Ulster Protestant and gone to live in Monkstown, County Antrim. He told Penrose he had been recruited by Army Intelligence in 1970 soon after the 'troubles' started. His job was to infiltrate extremist Protestant organisations, especially the UDA. He was quoted by Penrose as follows:

> I did a dangerous job over there for nearly five years and many UDA and IRA men went to prison as a result. But I could never understand why my case officers, Lt Col Brian X and George X, wanted the UDA to start a strike in the first place. But they specifically said I should get UDA men at grass-roots level to 'start pushing' for a strike. So I did.

Barrie Penrose went on to claim: 'Home Office officials working with MI5's legal adviser confirmed that Miller worked for the Northern Ireland security services.' He also reported that the Secretary of the D-Notices Committee, which vets newspapers for likely breaches of security, had asked the *Sunday Times* not to disclose Miller's whereabouts in Britain or the full identity of his case officers.

Miller's claims, according to Barrie Penrose, went even further:

> Miller said his MI5 case officers told him Harold Wilson was a suspected Soviet agent and steps were taken to force him out of Downing Street. Miller said that in early 1974 his case officers

instructed him to promote the idea within the UDA of mounting a general strike which would paralyse Northern Ireland.

None of these remarkable allegations was denied. Miller, who had told Penrose he was anxious to give his evidence to Merlyn Rees, the former Secretary of State, suddenly went quiet and did not continue with his allegations.

Colin Wallace recalls the great surge of confidence and enthusiasm when the Ulster Workers Council strike was won. 'Everyone seemed very pleased that the government had been forced to grovel,' he says. But military and civilian intelligence officers were worried that the staggering success of the strike had unified Protestant paramilitaries and provided them with a power base which could prove dangerous. 'We'd created a potential monster,' Colin says, 'and MI5 now felt that the extremist Protestants must he kept in check.'

In June 1974, as the dust settled after the strike, the security services hit out at the Protestants. They raided Orange Halls throughout the Province and found several arms caches. In the caretaker's house next to the West Belfast Orange Hall, for instance, they found fourteen pistols, eighteen rifles and shotguns, four home-made mortars, six smoke grenades and five thousand rounds of ammunition. Seven Orange Halls were raided, almost all of them leading to substantial arms finds.

MI5 set out to establish that the Orange extremists had been infiltrated by communists and left-wing revolutionaries. At Lisburn, Information Policy forged a leaflet entitled 'Workers Unite', illustrated with a photograph of a Kalashnikov rifle and followed by a few choice words calling on the Ulster people to free themselves from capitalist tyranny. The final slogan was appropriate: FREE THE PEOPLE.

This forgery convinced the correspondent in Belfast of the *Daily Telegraph*, 'the paper you can trust'. Kenneth Clarke wrote in the issue of 15 June 1974:

> The Orange Hall searches also yielded some evidence to support a feeling among the security forces that an unlikely alliance is being forged between Protestant and Catholic working-class groups. One poster depicting a hand clutching a Russian-made rifle states: 'Protestant and Catholic working people have the same common enemy: the Imperialist ruling class. Every blow struck against the capitalist state machine is a blow for a free and independent Ulster. Workers Unite.'

As the summer of 1974 wore on, two projects in particular caused Colin Wallace to reflect on what he was being asked to do. Both involved Northern Ireland politicians: John Hume, the prominent young Social and Democratic Labour Party leader from Derry; and Ian Paisley, the tub-thumping leader of the Protestant Democratic Unionist Party. The two men were on opposite sides of the political fence, but both were seen as enemies by the 'ultras' in Intelligence. Their chief crime was support for the Labour government. John Hume was a social democrat and a natural Labour Party supporter. Paisley's role was more complicated. He and his followers in the newly-formed Democratic Unionist Party were conservatives of the most extreme kind. But their party was not the poodle of the British Conservative Party as the old Unionist Party in the North of Ireland had traditionally been. The Democratic Unionists were renegades, prepared to vote for anyone who, in their view, might help their extremist cause. In 1974, in particular, when the Labour government was in a minority, Paisley and his colleagues were not averse to some tacit support for the Labour government.

This breach of loyalty to the Tories by the more extreme Ulster Protestant politicians infuriated the reactionaries in Intelligence. Colin Wallace was asked by the MI5 officer with whom he worked on Clockwork Orange, whom he knew by the pseudonym 'John Shaw', to produce an analysis of the likely consequences of the assassination of Ian Paisley. Several different situations in which this assassination might be planned were outlined, including a souped-up feud between rival Protestant factions quarrelling over the proceeds of Shankill shebeens or blackmailing each other over a homosexual vice ring. As part of this exercise Colin received a forged bank account, in Paisley's name, indicating substantial purchases of shares in two companies in Canada. Colin kept a copy of this forgery. It was published in the *Sunday Times* in 1987, and featured in a debate on the Thames Television programme, *This Week*. In the programme the Rev. Paisley denounced the forgery. He said it fitted precisely with all sorts of leaks and innuendoes which were made against him in 1974.

Colin also recalls (though he cannot find it in his papers) a forged bank account in the name of John Hume, which showed him receiving substantial sums from dubious charities in North America. John Hume, too, was obliged to deny allegations based on this wholly false document. [...]

Throughout his first few months in office Rees was plagued by leaks. These leaks were especially destructive of any initiative he took to lower the tension between the British government and the Catholic community. Through the early summer of 1974, for instance, he worked to set up an 'auxiliary police force' in Catholic areas. Citizens would be recruited as special constables on an unpaid, voluntary basis, and would have police powers. The auxiliary police force was designed to restore some semblance of respect for law and order in those areas where the Royal Ulster Constabulary was regarded, with every justification, as a sectarian force, defending only Protestant laws and Protestant order. The plans were to be announced at a special press conference in late July. Its success depended on catching the parties by surprise. If the case for the new police force could be put as persuasively as possible before the Royal Ulster Constabulary or the Protestant 'loony right' was able to get into the television studios, they would get a head start.

Imagine Rees's consternation, therefore, when the full plans were laid out on 23 July, on the morning before his proposed Press conference, in *The Times* under a big heading: 'Government Considers Volunteer Community Police Force for Hard-line Areas in N. Ireland'. The whole initiative was spiked. The auxiliary force never emerged. Merlyn Rees admitted to me several years later: 'Oh, there's no doubt the leak torpedoed the plan.' (*Daily Mirror*, 9 April 1987.) But no one ever found out where the leak came from - until Colin Wallace confirmed that the source was Information Policy.

Merlyn Rees himself is the best witness to the way in which his conduct of the Northern Ireland Office was constantly sabotaged by the Army Information Service. In the middle of the Ulster Workers Council strike, for instance, he decided on a secret visit by aeroplane to the Prime Minister who was holidaying in the Scilly Islands. He wrote in his book, *Northern Ireland: A Personal Perspective*:

> I felt it important for my journey not to be publicised and asked Frank King [Commander-in-Chief of Northern Ireland forces] to accompany me in my helicopter as far as Aldergrove so that it would look at the [Stormont] Castle as if I was going back with him to Lisburn. However, when I arrived at Culdrose (Cornwall), after a nostalgic flight over the valleys of South Wales where I was nurtured, it was to find that my trip had already been announced on BBC News. Was the leak from prying eyes at the Castle or from Aldergrove? Or was it from other sources? (*op. cit.*, p. 81.)

The leaks about rows within the Army during the strike, wrote Rees,

> came from Lisburn, from those in the Army Information Service with press contacts, and not from the Army staff who knew the facts. [...] (*ibid.*, p. 84.)

It was to try to stop these leaks and restore some semblance of responsibility and loyalty to the government in the Army Information Service that Michael Cudlipp, a former Fleet Street journalist, was appointed to take charge of Northern Ireland information services on 25 July (two days after the leak to *The Times* about the auxiliary police). But Cudlipp could do little to stop it.

In October 1975, writing in the Irish paper *Hibernia*, Robert Fisk reflected on the previous two or three years of information policy and news management. He concluded:

> Rees's men have found that far from smothering the Army's dissatisfaction, they have only driven it underground. Instead of the Press officer's unhappy briefing they now have to cope with the embarrassing leak. They have to face the reality that there are a number of fairly senior soldiers who want to destroy Merlyn Rees's political integrity. These soldiers want Mr Rees to go ... this must be

the first time in history that British Army officers, however few in number, have distrusted a British Minister more than have the IRA.

By early September 1974, almost all the information which came to Colin Wallace concentrated not on terrorists, but on politicians. A lot of the information, which was uncheckable, was gossip about the personal lives and sex habits of prominent politicians. Wallace's instructions were to circulate as far as possible rumours about the alleged homosexual inclinations of Northern Ireland ministers and politicians. He noticed, to his surprise, that the politicians he was being asked to smear were not only, nor even mostly, in the Labour Party. Edward Heath, leader of the Conservative Party, was high on this list. So was William Van Straubenzee, Heath's Minister of State in Northern Ireland until March 1974. [...]

Throughout that turbulent year, the situation in Northern Ireland had steadily deteriorated. Colin noticed that in 1974, as in every other year, there were more assassinations of Catholics by Protestants than vice versa, and for the first time began to worry about the close connections between the intelligence services and the extremist Protestant organisations. He learnt for the first time in September, for instance, that the explosives used to kill nineteen people in the indiscriminate bombing of a main Dublin street during the UWC strike might have been supplied by British Intelligence. He suspected too that some personal assassinations carried out by the UDA or the UVF had been inspired by British Intelligence. He was concerned in case the huge increase in assassinations in November had been planned to coincide with the secret ceasefire talks between the government and the paramilitaries of both sides. [...]

'I wondered about how badly we were doing,' Colin says now. 'We didn't seem to be getting anywhere. I'd come into this business to fight terrorism, but terrorism was on the increase and, in some respects, we seemed to be helping it along. My own friends and colleagues were being killed. We should have been concentrating all our efforts on sniffing out the terrorists and making life difficult for them. But we weren't. We were told more and more about these politicians, what they felt about communism, what shares they'd got in Canada, even what they did in bed. The situation was getting very serious by the middle of 1974 and I felt I'd had enough. I was genuinely anxious to get back to the basic business of fighting terrorism and I decided that Clockwork Orange didn't have much to do with that any more.'

'One afternoon early in October I saw "John Shaw" from MI5. I sat having a quiet drink with him at the White Gables Hotel, near Hillsborough. At one stage, I told him I didn't want to go any further with Clockwork Orange without political clearance. He seemed surprised and suggested that I already had clearance. But I made it clear I wanted some proof that the whole programme had been seen and approved by a minister.

'Of course I was pretty certain that "Shaw" couldn't get ministerial clearance for Clockwork Orange. I was pretty sure that no minister had a clue that Clockwork Orange even existed. But I knew I couldn't go on doing it, and I wanted to get on with other things.'

'John Shaw', Colin recalls, appeared to be sympathetic. He agreed to put Colin's proposal to his superiors. On 16 October, Colin was summoned to Stormont Castle and offered a job in the government's information office. He turned it down. He wanted to be with the Army, of the Army. Indeed his main reason for wanting to stop working on Clockwork Orange was that it was too political. At the end of October, he handed back to 'John Shaw' the voluminous files of information he had compiled under the code-name Clockwork Orange. He kept only his own handwritten notes.

He never saw 'Shaw' again. In some relief he went back to his more formal duties in the information office. He did not know how seriously his refusal over Clockwork Orange would affect his future. Indeed, he had little time to reflect on it. For before a few days had passed he was writing a memorandum to complain about an even more serious matter. It concerned a Belfast boys' home with a fine old Irish name: Kincora.

12.

Duncan Campbell

STILL DARK IN PARANOIA GULCH

(*New Statesman and Society*, 9 February 1990, pages)

Dark shadows that were first cast in 1975 still loom over the British political landscape. The leaders of both major political parties changed, and with them the course of national politics. The case that the secret worlds of British and American intelligence intervened to change the course of our history has yet to be proven. But in the past 15 years, such theories have moved from being fashionably left-wing - originally best recounted in Martin Walker's *Guardian* diary reports about goings-on in 'paranoia gulch' - to providing a more than ample case for the intelligence services to answer.

[...] What has become clear is that reports from paranoia gulch [...] were not odd ephemera conceived in distant shires, but were the public face of intelligence and military planners who had come to believe that Britain had to be saved from its elected government. Colin Wallace was provably aware of all this plotting, including the details of the security service (MI5)'s smears and fears about Harold Wilson. Was he - and the entire intelligence apparatus - as much involved in Wilson's 'destabilisation' as he now implies?

A shadow was cast over Wallace's life at the same time. In January 1975, he was posted away from his job as a Ministry of Defence senior information officer in Northern Ireland after his propaganda activities had become a source of both embarrassment and anger to the Northern Ireland Office. Although Wallace has given different accounts of the circumstances surrounding his work and his departure, one feature has never been in doubt: 'disinformation' was part of his job, indeed, he had attended a special MoD training course in 'psychological operations' to learn how to do it better.

British government 'disinformation' activities go back to the second world war, when many writers and intellectuals worked in secret operations for the Political Warfare Executive. PWE's methods were quickly revived in the Cold War. In 1947, Labour junior minister Christopher Mayhew authorised the establishment of a secret 'Information Research Department' inside the Foreign Office, and ordered it to conduct secret propaganda operations against communist governments. In colonial counterinsurgency campaigns, psychological operations - Psyops - became, as in Vietnam, an integral (if in the end a fairly worthless) part of the battle for local 'hearts and minds'. Military officers and civil servants were given special training courses in Psyops at the MoD's Joint Warfare Establishment near Salisbury.

The British government defines Psyops as 'planned psychological activities in peace and war directed towards enemy, friendly and neutral audiences, in order to create behaviour favourable to the achievement of political and military objectives'. In September 1971, the Army set up a Psyops unit at its Lisburn headquarters, near Belfast, under the cover title of 'Information Policy Unit'. Wallace worked with it and its first boss, propaganda specialist Colonel Maurice Tugwell, and later gained a senior post in the unit. Until this week, both the Army and the government had pretended that the unit simply gave official information to the press. Now it has been admitted that the unit - and the government itself - does conduct 'disinformation' activities using covert propaganda.

Tugwell (and Wallace) were responsible for Army press activities on, among other occasions the Widgery Tribunal into the Bloody Sunday killings in Derry in 1972. From London, the Foreign Office's Information Research Department played a prominent role in the establishment of psychological operations in Ireland. In November 1972, an IRD official, Hugh Mooney, was dispatched to work with Tugwell at Lisburn. Tugwell and Mooney's arrivals followed official fears that, after the introduction of internment, Britain had begun to lose the public and press relations battle with Sinn Féin and the IRA.

The intelligence scene in Northern Ireland in 1973 was a nightmare. The MoD ordered a new head of Army information services to take joint control both of public relations and Psyops. Whitehall wanted propaganda in the province under control. But the Psyops unit was also working with and to the instructions of MI5 and the Secret Intelligence Service (SIS or MI6) officials in the North, who were openly at war with each other as well as, often, the civil ministries.

Between 1973 and 1975, MI5 was temporarily in charge of intelligence. A senior MI5 official, Denis Payne, was posted to Stormont Castle as Director of Intelligence, Northern Ireland. But SIS had its own teams at Northern Ireland Office premises at Laneside (one of whose officials, Michael Oakley, conducted direct negotiations with the IRA), and at Army HQ Lisburn, where a 'political secretariat' was under the control of SIS officer Craig Smellie (now deceased).

There were fierce battles between the different intelligence factions. MI5 officers accused SIS of harbouring homosexuals who were alleged to be security risks. SIS put it about that the arrival of the MI5 team at Stormont had resulted in the betrayal and death of a dozen agents and informers. The press and the public harvested the results of disinformation. [...]

After formally becoming a member of the Lisburn Psyops unit, Wallace helped devise a plan to undermine extremist politicians by black propaganda techniques. He gave me (and others) this written account of what Clockwork Orange was about. MI5, says Wallace, 'asked me to undertake a project ... designed to cause major dissension within the loyalist leadership ... I was given a file containing extracts from Intelligence reports and other documents from which I was to construct and write in the Ulster idiom, two or three "personal" accounts by non-existent people giving details of the homosexual activities, etc of well known political figures and to link these activities to other political figures in London. The technique was simple in that accurate intelligence was to be reconstructed and collated in such a way that it would appear to be the personal experience of individuals. The object of the scheme was to put pressure on a number of key people who might play a major role in the unrest, particularly those whom Intelligence believed might have influence or control over the Loyalist paramilitaries.'

Wallace later enlarged on this account and has suggested that the Labour Party, rather than Loyalist politicians, was the major target of this secret work. There were three categories: 'Leaking information to the press to embarrass the Labour government or to create public hostility to the Labour Party in the run up to the 1974 general elections; the manufacture of false intelligence to influence political policies; the planting of manufactured intelligence to show links between Soviet and other communist agencies and the terrorists.' Wallace can show he was privy to many of MI5's extraordinary suspicions about Wilson and others. But he has not been able to demonstrate that they went beyond subversive chatter between himself and MI5 officers like Denis Payne.

It is clear, however, that by the middle of 1974, Wallace and the Army were running their own war against Merlyn Rees and the Northern Ireland Office. In July 1974, Army officials told the press concerning Rees's release of internees that 'well over half of any men released are reinvolved ... in violence within a couple of months'. Joe Haines, then Harold Wilson's press secretary, said soon afterwards that 'we felt that elements in the Army were working against us'. Wilson's response was to place the control of all Army press activities under a new information policy committee run by former *Times* journalist Michael Cudlipp.

During the 1970s, Wallace told journalists on several occasions that the Cudlipp committee had been created in order to run black propaganda in the province. The evidence suggests the opposite - that it was created to bring the tide of black propaganda and the 'Lisburn lie machine' to an end, and to place the Army's press work under the political control of the

Northern Ireland Office. In December 1974, Wallace was summoned to London to be told that he was to be moved to a mainland army HQ.

Wallace was required to resign in 1975, after admitting leaking a restricted document to *Times* reporter Robert Fisk shortly before he left the North. The document, which was relatively innocuous, gave a disguised account of the work of the Information Policy Unit, and was intended for the consumption of Army and police officers who did not 'need to know' what was really going on. It is still a mystery why the MoD took so harsh a view of this lead as to sack Wallace; rather more must have been at stake.

Wallace got a new job working for Arun District Council - and continued leaking. In October 1976, he gave Conor O'Clery of the *Irish Times* details of the Joint Warfare Establishment and its Psyops courses, which he had attended. Clery's reports provoked a major parliamentary row, in which the government admitted that 262 civil servants and military officers had been trained in Psyops.

When the scandal over a child sex abuse ring at the Kincora boys' home developed three years later, Wallace reminded journalists that he had passed out warnings as early as 1973. But Wallace was soon in trouble himself. Following the death in August 1980 of Sussex antiques dealer Jonathan Lewis, whose wife was Colin Wallace's assistant, he was convicted of manslaughter and sentenced to ten years imprisonment.

He remained in prison for six years, but continued to pass out selected information about his time in the North. In 1982, as the Kincora scandal grew, he was in touch with MP Gerry Fitt and the *News of the World*. In May 1984, after the *New Statesman* had reported on similar 'dirty tricks' reminiscences by former Army intelligence officer Captain Fred Holroyd, he wrote to me and Holroyd. We visited him repeatedly in Lewes prison in 1984. Holroyd then dedicated himself to overturning his conviction until Wallace's release three years later.

Wallace's Kincora allegations - that the intelligence services used their knowledge of the homosexual abuses at the home to blackmail and thus control leading protestant figures - did not receive great attention in last week's scandal, yet they are the most important and best proven aspects of what he has to say. Wallace's briefings about Kincora appear in a note on the small protestant extremist group TARA, and its links to Kincora housefather and TARA leader William McGrath. The note was seen - and reported - by many journalists during 1974-77, long before the scandal came to light. The *Sunday Times* reported in 1977, for example (avoiding naming names and with a legal disclaimer), that McGrath was 'said to be a homosexual' who was 'thought to owe more allegiance to the Red Flag than either the Union Jack or the Tricolour'.

A longer document, a copy of which Wallace smuggled to me during a visit to Lewes prison in the summer of 1984, gives many more details of activities at Kincora. If authentic, it establishes beyond any doubt that the authorities were well aware of what was occurring at Kincora, and contrived to ignore the matter for more than five years. Some experienced journalists reporting on Ireland point out, accurately, that Wallace did not supply copies of this material to anyone before much of the Kincora scandal became known. The more recent judicial inquiry into Kincora, by Judge William Hughes, scrupulously avoided finding out whether or not Wallace's document was genuine.

It should not be too difficult for the RUC and MoD, noting the extent to which ministers have already been embarrassed by being misled, to give a truthful answer as to whether or not this key document is genuine. So far, they have equivocated. In April 1986, defence minister Lord Trefgarne wrote to Peter Archer MP to say that the RUC inquiry 'did not establish its authenticity'. A forensic report was 'inconclusive as to authenticity'. None of these statements say that the document is a fabrication. And the Hughes inquiry team did not ask the MoD itself, or the Army, or Wallace's former colleagues whether it was genuine.

Other information suggests that the material is indeed genuine. For example, intelligence notebooks kept during 1974 by Holroyd refer to the Kincora hostel by name, and say of leading protestant politicians that they were 'all queers'. Holroyd also says that he was told that the TARA organisation was in effect controlled by British intelligence, and was not a real security threat - implying that McGrath had indeed come under intelligence control by 1973. When Wallace sent this and other papers to the Prime Minister's office in 1984, the originals were never returned. Pencil markings on the copies returned by mistake show whoever made them was closely attentive to any publicity that might affect the intelligence services.

Two years after the Cudlipp committee took control of information policy in Northern Ireland, David Owen ordered changes to Whitehall's own secret propaganda unit, the Foreign Office Information Research Department. It was closed in 1977. But many of its activities were continued by a new Overseas Information Department. Since 1980, confidential briefings distributed by this department have misled journalists into confusing disarmament campaigners with supporters of the Soviet Union, or critics of the police with supporters of the IRA. The government now says that its policy is not to use disinformation 'to denigrate individuals'. This is untrue. Not only do the briefings continue to denigrate individuals, the Foreign Office has had to apologise for getting some of the smears wrong. [...]

There should also be concern about the recent award of a knighthood for 'services to the military' to Colonel David Stirling, who established the GB-75 organisation and whose name featured prominently in several reports about planned right-wing interventions. Although Stirling's award was for military services, it was made in the civil division of the honours list, and on the recommendation of the Prime Minister. This was odd, as was the timing of the award, decades past any time when Stirling's services to the military (in helping found the SAS) when it would have been appropriate. It is also many years since Stirling has been politically active. The reporter in paranoia gulch must wonder if the knighthood was awarded in the hope of buying the old boy's silence between now and when he passes away.

In asking David Calcutt QC to investigate the circumstances of Wallace's dismissal from the MoD, one issue must be fairly clear. Although Calcutt will act independently, ministers will have wanted to be assured that his findings are predictable - or at least, controllable. This is not as clear as it seems from his limited terms of reference. The explicit reason why Wallace was dismissed was the leaking of a 'restricted' document about Army information. Wallace's motivation for and authority to leak such a document, as well as its contents, will be central to the argument.

Wallace claimed at the time that giving such information to reporters was part of his job, and that the leak was 'designed to clear his name of an accusation by a terrorist group' that he was engaged in 'black propaganda activities'. He argued (through his union, IPCS) that by providing a copy of the false description of his unit's activities, he would head off press suspicions that he was engaged in black propaganda work. Now he has succeeded in proving that the opposite was true, and claims that he was really dismissed because he objected to carrying out MI5's Clockwork Orange programme. This does not ring quite true - yet the government does not deny his story for fear of having to come clean about MI5's enthusiastic role in the whole affair.

Calcutt will also have to review the MoD's severe reaction to the leak, which seems disproportionate in scale. What obviously lies behind such a reaction is the Northern Ireland Office's battle to bring Army propaganda to an end. Calcutt may very well find that Wallace was moved out of Ireland because of his enthusiasm to pursue plots like Clockwork Orange II, not because of his desire to stop it. If he also finds that Wallace's dismissal for a minor leak was excessively punitive, he can recommend compensation. In this way, it may be hoped, Wallace himself may be more tarred with disinformation plotting than the MoD. MI5's larger hand will remain unseen, and dawn has yet to break in paranoia gulch.

13.

Liz Curtis

Republican publicity

(From *Ireland: the Propaganda War*, London, Pluto Press, 1984, pages 262-271)

In the years before 1981, journalists very occasionally gave their readers glimpses of republican publicists, usually in articles describing the public relations efforts of all sides. Thus in 1970, implying that reporters are subjected to equal pressure from all quarters, *The Guardian's* Anne McHardy wrote, 'Spokesmen from all sides offer chatty company and hospitality and expect sympathetic reporting in return. The Provisionals and the UDA offer tea and buns, the NIO and the Army gin and tonic and dinner.' She added that the Provisionals were better publicists than other paramilitaries, since they 'have the advantage of a romantic history and a fund of well-known traditional songs to soften people up.'[1]

During the 1981 hunger strike, however, as Bobby Sands neared death, the British authorities and media invested the republican publicists with extraordinary powers, crediting them with having concocted almost from nothing the enormous local and international sympathy for the hunger strikers. The notion of the 'Provisionals' propaganda machine - indefatigable, never resting', as *The Observer* described it,[2] was itself a propaganda device, designed to reassure the world that the British government was in the right, but helpless against the duplicity and superhuman efficiency of the 'enemy'. Concrete descriptions of the 'machine', which would have spoilt the impression by revealing the mundane reality, were eschewed.

Development of the press centre

The republican movement has its headquarters in Dublin, but Belfast republicans inevitably became the more important source of information on day-to-day developments. They were in the thick of things and, unlike their colleagues in other parts of the North, were close to the offices of the main media organisations. Their publicity work, however, developed in an ad hoc manner and was not treated as a priority.

The Belfast Republican Press Centre and the paper *Republican News* were started in 1970 by a handful of people centred around veteran republican Jimmy Steele.³ Steele died in August the same year. The Press Centre was a very loose arrangement, with no fixed headquarters nor formal meetings. It put out statements to the media which were delivered by hand to the various offices in the city.⁴ Reporters relied for information mainly on informal contacts with leading republicans such as Sinn Féin Vice-President Maire Drumm, who was assassinated by loyalists in 1976, and in the mid-seventies with Belfast organiser Seamus Loughran, who fell from grace within the movement when radicals gained the ascendancy in Belfast.⁵ There were occasional IRA press conferences, clandestine affairs which were, according to *Guardian* reporter Simon Hoggart, 'usually marked by considerable confusion'.⁶ Hoggart described one such press conference in 1972, when the Provisionals invited the Irish press and two British papers to meet Seamus Twomey, then the officer commanding the Belfast Brigade:

> This was a great cloak and dagger operation, with people arriving at staggered times, and ostensibly going to see a homeless family's relief centre. Unfortunately for the IRA, the word got out, and so the hall was besieged with reporters, making it quite obvious to any passing army patrol what was going on. Mr Twomey arrived very late, and seemed not quite aware of what he was supposed to do.⁷

After Operation Motorman in July 1972, when the British army moved in strength into the nationalist districts and destroyed the no-go areas, press conferences were generally restricted to Dublin.

The first issue of *Republican News*, then a monthly bulletin with eight A4-sized pages, appeared in June 1970.⁸ The main 'Provisional' republican paper was the Dublin-based *An Phoblacht*, which started after the movement split at the end of 1969. The 'Officials' retained the original paper, *United Irishman*. *Republican News* was started to cater for Belfast republican circles. As its first editorial pointed out, it followed a long tradition of Belfast republican journals, most of which were eventually banned under Special Powers legislation.⁹ The editorial, written by Jimmy Steele, promised:

> We shall preach the Gospel of Tone in seeking to unite all our people, Protestant, Catholic and Dissenter in the common cause of our Nation's unity and independence. We shall condemn and denounce from whatever quarter it may seek to raise its ugly head, the monster of religious bigotry and intolerance.

> The socialism of James Connolly, the idealism of Patrick Pearse and the unrepentant Republicanism of Tom Clarke, we shall try to inculcate into our people - pointing out to them the rugged freedom road which they travelled in that service.¹⁰

The paper was produced and printed secretly. Production and distribution difficulties increased after the internment swoops of August 1971, in which some members of the paper's editorial board were arrested.[11] Nonetheless, the two remaining board members started producing the paper weekly from the end of September 1971.

By August 1972 the paper was extending its appeal beyond Belfast, calling itself the 'voice of Republican Ulster'.[12] In April 1974 it changed to newspaper format, with eight large pages.[13]

The years 1974 and 1975 brought developments that had a significant impact on republican publicity. In the early years, the nationalist community had been relatively monolithic, with members of the middle class making militant gestures - the SDLP, for example, initiated the rent-and-rates strike against internment - and taking an ambivalent attitude towards the IRA except when its operations had particularly horrendous results. The SDLP's participation in the power-sharing executive meant the end of nationalist homogeneity. Papers such as *The Irish News* followed the SDLP line, and some republicans felt it necessary to mount a more effective challenge to them.[14]

At the end of the summer of 1974, Belfast republicans took over the first and second floors of a dilapidated building in the Falls Road, number 170. This was to become their main Belfast office, and remained so until the Northern Ireland Housing Executive, which owned the building, evicted them and they moved across the road to an equally ramshackle building in June 1980. In the autumn of 1974 a telex machine was installed in number 170, which became known as the Republican Press Centre, and by mid-1975 was the official address for *Republican News*.

The truce between the British army and the IRA, which began on 11 February 1975 and petered out at the end of the year, brought more changes. During 1974 detainees, politicised by their experiences, had begun to be released from the internment camps. With the truce, a few of the radicals who might otherwise have centred their activities on the IRA, became involved in agitational work.[15] At the same time, the Press Centre, along with other republican offices in the North, acquired a new status when it became the main Belfast 'incident centre' for monitoring truce violations, equipped with a direct telephone line to British officials.

The office, run at the time by Tom Hartley, began to be a focus for the press and for foreign support groups, supplanting the previous informal network. The telex machine was put to increasing use, and became a crucial tool, allowing republicans to convey their version of incidents immediately to the press, and for the first time enabling them to compete seriously with the various British public relations operations.

Republican News also underwent changes. These were in part the result of the developing polarisation of the 'Provisionals' into left-wing and right-wing camps. The dispute focused on the right's support for federalism, a policy which advocated that the government of Ireland should be based on four regional parliaments, one in each of the historic provinces. This arrangement would leave loyalists with considerable power in Ulster - an idea which pleased the right and alarmed the left. There were clashes over the content of *Republican News* between the Belfast republican leadership and its editor, Sean Caughey. On one occasion, apparently, a whole edition of the paper was burned on IRA orders because Caughey had printed a claim from an anonymous Catholic paramilitary group that they would bomb Protestant schoolchildren. The printing plates were then altered and the paper was reprinted without the offending piece.[16] In mid-1975 Sean Caughey lost his job and Danny Morrison, who had been among the internees released in 1974, took over as editor.

Raids on *Republican News*

In December 1977 the British authorities, by now intent on presenting republicans as 'criminals', launched the first in a series of raids on *Republican News*. At around 2.30 a.m. on Thursday 15 December, some 400 RUC men raided several Sinn Féin advice centres in Belfast, the press in Lurgan where *Republican News* was printed, and the homes of 36 republicans. Fifteen people were arrested, including printer Gary Kennedy - a member of the SDLP - and several senior Sinn Féin personnel. Danny Morrison and Tom Hartley, the editor and business manager of *Republican News*, were 'not at home' and escaped arrest.

RUC men, accompanied by British soldiers, stripped the Press Centre, removing all the office equipment, posters, and the paper's photo-library. The telex machine - which, fortunately for the republicans, was hired from the post office - was thrown out of an upstairs window into an army truck. At the printshop in Lurgan, the RUC seized that week's edition of *Republican News*, along with the following week's edition, which had been prepared early for Christmas, and 12,000 1978 republican calendars.

Labour Northern Ireland Secretary Roy Mason had repeatedly attacked the media that year for allegedly assisting the republicans, and in the same week as the raids he lambasted a BBC *Tonight* report on the IRA.[17] David McKittrick, then Northern editor of *The Irish Times*, wrote in a report on the raids that 'according to reliable sources in Belfast' the British authorities were hopeful of bringing charges against some of those arrested and also hoped that *Republican News* could be closed down. 'Mr Mason,' noted McKittrick, 'appears to take exception to the existence of a fairly well-produced Provisional Republican weekly newspaper.'[18]

But the paper re-emerged the same week with a defiant, one-page edition.[19] The next week, a replacement for the confiscated Christmas edition was on the streets.[120] All those arrested were released after three days without charge. There were two further raids in the next fortnight, in which Danny Morrison and Tom Hartley were among those arrested. Both were released after being held for some days in Castlereagh interrogation centre.

There was another major raid in the early hours of 27 April 1978 - again a Thursday, the day the paper came off the presses. Again the targets were republican personnel, Sinn Féin offices, including the press centre, and the press in Lurgan. Fifteen people were arrested, of whom 12 were charged with either or both IRA membership and conspiracy to pervert the course of justice - a reference to plans to set up a system of community courts. Those charged included the entire officer board of Belfast Sinn Féin, *Republican News* workers, printer and SDLP member Gary Kennedy, and a French photographer, Alain Frilet. The RUC confiscated 30,000 copies of a four-page *Republican News* supplement on the H Blocks from the printshop.

Again, *Republican News* reappeared immediately with an emergency edition,[21] and by the end of April was again coming out weekly. It was now being produced 'on the run', from the houses of sympathisers. Gary Kennedy's printing business was now in jeopardy - advertising from unionist sources had stopped[22] - and the printing of *Republican News* was shifted to the South. Those arrested were eventually released on bail, and in February 1979 the charges against them were dropped for lack of evidence.[23]

As *Republican News* developed it had come into increasing competition with the official paper of the movement, *An Phoblacht*. The latter was far less militant, and the existence of the two papers emphasised the division between the Northern radicals and the more conservative Southerners. By the end of 1977, the Belfast team were pushing for a merger, but the raids and arrests delayed the negotiations. The two finally merged in January 1979, with the Northerners taking over the editorial direction of the new paper. In effect, *Republican News* swallowed up *An Phoblacht*.[24]

The setting up of the Falls Road centre also stimulated the production of other publicity material, especially posters. During the hunger strikes of 1980 and 1981, output increased. At the end of 1980, republicans produced their first video, an hour-long exposition of the background to the prison protest. This was shown in republican clubs and at meetings north and south of the border. This increase in the production of posters, badges and pamphlets in 1981 led to the formation of a new department, Republican Publications, to handle distribution. Staffed by two or three volunteers, Republican Publications is housed in a bunker-like shop in Turf Lodge. The material is produced almost entirely for local use, and most is not subsidised. As with *An Phoblacht/Republican News*, costs are expected to be met through sales.

Veracity

There have been far fewer specific complaints by journalists about the accuracy of republican statements than about the accuracy of statements from the British army press office in its heyday. Nor is there any evidence that republicans have engaged in 'black propaganda' operations.

Republicans freely admit that until the mid-seventies the IRA issued exaggerated claims about the numbers of soldiers they had killed or injured in particular incidents. These, they consider, were partly due to over-optimistic assessments by the IRA personnel involved, compounded by the confusion that surrounds such incidents. Eventually *Republican News* began refusing to publish such claims unless the number of victims was confirmed by other sources.[25]

However from the early days republicans appear to have adopted a policy of admitting to violent actions that had 'gone wrong', despite the negative propaganda effects. A senior republican said, 'The IRA realised very early on that telling the truth was the best policy because it gave them credibility. The IRA claimed actions that went wrong, so people believed them when they said they had not done something.'[26]

That this policy existed in the early seventies is supported by a front-page editorial in *Republican News* following the Abercorn restaurant bombing in March 1972. The authorities blamed the IRA for the bombing, in which two people were killed and some 130 injured, but both the 'Official' and 'Provisional' IRA denied it. *Republican News* printed an impassioned article condemning the 'horrible crime'. It supported the IRA's denial by listing several actions which the 'Provisional' and 'Official' IRAs had admitted though the actions 'were liable to be misunderstood by their own supporters and ... were bound to be misrepresented by their enemies.'[27] These included a 'Provisional' shooting of a member of a wedding party and the bombing by the 'Officials' of a barracks at Aldershot in which seven civilians were killed. *Republican News* went on to contrast this 'record of truth' with a series of lies told by the British army and RUC. Inside, it reproduced a page from a bulletin issued by the loyalist UDA, in which the Abercorn was mentioned as one of many 'rebel establishments' in which the national anthem was not played and which loyalists were asked to boycott.[28]

The same month, the 'Provisionals' admitted responsibility for the widely condemned Donegall Street bombing and in July said they were responsible for the 'Bloody Friday' bombings which again resulted in civilian deaths and many injuries. In both cases the IRA said that warnings had been given. Down the years, the IRA continued to admit to such tragedies - though the circumstances of the 1974 Birmingham bombings remain unclarified - despite the fact that they alienated its supporters and provided ammunition for the British propagandists: the Central Office of Information film, *Northern Ireland Chronicle*, for example, is punctuated by gruesome footage of the aftermath of bombings such as those of Bloody Friday and the incineration of the La Mon restaurant in February 1978. Following La Mon, the IRA said in a statement that 'our supporters ... have rightly and severely criticised us.'[29]

There were exceptions, however. These appear to have been mostly in the early seventies, and mainly concerned killings of alleged informers and, during the spate of sectarian killings in 1975, those of Protestants.[30] The IRA did not deny such killings, but simply refrained from claiming them. In later years there were far fewer incidents in which Protestants were killed solely on sectarian grounds, and the IRA began more often to claim killings of alleged informers. A departure from this was the killing of Peter Valente in November 1980. Valente was killed during the first H Block hunger strike, and had a brother 'on the blanket' in the H Blocks. Apparently in order not to cause demoralisation among anti-H Block campaigners, the IRA said nothing at the time, and did not contradict the general belief that he was a victim of loyalists.[31] Soon after the start of the 1981 hunger strike, Chris Ryder revealed in a *Sunday Times* piece, evidently based on information from the RUC, that Valente had been an informer.[32] Ten months later the IRA - then offering an amnesty to informers - finally admitted they had killed Valente, 'an IRA volunteer ... who was a central RUC informer for a number of years'.[33]

Republican publicists working from the Belfast press centre appear to have a reasonably good reputation for veracity among journalists, though qualified by the acceptance that any organisation is bound to attempt to present its affairs in a favourable light. A journalist who reported for some years from Belfast for a British paper said that while he rarely spoke to the British army, neither the RUC nor the republicans had ever to his knowledge given him a 'bum steer'. An Irish journalist said, 'Sometimes they won't tell you things, but what they tell you is almost always true.' But one said bluntly, 'There's nobody in Northern Ireland who's going to tell you the truth - they'll all tell you from the point of view of their agency,' while another Irish reporter complained that the republicans, like the Northern Ireland Office, had given him misleading information during the 1981 hunger strike.[34]

Such complaints, heard during both the 1980[35] and 1981 hunger strikes, centred on republicans glossing over their difficulties and, in particular, saying that the 1981 hunger strike was not coming to an end at a time when in fact it was. Questioned about this, a republican spokesperson responded with some amusement:

> I see nothing wrong with that. I mean you have to have an expedient position if you're trying to hold a line. You have the position where every year, absolutely every year, reporters come to you after the closed session of the ard fheis [annual conference] and say, 'Was there a statement from the IRA read out?' And everybody categorically denies it. It's routine. Now that's stating that without prejudice to the fact whether or not a statement is actually read out! There you have a perfect paradox!

> You have to operate like that. It's like the Official Unionists saying there's no split inside the Official Unionists - when Harold McCusker is challenging Molyneaux for the leadership.

It's obviously for defensive reasons that one gets into ambivalence. Where it's more important to hold the organisation together, you may have to brazen your way through something expediently, but in the overall interests of the struggle or of a particular section of the movement.[36]

Relations with journalists

In his book *The Media and Political Violence*,[37] former British army major-general Richard Clutterbuck asserts: 'the investigative reporter can probe the army or police with no risk more serious than forfeiting their co-operation, but if he attempted a similar probe into a terrorist organisation he would forfeit his life.'

In fact no journalists have been killed in the North by 'terrorists', and there are no recorded instances of any being injured by the Provisional IRA. Indeed, the British army has arguably proved more dangerous to journalists, by using undercover operatives equipped with phoney press cards and by shooting photographers with plastic bullets.

When, in an isolated case, a reporter was beaten up in Belfast in March 1983, the violence came from another source. Alan Rusbridger reported in *The Guardian*,

> John Hicks of the *Daily Mirror* was attacked by three men as he was drinking in a bar and severely knocked about. It is thought this was in retaliation for an article he had written about Mr Eamon 'Hatchet' Kerr, a Worker's Party member who was shot dead in his bed at the end of last week. Mr Hicks had not been too respectful towards Mr Kerr, a renowned hit man in his day.

> NUJ officials are extremely disturbed at the attack, for, although many journalists working in the province have been given verbal threats, it has been very rare for any kind of physical violence or intimidation to have been used.[38]

One journalist who was threatened by the Provisionals was Chris Ryder of *The Sunday Times*. His colleague David Blundy, testifying in his defence in a libel suit taken by the Andersonstown Co-operative, said that in late 1976 or early 1977 Seamus Loughran had told him 'that Mr Ryder's presence would not be welcome and said if he came into the area he would get his head blown off.' Blundy explained, reported *The Irish Times*, that 'The Provos had been unhappy about articles written by Mr Ryder about IRA extortion.'[39]

Since then, with the centralisation of press relations in the Falls Road centre, it seems there has been no repetition of such incidents. Republicans stress that they will assist any journalist, even those who are flagrantly pro-British, but with the reservation that they would not help a reporter whom they believed to be a 'Brit agent'.

Improvements

Ironically for the British, the raids in 1977 and 1978 inadvertently contributed to improving the republicans' public relations work. Before the raids, people who worked in the press centre had kept their identities secret from outsiders, refusing to give their real names to journalists or to be photographed. Now, however, their names were in the newspapers. Danny Morrison explained:

> Up until then, for the sake of one's family, for the sake of one's personal security, we had been operating with aliases. So the Brits actually forced our hand ... and of course once it was done, we saw the advantages of it, in terms of increasing our credibility, increasing our profile, especially in the media, because they would now come and talk to a named, known person ... It was a centre of gravity for them, and they could relate to that.[40]

The prospect of being in the spotlight did not make liaising with the press a popular area of work. Richard McAuley, who took over from Joe Austin as the movement's Belfast press officer in 1980, said:

> Most people don't want to do PR work because it's very dangerous. It's dangerous in two senses. It heightens your public profile and could lead you to getting stiffed by loyalists or put out of the road by the Brits. It's also dangerous in that if you say the wrong thing - and I have made some cracking boobs over the years - you can embarrass yourself and embarrass the movement.[41]

From mid-1980, the press centre was located in a small, Spartan room in number 51-53 Falls Road, a shabby building with minimal facilities. It shared the upper floor with the Belfast Sinn Féin office and the prisoners' welfare department, while the ground floor was used as a waiting room for prisoners' relatives and friends awaiting transport to the prisons. The press centre's equipment was limited to a desk, a phone - the bills apparently paid by *Republican News* as the centre has no funds allocated to it[42] - and a telex machine in a tiny room nearby. It had one volunteer staffing it full-time, though other senior Sinn Féin personnel could be called on to do interviews, and other workers in the building assisted in answering the phone. Richard McAuley was scarcely exaggerating when, during the 1981 hunger strike, he said to American journalist Neil Hickey' 'Do you know the sum total of the famous Republican propaganda machine that everybody talks about? ... I'm it.[43]

The movement's press officer works in the same way as any other public relations person, answering queries from reporters, giving interviews, and arranging for journalists to meet other people or visit different areas.

One difference, however, from the usual public relations pattern is that neither the press officer nor leading republicans will accept invitations from journalists for meals. Although some journalists have expressed resentment of this, evidently feeling snubbed by such refusals, republicans say that to accept such invitations would not only put them under an obligation to the journalist concerned, but would compromise them in the eyes of the movement if the reporter subsequently produced a hostile story or damaging 'leak'...

Republicans have never prioritised press relations. The improvements they have made - except for the acquisition of the telex machine - have been largely a by-product of other developments. Such publicity as they have won has come less through the publicists' efforts than through the impetus of events: the 1981 hunger strike went virtually disregarded until Bobby Sands' election to Westminster...

Republicans cannot, in any case, hope to match the facilities and finance available to the Northern Ireland Office, RUC and army press offices. Even if they could, it is doubtful whether this would win them a good press in Britain: the ties between the media and the authorities are too strong. In Ireland, as elsewhere, the anti-colonial cause is unlikely to win the British media's respect until it is on the verge of victory.

Endnotes

1. *The Guardian*, 23 February 1980; see also Andrew Stephen in *The Observer*, 29 February 1976.
2. *The Observer*, 3 May 1981.
3. *Republican News*, vol. 4, no. 24, 15 June 1974.
4. Interview with former Press Centre member by the author.
5. See *The Observer*, 29 February 1976.
6. *The Guardian*, 14 June 1974.
7. *Ibid*.
8. An almost complete collection of issues of *Republican News* is held in the Linenhall Library, Belfast.
9. *Republican News*, vol. 1, no. 1, June 1970.
10. *Ibid*; also quoted in vol. 4, no. 24, 15 June 1974.
11. *Republican News*, 4, no. 24, 15 June 1974.
12. *Republican News*, 2, no. 48, 18 August 1972.
13. *Republican News*, vol. 4 no. 14, 16 April 1974.
14. Interview with a republican spokesperson by the author.
15. *Ibid*.
16. *Ibid*.
17. Shown on 15 December 1977.
18. *The Irish Times*, 17 December 1977.
19. *Republican News*, undated, appeared on Saturday 17 December 1977.
20. *Republican News*, vol. 7, no. 49, Christmas 1977.
21. *Republican News*, vol. 8, no. 17, 29 April 1978.
22. *Hibernia*, 11 May 1978.
23. For an account of the raids on *Republican News*, see Danny Morrison, 'Censorship at source', in ed. Campaign for Free Speech on Ireland, *The British Media and Ireland: Truth the First Casualty*, London, Information on Ireland, 1979, pp. 45-46.

24. The first edition of *An Phoblacht/Republican News*, vol. 1, no. 1, came out on 27 January 1979.

25. Interview with a *Republican News* journalist, by the author.

26. Interview by the author.

27. *Republican News*, 12 March 1972 .

28. Facsimile of *UDA*, No. 17 reproduced in *Republican News*, 12 March 1972.

29. *Republican News*, 25 February 1978.

30. See Jack Holland, *Too Long a Sacrifice*, New York, Dodd, Mead and Company, 1981, p. 138.

31. See *An Phoblacht/Republican News*, 22 November 1980.

32. *The Sunday Times*, 22 March 1981.

33. *An Phoblacht/Republican News*, 28 January 1982.

34. Interviews by the author, 1982.

35. Alan Murray of *The Irish Press* speaking at the NUJ/ACTT conference on media censorship of Northern Ireland, 28 February 1981.

36. Interview by the author, 1982.

37. London, Macmillan, 1981, p. 107.

38. *The Guardian*, 18 March 1983.

39. *The Irish Times*, 10 October 1979.

40. Interview by the author, 1982.

41. *Ibid*.

42. *Ibid*.

43. Neil Hickey, 'The Battle for Northern Ireland: How TV tips the balance', *TV Guide*, 26 September 1981, USA.

14.

David Miller

THE NORTHERN IRELAND INFORMATION SERVICE AND THE MEDIA: AIMS, STRATEGY, TACTICS

(From Glasgow University Media Group, *Getting the Message*, London, Routledge, 1993, pages 73-103)

[...]

The Northern Ireland Information Service (NIIS) is the press and public relations division of the NIO, the British government department responsible for running Northern Ireland. The Information Service is a major source of political news on Northern Ireland. It delivers press releases to news desks in Belfast three times a day and in 1991-2 employed fifty-eight staff in its Belfast and London offices (*Hansard,* 7 May 1991: 429 (w)). In 1989-90 it spent £7.238 million on press and PR, administering a population of 1.5 million (*Hansard,* 2 April 1991: 451-2 (w)). In the same year, by comparison, the Scottish Office, which administers 5 million people, spent £1.1 million (*Hansard,* 30 April 1991: 158-9 (w)).

This chapter will examine NIO public relations aims, strategy and tactics.[1] First, after a short introduction to interpretations of the conflict in Ireland, I will look at the broad strategy of the Information Service. Using the example of a publicity booklet issued in 1989 I will illustrate the general picture of the conflict the NIO attempts to paint. Second, I will examine some key themes which have been emphasized by the NIO and demonstrate how they are targeted. Third, I want to look at the different tactics the NIO uses in its relations with different sets of journalists. A key problem for much contemporary media research is the assumption that the media are homogeneous. In this view the process of news negotiation is similar regardless of the type of news outlet or source organization(s) involved (Ericson, Baranek and Chan 1989: 24). But as Ericson, Baranek and Chan note, different sources have different requirements of publicity and secrecy.

I will suggest that it is also the case that the NIO operates a 'hierarchy of access' in relation to different groups of journalists in order to influence various audience agendas.

Legitimacy and the State

The central dispute in interpretations of the conflict in Ireland is the question of the legitimacy of the Northern Ireland state and of the British presence. The official view of the conflict is based on an assumption, rarely made explicit, that the state is legitimate. While it acknowledges that the civil rights protests in the late 1960s against the systematic discrimination, gerrymandering and repression of the Unionist government had some justification, it sees the introduction of Direct Rule in 1972 as having fundamentally reformed the Northern Ireland state. From that point on the causes of the conflict had been removed and any manifestations of unrest could only be explained as emanating from 'extremists'. This view denies the political motivation of the Irish Republican Army (IRA) who are seen simply as 'terrorists'. The IRA is held to be a criminal conspiracy which is similar to organized crime networks such as the Mafia (thus the use of the term 'godfathers' in some official propaganda). It is also presented to some audiences as part of an international network of 'terrorists' with connections to Marxist revolutionaries in Europe, anti-western feeling in the Middle East, particularly Libya, and was until recently linked to the global ambitions of the Soviet Union.

The role of the British army and Royal Ulster Constabulary (RUC) in all this is seen as being to counter the 'terrorist threat' and keep the peace between the warring factions. The governmental apparatus exists solely to oversee a return of 'normality'. Thus we have seen media coverage of a large number of attempts by the British to 'facilitate' a negotiated settlement between the two communities. When these fail the responsibility rests, in the official version, solely with the deep and irreconcilable historical antagonisms which bind the unionist and nationalist communities in conflict.

But there are other views of the conflict. The most widely held of these stresses that Britain is not 'above' the conflict but is actually an intimate part of it. In this view the question of the legitimacy of the state is central. The conflict in Ireland is seen as rooted in the creation of the statelet of Northern Ireland in 1921 specifically to ensure a Protestant majority in perpetuity. The cause of the conflict in Ireland is therefore seen as the existence of the border. In this view the maintenance of the border is guaranteed by both the presence of British troops and the funding of the current administrative set-up by the British government. The cost of this British subvention to Northern Ireland in 1988-9 was £1.9 billion (Gaffikin and Morrissey 1990: 49). Versions of this view are shared by many politicians in the south of Ireland, the Social Democratic and Labour Party (SDLP) in the north as well as by some politicians in Britain. It is also current in some parts of the media. The *Daily Mirror,* for example, has put this view since 1978. In an editorial, signed by former proprietor Robert Maxwell, following the collapse in the summer of 1991 of the latest round of talks sponsored by the NIO, the *Mirror* repeated its view that the conflict continues because it is funded and underwritten by Britain:

> Once again, a well-meaning attempt by the British government to solve the unsolvable in Ulster has ended in failure. It will always be so. The Northern Ireland Secretary, Peter Brooke, as so many decent men before him, tried to win from the leaders of the Protestant majority and the Catholic minority an agreement on some measure of power sharing. *He was doomed to failure as were all the other Government Ministers who have tried before him.* The Protestant Unionist leadership will never concede an inch to the Catholic republicans as long as they believe they have a Big Brother in Britain to protect and finance them. The nationalists will remain obstinate while they believe the Dublin Government is always in their corner. (*Daily Mirror,* 5 July 1991: emphasis in original)

Arguments like these recognize that the conflict in Ireland is essentially a political one for which there is no military solution. Contrary to the logic of much *public* official thinking some senior figures in the British establishment also accept that this is the case. General Sir James Glover, the former Commander-in-chief UK Land Forces, who had previously served as an intelligence officer in Northern Ireland, has put this view:

> In no way can, or will, the Provisional IRA ever be defeated militarily ... The long war will last as long as the Provisional IRA have the stamina, the political motivation - I used to call it the sinews of war - but, the wherewithal to sustain their campaign and so long as there is a divided island of Ireland. (*Panorama,* BBC 1, 29 February 1988)

Some unionists in Northern Ireland also question the idea that Britain is neutral in the conflict. Many are distrustful of the motivations of British policy and often suspect their interests are being ignored or that they will be 'sold out' to the south. This was one of the main loyalist objections to the Anglo-Irish Agreement of 1985. As a result of such uneasy feelings some unionists now advocate either an independent Northern Ireland or closer integration with Britain in order to lessen the chances of being 'cut loose'.

The NIIS has sought to present its view of the conflict as the legitimate and rational perspective in opposition to that of the paramilitaries and other 'extremists'. Yet it is clear that both nationalists and some unionists in Ireland as well as some powerful voices in the media and, indeed, the

British military do not altogether share their perspective. Instead they see the presence or role of the British as part of the problem.

'The Wickedness of Terrorism' Vs 'A Community on the Move': the Strategy of the NIO

The central strategy of successive British Governments in Northern Ireland has been one of containment. Home Secretary Reginald Maudling provided an early illustration of this when he memorably revealed that the aim of the British government was to reduce the violence to 'an acceptable level' (*Sunday Times* Insight Team 1972: 309). But as O'Dowd, Rolston and Tomlinson have pointed out the strategy of containment is not simply one of repression or counterinsurgency. When the British introduced Direct Rule to Northern Ireland in 1972 they followed a dual strategy in which they 'accelerated the drive for reforms and the reconstitution of the rule of law, while at the same time drawing upon the latest repertoire of counterinsurgency thinking and practices derived from colonial experiences elsewhere' (O'Dowd, Rolston and Tomlinson 1980: 201). This strategy developed over time and has been inflected according to both the party in power and perhaps more importantly the balance of forces at any one time. [...]

Most research studies which have concentrated on the analysis of news coverage or on the production of news have tended to ignore or play down attempts to communicate the reform part of the NIO strategy. Nevertheless, it has assumed a very important role in the approach of the NIIS which stresses two basic messages: on the one hand, that the problem is the terrorist 'assault on democracy' (NIO 1989: 20), and, on the other, that the people of 'Ulster' are 'a community on the move' in which local 'entrepreneurial flair' and 'Ulster generosity' are 'rendering bigotry irrelevant' (*ibid*: 72). The attempt to convince the world that Northern Ireland is getting 'back to normal' has been massively funded. A large proportion of all NIO expenditure on press, public relations and advertising is spent on this approach.[2]

Because of the perceived difficulty of getting good news into the media, the Information Service itself has two staff who produce 'good news' stories for an international market, partly working through the Central Office of Information (COI) and their London Press Service. They attempt to 'place' these stories in suspecting and unsuspecting magazines and newspapers. Naturally, they are free of charge or copyright restrictions. Additionally, in 1990 the Industrial Development Board replaced their PR consultants Burson Marstellar with PR firm Shandwick and paid them £3.5 million for the first year of a contract, which included supplying the world's media with good news stories from a news bureau set up in Belfast.

The day of the men and women of peace

To illustrate the dual approach of the NIO I want to give some examples from the publicity booklet produced by the Information Service, in July 1989, for the twentieth anniversary of the redeployment of British troops.[3] Ten thousand copies were produced and, according to the NIO, distributed to 'MPs, the media, opinion formers and those interested in Northern Ireland' (*Fortnight*, September 1989). It is a large glossy publication full of photographs and reproductions of press clippings and is divided into five chapters which address the 'perceptions and realities' (NIO 1989: 1) of Northern Ireland. Opening with a review of the civil rights campaign of the 1960s, a list of campaigners' demands is counterposed with a list of 'reforms' to suggest that civil rights grievances have been met (Figure 1).

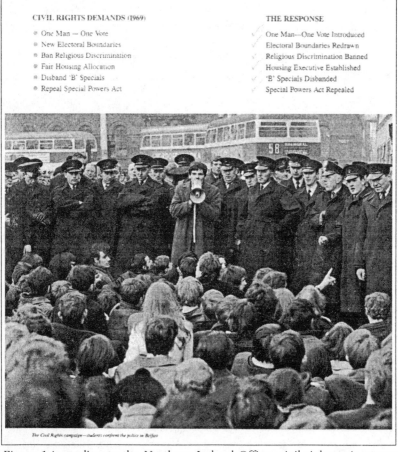

CIVIL RIGHTS DEMANDS (1969)	THE RESPONSE
One Man — One Vote	One Man—One Vote Introduced
New Electoral Boundaries	Electoral Boundaries Redrawn
Ban Religious Discrimination	Religious Discrimination Banned
Fair Housing Allocation	Housing Executive Established
Disband 'B' Specials	'B' Specials Disbanded
Repeal Special Powers Act	Special Powers Act Repealed

The Civil Rights campaign—students confront the police in Belfast

Figure 1 According to the Northern Ireland Office, civil rights grievances have been met.

Since then British governments have worked to create sufficient cross community consensus to restore 'an agreed measure of self-government to Northern Ireland' (*ibid*: 7). Once it has been established that the British are simply trying to bring the two sides together we can move on to the 'real' problem of Northern Ireland which is 'terrorism'.

In chapter 2 ('Attacking the community') the message on the 'terrorists' comes to the fore with a series of images of the death and destruction caused by the IRA (although loyalist 'terrorists' are mentioned there is only one photograph of identified loyalist violence compared with eighteen of victims of the IRA) (Figure 2). The conflict in Northern Ireland is due, in this version, to the 'evil dreams of evil men' who manipulate people so that:

> Young men and women with the normal aspirations of marriage and family and the ability to hold down good jobs needlessly spend years in prison as the penalty for listening to the evil dreams of evil men. And some die. That, too, represents part of the tragedy of Northern Ireland. Not only do PIRA kill, they do so with a cynicism which is a total perversion. (NIO 1989: 14)

We might then ask what the government is doing to combat these 'evil' men. Chapter 3, 'Protecting the community', gives us the answer: 'keeping the peace and maintaining law and order' (*ibid*: 32). The 'wickedness of terrorism' requires that the police and army be portrayed as able to deal adequately with the 'terrorist threat', while at the same time the presentation of the army and police as peacekeepers requires that the police are seen as part of 'the community'. As one commentator noted: 'The major problem for the authors of chapter three was how to make the RUC appear tough enough to cope with the boys in chapter two and still be friendly local bobbies' (Odling-Smee 1989: 14-15). The way the NIO tries to resolve this tension is to deploy visual images of friendly, helpful-looking police men and women. As well as one photo of policemen carrying a coffin there are four of officers helping children or giving directions, patrolling the streets or chatting with pedestrians (Figure 3). There is only one photograph in the whole booklet in which members of the police appear armed. In a bizarre expression of this tension between the 'anti-terrorist' and 'local bobby' images, the officers are seen wearing plastic red noses and laughing as they point their guns at the camera.

The point of such images, as the text makes clear, is to reinforce the notion that Northern Ireland is a society getting back to 'normal'. This is why there is such an emphasis on the low crime rate and the repetition of a common official normalizing anecdote about deaths on the roads being twice as common as deaths 'at the hands of a terrorist' (NIO 1989: 36).

By the end of chapter 3 we have already started to shift to the images of what is called a 'community on the move'. Chapter 4 deals with Ulster's achievements in industrial development and employment, agriculture,

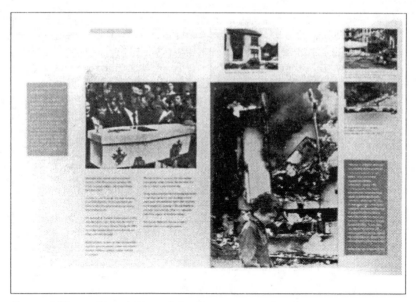

Figure 2 The 'evil' activities of the IRA contrasted with,
Figure 3, the friendly bobbies of the RUC.

innovation and culture. It argues that successive British governments have shown a 'high degree of commitment' to Northern Ireland by subsidizing public expenditure and trying to attract overseas investment (*ibid.*: 44). There are many colour photographs showing some of the developments supported by the Industrial Development Board (Figure 4) while the text reveals the 'excellent job' done by the board in attracting investment. There are no images of poverty or underdevelopment in this section. What is not mentioned is that, according to the Northern Ireland Economic Council, much United States investment is short term and that investment by some companies, for example the Ford Motor Company, has led to net job losses (Obair 1991). Ironically for a chapter titled 'a community on the move' there is no room to mention the problems caused by the large physical movement of population out of Northern Ireland via emigration.[4] Chapter 5 relays rosy images of the 'new spirit' through which 'new attitudes and new frameworks for equality and mutual understanding' (NIO 1989: 64) will be created with the help of the British government.

The conclusion sums up the twin approach. After arguing that the public, media-induced, perception of Northern Ireland is wrong, it goes on to stress the official version of the counterinsurgency strategy of the state:

> In reality, the community, together with Government and the forces of law, order and justice, is determined to succeed. It resists the small band of terrorists with a resilience which is impressive. It is coming to grips with its historic legacies, resolved to break their stranglehold. The economic and sectarian chains which have bound it for too long are slowly but inexorably being loosened. (NIO 1989: 72)

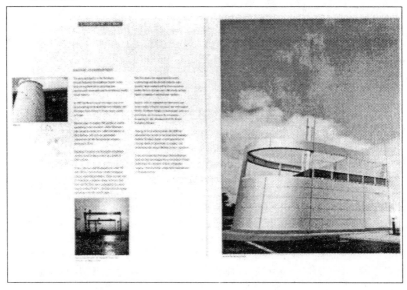

Figure 4 'A community on the move'

Here we have the familiar themes of the 'community' upon whose backs the 'small band of terrorists' prey. The government in this construction is on the same side as *'the* community' which is coming to grips with *'its* historic legacies'. The key proposition here is that the problems of Northern Ireland are nothing to do with the British government or the NIO. The position of the NIO in all this is that of a neutral observer or at most a facilitator for the Irish to sort out *their own* problems. The only reason for the continued British presence is the democratic wish of the Protestant majority to remain British.

Once this definition of the British role is laid out the argument moves on to the reform strand of NIO strategy emphasizing the 'nice' side of 'Ulster':

> The future begins to look brighter. Civic, family and personal pride are still intact. Space is being created to allow Ulster generosity to express itself in an ever increasing number of ways. Mutual respect and a willingness to appreciate the other's point of view are rendering bigotry irrelevant.

> Faith in the future is stronger than ever. (*ibid:* 72)

In this view the solution to the conflict is an end to bigoted attitudes which are to be replaced by cross community co-operation. The existence of the border, the presence of British troops and indeed the overall role of Britain in Ireland are evidently not at issue.

Some Key Themes

A key claim of official propaganda and of counterinsurgency theorists has been that IRA propaganda delivers variable messages to variable audiences (e.g., Tugwell 1981). The evidence for this is often Maria McGuire's 1973 memoir, *To Take Arms: A Year in the Provisional IRA*. It is quoted, for example, in an unattributable Foreign and Commonwealth Office (FCO) briefing paper which starts by arguing that:

> The claim of the provisional IRA to be the champion of Irish Nationalism overseas is accepted by many Americans of Irish origin from whom it derives considerable support ... Elsewhere, however, support comes largely from Communist, Trotskyist and other extremist and anti-western groups - a fact which the Provisionals are careful not to publicise in America. (FCO 1981: 1)

Some politicians apparently believe the briefings they are given and reproduce them in their memoirs. Jim Prior for example, who was Secretary of State for Northern Ireland from 1981 to 1984, has argued that what the IRA 'really want' is: 'The destruction of Democracy, and its replacement by a Marxist Irish state, which in time might threaten the whole of Western security' (Prior 1986: 221). But claims like this were apparently only meant for certain eyes. The case of the 'Marxist conspiracy' was, according to a senior information officer, 'a purely American oriented projection', which:

was fairly calculated and cool, simply that just telling America that an actor, for example, has communist tendencies, and he ain't going to work any more. Tell them that the IRA is a Marxist-Leninist conspiracy and people are going to say 'Well ...' (interview with author, December 1990)

The aim of this type of material is clearly to suggest the dishonesty and hypocrisy of the republican movement. It is ironic that briefing documents like this one are themselves mainly intended for United States and international distribution and that the Marxist revolutionaries line is not for distribution in Britain or Ireland nor is it promoted by the Information Service to British journalists (see also Rolston 1991: 161).

Another view promoted by the FCO and NIO has been the 'terrorist international' favoured by some counter-insurgency theorists (Sterling 1981; Wilkinson 1977). An analysis of unattributable briefing papers issued by the information department of the FCO reveals that this theme is often returned to (see, for example, FCO 1981, 1984, 1988b). This view tends to rest on two sorts of evidence. First, when the IRA were found to be in possession of weapons manufactured in the (former) eastern bloc it was implied that these countries supported the IRA (McKinley 1987), although when the IRA use arms manufactured in western countries this argument is not advanced. Second, the existence of 'Irish solidarity' groups in European countries is often taken to imply connections between 'terrorist' groups in France, Spain, Holland or Germany and the IRA.[5]

Following the killing of WPC Fletcher outside the Libyan Peoples' Bureau in London in 1984 and the United States bombing of Libya in 1986, the Libyan connection became one of the major themes of official propaganda (FCO 1984, 1986a, 1986b, 1988a, 1988b). Evidence of IRA attempts to obtain arms from Libya first surfaced in 1973 with the interception of arms aboard the *Claudia*. In the run up to and aftermath of the 1986 bombing of Libya, the United States government had constructed Libya as a major threat to western security. President Reagan had included Libya in his list of 'outlaw states' run by the 'strangest collection of misfits, loony tunes and squalid criminals since the advent of the Third Reich' (cited in Jenkins 1988: 7).

At the NIO and FCO the climate in the United States was seen as a good opportunity to influence United States opinion. As one information officer observed, the Libyan connection had 'bugger all to do with internal government or policy' (interview with author, December 1990). The capture of the *Eksund* in 1987, followed by reports that between 1985 and 1987 four shipments of arms and explosives had reached the IRA, gave a further boost to the campaign (Taylor 1988). The fact that these shipments included arms and plastic explosive of Czech manufacture allowed the NIO and FCO to imply eastern bloc involvement although there was, and remains, precious little evidence of this. The Libyan/Czech connection [...] was used in Britain [...] partly in order to maintain the belief in the United

States that it was not simply a 'line'. As one information officer argued: 'It was more or less to give credibility to emphasising it abroad ... It would look bloody stupid if we were talking about Libya and Czechoslovakia in America and nobody here [in the UK] was informed about it' (interview with author, December 1990). [...] As well as targeting different audiences through different groups of journalists and emphasizing different themes (where appropriate) to each, a long established technique of NIO publicity has been the importance attached to who is perceived to be delivering a message. It is to this approach that we now turn.

Who speaks?

If the lobby system or off-the-record briefings are useful in disguising the source of an official statement, they may still indicate that information emanates from official sources and as such, to a suspicious audience, they may be tainted (Cockerell, Hennessy and Walker, 1984; Margach 1978). The public words of other people who might be thought to be independent or even critical of the state are a different matter. Early NIO broadsheets and leaflets often used this device to attempt to show that influential opinion was on their side. For example, the then director of British Information Services in New York told the expenditure committee of the House of Commons in 1973 that:

> Some of the most effective material in this context comes from Dublin: from the statements of the last Prime Minister, Mr Lynch, the Cardinal, Cardinal Conway, and the former Irish Minister of Justice, Mr O'Malley, particularly on such matters as denouncing the support given in the USA to the IRA in way of funds. (Commons Expenditure Committee 1973: 18)

More recently, the glossy booklet issued by the NIO in July 1989 for the twentieth anniversary of the redeployment of British troops in Northern Ireland uses an assortment of quotes from politicians, religious figures, an American businessman and even George Bush. The title itself uses the words of Cahal Daly the then Bishop of Down and Connor: 'The day of the Men and Women of Peace Must Surely Come' (NIO 1989).[6] The philosophy of this approach was explained in the confidential planning notes of the film *Northern Ireland Chronicle* which were leaked in 1981. It argued that statements about the criminality of those convicted for 'scheduled' offences would be: 'far more cogently made by, say, a Catholic bishop than ... by any on-or-off-screen Government spokesman'. But it was not just interviewees from the British government who might not be convincing. Unionist politicians too were out, particularly since the target audience for the film was (and remains) the United States.[7] The unionists:

> are the people whom the film's target audience ... would be most inclined to reject. That Molyneaux would speak out against the IRA

is obvious: that, say, John Hume or Bishop Daly would might be a revelation. These are the people who, in terms of the film, will carry the most authority and have the most muscle. (cited in Curtis 1984: 200)

More recently the Information Service has attempted to have their message carried by Irish diplomats, SDLP politicians and Northern Ireland trades unionists as well as former politicians such as Paddy Devlin, particularly in relation to the British campaign against the MacBride principles of fair employment. Sometimes these approaches are done without the permission of the people who are used. Curtis notes that John Hume and Edward Daly were 'furious' when they found out they were being used in *Northern Ireland Chronicle* (Curtis 1984: 201).

Academics are another potentially valuable resource for the information manager. If they can be supplied with detailed information which is then reproduced in books this lends more credibility to the arguments of the Information Service. Many of these writers are ex-military and some have had first-hand practical experience of 'psychological warfare' campaigns in Ireland (see, for example, Clutterbuck 1981; Evelegh 1978; Hooper 1982; Kitson 1971, 1987; Tugwell 1973, 1981, 1987). The reproduction of the arguments of the NIO or FCO is sometimes not even accompanied by rewriting and whole passages of briefing documents have found their way verbatim into published work. For example, volume I of Barzilay's four volume study of the *British Army in Ulster* (Barzilay 1973) includes large sections of a Foreign Office, Information Research Department (IRD) briefing *The IRA: Aims, Policy, Tactics*.[8] The NIO or the FCO can then use the writings of academics as impartial and independent commentaries. The academics themselves may then be called upon by journalists as 'experts' on 'terrorism' (see George 1991; Herman and O'Sullivan 1989, 1991; and Schlesinger 1978, for more details on 'terrorology'). [...]

For many years the perceived problem for both the Northern Ireland government and latterly the NIO in presenting themselves in the United States was that there was no full-time officer devoted to Northern Ireland in the diplomatic service. In addition the officers who did deal with Northern Ireland were British. In the late 1940s the Unionist administration of Basil Brooke attempted to have an 'Ulsterman' positioned in the United States in an information role in order to mitigate these two obstacles. The Foreign Office was not keen and rejected the advance. It was not until the H-Block crisis in 1980 that the FCO relented. According to its then head, Patrick Nixon, this was partly because British Information Services in New York found that Northern Ireland became 'the biggest single item of government policy' they were called on to explain ('File on Four', BBC Radio 1, 23 November 1982). As Jenkins and Sloman point out: 'For years the Foreign Office was criticised for failing to put across the government's case on Ulster, sending diplomats with plummy accents to defend the thesis that Ulster people really did want "the British to stay"' (1985: 83). The solution was to send the press officer from the Northern Ireland Department of the Environment in Belfast on a four-year secondment. Cyril Gray was clear about the advantages of not having a plummy accent:

> I find it quite remarkable the impact that an obvious Irish accent has on often very difficult Irish-American audiences. They may be many generations out from Ireland, they have a very imperfect, inaccurate knowledge of Ireland. Nonetheless, they do ask very detailed questions at all times and, to be frank, it's the only kind of detail you could know if you are yourself Irish and have been there. (cited in *ibid.* 83)

Tactics - Targeting the Audience

The differential targeting of some messages implies that the NIIS recognizes and exploits the varying work routines of different groups of journalists. It operates what we might call a 'hierarchy of access'. However, this general hierarchy is traversed by media type and by professional and personal relationships. For example, there have periodically been complaints from writing journalists that better facilities are offered to broadcast journalists. Indeed, in late 1981 the then Northern Ireland Secretary Jim Prior was threatened with a news black out by the National Union of Journalists if the practice continued (*Belfast Telegraph*, 30 September 1981; *Sunday World*, 1 November 1981). Additionally, there are clear differences within as well as between media types, for example, between news reporters and features writers or tv documentary-makers. Journalists may move between different positions as their careers progress or they may be simultaneously working in more than one capacity. The relationship of any given group of journalists with the NIO is also constantly in flux. Nevertheless it is possible to categorize four main politico-geographical groups of journalists who are treated in distinct ways in relation to the hierarchy operated by the Information Service: Dublin journalists; local journalists, who work for regional newspapers or broadcast outlets; journalists for London-based media outlets (including both Belfast and London resident news reporters and TV current affairs and documentary-makers); international journalists both London- and home-based.

Dublin

Carrying on a tradition which goes back at least thirty years, Dublin journalists seem to be the least favoured of all those who cover the situation in Northern Ireland. This can perhaps best be illustrated by the treatment accorded to Garret Fitzgerald, the former Taoiseach (Prime Minister) of the Republic of Ireland, when he worked as a journalist. In 1960 the NIIS was approached by Fitzgerald in his position as the Dublin correspondent of the *Financial Times* for information on economic affairs in Northern Ireland. The Information Service was not keen and tried to exert pressure on the *Financial Times* to drop Fitzgerald in favour of their existing Northern Ireland correspondent, who unsurprisingly worked for a unionist paper in Belfast. The director of the Information Service was moved to write a memorandum for the Cabinet Publicity Committee of the Northern Ireland government giving details of Fitzgerald's background and arguing that:

> Any Dublin writer wishing to become a commentator on Northern affairs should be discouraged as far as can tactfully be managed and that no special arrangements should be made to supply him with press releases. The fact that Fitzgerald is a very able economist and writer and that he has got a firm foothold in the *Financial Times* and the *Economist* Intelligence Unit as well as a link with overseas papers makes it all the more important that we should keep our services to him to a minimum in an effort to restrict his scope to the South. Whatever about economics being non-political, Fitzgerald's viewpoint and sympathies are Southern and this must colour all his writings. (Public Record Office of Northern Ireland CAB9F/123/72 Memo from Eric Montgomery, 18 March 1960)

The publicity committee chaired by the Prime Minister Basil Brooke agreed with the Director of Information and concluded that: 'the Director should continue to provide only the basic minimum co-operation with Dublin writers as at present'. (PRONI CAB9F/123/72. Minutes of 97th Cabinet Publicity Committee meeting, 23 March 1960)

In the last twenty years there have been many allegations from Dublin journalists that they are denied information given to others. When the Director of Information Services tried to set up a lobby system in the mid-1970s it was Dublin journalists who got the blame for breaking it up. From the point of view of the NIO, a group lobby system was impossible because while: 'the locals and to a great extent the Nationals obeyed the rules ... there were others, particularly from the South of Ireland who simply didn't obey the rules and you got shopped' (interview with author, August 1989). The practice of the Information Service has been shaped by the perception that Dublin journalists are more likely to be critical of the NIO. They are, in effect, a lost cause. This perception is related to the history of the Information Service as much as it is to the practice of Dublin journalists. In 1970, for example, four new appointments were made to the Information Service. Three of the four were reported as having family connections with either the ruling Unionist party or with existing information officers. *Private Eye* reported scathingly that their job would be 'to tell the world that the days of Government-sponsored favouritism, discrimination and nepotism are over' (2 February 1970). By 1972 there was apparently only one Catholic member of staff in the Information Service (*Irish News*, 9 May, 1972) The NIO, perhaps more than any other government department has had great continuity of staffing in its press office. In 1987 when the director, David Gilliland, retired, the top four posts at Stormont were occupied by information officers who had been in the Information Service since at least 1970 when the Northern Ireland government was still in existence. Nevertheless one experienced British journalist has recounted his 'shock' when he encountered 'what I would call racism from the Northern Ireland Office in the way they spoke about Dublin journalists ... Oh "it's him from another country" sort of old-fashioned Protestant racism really. Their calls aren't returned. I witnessed that' (interview with author, January 1991). [...]

Local vs British journalists

When journalists who work for media in the north of Ireland are denied access by the NIO it is often in favour of journalists working for British national outlets, particularly TV current affairs or lobby journalists. I will therefore deal with local and British journalists together. Because the audience for the local media is by and large limited to Northern Ireland a journalist on a local paper is likely to be well down the hierarchy of access of the Information Service. As one senior information officer related:

> Local journalists with the best will in the world are simply local journalists. Their interests are in the Northern Ireland scene and just occasionally they will ask, how is Northern Ireland going to be affected by nuclear legislation, or whatever, and so briefings for local journalists were simply about the nitty gritty of everyday Secretary of State and Ministerial life and there was never any deep political probing ... I haven't met one single Northern Ireland journalist who was worth five minutes of my time. (interview with author, August 1989)

In an early, and less than subtle, example of the practice that goes with this view, recounted here by Henry Kelly, William Whitelaw's PR officer Keith McDowall, attempted to exclude all but correspondents for London papers.

> For several days towards the end of last week, Mr McDowall gave confidential 'lobby' briefings about what the Secretary of State had been doing during the day. But these were confined to English reporters only. No Belfast based papers were invited to send reporters, never mind Dublin based Irish dailies or evenings. (*Irish Times*, 6 April 1972)

Local journalists often resent this treatment. Some protest to the NIO about the facilities they are offered. For example, in 1989 one Belfast-based journalist proposed a TV programme which would have involved filming on patrol with the Ulster Defence Regiment (UDR). Following initial briefings the proposal was apparently referred to the top of the UDR and then to the NIO, who turned it down. Some months after this BBC1's

Panorama team were allowed the access to the UDR denied to the local journalists. But they did not come up with a cosy portrait, suggesting instead that members of the UDR have close links with loyalist paramilitaries. The programme revealed that at least 197 members of the overwhelmingly Protestant regiment had been convicted for 'terrorist', sectarian or other serious offences, including seventeen convicted of murder (*Panorama*, BBC1, 19 February 1990). *Panorama* also revealed that only NCOs and above are briefed on loyalist paramilitary suspects, 'on the grounds that if the Other Ranks were given the information they would tip off the suspects' (*Observer* 25 February 1991). The Secretary of State for Northern Ireland, Peter Brooke, was moved to write to the UDR commanding officer and release the letter to the press, arguing in morale-boosting fashion that the programme was a smear on the whole regiment (*Guardian*, 20 February 1990). The access given to *Panorama* led to complaints to the NIO by local journalists. One recounted: 'My argument was that we were much more sympathetic to the local situation, from whatever side, simply because we knew the nuances and the delicacies of the situation much better' (interview with author, August 1990).

The proximity of local journalists to the NIIS means that they are much more often in touch with it as a regular source than journalists who work for network current affairs programmes. Because of their work-cycle with daily deadlines, news reporters on the three Belfast dailies are more frequently in touch with their major sources than their colleagues who work on BBC Northern Ireland or Ulster Television current affairs programmes or even on the Belfast Sunday press. Local daily news reporters tell of their daily routine involving the regular 'ring-round' of sources and half-hourly 'check calls' to the police press office.

This close daily contact for staple items of news and the latest events to follow up means that the availability of a regular flow of news items is more crucial on a day-to-day basis. This often means that British or overseas journalists view local journalists as more easily manipulated. As one London-based television producer put it:

> Sometimes you do upset them [the NIO], and we can afford then to let them go and not talk to them for a year, that's happened ... If you're local, you have to deal with them on a daily basis, you can't do it. Therefore the room for manipulation and abuse by the Northern Ireland Office with local journalists is much more acute. (interview with author, January 1991)

Indeed, in his study of the Information Service, Hardy found that, over a three-month period, the three Belfast dailies used between 57 and 68 per cent of NIO press releases as the basis for news stories (Hardy 1983: 49), and that the transformation process they were put through was often slight. As he has related:

Attached to each press release there are things called Notes to Editors, which are supposed to be a government analysis of its own facts and figures and quite often I found that, in fact very often, you have journalists using these Notes to Editors as their own analysis. (*Hard News*, Channel Four, 19 October 1989)

When access is denied to local journalists, it may be in favour of London-based media outlets, with the emphasis on television current affairs programmes. In the hierarchy of access, media outlets which cover all of the 'United Kingdom' are more important for many messages. But public opinion in general may sometimes be an incidental target for image-conscious ministers. The suspicion of thwarted local journalists is that Northern Ireland ministers, none of whom are actually elected by Northern Ireland voters, can sometimes be more interested in their profile in government or in their own political party or constituency than the content of the message. More centrally, though, the local media in the six counties of Northern Ireland is not read by the British establishment or the 'opinion formers' which the Information Service targets.

But 'national' newspapers are not such a captive market for regular press releases. Because they devote less coverage to Northern Ireland they are also likely to put a press statement through a greater process of transformation before it hits the paper. Other researchers have pointed out that journalists throw most press releases in the bin (Tiffen 1989: 74), but it also depends on which journalists and whose press releases they are.

In London being frozen out from a particular government department is not nearly as great a hardship as it is in Belfast. According to some journalists this *relative* lack of power is recognized by the Information Service who are 'more cautious' with London journalists 'because [the journalists] would write the story of how the Northern Ireland Office tried to manipulate me. [The Information Service] don't want that story. They are very sophisticated in their judgement' (interview with author, January 1991). Nevertheless, this does not mean that British reporting *is* more critical than local reporting. Some researchers have pointed to the relative openness and higher proportion of political news in the local news media compared with national news (Elliot 1977). Indeed, Belfast-based journalists (on the local media as well as for London outlets) are often sceptical about their London-based colleagues' lack of knowledge about Irish events or the ease with which they are taken in by official briefings. In this view London journalists who fly in for irregular and brief assignments are referred to as 'fire brigade' units or 'parachutists'. [...]

The point is not whether journalists on national media do or do not push harder for information, nor is it a question of which group of journalists are the 'best'. These differences between the various local and national media can be partly explained by the strategies and priorities of sources like the NIO which release information selectively. Thus a front-page lead on

Northern Ireland in the *Belfast Telegraph* might not be accepted by the *Daily Telegraph* which would require a different type of Northern Ireland story to feature it on the front page.

International journalists

A final key area of interest for the NIO is international opinion. Information work for journalists from other countries involves additional tactics not used for British or Irish journalists as well as messages which emphasize more heavily the 'positive aspects' of Northern Ireland.

Interest in overseas journalists is again subject to a hierarchy of access. Journalists from western countries are seen as more important than journalists from what was the eastern bloc or the Third World. Indeed, journalists from eastern Europe have, on occasion, even been refused official cooperation and prevented from setting foot in Northern Ireland. At the time of the H-Block protests two Soviet journalists were told by the British authorities that they were 'unfortunately unable to make available the facilities for interviews at the time requested and, in these circumstances ... it was probably best that they should not make the trip' (*Irish Times*, 19 March 1980). Even among western journalists degrees of access can depend on the importance to the British government of the country they are from. French and German journalists, for example, are higher up the priority list than their counterparts from Norway, Denmark, Sweden or Finland. When confronted with a Scandinavian TV crew, one information officer explained:

> That gave me a real pain in the head, because I had no interest in what Sweden or Norway thought. I really didn't care, because it wasn't going to affect the situation of HMG one little bit... But Paris is different. French, Germans, in particular Parisian journalists, I used to make a fair bit of time for. (interview with author, August 1989)

But the main target for information efforts overseas has long been the United States of America. This is because of the large Irish-American community in the United States and its effect through elections and lobbying on United States politics. America is an ally and can exert some influence on British government policy. It is also because the republican movement has many supporters in the United States. One information officer explained the thinking of the Information Service:

> The prime target as far as I was concerned were American journalists, because they were the people ... we had to get to ... because they really could influence policy in terms of [the] United Kingdom. Because here was the leading nation in the Western world and if the US government had thought that the United Kingdom was wrong in their policy towards Ireland ... then somehow one had to

get the opinion formers onside. And so I devoted a great deal of my time to the American journalists ... to see if we couldn't possibly influence opinion there. And if you could influence the media then you could influence the senators, Congress and, eventually perhaps, the White House. (interview with author, August 1989)

In London the major targets among American reporters were the heads of bureaux because:

I took the view that ... they were high flyers in their own papers and if one got to know them while they were in London and if you never sold them a bum steer - some day somewhere at some time you might get to see them in America when they were bigger guys ... And I must say that proved a very effective thing to do. (interview with author, August 1989)

Activities in the United States

In the United States itself editorial boards of the major newspapers and business people have been the most visible targets of information officers and politicians. One typical journey for Tom King, when he was secretary of state, took him from 'the World Trade Centre, where he hosted a lunch for businessmen in the 107th-floor restaurant, downtown to meet the editorial board of the *New York Times*' (McKittrick 1989: 21). The targeting of editorial writers, rather than news journalists who visit Northern Ireland more routinely, has meant many trips by successive secretaries of state to the United States accompanied by press officers and other officials. In the view of the Information Service this tactic has been a great success. The long-time director of the Information Service, David Gilliland, has argued that:

Although the wire service reporting of events in Northern Ireland still tends to concentrate on the sensational, the *editorial* comment which is very important in the United States in the more serious newspapers and indeed on television and radio displays a much greater understanding of the problems and a greater sympathy with the policies of Her Majesty's Government than was apparent in previous times ... Where, as we frequently have done, we have sat down and patiently explained the background to the problems and the policy measures that have been adopted, we have found a sympathetic and responsive audience and that has been reflected in editorial comment throughout the United States. (Gilliland 1983: 7)

Discussion - Problems of Containment

I have argued that the approach of the NIIS embodies the dual strategy of the British state to the Northern Ireland problem. There are a variety of public relations techniques available to any organization, but while I have not explored many of the techniques used by the NIO, I have tried to explore the broad tactical way in which they are used. However, even the most powerful source cannot always be guaranteed the profile in the media that it would like. The NIO experiences many problems in its encounters with the media even at the broadest level of strategy. While strategy is inflected according to the government in power or in relation to the balance of forces at any given time, there is a sense in which the major contradiction at the heart of NIO public relations remains the same. It is to this problem that I now turn.

Figure 5 The Terror and the Tears: British officials thought it distasteful

There is a practical difficulty for media strategies in the dual approach which simultaneously emphasizes the 'wickedness of terrorism' and a 'community on the move'. There is evidence that this was recognized by the NIO in the month of its creation in March 1972. The first (and last) major piece of propaganda produced by the NIIS for the Unionist government was a booklet, *The Terror and The Tears* (Figure 5). It was published in March 1972 in the aftermath of Bloody Sunday when British troops shot and killed thirteen unarmed civil rights marchers. In the words of one information officer: 'We thought that the IRA were being portrayed as freedom fighters - glamour boys in trench coats. We hope this dossier will show them to be what they really are - thugs with blood dripping from their hands' (*Daily Mirror*, 4 March 1972). The sixteen-page booklet did this with a series of photographs of victims of the IRA.[9] Around 100,000 copies were printed with the Unionist government ordering a further 150,000 just before Direct Rule was introduced (*Irish Times*, 22 March 1972). One hundred and twenty thousand copies were distributed much to the apparent 'distaste' (*The Times*, 27 August 1974) of the British government, which ceased general distribution of the booklet from 24 March, the very day of the introduction of Direct Rule. Loftus reports that advertisers were then 'restrained' by a government/army/police committee which believed that 'at times overstressing security gave the government a poor image and that it was advisable to soft pedal' (Loftus 1980: 73).

More recently in a rare public speech in 1983 the then director of the Information Service spelt out the tensions within their approach:

> If we are to impress upon people abroad that the channelling of money or equipment to organisations within the province on one side of the community or the other which will contribute to violence is wrong, then we do have to show publicly the uses to which that money or equipment is put. By doing so we run the risk of leading people in industry or business to conclude that Northern Ireland is not a sufficiently stable community within which to commit their resources. It is a very real dilemma. (Gilliland 1983: 7)

In practice the attempt to resolve this dilemma is to emphasize that the 'terrorists' are only a tiny minority. It was something of an embarrassment then, when in the early 1980s Sinn Féin started contesting elections and winning around 40 per cent of the nationalist vote. Despite these difficulties of strategy the NIO and other official sources (most notably the RUC) continue to promote the anti-terrorist image. It is therefore somewhat disingenuous of the NIO to omit to mention their role in the creation of the 'bad image' of Northern Ireland when they argue that 'the violent images that have shaped the world's perception of the Province have also made it more difficult to achieve economic and industrial regeneration' (NIO 1989: 44).

Conclusion

While there may be a range of techniques and tactics available to source organizations, the evidence here suggests that the particular tactics used depends partly on the aim and strategy of the source rather than on which techniques are available. Some research attempts to catalogue the skills and stratagems sources use (even if they explicitly reject such an approach) (Chibnall 1977; Tiffen 1989). But these general pictures of the available range tend to see the media as homogeneous and do not differentiate between the different audience agendas which sources attempt to influence. We have seen that the NIO adopts quite distinct strategies and themes for dealing with distinct groups of journalists and operates what I have called a hierarchy of access.

One advantage of an approach which analyses the strategies of particular government departments or power blocs in parallel to considerations of their media profile is that we can much more clearly assess their relative strengths and, at least as importantly, their relative weaknesses (Bruck 1989). This approach also allows for a consideration of the *developing* strategy of the NIO and moves us away from the narrow and static snapshot which is the result of some theoretical approaches based on content analysis.

The NIO does not just highlight violence. They also want 'good news' coverage which does not automatically fit with the news values operated by many media outlets. In other words there are real problems and dilemmas of strategy for the NIO. In addition there are a number of factors which potentially limit the ability of the NIO to dominate the news in all the ways they would wish.

More broadly, though, the fact that the war is not called a war is testament to the power of official sources. The NIO is not above the fray. Instead it has pursued a strategy which bolsters certain conceptions of the conflict and marginalizes others, such that certain solutions follow. The presentation of Britain as neutral in the conflict is part of a deliberate counterinsurgency strategy in which the NIIS plays a key role. However successful the Information Service is in managing the media, in the end the political problem of the legitimacy of the state remains. It is precisely this problem which the information management of the NIO attempts to obscure. In as much as it is a diversion from the question of legitimacy the strategy of containment is itself a major obstacle to peace in Ireland.

Acknowledgements

Thanks to all the journalists, information officers, civil servants and other sources who spared the time to talk to me. Thanks to Robert Bell and Bern Kane at the Linenhall Library in Belfast for being a continuous mine of information and to Kevin McNamara MP. Thanks also to Kevin Williams, Liz Curtis and Mike Tomlinson and my colleagues at Glasgow University, John Eldridge, Jenny Kitzinger, Greg Philo and Jacquie Reilly, for comments on earlier drafts. Finally, thanks to the Deputy Keeper of the Records, Public Record Office of Northern Ireland for permission to publish from Crown papers.

Endnotes

1. These findings are based on over fifty interviews and conversations with, first, former and serving civil servants and information officers in the Northern Ireland Office, Foreign and Commonwealth Office (FCO), Central Office of Information (COI) and Ministry of Defence and, second, journalists from media outlets in Belfast, Dublin, London and internationally. I have also drawn on newspaper cuttings and other documents including publicity material and press releases issued by the NIO, COI and the FCO.

2. Details of expenditure in 1989-90 are as follows:

    NIO
    'Press, PR and advertising'   £12,276,545
    Industrial Development Board
    'Promotional expenses'   £5,234,000
    Northern Ireland Tourist Board
    'Press and public relations'   £976,181
    Total spending   **£18,486,726**

    Adding the spending of the IDB and tourist board to the press and PR spending of the Department of Economic Development (DED) (£3,477.000), the department concerned both with running IDB and countering the MacBride principles campaign in the United States gives a total of £9,687,181 which is over half the total of NIO spending. Obviously we should be cautious about these figures because those given for advertising by NIO are not broken down by department, nor is there any indication of the use to which other funds are put. Additionally the only data available on the RUC, recently released in a parliamentary answer, is not comparable. The RUC press office was merged with its command centre in 1982 to create the Force Control and Information Centre (FCIC) and figures given do not indicate the amount of expenditure specifically on press and PR work. The figures given are an estimate for the whole of FCIC and cover the whole year of 1989 rather than the financial year 1989-90. The figure for advertising is given for the financial year:

    Royal Ulster Constabulary
    Force Control and Information Centre   £2,380,000
    Advertising   £22,000

    (Sources: *Hansard* 2 April 1990, col. 451-2: Industrial Development Board, Northern Ireland 1990: 93; Northern Ireland Tourist Board 1990: 21; *Hansard* 9 December 1991, col. 454-5).

3. Publicity broadsheets were a favoured form of communication with journalists and others in the 1970s. During the time of the H-Block crisis a large number of glossy booklets and fact-sheets were issued (see NIO 1980a, 1980b, 1981a, 1981b, 1981c, 1981d), but more recently less of such material has emerged (see

NIO 1985a, 1985b). What has been published has mainly followed a theme of normalization in playing down violence and emphasizing the 'nicer' side of Northern Ireland (NIIS n.d.; NIIS/Arts Council of Northern Ireland 1985; NIO 1989). Much 'grey' propaganda in the form of unattributable briefing papers is also issued, mainly produced by the Foreign and Commonwealth Office (see for example, FCO 1981, 1983, 1984, 1986a, 1988b).

4. Thanks to Mike Tomlinson for this observation.

5. Thus a January 1988 briefing document, 'The Provisional IRA: international contacts outside the United States', from the information department of the FCO includes information about support groups in, for example, the Netherlands. Some of this information was then reproduced by counterinsurgency journalist Christopher Dobson (see *Irish Independent*, 2 May 1988; *Daily Telegraph,* 3 May 1988; cf. Dobson and Payne 1982). Much of the information was inaccurate and the Foreign Office was forced to withdraw some of it. British author Liz Curtis was among those named in the document (see Curtis 1984). Although inaccurate information about her was withdrawn, the Foreign Office refused to remove her name from the briefing, thus smearing her as an 'international contact' of the IRA (*Guardian*, 11 May 1988; *New Statesman and Society*, 1 July 1988).

6. This phrase is an inversion the Irish republican slogan 'Tiocfaidh ar la!', which translates as 'Our day will come!'.

7. An updated version of *Northern Ireland Chronicle* was made after the signing of the Anglo-Irish Agreement in 1985 and is still in the catalogue of the London Television Service at the COI which produces films for the FCO to distribute overseas.

8. This briefing document which is ostensibly anonymously produced was among others circulated to selected journalists. Pages 119-24 of Barzilay's *British Army in Ulster*, vol. 1 (1973) are lifted almost verbatim from the IRD-produced document, sometimes with only spelling mistakes or typographical errors to distinguish it from the original (see also *Time Out*, 14-20 October 1977 - thanks to Duncan Campbell for pointing out these passages). IRD subsequently became the Overseas Information Department and then the Information Department. The present day Information Department still produces 'grey' propaganda material similar to that produced by IRD. See Bloch and Fitzgerald 1983; Dorril and Ramsay 1990; Fletcher 1982; Smith 1979 for material on IRD.

9. Although not all of the victims were actually killed or injured by the IRA. A photo of the bombing of McGurks bar was included. McGurks was bombed by a loyalist group, but was blamed on the IRA by the army and police (see Curtis 1984: 91-2 for a full account). *The Terror and the Tears* is introduced with photographs of two very young children, one catholic, the other Protestant, who are described as 'only two of the tragic victims of the indiscriminate terrorism of the IRA. Altogether 252 people have died. Hundreds more have been injured, some of them seriously'. There is no mention of deaths caused by either loyalist groups or by the army/RUC, although these accounted for a significant portion of the 252 dead. The message is plain - any violence is the work of the IRA, the army only responds to the situation.

References

Barzilay, David, *The British Army in Ulster*, vol. 1, Belfast, Century Services, 1973.

Bloch, Jonathon and Fitzgerald, Patrick, *British Intelligence and Covert Action*, London, Junction Books, 1983.

Bruck, Peter, 'Strategies for peace, strategies for news research', *Journal of Communication* 39(1),winter 1989, pp. 108-29.

Chibnall, Steve, *Law and Order News*, London, Tavistock, 1977.

Clutterbuck, Richard, *The Media and Political Violence*, London, Macmillan, 1981.

Cockerell, Michael, Hennessy, Peter and Walker, David, *Sources Close to the Prime Minister*, London, Macmillan, 1984.

Commons Expenditure Committee, *First Report from the Expenditure Committee: Accommodation and Staffing in Ottawa and Washington*, 22 November, HC 29 London, HMSO, 1973.

Corner, John, 'Meaning, genre and context: the problematics of "public knowledge" in the new audience studies', in James Curran and Michael Gurevitch (eds) *Mass Media and Society*, London, Edward Arnold, 1991.

Curtis, Liz, *Ireland: The Propaganda War*, London, Pluto Press, 1984.

Dobson, Christopher and Payne, Ronald, *Terror! The West Fights Back*, London, Macmillan, 1982.

Dorril, Stephen and Ramsay, Robin, 'In a common cause: the anticommunist crusade in Britain, 1945-60', *Lobster* 19, May 1990, pp. 1-8.

Elliot, Philip, 'Reporting Northern Ireland: a study of news in Britain, Ulster and the Irish Republic', in UNESCO (ed.) *Media and Ethnicity*, Paris, UNESCO, 1977.

Ericson, Richard, Baranek, Patricia and Chan, Janet, *Negotiating Control: A Study of News Sources*, Milton Keynes, Open University Press, 1989.

Evelegh, Robin, *Peace-Keeping in a Democratic Society: The Lessons of Northern Ireland*, London, Hurst and Co., 1978.

Fletcher, Richard, 'British propaganda since World War 11- a case study', *Media, Culture and Society* 4, 1982: 97-109.

Foreign and Commonwealth Office, 'Irish terrorism's overseas supporters', *Greyband Brief*, October 1981.

– 'The IRA and Noraid', *Greyband Brief*, October 1983.

– 'Libya and Irish terrorism', *Background Brief*, June 1984.

– 'Libya Second International Conference Against Imperialism', *Background Brief*, April 1986 (a).

– 'Qadhafi and Irish terrorism', *Background Brief*, April 1986 (b).

– 'Libya: external relations and activities', *Background Brief*, October 1988 (a).

– 'The Provisional IRA: international contacts outside the United States', *Background Brief*, January 1988 (b).

Gaffikin, Frank and Morrissey, Michael, *Northern Ireland: The Thatcher Years*, London, Zed Press, 1990.

George, Alexander (ed.), *Western State Terrorism*, Cambridge, Polity Press, 1991.

Gilliland, David, speech to Meeting of the Belfast Chamber of Commerce and Industry, Forum Hotel, Belfast, 31 January 1983.

Hardy, Eamon, 'Primary definition' by the state: an analysis of the Northern Ireland Information Service as reported in the Northern Ireland press', unpublished dissertation, Queen's University, Belfast, 1983.

Herman, Edward and O'Sullivan, Gerry, *The Terrorism Industry*, New York, Pantheon, 1989.

– '"Terrorism"' as ideology and cultural industry', in Alexander George (ed.) *Western State Terrorism*, Cambridge, Polity Press, 1991.

Hooper, Alan, *The Military and the Media*, Aldershot, Avebury, 1982.

Industrial Development Board, Northern Ireland, *Annual Report and Accounts,* 1989-1990, Belfast, IDB, 1990.

Jenkins, Philip, 'Whose terrorists?' Libya and state criminality', *Contemporary Crises*, 12, 1988: 5-24.

Jenkins, Simon and Sloman, Anne, *With Respect Ambassador: An Inquiry into the Foreign Office*, London, BBC, 1985.

Kitson, Frank, *Low Intensity Operations,* London, Faber and Faber, 1971.

– *Warfare as a whole,* London, Faber and Faber, 1987.

Loftus, Belinda, 'Images for sale: government and security advertising in Northern Ireland, 1968-1978', *Oxford Art Journal,* October 1980: 70-80.

McGuire, Maria, *To Take Arms: A Year in the Provisional IRA*, London, Quartet 1973.

McKinley, Michael, 'The Irish Republican Army and terror international: an inquiry into the material aspects of the first fifteen years', in P. Wilkinson and A. Stewart (eds), *Contemporary Research on Terrorism*, Aberdeen, Aberdeen University Press, 1987.

McKittrick, David, *Dispatches from Belfast*, Belfast, Blackstaff, 1989.

Margach, James, *The Abuse of Power*, London, W. H. Allen, 1978.

Miller, David, 'Understanding "Terrorism": Contrasting audience interpretations of the televised conflict in Ireland', in M. Aldridge and N. Hewitt (eds), *Controlling Broadcasting: Access, Policy and Practice in North America and Europe*, Manchester, Manchester University Press, 1993.

– *Don't Mention the War: Northern Ireland, Propaganda and the Media*, London, Pluto, 1994.

Northern Ireland Information Service, *Northern Ireland Observed*, Belfast, NIIS, n.d.

Northern Ireland Information Service/Arts Council of Northern Ireland, *Images: Arts and People in Northern Ireland*, March, Belfast, NIIS/Arts Council, 1985.

Northern Ireland Office, *H-blocks: The Facts*, October, Belfast, NIO, 1980 (a).

– *H-blocks: The Reality*, November, Belfast, NIO, 1980 (b).

– *Day to Day, Life in Northern Ireland Prisons*, March, Belfast, NIO, 1981 (a).

– *H-blocks: What the Papers Say*, July, Belfast, NIO, 1981 (b).

– *Scope for Further Improvements in Prison Life*, July, Belfast, NIO, 1981 (c).

– *The Tragedy of Terrorism*, October, Belfast, NIO, 1981 (d).

– *Armagh Prison Strip Searching: The Facts*, Belfast, NIO, 1985 (a).

– *Life Sentence Prisoners in Northern Ireland: An Explanatory Memorandum*, January, Belfast, NIO, 1985 (b).

– '*The Day of the Men and Women of Peace Must Surely Come ...*', July, Belfast, NIO, 1989.

Northern Ireland Tourist Board, *Annual Report*, 1989, vol. 42, Belfast, NITB, 1990.

Obair, The Campaign For Employment in West Belfast, 'US investment in the North of Ireland', *Briefing Paper No. 5*, June, Belfast, 1991.

Odling-Smee, James, 'Making histories', *Fortnight*, September 1989: 14-15.

O'Dowd, Liam, Rolston, Bill and Tomlinson, Mike, *Northern Ireland: Between Civil Rights and Civil War*, London, CSE Books, 1980.

Prior, James, *Balance of Power*, London, Hamish Hamilton, 1986.

Rolston, Bill, 'Containment and its failure: the British state and the control of conflict in Northern Ireland', in Alexander George (ed.), *Western State Terrorism*, Cambridge, Polity Press, 1991.

Schlesinger, Philip, 'On the scope and shape of counterinsurgency thought', in G. Littlejohn et al. (eds), *Power and the State*, London, Croom Helm, 1978.

– '"Terrorism", the media and the liberal-democratic state: a critique of the orthodoxy', *Social Research*, 48 (1), spring 1981: 74-99.

Smith, Lyn, 'Covert British propaganda: the Information Research Department: 1917-1977', *Millennium: Journal of International Studies*, 9 (1), 1979: 67-83.

Sterling, Claire, *The Terror Network*, New York, Holt, Rhinehart Winston/Reader's Digest, 1981.

Sunday Times Insight Team, *Ulster*, Harmondsworth, Penguin, 1972.

Taylor, Peter, 'The unanswered questions about the IRA's Libyan connection', *Listener*, 3 March 1988: 4-5.

Tiffen, Rodney, *News and Power*, Sydney, Allen and Unwin, 1989.

Tugwell, Maurice, 'Revolutionary propaganda and the role of the information services in counter-insurgency operations', *Canadian Defence Quarterly* 3, autumn 1973: 27-31.

– 'Politics and propaganda of the Provisional IRA', *Terrorism* 5 (1-2), 1981: 13-40.

– 'Terrorism and propaganda: problem and response', in P. Wilkinson and A. Stewart (eds) *Contemporary Research on Terrorism*, Aberdeen, Aberdeen University Press, 1987.

Wilkinson, Paul, *Terrorism and the Liberal State*, London, Macmillan, 1977.

Section Three Introduction: Censorship

In Britain throughout the 1970s and early 1980s the debate about censorship and Northern Ireland surfaced periodically. Yet for most of this period direct state censorship in the classical sense did not exist. Instead, there were a variety of ways in which pressure was exerted. **Bill Rolston** surveys the British and Irish approaches to policing the media in the first piece in this section. He details the variety of laws which can be used against the media and the techniques of state pressure and intimidation, together with the evolution of processes of self-censorship.

In the Republic of Ireland from the mid-1970s and in Britain from 1988 direct censorship did exist in the form of restrictions on interviewing representatives of political and paramilitary organisations. **David Miller** examines the lineage of the British broadcasting ban, while **Betty Purcell** narrates the history and explains the workings of Section 31 of the Republic's Broadcasting Act.

Since these pieces were written, both the British and Irish bans have been lifted. Following a ruling of the United Nations Human Rights Committee in July 1993 that Section 31 contravened Article 19 of the International Covenant on Civil and Political Rights, the order was allowed to lapse in January 1994. RTE, the Republic's state-appointed broadcasting authority, then immediately introduced a 'reference-upwards' system to govern Sinn Féin appearances (see O'Farrell 1994). The decision to withdraw Section 31 was also made in the context of the then emergent 'peace process', which, somewhat later, led to the lifting of the British ban. On 16 September 1994, two weeks after the IRA ceasefire, John Major announced in Belfast that the ban was to be lifted.

> I believe the restrictions are no longer serving the purpose for which they were intended... Most importantly, we are now in very different circumstances from those of 1988 when the restrictions originally came in.

The peace process has had a marked impact on the coverage of Sinn Féin, but although direct censorship is gone, other pressures remain to constrain broadcasting (see Miller 1995). The known effect of both censorship and other pressures on particular programmes is listed in the final piece in this section. It reproduces **Liz Curtis**' meticulous compilation of programmes on Ireland which were banned, censored or delayed on the British networks between 1959 and 1993.

References

Miller, David. 'The media and Northern Ireland: Censorship, information management and the broadcasting ban', in Greg Philo (ed), *The Glasgow Media Group Reader, Volume II*, London, Routledge, 1995

O'Farrell, John. 'Sectional interests', *Fortnight*, no. 325, February 1994: 16

15.

Bill Rolston

POLITICAL CENSORSHIP

(Originally delivered to conference at Trinity College, Dublin, January 1993; published in E. Hazelkorn and P. Smith (eds), *Let in the Light: Censorship, Secrecy and Democracy*, Dingle, Co. Kerry, Brandon Books, 1993, pages 161-168)

The Troubles in Northern Ireland are at the core of censorship policy in these islands. Philip Schlesinger, a sociologist who researched the BBC and wrote a definitive book on media coverage of Northern Ireland in 1978, said:

> Ministerial intervention has been elusive and there was nothing in the BBC's approach to editorial control which approximated to the popular image regarding classic totalitarian censorship with its directives and specially planted supervisory personnel.

While Schlesinger is not suggesting this, there is a danger of concluding from this that the term 'censorship' only applies to the classic totalitarian form. I am arguing that there are more subtle and often more efficient ways of censorship in democratic societies and the case of broadcasting in these islands shows that very clearly. These laws have been mentioned often. It seems to me that the states in Ireland and Britain have enough legal instruments at their disposal to ensure that something approximating classic totalitarian censorship of broadcasting could actually exist. If we start with Britain in Northern Ireland, there is direct legal regulation of broadcasting through the BBC licensing agreement and the Broadcasting Act of 1981. There is also legislation not directly designed to control broadcasting but which can affect broadcasting. For example, the Official Secrets Act 1911; Section 2 created over 2,000 offences, many of which can be applied to journalists and broadcasters. Section 1 allows for prosecution for possession of material prejudicial to the security of the state. The

Northern Ireland Criminal Law Act 1967 makes it an offence for anyone, including a journalist or broadcaster, to refuse to give information to the police which the latter may wish to know. The British Contempt of Court Act 1981 prohibits the disclosure of any information or speculation which might be prejudicial to a current or pending court case. The Police and Criminal Evidence Act 1984, in Britain, says that the police can seize documents. Journalistic material is specifically excluded from that power; however, photographs are not and, in particular, photographs of any public event - for example, a march or a demonstration.

In Britain and Northern Ireland there is emergency legislation which can be used against broadcasters and journalists. The two most obvious acts are the Emergency Provisions Act 1978, which prohibits collecting, recording, publishing or attempting to elicit information, including photographs, concerning the army, police, judges, court officials or prison officers which could be of use to terrorists. The Prevention of Terrorism Act 1989 says that citizens have a duty to tell the police anything which might prevent an act of terrorism or might help the police apprehend a terrorist.

In the Republic of Ireland, the Broadcasting Act 1960 and amended in 1976, seeks to control broadcasters. The Wireless and Telegraphy Act and the Radio and Television Act extend these controls to the commercial sector. Beyond direct laws for broadcasters there are other laws which are usable. The Offences Against the State Act 1939 and the Defamation Act 1961 can be used against broadcasters and journalists. The Official Secrets Act 1963 was modelled on the 1911 British Act, the only difference being now that the British, realising how bad it was, updated and amended theirs in 1989. There is no contempt of court act but there is the force of Common Law, and search and seizure provisions under a number of acts such as the Offences Against the State Act.

These laws are not mere sabre rattling on the part of the states in Britain and Ireland. These laws can be and are used ... In 1971, a journalist from Britain [Bernard Falk] was jailed for four days in Northern Ireland under contempt of court legislation for refusing to identify someone he had interviewed as being the person before the court. The Official Secrets Act in Britain has been used against civil servants, but also against journalists such as Duncan Campbell and others in 1979 who were, interestingly, charged not just under Section 2 - possession of official information - but under Section 1 - treason. In fact, the Section 1 case collapsed, and under Section 2 they received very light sentences. But that is not the point.

Emergency legislation has been used in Northern Ireland to detain broadcasters and journalists and, in particular, photographers. A fairly recent example was in 1988: a German freelance photographer, Nick Vogel, was arrested under the Prevention of Terrorism Act after taking photographs of the police in action. He was charged with possession of arms, and let out on bail on condition that he would leave the country. The case was later dropped.

Use of the Prevention of Terrorism Act was threatened in an attempt to acquire film from broadcasting organisations regarding the Carrickmore IRA road block in 1979, and the killing of the two British army corporals in Andersonstown in 1988. It was successfully used to bring Channel 4 to court in 1992 over a *Dispatches* programme alleging loyalist and police collusion. A researcher for that programme, Ben Hamilton, was later arrested for perjury on the basis of an affidavit he made in that case. And finally, under the Criminal Evidence Act, it is now commonplace for police to ask for and get photographs and footage from photographers after every demonstration or march.

In the Republic, Section 31 has allowed for the dismissal of the entire RTE Authority in 1972. In 1972 Kevin O'Kelly was sentenced to three months in prison under almost identical circumstances as Bernard Falk had been in Northern Ireland - refusing to identify someone he had interviewed. It also enabled the sacking of Jenny McGeever in 1988. The Offences Against the State Act was used in 1988 to impose a five-year prison sentence on Don O'Leary for possession of a republican poster, sold openly.

There is a remarkable range of repressive legislation in Northern Ireland and Britain, and a wide and unspecific set of powers for one particular law in the South. But to play devil's advocate for a second, Section 31 and the British broadcasting ban notwithstanding, the amount of direct control of broadcasters through such repressive legislation is, on a world scale, relatively light. The laws are not designed for control of broadcasters and are rarely used to do so. When they have been used, as in the case of the Official Secrets Act in Britain, they have been remarkably ineffectual. As for legislation directed specifically at controlling broadcasters, only one broadcaster in the North and one in the South have been jailed in the entire two decades of coverage of the Northern troubles. Only two broadcasters in the South have been sacked and none in the North. Broadcasting law does not operate through the daily intervention of state censors, the daily involvement of state imposed officials in decision-making within the broadcasting organisations, or the continuous daily axing of programmes after they have been made.

This is not the stuff of classic totalitarian censorship, yet this is not the end of the story. The laws work at a number of levels to control broadcasting. First, they are a constant backdrop, influencing consciously or otherwise decision-making and distorting professional practice. Their use is frequently threatened in no uncertain terms. For example, in a series of battles between Thatcher and broadcasters in the 1980s, the use of the Prevention of Terrorism Act was frequently threatened against broadcasters and the Act was finally used in the case of Channel 4.

Second, even though the actual use of these laws has been relatively infrequent, there have been some spectacular outcomes. There are frequently differences between broadcasters and governments in any country, but as Betty Purcell has said in relation to RTE:

> In the atmosphere of daily censorship, managers learn that most conflicts blow over. Only on the sensitive subject of Northern Ireland have heads rolled and these were the most important heads in the organisation. Those of the RTE Authority itself.

Such cases act as exemplars and become part of the folk memory in broadcasting organisations. It only takes one such case every decade or so to remind everybody to be cautious.

Third, the main control of broadcasters now is through directives which are relatively imprecise, in both their content and their threatened sanctions. Section 31 and the British broadcasting ban do not operate by involving the state directly in the day to day running of these organisations. Rather they issue a blanket warning and leave both the implementation and the policing to the organisations themselves. A prime example here is the sacking of the RTE Authority in 1972. It was issued with a directive which was imprecise; it asked for further clarification, did not get it, and then when a report of an interview with Seán MacStiofáin was carried, it was sacked. In effect, the message of the state was, we will not tell you what the limits are, but we will let you know forcibly enough if and when you transgress them. Article 19, the anti-censorship organisation, refers to this as a form of prior restraint censorship: it threatens action if a ban is broken rather than responding to specific broadcasts. That is an incredibly powerful control mechanism. It works by imposing caution on the broadcasting organisations themselves. It must be remembered that there was already a high level of caution within the organisations before such directives were issued in Ireland or Britain. In a very general sense, this caution is part of the trade-off which professional journalism and broadcasting has had to make historically with the state. Its independence from the state is predicated on the promise of 'responsible behaviour'.

Additionally, caution is needed when covering the issue of violence and, particularly, violence against a state which is seen to be democratic. Caution can be relaxed a bit if consensual opinion has it that the state concerned is not democratic and even more if it is far away. Thus, Sandy Gall can rough it with the Mujahadeen in Afghanistan, but what if it is an IRA active service unit in South Armagh?

In RTE the caution was formalised and institutionalised under Section 31. In fact, ritual references to the existence of Section 31 have allowed top management in RTE to take a very inflexible line. Government directives ban interviews or reports of interviews with spokespersons of a number of organisations including Sinn Féin. But RTE has gone far beyond the spirit of the law to ban not just spokespersons but members. In addition, it has also been very quick to apply the ban to people under Section 18 of the Broadcasting Act who are not Sinn Féin members: Martin Galvin of

NORAID and Nell McCafferty. Furthermore, RTE has acted ruthlessly and almost without fail against those who have broken the rules, even inadvertently or technically. The guidelines of RTE are very threatening in this respect:

> The strictest care must be taken in these matters and action will be called for where individuals are seen to have disregarded the guidelines or to have been careless in observing them.

As Jenny McGeever found out in 1988, that was no idle threat.

How can management justify this unprecedented interference with the freedom of the media? There is a paradox here. It is they who interpret the law inflexibly. They who police the restrictions on a daily basis. They who appeal court cases which might lead to liberalisation, thus reinforcing inflexibility. They who sack the offenders, and yet they, as part of the professional ideology of broadcasters, are the ones to whom censorship is anathema. To me this is a paradox; to Wesley Boyd, Head of News, it is not. As he told the International Federation of Journalists:

> We have been told we could interpret the law more liberally. We find that by sticking to the letter we can show how stupid it is.

The end result is that there is very little scope for challenge or subversion within RTE. I refer again to Betty Purcell:

> The question automatically asked is not who is in Sinn Féin but who is definitely not in Sinn Féin.

To challenge this ritual is to run the risk of being labelled a 'Provo-lover'. The bottom line is that when this happens it is not just the grand ideals of democracy, freedom of the media or freedom of expression which are at stake, it is much more the down to earth reality of pay and promotion.

The case is somewhat different with the BBC, ITV and Channel 4. The broadcasting ban has been formalised relatively recently but it has served to emphasise that it works by emphasising a caution which is already built into the British broadcasting system over two decades. In the initial flurry of enthusiasm over civil rights, British broadcasters quickly found that covering Northern Ireland led to confrontations with the Right, both inside and outside government. After a number of run-ins, most notably and most spectacularly over a programme called 'A Question of Ulster', in late 1971, an institutionalised caution, called a reference-up system, was introduced into the BBC and ITV. All items on Northern Ireland were to be referred to high levels of management, sometimes even to Director Generals or the Independent Broadcasting Authority itself. Liz Curtis described this system:

> On virtually every other topic, programme editors, producers, and journalists are trusted to make appropriate decisions about what subjects to select and how to present them. They are expected to refer to their superiors for guidance only in cases of real doubt or difficulty. On Ireland, however, no one was to be trusted.

Roger Bolton, as a nuance to Curtis's general conclusion, claimed that such a massive amount of output meant delegation was inevitable, with referencing up only when necessary. This system did allow senior management a way out. If there was no trouble, reference up worked perfectly. If there was, they had not been sufficiently put in the picture and assistants' heads must roll.

This control, this reference-up system, covers a whole set of guidelines. BBC guidelines on the use of language are among my favourite:

> We call it the army and its personnel soldiers, not the British army or British soldiers when they are in Northern Ireland. The Irish Republican Army: it is never acceptable to call them that, it is acceptable to call them the Provisionals but never the Provos. Don't give pet names to terrorists... don't speak of IRA volunteers, we don't know why they joined.

Despite these guidelines, people like Roger Bolton, Paul Hamann and others ran into trouble at various points throughout the 1970s and 1980s. The official broadcasting line is that they won some battles and lost others; key to this folklore is a 1971 programme ['A Question of Ulster'] about which the BBC said they stood up to Tory assault and broadcast the programme anyway. But the folklore misses the point. Whether there was success or failure, each skirmish has led to increased caution, making it more difficult to make the next programme which may lead to confrontation with the state.

This leads to distorted coverage. For example, there are very few interviews with anybody who claims to speak on behalf of the IRA, INLA, etc. The last one was in 1979; before that, throughout the 1970s, there were only six each for ITN and the BBC. This extends to a lack of coverage of what Sinn Féin has to say. John Conway, former Head of BBC News in Northern Ireland, said, 'We use sparingly the opportunity we have to interview Sinn Féin members and we never forget their links to violence.'

In fact this was one of the arguments that the NUJ in Northern Ireland used in opposition to the broadcasting ban - the fact that they had not interviewed many republicans before the ban. Richard Francis, former BBC Controller in Northern Ireland, summed up the official attitude of the BBC when he said, 'We do not deal impartially with those who step outside the bounds of the law and decent social behaviour. Not only do they get very much less coverage than those who pursue their aims legitimately, but the very manner and tone that our reporters have dubbed makes our moral position quite plain.'

Finally, there is more leeway in the British legislation, in the British ban, than there is with RTE. Interestingly, that scope was underlined by the Home Office itself. The BBC fell over itself to be the most inflexible in interpreting the ban while Channel 4 pointed out initially that it also applied to works of fiction including feature films. The Home Office, however, claimed that 'genuine works of fiction were not covered by the ban' and that 'a member of an organisation can't be held to represent that organisation in all his (sic) daily activities'. Unfortunately broadcasters have not used that scope, with the exception of Mary Holland, who interviewed Gerry Adams on Channel 4's *Dispatches;* during that programme, Adams's words were spoken by Stephen Rea. Because it was so electronically synchronised that the join was unseen, it showed the ridiculousness of the ban in ways that Wesley Boyd's earlier statement does not.

To sum up. First, this may not be classic totalitarian censorship, but it is still censorship, and it works. It is a peculiarly democratic form of censorship. Second, Northern Ireland is central to this discussion. Despite all the run-ins that the British government had with broadcasters over the Belgrano, over *Spycatcher,* over Libya, over Zircon, at the core of most of these cases and the use of most of these laws is the question of Ireland. And third, censorship is derived from and enhances a censorship culture, especially in Ireland. It is not just that bans are extended beyond where they were intended to go. It is the fact that individuals and whole classes, whole communities of people are demonised and disenfranchised. The question of *The Street,* Gerry Adams's short stories, has been mentioned. In relation to RTE's refusal to advertise the book, it has been said:

> By depicting him solely as a beast, RTE is denying him his humanity and contributing to a climate of opinion whereby his murder will be welcomed.

That quote is not from *An Phoblacht,* but was written by Nick Garbutt, editor of the *Irish News.*

The measure of democracy is how society handles the extremes, not the every-day. How it encourages citizenship and a sense of belonging to minorities and those in the margins. In this sense, despite the sterling efforts of people like Roger Bolton, Ian Studdart and Mary Holland, democracy has been very badly served by the states in these islands and their respective broadcasting organisations.

16.

David Miller

THE HISTORY BEHIND A MISTAKE

(From *British Journalism Review*, 1(2), 1990, pages 34-43)

On October 19 1988 Douglas Hurd issued a notice, under section 29 (3) of the Broadcasting Act 1981 and Clause 13(4) of the BBC Licence and Agreement, restricting interviews with eleven Irish organisations. His action was widely reported as an unprecedented restriction in peace time. In one sense - the breadth of the directive in excising a whole swathe of elected opinion - it is. But the power of the Home Secretary to require the broadcasters in writing 'to refrain at any specified time or at all times from sending any matter or matters of any class', had been used on five previous occasions.

The Postmaster General issued two notices on November 15 1926. The first forbids 'any broadcast matter expressing the opinion of the Corporation on current affairs or on matters of public policy.' (*BBC Handbook* 1956, p. 12) It is now clause 13(7) of the Licence and Agreement. The second notice directed the BBC to refrain from broadcasting on matters of political, industrial or religious controversy. The next two notices were introduced on July 27, 1955 by the then Postmaster General, Charles Hill, the late Lord Hill. The 'Fourteen Day Rule' was a restriction which prevented the discussion of any matter likely to be debated in Parliament in the succeeding fortnight. The rule which the BBC had 'imposed upon itself' (*BBC Handbook* 1966, p. 143) since 1944, was given the force of law after the BBC announced that it would no longer abide by it. The second directive prohibited the broadcast of party political broadcasts on behalf of any political party other than those arranged with the main political parties. This came into effect after it was proposed that Plaid Cymru and the Scottish National Party should be allowed broadcasts on the Welsh and Scottish Home Service. It was withdrawn in 1965 after the main parties agreed to allow broadcasts.

Tony Benn introduced the fifth directive, banning subliminal broadcasts on the BBC, in 1964 when he was Postmaster General.[1] [...]

Self restraint

The history of the relations between the Broadcasters and the State is one of government pressure and 'voluntary self restraint' by the broadcasters. An early example was the General Strike, during which there was pressure for the government to take over the BBC. In the event they decided not to. But as Lord Reith, the first Director-General of the BBC, recorded in his diary: 'The Cabinet decision is really a negative one. They want to be able to say that they did not commandeer us, but they know that they can trust us not to be really impartial.' (Stuart, 1975 p. 96) When the second directive of 1927 was withdrawn in 1928 the BBC itself decided 'to continue to exclude the discussion of certain subjects so as not to offend religious or moral susceptibilities'. (*BBC Handbook* 1956, p. 16).

In the Second World War the BBC saw itself as having a central role in fighting the enemy and was subject to strict control of all news bulletins by the Ministry of Information, although the BBC was not simply the mouthpiece of the government. During the Suez crisis in 1956 the BBC came under very heavy government pressure. Prime Minister Eden regarded Suez as a war situation and expected internal criticisms of the government to be suppressed. When the BBC gave the opposition the right to reply to ministerial broadcasts and refused to excise critical comments from its overseas bulletins, the government made threats of financial cuts and planted a Foreign Office Liaison Officer in Bush House to vet the external services.[2] The BBC managed to resist government pressure partly because Suez was not a national emergency but also because there was a deep division in the press and in politics, a division which, we now know, stretched to the cabinet itself (*The Times* 1.1.87). In August of 1956, over two months before the crisis came to a head the BBC had already come under pressure from Eden who objected to an Egyptian Major being interviewed. The BBC rejected his complaints and following this Eden's Press Adviser, William Clark, wrote to the Prime Minister advising on the powers that could be used against the BBC. Clark noted that every dispute with the BBC has 'been settled by persuasion so far' (*Guardian* 2.1.87).

Again, the credibility of British broadcasting and of the BBC in particular was a key reason for the reluctance of the government to take over the BBC. This thinking was shared by the broadcasters. In the aftermath of Suez, Charles Hill, as PMG, argued this point with the cabinet:

> In my view, the gain to Britain from the BBC's high reputation is immense, far outweighing any confusion which may occur through failure to understand its relationship to government. The independence which the corporation has should always be kept

inviolate. Once this issue was decided little more was heard of the agitation to destroy or to reduce the BBC's independence. (Hill, 1964, p. 188).

Informal chats

Interestingly, two years later the issue of controlling the BBC's coverage came up again. This time it was the crisis in Cyprus and the proposed visit of Archbishop Makarios to London which prompted the Foreign Secretary, Selwyn Lloyd, to write to the BBC expressing his concern. Charles Hill, who by now was the Chancellor of the Duchy of Lancaster, then went to visit Harman Grisewood, Chief Assistant to the Director General, for what he called 'one of our informal chats.' (Quoted in the *Irish Times* 2/3.1.89) Grisewood resisted the attempt to keep Makarios off the air, but nevertheless Hill:

> was left with the impression that if they did put Makarios on, they would make it the occasion for severe hostile questioning of the gentleman. (Quoted in the *Irish Times* 2/3.1.89).

Hill then wrote to Macmillan that 'there is no power to prevent such an appearance either on the BBC, or ITA'. (*Irish Times* 2/3.1.89). It is curious that Hill should give this advice, since only three years previously, as Postmaster General, he had issued two directives to the broadcasters prohibiting certain 'matters' from being broadcast. A number of possible explanations come to mind. He may simply have forgotten that the Postmaster General had the power, or he may have deceived Macmillan in order to smooth a 'voluntary' agreement with the BBC. A more interesting possibility is that the government interpretation of the PMG's power to limit 'matters of any particular class' did not include banning individuals from being interviewed. This is in contrast to the interpretation contained in Douglas Hurd's directive of October 1988. Of course, there have been many armed conflicts and other incidents in British history, in the last seventy years, with the potential to become controversies. A key reason that some don't is that techniques of censorship, news-management and 'voluntary responsibility' have worked. One example is the coverage of the civil war in Oman between 1965 and 1975. Fred Halliday records that 'For the first five years of the war, as the conflict gathered force, up to the 1970 coup, not a single on-the-spot report was filed by any reporter from the British side.' (1987, p. 186) The result of this was that very little information about British involvement in Oman was available in Britain, information like the presence, in a combat role, of 200 SAS men and 2000 British personnel. But even when there was coverage of Oman it was difficult for some journalists to paint a full picture. Halliday notes that:

> For some years prior to the outbreak of the ... war, the BBC had used, for its overseas transmissions, a relay station on the Omani

island of Masira. While nothing was, it seems, written down, it was well 'understood' by the BBC that one of the conditions for continued use of the facility was that it did not publish broadcast material unwelcome to the Sultan of Oman. (1987, p. 196).

The lack of coverage of conflicts like Oman was paralleled in the case of Northern Ireland.[3] Rex Cathcart, the historian of the BBC in Northern Ireland, notes that:

> Until 1951 the BBC (in Northern Ireland) sought to portray a society without division: the very mention of 'partition' was precluded. (*Fortnight*, November 1988)

It wasn't until the Civil Rights Association took to the streets in 1968 that Northern Ireland began to feature on our TV screens. In 1971, Lord Hill, by then Chair of the BBC, wrote to the Home Secretary, defining the relationship between broadcaster and state. 'In terms which accorded with the state's definition of the situation', (Schlesinger, 1987, p. 212) he agreed that 'as between the British Army and the gunmen the BBC is not and cannot be impartial'. (Schlesinger, 1987, p. 212.) During the Falklands episode the broadcasters again found it difficult to admit critical or oppositional views to news programmes and they were attacked for being 'traitorous' when they did. In Suez the BBC had managed to resist government pressure but during the Falklands it is clear that much news was shaped to support government policy.

BBC reporting

After the *Panorama* programme, which included criticisms of government policy, was branded 'a subversive and odious travesty', the BBC's top executives discussed dispensations from the normal criteria of 'balance' and 'impartiality'. In the confidential News and Current Affairs (NCA) meeting, broadcasters were cautioned:

> It was vital that BBC reporting was sensitive to the emotional sensibilities of the public. The truth had been told well so far, especially by those on the ground, but there had been some mistakes - the BBC was not infallible. The Director General advised that, with the public's nerve endings raw, the best yardstick to use would be the likely general susceptibility. (Glasgow University Media Group, 1985, p. 14).

When Douglas Hurd announced the British ban he acknowledged that 'These restrictions follow very closely the lines of similar provisions which have been operating in the Republic of Ireland for some years' (*Hansard* 19.10.88 col 893) and to a large extent the wording of the notice 'is drawn from the Irish wording' (col 901). The power to restrict broadcasting in the South of Ireland is vested in the Minister for Posts and Telegraphs under Section 31 of the Broadcasting Authority Act 1960. Ironically the wording of this power is based on the BBC Licence and Agreement. It states that 'The Minister may direct the Authority in writing to refrain from broadcasting any particular matter or matter of any particular class, and the Authority shall comply with the direction.' Historically government intervention in Radio Telefís Éireann (RTE) has been more direct and overt than in Britain. In Britain the BBC's reputation for 'independence' has been acknowledged as of crucial importance by both the broadcasters and successive governments. RTE does not have the same reputation either internally or internationally and governments have been less concerned about being seen to control and constrain broadcasting output. [...]

The British ban

Section 31 is stricter than the British legislation in a number of ways. It not only bans the broadcast of interviews but also reports of interviews with listed organisations. It prohibits Party Political Broadcasts and election coverage as well. The British ban allows exemptions for Party Political Broadcasts. The Broadcasting ban also allows for transmission of actuality from inside the Houses of Parliament, but not from the European Parliament. Section 31 allows neither of these. One interesting anomaly is that while the British legislation applies to historical footage the Irish ban does not. In practice Section 31 is interpreted over-cautiously by the broadcasters. Whilst the order speaks of 'spokesmen' or 'representatives', RTE actually bans people who are simply members of Sinn Féin. [...]

British broadcasters have also been cautious in their interpretation of the ban. A series of guidelines were issued by BBC, ITN and C4 (at least nine by my calculations) and working practices fell into shape on a case by case basis. Lord Donaldson, the Master of the Rolls, has argued that 'If broadcasters took enough trouble they could "totally defeat" the ban'. (*Independent* 22.11.89) But it is clear that this has not been the broadcasters' main concern. The broadcasters approached the Home Office for clarification of the notice. The Home Office indicated that 'A member of an organisation cannot be held to represent that organisation in all his daily activities.' This allowed journalists to broadcast the sound of an interview with a Sinn Féin representative in their capacity as a council or committee chairperson. The BBC did this for the first time on February 16, 1988 when they interviewed Gerry Adams about jobs in West Belfast.[4] Thirty seconds of sound on film was broadcast in Northern Ireland, with Adams speaking as MP for West Belfast rather than Sinn Féin MP for West Belfast. The Home Office showed it was keeping an eye on things when it phoned the BBC in London for an explanation.

News bulletins from South Africa have regularly been prefaced by blanket warnings that, for example, 'This report ... has been prepared under reporting restrictions imposed by the South African government' (BBC1 1300 30.8.89) but health warnings on Ireland have only been used when Sinn Féin have been interviewed and they have been woven into the text of reports at the point that an interview occurs. Indeed the confidential minutes of the BBC's fortnightly Editorial Policy Meeting (EPM), which we have obtained, show that senior BBC executives have explicitly eschewed a blanket warning because 'it could sound propagandist' (EPM Minutes 15.11.88). The same concern surfaced after BBC Northern Ireland subtitled an interview with Danny Morrison (*Inside Ulster* 24.1.89). The BBC decided that subtitles would no longer be used on the local news because, in the words of one senior executive 'It looked so dramatic. It looked like we were seeking to make a point.' This decision was endorsed at the Editorial Policy Meeting and the Controller Editorial Policy, John Wilson, indicated his preference for it to be extended to network news. But the BBC have not been alone in being cautious. The IBA banned a song by the Pogues which simply proclaimed the innocence of the Birmingham Six and the Guildford Four. They argued that this contention might 'support, or solicit, or invite support' for a listed organisation. [...]

Legal advice

The caution of the broadcasters has also meant that they did not raise actions in the courts or apply for a judicial review. Their stated reasons are that their legal advice indicated that they would not win and that they could not waste licence payers'/public money in a losing battle. They also argue that a failed case would consolidate the Ban. But there are indications that not all the advice given to the broadcasters was uniformly pessimistic. According to Channel Four their advice was less pessimistic than that of the IBA and gave them a better chance of winning at the European Court. Lord Bonham Carter, former BBC governor, has reportedly been advised by at least two counsel that the case has a 'high chance of success in the European Court' (*Guardian* 20.11.89). But even then there are indications that for some broadcasters the legal advice was not the only criterion of whether to proceed. At Channel Four and the IBA other policy and political matters were taken into account. According to one senior IBA source, part of the reason that they did not proceed was because it was not the place of a statutory body to take the government to court:

> For the IBA as a statutory authority operating under the Broadcasting Act, the Home Secretary was operating legally and, therefore, legally, we didn't have a leg to stand on. Other people of course had wider interests - the NUJ and so on, who are not subject to the Broadcasting Act.

Even though, as we have seen, Section 31 is wider than its British equivalent and it is interpreted over-zealously by the Broadcasters, RTE executives including the Director General, TV Finn, have felt able to supply the NUJ with affidavits for their application to the European Court. The BBC and IBA have refused to do so.

Journalists have tended to use two main arguments when discussing the ban. One is that it limits understanding of the conflict in Ireland and is bad in principle. Michael Checkland, Director General of the BBC, has recently argued this in a speech in New York in November 1989. He said:

> We have protested and we continue to protest at this measure because it interferes with our task of reporting current events fully and fairly and sets a damaging precedent. Although there is no sign that the government is ready to change its mind, it will look increasingly strange as the movement for freedom of expression gathers momentum throughout Eastern Europe and the Soviet Union. (BBC News Release, 22.11.89)

A corollary of this argument is that the conflict in Ireland is not going to go away by simply ignoring it. As Liz Forgan, Director of Programmes at Channel Four, has argued.

> If I thought it would save a single life I would be talking differently. I don't think that ... I don't think it will help the situation in Northern Ireland by one tiny bit. (*Media Show*, Channel 4, 15.10.89).

A mistake?

The second argument is that the ban is a tactical mistake. Journalists who use this argument implicitly agree, along with journalistic supporters of the ban, that the main object of covering Sinn Féin and the IRA is not to explain why people are fighting, but to discredit the Republican Movement as part of the campaign to defeat 'terrorism'. Their difference with the supporters of the ban is that they see the ban as a means of inhibiting the 'exposure' of Sinn Féin. An editorial in the *Independent* put this case, arguing that:

> The wickedness of their arguments can best be exposed by allowing these to be voiced, especially in the aftermath of some particularly horrifying atrocity. (20.10.88).

This argument has uncomfortable echoes of Lord Reith's note in his diary at the time of the General Strike, that the government could trust broadcasters 'not to be really impartial'. Top broadcasters are often ambivalent or undecided about which of the arguments they favour. When Norman Tebbit attacked the BBC's coverage of the US bombing of Libya he argued that the BBC had emphasised the civilian casualties and that this operated in 'Libya's interests'. There are indications that this perspective is taking hold in broadcasting. In the aftermath of the IRA bombing at Deal in Kent, the BBC dispensed with their signature tune and closed their main evening news bulletin with the Marines band playing over slow motion footage of a young boy in uniform laying a wreath to the dead. (BBC1 20.55 23.8.89). When a contributor to *Right to Reply* complained that this was not news but 'pure emotionalism', the BBC responded that:

The day before this item was broadcast ten Marine bandsmen had been murdered and around 20 injured. We are satisfied that the item properly reflected the feeling of many people in the aftermath of such an event. (*Right to Reply*, Channel 4, 7.10.89)

This simply assumes that the BBC is in the business of reflecting the perceived feelings of the nation, rather than that of reporting events.

But it need not be like this. There were two strands to the BBC reply to Tebbit. One was that they were wrongly accused, that they had in fact excluded much coverage of Libyan casualties because it would have suited 'Gadaffi's propaganda purpose extremely well'. The other was a much stronger argument for the independence of broadcasting. The BBC argued that it was not their

function to decide whether some facts are too 'damaging' or too 'callous' to be broadcast, and if we were to take that decision we would indeed be open to the accusation of manipulating the news for political purposes.

When it comes to Northern Ireland the broadcasters have tended to duck this more resolute line in favour of being in touch with the 'national mood'. But, from their own point of view, this can only be a short sighted policy if, as Rex Cathcart has argued:

Northern Ireland has provided the means by which the professional broadcasters have steadily been brought to the government's heel (*Fortnight*, November 1988).

Endnotes

1. Ironically a recent casualty of this ruling was the Northern Ireland Office. When the NIO produced an advertisement inviting people to use the confidential telephone, the IBA insisted that one 'image of brief duration' be 'increased from four frames to eight to remove its subliminal character.' (*Fortnight*, March 1988).

2. There is some dispute over whether Eden intended to 'take over' the BBC during the crisis. See Harman Grisewood, *One Thing at a Time*, Hutchinson, 1968, and F. R. MacKenzie, 'Eden, Suez and the BBC - A Reassessment', *The Listener*, 18 December 1969.

3. According to the British Army's handbook, *Land Operations: Volume 111-Counter Revolutionary Operations*, between the Second World War and August 1969, the army had experience of 53 'operations of the counter revolutionary type'.

4. Although a Sinn Féin councillor's voice had been heard prior to this on independent radio. Mairtín Ó Muilleoir was interviewed as a language activist about the Irish language on Downtown Radio on November 1, 1988. The BBC had also broadcast sound of an interview with Sinn Féin councillor Francis McNally after his brother was shot dead by loyalists in mistake for him. He was interviewed in his role as a relative of the murder victim. (BBC 2100, 25.11.88).

References

Glasgow University Media Group, *War and Peace News*, Open University Press, 1985

Halliday, Fred. 'News Management and Counter-insurgency: The Case of Oman', in Jean Seaton and Ben Pimlott (eds), *The Media in British Politics*, Avebury, 1987

Hill, Charles. *Both Sides of the Hill*, Heinemann, 1964

Schlesinger, Philip. *Putting 'Reality' Together*, 2nd Edition, Methuen, 1987

Stuart, Charles (ed), *The Reith Diaries*, Collins, 1975

17.

Betty Purcell

THE SILENCE IN IRISH BROADCASTING

(From B. Rolston (ed), *The Media and Northern Ireland: Covering the Troubles*, London, Macmillan, 1991, pages 51-68)

> 'Are you sure you want to go ahead with this interview with Martin Galvin of Noraid?'
> 'Yes, I'm sure; why?'
> 'Well, I just wondered, well, is he intellectually worthwhile interviewing?'
> 'That never stopped us doing interviews before; in fact, if intellect had anything to do with it, we'd be out of broadcasting very quickly.'
> 'I don't think it's worth going ahead with this interview; I'd rather you withdrew the invitation.'
> 'Look, is the interview being banned, because if so I'd rather be told straight. I've already asked Galvin in, and I'm not withdrawing the invitation on some spurious pretext.'
> 'We'd rather not have to ban it, but we may have to.'

This exchange actually took place between a senior radio executive and myself in August 1984. I quote it to demonstrate the fear and self-deception that any censorship law brings with it. Martin Galvin, of the Irish-American organisation, Noraid, was at the centre of some controversy that summer. He had been excluded from Britain and Northern Ireland, but had announced his intention to breach the order excluding him. Neither he nor his organisation were banned from the air waves under Section 31 of the Broadcasting Act, yet his views would be close enough to those of Sinn Féin. It was clear that he was being banned under the spirit of Section 31 yet, when the ban came down to me, the Section cited was Section 18(i), which, among other things, bans interviews avowing violence against the state. Since the interview was now being banned not on the basis of

253

Galvin's person but on the basis of what he might say, I suggested that we pre-record the interview and then judge whether there was in fact a breach of Section 18(i). No, I was told, the interview was not going ahead, and that was that. (I should point out that we have interviewed, in the course of programmes over the years, self-confessed Nazis and racial bigots, but none of these has been stopped under the Section invoked against Martin Galvin.)

Then there was the case of Nell McCafferty. Nell is a well-known writer and feminist, who first came to prominence with a weekly column in the *Irish Times,* 'In the eyes of the Law'. It showed the lives of the poor and those who had broken the law, and their relationship to justice, through simple observation of the daily cases in Dublin's district court. Nell was from Derry, and was a witty and individualistic commentator on Irish life right through the 1970s and 1980s. She spoke about the denial of contraception and divorce, occupied the Federated Union of Employers over the denial of equal pay, and supported through her writing prostitutes, street traders and travellers, all of whom had their problems with the law. She also had strong views about Northern Ireland. In this she reflected the sympathies of many Derry people, who had lived through the Battle of Bogside in 1969 or Bloody Sunday in 1972. While she was not a member of Sinn Féin, and was often critical of them and of the IRA in her writing, she could understand why people from her own home town got involved in military activity.

One Saturday Nell McCafferty was invited, as she often was, to appear on the radio discussion programme, 'Saturday View'. The occasion was the seventieth birthday of former Minister for Posts and Telegraphs, Dr Conor Cruise O'Brien, who had extended Section 31 while he was in office. It should be pointed out that O'Brien was somewhat of a *bête noire* to northern nationalists due to his hardline anti-nationalism while in government, and because of a revision of the teaching and view of Irish history spearheaded by him which began the downplaying of the conflict between Ireland and Britain. In a manner for which he was well known, he immediately went on the offensive with his 'guests', asking each of them in turn to answer yes or no to the question, 'Do you support the Provos?'. When it came to Nell McCafferty, she attempted to qualify her reply. A yes or no answer was again demanded. She replied 'Yes, I do.' The technique used by O'Brien was reminiscent of the repetitive questioning of witnesses in the McCarthy period of the United States; 'Are you, or have you ever been, a member of the Communist Party?' No room was left for development of the rather grey area of northern nationalist unhappiness, mainly with the state but also with the IRA, which would have modified her position. Her affirmative answer was noted. Next day came the horrific bombing at Enniskillen. An understanding, and later a written note came down. Nell McCafferty was not to be used in live programmes.

Nell McCafferty was cut off from a large part of her livelihood, and programme makers were deprived of one of the liveliest contributors around. Nell's rehabilitation was slow, and is even yet not complete. Her first permitted broadcast, nearly a year after she was banned, was on the subject of Mother's Day cards and the sentimental and amusing verses that go with them. This interview had to be referred up through RTE from the producer, to the Head of Features and Current Affairs, and through him to the Controller of Radio, and the Director of Radio, right as far as the Director General's office. It was decided to allow the interview. Since then, Nell McCafferty has begun to make appearances - reviewing newspapers, doing a weekly social gossip column and contributing once again to radio and television panels. But the lesson of her ban had remained. Although she was not covered by Section 31 of the Broadcasting Act, she was considered to have breached its spirit. Everyone, including I imagine Nell McCafferty herself, will be very careful in the future.

Another example springs to mind. In 1983 Gerry Adams and Joe Hendron ran for election for the constituency of West Belfast. I was there with a reporter colleague covering the event for the daily current affairs programme. The count was tense. It was a close-run contest. The supporters of both camps kept coming out of the closed counting room in Belfast City Hall to give us indications of what the result might be. Eventually, the doors flew open. 'Adams has it.' The international press gathered with their microphones, cameras and notebooks to interview the winning candidate. I looked to my RTE colleague and he shrugged. We got on to our studio in Dublin to offer a Q. and A. (question and answer), and an interview with Joe Hendron, the defeated candidate. The same hopeless exercise was repeated on RTE television news that night.

So what is Section 31? RTE (Radio Telefís Éireann, the Irish national broadcasting service) was set up as a public authority under the Broadcasting Act of 1960. It was charged with presenting news and current affairs 'in an objective and impartial manner and without any expression of the Authority's own views.' It was to be 'fair to all interests concerned' in the reporting of stories and was restricted by all of the legal rules, such as libel and official secrets, which applied to the newspapers. In addition, Section 31 allowed the Minister responsible for Communications to prevent 'the broadcasting of a particular matter or any matter of a particular class [which] would be likely to promote or incite to crime or would tend to undermine the Authority of the state.' This was later concretised in an order which prevents interviews, or reports of interviews with spokespersons for Sinn Féin, the IRA, the UDA, Republican Sinn Féin, the INLA and all organisations proscribed in Northern Ireland.

The political context in which the censorship has been operated is of paramount importance. Various Irish governments and responsible ministers have stated their view that RTE should act in their support. This was put most notoriously by the Taoiseach (Prime Minister) of the day, Mr Séan Lemass, in October 1966: 'The government rejected the view that RTE should be either generally or in regard to its current affairs programmes completely independent of government supervision.' The broadcasting organisation was, in his view, 'an instrument of public policy', that policy being decided by the government of the day. These rather heavy-handed remarks could have remained in the realm of aspirational guidance. But they did not. The very birth of Irish current affairs television was marred by a series of battles for autonomy from government. The then Minister for Agriculture, Charles Haughey, complained about his treatment in the news and had the item changed in subsequent bulletins. A news programme to be filmed in North Vietnam was cancelled after government intervention. Similarly intervention stopped a 'Seven Days' film crew going to Biafra in 1968.[1] These were the public government involvements. Behind the scenes there was constant pressure on programme makers, to 'go easy' on ministers, to play down controversies and to avoid subjecting the government to the full rigours of a debate format. Sometimes the government won, at other times the programmes did. But these were battles; the decisive one was to come on a specific issue.

The government was sensitive enough about its image in the period of relative stability of the late 1960s. When Northern Ireland erupted at the end of that decade the censorship allowed under the Broadcasting Act was seized like clifftop scutch in the slipping man's grip. An order was issued under Section 31 of the Broadcasting Act preventing broadcasts which 'could be calculated to promote the aims or activities of any organisation which engages in, promotes, encourages or advocates the attaining of any particular objectives by violent means'. The RTE authority asked for further detail but it was not given. The scene was being set for a nervous government to overreact to the next controversial item concerning Northern Ireland. It came, in the form of a report of an interview with the IRA Chief of Staff, Séan Mac Stiofáin. The authority was sacked and the journalist involved was jailed. The shock waves in RTE were enormous and are still felt. In the atmosphere of daily controversy in RTE, managers learn that most conflicts blow over. Only on the sensitive subject of Northern Ireland have heads rolled. And they were the most important heads in the organisation, those of the RTE Authority itself.

Things were not to improve with changes of government. If anything they got worse under the Coalition Minister of 1974-7 Dr Conor Cruise O'Brien. In his first year in office he invited a group of Ireland's top political journalists to a dinner in one of Dublin's top hotels. After the meal, he proposed a toast: 'To our democratic institutions, and the restrictions on the freedom of the press which may become necessary to preserve them.' He later went on to attack the journalists present, and to call them 'Provo stooges' (Provo = Provisional IRA). Not surprisingly journalists became apprehensive about writing articles or broadcasting programmes which could be seen in any way to lend support to Sinn Féin or the IRA. As Mary Holland, one of Ireland's foremost political commentators, put it in writing about the O'Brien years in an article in the *Irish Times* in April 1978: 'Self-censorship had been raised to the level of an art. Caution lay like a thick cloud over everything.'

In between his more paranoid acts - on one occasion he announced that he was maintaining a copy of letters to the *Irish Press* on the subject of Northern Ireland 'for future reference' - Conor Cruise O'Brien set about reformulating Section 31, specifying the organisations from whom spokespersons were banned. These included Sinn Féin, the IRA and the UDA, along with any organisation proscribed in Northern Ireland. (This rather strange formulation hands a major power in Section 31's implementation to the government of Northern Ireland. If any organisation were banned there, they are then automatically excluded from RTE programmes. This is doubly strange since the Constitution of the Republic does not recognise the *de jure* position of the state of Northern Ireland.) Conor Cruise O'Brien was most anxious that the spokespeople of the republican side in Northern Ireland were covered by the ban. He stated his view in an address to the Independent Broadcasting Authority in March 1979.[2] He described viewing a programme on violence in Northern Ireland which in his view concentrated on violence perpetrated by the British army, and did not show IRA violence:

> I viewed the programme in the presence of the then Chairman of the authority and the then Director General. At the end of it I enquired whether the IRA had been in actual physical occupation of the station when the programme was made and when it was broadcast. It transpired that this was not the case. But the IRA propagandists had contrived ... to penetrate the station and attain a spiritual occupation sufficient to secure the making and transmission of such a programme ... I directed the Authority to refrain from broadcasting interviews with spokesmen for the IRA (both wings) and for Provisional Sinn Féin ... I could have left that decision to the authority itself ... In the circumstances I have described I thought it safer to act myself.

Section 31, as implemented by Conor Cruise O'Brien, has remained virtually unchanged for fifteen years. Every year it is formally renewed in the Dáil without any debate. For programme makers in RTE it has become almost second nature. And the influence of the censorship is evident not just in relation to Northern Ireland.

One of the biggest and most tragic stories to hit Dublin in the 1980s was an epidemic of heroin addiction among young people in working class areas. Every woman you would go to talk to about another issue would end up saying: 'But what can we do about the drugs?' The gardai did not appear to have the means to arrest and charge the drug barons and they continued to operate openly. In the end the communities started to take action among themselves. They set up groups known as Concerned Parents Against Drugs, and they confronted the pushers in their localities and drew them into the open. Sometimes the vigilante-type methods they used pitched people into open battle with the drug dealers. But they succeeded in flushing out the problem, and the pushers were put behind bars, as the problem was driven out of an area. Often it would surface elsewhere, as the drug-dealing families sought out new territory. But at least they were no longer allowed to ply their trade unimpeded in many poor parts of the city.

Although RTE covered these developments at their outset, it became clear that Sinn Féin members, many of whom lived in the working class flats complexes, were involved in Concerned Parents Against Drugs. Extreme caution had to be exercised in the treatment of the subject. Reporters being sent to cover the story had to be instructed to specifically ask each interviewee whether he or she was a member of Sinn Féin. Often this led to hostility from members of the public who were not so involved, but resented being asked the question. The difficulty of finding non-members, along with the inevitable annoyance our question would raise, led to the story of the Concerned Parents Against Drugs being covered less and less by RTE. The story did not go away, but we went away.

The issue of sexual morality and Irish schools raised its head in the case of Eileen Flynn. She was a Co. Wexford teacher who was living with a married man and was pregnant by him. The nuns who ran the school she taught in did not approve. They sacked her. A huge public debate raged. She was a competent teacher, as many of the schoolchildren's parents evidenced. The nuns agreed that this was so. The issue to be decided was whether what a teacher did in her own life might give scandal and bad example to the children under her tutelage - or whether she was entitled to work teaching as long as she was able to fulfil that function. There was a complication as far as RTE was concerned. The man Eileen Flynn was living with was a member of Sinn Féin. A question mark was placed over whether she was also a member. I wrote to her requesting an interview for the programme 'Women Today'. Before I rang to see whether she would talk to us, I was told by my line manager that she would have to be asked whether she was a member of Sinn Féin or not. We could not risk carrying an interview to discover later that we had breached Section 31. I telephoned, rather gingerly, because I was aware that she was suspicious of media interest in her story. She was not inclined to do the interview, but I was convincing her, I felt. I took a deep breath and asked the question. There was a silence, and then she said: 'Look, I think I'd rather not talk on the radio.' That was that. The pros and cons of her case were debated by all and sundry. But our chance of getting the story directly from the principal herself had been jeopardised by censorship relating to issues totally removed from those of sexual morality. It transpired, when the heat died down, that Eileen Flynn was not a member of Sinn Féin, nor had she been. But her association with a member had spread a web of suspicion and difficulty about her case which was entirely unnecessary.

Gay Health Action was a campaigning group which strove to have the reality of homosexuality recognised in order for preventive health care to take place in relation to the new phenomenon of AIDS. Its main spokesman was a member of Sinn Féin. On a live phone-in with the Minister of Health he attempted to open up this area of debate before AIDS could establish its grip on the vulnerable sections of the community such as homosexuals. He was specifically objecting to the closure of clinics dealing with sexually transmitted diseases, as part of government cutbacks. The phone call had to be hurriedly cut off.

Meanwhile, in 1987, the government was involved in talks with the Irish Congress of Trades Unions with a view to reaching a national understanding which would decrease the number and frequency of strikes in exchange for commitments on pay and redundancies. The President of Congress and chief spokesman for the public sector unions, Phil Flynn, was also stated to be a vice-president of Sinn Féin. He was listed as such in the party newspaper and list of officers, and had never denied the role. News and current affairs programmes were in a dilemma. This major story had to be covered, but this question mark sat over the chief negotiator on the trade union side. In the event, different programmes decided on different strategies. The newsroom covered the story by way of pieces to camera by the economics correspondent and the political correspondent. 'Today Tonight', the current affairs television programme, interviewed Flynn. No government questions were asked. Indeed it would have been fairly ridiculous if the government, which was itself talking to Flynn, were to ask questions about RTE talking to him. Nevertheless the interview was raised in the newspapers, and the editor of the 'Today Tonight' programme was quoted as saying that he was not aware that Phil Flynn was a member of Sinn Féin. There it ended. The programme survived its indiscretion. Could it have gone the other way? Surviving censorship is a risky business.

In the autumn of 1987, a period of tension between Dublin's street traders and the gardai reached its height. The traders were unauthorised, but had for years been making their living by selling goods such as fruit, flowers and jewellery from prams around the city centre. They were constantly being moved on by the gardai, who were receiving pressure from the shops whose business was affected by the street traders. Two public representatives in particular had taken up the cause of the street traders, Dáil Deputy Tony Gregory and Dublin city councillor Christy Burke. The former is an independent TD (member of the Dáil) for Dublin Central, the latter a member of Sinn Féin. They were imprisoned along with the women traders for their part in protests about the situation. They spent 14 days each in prison, and when Tony Gregory was released he was on 'The Late Late Show' (Ireland's premier television talk show) describing conditions, including his fear of the AIDS virus which was rampant in the jail. Gregory is someone who might be judged to have something to gain from Section 31. He appeared on prime time television, whereas Christy Burke received no publicity for his prison period. Yet he had this to say when I contacted him about the street trader episode: 'The application of Section 31 to Christy Burke is particularly ludicrous, because the issues he is involved with in his constituency are of a social nature and have nothing to do with the North. The ban on him is illogical and bears no relation to the purpose for which it was first introduced.' Tony Gregory is the only TD who opposes Section 31 on the grounds that he is against censorship and for free speech. The point he makes about fellow inner city politician Christy Burke applies to all of the above instances, where the broadcasting ban, introduced to deal with a situation of armed conflict in Northern Ireland, has had much wider implications. The theory of the ban makes credible coverage of northern politics very difficult. The reality of the ban makes all programmes restricted and nervous.

The number of examples of the effect of Section 31 in areas not remotely connected to the conflict in Northern Ireland are too great to mention - for instance, the continuing problem of housing in the inner city. I remember one morning such a housing problem featured as a prominent news story. I dispatched one of our younger reporters to the area to see what she could get on tape for the current affairs programme beginning at 11 o'clock. She arrived back shortly after 10, shaking her head. 'They're all Provos out there,' she said. Not one to be daunted, she had managed to track down an individual who was not 'a Provo' and whom she could therefore interview. But she'd had to work hard. Another example from the newsroom was that of a large fire in Bundoran in which quite a few people were killed. The only actual eye witness to the fire turned out, by coincidence, to be a member of Sinn Féin. He could not be interviewed on the subject of the fire, and the attempts of those inside to escape. Another example was slightly mischievous, but nevertheless showed the ridiculous nature of the restrictions. The 'Liveline' programme was doing a phone-in on gardening. A listener rang to ask a question about mushroom growing. Having asked it, he went on to point out that he was a member of Sinn Féin. The presenter, Marianne Finucane, had to truncate the call immediately, pointing out that this was a breach of Section 31. It transpired that the caller was not a member of Sinn Féin at all, but [...] was making a point about the censorship. Such items severely damage the credibility of RTE as an organisation with an important and responsible job to do in providing informational programming.

If RTE as an organisation is damaged by the ban, individual broadcasters have suffered too, to various degrees. People have items placed in their personnel files, have been moved sideways, denied promotion, and caused huge stress and extra work as a result of the breach or near breach of Section 31. But the ultimate sanction, that of dismissal, has also occurred. It happened to news reporter Jenny McGeever in March 1988.

Three IRA members had been shot dead in Gibraltar in controversial circumstances. They were unarmed at the time and witnesses had suggested that no attempt was made to arrest them as an alternative to killing them. The bodies were flown back to Ireland, to Dublin airport, where they were to be brought to Belfast for burial. Tension was high, and it was believed that there might be trouble on the journey north. Jenny McGeever was sent by the 'Morning Ireland' news programme to meet the coffins and to travel 'as closely as possible' to the funeral cortège to cover any signs of trouble. It was an assignment fraught with difficulties. Most of the people concerned with the funeral and its arrangements were banned under Section 31.

McGeever travelled with the funeral all night. She witnessed the flash points, recorded material, and headed straight back to Dublin. She arrived in to 'Morning Ireland' exhausted and frazzled, saying she had not enough material for a report but could do a Q. and A. (question and answer). No, she was told, do up a report. She then edited the tape, including a piece in which Sinn Féin member Martin McGuinness stated the accommodation which had been reached with the RUC over the question of berets and gloves on one of the coffins to ensure the peaceful passage of the funeral. It was a fairly nondescript statement. But it was a breach of Section 31. 'The voice' had been heard by the sleepy Irish public over their cornflakes and toast. Things would never be the same again!

It is hard not to be ironic in looking at what was involved. If McGuinness had been urging people to join the IRA or had even been commenting on events in Gibraltar, things would have been clear and unequivocal. As it was, it was a technical breach but nevertheless a breach. Jenny McGeever had her contract terminated there and then. RTE management announced this to the press in an attempt to prevent any blame attaching to the incident spreading up the organisation. The attitude of McGeever's colleagues of the Broadcasting branch of the NUJ was most unsavoury. They took no action on her dismissal and concentrated their energies on defending the jobs and reputations of the editors working over her. She was to be the isolated scapegoat, and everyone breathed a sigh of relief. McGeever began proceedings to sue RTE over her dismissal, but was given a settlement in the region of £5000 out of court. It was money well spent to be rid of the problem, its perpetrator, and the possibility of ministerial questions about the breach. Everything settled back to normal.

The McGeever case shows the extent of compliance with Section 31. People were shocked that any broadcaster might break the ban. The extent of their horror underlines another aspect of the directive. People err on the cautious side where there is doubt. Whole neighbourhoods of people were silenced because they are too close to a possibility of breaking the ban. The question is not, 'Who is in Sinn Féin?' but, 'Who is definitely *not* in

Sinn Féin?' Issues go unaddressed. And the concept of ordinary trade union solidarity is undermined. RTE's guidelines to news and current affairs staff point out that Section 31 takes precedence over that other requirement of the Broadcasting Act, that of being fair and impartial in the treatment of issues. [...]

The other way self-censorship works is to damn all those who oppose the ban, and to ascribe sinister motives to that opposition. As a trade union activist I was one of those involved in organising a ballot around the question of a strike against Section 31. The issue was debated long and hard and eventually the secret ballot decided in favour of a 24-hour strike. That was in 1985. At the Christmas party at the end of the year, those of us who were still going when the bars closed ended up in a Dublin night club. A production assistant from television whom I barely knew came up to me and said: 'Is it true that you really are a member of the IRA, because everyone in television thinks you are?' I was highly amused at the time, and very glad that the issue had been raised straight to my face. But when I thought about it afterwards, I was disturbed. Such innuendo and gossip has ruined the careers of many in the world of information and ideas. The hunting of witches is by no means over.

There is an international dimension to all of this. A document as basic as the Universal Declaration of Human Rights, adopted in December 1948, states: 'Everyone has the right to freedom of opinion and expression; this right includes freedom to hold opinions without interference and to seek, receive and impart information and ideas through any media and regardless of frontiers.' Now consider the following statements:

> Everyone has the right to communicate. Communication is a fundamental social process which enables individuals and communities to exchange information and opinions. It is a basic human need and the foundation of all social organisation. The right to communicate is therefore a fundamental human right which belongs to individuals and the communities they compose.[3]

> The problem is to create machinery which will reconcile freedom with responsibility, and ensure that broadcasters are free from detailed interference, while at the same time remaining subject to broad direction and control in the public interest.[4]

The contrast of perspectives could not be sharper. The first is the view of the International Institute of Communications, a group formed under the umbrella of the United Nations. The second view is that of the Irish Broadcasting Review Committee set up by the Irish government and which reported to them in 1971. From the universality of the right declared in the first statement we get down to how broadcasting can be constrained without it being too obvious.

The view of the Irish Broadcasting Review Committee and of the Irish government is essentially an élitist and paternalistic one. They must decide what it is in the public interest for the public to know. This implies that there are certain conflicting ideas that the viewers and listeners can make up their minds about, and others that are too dangerous or too clever for them to truly judge. All totalitarian regimes use such arguments to prevent organisation and speech which is contrary to the *status quo*. It is only where the line is drawn which differentiates the censorship in Ireland (now both South and North). Trade unionists, farmers, tenants and business people may still air their views on Irish radio and television. But on the difficult question of Northern Ireland, which causes heated disagreement even among parties who are not banned, the ugly knife of censorship is seen. Lord Windlesham addressed precisely this issue in 1980:

> Most often it is at times of crisis or communal stress when issues are of vital importance that freedom of utterance is at risk. This is why some of the most difficult and controversial of recent clashes have related to the reporting of events in Northern Ireland, or interviews with IRA or Protestant extremist leaders. Earlier, Suez, and in America Vietnam, were examples of international crises where critical comment was unwelcome to government. Nonetheless, it is precisely in situations of this sort that public discussion is needed most. Arthur Schlesinger, historian and White House advisor, has put it vividly: 'the cry of national unity has been used before to cut off debate and to conceal error. Democracy is not something to be suspended in an emergency'.[5]

Even though the situation in Northern Ireland is an extremely difficult one for Irish governments, I believe that they have taken the wrong step in curtailing people's right to hear all views in that situation. The Irish electorate is extremely sophisticated politically, and is capable of judging issues on an intelligent basis for itself. In fact, up until the recent broadcasting ban in Britain, half of the Irish viewers living in a multi-channel land were able to see interviews with the very people who were banned from RTE. This did not lead to mass defections to Sinn Féin, though, even if it did, I believe that would not be reason enough to operate a ban.

And so we come to another major inconsistency in the operation of the censorship. The ban applies only to radio and television. The logic is that they are such persuasive media that special rules must apply to protect the public from their influence. The influence of self-censorship among newspaper editors has led effectively to the non-publication of material which would be banned in broadcasting. Yet occasionally, the implicit ban is ignored, as it may be, and material of great public interest can be published by the newspapers. But the application of the ban leads to an unhappy separation between the broadcasting media and the printed press. Again to quote Lord Windlesham:

> As with newspapers and publications, where the battle for editorial freedom was fought over a long period, so with broadcasting. There cannot be one measure of freedom for what is broadcast and

another for what is printed ... A multiplicity of sources, and a multiplicity of media from which reporting and comment can originate, are the most effective counters to autocracy.[6]

Down the years, little blame has attached to various Irish governments for their implementation of censorship, because the opposition to it has been sporadic and without a parliamentary leadership. The only derogation from the ban allowed in the period during which I have been working in RTE was to allow the unedited broadcast of a series made by British broadcaster Robert Kee and co-funded by RTE. That was to save the Irish state embarrassment in the international arena. But for those of us who as broadcasters have had to be the unhappy implementors of the silence, there is a continuing awareness of something amiss, like a wound that has never healed. We wait from day to day for it to flare up again, to prevent a programme plan. As Professor John A. Murphy put it in reflecting on the censorship of the 1950s:

> However one regards the story of the effort to protect the national community against alien influences considered to be understandable, nothing can be said, then or now, in extenuation of the attempt to silence the nation's own voices simply because the state did not like the sound of them. That was the abomination of the age of Irish censorship.[7]

And so it remains to this day. [...]

Endnotes

1. Quoted by Muiris Mac Conghail in 'The Creation of RTE and the Impact of Television', in Brian Farrell (ed.), *Communications and Community in Ireland*, Dublin, Mercier Press, 1984, p. 70.
2. *Irish Times*, 19 March 1979.
3. From *The Right to Communicate: A New Human Right*, Dun Laoghaire, Boole Press, 1982, p. 19. This was a formulation agreed between the International Institute of Communications and members of UNESCO at a meeting in Strasbourg in September 1981.
4. *Report of the Irish Broadcasting Review Committee*, Dublin, Government Publications, 1974.
5. Lord Windlesham, 'The Case for Press Freedom', *Broadcasting in a Free Society*, Oxford, Basil Blackwell, 1980, p. 15.
6. *Ibid.*, p. 16.
7. John A. Murphy, 'Censorship and the Moral Community', in Brian Farrell (ed.), *Communications and Community in Ireland*, Dublin, Mercier Press, 1984, p. 63.

18.

Liz Curtis

A CATALOGUE OF CENSORSHIP 1959-1993

(From L. Curtis and M. Jempson, *Interference on the Airwaves: Ireland, the Media and the Broadcasting Ban*, London, Campaign for Press and Broadcasting Freedom, 1993, pages 42-92)

The list of programmes from 1959 to October 1983 was published in *Ireland: the Propaganda War* (Pluto, 1984) and Liz Curtis drew partly on the chronology by Paul Madden in *The British Media and Ireland: Truth the First Casualty* (Information on Ireland, 1979) to compile it. The listings since 1983 have been compiled by Liz Curtis for Information on Ireland briefings. They include some items which were important but did not involve censorship and these are indicated by **.

BEFORE THE BAN

1959 - BBC
SEE IT NOW (Ed Murrow talk show)

Lord Brookeborough, then Prime Minister of Northern Ireland, personally intervened to secure the dropping of the second of two interviews with actress Siobhan McKenna. He did this because she had, in the first interview, referred to IRA internees in the Republic as 'young idealists'.

1959 - BBC
TONIGHT

Seven 10-minute reports by Alan Whicker about the Six Counties were dropped after the personal intervention of Lord Brookeborough. Eight reports were planned, but only the first was transmitted; its subject was betting shops. but passing references to the political situation led to a major row and the banning of the succeeding reports.

July 1966 - ITV
THIS WEEK

A programme which depicted Ian Paisley as a tub-thumping bible basher was not allowed to be shown in the North of Ireland.

June 1968 - BBC
The BBC refused to do a feature programme about Austin Currie's protest occupation of a Dungannon council house which had been allocated to an unmarried Unionist. This became a *cause celebre* within the BBC.

1970 - BBC
The BBC commissioned Jim Allen to write a contemporary play about the North of Ireland, to be directed by Ken Loach and produced by Tony Garnett. The BBC stopped the project when the script was partially written. The play was about the politics of the Officials and the Provisionals. (Jim Allen went on to write a film script for Kestrel Films about the 1919-21 war against Britain, to be called *The Rising*; a Swedish company agreed to put up more than half the money providing some money could be raised in England, but no English company would finance it.)

July 1970 - BBC
PANORAMA

The programme included interviews with relatives of six people killed in Belfast. BBC Northern Ireland 'opted out' on the grounds that the programme was inflammatory. This was the first such 'opting out'. (BBC policy was that programmes should be identical in Britain and the North of Ireland.)

February 1971 - BBC
24 HOURS

A film which showed widespread disenchantment among Unionists with Northern Ireland Prime Minister Major Chichester Clark. The film was delayed by BBC Northern Ireland Controller Waldo Maguire. When the predicted resignation took place, the film became superfluous and was never shown.

August 1971 - BBC
24 HOURS

Senior BBC executives prevented *24 Hours* from doing an in-depth programme about the IRA. The Chief Assistant to the Director-General,

John Crawley, said, 'Such a programme setting out the roots of the IRA would not be acceptable.' (See *Private Eye*, 15 November 1971.)

October 1971 - BBC

The BBC filmed the proceedings of the Assembly of the Northern Irish People, which had been set up by the SDLP and the Nationalist Party as an alternative to the Stormont Parliament. The footage was never shown, possibly because it was deemed 'unbalanced' (*The Sunday Times*, 2 January 1972).

November 1971 - Granada
WORLD IN ACTION: 'South of the Border'

Granada wanted to do a programme showing how the 'troubles' in the North were building up pressures in the South of Ireland. The film included Seán MacStiofáin (Provisional IRA Chief of Staff) and Ruairí Ó Brádaigh (Provisional Sinn Féin President), and also Dublin politicians who were hostile to the IRA. The Independent Television Authority banned the programme before it was completed. ITA Chairman Lord Aylestone felt it was 'aiding and abetting the enemy'. Granada went ahead and completed the programme, but, on viewing it, the ITA confirmed the ban.

1971 - ITN

ITN suppressed a film about an army post surrounding a lone policeman on the Creggan estate in Derry.

November 1971 - BBC
24 HOURS

The BBC filmed a number of statements by ex-internees about their treatment at the hands of the British army during detention. Despite the mounting evidence of the torture carried in the press, the BBC delayed screening the films until after the publication of the Compton Report. The films were balanced by a discussion between a Tory MP, Anthony Buck, and former Labour Defence Minister, Roy Hattersley.

February 1972 - Thames
THIS WEEK: 'Aftermath of Bloody Sunday'
(also titled, 'Bloody Sunday - Two Sides of the Story')

Thames was preparing a programme piecing together, through interviews with witnesses and soldiers, the story of Bloody Sunday, when paratroopers shot dead 13 civilians in Derry. With the announcement of the Widgery inquiry, 10 Downing Street sought a blanket ban on media coverage. Thames compromised by showing a complete unedited roll of an interview with a Welsh ex-warrant officer, who lived in the area, balanced by a complete roll of accounts by Scottish paratroopers (one of whom, a lieutenant, later admitted to the Widgery Tribunal that his statement in the film that he had seen a gunman, was a lie). Twenty rolls of film, including interviews with Catholic Bogsiders, were never used: these contained more damaging material.

August 1972 - BBC
PANORAMA: 'Operation Motorman'

A Panorama team went into Creggan Heights in Derry alongside the Coldstream Guards during Operation Motorman, 31 July 1972, when the British army stormed the no-go areas in the city, dismantling the barricades put up by nationalist residents. Later that day the team - with reporter Alan Hart and producer Bill Cran - interviewed local people about their reactions. The film was suppressed on the orders of a senior BBC executive.

October 1972 - BBC
PLAY FOR TODAY: 'Carson Country'

This play by Dominic Behan was postponed from May, and finally transmitted on 23 October, 'to avoid provoking possible trouble during the marching season' (*Evening Standard*, 11 May 1972). The postponement was decided on by David Attenborough, Controller of TV programmes, and Northern Ireland Controller Waldo Maguire. The play was about 'the origin of the Stormont state'.

October 1972 - Thames
ARMCHAIR THEATRE: 'The Folk Singer'

The IBA asked to view this play by Dominic Behan, about a Liverpool folk singer who visits Belfast, before its proposed transmission date on 7 November. The IBA granted permission, but Thames chose to transmit it at 10.30 pm, instead of in *Armchair Theatre's* usual nine o'clock slot.

November 1972 - BBC
A SENSE OF LOSS

The BBC refused to screen this film by Marcel Ophuls on the grounds that it was 'too pro-Irish' (*The Sunday Times*, 5 November 1972). The BBC had a financial involvement in the film, following their screening of Ophuls' *The Sorrow and the Pity,* which was much acclaimed. The film consisted of interviews with ordinary Protestants and Catholics as well as politicians and soldiers. The film was, by implication, critical of the Unionist case, and was also against violence from any quarter.

February 1973 - ATV

HANG UP YOUR BRIGHTEST COLOURS: The Life and Death of Michael Collins

Following the success of Kenneth Griffith's BBC film on Cecil Rhodes, ATV commissioned him to make a historical documentary in the same vivid storytelling style. Griffith chose as his subject Michael Collins, IRA leader in the war against Britain in 1920 and a signatory of the treaty which led to civil war. A deeply committed film, possibly the best Griffith has ever made, it examines a crucial period of Irish history and condemns Britain's role. Sir Lew Grade, ATV's Managing Director, banned the film. It has never been shown, and even Kenneth Griffith does not have access to it.

March 1974 - BBC

CHILDREN IN CROSSFIRE

The Tory Northern Ireland Secretary tried to get this film stopped. BBC Northern Ireland Controller Dick Francis ordered major changes in the film. Not satisfied with the changes made, he had its transmission stopped twice. When it finally went out on 12 March, it had a one-minute announcement appended at the start implying that the government's Sunningdale policy had eased the tensions, depicted in the film, between the British army and people in the republican areas of the North. The film's message was that children there were growing up psychologically disturbed; this thesis was undermined by a follow-up film, *A Bright Brand New Day...?*, transmitted in January 1982 after a repeat of the first film.

November 1974 - Bristol Channel (Cable Television channel)

NEWSPEAK

On 29 November, when this local news programme had started, a ban came through from the Home Office on an interview with Adrian Gallagher, South-West organiser of Clann na hÉireann (the equivalent of Official Sinn Féin). He was to discuss the Birmingham bombings. The Home Office regulated this and four other cable television experiments, and outline programme schedules had to be submitted to them at least two weeks in advance.

May 1975 - Thames

THIS WEEK: 'Hands Across the Sea'

This programme, about fund-raising for the IRA in America, was postponed for a week by the IBA. The programme was originally timed to be shown on the day of the elections for the Northern Ireland Convention, but would have gone out half-an-hour after the polls had closed. The IBA postponed it because, they said, 'the subject matter could have an unfortunate impact on opinions and emotions in the North of Ireland.'

January 1976 - BBC
NATIONWIDE

On 8 January *Nationwide* showed a film on the SAS training, which had been on the shelf. Both negative and print were apparently later destroyed on 'advice' from the Ministry of Defence.

March 1976 - BBC
ARTICLE 5

A play commissioned by the BBC from Brian Phelan about three mercenaries/ torturers, who are commissioned by an Englishman to protect his interests in an unspecified country. The message of the play, written with the assistance of Amnesty International, was against the use of torture; the North of Ireland was mentioned in passing as an instance of the use of torture by governments. The play was recorded in January 1975 and banned by the BBC.

October 1976 - BBC Scotland
THE SCOTTISH CONNECTION

The BBC Northern Ireland Controller insisted that an interview with a Provisional IRA man be dropped from this film about the cultural and political links between Scotland and the North of Ireland. The cut was confirmed by Director-General Charles Curran. The producers intended to insert a statement saying that they could not show an interview with a Provisional IRA spokesman because it was against BBC policy, but that interviews with the legal Ulster Defence Association were permitted. This statement was omitted when the film was shown in Scotland on 23 October 1976 and on the network on 5 January 1977.

February 1977 - London Weekend
EIGHTEEN MONTHS TO BALCOMBE STREET

Shane Connaughton, the writer, asked for his name to be withdrawn from this reconstruction of the Balcombe Street siege because it had not been produced as he intended. 'I wanted to explain why the bombers were there,' he said (*The Irish Post*, 26 February 1977).

March 1977 - BBC
TONIGHT: Interview with Bernard O'Connor

Keith Kyle's interview with Bernard O'Connor, a Catholic school-teacher who alleged he had been ill-treated by the RUC at Castlereagh holding centre, was transmitted a week later than scheduled. The BBC governors thoroughly investigated the film before allowing transmission. In July 1980 O'Connor won £5,000 in compensation as exemplary damages for maltreatment. Both Roy Mason, then Northern Ireland Secretary, and Tory spokesperson Airey Neave condemned the BBC for showing the programme, and some newspapers blamed it for the killing of an RUC man by the IRA a few days later.

1977 - BBC
MAN ALIVE: 'A Street in Belfast' (also known as 'Short Strand')

The BBC commissioned this film from Eric Durschmied, a freelance film-maker, then refused to show it. The film focused on the daily lives of three families in the Short Strand, a small Catholic enclave in an overwhelmingly Protestant area of Belfast.

August 1977 - Thames
THIS WEEK: 'In Friendship and Forgiveness'

Peter Taylor, the reporter, described this film as 'an alternative diary' of the Queen's Jubilee visit to the North of Ireland. It challenged the pervasive media picture of a pacified province by showing that the visit had in fact heightened the political divisions there. The IBA took exception to several sections of the film and banned it two minutes before transmission on 17 August. The film was eventually transmitted, with small alterations, two weeks after the visit, when its topicality was lost, at a variety of times in the various ITV regions.

October 1977 - Thames
THIS WEEK: 'Inhuman and Degrading Treatment'

This Week investigated 10 cases of alleged ill-treatment of people held by the RUC for interrogation. The IBA insisted that the RUC be represented, but the RUC refused to cooperate or to be interviewed. The Chief Constable offered, the day before transmission, a five-minute RUC statement to camera, which would not allow the reporter to question him. *This Week* was forced to accept this, because otherwise the IBA would not have allowed the programme to be shown.

February 1978 - Thames
THE GREEN, THE ORANGE AND THE RED, WHITE AND BLUE

David Elstein, *This Week* producer, and Peter Taylor, *This Week* reporter, offered Thames a historical project on the North of Ireland which would have mixed documentary with dramatised reconstruction. Thames refused the project, probably because Elstein and Taylor had previously been involved in controversy, and it might have once again brought Thames into conflict with the IBA. Elstein offered it to the BBC, who also turned it down.

May 1978 - London Weekend
WEEKEND WORLD

Soon after *Weekend World* started making this film assessing the current strength of the Provisional IRA, the IBA ordered them to scrap the whole programme. The team still went ahead, though dropping film of IRA training sessions and a mooted interview with IRA leader David O'Connell. The IBA again banned the newly completed film. IBA Chairperson Lady Plowden finally decided to allow it to be transmitted on 21 May, three weeks after its planned transmission date.

May 1978 - BBC
THE CITY ON THE BORDER AND THE IRISH WAY: 'A Bridge of Sorts'

The City on the Border, about Derry, was intended as a preface to the seven-part series, *The Irish Way*. Director Colin Thomas was already worried about the fact that the role of the British army went unquestioned in the film, when he learnt that two sections had been cut: one showed a tombstone which read 'Murdered by British Paratroopers on Bloody Sunday'. In the meantime, one of the two films Thomas had directed in *The Irish Way* series 'A Bridge of Sorts', had been referred to BBC Northern Ireland, who said the film and commentary had to be substantially changed before transmission. Thomas refused to make the changes, and resigned. The film was transmitted under a new title, 'A Rock in the Road', with the changes.

June 1978 - Thames
THIS WEEK: 'The Amnesty Report'

Thames planned to transmit on 8 June a programme about the Amnesty report on the ill-treatment of suspects by the RUC. The report had already been widely leaked. The IBA banned the programme. The local ACTT union shop blacked the screening of a substitute programme, and the TV screen remained blank. Extracts from the shot film were subsequently shown on the BBC's *Nationwide*.

August 1978 - Southern
SPEARHEAD: 'Jackal'

Ulster TV refused to screen the fourth episode of this seven-part drama series about an army battalion. Like the first episode, which Ulster TV had screened, the fourth episode was set in the North of Ireland. The network transmission date, 8 August, coincided with the anniversary of the introduction of internment. This was the first time a drama programme, as opposed to current affairs, had been dropped by Ulster TV.

August 1978 - BBC
PLAY FOR TODAY: 'The Legion Hall Bombing'

This play, showing the operation of the Diplock Court system and based on the transcripts of the trial of Willie Gallagher, was scheduled for transmission on 23 February and was repeatedly postponed. The BBC insisted on commentary changes and that the epilogue be completely dropped. The play was meant to be followed by a discussion, but this too was dropped. The play was transmitted on 22 August at the late time of 10.25 pm, instead of the usual *Play for Today* time of 9.25 pm. The director, Roland Joffe, and writer Caryl Churchill requested the removal of their names from the credits.

1979 - Granada
WORLD IN ACTION

An interview with republican spokesperson Danny Morrison was dropped from a *World in Action* film on the North after Northern Ireland Secretary Howard Atkins said he would refuse to appear unless the interview was excluded.

May 1979 - Yorkshire TV
GLOBAL VILLAGE

IBA and Yorkshire TV officials forced the removal of an interview with Sinn Féin President Ruairí Ó Brádaigh from David Frost's *Global Village* programme on Northern Ireland. The cut was made because several Westminster MPs had walked out when they heard that Ó Brádaigh was due to appear. The programme normally went out live but this one was recorded and previewed by the IBA because it dealt with the North of Ireland.

August 1979 - BBC
THE VANISHING ARMY

A repeat showing of this play about an army sergeant who had become disillusioned after being wounded in the North of Ireland was cancelled because of the Mountbatten and Warrenpoint killings. Playwright Robert Holles described the cancellation as 'a crude and crass piece of censorship'. The play was eventually repeated on 3 April 1980.

November 1979 - BBC
PANORAMA

As part of a film assessing the Provisional Republican movement on its tenth anniversary *Panorama* filmed an IRA roadblock in Carrickmore Co. Tyrone. This led to an outcry in Parliament and in the press. The film was seized by Scotland Yard acting under the Prevention of Terrorism Act. The

BBC fired the *Panorama* editor Roger Bolton, reinstating him after union pressure. The programme was never completed.

November 1979 - BBC Northern Ireland
SPOTLIGHT

Spotlight, a BBC Northern Ireland local current affairs programme, planned to look at the implications of the *Panorama* 'Carrickmore' affair. The programme was banned at the last minute. *Spotlight* intended to bring together three journalists and three politicians to discuss the issue. Ironically, the official reason for the banning was the BBC's refusal to provide a spokesperson.

March 1980 - Harlech
CURIOUS JOURNEY

Harlech TV banned Kenneth Griffith's documentary *Curious Journey,* which centred on interviews with Irish veterans of 1916 and 1918. Harlech wanted Griffith to cut several quotations from historical figures: one such was from the British Prime Minister William Gladstone roundly condemning the 1800 Act of Union between Britain and Ireland. Griffith refused to make the cuts and Harlech eventually sold him the film rights for £1.

March 1980 - BBC
GONE FOR A SOLDIER

On 9 March Philip Donnellan's film about the history of the British army seen through the eyes of ordinary soldiers and including sequences in the North of Ireland was shown on BBC2. An ensuing row in the House of Commons led to the BBC banning both repeats and foreign sales of the film.

June 1980 - Thames
CREGGAN

Transmission of this film about Derry, by Mary Holland and Michael Whyte, was delayed nearly a year. It was finally shown on 17 June with two cuts and a commentary alteration. Although it won the prestigious Prix Italia and was named the best documentary of 1980 by the British Broadcasting Guild, it has not been repeated.

April 1981 - Thames
TV EYE: 'The Waiting Time'

This film, shown on 30 April, was about events immediately preceding the death of Bobby Sands MP. The IBA forced the producers to cut a 33-second sequence showing IRA members making a statement in a West Belfast social club and receiving rapturous applause.

June 1981 - Granada
WORLD IN ACTION: 'The Propaganda War'

Granada withdrew this film rather than comply with the IBA's command to excise a 27-second sequence showing hunger striker Patsy O'Hara lying in his coffin surrounded by an INLA guard of honour. The IBA apparently felt that the pictures might have invested those shown with a status they did not merit and would have given the 'wrong impression' to a British audience. Ironically part of the offending sequence was transmitted several times in an advance promotion for the programme.

September 1981 - BBC
TOP OF THE POPS

The BBC banned a video made by the rock group Police to accompany their single *Invisible Sun* and due to be shown on *Top of the Pops* on 24 September. *The Times* described it as 'A collage of Ulster street scenes incorporating urchins, graffiti, Saracens and soldiers ... it seemed good-hearted and utterly uncontentious' (16 December 1981). ATV showed a short clip of the video on *Tiswas*, omitting all references to Belfast.

January 1982 - BBC
OPEN DOOR

Senior BBC executives banned the Campaign for Free Speech on Ireland from making a programme for the BBC2 access slot, *Open Door*. The *Open Door* selection committee had approved the Campaign's application in November 1979. The project was 'referred up' to senior executives, including the Managing Director of BBC TV, the Controller of BBC2, and the Director of News and Current Affairs and Controller Northern Ireland. Three independent observers who sit on the *Open Door* selection committee wrote to the BBC to complain about the ban.

March 1983 - Yorkshire Television
FIRST TUESDAY

Yorkshire Television management ordered an end to work on a *First Tuesday* documentary on plastic bullets. Several months research had already been done and filming was due to start the following week. The ban came after the RUC and the IBA had put pressure on Yorkshire TV, following the appearance of an article about the programme in the Belfast paper, *The Irish News*.

October 1983 - Channel 4
THE CAUSE OF IRELAND

Shown in the *Eleventh Hour* slot on 3 October, *The Cause of Ireland* was largely funded by Channel 4. Made by Chris Reeves, a main theme was that

Catholic and Protestant workers in the North cannot be united prior to reunification. Jeremy Isaacs, head of Channel 4, approved the completed film, but members of the IBA personally asked to see it and subsequently demanded that two pieces of commentary and two sequences be cut: a total of six minutes. The first commentary cut was: 'For, while the firepower of republicanism is usually aimed at the security forces or public representatives of the British state, loyalist violence has been directed indiscriminately at the Catholic community.' The second referred to the possibility of bloodshed after a British withdrawal: 'those Protestants who have been trained in the UDR and the RUC would remain a real threat to Catholics in the North of Ireland.' The two sequences are believed to have been removed after Northern Ireland CBA chief Richard Gordon and landowner Bill Montgomery put pressure on the IBA. The first, demonstrating the gap between rich and poor in the North, showed Montgomery and other gentry foxhunting in County Down. The second was an interview with Gordon, who stressed that normal activities like 'playing golf' continued despite the troubles.

1983 - Thames

According to a report in the Dublin *Sunday Tribune*, Thames TV's *TV Eye* compiled a programme in 1983 on cross-border activities by the British army and RUC, including alleged murders and attempted kidnappings. At the time, the *Tribune* reported, it was suspected that political pressure from prime minister Margaret Thatcher's office was responsible for blocking the programme. But this was denied by Barry Sales, Thames TV's news and current affairs director [...] (*Sunday Tribune*, 29 April 1984).

December 1983 - Channel 4
RIGHT TO REPLY

The week before Christmas, Channel 4's *Right to Reply* planned a studio confrontation between Gerry Adams MP and John Ware of Granada TV's *World in Action*, in which Adams would have made detailed criticisms of a film about himself made by Ware. Titled 'The Honourable Member for West Belfast', Ware's film was transmitted on ITV on 19 December 1983, two days after the IRA's bombing of Harrods. But as Philip Schlesinger explained in the *New Statesman*, 'In the aftermath of the bombing it was decided no such programme could be screened, thus forestalling a major political row in which the channel would undoubtedly have faced accusations of treason' (*New Statesman*, 6 January 1984).

December 1983 - Channel 4
SATURDAY NIGHT AT THE LONDON PALLADIUM, BEAT THE CLOCK and ENGLAND

Also in the aftermath of the Harrods bombing, Channel 4 banned several comedy sequences. Two cuts were made to old programmes featured in the *Comedy Classics* slot on 27 December 1983. A running gag featuring Norman Wisdom and Bruce Forsyth, during which Wisdom made repeated attempts to sing 'When Irish Eyes are Smiling', was cut from a rerun of *Saturday Night at the London Palladium* from 1961. Also cut was part of *Beat the Clock*, in which a passing reference was made to the North of Ireland.

Another comedy show to be cut was Paul Hogan's *England*, shown on 30 December. A sequence in which someone tried to steal a Harrods bag was removed, as was another in which a tourist asked the way to Harrods (*New Statesman*, 6 January 1984).

January 1984 - Yorkshire TV
JIMMY YOUNG SHOW

The producers of Yorkshire TV's Jimmy Young chat show arranged for Gerry Adams MP to appear as a guest on the programme to be transmitted on 15 January. According to the *Sunday Times,* 'although Adams's contribution was going to be carefully balanced with other political views, Young refused to do the interview on the grounds that Sinn Féin should not he allowed airtime on British TV' (*Sunday Times*, 15 January 1984). [...] Following the Jimmy Young ban, Gerry Adams was invited for an interview on David Frost's breakfast programme on TV AM - an invitation which was angrily attacked by Tory MPs - and appeared on 15 January 1984.

January 1984 - Channel 4
GREEN FLUTES

Another victim of Channel 4's post-Harrods panic was *Green Flutes*, a documentary by Nancy Schiesari about a republican flute band from Glasgow, which was scheduled for transmission in the *Eleventh Hour* slot on 16 January 1984. Channel 4 executives decided - apparently when the commissioning editor was away - to take the film out of the schedules, and it was finally transmitted on 5 March. The film had previously been delayed twice. A transmission date was first promised for September 1983, but then cuts were demanded - and made - in sequences shot in the North of Ireland. It was then due to be shown in December 1983, but was replaced by a programme about the Clyde, which was then topical.

September 1984 - London Weekend
WEEKEND WORLD: 'From the Shadow of a Gun'

On Sunday 16 September 1984, London Weekend's *Weekend World* slot carried the fourth and final part of a documentary titled 'From the Shadow of a Gun', presented by Mary Holland. The planned format was that former diplomat Nicholas Henderson would take the role of honest broker and interview members of the various political parties in the North of Ireland. But Henderson refused to sit down with Sinn Féin, so LWT offered Sinn Féin a separate interview, done by Mary Holland. Sinn Féin decided not to appear on this basis, and issued a statement on 14 September 1984 saying, 'Sinn Féin sees no reason why it should participate in this programme in a way which depicts republicans as political lepers, and considers that *Weekend World* has surrendered objectivity and independence to the political narrowmindedness of Nicholas Henderson.'

February 1985 - Channel 4/RTE
THE PRICE

The Price was a six-part thriller, shown on Channel 4 and RTE in January and February 1985, about a woman being kidnapped by a republican 'terrorist' organisation. Top Belfast actor Mark Mulholland played the part of an RUC Special Branch detective. In the last episode, according to the script, the detective took part in a shoot-out south of the border. But then, according to Mulholland, his part was dropped from the last episode on RUC instructions, because they did not want even a fictional character acting the part of an RUC officer to be seen operating south of the border. 'I was contracted to do the final episode,' said Mulholland, 'but I was told by the executive producer that the RUC didn't want me in it' (*Sunday Press*, 17 February 1985).

May 1985 - BBC
PANORAMA

A *Panorama* programme critical of policing in the North of Ireland was delayed for a year. The *Irish News* of 12 August 1985 reported that the BBC had 'torpedoed' the programme some three months earlier, on advice from its lawyers. The paper said that the programme 'dealt with Catholic claims that the RUC operated a shoot to kill policy.' The journalists were looking at 'the controversial double killing of Armagh INLA members Seamus Grew and Roddy Carroll in December 1982', and 'were also probing the Stalker Report on the RUC which had been leaked to them.' The programme was finally shown on 16 June 1986.

July 1985 - BBC
REAL LIVES: 'At the Edge of the Union'

One of the biggest rows of the 1980s was over this *Real Lives* programme about the political and personal lives of two Derry politicians, republican Martin McGuinness and loyalist Gregory Campbell. The programme, produced by Paul Hamann, was scheduled for 7 August 1985. On 28 July the *Sunday Times* carried a report titled 'Thatcher slams IRA film', and alleged that McGuinness was chief of staff of the IRA. The BBC had vetted the film through its internal censorship procedures, and executives defended the decision to show it. Then on Monday 29 July the home secretary, Leon Brittan, wrote to the BBC saying the film - which he hadn't seen - was 'contrary to the national interest' and likely to give 'succour to terrorist organisations'.

On Tuesday 30 July the BBC's governors held a special day-long meeting, viewed the programme, and decided to ban it, thus violating the usual relationship between them and the board of management. [...]

The National Union of Journalists called a 24-hour protest stoppage on 7 July, and won almost total support from broadcasters. No national news was broadcast in Britain on 7 August, and the BBC World Service broadcast music all day. The *Times* reported:

> 'The walkout by journalists and technical staff represented the most serious industrial action ever undertaken in British television, and attracted more support than has ever been won by a pay claim or a call for conventional industrial action.' [...]

On the day of the strike, BBC director general Alasdair Milne said that the film would be shown in due course, but needed some amendment. On 5 September a joint statement from the governors and the board of management announced that the film would be shown in October with three small amendments. The main amendment was the addition of a 20-second colour film sequence of the aftermath of the IRA's 'Bloody Friday' bombings in Belfast in 1972, showing bodies being carried away. Two amendments concerned changes to captions. No cuts were made. The film was eventually transmitted on 16 October 1985.

July 1985 - BBC
OPEN SPACE: 'On the Word of a Supergrass'

An article in the *Guardian* on 31 July, in the middle of the *Real Lives* controversy, revealed that Brian Wenham, the BBC's director of programmes, had told the independent producers of 'On the Word of a Supergrass' that the programme would be postponed from its scheduled date of 14 August, possibly to 18 September. The *Guardian* reported: 'It is understood that Mr Wenham was concerned that, whether or not the interview with the alleged IRA chief of staff, Martin McGuinness, was allowed to be shown, a programme on the sensitive subject of supergrasses should not go out only a week later.' 'On the Word of a Supergrass' was eventually transmitted on 19 September.

July 1985 - BBC Scotland
OPEN TO QUESTION

In the midst of the *Real Lives* row, on 31 July 1985, Sinn Féin publicised the fact that Gerry Adams had been sent an invitation by a researcher at BBC

Scotland to appear on *Open to Question,* a discussion slot in which public figures were questioned by teenagers. Sinn Féin announced that Gerry Adams was accepting the invitation. A BBC spokesman told the press that the programme's producers had failed to follow the procedure of referring upwards any programme in which a member of Sinn Féin was to appear, to obtain the approval of senior management (*Daily Telegraph, Star,* 1 August 1985). *Open to Question* never subsequently made a programme featuring Gerry Adams.

August 1985 - BBC Radio Manchester
IRISH LINE

Four members of the production team of *Irish Line,* a weekly programme made (without pay) by the Irish in Britain Representation Group for BBC Radio Manchester, accused the BBC in August 1985 of censoring the programme. In a letter to *the Irish Post,* the paper of the Irish community in Britain, they listed items that had been censored. These included the cutting of two questions from an interview with an Irishwoman who was chairperson of the SDP in Manchester: one asked why she had joined the IBRG, while the other asked what was SDP policy on the presence of British troops in the North of Ireland. The BBC also cut out of a 'What's On' section an announcement of a Labour Party Young Socialists public meeting on strip-searching in Armagh jail. The BBC also cut completely a prerecorded interview about strip-searching with Bernadette Hyland, an IBRG member of the International Women's Day delegation to Armagh, which made an annual protest outside the then women's prison. This item was cut on 24 April, and the programme started six minutes late as a result (*Irish Post,* 10 August 1985).

November 1985 - UTV
WITNESS

On 29 November 1985, UTV refused to screen a five-minute religious broadcast by David Bleakley, general secretary of the Irish Council of Churches. In the broadcast, he warned of the dangers of endemic fear in Northern Ireland and said that what was needed was 'a politics of doing things together'. UTV said that the programme was in contravention of a section of the Broadcasting Act and said it hoped to screen the edition in a later subsequent current affairs programme. David Bleakley said he was 'dumbfounded' at the decision. He was trying to provide a 'vision of reassurance and reconciliation' (*Irish Times,* 30 November 1985).

December 1985 - ITV
CHRISTMAS EVE MASS

Christmas Eve Mass, celebrated by Bishop Cathal Daly, was due to be broadcast from the Mater Hospital, Belfast. Shortly before transmission time, it was announced that the programme had been changed and another programme, recorded a year or two previously, was screened instead. No reason was given for the change.

December 1985 - BBC
SONGS OF PRAISE

Angry Protestants forced the BBC to scrap plans for a cross-community edition of *Songs of Praise* from Dungannon, County Tyrone. The BBC's plan was for Dungannon Protestants and Catholics to join together in a service in the Catholic Church of St Patrick. The BBC had planned to record the programme on the two days immediately prior to the 23 January 1986 by-elections, sparked by the resignation of the Northern Unionist Westminster MPs, who were protesting against the recently signed Anglo-Irish Agreement. Anger at the Anglo-Irish Agreement was thought to be the cause of the Protestants' unwillingness to co-operate with *Songs of Praise*. Father Skelly, head of religious programmes for BBC Northern Ireland, said that Dungannon was the first area where he had found any opposition to the programme, which had been recorded in Larne, Limavady, Strabane and Letterkenny 'with good support from both sections in the community' (*Irish News*, 31 December 1985).

January 1986 - BBC
QUESTION TIME

The BBC scrapped plans for a *Question Time* to be broadcast from Belfast on 30 January 1986, shortly after the by-elections provoked by Unionist MPs resigning in protest at the recently signed Anglo-Irish agreement. Those invited to take part included Tom King, the secretary of state for Northern Ireland, and Peter Barry, minister for foreign affairs for the Republic of Ireland. The *Irish News* reported: 'It is thought that unionist politicians, currently refusing to speak to Mr King, would have been reluctant to take part in the broadcast, leaving the programme-makers with problems over balancing content' (*Irish News*, 18 January 1986). [...]

December 1986 - Channel 4
ELEVENTH HOUR: 'Turn it Up/They Shoot to Kill Children'

On 8 December 1986 the IBA, with the agreement of Channel 4's management, banned a 14-minute video about the use of plastic bullets in the North of Ireland. The video, titled 'They Shoot to Kill Children', was due to be shown late that night in the *Eleventh Hour* slot at the end of a compilation of videos made by groups of young people. The compilation, titled 'Turn It Up', was put together by the Birmingham Film and Video Workshop. The banned video included an interview with Paul Corr, who was hit in the face by a plastic bullet in 1981 when he was 12 years old, and a song which mentioned 14 of those killed by rubber and plastic bullets.

March 1987 - BBC
CROSSFIRE

This five-part thriller serial was referred back to the BBC in London for changes by James Hawthorne, the BBC's Northern Ireland controller. He was believed to have asked for the series' final two parts to be reshot. He said he had not previously been consulted by the programme's makers and, having viewed it, found it gave too sympathetic a portrayal of the IRA and an unfavourable depiction of the security forces. The programme had taken over two years to make, at a cost of over £1 million. Due to be screened from 6 March 1987, it finally went out from 15 March 1988.

In April 1988 actor Tony Doyle, who played the IRA chief of staff in the series, revealed that he had to redub certain lines in the script on the insistence of the RUC. He said: 'In one line I said "The organisation has safe houses in Belfast." I had to change that to "The organisation has bridgeheads in Belfast." They are of the opinion that there are no safe houses in Belfast' (*Sunday Press*, 10 April 1988).

December 1987 - Channel 4
COURT REPORT: 'The Birmingham Six'

On 3 December 1987, the attorney-general was granted an injunction by the Court of Appeal preventing Channel 4 from broadcasting that night a dramatised version of the appeal hearing of the Birmingham Six. The Court of Appeal, which consisted of the lord chief justice, Lord Lane, and two other judges, was the same court that was currently hearing the Birmingham Six's appeal, depicted in the dramatisation. On 16 December, the three judges refused to lift the injunction. They finally lifted in on 29 January 1988, after they had rejected the Birmingham Six's appeal, and Channel 4 cleared the schedules to show the two-hour programme that evening.

January 1988 - Channel 4
ACCEPTABLE LEVELS

Channel 4 chief Michael Grade pulled *Acceptable Levels* from the schedules on 28 January 1988 because he felt it would be 'inappropriate' to screen it on the day of the verdict in the Birmingham six appeal. Ironically the film examines media self-censorship: it tells the story of how a TV team reacts when a child they are filming in Divis Flats is killed by a British soldier's plastic bullet. *Acceptable Levels* had been shown before on Channel 4, on 30 April 1984. Its suppression was discussed in a *Right to Reply* programme in February 1988. It was finally transmitted on 18 February 1988.

April 1988 - London Weekend
ABC OF BRITISH MUSIC

A scene showing the killing of a British soldier was removed from the *ABC of British Music,* directed by Ken Russell, after the killing of two soldiers who drove into a republican funeral parade in Belfast. The scene accompanied the Pogues singing 'The Ballad of the Gentleman Soldier'. It depicted a soldier bringing a girl into a sentry box. Soon after the girl leaves, the sentry box explodes. Instead the scene, to be shown on Easter Saturday, just showed the sentry box 'wobbling about a bit'. The Pogues were included under I for Ireland.

April 1988 - Channel 4
FRIDAY NIGHT LIVE: The Pogues

The Pogues accused Channel 4 of censoring one of their songs and said they would not appear on the channel again. They were performing their song 'Streets of Sorrow/Birmingham Six' live when they were cut off two-thirds of the way through by a commercial break. The programme's producer denied that it was censorship and said the artists had to be kept to a very exact time. The Pogues' manager complained that no-one cuts off comedians before the punch-line, nor are boxing or football matches cut off before the end just because a commercial break was on the way. He said he believed the programme had several minutes to spare before the end, which the presenters had to fill by ad libbing (*Irish Post,* 7 May 1988).

** A major storm blew up in April and May 1988 over Thames TV's *This Week* programme 'Death on the Rock', which cast doubts on the government's version of what happened when the SAS killed three IRA members in Gibraltar in March 1988. On 28 April foreign secretary Geoffrey Howe asked Lord Thompson, chair of the IBA, to postpone the programme until after the inquest in Gibraltar. The IBA refused, and the programme was broadcast on 5 May. Following transmission, prime minister Thatcher, Northern Ireland secretary Tom King, and much of the press, accused Thames TV of 'trial by television'. Thames TV subsequently initiated an independent inquiry into the programme under Lord Windlesham: the inquiry concluded that it was appropriate that the programme was made.

June 1988 - Channel 4
NETWORK 7

When *Network 7*, a trendy Channel 4 magazine programme which was normally transmitted live, planned to broadcast a live discussion on 'Should the troops remain in Ireland?', the IBA demanded that the programme should be prerecorded a few hours earlier to allow them to vet the tapes before transmission. The programme had commissioned a poll on 'troops out' that revealed 57 per cent in favour and 43 per cent against. A planned live phone-in poll was dropped after pressure from the IBA, who claimed it would be 'open to abuse by unrepresentative opinion'. Such polls were standard practice on *Network 7.*

August 1988 - BBC
ELEPHANT, MONKEYS and NIGHTWATCH

In the wake of the Ballygawley bus bombing, in which eight British soldiers were killed, the BBC announced on 23 August 1988 that it was postponing three plays made by BBC Northern Ireland, saying it was 'inappropriate to allow such plays at this time'. *Elephant* was a play without dialogue, reenacting a series of killings in the North of Ireland. *Nightwatch* was about freelance intelligence services in Amsterdam and mercenaries in Africa. *Monkeys* reproduced parts of the court hearings of failed car manufacturer John de Lorean, when he faced charges of drug dealing. The three plays were finally shown over three weeks starting on 25 January 1989.

September 1988 - Channel 4
AFTER DARK WITH GERRY ADAMS MP

On 8 October 1988 Professor Paul Wilkinson of Aberdeen University publicised and protested against the fact that Gerry Adams MP was to appear in *After Dark's* live late-night discussion show on 10 October. The programme-makers had asked Wilkinson for advice on contacts, but had not asked him to appear. Wilkinson's protest led to angry attacks on Channel 4 by Tory MPs. Liz Forgan, Channel 4's director of programmes, decided that the programme should be abandoned, claiming that a 'satisfactory context' for Adams' appearance could not be found at such short notice. Forgan thus avoided a confrontation with the IBA, which said that if necessary it would have used Section 4 of the Broadcasting Act to stop Adams appearing (*Guardian,* 19 September 1988).

October 1988 - BBC
PANORAMA ON THE SAS

A *Panorama* programme on the role of the SAS in the North of Ireland, due to be shown on 3 October 1988, was postponed after the BBC's director general Michael Checkland and his deputy John Birt had viewed it. A BBC spokesman said that they had taken the decision on the grounds that the programme 'needed a bit more doing on it' (*Guardian,* 3 October 1988). The programme was shown on 17 October after cuts and changes had been made. Part of an SAS training video showing an exercise in the regiment's 'killing house' was removed on the advice of Admiral William Higgins, secretary to the D-notice committee. The scene showed SAS soldiers in balaclavas using live bullets to rescue a hostage held by the IRA.

THE BROADCASTING BAN

The broadcasting ban on eleven Irish organisations was formally announced by the home secretary, Douglas Hurd, on 19 October 1988. [...]

The ban prevents the broadcasting of words spoken by representatives of eleven organisations, and of words spoken in support of those organisations. When the ban was introduced, three of the affected organisations were legal - Sinn Féin, Republican Sinn Féin, and the Ulster Defence Association - but the UDA was subsequently outlawed. The ban also covers all organisations banned under the Emergency Provisions Act or the Prevention of Terrorism Act. These are now: the IRA, the INLA, Cumann na mBan, Fianna Eireann, the Red Hand Commandos, Saor Eire (long since defunct), the Ulster Freedom Fighters, the Ulster Volunteer Force, and the UDA. [...]

In the immediate aftermath of the ban, local radio stations both in the North of Ireland and in Britain applied it indiscriminately. Those who found themselves silenced included not only representatives of Sinn Féin, but also Errol Smalley, uncle of Paul Hill of the Guildford Four; Bernadette Devlin McAliskey; Richard Stanton, a Brighton Labour councillor and member of the Troops Out Movement; and US author Margie Bernard, author of *Daughter of Derry*, and the subject of her book, Brigid Sheils Makowski. [...]

Most interviews with Sinn Féin representatives are now broadcast with the person's original voice removed, and replaced either with a reporter's voiceover, or with subtitles, or with an actor's voice. In some cases, programme-makers have gone to great lengths to ensure that the actor's voice is accurately dubbed and similar to the original. [...]

October 1988 - Channel 4
MOTHER IRELAND

Mother Ireland, a 52-minute video made by Derry Film and Video and funded by Channel 4, was the first television programme to fall victim to the ban. The video explores the personification of Ireland as a woman in Irish culture and nationalism. Among the many women interviewed are historian Margaret MacCurtain, journalist Nell McCafferty, film-maker Pat Murphy, Cumann na mBan veterans Sighle Humphries and Miriam James, and Mairead Farrell (shot dead by the SAS in Gibraltar in March 1988). [...] For several months before the ban, Channel 4 had been requesting alterations to the video. They wanted the removal of film of Emma Groves immediately after she was shot in the face by a rubber bullet fired by a British soldier in 1971, and also of Christy Moore's song 'Unfinished Revolution', and of a montage of Irish women in resistance roles. Just before the ban, Channel 4 demanded more changes, including the removal of the interview with Mairead Farrell.

On 2 November Channel 4 issued a statement saying that the ban 'made further discussion on such a version academic, for it was clear that under any legal interpretation, the ban would rule out many other sections of the programme, including contributions from elderly participants in the 1920s Civil War'. [...]

In February 1989, *Mother Ireland* won the 'best documentary' award at a major international women's film festival, Femmes Cathodiques, in Paris. It was shown widely in Europe, the USA, Australia and New Zealand, and was bought by the West German station WDR and by Basque television. The footage of Emma Groves after she was shot by a rubber bullet was shown on BBC2 in May 1989 in the *Split Screen* slot, in a film made by Ken Loach for the Time to Go campaign.

Parts of Derry Film and Video's interview with Mairead Farrell - sections which had not been used in *Mother Ireland,* were shown on US television in June 1989, in the film *Death of a Terrorist* (see below). *Mother Ireland* was eventually transmitted - although with alterations - by Channel 4 in April 1991 as part of its banned season (see below).

October 1988 - Channel 4
THE MEDIA SHOW

On 30 October 1988, Channel 4's *Media Show* carried an examination of the effects of the broadcasting ban. This included an interview with Derry Sinn Féin councillor Dodie McGuinness, whose voice was silenced and replaced with another voice repeating exactly what she had said. Cllr McGuinness had explained how the ban made it impossible for her to use the media to get publicity for the council's campaign against the closure of a local maternity unit. [...]

The local BBC radio station, Radio Foyle, took a different line, broadcasting an interview with Cllr McGuinness on 16 November 1988 with sound intact.

October 1988 - BBC Northern Ireland
SPOTLIGHT

On 19 October 1989, *Spotlight* carried an interview with Tommy Lyttle, a leader of the Ulster Defence Association. His voice was silenced and a reporter read an exact transcript of his words.

November 1988 - Commercial TV and radio
THE POGUES: 'Streets of Sorrow/Birmingham Six'

On 20 November 1988 the *Observer* revealed that the Independent Broadcasting Authority had issued a circular to all commercial radio stations saying that the Pogues' song 'Streets of Sorrow/Birmingham Six' should not be played. The song supported the pleas of innocence by the Birmingham Six and Guildford Four, who were then still imprisoned. The

IBA said in a statement that, 'The song alleges some convicted terrorists are not guilty and goes on to suggest that Irish people are at a disadvantage in British courts of law. That allegation might support or solicit or invite support for an organisation proscribed by the Home Secretary's directive, in that they indicate a general disagreement with the way in which the British government responds to, and the courts deal with, the terrorist threat in the UK'.

The IBA's ban was made by its radio division and followed a request for a ruling on five songs by executives at Manchester's Piccadilly Radio. The IBA cleared the other four songs, one of which, ironically, was Paul McCartney's 'Give Ireland Back to the Irish', which was banned by the BBC in 1971. The IBA's director of television followed the ruling made by the radio division. [...]

December 1988 - BBC
40 MINUTES: 'Greenfinches'

After consultation with the Ministry of Defence, the BBC cut part of 'Greenfinches', a documentary about three women members of the Ulster Defence Regiment, transmitted on 1 December 1988. A BBC spokesman told the press that the programme could not have been made without the cooperation of the MoD: 'As a courtesy they were shown the film and voiced concern about the security aspects of one aspect of the programme. After due consideration we agreed to trim the voiceover' (*Irish News*, 25 November 1988). One section cut was reportedly a suggestion made by one of the UDR women 'that some UDR members join purely to get firearms training to fight a civil war against the Catholics, should the army be withdrawn' (*Independent*, 24 November 1988).

1989 - Channel 4
THE SILENT SCREAM (Originally 'Sixteen Dead')

The Silent Scream was a documentary about the use of plastic bullets in the North of Ireland commissioned by Channel 4 from Belfast Independent Video (now Northern Visions). It was made in close collaboration with relatives of those killed or injured by plastic bullets. All stages of production were monitored by Channel 4, to a second 'rough cut' edit, and pronounced satisfactory. But Channel 4 decided not to transmit the programme, giving as an official reason its 'lack of structure'. Unofficially, the programme-makers were told, 'We have to keep our heads low,' and 'Ireland is a sensitive issue'.

1989 - All channels
DEATH OF A TERRORIST

Death of a Terrorist is a documentary about the life of Mairead Farrell, one of three IRA members killed by the SAS in Gibraltar in March 1988. It was made by William Cran - a former BBC producer - for the Boston station WGBH's *Frontline* slot. WGBH is part of the Public Broadcasting Service network, which includes more than 200 US television stations. *Death of a Terrorist* was shown on the PBS network on 13 June 1989. It was subsequently shown on NHK - Japan's equivalent of the BBC - and in some European countries.

Executives from the BBC, Channel 4 and Thames TV asked to see *Death of a Terrorist*. All said they liked the programme and that it was a pity that it was unbroadcastable in Britain under the present rules. (See article by Roger Bolton in the *Listener,* 3 August 1989.) [...]

March 1989 - BBC
HERE IS THE NEWS

The BBC ordered cuts in *Here is the News,* a thriller by G.F. Newman, which was transmitted on Sunday 5 March 1989. One section cut was a fragment of conversation between the attorney-general and a journalist which suggested that the prime minister knew the truth about the SAS killing of three members of the IRA in Gibraltar (*Guardian,* 3 March 1989).

May 1989 - Channel 4
ELEVENTH HOUR: 'Trouble the Calm'

'Trouble the Calm', a film by Faction Films about political attitudes in the South of Ireland, was shown in Channel 4's *Eleventh Hour* slot on 8 May 1989. Channel 4 insisted that the film-makers cut about two minutes of an interview with a woman whose husband was imprisoned in Portlaoise, in which she explained why he had been jailed. The film-makers persuaded Channel 4 to allow them to replace the excised section with a caption, which read: 'Under government broadcasting restrictions, in force since October 1988, this woman cannot explain her husband's beliefs and motivations which led to his imprisonment in Portlaoise goal'.

June 1989 - Channel 4
DISPATCHES: 'A State of Decay'

This *Dispatches* programme, an assessment marking the twentieth anniversary of British troops being deployed in the North of Ireland, included a voiced-over interview with Gerry Adams MP. It was shown on 28 June 1989.

August-September 1989 - Thames
THE TROUBLES

From 17 August 1989, Thames TV repeated its acclaimed series on the history of the North of Ireland, *The Troubles,* in five weekly parts. The series had first been shown in January and February 1981. Due to the broadcasting ban six pieces of sound that had been transmitted in 1981 were excised from the repeat and replaced with subtitles.

The censored items included interviews with Gerry Adams and Joe Cahill, both of Sinn Féin. In the fourth programme, prisoners' voices were censored in film shot in 1979 during the 'no wash' and 'blanket' protests, as was the voice of hunger striker Raymond McCartney in an interview done by Granada TV's *World in Action* in November 1980. [...]

August 1989 - BBC
FOREVER DIVIDED

Forever Divided, shown on 13 August 1989, was a 90-minute programme by Jonathon Dimbleby marking the twentieth anniversary of the deployment of troops. It included a subtitled interview with Gerry Adams MP. [...] (*Independent,* 14 August 1989)

August 1989 - Channel 4
CREGGAN

On 22 August 1989, Channel 4 repeated the Thames TV film *Creggan* by Michael Whyte and Mary Holland, in a series of prize-winning Thames films. *Creggan,* about people on a Derry housing estate, had first been shown on 17 June 1980 after being delayed for ten months (see above). It won the Prix Italia but was not repeated at the time.The repeat fell victim to the broadcasting ban. Four sections of sound were cut, from interviews with two women, and replaced by subtitles. [...]

August 1989 - Visnews

On 23 August 1989, *Public Eye,* a current affairs programme on Australia's Channel 10, transmitted a critical film about the British broadcasting ban. It included a sequence showing how Maxine Mawhinney of the Belfast office of Visnews, the world's largest television news agency, now routinely made two versions of stories involving Sinn Féin. One version, without Sinn Féin voices, was for sale to Sky News for transmission to the UK. The other, with Sinn Féin voices, was for sale to television stations internationally. *Public Eye* used as an example Mawhinney's two versions of a report of Gerry Adams' address to Sinn Féin's annual conference.

September 1989 - BBC
BENTHAM/1996

The BBC insisted that G.F. Newman rewrite a play loosely based on the Stalker investigation of the RUC's 'shoot-to-kill' policy and the Kincora boys' home scandal. He had to change the setting from Ireland in the past to Wales in the future. The original version, a three-part series, was based on his book *The Testing Ground* and was titled *Bentham* after the central character. The new version, shown on 17 September 1989, was a single play titled *1996*.

September 1989 - Channel 4
DISPATCHES: 'A State of Decay' (repeat)

On 21 September 1989, Channel 4 repeated this *Dispatches* programme, first shown on 28 June, which included a voiced-over interview with Gerry Adams MP.

September 1989 - ITV
SARACEN

Following the IRA's bombing of a Marines barracks in Deal, Kent, on 22 September 1989, which killed 10 bandsmen, ITV postponed the episode of the thriller series *Saracen* due to be shown next night. The episode recounted events after one of the heroes, a former SAS man, took up with an Irish woman not realising he had killed one of her relations while serving in the North of Ireland. It was replaced by a story about a London bank robbery, and was transmitted later on 7 October.

September 1989 - BBC
THE SQUAD

This programme, about the West Midlands Serious Crimes Squad was scheduled for 28 September 1989, but was pulled that day after a High Court judge granted the Police Federation an injunction preventing its screening for seven days; this squad had been involved with the case of the Birmingham Six. The injunction was based on the alleged risk of serious prejudice to forthcoming criminal proceedings. The BBC applied to the Court of Appeal, which on 30 September gave the go-ahead for the programme to be transmitted. It was shown on 26 October 1989.

October 1989 - BBC
LATE SHOW

In a *Late Show* item on 19 October 1989 about the broadcasting ban, Sinn Féin councillor Mitchel McLaughlin was voiced over in sync by actor Harry Towb, who reproduced even the 'ums'. This had the strange effect of making McLaughlin, a Derry man in his early forties whose voice is familiar to listeners in the area, sound like a Belfast docker in his sixties.

October 1989 - Channel 4
MEDIA SHOW

In a *Media Show* programme on the broadcasting ban, shown on 15 October 1989, Derry Sinn Féin councillor Mitchel McLaughlin was silenced and subtitled.

October 1989 - Channel 4
HARD NEWS

In a *Hard News* item on media coverage of Ireland, shown on 19 October 1989, Danny Morrison, Sinn Féin's director of publicity, was silenced and subtitled.

October 1989 - BBC
QUESTION TIME

Jonathon Porritt and Paul Boateng MP recited the lyrics of the Pogues' song 'Birmingham Six' on *Question Time* on 19 October 1989. Unlike the IBA, the BBC had no ban on the song. Paul Boateng said, 'I felt it important to highlight the absurdity of the regulation,' and accused the IBA of 'cravenness' (*Sunday Correspondent,* 22 October 1989).

October 1989 - Channel 4
AFTER DARK

An *After Dark* programme on censorship, planned for 21 October 1989 and marking the first anniversary of the broadcasting ban, was scrapped when the IBA said it could not include members of organisations covered by the ban. The producers of the live late-night discussion programme had aimed to include Danny Morrison, publicity director of Sinn Féin, silencing his words and having a stand-in repeat them. An IBA spokesperson said, 'the voiceover method was thought unworkable in a live TV-interview situation. Technically, it might have been allowed, but in the context, it could have transgressed the guidelines' (*Sunday Correspondent,* 22 October 1989).

October 1989 - Channel 4
RIGHT TO REPLY

Two contributors to a *Right to Reply* programme on 28 October 1989 were voiced over. The first was Tony Doherty, a young man from Derry, who complained about the broadcasting ban in a 'videobox' item. Second to be voiced over was Mary Nelis, also from Derry, who participated in a studio discussion in Belfast about the BBC's *Families at War* series. She was introduced with the words, 'Now, Mary, you're a member of Sinn Féin, so we say again, people will not hear your voice.' She complained about the *Families at War* programme on ex-prisoner Shane Paul O'Doherty.

January 1990 - UTV
COUNTERPOINT

A *Counterpoint* programme on 18 January 1990 on the planned conference/ concert hall for Belfast included an interview with Sinn Féin councillor Mairtín Ó Muilleoir, but without using his voice. Ó Muilleoir afterwards accused UTV of broadening the scope of the broadcasting ban. He said that a *Counterpoint* reporter had agreed his comments should be broadcast, but that his interview had subsequently been presented as one given by a representative of Sinn Féin rather than as by a councillor for Upper Falls. He pointed out that former Home Secretary Douglas Hurd had said Sinn Féin councillors could be interviewed if they were speaking as members of a council rather than as members of Sinn Féin (*Irish News*, 22 January 1990).

February 1990 - BBC
ON THE RECORD

Three Sinn Féin spokespersons were silenced and dubbed over by actors' voices in *On the Record* on 18 February 1990. The programme included an assessment of Northern Ireland Secretary Peter Brooke's current initiative. Those voiced over were Sinn Féin president Gerry Adams, Sinn Féin councillor Mairtín Ó Muilleoir, and party spokesperson Richard McAuley.

March 1990 - BBC Northern Ireland
MURDER OF SAMUEL MARSHALL

On 7 March 1990 Samuel Marshall was shot dead by loyalists as he walked away from a Lurgan police station where he reported as a condition of bail. Next day Sinn Féin held a press conference to be addressed by two witnesses to the killing, neither of whom were members of Sinn Féin. But while Ulster Television News carried comments by one of the men, the local BBC news did not broadcast either man's comments. [...]

April 1990 - UTV
THE STRUGGLE FOR DEMOCRACY

Ulster Television pulled this documentary made by Central Television from the schedule on 9 April 1990, when it was due to be shown, after four UDR men were killed when a bomb blew up their landrover on the outskirts of Downpatrick. The programme included references to the Enniskillen Remembrance Day bombing and to Bloody Sunday in 1972. [...] The programme was shown elsewhere on the ITV network on 9 April as scheduled.

April 1990 - Channel 4
DISPATCHES: 'Terms for Peace'

This *Dispatches* programme, by journalist Mary Holland, shown on 11 April 1990, included a 16-minute interview with Gerry Adams, MP for West Belfast and president of Sinn Féin. His voice was dubbed over in lip-sync by actor Stephen Rea. Leading republican Martin McGuinness was also dubbed in lip-sync. *Observer* TV reviewer John Naughton wrote that by this device, *Dispatches* 'drove a coach and horses through the Government's fatuous ban on Sinn Féin and other prohibited spokespersons' (*Observer,* 15 April 1990). *Guardian* reviewer Hugh Hebert wrote that it was 'the ultimate demonstration of the total stupidity of the ban' (*Guardian,* 12 April 1990).

June 1990 - UTV
SHOOT TO KILL

Ulster Television refused to screen *Shoot to Kill,* a four-hour documentary drama reconstructing the RUC killings of six unarmed men - five of them paramilitaries - in County Armagh in 1982. The programme, made by Yorkshire Television, was due to be screened throughout the ITV network on 3 and 4 June 1990. UTV claimed to be acting on legal advice, that to show the programme would be contempt of court. The Belfast *Irish News* suggested this might refer to a Court of Appeal hearing currently being brought by relatives of four of the dead [...] The Committee on the Administration of Justice, a Belfast-based pressure group, organised a screening of *Shoot to Kill* to an invited audience on 17 June at the Queen's Film Theatre.

July 1990
DEAR SARAH - ITV

Written by journalist Tom McGurk, *Dear Sarah* was a television drama based on the love story of Sarah Conlon and her husband Giuseppe Conlon, one of the 'Maguire Seven', arrested in 1974 and imprisoned for explosive offences.

Giuseppe Conlon had died of tuberculosis in 1980 in the hospital next to Wormwood Scrubs prison, still protesting his innocence, and was only vindicated in 1989 when the Guildford Four - one of whom was his son Gerry - were released.

McGurk originally wrote the script as a one-hour BBC drama in 1986, but the BBC rejected it. Then David Elstein at Thames TV recommissioned it as a 90-minute film, bringing in Frank Cvitanovich as director. The project then had a bumpy ride, first rejected by Thames TV's board - apparently unnerved by the *Death on the Rock* controversy in 1988 - then approved by them in the autumn of 1989, only to be vetoed again a month later. Thames had by now set up a co-production deal with RTE, the Irish broadcasting company. After Thames' withdrawal, RTE tried to interest Ulster Television and Channel 4 but without success. Finally RTE took over the entire production, financing it by pre-selling it to the ITV network. The finished film was shown on ITV on 2 July 1990.

July 1990 - Yorkshire
FIRST TUESDAY: Joyriders

In this programme on joyriders, shown on 3 July 1990, Alex Maskey of Sinn Féin was silenced and dubbed over by an actor's voice.

** July 1990 - Sky TV
NBC NIGHTLY NEWS: Interview with Richard McAuley

On 20 July 1990 the satellite channel Sky TV breached the broadcasting ban by transmitting an interview with Sinn Féin spokesperson Richard McAuley. He had been interviewed by the American *NBC Nightly News* programme, which Sky TV regularly transmits live at 11.30 pm. [...]

October 1990 - BBC and ITN
NEWS

On Sunday 30 September 1990, joyriders Martin Peake and Karen Reilly were shot dead by British soldiers in West Belfast. Next day, Gerry Adams, MP for the area, was interviewed by various TV and radio programmes, which varied in how they transmitted the interview. On BBC Radio 4's one o'clock news, Gerry Adams' words were spoken by a reporter, with the interviewer's questions inserted. But BBC television's six o'clock and nine o'clock news that evening carried Adams' own voice, saying, 'I will be asking how many shots were fired, why has no one seen the car, why don't the British Army put forward spokespersons, how many soldiers were involved?' (*Daily Mail,* 2 October 1990). By contrast ITN used a reporter to paraphrase Adams' words, stating, 'In comments which can't be broadcast under government restrictions, West Belfast MP Gerry Adams claimed the security forces knew the area was a race-track for joyriders'.

The BBC told the press it had taken legal advice before screening the interview, and that the broadcast did not contravene the guidelines because 'Mr Adams was speaking as MP for the constituency where one of the victims lived' (*Daily Mail,* 2 October 1990). Tory MP Ivor Stanbrook called the incident an 'outrageous breach' of the government's ban, and Democratic Unionist MP the Rev William McCrea also complained, but the Home Office said it would not investigate it (*Irish News,* 2 October 1990).

October 1990 - BBC
THE MARY WHITEHOUSE EXPERIENCE

According to the *Sun,* the BBC banned a comedy sketch of Terry Wogan 'dressed as an IRA terrorist' from the *Mary Whitehouse Experience* on the advice of its lawyers. The *Sun* wrote: 'The tasteless gag had a Wogan impressionist wearing a black balaclava, camouflage clothing and toting a machine gun' (*Sun,* 3 October 1990).

October 1990 - BBC

STAR TREK

The *Daily Mail* speculated on 17 October 1990 that the BBC might censor a future series of *Star Trek*. The BBC bought a package of more than 80 episodes of *Star Trek* from its American makers. The *Mail* reported: 'In one episode, mention is made of British forces quitting Ulster in the 21st century after an IRA victory. "Characters refer to the Army pulling out because they couldn't win," a BBC insider revealed last night'. [...] Rumour has it that this episode was made in response to Irish American complaints about a previous edition featuring drunken, violent people with Irish accents! [...]

October 1990 - Channel 4

TERROR: 'The Decay of Democracy'

The last episode of this three-part documentary series, transmitted on 29 October 1990, used an actor's voice to dub over Sinn Féin spokesperson Jim Gibney.

November 1990 - BBC

QUESTION TIME

The BBC pulled out of broadcasting *Question Time* from Belfast City Hall on 8 November 1990 because of the Unionist-dominated city council's policy not to allow British government ministers onto the premises - a protest against the Anglo-Irish Agreement of 1985. The programme was broadcast from Bradford instead.

November 1990 - BBC

INSIDE STORY: 'The Maze - Enemies Within'

'The Maze - Enemies Within', transmitted on 20 November 1990, showed the daily lives of republican and loyalist prisoners in the Maze prison, formerly Long Kesh. Where prisoners were speaking in a personal capacity, their own voices were heard, but where they were speaking as IRA representatives, their voices were dubbed by actors. One of those affected was the 'IRA spokesman on food': his words, spoken by an actor, were. 'Well, the thing about the sausage rolls ... they're getting smaller, in terms of size and all that there, y'know. The quality is still all right' (*Independent* 21 November 1990).

February 1991 - BBC

CHILDREN OF THE NORTH

Children of the North, a four-part thriller set in the North of Ireland, was due to be shown in February 1991, but the BBC withdrew it because, in the words of the *Observer*, it decided 'it was inappropriate to air a programme whose theme was violence when British troops were fighting in the Gulf' (*Observer* 27 October 1991). The series was finally shown in the autumn, starting on 30 October 1991.

** March 1991 - IBA
STREETS OF SORROW/BIRMINGHAM SIX

The Belfast *Irish News* reported on 21 March 1991 that the IBA had lifted its ban on the Pogues' song 'Streets of Sorrow/Birmingham Six', which proclaimed the innocence of the Birmingham Six and Guildford Four. The IBA said, 'Now that the Birmingham Six are obviously not convicted terrorists, the record can be played again'.

April 1991 - Channel 4
'BANNED' SEASON

Channel Four ran a three-week season titled *Banned,* from 8 April 1991, featuring controversial television programmes. Several of these were on Ireland: *Mother Ireland, World in Action's* 'The Propaganda War', *This Week's* 'Death on the Rock', and *Dispatches'* interview with Gerry Adams. Ironically, every one of these was censored as a result of the broadcasting ban.

April 1991 - Channel 4
'BANNED' SEASON: *Mother Ireland*

This was the first screening for Derry Film and Video's *Mother Ireland,* which was the first television programme to be banned after the introduction of the broadcasting ban (see above, October/November 1988). [...]

The version shown by Channel 4 in its *Banned* season, on 11 April 1991, was, however, itself censored. Some of the alterations were those demanded by Channel 4 before the introduction of the broadcasting ban. The programme-makers had to remove footage of Mrs Emma Groves filmed immediately after she had been shot in the face - and, as it turned out, blinded - by a rubber bullet in 1971; paradoxically this sequence had been shown by the BBC on 9 May 1989, in a short film for *Split Screen* by Ken Loach. They also had to remove Christy Moore's song *Unfinished Revolution,* and footage of a group of women in the IRA.

Additional changes were made because of the broadcasting ban. An interview with Mairead Farrell was dubbed over in lip-sync by an actress; Farrell was one of the three IRA members shot dead by the SAS in Gibraltar in 1988, and the interview had been filmed after her release from Armagh gaol. But an interview with Rita O'Hare, a leading Sinn Féin member in Dublin, was not voiced over; her affiliation was not mentioned, and she was simply captioned by her name.

April 1991 - Channel 4
RIGHT TO REPLY

Complaints about the censorship of *Mother Ireland* were voiced on *Right to Reply* on 13 April 1991. This programme repeated parts of the interview with Mairead Farrell dubbed over with an actress' voice. *Right to Reply* showed scenes from two sequences which had been cut from the programme: a group of women IRA members, and Mrs Emma Groves after she had been hit in the face by a rubber bullet.

April 1991 - Channel 4
'BANNED' SEASON: *This Week*: 'Death on the Rock'

Thames TV's 'Death on the Rock', which had provoked government fury by asking questions about the SAS killings of three IRA members in Gibraltar in March 1988, was shown for the second time on 18 April 1991, as part of Channel 4's *Banned* season.

But this screening, unlike the first one, was censored. Because of the broadcasting ban, Channel 4 replaced a sound recording of the voice of Mairead Farrell, one of the Gibraltar victims, with subtitles. [...]

April 1991 - Channel 4
'BANNED' SEASON: *World in Action*: 'The Propaganda War'

This screening, on 23 April 1991, was the first for Granada's 'The Propaganda War', made during the 1981 hunger strikes. Granada withdrew the film in June 1981 rather than comply with the IBA's command to excise a 27-second sequence showing hunger striker Patsy O'Hara in his coffin. [...] For this screening, the disputed sequence was reinstated, but, because of the broadcasting ban, Sinn Féin spokesman Joe Austin was dubbed over by an actor in lip-sync, as was an H Block blanket protester, who shouted, 'We're political prisoners. We want political status'. The H Block sequence had been shown intact on television in 1981.

April 1991 - Channel 4
'BANNED' SEASON: *Dispatches*: 'Terms for Peace'

This showing, on 22 April 1991, was a repeat of the *Dispatches* programme which included a long interview with Gerry Adams MP, meticulously dubbed over in lip-sync by actor Stephen Rea. The programme was previously shown on 11 April 1990 (see above).

June 1991 - BBC Northern Ireland
SPOTLIGHT: The Official IRA

The Irish Republican Socialist Party claimed that BBC governors in Britain had pressurised the *Spotlight* team to drop this programme, which featured claims that the Official IRA (in theory disbanded) had carried out racketeering, fraud and armed robberies, and that some of those convicted of such crimes were members of the Workers Party (formerly Official Sinn Féin).

Kevin McQuillan, a spokesperson for the IRSP, which split from the Officials, claimed that the programme had been scheduled for May 1991, then rescheduled for 13 June, then stopped again. The BBC rejected allegations of pressure either from the BBC or from the Northern Ireland Office to stop the programme. It was finally shown on 27 June 1991 (*Irish News*, 14 June, 28 June 1991).

** In October 1991 the Independent Television Commission (replacement of the IBA) refused to renew the franchise of Thames Television. This was widely seen as a punishment for Thames for showing ' Death on the Rock', about the SAS killings in Gibraltar, in 1988.

October 1991 - Channel 4
Dispatches

A Channel 4 *Dispatches* programme, alleging high-level RUC involvement in a loyalist committee which planned the murder of Catholics, led to a long-running battle between the RUC and Channel 4. Made by Box Productions the programme was transmitted on 2 October 1991. The RUC investigated, and the Metropolitan Police Special Branch obtained orders under the Prevention of Terrorism Act requiring Channel 4 and Box Productions to hand over files and other materials relating to the programme. Both companies refused to comply with the orders, because they had promised a source - known as 'Source A' - that they would protect his identity. Instead, they destroyed or sent abroad material that could have compromised him. Channel 4 and Box Productions were then charged with contempt of court, and on 31 July 1992 were fined £75,000. There was relief that the fine was relatively low, but concern that the judgement denied programme-makers the right to give an unqualified undertaking to a source to protect their anonymity.

Two months later, on 29 September 1992, the researcher for the programme, Ben Hamilton, was arrested at his home in London. He was held for questioning, then charged with perjury. The charges were dropped two months later.

November 1991 - BBC
OMNIBUS: 'Ulster Says Ho Ho Ho'

Ninety seconds of a comedian's Ian Paisley routine were cut from this programme on humour in the North of Ireland, and the majority of his expletives were bleeped. [...]

January 1992 - Channel 4
FREE FOR ALL: '20 Years After Bloody Sunday'

This programme included an interview with Raymond McCartney, captioned 'Officer Commanding Republican Prisoners, Maze Prison', who was, as the second caption put it, 'Re-voiced due to government broadcasting restrictions'. [...]

March 1992 - BBC Radio 4
AFTERNOON STORY: 'We've Got Tonite' by Danny Morrison

The BBC banned a short story by former Sinn Féin publicity director Danny Morrison [...] from being read on Radio 4's *Afternoon Story* slot. Titled 'We've Got Tonite', the story was an innocuous tale of suburban love and adultery, with no mention of Ireland, and with no political content. The story was recorded in February 1992, and was due for transmission on 12 March. Danny Morrison then received a letter saying it had been postponed. Further enquiries produced a letter from BBC Belfast stating that the broadcasting of the story would be 'inappropriate' and that there would be no payment. Morrison wrote again asking for explanation and guidance, because the previous year, in reply to an enquiry from him, Radio 5 had encouraged him to write a play. He received a letter, dated 22 September 1992, from John Wilson, the BBC's Controller of Editorial Policy. Wilson wrote: 'The problem is your close connection with terrorism, not criminal conviction as a generality. It would be inappropriate to have a broadcast for entertainment purposes based on your work when so many people are victims of terrorism and so many more detest and fear it. Many people would be deeply offended.

In view of that your short story should never have been accepted and in the existing circumstances you should forget any encouragement from anywhere in the BBC to write a play or other creative work for entertainment purposes' (see also the *Guardian,* 14 October 1992).

** June 1992 - Sky TV
HIDDEN AGENDA

On 29 June 1992, Sky TV, the satellite company owned by Rupert Murdoch, screened Ken Loach's *Hidden Agenda* uncut to European viewers. The film, loosely based on the Stalker shoot-to-kill enquiry and the Colin Wallace affair, includes a scene where a real life Sinn Féin Councillor, Jim McAllister, plays a fictitious Sinn Féin member. Ken Loach had said the previous year: 'Here you have a Sinn Féin councillor playing a Sinn Féin member espousing Sinn Féin policy. It'll be interesting to see how broadcasters in Britain and Ireland cope with it' (*Irish News,* 1 July 1992).

September 1992 - BBC
NATION: 'Killing for a Cause'

The BBC provoked widespread protests when it extensively subtitled the contribution of former MP Bernadette Devlin McAliskey to a pre-recorded discussion in the *Nation* series, transmitted on 1 September 1992. Other participants were also subtitled, including 77-year-old Brent trade unionist Tom Durkin. None of those subtitled was a member or representative of organisations covered by the broadcasting ban.

The gist of Bernadette McAliskey's contribution was that, while she did not support violence, she understood the reasons for it. [...]

The programme was made by Juniper Productions for the BBC's multicultural unit, based in Birmingham. The executive producer was David Cox, who in 1990 had produced *Dispatches'* 'Terms for Peace', which had achieved some notoriety by featuring a long interview with Gerry Adams dubbed in lip-sync by actor Stephen Rea (see above, April 1990). [...]

Before recording started, the participants were reassured that subtitling was unlikely. But when recording began, Trevor Phillips' introduction included this warning: 'A government order made in 1988 requires broadcasters to remove the sound when something is said which could be taken as supporting certain organisations involved in the Northern conflict, such as the Provisional IRA and the Ulster Defence Association. To comply with this order, we'll use subtitles when necessary'. Juniper Productions then edited the programme down from about 90 minutes to just under 40. [...]

The programme was recorded on 23 August and transmitted nine days later, on 1 September. Bernadette McAliskey only learned about the subtitling by an indirect route on the evening of 31 August. Next day, through solicitor Gareth Peirce, Bernadette made strenuous efforts to get the BBC to withdraw the programme or, failing that, to remove the subtitles or to remove her contribution, but to no avail. Gareth Peirce wrote to the BBC that the subtitling was defamatory, and that 'the clearest possible implication' of the subtitles 'as is spelled out by the presenter Trevor Phillips in the introduction ... is that either she or the words spoken by her lend support to the views and actions of proscribed organisations. This is most clearly not the position of Ms McAliskey and was not the view that she put forward on the programme'.

Trade unionist Tom Durkin also tried to get his contribution deleted, but was repeatedly fobbed off by BBC information officers. Various civil liberties organisations made protests about the extension of the ban. Following transmission, the BBC was inundated with telephone calls of protest. [...]

Subsequently Bernadette McAliskey - with solicitor Gareth Peirce acting on her behalf - applied for a judicial review of the BBC's action. This was refused by Mr Justice MacPherson, who ruled that a judicial review was not a correct remedy and that she should take an action for defamation. Bernadette then applied to the court of appeal, which in July 1993 overturned MacPherson's decision and gave her leave to obtain the review. [...]

September 1992 - BBC
BITEBACK: Bernadette Ban

On 17 September 1992 *Biteback,* which airs criticisms of BBC programmes, included a report on the 'Bernadette ban' affair. It featured interviews with John Wilson, Tom Durkin, David Cox, journalist Peter Taylor and David Miller of the Glasgow University Media Group. Bernadette McAliskey declined to be interviewed because she feared she might be subtitled again.

Biteback used extracts from the offending interview with Bernadette, with subtitles and missing voice, and also similarly dubbed footage of Tom Durkin and another member of the audience. The programme contrasted the subtitling episode with footage of Bernadette participating in an *Open to Question* discussion on 3 February 1992, saying something very similar but without interference with her voice.

Biteback also repeated a section of *Inside Story: Enemies Within,* about Long Kesh prison (aka The Maze), in which the IRA spokesperson on food was both subtitled and re-voiced by an actor as he discussed the quality of the sausage rolls.

October 1992 - BBC
EASTENDERS

Scriptwriter David Yallop lost his job on the television series *Eastenders* in November 1989 after he proposed killing off several members of the cast in an IRA bombing. He sued the BBC for breach of contract, and on 17 October 1992 won £68,195 High Court damages plus interest. The award represented money owed to him. The BBC faced a legal bill unofficially estimated at £250,000. [...]

** To mark the fourth anniversary of the broadcasting ban, Sinn Féin defiantly breached the ban by openly running a pirate radio station in West Belfast on Saturday 17 October 1992. The *Irish News* reported:

> 'Radio Free Sinn Féin, which could be picked up in most parts of Belfast on 106FM from 11 am to 4 pm, was broadcast from a purpose-built stage in Andersonstown. Sinn Féin members acted as DJs, reading out requests and playing music. Interviews were carried out with various party officials, including president Gerry Adams.
>
> 'A "Sinn Féin Radio Roadshow" was set up in conjunction with the broadcast. Children played on a bouncy castle in Avoca Park and took part in radio competitions' (*Irish News,* 19 October 1992).

October 1992 - BBC Northern Ireland and UTV
SINN FÉIN STATEMENT

Writing in the *Irish News,* Sinn Féin president Gerry Adams complained that: 'On Tuesday, October 20, the Church of Ireland Primate, Dr Eames, in a speech to his Synod, strongly criticised myself as Sinn Féin president. News management of Sinn Féin material ensured that neither BBC nor UTV carried any response from Sinn Féin on their evening news reports.

When contacted, the BBC reported that the statement had been "lost". If Dr Eames had made a similar outspoken criticism of the SDLP or Unionists, it would be unthinkable that they would not have been given an opportunity to respond - in fact the BBC would have gone looking for a response!' (*Irish News*, 10 November 1992).

October 1992 - BBC West
HERE ACROSS THE WATER

'Here Across the Water' was a documentary which traced the links between Ireland and Bristol by looking at the lives of four Irishwomen living in Bristol, of different ages and interests. The film was originally scheduled to go out in October 1992 during the Bristol Irish Festival, but was then postponed to 18 March 1993, the day after St Patrick's Day - not a move that the programme-makers approved of, because they felt that Irish material should not be ghettoised. The BBC publicised the date, as did the Bristol Irish Society - but the programme was pulled again, at the last minute, to make way for a story on local job losses at Rolls Royce.

After pressure from the local Irish community, the programme was finally shown on 29 April 1993, but the Bristol Irish Society found it difficult to publicise it effectively because this was the third time the programme had been promised. As a result, the follow-up phone-in on radio was something of a damp squib.

January 1993 - BBC
TIMEWATCH: 'The sparks that lit the bonfire'

This programme, shown on 23 January 1993, looked at the early days of the 'troubles' and the possible role of the Irish government in the formation of the Provisional IRA. It revealed a rather curious voiceover policy - two people each ended up speaking with two voices, one their own and the other an actor's. An early sound recording of IRA leader Seán MacStiofáin saying 'concessions be damned - we want freedom' was voiced over by an actor, but in an interview done for the programme, MacStiofain's own voice was used. Part of an interview done for the programme with Joe Cahill, former Belfast commander of the IRA, was used without interfering with his voice - when he was talking about the split between the Official and Provisional IRA; but part was voiced over - when he was talking about the Provisionals' military campaign. A short clip of Gerry Adams giving a speech was also voiced over.

** On 3 March 1993, BBC Wales gave the first British television screening to *Hang Up Your Brightest Colours,* Kenneth Griffith's long-banned documentary on the life and death of Michael Collins, a hero of the Irish war of independence of 1919-21. The film was banned in 1973 by ATV.

March 1993 - Channel 4
HIDDEN AGENDA

Ken Loach's award-winning feature film *Hidden Agenda,* about sinister undercover operations by the British state in the North of Ireland, was scheduled to have its first mainstream British television screening on 21 March 1993. (It had previously been shown on Sky TV on 29 June 1992 - see above.) But after the IRA's bombing in Warrington the day before, when a child was killed, Channel 4 decided to pull the programme, and was inundated with protesting telephone calls. Ken Loach told the press: 'Provided it didn't offend people's grief there's no reason to ban it. We have got to discuss the issues openly. The horrific events in Warrington were awful beyond words but people talk about it as though it bears no relation to British practices in Northern Ireland. Foremost among the men of violence are the British' (*Guardian,* 23 March 1993).

Hidden Agenda was eventually shown on 16 April 1993.

March 1993 - Channel 4
ANGEL

Angel, a non-realistic thriller set in the North of Ireland directed by Neil Jordan and starring Stephen Rea, was first shown on Channel 4 on 15 November 1984. It was scheduled to be repeated on 23 March 1993 but was pulled by Channel 4 in the wake of Warrington. Sources at Channel 4 said that the only reason it was pulled was that *Hidden Agenda* was being pulled, and to allow *Angel* to go ahead might have provoked allegations of double standards. It was finally shown on 8 June 1993. [...]

June 1993 - BBC Scotland
AXIOM

Sinn Féin councillor Mairtín Ó Muilleoir was among the panellists on the BBC Scotland discussion programme, *Axiom,* about the North of Ireland and its significance for Scotland. The programme was recorded on 3 June and shown the following day, with Ó Muilleoir's voice dubbed over by an actor's. Mairtín Ó Muilleoir subsequently received a substantial sum in an out of court settlement from the *Sunday Express,* which had published an article complaining about an 'IRA councillor' being brought to Scotland at the expense of the BBC (*Irish News,* 29 July 1993).

July 1993 - Channel 4
FRONTLINE

On 3 July 1993 *Frontline* featured a film by Belfast journalist Malachi O'Doherty about how the inquest system fails people whose relatives have been killed by the British army or Royal Ulster Constabulary. The voice of Sinn Féin spokesperson Richard McAuley was dubbed over by an actor's.

. **Acknowledgements**
Thanks to Helen Dady, David Miller and many more who have given information over the years.

SECTION FOUR INTRODUCTION: REPRESENTING THE TROUBLES

From an early stage, research on how the conflict in the North of Ireland has been represented, particularly but not solely in the British media, has consistently concluded that there has been an over-riding emphasis on violence in general, and republican violence in particular. This is a clear conclusion of all the chapters included in this section.

Liz Curtis argues forcefully that the British media's focus on violence as the preserve only of republicans has led to representations of republicans which were far from sympathetic. She also presents an astonishing array of supposedly factual stories which have appeared in the British print media, which range from the simply distorted to the fantastic.

Using the responses elicited from editors of British daily papers, and senior television executives in both Britain and Northern Ireland, **Peter Taylor** shows how language is 'policed' in ways that suit the British state's representation of the conflict and the protagonists in it.

In a wide-ranging survey **Philip Elliott, Graham Murdock and Philip Schlesinger** examine the official perspective of the British state in relation to the Northern Ireland conflict. While they acknowledge that this is closely reproduced in some television broadcasts, they add that there is scope for alternative, even oppositional views. Of particular interest is the way in which the authors draw out the parallels between representations in both actuality and fictional accounts of the conflict.

This chapter is an early version of material later published in *Televising 'Terrorism'*, which is now sadly out of print. This dealt with British television treatments of political violence in general, although there was, naturally, extensive consideration of the Northern Ireland case. There was one significant refinement which the authors made in the transition from the paper included here to the book. Here three general perspectives on 'terrorism' are identified - official, alternative and oppositional. In the later work, a fourth is added - the populist perspective. The official perspective emphasises that the struggle against 'terrorism' is like a war, yet simultaneously stresses the rule of law. It is here that the populist perspective comes in.

> The official perspective is open to a charge of inconsistency. If there is warlike talk, what about warlike action? Why not kill the terrorists, whether by military operations, or by imposing the death penalty after they have been captured and convicted. Proponents of this view take the metaphor of war seriously. We have labelled the framework in which it is developed the 'populist' perspective... Whereas those who pursue ... the official perspective continue to claim (however rhetorically) that the rule of law must be upheld, 'reactionary' populists are prepared to drop this caveat and call for a full-blooded 'war against terrorism' aimed at restoring order by whatever means may be necessary. Moreover, it is argued, if the state refuses to take such action, people are entitled to fight back themselves, by force if necessary. (Schlesinger, Murdock and Elliott, 1983: 24-25)

The authors argue that the populist perspective is not as central to television representations as the official and alternative approaches, but it does occupy a 'secure niche' in popular fiction. We might also note its presence in much (especially tabloid) newspaper reporting. It also sometimes finds expression in back-bench criticisms of Conservative policy and some ministers and prime ministers have given the impression that they are ambivalent about whether they favour the official or populist perspective. In the Northern Ireland context, loyalist paramilitaries and some unionist politicians are key sources for such sentiments.

The addition of the populist perspective does give a more adequate account of discourses on 'terrorism' generally. However, in relation specifically to the North of Ireland, the inclusion of unionist sentiment as populist does tend to submerge the important differences between both (official and populist) British and unionist perspectives. In an analysis of 'settler ideology', Clayton (1996) has shown the important divergences between 'settlers' (unionists) and the metropolis over the treatment of the 'natives'.

In the following chapter, **Jack Holland** looks at U.S. press coverage of the Northern Ireland conflict between 1969 and the early 1980s. Although he sees evidence of a somewhat critical approach during the 1981 republican hunger strike, his conclusion is that the U.S. media differ little from the British in their overall approach. (For how this process is viewed from the vantage point of a professional journalist from the U.S., see Thomas 1991).

Finally, **Bill Rolston** returns to fictional writing, examining how women are represented in the hundreds of novels of the 'troubles'. (For an account of how republican men are represented in popular fiction, see Titley 1980.)

The parallels between fictional accounts and actuality reporting, as observed by a number of the authors, are apparent. As Section 5 below reveals, actuality reporting has changed somewhat since the 1994 ceasefires.

There is no systematic body of work yet available which examines the ways, if any, in which fictional representations have changed since the ceasefires, but, as the stream of novels and feature films (see Hill 1987) shows little sign of abating, the question is one which deserves contemporary consideration.

References

Clayton, Pamela. *Enemies and Passing Friends: Settler Ideologies in Twentieth Century Ulster*, London, Pluto, 1996

Hill, John. 'Images of Violence', in Kevin Rockett, Luke Gibbons and John Hill, *Cinema and Ireland*, London, Croom Helm, 1987: 147-193

Schlesinger, Philip; Murdock, Graham and Elliott, Philip. *Televising 'Terrorism': Political Violence in Popular Culture*, London, Comedia, 1983

Thomas, Jo. 'Toeing the line: why the American press fails', in Bill Rolston (ed), *The Media and Northern Ireland: Covering the Troubles*, Houndmills, Macmillan, 1991

Titley, Alan. 'Rough rug-headed kerns: the Irish gunman in the popular novel,' *Éire-Ireland* 15(4), 1980: 15-38

19.

Liz Curtis

REPORTING REPUBLICAN VIOLENCE

(From *Ireland: the Propaganda War*, London, Pluto Press, 1984, pages 107-133)

Dominating the coverage

Violence dominates British media coverage of the Six Counties. In his survey, Philip Elliott found that most stories were about 'acts of violence or the enforcement of the law' and that only a third of stories dealt with politics and other subjects.[1] The Irish media had a different perspective: they carried about five times more stories on the North than the British media, and they were much more concerned about the political dimension.[2]

The British media not only concentrate on violence to the exclusion of politics, but they also, as critics have long pointed out, report violent incidents without giving any context or explanation for them. As far back as 1971, critics were observing that television news bulletins were not attempting to explain what was happening in the North: comment was rigorously excluded from the news, and was treated as the preserve of current affairs programmes.[3]

As Elliott noted, the British media's emphasis on 'factual' reporting of incidents, concentrating on the 'who, what, where, when' and leaving out the background and significance, appears to be objective and straightforward but in fact is very misleading. This type of reporting provides the audience with details of 'age, sex, occupation, type of incident, injuries, location and time of day.' But such information says nothing about the causes of the incident, making violence appear as random as a natural disaster or accident.[4]

309

Not only does violence, reported in a non-explanatory manner, dominate the coverage: it is also presented as if it were the almost exclusive preserve of republicans. Elliott contrasted the approaches of the British and Irish media:

> The overall tendency of the British press was to simplify by writing the IRA into the headlines ... Reports in the Irish papers were more complex. More attention was paid to the way in which any particular incident fitted in with current trends. More emphasis was placed on assessing responsibility, not simply in the sense of reciting alternative versions but in the sense of deciding which was more likely to be correct. The Irish papers were less likely to quote official sources unless they contributed to this process of validating a version of the event ... On occasions the Irish papers also provided a longer historical dimension.[5]

Blaming the IRA

The IRA has been blamed for numerous acts of violence perpetrated by the British army or loyalists. This process culminated during the 1981 hunger strike with the IRA being blamed for all the deaths in the troubles to date. Tory and Unionist MPs and Christopher Thomas of *The Times* asserted that the IRA had killed 2,000 people, while *Express* cartoonist Cummings marked the death of Bobby Sands MP with a drawing of a huge memorial inscribed '1969-1981 THEY HAD NO CHOICE 2094 MURDERED BY THE IRA'.[6]

Christopher Thomas began his front page *Times* report on the funeral of Bobby Sands thus: 'The Roman Catholics buried Robert Sands yesterday as Protestants lamented their 2,000 dead from 12 years of terrorism.'[7] He went on to refer to the '2,000 victims' of Bobby Sands' 'collaborators'. The implication was clear: that the IRA had killed 2,000 Protestants. Indeed, since the official figure for the number killed in the troubles since 1969 was just over 2,000, Thomas was in effect blaming the IRA for every single death.

London-based Irishman Donal Kennedy wrote to *The Times* to complain, pointing out that among the North's 2,100 dead were hundreds of Catholics killed in sectarian murders by loyalist paramilitaries, as well as hundreds of people, including IRA members, killed by the army and RUC.[8] He received a brief reply, saying that following the receipt of his letter 'our Northern Ireland correspondent has checked the figure and confirms it from several sources.'[9] Kennedy then made a complaint to the Press Council, which prompted *The Times* to publish a letter drawing attention to the inaccuracy. Some nine months later the Press Council finally reprimanded *The Times*.[10]

[...]

The fact that Thomas could confidently make such a grossly inaccurate statement without fear of rebuke from his editor testifies to the extent of the fact-rigging process that had gone on over the years. By May 1981, the army and police had been responsible for over 200 deaths, and loyalists for over 600. Further, loyalists had killed more civilians than nationalists had, and indeed virtually all of the victims of loyalists were civilians.

The IRA have not only been blamed for loyalist and army violence, but also for a ragbag of other incidents, some real, some half-imagined, that they had nothing to do with. In June 1977, for example, television news bulletins announced that a 17-year-old soldier, Peter Wright, was feared to have been kidnapped and murdered by the IRA. He later turned up in Dorset, in Scotland Yard's words 'alive and well'.[12] Then on 1 January, 1978, under the front page headline 'DEATH BOMB BLAST ROCKS MAYFAIR', *Sunday Express* journalist William Massie proclaimed, 'A Provisional IRA car bomb exploded in the centre of London last night killing the vehicle's occupant and another person.' In *The Sunday Times,* however, David Blundy established that the two dead men were Arabs and believed to be members of the Syrian embassy staff.[13] The police later concluded that the men had in fact been transporting the bomb themselves. Philip Elliott records how in 1974 the *Daily Express* immediately concluded that an army colonel, shot and injured at his home in Wiltshire by a single gunman, was an IRA victim. Yet other papers simply reported that police were looking for a motive, and *The Sun* said unequivocally that detectives and army chiefs 'do not believe the IRA were involved'.[14]

Similarly, when in February 1979 bombs exploded in the shopping centre of Yeovil in Somerset, the papers immediately headlined the news that the IRA was responsible, even though the police said it was too early to say who had planted the bombs.[15] The police rapidly established that a man from Gloucestershire who had been injured in one of the explosions, was responsible: he was able to tell them where to find six unexploded devices, and they found bomb-making ingredients at his home where an explosion had wrecked an outhouse two weeks before.[16]

Again, an arms raid on a barracks in Cambridgeshire in January 1982 led *The Sun* to announce on its front page 'TRAITOR IN ARMY CAMP' with the sub-headline 'Soldier stole guns for IRA'. Reporter Ian Hepburn told with complete conviction how 'A British soldier turned traitor to mastermind a daring arms snatch from an Army barracks. Then he handed the haul to the IRA.' *The Guardian* of the same day, however, put a different gloss on the story, quoting the policeman in charge of the inquiry as saying, 'It could be someone wishing to embarrass the Army or a criminal hoping to use the weapons or sell them. Of course, we cannot totally rule out the IRA.'[18]

The habit of writing the IRA into the headlines on the slightest excuse sometimes has ludicrous consequences. When former Northern Ireland Prime Minister Brian Faulkner died in March 1977, the *Daily Express* headlined the story 'Faulkner, target of IRA dies in fall from horse'.[19]

Bombs in Britain

The amount of attention paid to acts of violence that really were committed by the IRA depends on the circumstances. Attacks taking place in Britain, killings of prominent people - especially if they are British, and bombings that result in civilian deaths generate the most publicity. A journalist reporting from Belfast for a British paper said:

> The daily violence has got to be fairly exceptional to be a big news story ... You're fairly limited in what you can write about incidents of violence - bombs going off and assassinations - because you weren't at the scene at the time. If you jump into the car and rush down, you're held up - you can be held even with a press card - almost out of sight of the scene, so you're not going to see much of it. So my approach is to try and deal with it as quickly and efficiently as possible, to make use of the radio, the *Belfast Telegraph,* television, and then try and save time to do the more in-depth pieces.[20]

Philip Elliott found in his study that the bombing of two pubs in Guildford 'received nearly twice as much space in the British media as all the incidents which occurred in Northern Ireland taken together.'[21] Yet during that three-week period, nearly twice as many people were killed in the North of Ireland as at Guildford, and there were also numerous other violent incidents.[22]

Elliott also noted that the Guildford bombings were the only incident to become a running story in the British media. [...]

The prolonged attention given to the Guildford bombs did not, Elliott suggested, 'simply reflect the importance which British news editors attached to events on the mainland as against events in the province.'[23] It was rather as if British society, united against an external threat, was daily applying a new dressing to the wound it had received. [...]

Human interest

The media usually report violent incidents in terms of 'human interest', concentrating on the experience of individuals rather than of groups or classes, and dramatising the single event rather than looking at the background. This is part of the normal approach of the media, especially the popular press and television, and journalists are expected to report in this way. A textbook used on journalism training courses puts the patronising view that

> The bulk of readers of the bulk of newspapers are people who left school at 14 or 15. Their primary interest is in people or the doings of people; they are not so much interested in abstract concepts ... Readers are interested in how the news affects them and their

children, and how it affects other people. They readily identify themselves with people in trouble, with people engaged in controversy, with people at the centre of great events.[24] [...]

But the media are highly selective about whose lives they take an interest in. [...] Whereas victims of British or loyalist violence usually feature as little more than ciphers, nameless, ageless, without occupations or mourning relatives, victims of republican violence are fleshed out and given a human identity. The commentary on a BBC *Tonight* film neatly illustrates the contrasting treatment: over shots of Bloody Sunday, the audience was told that

> In January 1972 British paratroopers shot dead 13 unarmed civilians during a civil rights march in Londonderry. In retaliation the Official IRA bombed the paras' Aldershot headquarters. The explosion killed five women canteen workers, a gardener and a Catholic padre.[25]

[...] As sociologists Philip Elliott, Graham Murdock and Philip Schlesinger have pointed out, the suffering of these victims is reported in a way that carries a strong political message: 'that it is terrorism which is responsible for injury, death and increasing the sum of human misery'.[26]

The victims of 'terrorism' do not all, however, receive the same treatment. As Philip Elliott noted, 'The death of an ambassador, a judge, a magistrate, is worth more space than that of a 14-year-old mental defective, however heart-rending his story may be from a personal human interest.'[27] When a prominent person is killed, powerful sections of society respond with eulogies of the victim and condemnations of the killers: when an ordinary soldier or policeman is killed, they have little to say.

Lord Mountbatten

The assassination of Lord Mountbatten on 27 August 1979 provides a dramatic example. Within hours of Mountbatten's death, an IRA ambush near Warrenpoint in County Down killed 14 soldiers, with four more dying later. While the death of Mountbatten, whose grandson and boatman died with him, was given enormous coverage, the soldiers' deaths received much less prominence. *The Guardian*, for instance, on 28 August gave over the greater part of its front page to Mountbatten's assassination, and relegated the soldiers to a short column at one side.[28] The *Daily Mirror* devoted nearly eight full pages to Mountbatten: a note at the bottom of page two read '14 soldiers massacred - see back page'. Even then, the greater part of the back page featured an editorial on Mountbatten, alongside an item on his dead grandson, while the piece on the soldiers' deaths was in the bottom right hand corner. While all the *Mirror's* articles on Mountbatten were surrounded with the black lines of mourning, the item on the soldiers was not.[29] A few days later, the *Mirror* gave ten black-lined pages to Mountbatten's funeral.[30] The coverage had strong ritual overtones, with Mountbatten symbolising goodness, civilisation and the British nation at its mythic best, while the IRA were portrayed as the irrational forces of evil: the *Daily Mirror* headlined its leader 'LORD LOUIS and the enemies of man'.[31] As Philip Schlesinger wrote,

> [...] Mountbatten was presented as the epitome of the finest British qualities: soldier, hero, noble, statesman, family man *par excellence*. The newspapers and television programs ran stockpiled obituaries, interviews with acquaintances and friends and tributes from across the globe. The act of killing was widely interpreted as irrational, as that of 'evil men' (*Daily Mail*), 'wicked assassins' (*The Sun*), 'psychopathic thugs' (*Daily Express*), 'murdering bastards' (*Daily Star*), as 'cowardly and senseless' (*Financial Times*) and as the product of 'diseased minds rather than political calculation' (*Daily Telegraph*).[32]

The image of both the man and the nation had more to do with myth than reality. The *Daily Express,* for example, in a front page piece headlined 'THESE EVIL BASTARDS, contrasted the 'cowardly psychopaths' of the IRA with 'the British' who 'have never yielded to terror' and Lord Mountbatten, whom 'everyone loved'.[33] As journalist Geoff Bell commented,

> Obviously 'everyone' didn't 'love' Mountbatten, and obviously Britain has 'yielded to terror' on numerous occasions. Indeed probably no other ruling class in the world has negotiated with more of what it defines as 'terrorists'.[34]

The major controversies of his career were submerged in the tide of eulogies or transformed into great achievements. A *Daily Mirror* obituary, titled 'PROFILE OF A HERO', revealed in the small print that 'even today, in Canada, Mountbatten's name is reviled', on account of the 1942 Dieppe raid, which he planned, and in which 3,363 out of 5,000 Canadians lost their lives. The same piece noted that 'the biggest question mark in his life hovers over India ... He led it to freedom - but 200,000 people were killed in the riots that followed.' Reporter Terence Lancaster went on to comment, 'I believe Mountbatten was right.'[35] In *The Guardian,* Mountbatten's supervision of Indian independence and its partition became 'his greatest service'.[36] His vanity and arrogance went unremarked or were excused: an *Observer* 'appreciation' concluded that 'the touch of hubris in his nature was combined with so many glorious qualities that even the gods should forgive him.'[37]

Captain Nairac

Another person whose death became a conduit for patriotic sentiment was Captain Robert Nairac. Nairac received more coverage in death than probably any other soldier killed in the Six Counties since 1971. A Grenadier Guards captain, he was working undercover with the SAS in South Armagh when he was kidnapped and killed by the IRA in May 1977. The media immediately profiled him as a 'classic hero'.[38] Whereas most soldiers killed while on duty are described as having been 'murdered', Nairac was 'executed'. The notion that Nairac was executed rather than murdered was central to the portrait of a war hero, bravely sacrificing his life for his country: the *Mirror's* front page featured a large picture of Nairac in uniform with the headline 'Missing while on active service, believed EXECUTED'.[39] The media evidently reproduced without question the profile they had been supplied with by the military. ITN's *News at Ten* accorded his life and death a full five minutes, which, as journalist Steve Gilbert noted, was 'as substantial a report as would record the death of a major statesman.'[40] Gilbert described how

> Norman Rees, accompanied by two stills of Nairac as an adolescent, read a fulsome tribute: 'Captain Nairac was one of those people who, from an early age, combined academic brilliance with a love for tough and demanding physical sport. His big love was boxing. At Ampleforth, Britain's top Roman Catholic public school, he captained the boxing team while managing nine "O" levels, three "A" levels and a place at Lincoln College, Oxford. At university, he continued boxing and won a blue while studying history. Then it was off to Sandhurst and a commission in the Grenadier Guards, a commission that soon saw him on active duty in Northern Ireland'.[41]

The *Daily Mail* took up the same theme, titling its two page spread 'The boy who was good at everything'. The story opened, 'Robert Nairac was a genuine hero straight from the pages of the Boys' Own Paper ... tough, intelligent, always anxious to be at the centre of the action.'[42]

Sociologist Frank Webster has pointed out that there was nothing 'natural' about the way Nairac's death was reported: instead, it stemmed from the British media's particular perspective, 'which interprets the British army presence and fighting in Northern Ireland as unquestionably legitimate.'[43] He writes,

> A different culture, one that perhaps defined the army's role in Northern Ireland as a classically colonial one of holding down an unwilling populace, would see the disappearance of Robert Nairac rather differently to the British press ... Here what could well have been emphasised may have been Nairac's membership of the SAS (Special Air Service), his role as a 'spy' in Armagh ... Or a theme of the success of republican 'partisans' against a well-trained and equipped army could have been developed. Other media could have stressed Nairac's background ... as indicative of the British Army's class prejudices, which leads to the sort of amateurism that results in such loss of highly placed personnel ...[44]

Several of these angles were indeed featured in the Belfast weekly *Republican News*, which carried a comic strip profiling 'Captain Nervewreck', an incompetent ex-public schoolboy with a taste for adventure.

Sefton

Perhaps the most potent 'human interest' stories in the British media are those which do not feature people at all, but animals. British soldiers in Crossmaglen reportedly became somewhat disconsolate when the much-publicised dog, Rats, received a much greater volume of fan mail than they did themselves.[45] In the aftermath of the IRA's London bombings in July 1982, in which 12 soldiers died and numerous soldiers and civilians were injured, the image that was most strongly imprinted on the national consciousness was that of a horse, Sefton, who was soon being described as 'the most famous horse in Britain'.[46]

The day after the bombings, practically every British paper carried a photograph of Sefton. While he did not bulk large in the qualities, the popular press spotted the potential of the story immediately. [...] The *Mail* headlined its story 'The victim of savagery',[47] echoing the coverage of Mountbatten's death with its emphasis on civilisation versus the forces of evil. *The Sun* opted for another angle: 'SEFTON - THE HORSE THEY COULDN'T KILL'.[48]

The Sefton story ran and ran, on television as in the press. Sefton's wounds, his mountains of gifts and get-well cards, his convalescence, his return to barracks, were all recorded. The military arranged photo-calls and briefings on his condition, and the media responded. The horse rapidly attained symbolic status. A few days after the bombings, the *Daily Mirror* devoted its front page to 'The wonder horse that wouldn't die'. Concentrating on Sefton and how 'he battled back' and 'showed his spirit by tucking into a bunch of carrots', reporter John Jackson mentioned the death of a fourth cavalryman only in passing.[49] Next day *The Sunday Times* carried a front page feature headlined 'Sefton: symbol of suffering'. Racing correspondent Brough Scott told how 'Old Sefton stood bravely in his box, battered but unbowed, a superb dumb symbol of suffering.'[50] It was as if the horse had become a symbol of the British body politic, grievously injured through no fault of its own by savage outsiders, but battling through to survival despite the odds.

On the face of it, the avalanche of sympathy for Sefton might appear to be an innocuous expression of human compassion, unrelated to politics. In practice, however, it contained a political message that was all the more powerful for being concealed. As educationalist Albert Hunt put it, when discussing a BBC interview with two white Rhodesians whose relatives had died in a 'terrorist' attack, 'We're invited to identify with the characters, to share their suffering. But in sharing their suffering, we're also being invited

to identify with their view of the world ... But because it's presented in such a personalised way, it becomes hard to recognise as a political view at all.'[51] From Sefton's point of view, as interpreted by the British media, the IRA appeared as mindlessly cruel, while the British were innocent sufferers.[52]
[...]

Fantasies

Coverage of the IRA has produced a remarkable crop of stories with no foundation in reality. These fantasies both satisfy the popular papers' need for drama, and serve the propaganda purposes of the authorities.

Manufactured atrocity stories, often featuring women, children or animals, were common in the early years when the British army's 'Information Policy' unit was in its heyday. A spate of stories in 1971 alleged that IRA leaders were ordering children to riot and even training them to kill, though none of the reporters responsible said how they had come by this information. In a particularly garish piece in *The Sun*, titled 'FRONT LINE KIDS', Roger Scott claimed that

> IRA terror leaders here are now sending their shock troops to war - their own children. Bomb-throwing eight-year-olds are in the front line. They steal out at dusk to play games with death, trained to hate and kill. And the children at war chant obscenities to nursery rhyme tunes as the bullets fly.[53]

Of course, as anyone familiar with the nationalist areas knows, the children need no encouragement to riot: the problem is to dissuade them. As Eamonn McCann pointed out, 'No one who knows the areas or the people who live there could accept these reports.' But most British readers had no such background knowledge.[54]

The media can get away with such concocted stories not only because of their audience's lack of local knowledge but also because when they are caught out they are under no obligation to publicise the fact. On 23 August 1972 ITN carried as its second item a story about three tiny eight-year-old girls who had been used by the 'unscrupulous IRA' to push a pram containing a huge bomb towards a military post at the back of the Royal Victoria Hospital in Belfast. The *Daily Mirror* also headlined the story. Some days later the British army press office admitted that the entire story was untrue. But the media made no denials.[55]

1972 was a fruitful year for manufactured atrocity stories. John McGuffin recorded how, in the same week as ITN carried the story of the children's bombing expedition, London's *Evening News* and *The Sun* both carried lead stories about IRA men raping young girls at gunpoint in the Markets area of Belfast, and alleging that four of the girls had become pregnant. Subsequently, however, the RUC issued a statement admitting that the story was completely false.[56] Also in 1972, popular papers seized on a story that IRA members had been using dogs as target practice. Again, the story was false: as *Time Out* reported, dogs had been killed, but it was British soldiers who had shot them. They had done so while on night patrol in the nationalist Ballymurphy district of Belfast because they were afraid the dogs' barking would betray their presence.[57] *Time Out* attributed this and other horror stories of the period to army press officers Colonel Maurice Tugwell and Colin Wallace.

Another bogus story painting the IRA as cruel to dogs, and thus certain to arouse the revulsion of the animal-loving British, was promoted in 1974 through then Northern Ireland Secretary Merlyn Rees. *Sunday Times* journalist David Blundy has told how soon after prisoners burned down Long Kesh camp in October 1974,

> Rees made a powerful speech in which he condemned the 'sadistic' burning to death of four guard dogs by internees. However, an army officer has told the *Sunday Times* that Rees had been misled. No guard dogs had been killed. When a local paper called Army HQ and asked to photograph the dogs' burial there was, apparently, 'quite a laugh'. The army joked about burying sandbags instead.[58]

Other fantasy stories have linked the IRA with an international 'red' conspiracy. On 23 October 1971, a few days after *The Sunday Times* had published details of the torture of internees, the *Daily Mirror* printed what must rank as one of the most bizarre stories of the decade. Huge letters on the front page announced, 'IRA HIRE RED KILLERS', with the sub-headline 'Czech assassin is shot by troops'. The 'Mirror Exclusive', by Joe Gorrod and Denzil Sullivan, began: 'IRA terrorists have hired assassins from behind the Iron Curtain to gun down British troops in Northern Ireland.' They continued:

> The disclosure came last night after it was learned that a paid assassin from Czechoslovakia had been killed by troops in County Londonderry. The gunman had ambushed an infantry patrol. The troops stalked him and cornered him in a graveyard.[59]

The source for the story was an anonymous 'Army officer in Northern Ireland' who was quoted as saying that the gunman '"was dressed all in black and was a hired killer. He had been firing at the troops with a Czechoslovak rifle."' [...] Conveniently, the Czech's body had been taken away and there was no inquest. The troops 'were ordered not to talk about the incident,' and 'official Army sources refused to discuss the incident.' [...]

In fact, as the army later admitted in the Belfast paper, the *Sunday News*, the entire story was 'a bit of fantasy' which 'had been going round for the past year.'[60] But the *Mirror* hadn't finished there. A later edition offered further proof of Red infiltration, telling its readers that

> On 3rd July, 1970, security forces shot dead 21-year-old Ulik Zbigniew [sic], a naturalised Pole from London. He was killed

climbing over the rooftops dressed in a black sweater, with his face blackened and carrying a rifle.

Zbigniew Ulik (sic) was in fact a postman from West London, a British subject by birth. He supplemented his income from freelance photography, and in July 1970 went to Belfast where he was caught up in the Falls Road curfew. After spending some time in the house of a friendly local person, he decided to go back to his hotel to fetch another camera. Because the streets were still patrolled, he slipped out of the back over a shed. Some time that night British soldiers shot him dead. At the time, the army never said that he had been carrying a rifle, nor that his face was blackened, and a *Sunday Times* reporter who was present at the morgue when Ulik's body was brought in confirmed that his face was not blackened.[61]

Another 'red scare' theme concerns the alleged training of IRA members in countries such as South Yemen[62] or Libya. In September 1983, *The Mail on Sunday* carried a story dramatically headlined 'GADAFFI CAMP THAT TRAINS THE IRA KILLERS'.[66] The story, by Gloria Stewart, alleged that Libya had been secretly training 'hundreds' of IRA members at two camps near Tripoli. Freelance journalist Alan George investigated the story and found there was 'not a shred of evidence' to support Stewart's claims. The Foreign Office told him that it had 'no reason to believe that members of the IRA are being trained in Libya', and this was confirmed by the RUC and by 'security sources'. [...]

In a variant on this theme, stories have been concocted which linked the IRA with British left groups. Because the IRA's media image was so bad, such stories had the effect of discrediting the British groups. Thus in 1977 the *Daily Mirror* produced a piece titled 'Trots hire IRA to bomb English cities'. Reporter Joe Gorrod told how

> IRA-linked Left-wing militants are planning a bomb war on English cities. And it could lead to a winter of havoc and bloodshed if the scheme works. British Trotskyists and Marxists have spent two months forging links with wildcat IRA bombers. They are believed to have offered help to the bombers in organising a blitz of shopping centres, railway stations and other government offices.[64]

Gorrod offered no evidence for this tale, and did not even claim to have got it from the army or police. [...]

The same year, shortly after the major confrontation between police and anti-fascists at Lewisham, the *Mirror* carried an article headed 'THE MEN BEHIND THE MOB'. In this, reporter Alastair McQueen recounted how an 'Intelligence man' had told him that 'Maoists and Trotskyites' were studying the 'confrontation techniques' of the IRA and were using these 'to inflame Britain's latest series of race riots.' They had travelled to Ireland, he said, where 'They were billeted with families in the hardest-line areas of West Belfast and in Creggan and Bogside, Londonderry, to watch the IRA at work and learn.'[65]

In fact, the previous year the Troops Out Movement had taken a delegation of trades unionists to Ireland in order to give them first hand evidence of the need for British withdrawal. And, shortly before the article appeared, a small British delegation, which included pacifist Pat Arrowsmith, had travelled to the North to investigate allegations of army brutality. Both groups were put up in republican areas - but their purpose was to learn about Britain's activities, not the IRA's.

The same smear tactic has been used against the Irish community in Britain. In October 1976 the *Daily Express* published a front-page article alleging that Irish people were to the fore in a £200 million social security swindle: they were skimming off money to keep them and their often-bogus families, and millions of pounds were going to the IRA. Reporter Alan Cochrane cited as evidence a recent 'top-secret survey' done by the Department of Health and Social Security. Confronted by irate representatives of the Irish community, minister Stanley Orme stated categorically that the survey quoted by the *Express* was a myth. In August 1977, the Press Council upheld a complaint from the Federation of Irish Societies about the article.[66]

The Margaret McKearney saga

IRA activity in Britain has produced some spectacular tall stories. Steve Chibnall in his book *Law-and-Order News* tells how, after the trial in Winchester of those responsible for the Old Bailey bombings in 1973, a number of journalists collaborated to spin a yarn, that was carried in several papers, about an IRA plot to kidnap ten English villagers as hostages against the release of the convicted prisoners. According to Chibnall, the story was first floated by an Irish journalist.

A journalist who had covered the trial for a quality paper told Chibnall that a number of reporters thought it was a good story, 'but it was also a dodgy story so it needed more than one person to run it to give it credibility.' The reporters then put the idea to the police, who didn't discount it as a possibility: indeed they couldn't afford to dismiss the idea just in case it actually happened, in which case they would be in trouble. The journalist who spoke to Chibnall refused to write the story because it was ridiculous, and warned his news desk that there was likely to be 'a big flap on the night desk because we haven't got it'. His office agreed that they wouldn't carry the story whatever other papers did, but said 'If you prove to be wrong you'll have to answer for it'.[67]

Other dramatic scare stories, more dangerous because they targeted individuals, have been directly inspired by the police. At the end of August 1975 several bombs exploded in London and soon afterwards, on 4 September, Scotland Yard issued a press statement, accompanied by a photograph, identifying Margaret McKearney, a young woman from County Tyrone, as 'the most dangerous and active woman terrorist operating here'.[68] This dominated the front pages the following day, as the press unanimously convicted Margaret McKearney in their headlines.

'SHE IS BRITAIN'S MOST WANTED WOMAN TERRORIST', cried the *Daily Mail*. The *Mirror* described her as 'TERROR GIRL', as did the *Telegraph*, which sub-headlined the story 'Murder hunt for "most dangerous" IRA blonde'. *The Sun* called her not only 'DANGER WOMAN' but 'DEATH COURIER'. The *Express*, in a highly evocative piece titled 'THE MOST EVIL GIRL IN BRITAIN', told its readers, 'Her Irish eyes may be smiling but her trade is fear and death... Consider this female of the species... But keep well clear. For Margaret McKearney is certainly more deadly than the male.' *The Times* and *The Guardian* also carried the story and picture on their front pages, but unlike the other papers they attributed it to the police in their headlines.[69]

The media had, overnight, invested Margaret McKearney with notoriety. Within days the McKearney family were given police and army protection after a threat from the loyalist UVF 'to get your family - each and every one of you.'[70] It was no empty threat. On 23 October a woman and a man were found shot dead in a lonely roadside bungalow near Moy, County Tyrone. They were also called McKearney, and had evidently been mistaken for Margaret's family, who lived in the same area.

The evidence for Scotland Yard's allegations was shaky. As the Dublin-based *Irish Press* noted, some of the statements given by Scotland Yard in their list of reasons for wanting to interview Margaret McKearney were 'so unfounded that our Special Branch were able, through their own surveillance, to dismiss them as utter rubbish because she was in Ireland at times when the "Yard" alleged she was committing crimes in England.'[71] [...]

Bald Eagle and the white Opel

Another story sponsored by Scotland Yard turned into a wild goose chase of surreal dimensions. At around 2 a.m. on Sunday 17 December 1978, bombs exploded almost simultaneously in five English cities: Bristol, Southampton, Coventry, Manchester and Liverpool. The police went into overdrive, apparently desperate to demonstrate that they were doing something to counter the renewed IRA threat. First they arrested some 22 people, all of whom were later released, as they boarded the ferry for Belfast at the Scottish port of Stranraer. Then they cancelled all police leave in London and saturated the centre of the capital in a move dramatically titled 'Operation Santa'. In a masterstroke, the Yard also informed the media that they were looking for an Irishman called 'Bald Eagle'. The press seized on this with delight. 'FIND BALD EAGLE!' cried *The Sun's* front page on 19 December, and reporter Trevor Hanna told that 'A huge hunt was on last night for a fanatical Irishman believed to be masterminding the Christmas terror bomb blitz on English cities.' The *Daily Mail* explained, 'Bald Eagle is a Provo bomb expert who has vanished from Belfast ... He gained his nickname from his bald head which he invariably disguises with different wigs.'[72] Next day the *Mail* went a step further, naming Bald Eagle as Cornelius McHugh.

There was indeed a bald Belfast man of that name who answered to the nickname Bald Eagle. But on the day the *Mail* identified him as 'one of the most wanted men in Britain' he was in fact signing on the dole as usual in Belfast. That afternoon he gave interviews to Ulster Television and to journalists, explaining that he had never set foot in England and didn't intend to, and expressing himself mystified as to why, if half the policemen in England were looking for him, no policeman or soldier had come to his house. 'If they had,' he said, 'they would have found me at home with my wife and seven children.' He was also worried sick, said *The Guardian*, that all the publicity might lead to a 'trigger happy' soldier taking a shot at him.[73] The Belfast paper *Republican News* later reported him as saying that 'there is nothing more sinister about his bald head than the obvious dislike his hair has for staying with him; and he certainly never wears a wig.'[74]

Meanwhile back in England a new twist had been added to the plot. The Yard had issued another nationwide alert, this time for a white Opel Kadett, registration APU 827S. Over succeeding days there were a hundred or more reported sightings of this car, the most exciting of which was by Detective-Constable Ted Morley of Farnham in Surrey. '"I faced Bald Eagle"', was the London *Evening Standard's* dramatic headline. Kenneth Tew's report began, 'The detective who chased the IRA terrorist "Bald Eagle" today told how he found himself looking down two barrels of a sawn-off shotgun.' He went on to tell how Morley, 32 years old and father of two, had chased the white Opel for two miles until it stopped. Morley said, 'I had it in mind to ram their car. The passenger took a shotgun and leaned out of the window. When I looked down those two barrels I swerved, hit the brakes and then I hit the deck ... I was only on the deck for seconds but it had gone when I looked up.'[75] Morley then took an ITN camera crew in his car and re-enacted the drama for the benefit of the television audience.

Morley's Chief Superintendent stood staunchly by his account, and when asked why he thought the IRA were still driving the most wanted car in England said, 'Think of the worst Irish joke you know and draw your own conclusion.'[76] The joke was, however, to be on him. In mid-January the white Opel turned up in Ireland. It had been taken there via Holyhead on 24 November, nearly four weeks before Scotland Yard started looking for it in Britain.[77] The unfortunate Morley was then suspended from duty.[78] [...]

Not the day of the Jackal

Scotland Yard started another wild goose chase during the British general election campaign in 1983. On Friday 27 May the front pages of several papers were dominated by a story, released by the Yard the previous evening, about how two IRA men were planning to assassinate a leading British politician. [...]

The Yard had given the story first to the *Daily Mirror*, at about 6 p.m. on the Thursday, and later, at about 10.30 p.m. to the rest of the media.[79] Since the *Mirror* was the only national paper supporting Labour in the election, it is possible that the Yard's intention was to create a 'law and order' scare which would benefit the Tories.

The *Mirror* was the only paper to have the story in its first edition and billed it as an 'exclusive'. The front page headlines announced, 'IRA man's "Day of the Jackal" mission - "Kill a top politician"'. Reporter Sylvia Jones elaborated:

> The alert was sounded after a leading Provisional IRA terrorist slipped into Britain, apparently on a mission to kill. Police believe the aim is to bring chaos to the election with a real-life enactment of the Day of the Jackal assassination plot ... police have launched a nationwide hunt for 30-year-old Provo boss Sean O'Callaghan ... O'Callaghan, from County Kerry in the Irish Republic, arrived in England several weeks ago. He is thought most likely to be in London. Police warned that he is armed and dangerous and should not be approached.[80]

The other dailies carried the story on the front pages of their later editions. 'IRA "JACKAL" IN THREAT TO MAGGIE', cried *The Sun*. The *Mail* proclaimed 'ELECTION TERROR WARNING', while the *Daily Star* said, 'Yard alert as IRA squad slips in'.[81] That evening, television news bulletins carried a photofit picture of a second wanted man, John Downey. Scotland Yard said they wanted to question Downey about the previous year's Hyde Park bombings, and believed he might still be in Britain.[82]

Next day the *Mirror* carried another front page piece by Sylvia Jones headlined 'SAS alert in Jackal hunt': 'Special Air Service troops are on 24-hour alert in the hunt for the IRA "Jackal" believed to be stalking top politicians in Britain.' Alongside was a picture of Sean O'Callaghan, named by the Yard as 'the hit man'.[83]

The following day, the Sunday papers exhibited some confusion over who the IRA's intended victim was. 'TARZAN IS IRA TARGET', cried the *News of the World*, referring to Defence Secretary Michael Heseltine,[84] but *The Mail on Sunday* proclaimed, 'Jenkins target of IRA Jackal'. That day Scotland Yard's story began to fall apart. The first wanted man, Sean O'Callaghan, turned out to be in his home town, Tralee in County Kerry, where he was photographed holding a copy of *The Mail on Sunday*. A spokesman for the garda, the Irish police, said that O'Callaghan was not under surveillance and that, to the best of his knowledge, no request had been received from the British police to bring him in for questioning. The Irish police also said they were satisfied that he had not been out of Tralee for a month.[85] Then on the Monday the second named man, John Downey, telephoned journalists from Ballyshannon in County Donegal and said he had never been to England in his life.[86] The Irish police said that the previous Thursday, the day Scotland Yard had named him, Downey had been seen collecting his dole in Ballyshannon.[87]

'Godfathers'

The media have always endeavoured to depict the IRA as external to, and unrepresentative of, the nationalist community. In the early years, nationalist riots against the British army were often ascribed to IRA 'agitators' or 'infiltrators',[88] and newspaper stories linked the IRA to a Soviet-led communist conspiracy. Later the IRA were widely described as 'a small band of gangsters and thugs', while during the 1981 hunger strike they metamorphosed into masters of psychological manipulation, the possessors of a powerful 'propaganda machine'.

The word 'godfathers' entered the lexicon of reporters describing the IRA in the mid-seventies. This mafia metaphor gained currency during the term of office of Labour Northern Ireland Secretary Roy Mason, whose strategy was to deal with the IRA revolt as if it were purely a criminal matter.

Stories about IRA 'gangsterism' reach journalists through the RUC and army. One distinguishing feature of such stories is that they are generally impossible either to prove or to disprove - for which reason some journalists steer clear of them. A second is that the activities cited as 'evidence' are often open to contrary interpretation. For example, the black taxi service run by ex-internees in West Belfast has been portrayed by the army and RUC as a means by which the IRA brings an unwilling community under their control, but is seen by many locals as a welcome alternative to the expensive and frequently disrupted bus service. Similarly, social clubs where people go for an evening out were described by a police officer quoted in *The Sunday Times* as places where 'witch doctor' techniques are used to 'hypnotise' the young with republican songs: 'Then the next day the godfathers put a gun or bomb in their hands and send them out to kill somebody.'[89] As well as being unsubstantiated, this account excludes the possibility that republican culture has developed as the product of a community, and that young people might wish to join the IRA of their own volition.

Two articles on the 'gangster' theme written in 1975 and 1976 by Chris Ryder, a Belfast-born journalist, resulted in a partially successful libel action against his paper, *The Sunday Times*. The first, a full-page piece headlined 'When a city falls to gang rule' [...] began by describing two UDA killings and a series of armed robberies, almost all, again, done by the UDA. Then, to illustrate alleged IRA 'rackets', he turned to the Falls Road taxi service, social clubs - which he described as 'drinking clubs' - and the Andersonstown Co-operative Society, which runs various shops. The Co-op, said Ryder, was 'a key front organisation for the Provos'.[90]

The second article, titled 'Belfast's new godfathers', continued the gangland theme. [...]

> Knowing they will never persuade the Catholics to vote for them at the ballot box, the Provos have resorted to controlling essential community needs, legally where possible, illegally where necessary, and in the process have created a new dimension to urban terrorism. Military intelligence analysts believe that the Provisionals could one day use their power over the supply of vital necessities, like food, to force the Catholic community to support them.[91]

The Andersonstown Co-op and its former Secretary, Seamus Loughran, and former Chairperson, Gerry Maguire, sued for libel. The case was heard in the Belfast High Court in October 1979, and the jury found that *The Sunday Times* had libelled the Co-op by describing it as a Provisional IRA front, and awarded it £200 damages against the paper. At the same time, however, the jury found that the article did not 'materially damage' the reputations of Loughran and Maguire by associating them with the IRA, and they were ordered to pay the newspaper's costs and their own.'[92]

In March 1977 Ryder produced another sensational story, titled 'How IRA siphoned off £1m government cash in housing swindle'.[93] The article held that in 1975 'the Provisional IRA and, to a lesser extent, the Official IRA' had diverted money from building firms [...] A police investigation later concluded that little or no money had gone to the Provisional IRA, but that a building firm had paid £5,000 to the Official IRA. A Commission of Inquiry did not recommend any prosecutions and its report said, 'We accept that paramilitary influence dictated who could work on the sites, but the loss of money was due mainly to the weak contract ... rather than to organised fraud.'[94] [...]

The problem with such an approach is not only that it involves unprovable assertions and a contentious interpretation of the IRA's relationship to the nationalist community, but that, by reducing analysis of the IRA to the concept of gangsterism, the political issues are obscured. [...]

Endnotes

1. Philip Elliott, 'Misreporting Ulster: news as a field-dressing', *New Society*, 25 November 1976.
2. *Ibid.* Elliott deliberately chose two three-week periods which each contained a major election in the Six Counties because he wanted to 'maximise the level of political reporting'.
3. Jay G. Blumler, 'Ulster on the small screen', *New Society*, 23 December 1971.
4. Philip Elliott. 'Misreporting Ulster', *op. cit.*
5. Philip Elliott, 'Reporting Northern Ireland: a study of news in Britain, Ulster and the Irish Republic', Centre for Mass Communication Research, University of Leicester 1976; later published in *Ethnicity and the Media*, UNESCO, 1978.
6. *Daily Express*, 6 May 1981.
7. *The Times*, 8 May 1981.

8. In November 1983 the New Ireland Forum released a report on the 'costs of violence' in the North. This included statistics which showed that 2,304 people had been killed in the North between 1 January 1969 and 30 June 1983: republican paramilitaries were responsible for 1,264 of these deaths, loyalist paramilitaries for 613, and the 'security forces' for 264, while 163 were 'non classified'. Other statistics showed that of the 1,297 civilian victims, 773 were Catholics, 495 were Protestants, and 29 were not natives of the North. The report was printed in full in *The Irish Times*, 4 November 1983.

9. *The Irish Post*, 23 May 1981.

10. *The Irish Post*, 20 February 1982. In August 1982 the Press Council upheld similar complaints against the *Daily Star* and the *Daily Express*: see *The Irish Times*, 16 August 1983. See also *The Daily Telegraph's* leader attacking the Press Council, 17 August 1983.

11. From statistics supplied by Fr Raymond Murray of the Association for Legal Justice.

12. *The Sunday Times*, 26 June 1977.

13. *The Sunday Times*, 1 January 1978.

14. Philip Elliott, 'Reporting Northern Ireland', *op. cit.*

15. *The Daily Telegraph*, 24 February 1979.

16. *The Guardian*, 26 February 1979.

17. *The Sun*, 12 January 1982.

18. *The Guardian*, 12 January 1982.

19. *Daily Express*, 4 March 1977.

20. Interview by the author, April 1982.

21. Philip Elliott, 'Misreporting Ulster', *op. cit.*

22. Philip Elliott, 'Reporting Northern Ireland', *op. cit.*

23. *Ibid.*

24. Harris and Spark, *Practical Newspaper Reporting*, quoted in Tim Gopsill, 'Anatomy of a hack', *The Leveller*, January 1978.

25. *Tonight* report on the IRA, transmitted 15 February 1977, quoted in ed. Campaign for Free Speech on Ireland, *The British Media and Ireland: Truth the First Casualty*, London, Information on Ireland, 1979, p. 29.

26. Philip Elliott, Graham Murdock, Philip Schlesinger, 'The State and "Terrorism" on British Television', published in English in *L'imaggine dell'Uomo*, vol. 1, no. 2, Florence, and in Italian in *Dati per la Verifica dei Programmi Transnessi*, RAI, Rome, 1982.

27. Philip Elliott, 'Reporting Northern Ireland', *op. cit.*

28. *The Guardian*, 28 August 1979.

29. *Daily Mirror*, 28 August 1979.

30. *Daily Mirror*, 6 September 1979.

31. *Daily Mirror*, 28 August 1979.

32. Philip Schlesinger, '"Terrorism", the media and the liberal-democratic state: a critique of the orthodoxy', *Social Research*, Spring 1981, vol. 48, no. 1.

33. *Daily Express*, 28 August 1979.

34. Geoff Bell, 'Out of the gutter - the press and Mountbatten', *Socialist Challenge*, 20 September 1979.

35. *Daily Mirror*, 28 August 1979.

36. *The Guardian*, 28 August 1979.

37. *The Observer*, 2 September 1979.

38. *Daily Mail*, 17 May 1977.
39. *Daily Mirror*, 17 May 1977; see also *Evening Standard*, 16 May 1977.
40. W. Stephen Gilbert, unpublished article.
41. ITN, 16 May 1977, quoted in W. Stephen Gilbert, *op. cit.*
42. *Daily Mail*, 17 May 1977, quoted in Frank Webster, *The New Photography: Responsibility in Visual Communication*, London, Platform Books/Calder, 1980.
43. Frank Webster, *op. cit.*, p. 243.
44. *Ibid.*
45. Max Halstock, *Rats: The Story of a Dog Soldier*, London, Gollancz, 1981.
46. *The Sunday Times*, 25 July 1982.
47. *Daily Mail*, 21 July 1982.
48. *The Sun*, 21 July 1982.
49. *The Daily Mirror*, 24 July 1982.
50. *The Sunday Times*, 25 July 1982.
51. Albert Hunt, *The Language of Television*, London, Eyre Methuen, 1981, p. 23.
52. In 1983 Souvenir Press released a book about Sefton, *The Story of a Cavalry Horse*, by J.N.P. Watson: the blurb described Sefton as 'the equine hero whose bravery and character captured the hearts of millions'. The same year Quiller Press published *Sefton: 'The horse for any year'*, edited by Brigadier General Landy, proceeds to the Army Benevolent Fund.
53. *The Sun*, 8 February 1971, quoted in Eamonn McCann, *The British Press and Northern Ireland*, Northern Ireland Socialist Research Centre 1971.
54. Eamonn McCann, *op. cit.*
55. John McGuffin, *Internment*, Ireland, Anvil, 1973, p. 189; *Time Out*, 13-19 October 1972.
56. John McGuffin, *op. cit.*, p. 189.
57. *Time Out*, 13-19 October 1972.
58. *The Sunday Times*, 13 March 1977.
59. *Daily Mirror*, 23 October 1971; see also *Private Eye*, 15 November 1971.
60. *Sunday News*, 24 October 1972, quoted in John McGuffin, *op. cit.*, p. 150.
61. *Private Eye*, 15 November 1971.
62. See *The Sun*, 18 June 1979.
63. *The Mail on Sunday*, 25 September 1983, quoted in *New Statesman*, 28 October 1983.
64. *Daily Mirror* article reproduced in *Big Flame*, October 1977.
65. *Daily Mirror*, 2 September 1977.
66. *Daily Express*, 28 October 1976; *The Irish Post*, 26 February 1977, 20 August 1977; *The Irish Times*, 18 February 1977; see also *The British Media and Ireland: Truth the First Casualty*, *op. cit.*, p. 44.
67. Steve Chibnall, *Law-and-Order News*, London, Tavistock, 1977, pp. 42-43.
68. Quoted in the press on 5 September 1975.
69. *Daily Mail, Daily Mirror, The Daily Telegraph, The Sun, Daily Express, The Times, The Guardian*, 5 September 1975.
70. *The Guardian*, 9 September 1975.
71. Quoted in unsigned article by Liz Curtis, 'The case of Margaret McKearney', in *The British Media and Ireland: Truth the First Casualty, op. cit.*, p. 38.
72. *Daily Mail*, 19 December 1978.
73. *The Guardian*, 21 December 1978.

74. *Republican News*, 6 January 1979.
75. *Evening Standard*, 20 December 1978.
76. *The Guardian*, 21 December 1978.
77. *The Irish Times*, 19 January 1979.
78. *The Guardian*, 8 February 1979; *Daily Mirror*, 19 May 1979. For accounts of the 'Bald Eagle' saga, see Belfast Workers Research Unit, *Belfast Bulletin*, no. 6, Spring 1979; *Republican News*, 6 January 1979; cartoon by Christine Roche in *The British Media and Ireland: Truth the First Casualty, op. cit.*, p. 39.
79. Alan Rusbridger, *The Guardian* diary, 31 May 1983.
80. *Daily Mirror*, 27 May 1983.
81. *The Sun, Daily Mail, Daily Star*, 27 May 1983.
82. BBC1, 5.40 p.m., 27 May 1983.
83. *Daily Mirror*, 28 May 1983.
84. *News of the World*, 29 May 1983.
85. *The Irish Times*, 30 May 1983; see also *Daily Mirror* and *The Guardian*, 30 May 1983, and Mary Holland, *What the Papers Say*, Channel 4, 3 June 1983.
86. IRN News, 30 May 1983; ITN, 5.05 p.m. (sic: it was a bank holiday), 30 May 1983.
87. *The Guardian*, 31 May 1983.
88. See Eamonn McCann, *The British Press and Northern Ireland, op. cit.*
89. *The Sunday Times*, 22 August 1976.
90. *The Sunday Times*, 3 August 1975.
91. *The Sunday Times*, 22 August 1976.
92. *The Irish Times*, 4 October 1979, 9 October 1979, 10 October 1979, 25 October 1979; *The Guardian*, 25 October 1979.
93. *The Sunday Times*, 27 March 1977.
94. Belfast Workers Research Unit, *Belfast Bulletin*, no. 8, Spring 1980.

20.

Peter Taylor

THE SEMANTICS OF POLITICAL VIOLENCE

(From P. Golding, G. Murdock and P. Schlesinger (eds), *Communicating Politics: Mass Communication and the Political Process*, Leicester University Press, 1986, pages 211-221)

Above a photograph of the fractured spine of the Grand Hotel, Brighton, the headline in *An Phoblacht/Republican News* on 18 October 1984 proclaimed 'IRA Blitz Brits'. In an interview in the same issue a spokesman authorized by the General Headquarters of the Irish Republican Army (IRA) warned: 'Britain's occupation of Ireland is going to keep on costing her dearly until she quits.' 'Murder' was the verdict of the *Daily Mirror.* 'Unbowed', declared a defiant *Daily Express* headline the same day above a photograph of Mrs Thatcher; 'She flung defiance at terror with the words "Democracy will prevail".' The *Sun* demanded that those responsible 'must be hunted remorselessly and exterminated like rats'. Without doubt it was the most sensational attack the IRA had launched in its 15-year campaign, not to mention the most determined attempt to wipe out a British government since the Gunpowder Plot. The reaction of the media was akin to what Philip Elliott described as 'the affirmatory ritual' which followed the assassination of Lord Mountbatten: in this ritual, according to Elliott (1980), press and broadcasting emphasized the integrity of the social order and represented terrorism as the inhuman and irrational embodiment of encroaching chaos. Thus in the aftermath of Brighton, Fleet Street declared that Britain would not be bombed out of Ulster and would emerge with renewed determination to defend democracy against the men of violence. The *Daily Mail* summed up the mood on 14 October as 'This outrage that unites the nation against terrorism'.

There is no doubt that the IRA poses a threat to the existence of the state because its campaign is directed at the severance of one part of it from the main body. Government has to counter the threat not only by taking direct measures against those who seek to subvert it but by enlisting the support of the media in what it calls 'the battle against terrorism'. In its use of language and interpretation of events, the media helps to condition the way that 'battle' is perceived. This leads in turn to the synthesis of the political and public perception of the state's enemy. This is why words are so crucial in describing and defining the contemporary phenomenon of political violence not just in Northern Ireland but worldwide. These words can be an aid to understanding or a distortion of it. They not only reflect the journalist's perception of a particular situation but condition the way his report is received. The problem remains one of definition. As the BBC cautions on page 75 of the 1984 edition of its *News and Current Affairs Index*, 'some terrorist activity enjoys virtually no popular support and is totally reprehensible. But it is also true that sometimes yesterday's terrorists have become today's prime ministers, and that one man's terrorist may be another man's freedom fighter.' No doubt the deaths and injuries of 200 British officers and civilians in the bomb attack on Jerusalem's King David Hotel in 1946 provoked a reaction not dissimilar to Brighton. The fact that Menachem Begin, the leader of the Irgun, the Jewish resistance group responsible, went on to become the Prime Minister of Israel was not a consideration in the minds of British people who reacted with horror at the time.

So what is a terrorist? What is a guerrilla? What is a freedom fighter? The great dictionaries at least offer a starting-point. The *Concise Oxford English Dictionary* (1982) defines terrorist as 'one who favours or uses terror-inspiring methods ... of coercing government or community'; *Chambers* (1983) says a person involved in 'an organised system of intimidation, especially for political ends'; *Websters* (1983) has one who systematically uses 'terror especially as a means of coercion'. On this reading, the IRA and every other organization involved in political violence would fall into this category. What of guerrilla? According to the *OED*, he (or she) is a person taking part in 'irregular fighting by small independent acting groups'. *Chambers* says 'one who takes part in ... harassing an army by small bands: petty warfare'; and *Websters* has 'one who engages in irregular warfare especially as a member of an independent unit carrying out harassment and sabotage'. Under this definition, the IRA and most other groups around the world (with the exception of those like the Red Brigades, Baader Meinhof and the Red Army Fraction) would also fall into this category. And what of freedom fighter? The *OED* says 'one who takes part in resistance to an established political system'; *Chambers* 'one who fights in an armed movement for the liberation of a nation ... from a government considered unjust (or) tyrannical'; *Websters* has no listing. All armed groups would see themselves in this category although none of their opponents and few of their recorders would grant their inclusion. But such dictionary definitions only tell us what the terms mean and do not offer a guide for their common usage. Each word now carries a particular nuance which cannot be divorced from the society in which it is used. It may depend on the circumstances of the particular event, whether the target is military or civilian (a distinction not specified in the dictionaries); or on the political circumstances surrounding it, for example, the political colour and nature of the regime under attack; or, perhaps most important of all, on the proximity of the events being reported. It remains a fact of life for journalists reporting the conflict in Ireland that the terminology used is not that which may be accorded to similar conflicts further from home. When I filmed the African National Congress training in the bush in a country outside South Africa, I was able to refer to them as 'guerrillas' - which is what I believed they were. Whilst in South Africa preparing the same report at the time of the Hunger Strike, I noted that Bobby Sands's status was defined in some of the South African press as an 'IRA guerrilla'. If I had been allowed to film a similar sequence with the IRA - which for legal and political reasons I would not - I doubt if I would have been able to refer to them as 'IRA guerrillas'. I have, on occasions, without problem, referred to the IRA as a 'guerrilla army' - which, of course, is what it is. Although logic demands that members of a guerrilla army are, *ipso facto,* guerrillas, political circumstances dictate that in Britain in print and word they are not. Certainly, at the time of the Hunger Strike, it would have been unthinkable to refer to Bobby Sands as an 'IRA guerrilla'. Significantly, much of the foreign press do refer to the IRA as guerrillas: Colin McIntyre, for example, writing in *The Advertiser* (Australia) on 15 August 1984 of the 15 years of conflict in Northern Ireland, referred to the 'increasingly well-trained and armed republican guerrillas fighting British rule in the province'. Although in theory, guerrilla is a neutral word between terrorist (the preferred political term where domestic conflict is involved) and freedom fighter, its interpretation by those who see or hear the word is, in present circumstances, unlikely to imply any neutrality. As for 'freedom fighter', it stays firmly within the covers of the dictionaries.

In collecting material for this essay, I contacted most of the national newspapers and broadcasting organizations to establish what words they used to describe various aspects of political violence and its practitioners, in particular with regard to the IRA. What follows is based on their replies in personal interviews or correspondence during the second half of 1984. Was there a policy? Were there guidelines? Were there political considerations? I found to my surprise that, with rare exceptions, there were few guidelines and not many had even given the subject much thought. Most relied on the experience and good sense of their reporters and a 'feeling' for the subject and their audience's response to it. Some responses were blunter than others. The editor of the *Daily Star* Lloyd Turner, told me that instructions to his journalists reporting violence in Northern Ireland were 'clear cut'. He said:

> Those fighting to overthrow the State - and the democratically
> elected representatives of the State - are terrorists. There are no
> freedom fighters in Northern Ireland. The people living in Northern
> Ireland have freedom of choice. They have democratic elections.
> They are not prevented from leaving Northern Ireland to live
> elsewhere. Those who want to change Northern Ireland are given
> the opportunity to do so at the ballot box. In fact they resort to
> bullets instead. That is terrorism.

The editor of the *Daily Express,* Sir Larry Lamb, was more judicious. He
said the *Express* had no policy, just unwritten guidelines which 'every
experienced reporter applies to the reporting of sensitive situations'. He
concluded: 'As far as I am concerned there are no different rules for
different conflicts and Belfast is no different from Beirut.' The *Daily Mail*
replied:

> We do not issue any guidelines to our correspondents and reporters
> on the vocabulary to be used in reporting political violence. We
> leave it to their judgement on the spot in particular circumstances.
> I am afraid that the bustle of daily newspaper life does not always
> lend itself to neat academic pigeon-holing... Put certainly, we
> would regard the IRA and others, catholic or protestant, who use
> violence to further their political ends in Northern Ireland as
> terrorists.

The editor of the *Morning Star,* Tony Chater, was more terse. 'We try to
use words on violence that do not make the situation worse.' The editor of
the *Sunday Telegraph,* William Deedes, was almost as brief: 'I am afraid we
can offer very little guidance to assist you in these enquiries. We do not
issue guidelines here but rely on the professionalism of our staff to gather
and report the news as it comes.' The editor of the *Sunday Times,* Andrew
Neil, was more forthcoming. He said:

> You raise a very difficult issue and I am afraid there are no clear
> guidelines laid down by the *Sunday Times* for distinguishing
> guerrillas, terrorists and freedom fighters. It is a thorny problem
> which appears to be addressed through subjective convention
> rather than firm instructions from the editor. As a general guideline
> we believe a terrorist is an individual or member of a group that
> wishes to achieve political ends using violent means, often at the
> cost of casualties to innocent civilians and with little evidence of
> popular support among the people he claims to represent. On that
> basis we would describe the provisional IRA as a terrorist group
> and the PLO as a guerrilla group. However, the PFLP [the Popular
> Front for the Liberation of Palestine] we would describe as a
> terrorist organisation. These are naturally subjective interpretations
> but we feel they adequately reflect the situation.

The Times said: 'We have rules here which try to set out the circumstances
in which somebody should be described either as a guerrilla or as a
terrorist. Essentially, the difference should derive from the choice of target

or the tactics of that particular violence. Terrorism, in our view, is any act of violence perpetrated willingly or inadvertently against non-military targets. Guerrillas may be guerrillas, but they are also terrorists when they attack buses full of civilians.' The editor of the *Observer,* Donald Trelford, made broader observations.

> We do not have a 'policy' or 'guidelines' for writing about political violence. Each incident will dictate the choice of words - although we would never describe someone who throws a bomb into a busload of children as a 'guerrilla', still less a 'freedom fighter'. I rely on the feel for words of our writers and page editors, and their judgement. We prefer to avoid general words, and instead use phrases such as members of the IRA, etc. We would not hesitate to describe the perpetrators of the Brighton bombing as 'terrorists' but, to be specific, I find that in our issue after it, the word does not appear. (The leader has the expression 'cold-blooded IRA killer'.) In our follow-up to the storming of the Golden Temple in Amritsar the Sikh leader was described as 'the terrorist Bhindranwale'; the page editor deleted 'terrorist' in page-proof. In retrospect he has doubts about the deletion but stands by it on the grounds that Bhindranwale did not personally kill people. The November *Encounter,* writing about the Libyan People's Bureau incident this year, has the phrase 'Colonel Gaddaffi and other terrorists'. I would not have allowed that.

Mr Trelford also cited the experience of one of the *Observer's* former American correspondents, Charles Foley. In the 1950s Mr Foley was editor of the *Times of Cyprus* and had been on the 'hit list' of the EOKA leader, Nikos Sampson. Many years later, Mr Foley was consulted by the *Observer* colour magazine which planned to refer to Mr Sampson as a 'terrorist'. Although he had been one of Sampson's 'targets', Foley dissented and, after discussions with the sub-editor of the magazine, the word 'terrorist' was replaced by a phrase like 'EOKA gunman'. Retrospectively, although he admitted there was room for doubt on the issue, Donald Trelford felt that Foley's instinct was right. The most detailed Fleet Street response came from Geoffrey Taylor, the chief leader-writer on Northern Irish affairs for the *Guardian.*

> We have not made any rules about terminology because if we did we should find ourselves adjudicating on the exceptions. Obviously there is normally a case for using the least loaded and most objective word, but I doubt whether 'guerrilla' any more than 'terrorist' is now free of an ethical judgement by the writer or speaker. In the case of indiscriminate violence it seems unduly punctilious to use the word guerrilla if the immediate purpose of the operation was to spread terror, irrespective of what the ultimate textbook motive might be. Both words have emotional connotations: terrorist with the causing of random death or suffering and guerrilla with the nobility of a fight for liberation, as in France during the

war. If we are forced into adopting definitions then 'guerrilla' will come to mean 'not in our opinion bad enough to be called a terrorist' and 'terrorist' will come to mean, 'not in our opinion worthy to be called a guerrilla'. In practice the choice does not often have to be made at all because the purely descriptive words 'gunman' or 'bomber' can be used. The only neutral word I can think of (and it would not be neutral for long) is 'insurgent' because the IRA is in a state of insurgency against the governments of the United Kingdom and the Irish Republic. But 'insurgent' is part of a highly sociological language and a paper which wrote about insurgents blowing up a pub in Birmingham would have parted company with its readers. We try to avoid impaling ourselves on definitions, and sometimes criticise other people for doing so. This makes us chary of forbidding what may seem the right word to use for the occasion. I agree that there is bound to be some subjectivity about that. One cannot entirely cease to identify with the society one lives in, and adopt an attitude of celestial superiority towards most of its other inhabitants. Half the time the word 'terrorist' is used in quoted speech, and a newspaper would not be entitled to force its own linguistic standards on people being interviewed or reported. Again, there must be occasions when the reporter's own experience of an event makes him regard a clinical word as inadequate. If so we can't haul him before a thought-court, deliver a lecture on the history of Ireland, and ask him in future kindly to guard his language. Should the reporter at, for example, the Darkley Pentecostal Church ring up the desk and ask for guidance about whether the attackers were terrorists or guerrillas? And if he did, and an editorial committee decided they were guerrillas, could not the victims of the attack object to being identified as legitimate targets in a struggle for civil or political rights? Hard cases make bad law, of course, but all the cases we are discussing are hard to those at the receiving end, and that is why it is better not to have a law at all. I am surprised to find myself arguing for the retention of the word 'terrorist' as one of the options open to a writer. (It is not a word I use much myself, simply because of its emotional overtones.) But I find it profitless to look for the precise demarcation line between terrorism and guerrilla activity. Where, for example, would the Red Brigades or the Red Army Faction fit into a precise set of definitions? Neither could claim to be under the heel of an authoritarian regime which could not be changed by nonviolent methods.

I also conducted interviews with several senior television executives in Britain and Northern Ireland. The editor of Granada Television's *World in Action*, Ray Fitzwalter, said that in describing organizations like the IRA and the PLO and the ANC 'we prefer to avoid emotive descriptions, to avoid partisan expressions, to avoid descriptions which can change in their meaning according to the colour of the government or change through time. We usually use factual descriptions. Thus we would refer to the IRA, to IRA men, perhaps to gunmen, if it were appropriate, but we would not use phrases like terrorists, guerrillas or freedom fighters.'

The BBC, because of its unique position in broadcasting, shares the same problems as the other broadcasting organizations but perhaps feels them more acutely. As Philip Schlesinger, Graham Murdock and Philip Elliott observe in *Televising 'Terrorism'* (1983: 41), 'in Britain there is an important sense in which the BBC, in spite of its formal independence from the state is the national broadcasting organisation in a way in which the programme companies making up the ITV network are not'. The BBC does have guidelines which are updated from time to time by memorandum from senior executives. One such memo is referred to by Liz Curtis in her exhaustive study *Ireland: The Propaganda War* (1984). It concerns, however, not Ireland but the reporting of political violence in foreign parts. In 1974 a memo to BBC newsroom staff entitled 'Guerrillas and terrorists' said:

> 'Terrorist' is the appropriate description for people who engage in acts of terrorism, and in particular, in acts of violence against civilians, that is operations not directed at military targets or military personnel.
>
> 'Guerrilla' is acceptable for leaders and members of the various Palestine organisations of this kind, but they too become 'terrorist' when they engage in terrorist acts (unless 'raiders', 'hijackers', 'gunmen' is more accurate).

Liz Curtis also refers to the BBC's *News Guide*.

> Don't use 'commando' for terrorist or guerrilla. In the 1939-45 war, the word had heroic connotations, and it is still the name of units of the Royal Marines.
>
> Even so we still have problems with 'terrorist' or 'guerrilla'. The best general rule is to refer to 'guerrillas' when they have been in action against official security forces, and to use 'terrorist' when they have attacked civilians. Thus we should say 'Guerrillas have attacked an army patrol in the Rhodesian bush...', but 'Terrorists have killed six missionaries in Rhodesia...' (Curtis 1984: 135-6)

The Head of BBC Television News, Peter Woon, and his Deputy, Robin Walsh, admitted that in days gone by Television News had 'transgressed on the Middle East' by allowing the expression 'PLO guerrillas' to creep in: the terminology was changed after vigorous representations from the Israelis; now less emotive words were substituted like 'fighters'. Would they ever call the IRA 'fighters'? No, they replied. They pointed out that there was a danger in sticking to the Oxford English Dictionary and said they had to be aware of the public perception of an act of political violence. 'If we know that the use of "terrorist" or "guerrilla" divides our audience, [and we use it] then we are not getting our story across as well as we should. Why use words which have such a subjective interpretation when others - like "gunmen" or "bombers" - will do?' Sometimes, they said, you need use no such descriptive word at all when the initials of the organization would suffice without adding colour to the report: if an excessively neutral word were required, then there was always 'paramilitaries'. Wasn't 'guerrilla' technically a neutral word, I asked. No, they said, at least not in the eyes of their audience. 'Guerrilla still carries connotations of the "good guys" because of Yugoslavia.' Would they ever call the IRA 'guerrillas'? They said they could never see it happening. But wasn't the IRA a guerrilla army? They thought a while and then acknowledged that it was true to say that it was but added that the term 'guerrilla army' wouldn't have the same connotation as describing its members, on air, as guerrillas. They admitted it might be a 'cowardly' way, but they tried to avoid labels - just as they tried to avoid the terms 'militant' and 'moderate'. There were no written rules. 'At the end of the day, you can't have a glossary. You have to rely on experience and common sense.' But there was one clear distinction; if the action was directed against the civilian population, it was an act of 'terrorism'. But what if an IRA man killed a British soldier? They admitted that, technically, it shouldn't be described as an act of a 'terrorist'. They said they avoid the problem by using another word. There *was* a difference, they agreed, between Belfast and Beirut. 'Beirut is a long way away.' With candour they admitted: 'we do work slightly differently when it affects us. Whether subconsciously or consciously we differentiate.' In conclusion I asked whether the security forces were 'fighting terrorism'. Again they paused for reflection before saying that they never reduced it to one phrase. 'Maybe it's a great criticism of our output that we've never grappled with that one. We've never felt the need to express a verdict.'

My own experience confirms that at the BBC there are no specific guidelines covering the words its correspondents use to describe the actions of the IRA and other paramilitaries. But, for understandable reasons, one does have to exercise care. I recall a line of commentary I had written for the opening sequence of a *Panorama* programme on extradition which examined the significance of the political offence exception. The film showed two men walking in Phoenix Park, Dublin, where a century earlier some forerunners of the IRA (called the Invincibles) had assassinated Lord Frederick Cavendish, the new Chief Secretary for Ireland. The point of comparison was that the men now seen in the Park were former members of the INLA which had 'assassinated' Airey Neave. Alan Protheroe, the Deputy Director General of the BBC, saw the film prior to transmission and said that the word should be 'murder' not 'assassination'. I said I had used the word deliberately to draw the parallel between that and the incident which had happened one hundred years before at the same spot. Mr Protheroe took the point but insisted that 'murder' was the 'more precise and accurate word'. So 'murder' was used. But there remains some difference of view at the BBC over the use of those particular words. Both Peter Woon and Robin Walsh said they would have said the 'assassination' of Airey Neave - as they would of Lord Mountbatten or of Mrs Thatcher had the Brighton bomb killed the Prime Minister. 'We had no hesitation in saying it of Mrs Ghandi.' But in the end they would be governed by any guidance given by the Director General's Office.

ITN operates on much the same principles although structurally it enjoys a greater degree of independence. David Nicholas, ITN's editor explained that there are no written rules and that the use of these words had evolved over a period of time. 'We do refer to "terrorist explosions" in the UK', he said, 'but on the whole we prefer to say "bombers" or "gunmen". Occasionally we refer to the IRA as "terrorists". The IRA is outside the law - we have an anti-terrorist squad and anti-terrorist laws, so I wouldn't object to the use of the word. We never use the word "guerrilla", or "guerrilla army" - although that's what they might be. We try to find the most neutral word and that's not because we're impartial - we're not as far as the IRA is concerned.' Is there a difference between reporting political violence at home and overseas? 'I suppose there is a different standard when it applies in our own society', he admitted; 'we operate within the rules of a parliamentary democracy and we are observers of the laws passed by that democracy.'

I also spoke with those directly responsible for the local television output in Northern Ireland where every word is open to scrutiny by both communities and where the images and descriptions of political violence are redirected at the society from which it springs. Derek Murray, Ulster Television's Head of Local Programmes said: 'We have no policy, but it's probably true to say that we're less likely to use the word "terrorist" because they come from within our own society. We're more inclined to talk about "paramilitaries" or use the recognised title of the organisations involved. We tend to use impersonal terms like "a terrorist bomb" or "support for terrorism" rather than the personal term "he is a terrorist". We recognise that "terrorist" is a term used by those who don't agree and that those who do agree would call them "freedom fighters" - but it's a term we would never use.' Would Ulster Television ever refer to IRA guerrillas? 'No, it's just not part of the language. Those terms are much more easily bandied about at a distance.' Would you refer to guerrilla warfare? 'Yes, to describe the nature of the operation.' So aren't they guerrillas? 'Yes', he smiled, 'I can see the logic but words spin off a typewriter without contemplating your navel.'

At Broadcasting House in Belfast, James Hawthorne, the BBC Controller Northern Ireland, said it was general policy to offend the least number of people. He used the Hunger Strike in the H-Blocks as an example of the great sensitivity of language. Every time a reporter spoke, he risked offending one section of the community as Protestants said 'Aitch-Blocks' and Catholics said 'Haitch-Blocks'. For grammatical reasons, the BBC decided that the Protestant version should prevail. I asked Mr Hawthorne about 'terrorist' and 'guerrilla'. He said that 'terrorist' was now seldom used as it was a word which faded in and out. But it was, he admitted, a word which was affected by political change, notably the rise of Sinn Féin.

'Guerrilla would jar', he said; 'it would get in the way of understanding. To introduce it now would produce 50 phone calls and cause an unnecessary additional obstacle to our credibility.' What about 'murder' and 'assassinate'? 'Assassination bestows rank on the victim but it also confers respectability on the part of the perpetrators. We've used both terms in relation to Airey Neave. Murder is not a neutral term. But we would use the words "shot dead" to describe the killing by the RUC of two suspected INLA men in Armagh. The SDLP and Sinn Féin would say "murder". We try to be neutral whilst trying to reflect something which society demands of us.'

But perhaps the most sensitive problem of all arises when the media have to report actions of the security forces which lead to the death of civilians. It is true that the popular perception of the civilian death-toll in Northern Ireland is often that responsibility for it lies with the IRA. The figures should be carefully analysed before any such judgement is made. By November 1984 a total of over 2,400 people had been killed in Northern Ireland. Over 1,300 of them were civilians. These figures are furnished by the Irish Information Partnership which provided much of the statistical evidence for the New Ireland Forum report. The Partnership's definition of 'civilians' is 'persons without manifest connection with paramilitaries, security forces, police or prison services'. It is worth noting that the RUC's definition of 'civilians' includes *all* those who are not members of the security forces. This means that any paramilitary who is killed is recorded as a 'civilian' death, following the logic of the policy followed by successive governments that the security forces are not fighting armed revolutionaries (or guerrillas) but common criminals. The breakdown of the agencies responsible for these *civilian* deaths show that the IRA is far from being entirely to blame. Since 1969 it is estimated that loyalist paramilitaries have been responsible for over 560 'civilian' deaths, republican paramilitaries for over 490 'civilian' deaths and the security forces (British Army, UDR and RUC) for 160 'civilian' deaths. (In all, according to a parliamentary answer given in June 1985, the security forces on duty have shot and killed 253 people since 1969.) The balance is made up of over 140 'unidentified and others'. The Irish Information Partnership concludes: 'it appears that well over half of those killed by the security forces over the past 15 years have been civilians. In three of the last four years, two thirds of those casualties were civilians.'

So how do the media describe the innocent victims of what some would call 'state violence' like John Boyle of Dunloy shot dead by the SAS in 1978 or Patrick McElhone of Pomeroy killed by a British soldier in 1974? Boyle was a 16-year-old Catholic who found an arms cache in a local graveyard and informed the police. When he returned out of curiosity, he was shot dead by two SAS men who had staked out the hiding-place. McElhone was a 22-year-old farmer's son who had been questioned by an army patrol which was searching the family farm. After he was told he could go on his way, a soldier was sent to fetch him back for further questioning. The soldier called on him to halt. When McElhone started to run away, the soldier shot him dead, thinking, as he told the court, he was a 'terrorist' trying to flee. In both cases, the judges acknowledged that both Boyle and McElhone were completely innocent. No doubt most journalists would refer to them being 'killed' or 'shot dead' by the security forces. But to anyone else reporting outside the political consensus, these shootings, like the shootings on Bloody Sunday, would be seen as murder pure and simple and recorded as such. The fact that I use 'shot dead' and 'killed' to describe the deaths of Boyle and McElhone indicates the difficult path one treads in working within a political framework which is itself under strain from the events one is reporting. Unlike the definitions in the dictionaries, the semantics of political violence are neither pure nor simple. The best one can hope for is to free the vocabulary from subjective political judgement and keep the words as far as possible consistent, accurate and honest.

21.

Philip Elliott, Graham Murdock and Philip Schlesinger

THE STATE AND 'TERRORISM' ON BRITISH TELEVISION

(From *L'Immagine Dell'Uomo: Rivista del Festival dei Popoli*, 1, January-April 1982, pages 77-130)

Introduction

[...]

Within liberal-democratic political thought, the state is usually understood to derive its legitimacy from its constitutionality, from fair and free elections, its foundations in rational-legal norms respecting individual rights, and an adherence to the rule of law. Much less emphasised is the place of force, or of 'legitimate violence', in the preservation of the social order. [...]

[...] Such a perspective, as Sol Picciotto rightly notes, is but the starting-point for further investigation since 'the mere combination of the contradictory ideas of consent and coercion does not help to explain *what form* of coercion is involved, nor *how* the consent is obtained.'[1]

Nevertheless, those contradictory moments of force and fraud, of repression and ideological hegemony, while needing precise definition in any given set of circumstances, pose inherent problems for the system of ideological representations in a liberal democracy. For if the state swims in the seas of its own legality and legitimacy and emphasises the moment of consent, how then should politicians, intellectuals and the mass media represent the moment of coercion when the state has recourse to force? Moreover, how should violence which comes up against, or even transgresses the bounds of legality be handled? It is precisely this problem we seek to address in this paper, in which we focus upon how British television variously represents the question of 'terrorism'.

Discourses upon Terror: Official, Alternative and Oppositional

[...]

As an essential starting point we have to consider questions of definitional power, how what Chomsky and Herman call the 'semantics of terror'[2] are discursively organised. We will begin by suggesting that it is useful to analyse discourses about terrorism in terms of three ideal types, which we will label the *Official, Alternative* and *Oppositional.*

The *Official discourse* emanates from within the state and is further elaborated by intellectuals engaged in the propaganda war against 'terrorism'. Of particular importance in Britain has been the persistent effort to deny any political character to the armed struggle of Irish republicanism and the insistence upon its criminality. Mrs Thatcher, the British Prime Minister, made this point forcibly in a speech delivered in May 1981. Speaking of the killing of some British soldiers in Northern Ireland (she used the term 'murder'), Mrs Thatcher said:

> I hope that when their murderers have been tried and convicted, no one will claim that they are entitled to special privileges – which is what political status means – when they serve their prison sentences.

Of especial interest for our purposes is the way in which she linked her general characterisation of terrorism to a view of what a responsible press and broadcasting will do:

> They must, of course, report the facts. Nothing would be more damaging than misinformation and lack of balance. Yet the line is hard to draw for terrorism needs publicity. Newspaper and television coverage can provoke the very reaction the terrorist seeks. It can give the convicted criminals on hunger strike the myth of martyrdom they crave, *but the true martyrs are the victims of terrorism.*[3]

Mrs Thatcher defined a desirable focus away from the false martyrs to the true. It is surely no coincidence that [...] in the fortnight after Mrs Thatcher's speech a Granada television programme, *Lying in State*, which examined both the Provisional IRA's and the Government's propaganda campaign, was withdrawn after a radical change was demanded by the Independent Broadcasting Authority.[4] This instance illustrates how a given definition injected into public debate at the same time as state pressure, indirectly shapes what television is able to show. But because of the mechanisms employed, the state itself is not open to accusations of overt censorship.[5]

[...] a further dimension of the official discourse involves the association of terrorism with communist subversion. [...]

A particularly clear illustration of the claimed fusion between communism and terrorism was given by the Reagan administration, inaugurating its new tough-sounding anti-sovietism at the beginning of 1981. According to the US Secretary of State, Mr Alexander Haig, 'International terrorism will take the place of human rights in our concern because it is ultimate abuse of human rights.'[6] 'International terrorism' has done the rounds as a label ever since the early 1970s. Its mobilisation as part of the foreign policy rhetoric of the major Western power indicates a serious effort to market a new ideological tool – one which is monistic, ubiquitous, and conveniently off-the-shelf. Quite diverse manifestations of political violence around the globe, from El Salvador to Namibia, are interpreted as instances of global Soviet design for world domination. [...]

The threatening presence of outsiders to the democratic order justifies the search for subversives, and underwrites the state's right to respond with all means at its command, including the use of 'counter-terrorism'. The SAS's execution of several gunmen during the storming of the Iranian embassy at Prince's Gate in 1980 provides a good example, the more so as it occasioned little fuss, and some interesting fancy footwork to minimise what happened.[7] The 'war against terrorism' also justifies emergency legislation such as the Prevention of Terrorism Act, which withdraws certain basic civil liberties and increases the level of surveillance over ordinary citizens (through largely uncontrolled phone-tapping, computerised data collection and searches).[8] Such erosions of civil liberty are seen as regrettable but necessary. They are not represented as instances of *state repression* – a category absent from official discourse. Rather, in an interesting linguistic twist, they are encoded as the suppression or prevention of terrorism; it is the language of symptomatology, of the purgation of ills from the body politic, a language which implicitly denies causality.

[...] This perception plays itself out against the view of the state as the embodiment of constitutional practice. It is precisely at this point, however, that the problems of legitimation arise: for the picture of the benign state versus evil terror can be challenged by introducing the concept of state repression or even state terror.

It is here that *Alternatives* appear to challenge the Official discourse. These alternatives derive from civil libertarians, critical academics, foreign policy experts and opposition politicians. All accept the ideal of a non-violent, liberal-democratic state and reject the use of violence to pursue political ends. This means the alternatives do not offer a fundamental challenge to the claims to legitimacy found in the official discourse. Instead they develop piecemeal challenges at two points. First they question whether the state adopts repressive measures against its citizens the more do these ideals become tarnished. Second, alternative spokespeople question the official strategy of repressing and exorcising terrorism, advocating instead strategies of political and social engineering designed to defuse the violence and tackle its causes.

There are occasions when challenges under the first of these headings come close to a complete rejection of the legitimacy of the state. [...]

More often, however, the alternative views do not offer such a direct challenge but more specific criticism of particular aspects of the state's strategy. Whereas the official discourse appears to be a coherent whole, the alternatives are fragmented points of opposition. A case in point is the argument that a clear distinction needs to be made between criminality and politically motivated violence: that 'terrorism' needs to be placed in a socio-political context and the motivations of insurgents seriously addressed. In West Germany this 'sociological' argument has caused its protagonists to be accused of being terrorist sympathisers and in Italy to be seen as justifying terrorism.[9] Alternative spokespeople are particularly vulnerable to such accusations because of the coherence and relative simplicity of the official discourse. Rejection of the official strategies for dealing with political violence is interpreted as support for the violence and obscures the alternative spokespeople's acceptance of the legitimacy of non-violent politics.

The alternative attack is directed particularly against the state's response to political violence and the justifications of that response contained in the official discourse. Insistence upon the political character of insurgents rather than upon their criminality or external manipulation requires that political solutions be sought instead of repression based on a doctrine of national security. If insurgent terrorism is generated by structural conditions and contradictions *within* a given society, such as inequalities in the existing distribution of power or deficiencies in the representative institutions, the remedy is to be found in engineering appropriate social change. [...] Alternative spokespeople also direct attention to ways in which the state's response tends to violate its own principles. For example, it is argued that civil liberties may be eroded to such an extent by efforts to suppress and prevent terrorism that democratic institutions are undermined by the state which over-reacts in their defence.[10]

A crucial feature of the alternative perspective is the persistent attempt to realign the sign 'terrorism' and to contest the effort to locate it within the parameters of the official discourse, by drawing attention to instances of state-organised terror. This procedure may operate both at the national and at the international levels. In the case of Northern Ireland, for instance, there are the documented cases of systematic torture and ill-treatment in British interrogation centres, and the demonstration of how these violate internationally binding conventions on human rights, and therefore democratic norms.[11] [...]

On an international plane, the most elaborated counter-text, exposing the human rights pretensions of successive US administrations is the two-volume study by Chomsky and Herman, in which the United States is portrayed as the mainstay and organiser of 'Third World Fascism'.[12] In similar vein, when the Covert Action Information Bulletin talks of a 'new spate of terrorism' it explicitly denies that label to the left and rather points to US government complicity in right-wing terror networks.[13] Thus, the alternative view makes use of the term 'state terror' to refer, very occasionally, to the practice of liberal-democracies, and more frequently to the support which liberal-democracies (especially the US) may give to regimes in the Third World which users of the official discourse prefer to label 'authoritarian'.[14] [...]

The alternative perspective places on the agenda the notion of a security state contained within the forms of liberal democracy, and argues both for the exposure and the control of excesses of the 'state within the state'. This consequently poses an uncomfortable challenge to state secrecy.[15]

[...] Finally, we need to consider the ways in which these latter aspects of the alternative perspective are extended and developed into an *Oppositional* viewpoint which justifies the use of violence in the pursuit of political ends. Basically, there are two cases which have been argued by terrorists and their spokespeople or which they have attempted to demonstrate through their actions by 'the propaganda of the deed' or by exposing the hypocrisy of the state's claims to legitimacy. The first justification for political violence is that politically and/or economically the state is a repressive organisation practising state terror, and in these circumstances any other form of political action is impossible or ineffective. The second justification is national or sectional liberation in cases where the state can be said to have adopted a colonial role towards another people or towards a section of its own population. The subjugation of other peoples may take the form of economic imperialism rather than colonial administration and so be carried out through intermediaries such as client states and dependent governments. In this second case warfare becomes a realistic metaphor for the insurgents to adopt although it is continually rejected by the authorities. [...]

[...] Such distinctions are important in considering the cases made by different opposition groups but they are distinctions which are not drawn within the official discourse. Indeed the official discourse specifically rejects them, focusing instead on the violent quality of the acts involved and the loss of life or material and psychic damage which these entail.

'Open' and 'Closed' Presentations

The official discourse and the alternative and oppositional replies furnish the images, arguments and points of reference around which television's presentations of terrorism and the State's responses are organised. But they do not pass through the television system like a stone through water. The raw ideological material they provide has to be actively worked on and turned into watchable television. This production process is subject to a variety of constraints, ranging from political and market pressures, through restrictions of time and resources, to the limits set by the rules and conventions which define 'good' practice within particular programme forms. Since these constraints operate in different ways and with varying degrees of intensity in different parts of the programme system, presentations of terrorism turn out to be a good deal more diverse and complex than the simpler assumptions about television's relation to the state and to dominant ideology would predict.

Some types of programming (such as news bulletins and action-adventure series) are relatively *closed* and operate mainly or wholly within the terms of reference set by the official discourse. But other forms (such as 'authored' documentaries and single plays) are relatively *open* in the sense that they provide spaces in which the core assumptions of the official discourse can be interrogated and contested, and alternative and even oppositional themes presented and examined. Before we look at the mechanisms through which these openings and closures operate, however, we need to itemise the major forms of programming dealt with in this study, and to outline the conditions under which they operate.

Forms of Actuality Television

From the initial distinction between news and current affairs output, almost universal among broadcasting organisations, a variety of different forms have developed within actuality television, the main ones of which are set out in Figure 1.

Figure 1: *The Major Forms of Actuality Television*

Programme form	News bulletin	News magazine	Current affairs	Documentary
Examples	*News at Ten* (ITV)	*Nationwide* (BBC1)	*Panorama* (BBC1)	*Heroes* (John Pilger)
	BBC News	*Newsnight* (BBC2)	*TV Eye* (ITV)	
Frequency	Daily	Daily	Weekly	Irregular
Item length	Short (news item)	Short (programme item)	Long (programme theme)	Long (programme subject)
Presentation techniques	Visual clips, brief interviews	short film report/ studio interview	film report/ studio discussion	film report
Presenter's role	Reader	Reporter/ interviewer	Reporter/chairperson/ interviewer	Storyteller
Programme identified with	The broadcasting organisation	The production team	The production team	An individual presenter/producer

RELATIVELY CLOSED ←— — — — — — — — — —→ RELATIVELY OPEN

Because of the mass audiences it attracts and the potential influence on public opinion that this confers, broadcast news has, from the beginning, been hedged around with a powerful set of formal requirements. In Britain both the BBC and the commercial television companies are obliged to present all their news with due accuracy and impartiality and to preserve impartiality in all programmes dealing with matters of political controversy. Since it is news output that attracts the most attention and scrutiny from politicians it is here that the authority and credibility of the broadcasting organisations is most exposed. Consequently, adherence to the rubrics of objectivity and impartiality is as much a matter of institutional survival as of external pressure. By cementing an image of the broadcasters as politically responsible they help to strengthen their claims to autonomy and to forestall attempts to impose more stringent controls on their operations. This framework of constraints, however, produces a form of news which appears as a factual report of events happening in the world, rendered in a style that conceals the processes of selection and decision involved in the reports and allows the least room for comment and argumentation. The opinions of selected 'others' outside the broadcasting organisations are presented, but they are almost always confined to the holders of power in the major institutional domains [...] As a result, news is one of the more 'closed' forms of presentation and operates almost exclusively within the terms of the official discourse.[16]

News magazine and current affairs programmes have developed as a complement to the news bulletins and are designed to provide space for longer, more reflective treatment of the day-to-day issues of social management. Nevertheless, they remain closely tied to news and are subject to many of the same constraints. They generally take their topics from some recent or forthcoming news event, and they tend to draw on the same cast of spokespeople. Although the rubric of balance and the easing of time constraints ensures that a wider spread of opinions are presented, the range generally remains confined to the positions taken up within the main political parties and 'accredited' interest groups and comparatively little attention is paid to views falling outside this range. Occasionally, these bounds are broken as in the instance (discussed below) when a spokesman for the Irish National Liberation Army was interviewed on the BBC daily news magazine *Tonight*. But these cases are the exception rather than the rule and they invariably provoke heated debate on the legitimacy of giving air-time to enemies of the state.

Within the 'normal' confines of the standard news magazine and current affairs formats, however, there are still important variations of emphasis. These can be seen in the different ways in which presenters perform their roles of chairperson and interviewer. [...]

Nevertheless, this flexibility remains subject to the constraints which stem from the BBC's 'special relationship' with the state and with notions of nationhood. In Britain there is an important sense in which the BBC, in spite of its independence, is the national broadcasting organisation in a way in which the programme companies making up the ITV network are not. This means that the BBC's general current affairs and documentary output is more closely identified with the organisation, the organisation is more exposed to political and other criticism and its regular current affairs output is more closely tied to the political agenda of the day. The weekly *Panorama*, for example, is regarded as the BBC's 'flagship' in current affairs. Its topics and techniques are particularly exposed to political scrutiny and censure. It is expected to act as a national forum and deal with the important issues of the day. The regular current affairs output on ITV on the other hand has more freedom to select its own agenda.

At this point, however, we need to introduce a further distinction, between *'tight'* and *'loose'* programme formats. A *'tight'* format is one in which the evidence and argument is organised to converge upon a single preferred interpretation and to close off other possible readings. In a *'loose'* format ends are not fully resolved within the programme, leaving the audience with a choice of available interpretations.

This distinction cuts across our earlier dichotomy between 'open' and 'closed' presentations. A programme may be 'open' in the sense that it provides space for anti-official elements, but 'tight' in the way the material is mobilised on behalf of a particular reading. Usually tightness confirms the official discourse. An exception which developed alternative perspectives was John Pilger's documentary, *Heroes*, (which we discuss below). [...]

As we shall see, *Heroes* was unusual in being one of the very few actuality programmes to raise the issue of state terrorism. However, the fact that it did so in the context of a discussion of the situation in El Salvador, brings us to the operation of another important factor which we can call *proximity*. This operates along several dimensions, the first of which is time. Thus, it is possible to cast a dispassionate, even acerbic, eye over British activities in Ireland in an historical documentary series such as *The Troubles*, or a drama-documentary such as *The Crime of Captain Colthurst*. Historical distance allows for the portrayal of economic exploitation and military brutality, and for the admission of past mistakes and excesses on the part of the British state. In depicting the contemporary situation, however, programme-makers bump up against the operation of proximity in its other main dimensions – the geographical and ideological.

Actuality presentations are generally at their most 'closed' and 'tight' when dealing with contemporary terrorism within the boundaries of the British state. Where the imperatives of national security recede (and with them the concomitant threats of censorship or other state intervention) the possibilities of openness expand. Other state's problems with terrorism attract an altogether more critical gaze. However, this geographical factor is heavily overlaid by ideological criteria. Hence, television presentations are likely to be at their most a 'open' where insurgency takes place within non-democratic states in which legitimate channels of dissent are either restricted or closed and in which state repression is a prominent feature of the system of rule. In such cases, where violence against the state may be seen as justified as a tactic of last resort, the label 'terrorist' is likely to be replaced by that of 'guerrilla', 'freedom fighter' or member of the 'Resistance'. In other words, attitudes towards insurgencies are inextricably tied to attitudes towards the regimes in which they take place. [...]

The same is true of dictatorships such as El Salvador. But there is another reason why John Pilger's *Heroes* is more 'open' than the general run of actuality television. It is an 'authored' documentary. [...]

Whereas the news and most of the regular current affairs output are so closely identified with the broadcasting organisations as to be seen as 'their' products, for which they bear collective responsibility, 'authored' documentaries are ascribed to an individual reporter or producer and presented as their particular view of the subject. Accordingly, the commissioning organisation is usually at pains to distance itself from the programme, by, for example, announcing at the beginning and end that it represents the personal opinions of the makers. This disavowal in turn licences the presenters to ignore the normal constraints of balance, and to offer their individual views backed by whatever material they can command. In the process, they move out of normal roles of observer and reporter and into the role of 'author', a role they share with the creators of television fiction, and more particularly with writers of single plays.

Forms of Television Fiction

We decided to include the main forms of television fiction in the present study because taken together, they provide the largest single category of programme output and the bulk of the most widely viewed shows. Consequently, any analysis that fails to incorporate them can only ever produce a partial and limited evaluation of television's presentations of terrorism and of their potential impact on popular consciousness and action. But the inclusion of fiction has benefits for analysis beyond greater comprehensiveness. It also allows us to compare actuality and fictional forms and to begin exploring the continuities and breaks between them. As Bazalgette and Paterson have shown, certain narrative codes and ideological reference points cut across forms as varied as comic strips, news bulletins and realist drama.[17] However, as we shall see, fictional forms also allow for a range of representations which are largely excluded from actuality programming.

In the first place, television drama is not subject to the strict requirements of objectivity, balance and impartiality and is therefore able to be more partisan. In addition it is able to depict key groups of political actors who almost never appear in current affairs and documentary, and intelligence services with special responsibilities for counterinsurgency operations.

Indeed, the battle between the agents of terror and subversion and the forces of national security has been a stock theme of popular fiction since the turn of the century and still provides plots for television.[18] Moreover, as we shall see, certain fictional forms provide a good deal of space for probing the political motivations and rationales of terrorism and raising questions about the legitimacy and legality of the state's repressive responses. Unlike current affairs producers and documentary makers, writers of fiction can circumvent problems of access to clandestine state operations and high security institutions. And they can therefore explore the workings of the 'secret state' from the 'inside'. This is a crucial difference, which emerged particularly clearly in a televised discussion of a BBC play, *Psy-Warriors* (discussed below) which dealt with a secret anti-interrogation course employing the techniques of modern psychological warfare to test potential recruits to an élite anti-terrorist unit. As Roger Mills, one of the BBC's best known actuality producers, explained, although he had tried to get access to make a documentary programme about such courses, his request had been denied. [...]

Despite the potential advantage of circumventing such restrictions however, fictional presentations are still subject to a number of pressures and constraints stemming from the forms and genres they employ and from their position within the domestic and international market.

For several reasons, these factors exert their strongest pressures towards ideological closure on popular series that feature a stable set of characters over different, self-contained episodes. [...] Consequently, they tend to draw heavily on elements from the official discourse, since these are the most pervasive and best publicised. In the case of programmes like *The Professionals* which are aimed at international as well as domestic markets, this tendency to closure is reinforced. The producers have to find themes that will be intelligible across cultures and especially so in the United States, since it is American sales which are the major factor in profitability. The result is often a kind of 'mid-Atlantic' style which draws heavily on the themes and formats of the action-adventure series.[19] [...]

The plots revolve around the adventures of the core characters. They are the heroes. The villain's function is to disturb the social and moral order and to present the heroes with puzzles to solve and tasks to be accomplished so that normality can be restored. But the villains do not need to be rounded characters to fulfil this role. They simply have to personify threats to order in a readily recognisable form.[20]

Consequently, in the action-adventure series, the upholders of order and the agents of disruption are always unequally represented. We know a good deal about the heroes, their private lives, their personalities, past experiences, and existential doubts since each new story can trade off the knowledge presented in past episodes. But we usually know next to nothing about the villains. They appear abruptly at the beginning of the episode and they are purged from the body politic at the end. But they remain drastically under-characterised, and the action is presented almost exclusively from the heroes' point of view.

In terms of our previous distinctions then, the standard action-adventure series is both relatively 'closed' and relatively 'tight'. It tends to reproduce the emphases of the official discourse and to offer few spaces for alternative and oppositional viewpoint. And it tends to organise the narrative around a struggle between good and evil where the two sides are portrayed with little or no ambiguity or contradiction and where good always triumphs at the end of each episode. But within the general field of popular series and indeed within television drama *as a whole* there are significant variations of form and genre.

Take for example, the secret service thriller which is the genre used most often in presenting terrorism. This emerged in its classic form in Britain during the Edwardian era when the security of the nation was seen as under attack from enemies across the Channel represented firstly by the Germans and later by the Soviet Union, and alien forces within the state, most notably Irish Republicans and Anarchists. Within the genre, these threats were almost always opposed by English gentlemen who had been educated at Oxford or Cambridge, were well connected socially, and belonged to the most exclusive clubs.[21] They represented tradition and continuity, they personified the English way of life they sought to preserve, and they demonstrated the ruling class's capacity to fend off threats to these ideals from within and without. Some were amateurs, serving their country out of love and duty, others were professionals, members of the newly formed intelligence and security services, but all were gentlemen.

These basic elements of the genre have proved remarkably resilient and they still retain a strong presence in popular television fiction. As we shall see, the image of terrorism as an alien incursion, an 'invisible export' from Ireland or Germany is still a standard plot device. So is the characterisation of the secret service agent as English gentleman. It is most obvious in *The Avengers* where the main character, John Steed, displays his 'Englishness' by the universal signs of the gentleman – the bowler hat and rolled umbrella. [...]

The standard secret service plot is an instance of what Jerry Palmer calls the 'classic' thriller, in which a positive hero overcomes great odds to defeat the villains and re-establish normality. As the story ends 'we are left with the feeling that the evil has been expunged from the world, and that order, sweetness and light have been restored.'[22] But, Palmer argues, there is also a 'negative' variant of the genre whose hero is the antithesis of the James Bond figure. [...]

This 'negative' variant entered the general thriller genre through the 'hard-boiled' detective stories of Dashiel Hammet and Raymond Chandler of the 1940's. These centred around the figure of the down-at-heel private investigator, an image which found its full popular expression in Humphrey Bogart's portrayal of Chandler's Philip Marlowe in the movie version of *The*

Big Sleep. But despite their reduced circumstances, these new heroes remained absolutely honest and their integrity was pitted against the corruption to be found within the official agencies of law enforcement almost as often as it was against the villainy of the underworld. In presenting this negative image of the institutions of law and order, the genre drew on popular disenchantment with the growth of large organisations and on popular suspicions that the bureaucrats who ran them were not only inefficient but just as likely to be working against the public interest as for it [...].

This negative version of the genre gained ground within the secret service thriller in the early 1960's, as the already established themes were mobilised in relation to the altered political mood of the time to create a new variant. The characterisation of the seedy angst-ridden agent was clinched in John Le Carre's best selling novel, *The Spy Who Came In From The Cold*, which came out in 1962. In the James Bond books the secret service is presented as an exotic world where the business of defeating conspiracies is mixed with the pleasures of foreign travel and beautiful women. But Le Carre's 'service' is altogether bleaker, more mundane, and efficiency as an operative is often bought at the cost of destruction as a person, and even then professional failure constantly threatens. Indeed, the 'hero' of *The Spy Who Came In From The Cold* botches his mission and is shot by the 'other' side.

The early 1960's also saw an important shift in the public image of the 'secret state'. In the Bond books, the conspiracies which threaten democracy are always located *outside* the social order. They are the work of foreigners, agents of hostile powers, or people possessed of 'alien' political beliefs.[23] And the intelligence services appear as institutions of unquestioned integrity and patriotism, 'our' last line of defence against anarchy and subversion. However, with Kim Philby's defection to Moscow in January 1963 this image was severely dented. The discovery that a highranking intelligence officer had been a long-standing Soviet agent introduced a permanent note of suspicion and doubt which found its way into the thriller genre in two important themes; the possibility that conspiracies could originate inside the security services themselves, and the negative image of the English gentleman, as an agent of subversion and disorder rather than a bastion of decency and security. This image has been nourished by the fact that the most celebrated counter-agents of the post-war period, from Guy Burgess and Kim Philby to Sir Anthony Blunt, had all the educational and social qualifications of the perfect gentleman. As well as breathing new life into the thriller genre by providing novel plots, these elements enabled it to be partially deconstructed, both formally and ideologically. As we shall show with the television serial *A Spy at Evening*, they have made space for alternative and oppositional viewpoints and introduced elements of ambiguity and contradiction into the depiction of the 'secret state' and its agents. They therefore allow for the production of popular narratives which are relatively more 'open' and 'loose' than the standard action-adventure plot.

However, these possibilities are more likely to be actualised within popular *serials* where the plot develops over a number of weeks rather than in series where the action has to be resolved in the space of a single episode. The more relaxed narrative pace of the serial provides opportunities to develop more complex characterisations of terrorists and their motivations, and space to interrogate the nature and operations of the 'secret state'. Indeed, as we shall see with *Blood Money*, the military response to terrorism and the limits of its legitimacy can provide the central themes for popular television series.

This interrogation of the state's democratic credentials is most fully developed however, outside of popular form, in the single play. Unlike series and serials, television plays are not in the front line of the battle for audiences or programme exports and so they are not under the same pressure to work with the most prevalent ideological themes or to deliver predictable pleasures to the largest possible number of viewers. On the contrary, the producers of single plays are expected to fulfil the role of 'authors' and to express their own particular viewpoints and commitments in their own distinctive voice and style. This notion of 'authorship' gives them a licence to raise awkward political questions and to do so in forms that may disturb or even overturn the audience's expectations.[24] This potential for provocation is not always fully realised of course. Plays on sensitive issues (such as the situation in Northern Ireland) are subject to political pressures from inside and outside the broadcasting organisations, and cuts and cancellations are therefore a permanent possibility.[25] Moreover, by no means all television playwrights take advantage of the potential flexibility of presentational forms, to make space for diverse points of view. Nevertheless, a good deal of politically contentious material does get transmitted, and as we shall see in the case of *Psy-Warriors*, it is possible to mobilise alternative and oppositional perspectives in a single play in a more complete and sustained way than is generally possible in popular series and serials. They are therefore the most potentially 'open' and 'loose' form of television fiction.

Terrorism In Actuality Television

Two conclusions stand out from our survey of the treatment of terrorism in recent current affairs and documentary output of British television. First, the term terrorism and the meanings associated with it are openly contested in most of these programmes. In terms of the distinctions outlined above most programmes are open rather than closed. A variety of meanings and definitions are usually included even if the broadcasters, as interviewers, reporters or presenters, are working for closure in the terms of the official discourse. Second, the repertoire of meanings and definitions which is contested is remarkably narrow, mainly involving defining the violence as terrorism or not terrorism and weighing the reasons for violence against its consequences.

In the official discourse this balance is weighted heavily in favour of the consequences. [...] Those who engage in such behaviour do not have 'reasons' in the normal sense of the word. Their behaviour is senseless, irrational and inhuman.[26] [...]

An extreme example of this view that terrorists are not human shows one technique broadcasters use to re-establish the official discourse. After a filmed interview with a spokesman holding oppositional views, a spokesman for the Irish National Liberation Army, the organisation which killed the Conservative MP and Northern Ireland spokesman Airey Neave, the *Tonight* programme reverted to the studio so that a presenter and two Northern Irish politicians could put the interview into perspective. In the interview the INLA spokesman had denied that INLA had 'murdered' Airey Neave, saying instead that he had been 'assassinated' or 'executed'. Following the interview the studio presenter, Robin Day, re-established the point that it was murder before inviting the two MPs to comment.[27]

> [...] *Presenter* – Following that interview by David Lomax with one of the self proclaimed murderers of Mr Airey Neave I have with me the Rev. Robert Bradford, the Official Unionist MP for Belfast South who is in our Belfast Studio and here in the studio Mr Gerry Fitt leader of the SDLP and MP for Belfast West.
>
> Mr Bradford first of all may I ask you for your comment on that interview?
>
> *Robert Bradford MP* – Well I'd like to say first of all that my immediate reaction was to decline the invitation to join you on this programme because of the interview which we've just heard. But when, having established that I wouldn't actually have to talk to this creature, I think I should take the opportunity to say on behalf of all the people of Northern Ireland that this subhuman creature will be pursued by us, by the security forces, and we will do everything in our power to put this kind of people to death and make sure that they do not inflict the hurt and the death and the anguish on the community in Northern Ireland for a minute longer than is possible.
>
> *Presenter* – Mr Fitt what is your comment on that interview?
>
> *Gerry Fitt MP* – I don't think it was wise of the BBC to allow such an interview to take place. I know that in Northern Ireland the interview that has just gone out will have inflamed Protestant and loyalist opinion...

The charge Mr Fitt makes, that television itself would be responsible for suffering as the interview would inflame passions, is a point on which broadcasters are particularly sensitive. This interview was quoted two years later in a discussion programme on television's reporting of Northern Ireland as a prime example of the 'irresponsible and reckless use of the medium' in the words of Richard Clutterbuck, a counter-insurgency expert [...].

In the programme two journalists, one from print, the other from television, put their case for interviewing terrorists. As the interviewer makes clear questioning Jeremy Paxman, the television journalist, this case runs counter to the official discourse. If terrorists are criminals then there is no need for in-depth investigation of their motives. As the exchange develops so it becomes apparent that the alternative view put by the reporters is a challenge to the official discourse.[28]

Presenter – I'd like to ask you both, Anne McHardy would you yourself think it proper as a citizen as well as being a journalist to interview terrorists at length and frequently?

Anne McHardy, Guardian, Ulster Correspondent – Yes I think it's entirely proper. I've obviously thought about it long and hard and talked about it often. I don't think that I could possibly, as a reporter working for a British newspaper write about Northern Ireland with any kind of authenticity if I didn't talk to terrorists.

Presenter – Would you think that applied to television as much?

Jeremy Paxman, BBC *Panorama* – Absolutely. It seems to me that the basic perception of the problem in Northern Ireland is that it is a problem of irreconcilable political aspirations compounded by a problem of law and order. Now if that is the case you cannot have political dialogue without reporting political differences and therefore it seems to me absolutely essential that however much you may disagree with these people you have to talk to them. You have at the very least and at the most basic level to understand why it is that people are being killed.

Presenter – But that is making the assumption that they are not, as some people would argue, mere murderers or thugs as well as being enemies of the state and that you would then have an obligation to go to the security forces whenever you meet such people.

Jeremy Paxman – It is my judgment as a journalist that these people are not murderers and thugs, although they may be, solely, although they may be that as well. There are political motivations at work and that we have to understand those if we are to understand what is happening in Northern Ireland. And it seems to me if you are going to say that we should not be talking to these people then what you are really saving is that there is a state of war and that we should impose military censorship. And if that was the case, and it is the case in many other wars which I've covered then that's fair enough because we'll all know where we stand.

Another example from an interview with Provisional Sinn Féin spokesman Danny Morrison following the death of Bobby Sands on hunger strike shows the programme presenter working to establish the idea that terrorists are criminals against the oppositional definitions offered by Danny Morrison.[29]

> [...] *Presenter* – The question was put to Mr Atkins just now: Can the British government cope with three more Bobby Sands? Can the Republican Movement cope with three more Bobby Sands or even more?
>
> *Danny Morrison* – Well, the British government hasn't got a leg to stand on. This argument that these people are criminals without support among the local community.
>
> *Presenter* – (interrupts) Are they or are they not criminals first of all? Francis Hughes, can you really say that somebody who committed what he did deserves political status ... for the murder of a soldier?
>
> *Danny Morrison* – Well there's a war going on in the North of Ireland.
>
> *Presenter* – (interrupts) You say there's a war going on in the North of Ireland.
>
> *Danny Morrison* – The British, the British, well, Reginald Maudling, who was Home Secretary in 1971, declared war on the IRA.
>
> *Presenter* – That does not make it a war situation; that does not justify the use of violence in return, but still, I want to go on.
>
> *Danny Morrison* – (interrupts) In the legislation, in the legislation, which convicts these political activists in the non-jury courts, it is stated that what distinguishes them from ordinary prisoners is the fact of their political motivation. Margaret Thatcher voted for that legislation, and then she gets up and makes this stupid statement, makes an arse of herself: 'A crime is a crime is a crime ...'
>
> *Presenter* – But is that not the case, that, after all ...
>
> *Danny Morrison* – No.
>
> *Presenter* – ... that if soldiers are killed, are murdered, are you suggesting that somehow because you call that a political event that that gives you the right to move it into a different sphere of law altogether?
>
> *Danny Morrison* – Has the British Army ever murdered anybody in Ireland? Has the RUC ever murdered anyone in Ireland? You journalists are employed ... You won't tell the British public.

Presenter – That is, that is, that is not the question. These are the legitimately constituted forces. They are the legitimately constituted forces of the realm.

Danny Morrison – You won't explain to the British people what's going on over here ...

Presenter – (interrupts) That has often been explained plenty of times.

Danny Morrison – ... The interrogation centres, the prison camps full of young people.

Presenter – (interrupts) That has often been explained if you read the papers. But I want to hear what you have to say. Will the other three now go through with their strike?

Danny Morrison – Yes, they will carry it through because there was another republican hunger-strike, that of Terence McSweeney, who was MP for Mid Cork and died on hunger-strike in 1920. And he left the Republicans a saying: 'It's not those who can inflict the most, but those who can suffer the most who will win in the end'.

Presenter – Can you say to people what you think you have gained by this; what in hard concrete political terms do you feel that you are gaining, apart from losing people whom you see as comrades?

Danny Morrison – The spotlight is on the prison camp and the arguments which Margaret Thatcher puts for suggesting that these people are criminals, and that argument does not stand up, and all the journalists that I have spoken to from around the world are sympathetic and understand the situation. They've seen it before in Nicaragua, they've seen it before in Latin American countries, and they are sympathetic and they realise that Bobby Sands was a political prisoner.

Presenter – So you feel that you are getting the propaganda victory from this, you're getting propaganda mileage out of it?

Danny Morrison – Yes, there's publicity about this case, and Britain is a political leper in the eyes of the world.

Presenter – Danny Morrison, thank you.

We shall have more to say below about the oppositional definitions supplied by Morrison that Northern Irish violence is not terrorism but war. Continuing the theme of criminality and inhumanity consider this counter-example from a programme about violent opposition to the South African regime. In this case the reporter allows an alternative definition – terrorists are human – to prevail even though he rehearses the official argument. He pushes his respondent on the point that these men are terrorists even though in the rest of the programme he refers to them as guerillas.[30]

Peter Taylor, Reporter – (Suppose the guerillas came to you for) food, assistance, medical supplies. Would you encourage the mission to give them what they wanted?

Solomon Sente, Lutheran Bishop of Northern Transvaal – In a situation of need like that I think I would even not want to know who they are. I would simply see them as people, see the need that they require from me and we will do everything we can to assist them.

Peter Taylor – Even if you knew who they were?

Solomon Sente – Well I think it would still not change my attitude. They are humans and I'd give them the type of assistance they required.

Peter Taylor – Even if you knew they were terrorists?

Solomon Sente – (Embarrassed laugh) I think I would do that (more embarrassed laughter). It is a bit ... er ... difficult but if you start considering, that it may be your son, it may be your uncle, it may be your nephew. You would be bound from human compassion I think to do that.

Peter Taylor – That they are your people?

Solomon Sente – Because they are my blood. They are my flesh. They are part of my emotional experience. I think this is very important. In a way, one may not say very, very, very loudly but I think they are part of 'my agony'.

This interview is extremely unusual. Human compassion is rarely enlisted for people who in a more proximate context like Northern Ireland would be clearly identified as terrorists. [...]

The fact that state bullets inflict death and injury in just the same way as terrorist bullets does pose ideological problems for the dominant perspective. The weight of the argument against terrorism is that it causes suffering. If it can be shown that the state and its agents cause suffering there is some explaining to do. One answer is that given above, that state violence is legitimate. But this is relatively rare because it admits that state violence occurs and has nasty consequences. Even in discussions of the state's preparations for war against a conventional enemy euphemisms and technical terms are used to disguise the fact that war means death and injury starting from the initial and ubiquitous euphemism of defence. By comparison arguments that suffering caused by state violence was an isolated mistake, that under provocation some retaliation may be inevitable or more general attempts to deny that the incidents took place or that state forces were not responsible are more common. A favourite British device which has been used in cases like Bloody Sunday when British troops shot dead 13 demonstrators or following allegations of torture in Northern Ireland is to resort to Widgery, to set up legal enquiries which over a long period redefine the problems into acceptable terms. These the media can then report. In the case of Bloody Sunday Lord Widgery found there had been 'shooting by the army which bordered on the reckless'. Sir Edmund Compton redefined torture as physical ill-treatment.[31] [...]

On the question of what is to be allowed as real suffering an instructive comparison can be drawn between the treatment of two funerals, one of the hunger striker Bobby Sands in Northern Ireland, the other of Pallas Mallangu a black striker in South Africa.[32]

> BBC TV News, *Kate Adie*, 7.5.81. – To the tens of thousands who watched his coffin to the grave this was the burial of Bobby Sands, martyr. The full paraphernalia of an IRA military funeral. The Irish tricolour draped over the coffin after a funeral mass in St Luke's church, where the priest asked the congregation to pray not only for Bobby Sands but for two other men who died last night, a policeman and a terrorist bomber.
>
> The Massed Escort in combat uniform prepared to march the four miles to Milltown Cemetery. An army helicopter grinding relentlessly overhead all but drowned the tones of the Irish pipes and there were shouts by the stewards as they tried to supervise the coverage by the world's press. For this was both funeral cortège and demonstration. Tens of thousands of people from all over Northern Ireland and from the South, a grim-faced demonstration of support for the political aims of the hunger strikers, overtaking the private grief of the Sands family. Such a procession had to be prevented from having any contact with a Protestant area and huge screens had been erected to avoid the sight of the cortège provoking trouble. The security forces kept their distance as the procession passed the Protestant Suffolk district. Outside a shopping centre in Anderson's town [sic] came the symbolic moment for the Republicans. Three masked men stepped forward and obeyed orders in Irish to fire a three volley salute. Illegal uniforms. Illegal shooting. All grist to the mill for the convictions of republican and loyalist.
>
> Among the mourners the Vice Presidents of Provisional Sinn Féin, Gerry Adams and David O'Connell. There was a huge crowd at the entrance to the cemetery, perched on crosses and headstones. At the graveside in the pouring rain, Sands' mother, father, sister, and his 8 year old son. Sands, the elected MP for Fermanagh and South Tyrone, serving 14 years for the possession of firearms starved himself to death and into a place in republican history.

The Sands funeral is admitted to be a tragic symbol for his supporters but, according to the reporter it is a symbol arranged for the media which has no more than propaganda value for a cause which we, the reporter and her audience, cannot support. The Mallangu funeral on the other hand is a 'political demonstration'. In that case the reporter developed the story to show how workers and guerillas are united in the same movement, pursuing the same cause, the 'liberation of the black man'.

> *Peter Taylor*, against background of chanting mourners at funeral procession – Many black workers see themselves as comrades, fighting the same war as the guerillas. Pallas Mallangu's funeral became a political demonstration. To the crowds who followed his coffin Pallas Mallangu was not just a martyr to the workers' cause. He was a martyr to the cause of black liberation. It's the political message of scenes like this. A mixture of anger and grief which makes the government ever more anxious about the power of the black trade unions. Many black workers see themselves as comrades, fighting the same war as the guerillas. They share the same enemy, they share the same end. Only the means are different. [...]

Liberation is the oppositional justification which may be allowable in less proximate cases. In the programme from which this example is taken 'terrorists' became 'guerillas'. In the INLA interview quoted above however attempts by the INLA spokesman to claim liberation status for their actions in Ireland were vigorously denied by the interviewer. [...]

The official discourse only uses war as a metaphor. It denies the terrorist even the limited legitimacy of being a conventional enemy. It does allow the possibility however that they are the agents of a foreign power whose aim is to subvert our way of life. In the South African *Panorama* the red threat was rehearsed as the South African government's case against the guerillas but one not to be taken too seriously. [...]

In more proximate cases the red threat becomes much more serious however. The following extract is taken from a programme on the attempt on the life of the Pope. This set out to establish from circumstantial evidence and the supposition of the Italian right that the KGB was behind the attempt. The extract sets out the case which was then developed in the programme which was both closed and tight. With an agency so ideologically distant as the KGB all pretence was dropped that there were alternative views or an opposition case.[33]

> *Presenter* – Good evening. *TV Eye* returns tonight with an investigation into the attempt to kill the Pope. This photograph was taken a moment before the shooting. Close ups reveal the would-be killer waiting half hidden on the left. The face on the right, so police believe, was that of an accomplice. If there was an accomplice then there was a plot and the Italian authorities have told us they believe the KGB was involved. Julian Mannion reports.

Our other example of a tight programme, this time putting an alternative view, is an authored documentary in which John Pilger reported on the current plight of the Vietnam veterans in the United States and drew out the implications for current American policy in El Salvador. In the course of the programme Pilger dealt with the same repertoire of meanings and definitions as are to be found in the other coverage of terrorism which we have discussed. But he systematically inverted the official meanings and definitions and provided a clear statement of an equation which is the precise opposite of the dominant view of terrorism. In official discourse insurgent terrorism leads to unacceptable human misery. In Pilger's alternative statement it is state terror which produces unacceptable human costs.

This inversion is completed at the end of the programme by first underlining the human experience of war and explicitly decoding its jargon. Then the war aims which justified this suffering are shown to be spurious, unachieved and unachievable.[34]

> *John Pilger* – Missing from this film are other witnesses to the Vietnam period, the Vietnamese. We hear very little about them these days and the American veterans speak little about them perhaps because what was done over there was so terrible that only the victims can afford to speak about it. Such has been the politics of vengeance that the people of Vietnam are now almost completely isolated with only the waiting arms of the Russians to turn to whom they rightly distrust as much as they distrusted the Americans, the French, the Japanese and the Chinese who came to their country selling noble causes.
>
> So here is the news from Vietnam. In the wake of the war's devastation there is now famine. Rations are less than even during the war years, about half the food needed for a healthy survival. There is no milk any more for children over the age of one and unexploded mines and bombs kill children everyday.
>
> Like its refusal to help its own victims of the war the American government has denied all help to the people of Vietnam and so too has the British government. [...]

In an earlier sequence Pilger had pointed out the terror of war behind the sanitised and heroic images of the parades that ended earlier wars.

> *John Pilger* – Patton's Doughboys marched home from Europe in 1919. The military parade at the end of the war has always been a grand illusion. Especially in countries themselves not ravaged by war. Like TV movies in which blood and gore are never seen the parades of the past were great demonstrations of vital, victorious manhood. Vietnam changed all that, perhaps for ever and the longing of some Vietnam veterans for parades and flags can never be realised because they brought home the truth of war.
>
> Imagine a parade for them led by human crabs without limbs, men without faces, men with minds and testicles blown away. Frail young men addicted and dying from cancers caused by chemical

warfare and behind them in endless formation Vietnamese women and children and old men zapped by the friendly fire of Napalm.

In a third inversion Pilger redefined the concept of terrorism. He cited the US government view that international terrorism was Moscow inspired only to knock it down with CIA evidence. [...]

In drawing the parallel between Vietnam and El Salvador Pilger used US Ambassador White to redefine terrorism from insurgent terrorism to state terrorism. He then underlined the point by comparing the tragedy of the El Salvadorians and the Vietnamese, both victims of the state's military machine. [...]

> *John Pilger* – This book is a collection of *New York Times* front pages which trace the American involvement in Vietnam and reading it now is an eerie experience. The same headlines are appearing today. The same jargon such as escalation, and light at the end of the tunnel. The same delusions. Delete Vietnam and write in El Salvador and the stories seem almost identical. Like the politicians then, Kennedy, Johnson and Nixon, the politicians now, Haig and Reagan, see the world in the same arrogant, simplistic terms, speaking of dominoes as if nations were mere blocks of wood. Not societies riven with their own differences and animosities. Today as before honest men pay with their careers. The American Ambassador to El Salvador, Robert White, has said that the war in that country is caused by social injustice and that the real terrorists are the regime backed by Mr Reagan and Mr Haig and supported of course by the British government.

> *Robert White*, US Ambassador to El Salvador – The security forces in El Salvador have been responsible for the deaths of thousands and thousands of young people, and they have executed them just on the mere suspicion that they are leftists or sympathise with leftists. Are we really going to send military advisers in there to be part of that type of machinery?

> *John Pilger* – For speaking that truth the ambassador was sacked. Here is an announcement of US advisers going to Vietnam and US troops going to protect them. The advisers have already arrived in El Salvador. As in Vietnam the people who are dying in the streets and jungles of El Salvador are nameless stick figures on a television news or between the commercials in a re-run Hollywood movie. The American veterans of Vietnam have much in common with them for they too have been declared expendable.

This is a rare statement in actuality television of the thesis that there is a problem of state terrorism. In contrast, the nature and legitimacy of the state's use of violence is a central theme in television fiction dealing with terrorism, although the way it is handled varies considerably. To illustrate this range we have chosen four programmes which represent the major types of television drama we outlined earlier. They are: an episode from a top-rating action-adventure series, *The Professionals*; a thriller serial written especially for television, *Blood Money,* a series adapted from a secret service novel, *A Spy at Evening*; and a television play, *Psy-Warriors*. As with the actuality programmes just discussed, these instances can be arranged on a continuum running from relatively 'open' to relatively 'closed', as shown in Figure 2.

Figure 2

Intended Audience

Maximum ←— — — — — — — —→ Restricted

Actuality	News Magazines e.g. *Nationwide*	Current Affairs e.g. *Panorama*	'Authored' documentaries e.g. *Heroes*
Fiction	Action-adventure series e.g. *The Professionals*	Serials e.g. *Blood Money, A Spy at Evening*	Single plays e.g. *Psy-Warriors*

RELATIVELY ←— — — — — — — —→ RELATIVELY
'CLOSED'   'OPEN'

Terrorism in Television Fiction

The Professionals is one of the most successful action-adventure series produced in Britain in recent years. Almost all the episodes have featured in the top ten most popular programmes and the series has been sold in most of the major overseas markets. The action centres around Bodie and Doyle, the two top agents of CI5, a crack Criminal Intelligence unit which bears more than a passing resemblance to the SAS. According to the publicity blurbs for the series:

> Anarchy, acts of terror, crimes of violence – it's all grist to the mill of the formidable force who make up CI5.[35]

> CI5 breaks all the rules: no uniforms, no ranks and no conscience – just results. Formed to combat the vicious tide of violence that threatens law and order, its brief is to counter-attack. And when there's a hijack, a bomb threat, a kidnap or a sniper, men from CI5 storm into action.[36]

This brief underscores two key themes in the official discourse. Firstly, it places terrorism firmly within a criminal rather than a political frame and defines it exclusively in terms of the violence it entails. And secondly, it legitimates the state's use of violent countermeasures by arguing that exceptional threats to the social order require exceptional responses in which considerations of civil liberties, democratic accountability, and due process are held in abeyance in the interests of efficiency. Within this perspective the end of reestablishing order justifies the use of dubious and even illegal means, and licences the men of CI5 to use the same dirty tricks as their adversaries. We are told that Bodie and Doyle;

> Believe in fighting violence with violence. They are cold and ruthless. They would think nothing of kidnapping a kidnapper, or chaining a bomber to his own bomb and leaving him to defuse it.[37]

But, the fact that they are agents of the state means that popular support for these strong-arm tactics cannot be entirely taken for granted, as the unit's commander, Cowley, tells his men;

> Oh, there'll be squeals, and once in a while you'll turn a law-abiding citizen into an authority-hating anarchist. There'll be squeals, and letters to MP's but that is the price they, and we, have to pay to keep this island clean and smelling, even if ever so faintly of roses and lavender.[38]

Hence, while it operates firmly within the terms of the official discourse, the programme must also work actively to head off dissent and enlist the audience's support for powerful countermeasures by underlining the exceptional nature of the terrorist threat and pointing up the irrelevance of alternative and oppositional perspectives on state violence. This process of ideological mobilisation is well illustrated in the episode entitled *Close Quarters*.[39]

The episode opens with the assassination of a British politician, Sir Denny Forbes, at a check-in desk at London airport, killed by the leader of the Meyer-Helmut terrorist group with a syringe of poison. This precipitating incident introduces four central themes; the essential criminality of terrorism; its identification with the Left; its characterisation as an alien incursion originating outside Britain and the absolute contrast between the legitimate pursuit of interests through parliamentary representation and the illegitimacy of direct action. The assassination is a direct attack on the 'body politic' and on the 'British way of life'.

Having detonated these themes in the opening pre-credit sequence, the narrative immediately begins to elaborate them. The audience have already been invited to see Meyer's act as essentially criminal rather than political by the very fact that it is going to be tackled by CI5, a criminal intelligence unit. But to reinforce the point the scene immediately after the credits shows Cowley briefing his men in a style familiar from countless crime movies where the chief of police talks his officers through the 'most wanted' list. [...]

Although Bodie attends the briefing he is excused active duty because of an injured gun hand, and he decides to take his girlfriend Julie for a picnic on the River Thames at Henley. While on the water he recognises Meyer standing on the bank. He follows him to the cottage he is using as a 'safe house' and arrests him. But the other members of group arrive and give chase. Bodie eludes them and makes his getaway in a stolen car. The group pursue him and he barricades himself in a country vicarage which the group, heavily armed, surround.

The key visual images in this action sequence serve to underscore the essential alienness of terrorism by counterposing the menacing figure of the German, Meyer, with idealised representations of traditional England and the British 'way of life' – rowing on a sunlit River Thames at Henley (site of the famous regatta), and the elegant eighteenth-century vicarage set in the kind of rolling parkland familiar from the novels of Jane Austen.

After this action sequence the dialogue again takes up the two core themes: of the irrationality and criminality of terrorism and its essential alienness to the British way of life.

> *Bodie* (having burst into the vicarage and secured the doors and windows, turns to the vicar and his housekeeper) – In the heat of the moment I forgot my manners. This is Julie my girlfriend and I'm Bodie. May we have a drink. I think we all need one.
>
> *Meyer* (with heavy sarcasm) – May we have a drink vicar. So polite vicar. Let's all have a little tea party. You English are all insane.
>
> *Bodie* – Not like the Meyer-Helmut group eh? They just bomb and hijack and shoot the odd plane load of hostages.
>
> *Meyer* – It's a necessary part of our strategy.
>
> *Bodie* – The end justifies the means eh?
>
> *Meyer* – You don't understand. You will never understand.
>
> *Bodie* – No. Not if I live a million years.
>
> *Meyer* – We are the Meyer-Helmut group. We are not trash.
>
> *Vicar* – Who are those people outside?
>
> *Bodie* – He just told you, a bunch of killers.
>
> *Meyer* – We are a political force.
>
> *Bodie* – Forget the political vicar, just concentrate on the force. [...]

The group's utter ruthlessness is confirmed when they shoot the vicar in cold blood as he is climbing out of a window in an effort to reason with them. This incident clinches the central ideological theme of the narrative; that you can't bargain with terrorists and that faced with their arbitrary violence the State is justified in using similar tactics. Popular support for this position is mobilised through the common-sense response of the housekeeper and Bodie's girlfriend. The audience is invited to see its real-life position as analogous to the women's situation within the narrative; innocent by-standers who are caught up in events they do not fully understand but who can recognise the State's moral right to combat terrorism with all the weapons its commands.

> *Meyer* (addressing the girlfriend and the housekeeper) – How does this concern you? You have no conception of what this fight is about. It's not your fight.

> *Housekeeper* – I don't understand your politics, but I understand good and evil. You kill without cause. You kill people who cannot possibly stand between you and your ideas. You don't even know who they are.

> *Julie* (addressing Meyer) – You're right. I have no idea what you're fighting about. I just know it means violence and killing and someone's got to stop you.

Despite these protestations Julie still has reservations about the legitimacy of Bodie's use of violence (after he has shot two members of the group as they attempted to enter the vicarage).

> *Bodie* – I'm doing this to protect you, people like you.

> *Julie* – You live by violence, just like him (indicating Meyer).

> *Bodie* – Yes, well you fight fire with fire in this job.

But at the climax of the plot, when the chips are down, Julie overcomes her qualms. As the last member of the gang storms the room where they are hiding, Bodie is disarmed by Meyer and it is Julie who picks up his gun and shoots. The ideological circle is finally closed, around the official discourse.

By no means all popular television fiction is as 'closed' or as 'tight' as this however. Serials in particular, may provide spaces for a more critical appraisal of state violence and point to contradictions which may not be entirely resolved within the scope of the text. This was the case with a six part serial, *Blood Money.*[40]

The narrative opens with a scene set in an exclusive private boarding school for the sons of the rich. The boys are out on a cross-country run through the sunlit landscape. One of them, Rupert Fitzcharles, is the son of the Administrator General of the United Nations and because of his father's political status he is guarded by a plain clothes policeman working undercover as a school sports master. Suddenly, figures wearing gas masks spring out from behind the hedges, spray the boys with CS gas, abduct the diplomat's son and drive him to their 'safe' house in London. They intend to release him when the authorities agree to meet their demands, but if they refuse the group intend to kill him.

As in the initial scenes of *Close Quarters*, this opening sequence calls into play two of the central themes in the official discourse - the essential ruthlessness of terrorists and their disregard for human life - and their characterisation as an alien incursion. And as in *The Professionals*, this opposition between terrorism and the 'British way of life' is represented by idealised images of rural and upper class England on the one hand, and by making the terrorist leader a German (although in this case she is a blonde woman rather than a dark haired man, the model being Ulrike Meinhoff rather than Andreas Bader). As the narrative progresses, however the framework established by this opening is made increasingly problematic.

The fact that the narrative is less compressed than in a standard series episode provides space for a fuller characterisation of the terrorists and for some discussion of their motivation, and in the process tensions and contradictions begin to emerge. On the one hand, the characterisation of the group's leader, Irene Kohl, reinforces the terms of the official discourse. She is consistently depicted as fanatical and ruthless. She shows no sympathy whatever for the kidnapped boy and the fear he feels. She sees him simply as a bargaining counter, necessary for the achievements of the group's political aims, but dispensable if things go wrong. And the fact that she is a woman is constantly used to underscore the official view that terrorism is 'unnatural' and dehumanising. On the other hand, the characterisation of the Irish member of the group, Danny Connors, leads in the opposite direction. He shows considerable sympathy for the boy's distress and eventually establishes a friendly relationship with him. He is portrayed as an essentially decent man who has been led astray by political idealism, but his choice is presented as entirely intelligible given the history of the British ruling class's treatment of the Irish people. This point is made quite early on in the narrative as Danny is handing the boy his evening meal of meat and potatoes.

> *Danny* – That's yours. You should be grateful for it. At least it's cooked. During the famine in Ireland the people were eating potatoes raw and rotten, that's when they had any at all. The Brits, they owned all of Ireland, did you know that? And because the people couldn't pay their rents, 'cause they had nothing, no food, no clothes, nothing, they sent the troops to tear down their homes so that the landlords could have their land back to do what they liked with, Irish land. Didn't teach you that at school did they? No, I bet they didn't.

This contrast between the depiction of terrorists as fanatical and inhuman on the one hand and as human but politically motivated on the other is never resolved and remains a permanent tension within the text. But the larger and more significant fissure opens up around the presentation of the forces of law and order.

Since the kidnap is classified as a crime the investigation is the responsibility of the relevant section of the regular police force commanded by Chief Superintendent Meadows. But because of the political status of the boy's father, Captain Percival of the Secret Intelligence Service is also assigned to the case. Meadows represents the rule of law and due process. His overriding concern is to return the boy safely to his parents and bring the kidnappers to justice. Percival on the other hand, is primarily concerned with eradicating terrorism and he is quite prepared to go behind the back of the law to achieve this. In the ensuing conflict between the two men, the normal connections between law and order are prised apart and the effective maintenance of order is presented as potentially *at odds* with adherence to legal processes. This tension is made explicit in the scene which ends episode two, where Meadows' deputy, Inspector Clarke, hands Percival the ransom note the police have received from the terrorists.

Clarke – Sir, the actual ransom demands, they seem to me to be very moderate.

Percival – Oh indeed! Who apart from someone like myself isn't prepared to give a million pounds to Amnesty International and an awful lot of people would enjoy seeing the Prime Minister confessing on television to her crimes and those of her predecessors... whereas for the H-Blocks, no-one really cares about them except a few Irishmen who would support the kidnap anyway. So that's clearly a bargaining counter. Expendable, but that's their strength. The terrorist can compromise. The state cannot. The State can no more compromise a little bit than a woman can get a little bit pregnant... As you may be aware inspector, terrorism is about propaganda. Giving the impression that the state is unable to protect the things it cares for most. It doesn't matter too much what they are or who they are, politicians, or industrialists like Aldo Moro and Hans Martin Schleyer, a pub or a dance hall in Belfast, the Israeli athletes at Munich, even President Kennedy.

Clarke – All the same, you'd have thought they would have made better demands than, well, those.

Percival – Not at all. They don't want to change the state, they want to destroy it, or rather, make it destroy itself.

Clarke – Well then, why not ask for more?

Percival – Because if they make demands like these, which the man on the Clapham omnibus and even you regard as reasonable, the state in responding as it has to, must either disregard public opinion or surrender. Must either appear tyrannical or impotent.

Clarke – Yes, but even a democracy has an enormous amount of power.

Percival – Yes of course, but it must not be seen to use it. Democracy has deep roots but very delicate fruit.

Clarke – So delicate, that in the end terrorism is bound to win?

Percival – Not necessarily. The terrorists may choose the game, we make the rules.

Clarke – The fact that a child's involved, the Superintendent will want the heaviest sentence that the law can hand out.

Percival – Oh I do hope it doesn't come to that. After all, they specifically say they're at war with us and in a war one doesn't have to take prisoners.

This dialogue encapsulates the essential dilemma that democracies face in balancing force against consent, order against law. Either the state can play by its own rules and bring the terrorists to trial thereby giving them a platform for their views and an opportunity to mobilise public opinion. Or it can violate its principles, dispense with due process and eradicate the terrorists without a trial, thereby undermining the popular consent on which its legitimacy rests. The solution to this dilemma is to kill the terrorists clandestinely, away from the glare of publicity. [...] To retain popular consent the law must operate in public and justice must be seen to be done, whereas force is best exercised in secret so that the repressive fist within the democratic glove remains concealed.

This contradiction is central to the climax of the narrative and is strongly underscored in another interchange between Percival and a police inspector, just before the final action sequence.

Inspector – You'd rather they were all killed wouldn't you?

Percival – In an ideal world yes. I'd rather there wasn't a trial. Inspector Clarke knows my views. Acts of terrorism per se are quite pointless. Terrorism is about propaganda.

Inspector – Yes I know that.

Percival – So to give a highly articulate terrorist the publicity of a trial which would be the main story in the media for weeks is rather like giving a kleptomaniac free run of Harrods.

Inspector – Under the rule of law we have no alternative.

However, as Percival has hinted earlier, there is an alternative - licensed murder by agents of the state – and that is the solution he opts for.

The terrorists have been tricked into thinking that their demands have been met, by a fake broadcast by Meadows, who aims to arrest them as they leave the 'safe' house. But unknown to him, Percival has surrounded the house with a crack paramilitary unit. As the group step into the street, he gives the order to shoot them in cold blood. The boy is unhurt, but Meadows is outraged.

Meadows (to Percival) – You bastard!

Percival – Why? The woman was armed, she was going to kill the child.

Technically, Percival is correct, but since he has made it clear from the beginning that saving the boy's life is secondary to eliminating the terrorists, the audience is invited to read his remarks as a somewhat flimsy and inadequate justification for judicial murder and the abandonment of the rule of law. This is the last exchange of dialogue, and the narrative ends on an ambiguous note with Meadows turning his back on Percival and walking away. Although the tension between order and law is resolved, the nature of that resolution is presented as highly problematic and open to question. [...]

The possibility that the use of terror may be a normal and *systematic* feature of the democratic state's operations in periods of crisis, rather than the work of the occasional renegade functionary employed by a hostile power, is explored in *Psy-Warriors*.[41]

The play is set in a high security installation whose existence is known only to selected members of military intelligence and senior Ministry of Defence personnel. The action opens with two men and a woman being brought in for questioning. They are suspected of having left a bomb in an Aldershot public house, popular with soldiers from the nearby army camp (a scenario based on an actual incident). Within the unit normal legal rights are suspended. The suspects do not have the right to call a lawyer or to inform their family or friends of their whereabouts and they can be detained without being charged or brought to trial.

The play's opening scenes display the full range of disorientation techniques employed in modern interrogation. The group's leader is stripped naked and made to stand against a wall with his legs apart and a black bag over his head for hours on end. Later, he is led away blindfolded and taken up in an army helicopter and pushed out of the open door. In fact he is only a few feet from the ground but he is told he is over the Thames estuary. The second man is kept in a cage in a white-tiled room under constant glaring light and his regular patterns of sleep are interrupted by bouts of intensive interrogation. The woman's head is covered by a black bag smelling of vomit. She is forced to eat repulsive food, and when she asks to go to the toilet she is forcibly marched there. These techniques of sensory deprivation and psychological warfare are all drawn from official reports of the British army's operations in Ulster and elsewhere, but by displaying them in a particularly graphic way, the play forcefully raises the question of how far the state is justified in suspending basic human rights in the interests of securing confessions of information from suspected terrorists.

Thus the audience is invited to believe that they are watching a play about the way in which the state deals with possible terrorists, but the author then proceeds to overturn this assumption in order to raise less obvious questions about the legality and legitimacy of the State's operations in relation to terrorism.

After the initial interrogation scenes, the action cuts to a meeting between the directors of the unit and a visitor from the Ministry of Defence. It is revealed that the 'suspects' are not in fact terrorists at all, but army volunteers who are being tested for possible recruitment to an élite anti-terrorist unit. The training exercise the play presents requires them to assume the identity of terrorists in order to understand their situation and motivations from the inside so that they will be able to combat them more effectively. This phase of the training programme has culminated in them leaving a live bomb in the pub. But since the exercise is top secret, the police bomb squad were not informed, a fact which once again points up the tension within the state apparatuses revealed in *Blood Money* [...]

Group Leader – What if the bomb had gone off?

Interrogator – Then the Provisionals would have claimed responsibility. Well why not eh? We help keep the terrorist cause in the public eye and the terrorist helps us justify the need for greater security. What's called a symbiotic relationship I believe.

This scene points to several prominent themes within the alternative perspective. Firstly, it suggests that in certain circumstances security agencies are prepared to act as an agent provocateur and to instigate acts of terrorism. It also draws attention to the 'secret state's' use of 'black' propaganda which bends the truth to sustain the official discourse's more or less exclusive identification of Irish violence with the Republican cause. But perhaps even more significantly, it suggests that ultimately the security services may be less interested in defending democracy than in extending their reach and power, and that they may therefore have a vested interest in the continuation of terrorism; that their relation to terrorism is symbiotic rather than antithetical.

As well as raising questions about the legality of the 'secret state's' operations, the play's structure provides considerable space for the presentation of oppositional justification for terrorism. The aim of the exercise presented in the play is to get the volunteers to understand the experience and motivations of terrorists from the inside out. The narrative depicts two devices for achieving this. The first is to make them take on the persona of terrorists, act out these assumed identities, and experience the possible consequences. The other is to licence the interrogators to act as devil's advocates, putting the strongest possible oppositional case in order to deepen the recruits' insights into the terrorist's motivations and to toughen up their resistance to counter-propaganda.

The oppositional case for terrorism is particularly powerfully put in the scenes between the chief interrogator and the woman. She has begun to crack under the strain and he needs to push her to the limit ideologically in order to find out where her breaking point is. In one scene they discuss the rationality of Ulrike Meinhoff's abortive attempt to send her children to be trained as guerillas by the Palestinians.

Interrogator – A food parcel and a bag of salt are no longer the currency they used to be. For a Palestinian refugee they don't express compassion, only the privilege of the sender. We give them nothing, and we learn nothing. We know nothing of the life in the camps of the Palestinians. We choose not to know. But now, there is Black September. With Black September behind them, within them, they are no longer to be pitied but feared. They have a different identity. Not refugee. Not displaced person. The Palestinian has become a fighter. They have become the enemy. And these people the enemy, are committed to violence, to killing. It is their last line of defence. They are forced to answer violence with violence. They use their bullets to subdue the violence of the people who exploit them. They see the harvest of this exploitation every day in their refugee camps. They kill to breathe.

Woman – Thank Christ I don't have any children. I couldn't do it. To send your children into the care of people you don't know, foreigners, terrorists, refugees, knowing full well they are to be indoctrinated into the art of maiming, killing, terrorising. It's wrong, It cannot be justified. It's fanatical.

Interrogator – Perhaps it was an act of true compassion, an act of true responsibility. If you had been humiliated for over twenty five years... If you were persona non grata according to international law, no identity, no passport, cannot, must not travel, no rights, not even to work, how would you act? How do you think you would act if you were regarded as though you were not really a person at all?

Woman – I don't know how I would react.

Interrogator – That in itself is an expression of privilege. Perhaps Ulrike Meinhoff traded her privilege for compassion, sent her children to the Palestinians instead of a food parcel. What would you send?

[...] Also in *Psy-Warriors* however, was the presentation of the situation in Northern Ireland in terms derived from the rhetoric of militant Republicanism. This depicts it as Britain's last colonial war and presents the IRA's terrorist campaign as a guerilla offensive against an army of occupation who consistently violate human rights in the defence of an exploitative colonial power.

Chief Interrogator (addressing the woman volunteer) – Mau Mau, EOKA, the NLF, the IRA. I've spent the greater part of my working life watching British troops being pulled out of places they were never going to leave. A long hard line of colonial campaigns, and on every campaign the British used internment, concentration camps, and intensive interrogation, torture-sticks up bums, bums on blocks of ice, licking the lav bowl clean, nudity, humiliation, running round in circles and pissing in the wind. You name it, we've inflicted it, I've inflicted it, the Empire, your heritage... What you see in Ulster is the rear end of the crudity and exploitation of over thirty colonial wars. The last colonial battlefield. A dog devouring its own tail. When it reaches its arse it will be in England.

Faced with this ideological onslaught the woman has no defence and is dropped from the training programme. The second man is found to be unstable and untrustworthy and is also dropped. The group leader however comes through the ordeal with flying colours and is offered the job of heading the new anti-terrorist unit in the field. But he refuses and resigns his commission claiming that he no longer wants to be part of a service that does to people, even suspected terrorists, what has just been done to him.

Although *Psy-Warriors* was the most 'open' programme we looked at, as we have shown it was not an altogether isolated instance. Rather, it lies at one end of a continuum which runs from ideological 'closure' to relative 'openness', which operates in complex ways within the major forms of programming, and which provides space for rather more conflict and contestation than the prevailing wisdom of critical media research might predict. That this should be so came as something of a surprise to us, but it was also exhilarating, since it has opened up a whole range of issues for investigation and analysis which have barely been touched on by the work done so far.

Conclusion

In this analysis of terrorism on television we have tried to demonstrate some of the continuities and discontinuities to be found right across the output of the medium, embracing both 'actuality' and 'fiction' and the more popular as against the more exclusive forms. This we have done by looking at the ideological problems that political violence raises for the state and the contest over legitimation that is involved. Our approach, perforce, must challenge and extend the present orthodoxy in media sociology and cultural studies. This orthodoxy – one which we ourselves have helped to establish and develop – has concentrated almost exclusively on news. Factual programmes have come to be seen as virtual paradigms of how the national culture is represented. Consequently, news and current affairs programmes have had a heavy burden to bear. They have been taken by their critics to be a virtually self contained area which provides the most crucial social map made available by the mass media to the wider public, and therefore as the most important targets. As is plain from our analysis, the frameworks of interpretation which we have delineated play a structuring role in forms as varied as news, documentary, the drama series and the single play. Moreover, the precise ways in which a given form may be structured is illuminated by comparison with others. This enables us to be made much more aware of the possibilities and limitations available within each form when it comes to representing an issue such as that of 'terrorism', and the wider relationships of political violence to the state.

Much recent work has reproduced the structure of attention of the media themselves by an excessive concern with the representation of formalised conflicts in the parliamentary arena, industrial relations or process of law enforcement.[43] In these cases the system of representations to be found in broadcasting are heavily grounded in social institutions of conflict resolution and management, and reproduce the concerns of these institutions and their leaders. Nevertheless in the last two cases particularly much of the conflict in terms for example of unofficial strikes, demonstrative picketing, factory occupations, street demonstration, and riots occurs outside the frameworks consecrated by the established institutions of the state and civil society. Where conflict escapes the institutions it is characteristically handled as 'violence' which poses a fundamental threat to the stability of society. We recommend taking violence as the central focus because it is precisely at this point that the legitimacy of the state comes under most pressure. Even if spokespeople for the 'violent' are denied routine access to the centre of the stage though, as we have seen, their views do not go entirely unrepresented, those who exercise control in this area have to work hard to justify and legitimate repressive action and to maintain their indiscriminate condemnation of the violent, the criminal and the terroristic.

Instead of concentrating on those processes which affirm the stability of the state and civil society it seems fruitful to consider those which are deemed to pose a threat to their very existence. For one thing it brings another range of institutions into view, the apparatuses of the secret state. These are largely invisible in actuality programming but provide much of the substance of drama. An exclusive concern with factual representations is simply too narrow. What is needed is an awareness of the inter-relatedness of the components of the national culture. [...]

Endnotes

1. S. Picciotto, 'The theory of the state, class struggle and the rule of law', in Bob Fine et al. (eds.) *Capitalism and the Rule of Law*, London, Hutchinson, 1979, p. 165.
2. N. Chomsky and E. S. Herman, *The Political Economy of Human Rights*, 2 vols, Nottingham, Spokesman Books, 1979.
3. M. Thatcher, speaking at the 51st Annual Conservative Women's Conference 20 May 1981, emphasis added.
4. *Cf.* the reports in *The Guardian*, 'Thatcher warns on danger of media aiding Ulster terrors' (21.5.81) and 'Granada stops film on Ulster' (2.6.81); also *cf.* Peter Fiddick's article in the same paper, 'The Irish facts that are not fit to be shown' (9.6.81).

5. For a synoptic account of the British model of censorship on Northern Ireland and policing, and for a more general discussion, *cf.* Philip Schlesinger, 'Terrorism, the media, and the liberal-democratic state', *Social Research*, vol. 48, no. 1, Spring 1981.

6. *Cf.* 'Close Watch on Russian Conduct and 'Washington Chilled by Cold War Winds', *The Guardian*, 30.1.81 and 31.1.81.

7. For an account of how broadcasting handled the siege *cf.* Philip Schlesinger, 'Princes Gate, 1980; the media politics of siege management', *Screen Education*, Winter 1980/81 No. 37. The SAS (Special Air Service) are a counter insurgent force within the British Military. The Iranian embassy siege was their first acknowledged operation on the British mainland though they have been deployed in Northern Ireland. For a coloured and colourful account of the SAS see Tony Geraty, *Who dares wins: the story of the Special Air Service*, London, Arms and Armour Press, 1980.

8. For a useful source on this *cf.* Duncan Campbell, *Big Brother is Listening: Phonetappers and the Security State, NS Report* No. 2, 1981.

9. *Cf.* Marletti, *op. cit.*, and S. Cobler, 'The Determined Assertion of Normalcy', *Telos*, no. 43, Spring 1980.

10. A good instance of this is C. Scorer and P. Hewitt, *The Prevention of Terrorism Act: The case for repeal*, London, National Council for Civil Liberties, 1981.

11. *Cf.* P. Taylor, *Beating the Terrorists?*, Harmondsworth, Penguin, 1980.

12. *Op. cit.*

13. W. Schaap, 'New Spate of Terrorism, Key Leaders Unleashed', *Covert Action Information Bulletin*, No. 11, December 1980.

14. *Cf.* C. Maechling, 'Is the US about to export state terrorism?', *The Guardian*, 23.2.81; S. Lukes, 'Drawing fine lines around human rights', *The Times Higher Education Supplement*, 11.9.81.

15. For an influential polemic *cf.* E. P. Thompson, *Writing by Candlelight*, London, Merlin, 1980.

16. News has become the most studied of all televisual forms. For evidence on these points see *inter alia* Peter Golding and Philip Elliott, *Making the News*, Longman, 1979, and on the cast of accredited spokespeople, Stuart Hall *et al.*, *Policing the Crisis*, Macmillan, 1978.

17. C. Bazalgette and R. Paterson, 'Real Entertainment: The Iranian Embassy Siege', *Screen Education*, Winter 1980/81, No. 37.

18. On the origins of fiction dealing with terrorism and with the intelligence services see Walter Lacquer, 'Interpretations of Terrorism: Fact, Fiction and Political Science', *Journal of Contemporary History*, vol. 12, no. 1, January 1977 (especially pages 15-32); Bill Melman, 'The Terrorist in Fiction', *Journal of Contemporary History*, vol. 15, no. 3 July 1980; and David Stafford, 'Spies and Gentlemen: The Birth of the British Spy Novel, 1893-1914', *Victorian Studies*, vol. 24, no. 4, summer 1981.

19. On this point see Graham Murdock and James D. Halloran, 'Contexts of Creativity in Television Drama: An Exploratory Study in Britain', in Heinz-Dietrich Fischer and Stefan Melnik (eds.) *Entertainment: A Cross-Cultural Examination*, New York, Hastings House, 1979, pp. 273-285.

20. See Jerry Palmer, *Thrillers: Genesis and Structure of a Popular Genre*, London, Edward Arnold, 1978, p. 23.

21. See David Stafford, *op. cit.*

22. Jerry Palmer, *op. cit.*, p. 40.

23. On the xenophobia of the Bond books and their representation of 'Britishness', see Umberto Eco, 'Narrative Structures in Fleming', in his collection, *The Role of the Reader*, Bloomington, Indiana University Press, 1979, pp. 144-172; and David Cannadine, 'James Bond and the Decline of England', *Encounter*, vol. LIII, no. 3, September 1979, pp. 46-55.

24. The 'ideology of authorship' and its role in television fiction production is discussed in greater detail in Graham Murdock, 'Authorship and Organisation', *Screen Education*, no. 35, Summer 1980, pp. 19-34.

25. On the political sensitivity to television dramas dealing with Northern Ireland see Richard Hoggart, 'Ulster: a "switch-off" TV Subject?', *The Listener*, vol. 103, no. 2651, 28 February 1980, pp. 261-2, and Paul Madden, 'Banned, Censored and Delayed', in *Truth The First Casualty: The British Media and Ireland*, London, The Campaign for Free Speech on Ireland, 1979, pp. 17-21.

26. On the innuendos surrounding these terms see Phillip Elliott, 'Press Performance as Political Ritual', in H. Christian (ed.), *The Sociology of Journalism and the Press, Sociological Review* Monograph, no. 29, 1980.

27. *Tonight*, BBC1, 5th July 1979. We are particularly grateful to Mairaid Thomas and Paul Kerr of the British Film Institute for invaluable assistance in the preparation of the accompanying tape of illustrative excerpts and for helpful suggestions which started us on a number of fruitful lines of enquiry.

28. *The Editors*, BBC1, 28th June 1981.

29. *Newsnight*, BBC2, 6th May 1981.

30. *Panorama*, BBC1, 15th June 1981.

31. The relevant texts are: on Bloody Sunday, *The Report of the Widgery Tribunal*, HMSO, London, HC 220, 1972 and, on torture, *The Compton Report: Allegations against the Security Forces of Physical Brutality in Northern Ireland*, HMSO, London, Cmnd 4823, 1971. The interrogation techniques portrayed in the play *Psy-Warriors* which we discuss below are based on those whose use was confirmed by Compton. For an account of reporting in Northern Ireland in this period see Simon Winchester, *In Holy Terror*, Faber and Faber, 1974.

32. The *9 O'clock News*, BBC1, 7th May 1981 and *Panorama*, BBC1, 15th June 1981.

33. *TV Eye*, ITV, 3rd September, 1981.

34. *Heroes*, ITV, 6th May 1981 (produced by ATV).

35. *TV Times Extra: Who's Who Among the TV Super Sleuths*, London, Independent Television Publication 1979, p. 11.

36. Blurb on the back cover of Ken Blake, *The Professionals: Where The Jungle Ends*, a novel based on the original television screenplays by Brian Clemens and Anthony Read, London, Sphere Books, 1978.

37. *TV Times Extra, op. cit.*

38. *Where the Jungle Ends, op. cit.*, p. 19.

39. *Close Quarters*, written by Brian Clemens, directed by Williams Brayne, produced by Sidney Hayters. Broadcast of ITV Friday June 5th 1981, 9 p.m.

40. *Blood Money*, a serial in six episodes, written by Arden Winch, directed by Michael E. Briant and produced by Gerard Glaister. Broadcast on BBC1 from 9.35 to 10.05 p.m. on Sunday evenings from 6 September to 11 October 1981.

41. *Psy-Warriors,* written by David Leland, directed by Alan Clarke and produced by June Roberts. Broadcast on BBC1 as a 'Play for Today' from 10.15 - 11.30 p.m. on 12 May 1981.

42. For politics see Stuart Hall, Ian Connell and Lidia Curti, 'The "unity" of Current Affairs Television', *Working Papers in Cultural Studies*, no. 9, 1976, pp. 51-93, quotation from p. 61; on industrial relations the Glasgow University Media Group, *Bad News* and *More Bad News*, London, Routledge and Kegan Paul, 1976 and 1980, on law enforcement within the paradigm of news, Hall *et al.* 1978 *op. cit.*, and within the paradigm of election broadcasting, Alan Clarke, Ian Taylor and Justin Wren-Lewin, 'Inequality of Access to Political Television: The Case of the General Election of 1979', paper presented to the Annual Conference of the British Sociological Association, Aberystwyth, Wales, 1981.

22.

Jack Holland

COVERING THE NORTHERN CRISIS: THE U.S. PRESS AND NORTHERN IRELAND

(From *The American Connection: U.S. Guns, Money and Influence in Northern Ireland*, Swords, Co. Dublin, Poolbeg Press, 1989, pages 196-235)

[...]

Three things emerge from a review of the often extensive coverage Northern Ireland has received in the American press. The first is that there exists a general consensus on Northern Ireland among the major newspapers and magazines. Second, the consensus was basically the same as that of the British government. Third, this consensus was remarkably consistent until about 1979. Then, and increasing after the hunger strikes of 1981, a shift toward an attitude more critical of Britain's role can be detected.

Though Northern Ireland has received great attention, no newspaper except the *Christian Science Monitor* has ever had a full-time Irish correspondent. Northern Ireland was usually the responsibility of the London office, while reporting the day-to-day violence generally became the responsibility of the wire services – Associated Press (AP), United Press International (UPI), and Reuters. Press attention has, of course, experienced peaks and troughs, yet it has been fairly constant since 1969. As a gauge of this level of interest, in 1985 four papers – the *Chicago Tribune,* the *New York Times,* the New York *Daily News,* and the *Boston Globe* – accounted for at least a thousand pieces of commentary and analysis alone, not including reports.

Local U.S. newspapers, of which there are estimated to be almost 1,500, generally relied on wire services (either those just mentioned or those of the major newspapers) for the bulk of their coverage. More often than not they took their editorial line from big-city colleagues.

Like the British government's official 'line' on Northern Ireland, that of the major newspapers and magazines in the U.S. held the problem to be a sectarian conflict between recalcitrant religious groups kept apart only by the intervention of Britain acting as a kind of 'bobby.' The view of Britain was that of a detached, patient, and objective arbiter doing its best to convince two irrational, hate-filled communities to live together in harmony. Constantly undermining these noble efforts was the IRA, portrayed as a gang of mindless criminals and psychopaths bent on destruction. In later years, this portrait was touched up somewhat by the rising concern over 'international terrorism'; into the picture was dutifully painted various 'links' with other equally anathematized groups and individuals, such as the Palestine Liberation Organization and Colonel Qaddafi of Libya.

This consensus has excluded from serious debate on Northern Ireland the other view, what might loosely be termed the 'republican' analysis. In one form or another, this view is accepted by all the non-Unionist political parties in Ireland. It sees the Northern crisis as the offspring of the partition of Ireland, and the war as political rather than religious. It holds that as long as Britain maintains a presence in Ireland, the problem will never be solved, and argues that in the long term the only hope for permanent peace and stability is some kind of unified state. The moderate Social Democratic and Labour party (SDLP), the Fianna Fail party, the Fine Gael party, and the Irish Labour party all agree on this. So does the IRA. They differ in that the establishment parties do not think that violence is justified in achieving the goal they share; the IRA does.

In the pages that follow, it is not proposed to conduct a polemic on behalf of this view. Rather, it is hoped it will be shown that the U.S. press, by excluding it from its terms of reference, lacks not only explanatory power but reliability when covering the Northern crisis.

The 'Inexplicable Irish'

The Northern Ireland crisis first received extensive coverage in August 1969. [...]

Even at this early date, the *New York Times* quickly established certain stereotypes. Its reporter, Gloria Emerson, wrote: "In London there was a sense of something dark, inexplicable and strange in the Irish soul that foreigners cannot explain – or quite ignore."[1]

The 'inexplicable' Irish soon became a fixture of the coverage. Benignly, the inexplicable nature of the Irish could be expressed in terms of mystery. Or it could be seen malignantly, as an explanation for the religious hatred which the press regards as a cause of the violence. In early 1972, *Newsweek* lamented the prospect of England's being dragged into 'the deadly Irish quagmire' by 'two fanatical religious armies' – i.e., the Catholics and the Protestants. The image of the unreasoning, fanatical Irish (the negative side of the 'inexplicable' soul) suggested something primitive. *Time* wrote that the crisis was due to the 'truculent tribalism' of the Northern Irish.[2] Thus the magazine could imply that the Irish needed the British. After the failure of a British initiative, *Time* said, 'The trouble, as the past few weeks have tragically demonstrated, is that the Irish cannot run Ireland either.'[3]

Irrational sectarian hatred as the cause of the problem readily appealed to the *New York Times* reporter who wrote: 'As the demands for reform were being made, and beginning to be met, however, members of the lunatic fringe – which is quite a long, thick fringe in Northern Ireland – got going, and coerced their co-religionists into supporting them... Then the bomb-throwing and gun psychopaths of the Provisional IRA wing went to work.'[4] The *Boston Globe* writer concurred on the subject of the backwardness of the warring Irish tribes: 'The British army is separating the combatants in Ulster's guerrilla war because the people of Northern Ireland proved incapable of governing themselves...'[5] Obviously, victims of such tribal, irrational hatreds could not possibly run a modern state.

New York Times liberal columnist Anthony Lewis, espousing the more benign view of Irish irrationality, wrote: 'A mystic might say that there is some special fate bedeviling the two islands, close neighbors that need but cannot understand each other.'[6] He goes on to quote a British official as theorizing that there is 'too much myth in the way. Or perhaps too much history to let reason work.' Lewis continued: 'His voice sounded near despair as he discussed the alternatives open to Britain.' One year later Lewis came to the conclusion that the only hope for Northern Ireland was for Britain to pursue a policy of 'enlightened colonialism.'[7]

Lewis, a well-known defender of various liberal causes, had written the first piece quoted above a few days after British paratroopers gunned down thirteen unarmed civilians after a civil-rights demonstration in Derry. [...] As an explanation of a brutal mass murder it was hardly adequate. Yet that a prominent liberal could find it so is one indication of the lack of objective critical analysis by those in the press who evaluated the events in Northern Ireland. That a liberal could go on actually to hope colonialism would save the Irish might be thought extraordinary. [...] (The liberal American literary intelligentsia has generally shied away from the Northern Ireland issue. That bastion of enlightened and progressive thinking, *The New York Review of Books,* for instance, almost completely ignores Northern Ireland and the various issues involved, while providing regular features and reviews about other international crises.)

The 'inexplicable Irish' view of the crisis, though less obvious since the early 1980s, is still pervasive. In an article welcoming the Anglo-Irish Agreement, *Time* magazine's report opined: 'In another part of the world, it would be called tribal warfare. In Northern Ireland, the shootings and the bombings that have taken more than 2,500 lives over the 17 years are more primly referred to as "the troubles." The spasms of killing have followed the ebb and flow of ancient hates and fears that divide the British province's Protestant majority and its Catholic minority.'[8]

By reducing the problem to this level of 'ancient hates and fears,' the press succeeds in removing it from the realm of serious political debate. [...] In this way, the coverage reinforces Britain's propaganda that Northern Ireland's problem is a product of irrational fears and hatred manipulated by gangsters, deserving of little sympathy or concern among right-thinking, intelligent people.

The British 'Tommy' to the Rescue

Having established the truculent tribes of inexplicable Irish full of ancient hatreds, the press has conveniently opposed to them another stereotype: that of the patient, all-suffering Britisher. An internal memo sent between *Newsweek's* London and New York offices in July 1970 shows that this stereotype was set up from the very beginning. It read: 'We're particularly interested in putting together a separate sidebar on the impossible task of the British soldiers caught in the middle between the warring Catholic and Protestant communities.' That the role of the British soldier was that of a referee was taken for granted. And the use of the word 'Tommy' to describe the soldier conjured up a memory of the chirpy little World War II trooper in a soup-plate helmet – an anachronism that ignores the fact that the British army in Northern Ireland is an army of volunteer professionals, not of conscripts as was the case in the 1940s. 'The British army,' lamented one writer, 'continually deals with two potential enemies... The Tommy stationed in Ulster should have the two-faced head of a Janus as well as the patience of Job.'[9] After a series of bombings in Belfast that in one day (called 'Bloody Friday') killed eleven people, the *Boston Globe* reporter surmised: '... if British soldiers do not keep the Catholics and Protestants apart, "Bloody Friday's" 11 deaths and 130 injured from bombings will be only the beginning.'[10] [...] According to the *New York Times* reporter, the army was there as a 'neutral peacekeeping authority between the warring Protestant and Roman Catholic communities.'[11]

This is a constant refrain throughout the press coverage from the beginning of the conflict until today. It has withstood several shocks that ought to have been traumatic enough to make observers question it as a basis for understanding Britain and her army's role in Northern Ireland.

For instance, after internment was introduced – during which 342 men were arrested and held without trial – the press followed the government's line that internment was necessary to halt the violence. Even though it provoked the worst violence the state had yet seen – within four days twenty-two people died, all but three of them civilians, and by month's end there had been over one hundred explosions in Belfast alone – the coverage in general emphasized the British line.

'How can Catholics of this community,' fumed Anthony Lewis of the *Times,* 'be associated with protests that lead to the death of women and children – even last night to the fatal shooting of a priest as he gave the last rites to a wounded man ... ?[12] Lewis did not mention, or did not know, that the gunman who had killed the priest was a loyalist paramilitary, and the wounded man the priest had been attending was a civilian shot by the army. But the whole of the *Times* story is framed so that, despite the British action, blame is pinned only on the IRA. [...] 'The IRA fanned hatred by staging incidents and shooting isolated soldiers. The army, which showed incredible patience, was bound eventually to make mistakes and kill innocents...'[13]

Conveniently ignored [...] was the fact that since the summer of 1970 the army had (with Conservative government approval) adopted a much more aggressive counterinsurgency role, which was directed exclusively against Catholics. This role could not be maintained along with that of the objective referee keeping two sides apart, because it was predicated on the belief (either of mere convenience or of true conviction) that the Northern Ireland problem was not caused by discrimination and injustice against Catholics, but by left-wing IRA subversion. Such was the thesis of the Unionists, and when the Conservatives were elected in June 1970, they saw to it that it was acted upon. Though there is little hint of this in the *Times* coverage, a feeling of disquiet did manage to creep into the editorial page.

'It may be argued,' reflected the newspaper a few days after internment, 'that the Prime Minister acted unwisely in resorting to the arbitrary arrest of IRA leaders...'[14] Even here, the *Times* modifies its reservations in asserting the London line that in spite of the violent backlash from the Catholics the procedure had succeeded – at least to the extent of netting the 'IRA leaders.'

Yet, within days of internment, the IRA held a press conference in a school in the heart of the Falls Road area – the area worst hit by the swoop – at which the IRA's Belfast leadership was able to appeal for help. [...] internment not only led to an increase in violence, but blatantly failed in its original object of damaging the IRA through rounding up its 'leaders.' Yet no word of this is mentioned in the *Times* editorial.

Perhaps an even stronger jolt to the image of the imperturbable Tommy caught up in a religious war came with Bloody Sunday, and the shooting dead of thirteen civilians at the end of a civil-rights demonstration in late January 1972.

The following day – January 31 – the major newspapers led with stories (mostly from the wire services) reporting a shootout between Catholic gunmen and British paratroopers. The British army claimed that eight of the dead were wanted, and several had been found with weapons. Within hours, this story was withdrawn. Only four, it appeared, were wanted IRA men, and only one was said to have been carrying a weapon – a 'nail bomb.' However, over the next day or two, even this claim was abandoned, as it was gradually acknowledged that none of the thirteen dead was in the IRA, and none was wanted for any offense. The local people's assertion that the shooting had come solely from the army gained credence. However, the U.S. press, particularly the *New York Times,* continued to assert the army's original story. In early February, the week after the shooting, *Newsweek* described it like this: 'A Catholic demonstration in Londonderry degenerated into a mêlée of fighting with British troops, and in the confusion, thirteen marchers were shot to death.' The *Times* preferred the idea of 'misunderstanding' as the explanation for the butchery: 'Bloody Sunday, as it is being called, is likely to go down as another landmark in the long record of misunderstanding and hatred in British-Irish relations.'[15]

On the West Coast, the Irish case fared no better. The day after the shootings, an editorial in the *San Francisco Chronicle* blamed 'history' (repeating a familiar theme), but did not suggest that the British troops were responsible.[16] An editorial in the *Los Angeles Times* called for an 'international inquiry' and suggested a U.S. presence. It went so far as to blame the British government for allowing discrimination to continue. But the weight of its condemnation fell on the IRA, whose activities, it argued, had led to Bloody Sunday. The Irish government was also held to bear some of the responsibility. In general, while the horror of the killings was described effectively, neither in the reportage nor in the editorial comment was the culpability of the British 'Tommy' emphasized.

The *Chicago Tribune* took a somewhat different tack. Though never actually coming out and condemning Britain, its editorial held that 'defying prohibitions of street demonstrations, stoning British troops, and shooting civilians *with or without provocation* lead to no reduction of hostility' [my emphasis]. Thus it at least raised the possibility that the shootings were unprovoked. [...]

The *Chicago Tribune* was one of the only papers that in its actual reporting of the shootings featured strongly Catholic counterallegations. In the second paragraph of its front-page report it quoted Catholic leaders as calling the killings 'awful slaughter' and 'mass murder.'[17] [...]

In the days following the Bloody Sunday massacre, some papers amused themselves with discussing other sidelights rather than pursuing questions such as what had actually happened and whether or not the British account was the whole truth. Bernadette Devlin, the civil-rights activist, was at that time a member of the House of Commons for the Northern Ireland constituency of Mid-Ulster. [...] On January 31, the day after the shootings, during a debate in the House of Commons, she strode across to the government benches and struck the British home secretary, Reginald Maudling, accusing him of lying about the events in Derry. The *Chicago Daily News* reported: 'Bernadette Devlin, being female and Irish, is a mystery in her behavior to the British public. They are still mulling deeply over her indecorum in slugging Home Secretary Maudling, a genial, slow-spoken family type. Even more puzzling, Miss Devlin, after she cooled off, failed to do the gamesmanlike thing demanded of all Britons ... apologize and shake hands. She said she wouldn't mind another try. This simply isn't done, even in Parliament. To the puzzled British this failure makes more acute the question of what makes Bernadette run...'[18] [...]

The report, by George Weller, went on to quote the *Daily Telegraph* of London, which jokingly suggested that the cause of Devlin's impassioned attack on Maudling was frustrated love. The *Telegraph's* story, in the form of a letter to a woman's advice columnist, and her reply, were given at length in the *News*.

This was no more than a day after Ms. Devlin had been a witness at one of the most brutal shootings in recent Irish history – shootings carried out by troops answerable to the government of which Mr. Maudling was a prominent member. [...] Anyone reading such stuff would not have imagined that it was the Irish who had been at the receiving end of a recent and brutal attack. Later, Ms. Devlin – now Mrs. McAliskey – said that the British reaction showed a lot about their attitudes toward Ireland; the assault on Maudling was greeted by more outrage than the paratroopers' killings in Derry. [...]

The One-Sided Sectarian War

[...] Beginning with the riots of 1969, and continuing to date, the overwhelming impression is of violence between Catholics and Protestants. Most U.S. newspapers relied for their day-to-day coverage on wire-service reports. Brief, and without much embellishment, these stories used the sectarian model for such explanation as was offered. '[Police found] the body of a middle-aged man... The discovery raised the death toll in three and a half years of Catholic and Protestant strife in Ulster to 649.'[19] 'He was the 730th person killed in sectarian strife in Northern Ireland in three and a half years.'[20] 'He had been shot in the head – the usual method of killing in the silent clandestine struggle between the province's Protestant and Catholic communities.'[21]

Even when the victim is killed by the British army, the sectarian angle is still emphasized. Reporting the death of a Belfast teenager shot by troops at a checkpoint, the Associated Press summed it up: 'His death brought the toll since the outbreak of sectarian warfare in the British-ruled province in 1969 to at least 1,836. So far this year 35 persons have died in the fighting between predominantly Roman Catholic Irish Republican Army militants and Protestant extremists.'[22] When the *Los Angeles Times* came to do a retrospective history of the crisis, it explained the origin and nature of the violence in these words: 'What had been largely a civil rights movement deteriorated into guerrilla warfare, with Catholics and Protestants killing one another in ever increasing numbers.'[23]

The sectarian-war thesis is, of course, intimately linked to the view that the IRA is the villain and that Britain, represented by the anachronistic 'Tommy' image, is the patient and detached referee. When one reviews the coverage, it is noticeable that when sectarian warfare is mentioned, it is usually only one organization (if any) that is named as a participant in the war – the IRA. The IRA is referred to as the cause of the deterioration into violence, and is credited with perpetuating it. 'Rock-throwing rioters gave way to deadly snipers,' wrote *Newsweek,* explaining the development of the situation in April 1972; 'Pitiless terrorists from the Irish Republican Army (IRA) from the South began to infiltrate Ulster in specially trained bomb squads.' [...]

When Protestant paramilitaries have been dealt with, the treatment has usually followed lines rather different from those typically applied to the IRA. It is extremely doubtful, for instance, if even an attentive reader would be aware of the names of the Protestant paramilitary groups, never mind being able to discern from what he read their actual role in the Northern Ireland violence. The major Protestant paramilitary group is the Ulster Defense Association (UDA), a legal organization with headquarters in East Belfast. At one time in mid-1972 it claimed about 20,000 members, making it one of the largest paramilitary groups in the world. [...]

In the early 1970s, when sectarian violence was at a bloody peak, the UDA gave many interviews to visiting journalists. *New York Times* reporter Tom Buckley interviewed UDA spokesmen at length for an 'in-depth' article. 'I decided they were rather sinister,' wrote Buckley, 'and, for people who never tired of waving the Union Jack, crashingly un-British.' But his talks with them convinced him that, 'As I saw it, the degree of prejudice to which the Catholics were subjected had been somewhat exaggerated, and it seemed to me that they had brought a good deal of it on themselves by pretty much refusing, right up to the time of the first civil rights marches, to do anything for themselves...' So, he concluded, 'By the time I left I can't say that I became particularly fond of any of the militant Protestants I had met, but I was somewhat more sympathetic to their point of view.'[24]

A few months before, *Los Angeles Times* correspondent Tom Lambert spoke with a UDA representative and reported: 'But the UDA has nothing against Northern Ireland's Roman Catholics, and will only try and persuade them to repudiate the IRA, he promised.'[25] The story was headlined PROTESTANTS THREATEN WAR ON IRA, and continued: 'The threat ... raised the possibility of increased sectarian clashes in Northern Ireland...' He said, 'Some observers were inclined to take that threat seriously.' At the same time, the *Boston Globe's* man in Belfast, Jeremiah Murphy, was also talking to the UDA. He interviewed Ernie Elliott, a leading member of the organization from the loyalist Shankill Road area, who expressed his anxiety over the effect the IRA's campaign was having on his men. 'It's tough to hold the boys back now,' he told Murphy, 'they wanna have a go at them Catholics.' Murphy comments: 'If British soldiers do not keep the Protestants and Catholics apart ... that would just about complete the Northern Ireland tragedy.'[26] The UDA relied on the pretense that it was acting as a brake on sectarian violence, and the press repeated it for them. UDA leader Andy Tyrie told the *Christian Science Monitor's* Irish correspondent that 'the UDA would end its own ceasefire and retaliate with an all-out anti-terrorist drive' if the British gave concessions to the IRA.[27] And yet at the same time it was observed (being the substance of the daily reports of violence throughout the 1970s) that Catholics were suffering heavy casualties at the hands of Protestant extremists.[28] How did this fit into the UDA's constant claim, reported in the U.S. press, that it was doing its best to 'hold the boys back'?

In the beginning, if Protestant extremists were blamed, it was usually those belonging to the Ulster Volunteer Force (UVF) – a smaller, illegal group that predated the UDA. Indeed, at one time, AP pinned '97 percent of the Protestant violence' on the UVF.[29] Then, in 1973, the Ulster Freedom Fighters (UFF) emerged, claiming responsibility for killing Catholics. The authorities went ahead and outlawed it. But the UDA remained, issuing statements, meeting reporters and government officers, occasionally lamenting that it was doing its best to keep control of the beast of sectarian war but if there were any more concessions to the IRA, it couldn't guarantee what might happen. 'These men who are killing Catholics are just wildcats... They are not acting under UDA orders. We are trying to stop it, but we do not know who they are,'[30] Reuters quoted a UDA leader as saying in the aftermath of one of the most vicious bouts of sectarian bloodshed Ireland had ever seen.[31]

The UDA were not the only ones who affected puzzlement as to the identity of these 'wildcats.' The Northern Ireland police were equally stumped. 'We're getting these sectarian killings now that make no sense at all... As many Protestants as Catholics have been killed,' a police spokesman was quoted as saying in the *New York Times*.[32] In fact, the ratio of Catholics killed to Protestants has normally been two to one, though Catholics are a minority of the population. No matter. When it came to the actual sectarian killings of Catholics in the much-referred-to sectarian war, nothing seemed certain. When an old Catholic couple were machine-gunned to death, UPI's story in the New York *Daily News* ran: 'The Police said it was not yet known whether the killings were connected to the past four years of violence among Northern Ireland Catholics and Protestants.'[33]

An anomaly was becoming apparent in the way the authorities were treating the sectarian war, and in the way it was being reported. Though it was said to be two-sided (since every war needs at least two sides), only the actions of one side, the IRA, were attributable, while those on the other remained not only 'inexplicable,' but even 'motiveless' (a favorite word the police used to describe murders of Catholics). Though it is not clear how the killings of one side in any sectarian war can be called 'motiveless,' this police evaluation was allowed to go unchallenged by the press. The activities of the Protestant extremists were never brought into clear focus. [...]

The press, like the authorities, is capable of great tolerance when it comes to UDA disavowals. Take, for example, the period between December 1971 and December 1972. During that time, the press interviewed several UDA leaders, including Ernie Elliott, known locally as 'the Duke,' who told the *Globe* of his difficulties in 'holding the boys back.' One can estimate the extent of his difficulties by counting the number of sectarian killings for the period: 136, 96 of whom were Catholics and 40 Protestants. [...] Just how ineffective it was emerged in late December 1972, when Ernie Elliott's body was found in a box in the back of a car. He was one of the forty Protestants murdered that year. Superficially, his death would be attributed to the IRA-versus-Protestant-extremist bloodbath in which Northern Ireland is supposedly steeped. In fact, UDA men murdered Elliott in a drunken brawl in a Protestant club. In that, his death was no different from those of the other victims of the sectarian conflagration. For the truth is that the UDA is responsible for the bulk of all sectarian killings in Northern Ireland. [...]

During research completed in 1977 by this author and David McKittrick of the BBC for a history of the UDA, figures gathered showed some 540 Catholics were murdered by Protestant extremists between 1971 and 1977. Of those, the UDA was responsible for approximately 400. Since then, sectarian killings have been less frequent. But they still occur, and the UDA usually is responsible. As for the UFF, it is merely a name of convenience invented by the UDA in 1973.

What is remarkable is how little attention was paid to this murder campaign, at the same time that the press was writing about the 'Catholic-Protestant conflict,' which, the reader was told, the British were preventing from getting out of hand. Once again, the consensus the press adopted was that of the British government. The British chose to ignore the UDA as much as possible. In early 1973, after a bomb attack on a busload of Catholic workers, the authorities were forced to intern UDA men. They arrested two.

The *Wall Street Journal* observed: 'Until the two Protestants were jailed, only Roman Catholics had been singled out on terrorist charges.'[34] At the time, hundreds of Catholics were being held without trial, and the army constantly raided Catholic areas, arresting dozens of men. No more than a hundred Protestants were interned in the two years between that date and December 1975, when internment ended, compared with nearly two thousand Catholics.

Britain's reluctance to tackle the UDA was not based on ignorance of its activities. After all, the police came from the same community as the UDA; contact between them was frequent; information was exchanged; and by the mid-1970s the security forces had a wealth of often detailed data on the organization. The British view of the Northern crisis as a purely sectarian war initiated by the IRA allowed them to maintain that the Protestant violence was a product of IRA violence, so that it was essential to concentrate on stopping the IRA.

Time magazine summed it up: 'British army officers seem to agree that the Protestants will stop if the Catholics do. Lately, the British have been applying most of their weight against Ulster's Catholics.'[35] For the most part, the U.S. press accepted this as a justifiable explanation for the comparative lack of action against Protestant extremists [...].

Nor was the press given much pause for thought by the fact that during the two periods when the IRA called a truce and halted its campaign the sectarian violence actually increased dramatically. The *Christian Science Monitor* reported that politicians' fears of further violence 'are fed by sectarian killings of Catholics and the burning of Catholic-owned buildings, which have gone on almost daily since the IRA declared its latest ceasefire.'[36] While this seeming contradiction did not go unreported, it generally went unanalyzed. [...]

[...] the evidence has contradicted the theory of a Protestant-Catholic tit-for-tat sectarian war; instead, it has pointed to a different kind of sectarian war, in which the victims are mainly Catholic. This not only discredits the Catholic-versus-Protestant theory; it also threatens to undermine the whole consensus, which is based on the thesis that the British are in Northern Ireland to keep the two sides apart.

Naturally, then, the press showed great reluctance to examine the UDA's role, just as the British did. Nor did it deduce from the abundantly available evidence the sectarian nature of the Protestant commitment to Northern Ireland, though this was clear from the beginning. In August 1969 *New York Times* reporter Gloria Emerson had an encounter with a Protestant woman. '"We are not animals who need to be locked in, but they are, down there, the filthy scum, those papists," a twenty-seven-year-old housewife, with badly dyed blond hair and a torn raincoat, screamed at the top of her lungs.' In June 1972, Bernard Nossiter of the *Washington Post* observed: 'Protestants, particularly those in the upper class, have a contempt for Catholics that verges on racism.' He interviewed a UDA man, a small business contractor, who said of Catholics: 'IRA lazy fenian bastards don't want to work... they just want to stay in their bloody pubs and drink. There is no such thing as a good Catholic. They're a dirtier class of stinking people and I'm paying to keep them up. We could stop the IRA bombing in a month. We could shoot them. We don't need the uniform to do anything.' Such loathing is characteristic of the loyalist propaganda that emanated from the various paramilitary organizations. [...] It expressed itself most gruesomely in the tortures inflicted on some Catholic victims of the UDA and UVF before they were shot.

Though grisly killings of this kind were reported as common on both sides (as in the AP story that concluded: 'So far this year at least 105 others

– 70 Catholics and 35 Protestants – have been slain in much the same way, often after being bound and tortured, burned with cigarettes, branded or had bones broken'[37]), this was not the case. Such acts were exclusively the responsibility of Protestant extremists. Catholic anger was directed against the state, its security forces, and its various institutions, and did not involve the urge to degrade or humiliate the victim before killing him.[38] Did not the IRA take part in the sectarian violence also? Yes, it did, but only at certain times and then – ironically enough, in view of the press consensus that Protestant violence was a reaction to that of Catholics – generally as a retaliation against UDA or UVF attacks on Catholic areas. Only once, in the summer of 1975, can it be said to have become a part of IRA policy. On that occasion, during an IRA ceasefire, the IRA leadership did issue a statement warning loyalists that it would take retaliatory measures if their attacks on Catholics did not cease.[39] Unfortunately, the consensus in the American press imposed restrictions on its coverage that prevented such complex realities from being exposed. Without thorough reporting of these realities, the tangled nature of the Northern Ireland crisis cannot be understood.

Looking for Scapegoats

[...] Another aspect of the prevailing consensus concerned the IRA. Not only was it blamed for starting the 'troubles' – either by infiltrating the civil-rights movement or 'fanning' hatred of the British troops – but it was often described as coming from outside Northern Ireland to do so. The Republic of Ireland was either explicitly or implicitly held to be responsible for allowing the IRA to operate.

In 1972 there was a series of bombings in Dublin. *Newsweek* headlined its story IRELAND: THE BOMBS COME HOME – the clear implication being that the bombs that had been devastating Northern Ireland came from the republic. [...]

When bombers again attacked Dublin in 1974, the press attitude was that the South now knew what it felt like. Richard Eder at the *New York Times* reported from Dublin: 'The tendency here not to think about the problems of the North and the consequent lack of any strong public pressure to take action against the gunmen operating from the Republic's territory came from something more complex than complacency. Partly it was the residual sympathy for the tradition of violent action to obtain a united Ireland...'[40]

The following day Eder reported that the bombings were carried out by Protestant terrorists 'who wanted to give this predominantly Roman Catholic country a taste of the kind of violence served on the North by the Provisional wing of the IRA.'[41] A columnist in the paper had earlier suggested (July 9, 1972) that there was some equivalence between how the

Catholics were treated in Northern Ireland and how Protestants were treated in the South.[42] Already, the South had stood condemned at least for letting the 'pitiless terrorists' of the IRA 'infiltrate Ulster in specially trained bomb squads.'

It was convenient for the British government to find a scapegoat for the crisis in Northern Ireland. Not wanting to admit that its policy and the conduct of its security forces had something to do with the violence and Catholic support for the IRA, it turned to the south of Ireland. In the newspeak of the 1980s, it implied that the Irish Republic was a 'sponsor state' of terrorism. While there is no doubt that the IRA operated back and forth across the border between the two states, this was in spite of often massive Irish security operations. To suggest, as *Newsweek* and other reputable newspapers continually did, that the IRA was an outside force sent into Ulster was absurd. If the correspondents in question had merely visited Long Kesh internment camp and looked at the list of the inmates' home addresses, that particular theory would have been seen for the transparent propaganda it was.

When the Irish government brought a case against Britain before the Strasbourg Court on Human Rights, the British were outraged. Ireland alleged that British security forces had used illegal methods of interrogation on IRA suspects in August 1971, consisting of a series of sensory-deprivation techniques. The European Commission on Human Rights investigated the allegations to see if the Irish had a case to bring before the Human Rights Court. It produced one of the most detailed and exhaustive documents on the Northern Ireland situation ever published. It was also the first non-British enquiry into the Northern situation. The commission's report, 563 pages long, was released in September 1976. It found that the British forces were guilty of violating article 3 of the European Human Rights Convention, which states, 'No one shall be subjected to torture or to inhuman or degrading treatment or punishment.' The case was then allowed to proceed to the court at Strasbourg for judgment.

The British had attempted by various means to stall the commission's inquiry. They had also tried to undermine the Irish government's suit by alleging that it was detrimental to their fight against the IRA. And when the commission's result was revealed, the British attacked the Irish government. This is what the *New York Times* chose to emphasize, rather than the report's findings. Its story was headlined BRITISH ACCUSE IRISH ON TORTURE REPORT (September 6, 1976), a reversal of events that, though it must have pleased the British government, hardly constituted a fair or balanced assessment. The *Times* report ran: 'British officials today accused the Irish Republic of deliberately embarrassing the British Government and thereby endangering joint efforts by the two countries to combat terrorism in the United Kingdom.'[43] Only in the second paragraph was the Strasbourg report accusing Britain of using 'torture' on Irish prisoners mentioned [...]

'The report said that in 1971 special British instructors had briefed local police in Ulster in interrogation techniques that were eventually put into practice.' The report had said much more than that. The 'five techniques,' as they were known, had already been declared illegal by a British inquiry in 1972.[44] The Human Rights Commission found that their use had been approved at a very high level. That is, the five techniques constituted what is termed 'an administrative practice.' The implication was clear that the British government itself had authorized the use of illegal methods of interrogation in Northern Ireland. However, instead of pursuing this line of inquiry, the press for the most part preferred to lament the detrimental effect it would supposedly have on antiterrorist efforts. A combined wire-service story in the New York *Daily News* said, 'The action by the Republic of Ireland in pressing the charges before the Rights Commission strains its relations with Britain at a time when both Governments are battling terrorists.'[45]

The report in the *Christian Science Monitor* on September 6, 1976, headlined BRITAIN DISMAYED OVER TORTURE ISSUE, also stressed the British government's upset. A scandal of potentially Watergate dimensions involving British ministers authorizing army officers to break the law was lost in the rush to describe British government 'embarrassment' and annoyance at being pestered by the Republic of Ireland over such a matter.[46]

In January 1978, the Human Rights Court, after considering the report, passed its judgment. It found Britain guilty of violating article 3 of the convention. The judges found that the 'five techniques' constituted 'inhuman and degrading' methods of interrogation, but they did not consider them as 'torture,' in spite of the commission's finding. The reaction in the U.S. press was predictable: RIGHTS COURT ABSOLVES BRITISH IN IRA CASE proclaimed the headline in the Reuters story carried by the *New York Times* on January 18, 1972. 'The European Court on Human Rights cleared Britain today of charges that its security forces in Northern Ireland had tortured suspected members of the IRA.' Then the report went on to say that the court had found 'evidence' that the British had used 'inhuman and degrading treatment' in their interrogation methods in 1971. Only in the third and final sentence of the opening paragraph does the reader learn that the court actually found Britain guilty of breaking article 3 of the Human Rights Convention.

On the West Coast the coverage of the story gave a more balanced view. An AP report in the *San Francisco Examiner,* headlined COURT SLAPS BRITAIN FOR IRISH ACTS, said that the court had condemned the British for letting its troops use 'inhuman and degrading third-degree methods of questioning suspected members of the IRA in 1971.' AP said that the court had 'turned down a recommendation of its European Commission on Human Rights that the interrogation techniques be called 'torture.'[47] It went on to describe briefly the five techniques. Likewise, the *San Francisco*

Chronicle, under the headline COURT ASSAILS BRITISH TREATMENT OF
IRISH CAPTIVES, managed at least to convey that it was the British and not
the Irish who were on trial. The report quoted Irish government officials as
saying that the judgment was 'of major importance' because it formally
condemned the interrogation methods.[48] The *Los Angeles Times* ran a
report similar to that from AP in the *Examiner.* [...]

On a different level, the press has continually sought to blame Irish
Americans for Northern Ireland's troubles. It has also excoriated anyone of
any political standing who seemed to be pursuing a course more favorable
to the republicans. Congressman Mario Biaggi is a case in point.

In early 1978, when the Irish prime minister attacked the congressman in
a letter that was made public, the press eagerly joined in. '... the
encouragement of Ulster extremists by thoughtless and ill-informed
politicking in this country hurts the chance for peace over there,'[49] said the
editorial in the *Washington Star.* The *Baltimore Sun* denounced Biaggi's
association with the Caucus and Sinn Féin, which it claimed 'he has taken
as representatives of Ireland.' The *Sun* called Sinn Féin 'a handful of
people who could never get elected,' and accused Biaggi of 'spurning
those whose legitimacy like his own survives the test of fair and free
elections.'[50] One wonders if Sinn Féin's subsequent electoral successes
would cause the *Sun to* be less critical of any congressman who now chose
to meet with them.

The idea that a Bronx congressman should presume to concern himself
about Northern Ireland seemed to cause extreme irritation in editorial
offices all over the U.S. The only serious exception to this almost universal
condemnation was a significant one – the New York-based *Irish Echo,* the
country's largest Irish-American newspaper. Calling Biaggi a 'Friend of the
Irish,' the paper said that Biaggi had 'time after time on a variety of issues
... stood for what is right and just.'[51]

Few papers, apart from the *Echo,* paused to reflect on the extremely
unusual nature of the event on which they were editorializing. That is, a
head of a friendly government had publicly berated a member of the
House of Representatives. The *Manchester Union Leader* did refer to it as
an 'unprecedented step' and advised that 'private persuasion might have
been more in keeping with diplomatic niceties.'[52] Nor did the press take
time to consider the possibility that in order to understand a guerrilla war
it might be necessary to meet with and talk to all the participants. Whether
one condones their activities or not, getting 'the whole story,' as the *Echo*
put it, is a legitimate aim for anyone concerned with a situation like that of
Northern Ireland. It is ironic that it is the newspapers themselves who have
to be reminded of this.

However, the British consensus upon which much press coverage was
based did necessitate finding scapegoats. [...] The main purpose of the
consensus was to prevent the raising of certain questions potentially

critical of Britain. The dissenter must be slapped down, and the basis of the consensus protected, regardless of facts.

Blaming the Judge

The press reaction to the courts' refusal to extradite IRA fugitives has provided one of the most egregious examples of unbalanced coverage. But this bias has been drastically increased because although the press has generally reported and editorialized on each decision, none of the major newspapers has ever actually covered the hearings themselves. When the finding is announced, the reader has nothing to guide him other than a report outlining it and an editorial condemning it virulently. The detailed testimony preceding the judgment is never reported, probably because so much of it is unfavorable to the British and would certainly challenge the consensus that the American press generally relied on to guide its Northern Ireland coverage. But without that context, the editorial opinions condemning the judge's decision cannot possibly be fairly weighed by any reader not directly familiar with what went on in the courtroom.

Press hostility to the courts' continual rejection of extradition warrants against IRA fugitives reached a peak in late 1984 with the handing down of the Doherty decision. The editorial reaction to that decision will be looked at in detail, since it followed the lines of previous opinions on the outcome of earlier cases, except that over Doherty most of the major newspapers lost any semblance of fairness.

Manhattan Federal Court Judge John Sprizzo handed down his decision rejecting the British extradition request for IRA member Thomas (Joe) Doherty on December 13. [...] The *New York Times* headlined its December 14 report on the judgment: U.S. JUDGE REJECTS BID FOR EXTRADITION OF IRA MURDERER.[53] The New York *Daily News* story on the decision carried the headline: CONVICTED IRA KILLER WINS A COURT VICTORY.[54] And the *New York Post* greeted the decision with: GUNMAN CAN REMAIN IN U.S.[55] (The *Post* did not say that remaining in the U.S. meant continued incarceration without bail. Doherty's victory did not free him, and he has remained in jail since his arrest in 1983. William Quinn, fighting extradition since 1982, has never been released either.) On the West Coast, the *San Francisco Chronicle,* using an AP story, headlined it U.S. JUDGE BARS EXTRADITION OF IRA KILLER.[56] These set the tone for the editorials and generally unsympathetic coverage that followed. The New York *Daily News* was one of the first to editorialize on Sprizzo's finding. Entitling its piece FIGHTING TERRORISM – EVERYWHERE, the *News* began unequivocally: 'Thomas Doherty is an Irish terrorist who murdered a British soldier and ought to be extradited to face charges.' It went on, referring to Sprizzo's decision, 'It's a crazy ruling. Imagine the outcry if some foreign government refused to extradite an FALN bomber because it's a "political" struggle. The IRA members are terrorists just as much as the Puerto Ricans who tried to kill Harry Truman, or the Moslem fanatics who killed the Marines in Beirut, or the hijackers of the Kuwaiti plane who murdered two Americans.' The editorial then lists a series of acts committed by the IRA, including the 1984 bombing attack on the hotel where the Conservative party leaders were staying, and the bombing of department stores and restaurants. 'Sprizzo would presumably call all these "political" attacks... It's a ridiculous argument,' the *News* asserted. 'Terrorism is a plague, afflicting Americans as well as British, Irish, Israelis and Lebanese... The U.S. insists, rightly, that the nations of the world must unite to fight terrorism. It's a hollow protest if a U.S. judge can wrap an Irish murderer in the American flag.'[57]

Other editorials which followed in the *Wall Street Journal,* the *New York Post,* the *New York Times,* and the *Chicago Tribune* all made similar points [...] The *Wall Street Journal,* referring to Sprizzo's description of the IRA as a disciplined group, which he found distinguished it from amorphous terrorist groups, claimed the finding could be used to protect Mehmet Ali Agca, 'whose attempted assassination of the Pope has behind it the organization, discipline and command structure of the Soviet Government.' [...]

The *Chicago Tribune* accused Judge Sprizzo of misusing the power to forbid extradition. It acknowledged that he had 'acted within the law and his powers, but he certainly violated the clear rules of common sense.' It said the judge had 'conferred upon the IRA the political and military status that has been denied it' by both British and Irish governments, and 'gave blessing to the myth' that the IRA is involved in a struggle to free Ulster from British rule. '... in reality,' the *Tribune* explained – trotting out the well-worn consensus view that the press has followed from the beginning – 'the struggle there is tragically medieval... The IRA has exploited that strife to fight both the British and Irish Governments, to prey in street-gang fashion upon both Protestant and Catholics and to harass, frequently with violence, the chief Catholic political party in Ulster.'[58] Here the *Tribune* was referring to the SDLP. [...]

There were few papers that took any other line. Among those that hailed the Sprizzo judgment was the *Philadelphia Daily News,* which attacked 'the same newspapers that condemn repression in South Africa' for complaining about the judgment. It noted that the British used the same arguments against Doherty as they did when 'hunting down many of the men who became the leaders of Israel.'[59]

The weekly *Irish Echo* in New York defended the decision, calling it 'a very correct ruling.' 'Sprizzo ruled that Doherty could not be extradited because his was a "political offense." The judge is correct on the facts and correct on the law. His detractors should be ashamed of themselves. And they should try to get their facts straight.'[60] The *National Law Journal* agreed with the *Echo.* Its editorial, entitled FOLLOWING THE LAW, defended the judge against his detractors in the administration. For administration officials to attack Sprizzo, as they did after his finding was announced, the *Law Journal* said, was 'to demean the judicial process and the Justice Department itself.' It pointed out that Sprizzo's decision 'was fully supported by the facts and the law.'[61]

The exasperation and dismay expressed in the *Echo's* editorial is justified considering the quality of the major newspapers' response to the Doherty ruling. To draw analogies, as they did, with an attack on an abortion clinic, the attempted assassination of the Pope, and the various atrocities committed in the Middle East, was to show ignorance of the law on the matter, as well as apparent ignorance of the decision itself, that is truly inexcusable in any press organ with a reputation for serious reporting. [...]

As Sprizzo made clear in his very precise and pithy decision – all of 13 pages long – one of the factors necessary before the political-offense exception can be successfully appealed to is the existence of a widespread uprising or rebellion in which government authority is being challenged by the rebel group. Sheer indifference to the facts, or wilful ignorance, may not be sufficient to explain how editorial writers could pretend to find that factor in the acts of an abortion-clinic bomber or a fanatic assassin who tries to kill the pope. Obviously, as with the administration's policy toward the extradition law, there is a preconceived and weighty body of political opinion operating in the background to distort and warp the press's attitude toward, and reporting of, these judicial matters. Once more, and perhaps more blatantly with the extradition cases than with any other aspect of the Northern Ireland problem, the U.S. press showed itself to be almost an arm of the government rather than a mediator responsible for presenting its readers with a version of events approximating to the facts.

When the Senate Foreign Relations Committee met to consider the proposed revisions to the U.S.-U.K. treaty in the summer and fall of 1985, the press repeated its performance of December 1984. The new treaty proposed to make the political-offense exception inapplicable when the accused was alleged to have committed acts of violence, which the new clauses specified. The *Times* hailed the new treaty with the headline SEALING A TERRORIST FOXHOLE.[62] When the revision did not get the easy passage that was hoped for, the *Washington Post* called it 'disgraceful,' alleging that the impediments were due to a lobbying campaign by 'supporters of the IRA in this country.'[63] [...] The political point was the same as that made by the administration throughout all of the extradition cases: that it was politically and diplomatically embarrassing to have these fugitives described as political offenders, regardless of the nature of the struggle in which they were participants. The chief yardstick used was the political and diplomatic self-interest of the United States in relation to its ally the United Kingdom. Legal standards were ignored, or addressed without detachment, and the press was once more content to recycle the usual errors and misleading comparisons. The terminology of the editorials on the new treaty, as on the extradition decisions, was that of the administration, providing another unsettling example of the merging of press and government consensus in dealing with this controversial issue.

Sentimental Tough Guys – Hero Reporters

Among American journalists, few broke through these self-imposed limits and restrictions. There is, however, a group of Irish-American columnists who produce work which is decidedly more sympathetic to the Irish nationalist view. Indeed, Pete Hamill, who writes for the New York *Daily News* and the *Village Voice,* Jack McKinney of the *Philadelphia Daily News,* and Jimmy Breslin, a syndicated columnist with the New York *Daily News,* often write fiercely from that viewpoint. Unfortunately, they generally rely on stereotypes and use stylistic characteristics that throw little light on the situation. Rather, this style tends to throw light on the writers' connection with that situation, which they view through the eyes of a 'sentimental tough guy' persona derived, it would seem, from popular American detective fiction.

Breslin mixes the sentimental – which enables him to describe Northern Ireland in maudlin terms as 'a wet, soft, beautiful, bitter little country' – and the street-tough attitude, which views people from Belfast as hard-drinking, ballad-singing 'characters' obsessed with murder, or with talking about murder. For example [...] Breslin's version of a Belfast taxi driver is a ghoul who rambles on: '"On the Antrim Road we have "marder male" ["murder mile"], the one called Liam said. His words came out of a long, sad face.'[64] Such ghouls are as much a caricature as are the inexplicable natives and truculent tribes who typify the coverage of the *Times, Time,* and *Newsweek.*

The sentimental tough guy reaches something of an apotheosis in the work of Hamill. The most vigorously engaged in the Northern Ireland question of any American journalist, Hamill can be credited with hard-hitting work. When the *New York Times* was apologizing for internment, Hamill, writing in the *New York Post,* actually described an army raid on a Catholic home. He wrote about the horrors of the prison protests in the early 1980s. And he is probably one of the few American reporters to sit down and interview Gerry Adams, Sinn Féin president and member of Parliament for West Belfast.

On the debit side, however, Hamill's work is marred by sentimentalism. There is a vicariousness in his writing on the IRA, for instance, which tends to intrude constantly between the reader and the subject matter. Responding to Governor Hugh Carey's attack on the IRA in April 1977, Hamill wrote: 'In that province [Northern Ireland] I have met cowards and fools and liars. But I have also met some of the bravest men and women on this earth and all of them have been in the Provisional IRA.' He cannot resist injecting himself into the story. 'Twice,' he continues, 'on my visits to Northern Ireland, they saved my life. On more times than that, I listened to them as they discussed strategy and decided against actions that would have killed innocent people.'[65] He does not say how his life was saved by the IRA. But the article extols the IRA as model freedom fighters and ends in a blaze of sentimentality: 'I wish I could provide [Carey] with the names of some people to whom he could send his apologies. Unfortunately, most of them are dead. [...] They died without ever knowing whether their children would live in freedom. They died without ever seeing the tricolor billowing in the breeze over the rooftops of Derry. They died for Ireland. Maybe they were fools. But they were better men than Hughie Carey and it will take someone better than me to forgive him for this one.'[66]

The object is blurred by melodrama. The Northern Ireland issue becomes a backdrop to the drama of the journalist's feelings about it. In the process, negative stereotypes about the sentimental, maudlin Irish are reinforced. This of course does little to raise the level of debate on to the rational, critical plane where it has to be dealt with if any understanding is ever going to filter into the public awareness. Unfortunately, the arcadian disposition accepts this kind of sentimentality readily; sentimental reveries come more easily to it than analytical thinking. This partly explains the appeal of Hamill's writing on Northern Ireland to Irish Americans. Perhaps related to this is the fact that Irish-American writers have not managed to produce a sustained work of evaluation of the Northern Ireland problem. This indicates something about the Irish-American community's arcadian view of Ireland as a Garden of Eden spoiled only by the serpent England. Clearly, it is too narrow a basis on which to give a complex and stimulating analysis of the crisis.

The Post-Hunger Strike Coverage

In the late 1970s and early 1980s, two major factors influenced the U.S. press and made it somewhat more critical of the British government's role in Northern Ireland. The first was the growing access that the Irish diplomatic service had to the editorial rooms of major newspapers like the *New York Times* and the *Los Angeles Times*. [...] the other major factor was a powerful one: the hunger strikes of 1981 and the subsequent rise to political power of Sinn Féin, the political wing of the IRA. The hunger strike has undoubtedly been the major news story of the last sixteen years in Ireland. An estimated four hundred journalists were gathered in Belfast from all over the world, with a heavy representation from all the major U.S. newspapers and network television stations, to watch as Bobby Sands, the first of the hunger strikers, died.

The death of Sands, which was followed by the deaths of nine other prisoners (all of them either members of the IRA or INLA), provoked the most critical editorials the British had yet seen in papers like the *New York Times*. 'By willing his own death,' the *Times* wrote, 'Bobby Sands has earned a place on Ireland's long roll of martyrs and bested an implacable

British Prime Minister... Mrs. Thatcher deplores the IRA terror, but seems unable to address the grievances that make terrorists like Bobby Sands heroes to the Catholic minority. Power remains in the hands of an unyielding Protestant majority, whose leaders, in 1914, preferred mutiny against the Crown to Home Rule.'[67] The paper went on to advise Mrs. Thatcher to negotiate, as she had in Rhodesia.

In an editorial dated May 1981, the New York *Daily News* called for a British withdrawal and demanded 'a break-up of the covert alliances between Protestant paramilitary groups and military and police organizations in Northern Ireland.' This is remarkable, considering that the *Daily News* had almost completely ignored such stories in its regular reporting. Mike Daly, a *News* columnist, wrote about the UDA in the winter of 1980. This was one of the rare acknowledgments of the loyalists' contribution to the violence, and was probably the inspiration for the editorial's assertion. Even the *New York Post,* usually so pro-British and pro-Thatcher, exclaimed editorially: 'That Northern Ireland is now a colony is beyond argument. That is exactly how Britain treats and rules it, albeit prolonging the agony.'[68] And as another hunger striker neared death, the *Times* upbraided Thatcher for her intransigence, predicting: 'The cry of "Brits Out" may yet come true.'[69] The old consensus was broken; the idea that Britain was partly responsible for the Northern Ireland mess had taken hold.

The hunger strike set off a chain of events whose reverberations are still being felt. It created a power base for the politics of Sinn Féin. No longer could it be said – as the press had throughout the 1970s – that the IRA's cause had no support among nationalists. This in turn started a frantic effort in the moderate nationalist political camp to build a new platform on which to appeal to nationalist voters. From this came the 1984 New Ireland Forum, an attempt by the SDLP and the Dublin government under Garret Fitzgerald to present a reasonable nationalist alternative – or set of alternatives – to the 'Brits out' demands of Sinn Féin. When the Forum report was published in the early summer of 1984, the American press welcomed it wholeheartedly; in an editorial entitled 'Ireland makes its move,' the *Chicago Tribune* sympathetically reviewed the report's proposals. Margaret Thatcher was criticized for her 'great fondness for the status quo' in Northern Ireland, and for maintaining her position that 'nothing will be done without the approval of the province's Protestant majority.' The *Tribune* reminded Thatcher that 'the lack of a political solution has cost an insupportable price in violence, bloodshed, economic decay and loss of public treasure. Attempts to maintain the status quo have always led to a change for the worse. Ireland has made its move. Now, urgently, it is Britain's turn.'[70]

Equally positive about the report was the *New York Times,* which in a May editorial called UNDER TWO FLAGS suggested that the idea of joint authority, which was one of the alternatives discussed in the report, was a worthy one that deserved serious study in London.

Seven months later, Thatcher and Fitzgerald met in London. After the meeting Thatcher gave a press conference at which she dismissed in staccato fashion (the famous 'Out, out, out' speech), the three major alternatives described in the report. The U.S. press reaction was swift and hostile. Forty-seven editorials appeared, generally critical of Thatcher's position. THE IRA WINS AGAIN proclaimed the *Chicago Tribune*.[71] THATCHER SAID TOO MUCH was the response of the *San Francisco Examiner*.[72] In an editorial entitled THE INS AND OUTS OF IRELAND, the *New York Times* said of the British prime minister: 'No one doubts her courage in opposing the demonic fanaticism of the IRA. But she has yet to show the same resolve in dealing with Northern Ireland's Protestants who refuse to share power or even symbols with the oppressed minority.'[73] The *Washington Post* said that the bridge-building efforts of Fitzgerald and the New Ireland Forum had been 'undermined by Mrs. Thatcher's brusque and dismissive comments,' and warned that 'terrorists can only find comfort from the failure' of the cooperative efforts of Dublin and London.[74]

'Prime Minister Margaret Thatcher,' declared the *Boston Globe,* following the summit débâcle, 'rightly prides herself on her toughness and determination. Her grave mismanagement of affairs in Northern Ireland, however, calls into question her imagination and sensitivity. It does no good to have a will of iron if that will is in the service of an obtuse sensibility and a mind choked with prejudices...'[75] It was probably one of the most outspoken attacks on a British prime minister ever to appear in a major American newspaper.

The barrage of criticism had some effect. When Thatcher came to Washington early the following year to address both houses of Congress, she was a different figure from the Iron Lady usually presented to the press. Instead, she made conciliatory remarks on Northern Ireland, which emphasized the cooperative effort with Dublin. Later that year, she signed the Anglo-Irish Agreement with Prime Minister Fitzgerald, giving his government some role in the affairs of the North for the first time. Undoubtedly, the hostile response of the press to her earlier position played a part in that development.

The press universally welcomed the agreement. In doing so, however, they were occasionally involved in contradictions such as that demonstrated in the *Los Angeles Times*. The paper reported on the need for the agreement's provision to give Ireland a role in the North; this way, it was thought, the alienation of Catholics from institutions like the courts might be reduced. Yet in the same issue an editorial said, 'The system of British justice applied in Northern Ireland has shown every sign of working fairly.'[76] Presumably, if the courts were working fairly, there would be no need for said provision.

Overall, the agreement was greeted as a viable solution that would undermine support for Sinn Féin and the IRA. It led to a modification of the old consensus, which had already been revised after the 1981 hunger strikes. In the new, post-agreement consensus, the London-Dublin nexus, which the agreement holds up, is regarded as the only hope for peace. Therefore it has to be defended against the onslaught of the IRA and the intransigence of the loyalists, both of whom are viewed as twin enemies of the agreement; their every action is treated as if it were designed to thwart it. In the new alignment, the Protestant majority, which opposes the agreement, and whose rights as the majority have been for so long defended against nationalist claims to a united Ireland, are now being told that they have to accept the new plan – being a majority obviously no longer carries the democratic mandate it once did, an interesting shift which has generally not been commented upon in the eulogies of the agreement in the press.

Conclusion

[...] The remarkable thing about the American press is that in general it has stayed closer to the British government consensus than has its British counterpart. British reporters, in both print and broadcast media, have shown more willingness to question the British government's attitude to the Irish conflict than have American journalists, and have managed over the years to produce a respectable body of work delving into the genesis and development of the situation. The same daring cannot be said for their American counterparts. What is noticeable, even among the handful of reporters in America willing to break the mold, is the almost complete absence of any detailed or extended treatment of the complexities of the crisis. The consensus view - of religious fanatics held back by a kindly British referee – suffocated any intelligent discussion of Northern Ireland in the U.S. throughout the 1970s.

Such limitations took their toll. A *Time* magazine story began: 'By now the Ulster problem probably bores the world.'[77] Another commented almost petulantly, 'This time for what it was worth, the blame for the outburst of violence could be leveled at the Protestant side...'[78] Around the same time the *New York Times* reporter was also suffering from ennui: 'It is all old and stale: the army patrols, the stone-throwing – some of the 7-year-olds started when they were 4 – the resentment and weariness of the soldiers...'[79] [...]

As noted, things changed somewhat with events of the late 1970s, and the 1981 hunger strikes. By 1985, the *New York Times* had published a rare investigative piece on the alleged 'shoot-to-kill' policy of the Northern Ireland police by its reporter Jo Thomas. Yes, the old consensus was broken. But what of the new one taking shape? Whether it will prompt the U.S. press to do more challenging work on Northern Ireland remains to be seen. But one thing is clear: the acceptance in the press of the British government's consensus on Northern Ireland throughout the previous decade has provided a worrying example of how in democratic societies a free press can be used to stifle controversial matters and make sure that challenging questions about a tragic crisis are not admitted into serious political debate.[80]

Endnotes

1. *New York Times,* August 16, 1969.
2. *Time,* February 19, 1973.
3. *Ibid,* June 10, 1974.
4. *New York Times,* December 10, 1972.
5. *Boston Globe,* July 21, 1977.
6. *New York Times,* February 3, 1972.
7. *Ibid,* March 24, 1973.
8. *Time,* November 25, 1985.
9. *New York Times,* July 12, 1972.
10. *Boston Globe,* July 23, 1972.
11. *New York Times,* January 21, 1973.
12. *Ibid,* August 11, 1971.
13. *Ibid.*
14. *Ibid.,* August 12, 1971.
15. *Ibid,* February 1, 1972.
16. *San Francisco Chronicle,* February 1, 1972.
17. *Chicago Tribune,* January 31, 1972.
18. *Chicago Daily News,* February 1, 1972.
19. New York *Daily News,* December 4, 1972.
20. *Ibid,* February 23. 1973
21. AP, *New York Times,* May 14, 1973.
22. *New York Times,* May 8, 1978.
23. *Los Angeles Times,* Jan. 7, 1976.
24. *New York Times,* December 10, 1972.
25. *Los Angeles Times,* July 24, 1972.
26. *Boston Globe,* July 23, 1972.
27. *Christian Science Monitor,* June 6, 1975.
28. According to statistics compiled by the European Commission on Human Rights in the mid-1970s, of the 121 victims of sectarian murder in 1972, eighty-one were Catholics and forty Protestants; in 1973, the breakdown was fifty-six Catholics and thirty-one Protestants; in 1974 it was sixty-one Catholics and thirty-one Protestants. It has remained fairly constant at the rate of two Catholics for every one Protestant assassinated. The commission also categorized the data according to which section of the community was responsible for the murders. This was a much more uncertain undertaking, but it generally revealed that almost 50 percent of all Protestants assassinated were assassinated by Protestant groups. The percentage of Catholics killed by the IRA in factional or 'execution-style' murders was much smaller.
29. AP, November 19, 1973.
30. Reuters, July 8, 1972.
31. There were twenty-three assassinations between January and June in 1972, and thirty-six in July alone, the bulk of them the work of the UDA.

32. *New York Times,* July 14, 1972.
33. New York *Daily News,* July 8, 1973.
34. *Wall Street Journal,* February 8, 1973.
35. *Time,* November 4, 1974.
36. *Christian Science Monitor,* February 27, 1975.
37. AP, December 6, 1972.
38. IRA punishment shootings, such as kneecappings and the killing of alleged informers, are often horrific and brutal. This however, does not negate the validity of distinguishing between such violence and that motivated by the hatred of a dominant, repressive group acting out of insecurity when it believes that dominance threatened, which is the motivation behind Protestant sectarian killings.
39. Major bouts of IRA violence directed against Protestants have occurred on several occasions. In November 1974, a tit-for-tat pattern was established for a short time, mainly in North Belfast. Then, during the summer of 1975 and early in 1976, IRA members (acting either on their own behalf or with the sanction of local leadership) retaliated against Protestant targets. However, this was something of an aberration and was stopped in 1977 with the rise of new, left-wing leaders in Belfast.
40. *New York Times,* May 19, 1974.
41. *Ibid,* May 20, 1974.
42. 'In the South, Protestants are second-class citizens; in the North the Catholics are second-class citizens.... (July 9, 1972). Mr. Sulzberger ignored the fact that much of the wealth of the Irish Republic was and is in the hands of a rich Anglo-Irish Protestant minority.
43. *Ibid,* September 6, 1976.
44. The Minority Report of Lord Gardiner, March 1972.
45. New York *Daily News,* September 6, 1976.
46. A full description of the commission's inquiry and the British government's coverup of responsibility will be found in my book *Too Long a Sacrifice,* Dodd, Mead, 1981; Penguin, 1982, chapter 3.
47. *San Francisco Examiner,* January 18, 1978.
48. *San Francisco Chronicle,* January 19, 1978.
49. *Washington Star,* February 22, 1978.
50. *Baltimore Sun,* February 24, 1978.
51. *Irish Echo,* March 4, 1978.
52. *Manchester Union Leader,* May 9, 1978.
53. *New York Times,* December 14, 1984.
54. New York *Daily News,* December 14, 1984.
55. *New York Post,* December 14, 1984.
56. *San Francisco Chronicle,* December 14, 1984.
57. New York *Daily News,* December 16, 1984.
58. *Chicago Tribune,* January 11, 1985.
59. *Philadelphia Daily News,* December 19, 1984.
60. *Irish Echo,* December 29, 1984.
61. *National Law Journal,* December 31, 1984.
62. *New York Times,* July 11, 1985.
63. *Washington Post,* November 3, 1985.

64. *Daily Item,* April 1, 1977.
65. New York *Daily News,* April 27, 1977.
66. *Ibid,* April 27, 1977.
67. *New York Times,* May 6, 1981
68. *New York Post,* May 6, 1981.
69. *New York Times,* May 10, 1981.
70. *Chicago Tribune,* May 19, 1984.
71. *Chicago Tribune,* November 27, 1984.
72. *San Francisco Examiner,* November 26, 1984.
73. *New York Times,* November 24, 1984.
74. *Washington Post,* November 24, 1984.
75. *Boston Globe,* November 27, 1984.
76. *Los Angeles Times,* October 21, 1985.
77. *Time,* January 29, 1973.
78. *Ibid,* February 19, 1973.
79. *New York Times,* May 28, 1973.
80. Irish Americans have occasionally challenged the press on its Northern Ireland coverage. In 1982 a group called the American Irish Unity Committee filed a complaint before the National News Council in New York alleging that a *New York Times* report of a speech by Irish Prime Minister Garret Fitzgerald had seriously distorted the prime minister's remarks. It had done so, the committee complained, by omitting part of the sentence quoted. The *Times* reported the prime minister as having said: 'If I were a Northern Protestant, I cannot see how I could be attracted to getting involved in a state which in itself is sectarian. ' The qualifying phrase '... although not in the way Northern Ireland was in which Catholics were repressed' was omitted. This was pointed out to the *Times,* but no correction was offered and the quote was actually repeated in its truncated form. The News Council found that it was 'inaccurate and unfair' of the newspaper not to set the record straight. However, they found the failure to do so by the *Times* a matter of administration breakdown, not intent.

23.

Bill Rolston

MOTHERS, WHORES AND VILLAINS: IMAGES OF WOMEN IN NOVELS OF THE NORTHERN IRELAND CONFLICT

(From *Race and Class*, 31(1), 1989, pages 41-57)

Almost two hundred novels have appeared in English[1] since 1969 focusing on the current Irish conflict. The bulk of these have been by authors from outside the North of Ireland, many of whom are already established. More often than not, the conflict serves merely as the backdrop for their latest product. Thrillers lend themselves with ease to such transposition: whether the hero chases the villain and gets the girl in Belfast, Beirut or Moscow is irrelevant as long as all the elements of the thriller are present.

But not all the novels are thrillers. There are a number which the authors at least would prefer to catalogue as 'literature'. Such authors seem more concerned to 'make a statement' about the conflict, and in this way are noticeably different from the thriller authors. Despite such differences, there is an amazing similarity throughout the genre.

One common theme is that the problem of violence in the North of Ireland derives from republicans. They can be psychopaths, the most common representation (cf, as one of the best examples, Powers in *The Whore Mother),* or professionals (like Billy Downs in *Harry's Game);* they may even be depicted as idealists (like Martin Fallon in *Prayer for the Dying* or Binnie Gallagher in *The Savage Day).* But what is certain is that they are central to the novels of the conflict overall. By comparison, loyalists appear infrequently, and even then often as shadowy figures in the wings.[2] This is all the more amazing when one considers another general trend, namely, seeing the British army as a buffer between the warring tribes. It is depicted as such even in those novels which also ignore the presence of loyalists. In these ways the novels faithfully replicate dominant British explanations of the aetiology of the Northern 'troubles'.

The novels make explicit what is rarely said in polite company,[3] and this is true whether they are thrillers or aspire to literary excellence. Thus *Blood Sisters* (a book with aspirations to feminist literature) has American heroine Liz commenting on a bus queue in London.

> They were all pushing and yelling. This was no English queue; it was more like a swarm of ants on a melting chocolate bar ... The bus was packed now. Irish-looking men next to each other, stupefied from the fumes of their own beery breath and sweat.

Michael Nealis, the Derry-born hero in *With O'Leary in the Grave* (a thriller), knows similar Irishmen in Liverpool.

> They are a raucous, beefy race; unfashionably dressed and temporarily affluent, they are eager to get their money spent so that they may exchange the awful responsibility of having money for the uncomplicated pleasures of being poor.

Depicting men

Although the focus of this article is not the depiction of men, some mention has to be made of it. Women's roles and men's, in fiction as in real life, cannot be seen in isolation. Consequently, we shall look briefly at one category of men in the novels, 'republican villains'.[4]

As far as the novelists are concerned, men are for the most part into power. Take one example: Leamus, the republican killer in *Across the Water*, loves guns because 'anyone was yours to command when he knew he was in your sights, no matter how strong his physique, how great his wealth, how immeasurable his influence'. Jerry Palmer has analysed this relationship between men and power well in relation to thrillers: 'In real life political groups seek, and achieve, power in order to put policies into effect. In the thriller villains seek power as an end in itself.'[5] Yet this sense of the villain as an apolitical individual is also common in many of the non-thriller novels. The villain is a loner who acts out of personal need or psychological inadequacy; rarely is he portrayed as part of a collective capable of arriving at political conclusions through rational thought processes.

Inadequate men fall into two categories. First, there is the godfather, a well-known cypher of mainstream media accounts of the conflict. A typical example is Reilly in *The Killing of Yesterday's Children,* a smooth operator, part sleazy car salesman, part Mafia boss. Far enough away from killing not to be directly implicated in it, and claiming to dislike bloodshed, he has no qualms about ordering others to kill. In many instances, such dangerous hypocrisy is said to derive from sexual and, above all, homosexual repression. Thus, Hugh Ward in *The Fugitives* is a misogynist whose repressed homosexual tendencies lead him to believe in the cleansing nature of blood sacrifices - to the point that he is prepared to sacrifice the volunteer Paddy to a martyr's death in order to further the cause. Similarly Skeffington in *Cal* is an effete schoolteacher, fixated on his doddering father. The literary device used is to compare him with the 1916 leader Patrick Pearse in terms of looks, repressed homosexuality and the belief in the cleansing power of blood.

Godfathers are usually threateningly contained. But psychopaths are volatile, unpredictable and vicious. Unable to be leaders themselves, their energy can be harnessed by godfathers. For psychopaths there is also a behavioural connection to sexuality, though not in this instance repressed. Their sexual urges, like their character overall, are violent and hedonistic. As they are in sex, so they are in war. In *The Whore Mother,* Powers, the chief republican villain, has just raped and killed a woman. Asked by a minor villain: 'What'ye like best, fuckin' or killin?' 'Och', he replies: 'One's as good as the other.'

Sex is also depicted as a reward for violence. Billy Downs, the Provos' most professional killer in *Harry's Game,* needs to go home to his wife after a job to find relief from the tension of killing; his batteries recharged from sex with her, he can calmly go out and kill again. In similar vein, Frank McCrossan, the maverick republican in *The Price,* has to have sex after each job with a passionate local woman, not with his wife, who, he says, is 'always mute and passive'. 'It was always the same after a killing: first the running, then the exultation of escape, then the woman.'

[...] Similar characters appear in most thrillers and, indeed, in cowboy stories, detective novels and science fiction. They are there to excite and titillate us, not least because in moral terms they are beyond the pale. It is in this sense that such characters most resemble those in medieval morality plays. As evil incarnate they exist in order to deter the rest of us from sin. They are not intended to be real; the very uni-dimensionality of someone like Powers in *The Whore Mother*[6] reveals this. But in the absence of other political men with whom they can be compared, the effect is not only that they appear as real, but that their narrowness and psychopathology serve as the *total* explanation of the Irish conflict - it derives from men, violent men, especially violent republican men. Naked male power, expressed both sexually and militarily, is what women in the novels are up against.

If violence was confined to men, the analysis here would be relatively straightforward: women would be either victims or survivors. They are certainly depicted in both roles in the novels. As victims, they are raped, beaten, tarred and feathered, blown up, drowned, isolated as housewives or prisoners' wives, or forced by circumstances to trade sexual favours for survival in poverty-stricken ghettoes run by Mafia-like villains. As survivors, they are forced to stand on the sidelines while the men get all the central roles of godfather, gunman, bomber, renegade militant, informer; like the children who share the shadows with them, they have little to do, little to say; surviving is a full-time occupation in the madhouse of Irish violence.

But the misogynism in the novels is often also based on women's willingness to embrace violence. This could only be so if it is judged to be an unnatural choice for women. The novelists would have us believe that women are peace-loving by nature - or, more accurately, by biology. Motherhood, children and abhorrence of violence go hand in hand. If women reject one of these components, they reject the whole package, and, the authors assure us, become capable of the most horrific violence, as we shall see.

Women as mothers

It is an unwritten rule of these novels that women's most important role is that of mother. As mothers, women care for children: they attempt to protect children from the ravages that life, especially life outside the domestic sphere, can bring. Violence, in particular, threatens children and the stability of family life and as such is abhorrent to mothers. The more random the violence, the more abhorrent it is. To be the wife of a Provisional IRA man is problem enough, but at least his possible injury or death is an occupational hazard. However, the violence that is not directed against family members because of their specific role in political struggle, but blindly strikes out at whoever is within reach - the no-warning bomb, the sectarian assassination - is the mother's greatest fear. She will do anything to protect her children from that: keeping them locked in the house when things are bad, trying to get them educated out of their class and community, even - and this is the most difficult leap of all - breaking out of the privacy of the domestic world to oppose publicly those who so needlessly threaten her offspring. [...]

If the novels are to be believed, then, the division between men and women in relation to violence is not only biological, but almost metaphysical. Men come to represent violence and women peace with all the force of a Greek myth. The only proper, acceptable, natural role for a woman is that of mother - both in the domestic sense of caring, and in the more global or mythical sense of peace-loving. Because they care for children, women care about peace

The evidence for the above characterisation can be found in many of these novels. Mrs O'Meara in *Both Your Houses* has republican violence close to home in the form of her husband, Liam, an IRA godfather. She has no time for Liam's politics, at one point telling him that 'this angry nonsense of Ulster is above sense or family'. Similar fights are a daily occurrence in the Logan household in *Shadows on Our Skin*. The husband is not even a current hero, but his republican bravado in speech is a source of constant aggravation to his wife. When two British soldiers are killed, he is overjoyed. His wife is not only full of sympathy for the dead soldiers, but is enraged by her husband's easy acceptance of violence. 'Two of the enemy are dead.' 'Two children.' 'What do you mean, children?' 'That's all they were. Younger than Brendan.'

For women connected to republican activists, violence can be an unbearable burden. In *No Time for Love* the hero's wife, Brenda, is not unsympathetic to his politics. But the fact that he is the leader of a highly active republican group called Saor Eire means that he is constantly on the run, in jail or in hospital; at all those times, she has to suffer the constant police and army surveillance and harassment. She can take no more and, as much for the sake of their young son as for herself, heads off to London leaving behind a letter.

> I just can't stay. This society is so fucked up that it is going to take a lot of tears and blood to rectify it ... I don't want my children growing up to become part of that lake. I don't want to watch you becoming part of it. And I don't want to end up at the bottom of it myself. [...]

The welfare of children, even other people's, even if the woman has none of her own, thus becomes a source of grave anxiety to women. The unnamed heroine of *The Patriots* is a member of a two-person bomb squad. After the jailing of the Price sisters in 1974 for causing explosions in London, she and her male companion take over to wreak havoc in the capital. She is a competent and able bomber, but what proves the beginning of her psychological unravelling is when one of her bombs injures a young girl who later dies. Her determination is suddenly shattered. 'I didn't think to be ... to be waging war on their ... children.'

For women, children and violence cannot co-exist. As mothers, real or potential, women must eventually come to stand up against violence. In the case of Martha in *Give Them Stones,* her public stand takes a long time to emerge. She sees violence daily in her working class area of Belfast and escapes into her own little world by running a home bakery. Her main concern is that none of her sons become 'involved', and in this she is successful. But when a teenager is kneecapped beside her house for anti-social activities, she immediately refuses to pay any more protection money to the IRA. Despite threats, she maintains her stand. The IRA burns down her home. Her position is not rational, either in the sense of being carefully thought out in advance or of being in her own personal best interest. But it is a case of personal experiences being transformed into political stances. In this sense, Martha comes to stand for all women as represented in the novels - the caring, peace-loving mother. Her story is intensely personal, but her solution is of wider import.

This point is carried to cosmic bounds in *Too Long a Sacrifice*. Máire is a healer and Tadhg a bard in Cruithin Ireland. They are taken by the fairies below Lough Neagh and only released 1,500 years later in the 1970s. Tadhg swaps his harp for a machine-gun and Máire uses her supernatural powers to heal those injured in gun battles and explosions. Finally, they are metamorphosed into mythical pre-Celtic heroes, he Bealtaine, the god of winter, egged on to violence by the Hate-Beast, and she Samhain, the goddess of summer. They have a showdown at the site of the palace of the High Kings at Tara. Máire's elk kills Tadhg's Hate-Beast and he is thus freed from the spell of evil. Woman/peace has won out over man/war.

But it is not always so. Hate wins often, and is at its most vicious when the victim is a peace-loving woman like Aileen O'Meara in *Both Your Houses*. Aileen, daughter of the republican godfather, falls in love with and marries a young, innocent loner of a British soldier, appropriately named Tom Moody. In a riot Tom shoots dead Aileen's psychopathic cousin, but later the republicans have their revenge by killing Tom. At his funeral a crowd mounts an attack and throws Tom's coffin into a river. They then throw pregnant Aileen in too, and the book closes with her drowning. The frantic crowd is composed of women as well as men, and it is this which strikes Aileen in her last moments as being so strange and unnatural. The 'heavy woman' who attacks her, screaming that she is 'a sewer rat', 'should be darning socks or cooking children's dinner'. Once the role of mother is let slip anything can happen.

Women as seducers

Motherhood, however, is not a role without the possibility of contradictions. The most obvious is that it is men who are violent, yet they have been raised by women/mothers. How can this contradiction be explained?

Entrusted with the task of socialising the young, women can pass on to their offspring the wild stories of the past glories done by Ireland's heroes and the wrongs against Ireland that still need avenging. What matter that the heroes and avengers about whom the myths and stories, poems and songs have been created are male? It is women who perpetuate the mythology by telling them to the young, especially young males. In doing so, women can be at their most hypocritical. Accepting the role definition that they as mothers should not be involved in violence, they indulge by proxy. Like the terrorist godfathers, they incite others to carry out the violence they will not do themselves. No longer mothers, they are now godmothers.

As if to underline the unnaturalness of their behaviour, they must often resort to lies to give the myths a more striking legitimacy. But, lies or not, it is clear that in infecting the young with the disease of violence they have been traitors to the highest role to which women can aspire. They entice young men into sin, like prostitutes. But worse: as the young men are their own sons or grandsons, they are even worse than prostitutes. They are incestuous 'whore mothers', to use the title of Shaun Herron's novel.

Why should women behave so unnaturally? The most powerful explanation for their behaviour lies in the fact that their direct mothering days are over. They are older women, often grandmothers. Deprived now of what is supposedly their only real reason for existence they become cranky. Aged, asexual, unfeminine, they can become purveyors of violence against their previous natural instincts. As such, they become clones of old Mother Ireland herself, her complaints of past wrongs serving to stir her sons to vengeance. Ireland is the ultimate 'whore mother'.

This is the message of Shaun Herron's novel, a message brought home to its middle-class hero, Michael, in a very personal way. On the run from the IRA, he is befriended by Kate, the ageing widow of a famous author of erotic poetic novels. She takes him home and eventually entices him, a virgin, to be her lover. By day she reverts to being plain, potty and grandmotherly; she is 'mother in the day, mistress in the night'. One night she recounts one of her late husband's erotic poems. It is of a young man named McMorna who has a lover by night, but by day she becomes an old woman, 'her breasts the broken hills, her belly as creased and cracked as the Burren, her legs the dead willows'. Eventually McMorna asks her name. 'The name they call me is Cathleen the Whore-Mother.' The moral is not lost on Michael. Later, as he escapes from both Ireland and the IRA (although only temporarily from the latter), he talks ominously of his country. 'She's the whore we never leave ... Somebody called her the old sow that eats her farrow.'

The metaphor of Mother Ireland as a murderous seductress is not confined to this one novel. In *With O'Leary in the Grave,* the hero is on the point of being transformed from model Liverpool police superintendent to gunman preparing to avenge the death of - no coincidence - his quiet, innocent old mother. 'This bloody country reaches out and drags you into itself. Like an old whore she is hungry for men, and when she gets them, she drains them of their manhood. The Irish as a race are a nation of eunuchs and that's what it's all about.' Michael Nealis finds himself caught between the conflicting lures of the real mother and the whore mother.

It is the very asexuality of these women which makes them so dangerous. Their seduction is more threatening because they have become purveyors not of sex but of violence. Nowhere is this more obvious than in the curse of the Irish granny.

> I once met a man who told me that grandmothers were at the root of the trouble in Ireland. They keep them at home, the Catholics, I mean. No question of old people's homes. So there they sit by the fire, night after night, telling all the old stories, spreading all the old lies. That's why the different kinds of Irish go on hating each other.

These words are spoken by the Brigadier in *Vote to Kill.* If the character was a buffoon, it would be unfair to take his words at face value. But, although he is a minor character, he is the father of Clarissa, private secretary to the Tory Prime Minister. Interestingly he reveals that Clarissa herself had an Irish granny. So, it is no surprise when Clarissa turns out to be a traitor, lover of a top IRA man. She is later killed trying to assassinate the Prime Minister.

Grannies and lies also play a part in *The Price*. A kidnap for ransom has been witnessed by a young boy whose grandmother convinces him not to speak to the police because the kidnappers are carrying on the tradition of her dead IRA husband. But the boy recoils from her tales in the same way as he finds her physical presence overpowering. 'She drew him closer. He fought to hold his breath, in a panic lest she might kiss him', thus contaminating him with her republican ideals. It was for these her husband died, she claims. But not so; as her own daughter later reveals to a policeman, the husband had been shot for informing.[7]

In *The Price* the boy's mother is furious at her own mother telling lies to the child. But, the novelists assure us, other mothers are not so principled. Blinded by hate, wizened in mind if not also in body, they waylead their own children - mothers like Mrs McAteer in *Victims*. She has an iron hold on her adoring twin sons, Pascal and Pacelli, both of whom are in the same IRA kidnap gang as Bella Lynam, the middle-class graduate totally unsure of her ability to participate in violence. Everything about Mrs McAteer is repulsive to Bella. She is 'enormous ... all chin and breast'; she is quite literally short-sighted. And she is bed-ridden with some unexplained ailment which we are to assume is as incurable as her quasi-religious nationalism. 'Always wanted a daughter ... if I had one, she wouldn't be troubled like you ... too much learnin' is the ruination of the world. All a body needs is faith in God, his Blessed Mother, faith in your people and faith in your country.' It is that blind faith which she has passed on to her sons, the republican Tweedledum and Tweedledee. [...]

Pascal and Pacelli obediently and uncritically obey their domineering mother. So does Martin Dealey in *The Killing of Yesterday's Children*. After his father and brother are assassinated, his mother tells him: 'You're the man of the house now, Martin, now that your daddy's gone. It'll be on your shoulders to see that somebody pays.' And so Martin obediently joins the IRA. Maguire, one of the gang which kidnaps the Queen of England in *The Minstrel Code*, also joins up because of his mother's influence.

> He knew the republicans owed a lot to the way some Arabs supplied the IRA with arms; as for the Israelis, all he knew about them was that they were Jews. And Maguire's mother had taught him to hate Yids as Christ-killers as early as she'd taught him to hate the English for keeping Ireland enslaved.

Where words lead, actions follow. Having abandoned the proper role of mother so completely, such women are not averse to allowing their children to witness brutal violence at first hand. In *The Outsider*, Michael Flaherty, an American who joins the IRA, is hiding out in the Falls Road. A premature explosion kills a woman and Michael leaves the safe house to see what has happened. A stranger in the area, he is attacked by a crowd of women. The local IRA commander succeeds in calling them off.

One by one they fell back. The last to do so, a young mother whose child watched it all from beside the bled-white body of the dead woman twelve feet away, turned and spat in his [Michael's] face. 'Bastard.' Her mouth was deformed in a snarl as she turned to take the child's hand.

Where the bond of love is used to foster hate, the role of mother becomes as deformed as this woman's face. Women can educate children to violence in the most definitive way possible - through their own participation in it.

Women as villains

Once women have taken the plunge into the unnatural and rejected their prime role of mother, anything is possible. For a start, women embrace violence with a passion exceeding that of men. Men are cool when they are violent; even the psychopaths are completely in control, quivering on the edge of climax. Violent women, on the other hand, represent raw, unadulterated emotion. They tremble with rage, shake with anger, get carried away in emotion. There is no control, no standing back a little to savour the power of violence. Instead, there is total immersion. The violence of women is thus valuable in certain circumstances to paramilitary organisations, but it is dangerous in as far as it threatens to break away from all control. Cool men are needed to manage such women; but they never rely on them.

The metaphor is undoubtedly sexual. Men are attracted to these violent women in as far as their raw emotion can be presumed to translate into sexual abandonment. Yet they are simultaneously repulsed by women who show such strength, fearing sexual and political emasculation.

Emotional women are not to be trusted. For this reason, very few of them ever make it to positions of power in the male world of revolutionary warfare. But, for those who do, behind the bravado and professionalism lurks psychosexual disorder, bound up, according to the novels, with their relationship to their fathers. For some, the rejection of the father is a form of seeking his attention. For others there is a pathological need to please him. For both sets of women male leaders in the organisations become surrogate fathers, and often lovers. Men may follow visions, manifestos and ideals, but 'career terrorist' women have little of this to keep them going - sexual hang-ups are at the root of their involvement. They often do not believe in the cause, do not accept the stirring rhetoric and despise men for playing these male games of mental and rhetorical self-abuse. They do not choose revolution, but are trapped in it.

Women revolutionaries are thus basically sad specimens of womankind. As such, they have a fatal attraction to male revolutionaries who can see the little girl inside the woman in need of the care of a surrogate father. This is a long way from being a comrade, on equal footing with such men.

[...] When the chips are down, such women are not trusted by male colleagues; no man wants to leave his life in the hands of a disturbed woman.

And this is the ultimate loneliness and isolation of revolutionary women. Their curse is that, having abandoned their natural vocation of motherhood, they can never be real 'terrorists' like men. Stuck in the middle, they do things which neither mothers nor men would do. As 'terrorists', they often wilt under fire, becoming filled with self-doubt, prone to tears and capable of the most unrealistic of expectations. That merely makes them second-class 'terrorists', not 'mothers', for it is also clear that they do not care about harming children, even when men do.

Such alienation probably accounts for the fact that, when women embrace violence, it is with an intensity that is frighteningly demonic. Take this scene from *The Whore Mother*. A republican gang is about to tar and feather a young woman for dating a British soldier. The gang is aided by a large group of women and girls.

> A large fat woman took handfuls of Mavis's soft auburn hair in her big fist, slapped the girl's head back against the lamp-post, and snipped the hair off close to the scalp ... When that work was done an angular woman with the face of a bitter man took the can of black paint ... and upended it above the bound girl's head ... On the edge of the ring her father fought furious women to reach his child and was battered again with his own club. They tore at his head, clawed his face, and gathered his flesh under their nails, beat him again to the ground, kicking him in the stomach, the back, the face, the groin, jumping on his feet and ankles, hooting, howling, screaming in deranged triumph. The man lay still. The circle danced; fat women jigged around the lamp-post and the girl, their skirts hauled high, big putty thighs bouncing and jiggling like sows' bellies.

In similar vein, Ned Galloway, the loyalist hitman in *Silver's City*, discovers the viciousness of women. He takes a young man and woman with him to rescue a fellow loyalist, Silver Steele, from his guarded hospital room. During the operation, Ned allows the young cubs to release pent-up energy by beating up one of the police guards. 'The girl, he noticed, was particularly vicious, but, then, they always were.' He has to pull her off, slapping her in the process. Later, when Galloway himself is being punished by the organisation, the girl has her revenge.

> 'That fucker hit me once', she shrieked, clawing at his cheeks, before the others [men] threw her aside, for she interfered with their more careful workmanship. Towards the end, however, just as in the movies, the squaw was to have her way again. While the others passed a bottle, she went for his face again. He managed to turn his head, but those nicotine-stained baby fingers ripped the single earring he wore from the flesh.

Revenge is an important element in the explanation of women's violence, an instant reaction to the hurt inflicted on a loved one. Thus, Billy Downs's wife in *Harry's Game,* despite her abhorrence of violence, has no hesitation in killing the British agent, Harry Brown, with his own gun in return for his killing Billy in her presence.

Even if revenge is not involved, the explanation of women's violence is always at the emotional level. Thus, loyalty to family or lovers can involve women in violence with uncharacteristic ease. Jenny, the anti-violence widow of an IRA man in *Hennessy,* abhors Hennessy's violent mission in England. Yet, because 'one never quite gets used to living alone', she falls for him, drops her objections and agrees to help him out. Caragh Hughes is the sister of Con Michael who is the intellectual force behind a republican group (called Sullivan's Volunteers) in *In Connection with Kilshaw*. She becomes involved in providing safe houses for the Volunteers and ferrying them here and there. 'I started doing it because my brother asked me to', she tells Harry Finn. Finn is an ageing British agent sent to uncover a gun-running operation by a loyalist politician. Politically speaking, Caragh should avoid him like the plague. But within no time it is the British agent she is sheltering, ferrying about and eventually bedding.

The ease with which women embrace violence out of emotional loyalty is thus matched by easy switches in allegiance when emotional connections change. Deirdre O'Shaughnessy, the highly capable Official IRA woman in *The Extremists,* switches her allegiance to British officer Lieutenant Giles Fleming about as quickly as she climbs into bed with him. Similarly, Siobhan, the peace-loving, anti-republican university student, tells the American Michael Flaherty (in *The Outsider):* 'Go home with youse. We don't need any more gunmen here.' But soon she falls in love with him and immediately is pro-violence. 'I was wrong. Here I am, a university student, and about the last to see the truth. Even this bloody foreigner knew the truth before me.'

When women are on the edges of violence, as is mostly the case, their fickleness is of no great account. But when they are actually involved as guerrillas, then the problems of women's unreliability are imported into the very heart of the struggle.

Bella Lynam (in *Victims*) is a member of a five-person team which kidnaps an Anglo-Irish family as ransom for the release of three top IRA men from prison. A university graduate, she is ill at ease with the other less well-educated members of the unit, all of whom are men. They are certain of their roles and the need for military action. They have political commitment. But her involvement derives from a need to strike back at her father. Out of place and out of her depth, she is filled with a constant sense of doom. The foreboding is justified as the kidnap eventually goes wrong, and at the point of deepest crisis her response is utterly irrational. She turns to Martin Leonard, the officer in charge of the kidnap team, a man she does not particularly like, and states: 'I want to make love.' Bella's hang-ups are ultimately sexual; she seeks to punish her father by joining the IRA and then craves the attention and love of the father substitute.

Her problem is similar to that of the unnamed IRA woman bomber in *The Patriots*. She is a graduate and student teacher, involved because of her fixation on her dead father. She constantly thinks of him, remembers his words, talks to him, not least when she successfully plants a bomb and thinks: 'Father, look down on your daughter now! Who's doing the grand work for Ireland, boy or not!' This need to please her father is extended to father figures in the movement. After one explosion goes wrong, she meets a godfather and expects a reprimand. Instead, he comforts her: '"Easy, cushla, be easy!" And it was her own father speaking, surely!' While she listens to his instructions for the next job 'her heart began to pound'. 'And then, as her father used to do, he put his left arm around her shoulders' and her bliss is complete. Yet, in the very midst of her joy, she experiences total disillusionment about the political cause which he represents. 'I'm thinking most men are proud of the words they fight and die for', she dares to tell him, implying that she as a woman could never be so waylaid. In the end, all she can hear from him/her father is 'the chattering of words, their emptiness, their hollowness'. This woman can never be like her male colleagues, even though she is technically as capable as they.

To first appearances Maureen, the heroine in *Maureen's Ireland*, is the equal of any man. Twenty-four years old, she is in charge of an IRA Active Service Unit. Into that unit comes Sean, mid-50s, returning to Ireland from the US after thirty years, with a broken marriage behind him. He cannot handle the fact that the boss is a woman half his age, but quickly gets things into perspective by sleeping with her. The chink in her armour is thus revealed. 'She had a thick skin, but underneath her heart was warm ... She was so vulnerable now.' Eventually he is 'able to see Maureen as a loving, caring person instead of the leader of a terrorist band'. The armour, once pierced at the emotional level, is thus penetrated at the political level. Soon Sean becomes the *real* leader; *he* thinks of using mortars where she never has, and *he* leads the mortar attack on an army barracks when six IRA volunteers kill sixty-eight soldiers and injure 180! At one point, Maureen breaks down when she thinks of her own father, tortured and killed in prison, and of all the repression caused by the British army. 'Her whole body shook with great heaving sobs ... "I need you, Sean", she whispered in an odd, little girl voice. "I can't live without you anymore - I'm just not strong enough." "I know", I said', and it is clear that her admission of inferiority and his arrogant answer are as much political statements as sexual ones.

Without the saving presence of a man, women 'terrorists' go over the edge. Having abandoned all maternal instinct, they have no qualms about hurting children. In *The Price,* the kidnap is witnessed by a young boy. Frank, the kidnap gang leader, does not want to shoot the boy, but Kate, a middle-class graduate, goes berserk and wildly opens fire. Norah Murphy in *The Savage Day* is a cooler customer altogether, but, like Kate, more prepared than the men around her to kill children. She and her ever-faithful sidekick, Binnie Gallagher, are on the side of the good republicans who 'kill soldiers, but not children - never that'. As such, they are pitched against a breakaway republican group led by Frank Barry, the Sons of Erin, who are into mindless violence, bombing city centres and killing women and children. In the end, Binnie discovers that Norah actually belongs to the Sons of Erin.

> 'You mean you're one of them? You've been working with Frank Barry all along? A man who would murder - has murdered women, kids ...' 'Sometimes it's the only way, Binnie. We can't afford weakness now. We must be strong.' 'You bloody murdering bitch', he cried and took a step towards her, the sten coming up. She shot him twice at close quarters.

Conclusion

There are aspects of the novels which are all too accurate, regrettably, in their depiction of the oppression of women. In particular, those which set out to use the political 'troubles' as a metaphor for women's particular suffering - such as *To Stay Alive* and *Troubles* - strike close to home at numerous points. Similarly, *Dreams of Revenge* intertwines the personal and the political. The relationship between Michael and Barbara develops and disintegrates as do the Northern 'troubles'; both situations consist of a constant tension punctuated by a series of violent outbursts.

In addition, some of the novels manage to capture the way in which patriarchy is compounded by political conflict. Nora, the prisoner's wife in the novel of the same name, is trapped both by marriage and the worship of the community. Her husband is a prisoner and a hero. Consequently, 'Long Kesh kept them together; its walls, wire fences and watchtowers held them more securely than any marriage vows. Now her marriage had entered the public arena of ghetto politics and it was impossible for her to take any steps to break with him.'

But, true as these insights may be, they only tell part of the story. And it is the absence of the other parts which is the fundamental problem of these novels. There are few positive images with which to compare the women in these pages. Yet, in reality, there are *other* women with whom the women here can be compared - neither victims nor survivors, but active initiators, whether at the domestic level, in community politics or in rational and committed participation in armed struggle. Such women exist; proof of this is the delight with which they are seized on by visiting feminists eager to find evidence of women's changing role in the midst of war.[8] But they do not have fictional sisters. The peppering of the novels with occasional valuable insights into women's oppression is not enough to salvage the genre.

This is not to conclude that the novels are irretrievably woeful. Some are better than others, sometimes despite themselves. Both *Troubles* and *You're Welcome to Ulster* appear to capture well the insularity of the North's Protestant and Catholic bourgeoisies respectively, the former out of previously unchallenged authority, the latter out of fear of rocking too many boats. And class is the theme of what is perhaps the best of the novels, *The Price of Chips* - it poignantly captures the way in which the 'troubles' have been more painful for the Catholic working class than for the bourgeoisie. Similarly, in relation to women, some novels have succeeded well. *Blood Sisters,* an otherwise overly-didactic story, at least has captured a debate which has possessed, and divided, the Irish women's movement, that of feminism versus republicanism. *The Streets of Derry* is excellent in conveying the fact that what women do anyway in a tight working-class community in terms of support becomes translated, in a war situation, into political action. And *Give Them Stones* is poignant in its representation of a woman whose husband turns out to have married her to take the place of his ageing mother. She has four sons and is trapped in the all-male household. After the birth of her first she thinks, 'I didn't feel any of this wonderful joy I'd read about. I felt as if somebody had kicked me up the Cave Hill and down again and I was cold and hungry and I was landed with a big son. No wee dresses and again nobody to talk to.'

Finally, it must be emphasised that, in as far as they are woeful, the novels have echoes in non-fictional representations of women in the Irish conflict. One has only to remember the British media's view of Máire Drumm, the vice-president of Sinn Féin assassinated in 1976, as 'the grandmother of hate', or of Mairead Farrell, assassinated in Gibraltar in 1988, as 'the angel of death', to realise that the fictional accounts are based on stereotypes which are well established in popular culture. The novelists are allowed more license in using the stereotypes, but they are following a common script. Or, as Ward and McGivern put it in relation to non-fictional accounts:

> Passive victims of the troubles, viragos of the barricades, advocates of a messianic peace. Our contention is that none of these stereotypes reveal the true situation of women living in a socially deprived, war-torn, rigidly patriarchal society.[9]

Endnotes

1. There are at least two novels in French, and a number of the English novels have been translated into other languages. For example, *Harry's Game* is also available in Spanish and Norwegian, and *The Whore Mother* in Danish, German and Turkish. Novels cited in this article are listed in the bibliography alphabetically by title.
2. Exceptions which put loyalist protagonists centre stage are *In Connection with Kilshaw,* where the loyalist politician Kilshaw is aiming for a right-wing

take-over and *Silver's City*, which depicts the clash between idealist loyalist Silver Steele and psychopath Ned Galloway. *Across the Water* has a loyalist central character, Robert, who seems to exist merely so that he can end up pitched in mortal combat with his alter ego, the republican Leamus.

3. For numerous examples of stereotyping and anti-Irish racism, see Liz Curtis, *Nothing But the Same Old Story: the roots of anti-Irish racism*, London, Information on Ireland, 1984.

4. For an excellent account of representations of republican men in novels, see A. Titley 'Rough rug-headed kerns: the Irish gunman in the popular novel', *Eire-Ireland*, Vol. 15, no. 4, 1980, pp. 15-38.

5. Jerry Palmer, *Thrillers: genesis and structure of a popular genre*, London, Edward Arnold, 1978.

6. The reference to religious morality plays is perhaps not as far-fetched as it appears. Shaun Herron, author of *The Whore Mother*, was born in Carrickfergus, but is currently a minister in Canada.

7. In *The Outsider* it is the influential grandfather who turns out to be a liar and informer.

8. Cf., for example, Judy Ezekiel, 'Women in Northern Ireland', *Radical America*, Vol. 14, no. 6, 1980, pp. 57-65.

9. Margaret Ward and Marie-Therese McGivern, 'Images of women in Northern Ireland', *The Crane Bag*, Vol. 4, no. 1, 1980, pp. 66-72.

References

Across the Water, Stewart Binnie, London, Alison Press, 1979
Blood Sisters, Valerie Miner, London, Women's Press, 1981
Both Your Houses, James Barlow, London, Pan, 1973
Cal, Bernard Maclaverty, Belfast, Blackstaff Press, 1983
Dreams of Revenge, Kevin Casey, Dublin, Wolfhound Press, 1987
The Extremists, Peter Leslie, London, New English Library, 1970
The Fugitives, John Broderick, London, Pan, 1976
Give Them Stones, Mary Beckett, London, Bloomsbury, 1987
Harry's Game, Gerard Seymour, London, Fontana, 1977
Hennessy, Max Franklin, London, Futura, 1975
In Connection with Kilshaw, Peter Driscoll, London, Sphere, 1975
The Killing of Yesterday's Children, M.S. Power, London, Chatto and Windus, 1985
Maureen's Ireland, Sean Patrick, USA, Author, 1986
The Minstrel Code, Walter Nelson, London, New English Library, 1980
No Time for Love, Hugo Meehan, Dingle, Brandon, 1987
The Outsider, Colin Leinster, London, New English Library, 1980
The Patriots, G.W. Target, London, Duckworth, 1974
Prayer for the Dying, Jack Higgins, London, Coronet, 1975
The Price, Peter Ransley, London, Corgi, 1984
The Price of Chips, Walter Hegarty, London, Davis-Poynter, 1973
The Prisoner's Wife, Jack Holland, London, Robert Hale, 1982
The Savage Day, Jack Higgins, London, Coronet, 1974
Shadows on Our Skin, Jennifer Johnston, London, Coronet 1977
Silver's City, Maurice Leitch, London, Secker and Warburg 1981

The Streets of Derry, Albert J. Countryman, Palmyra, New Jersey, Countryman Publishing, 1986

To Stay Alive, Linda Anderson, London, Bodley Head, 1974

Too Long a Sacrifice, Mildred Downey Broxon, London, Futura, 1981

Troubles, Naomi May, London, John Calder, 1976

Victims, Eugene McCabe, Dublin, Mercier, 1979

Vote to Kill, Douglas Hurd, London, Collins, 1975

The Whore Mother, Sean Herron, London, Coronet, 1975

With O'Leary in the Grave, James Carrick, London, Heinemann, 1972

You're Welcome to Ulster, Menna Gallie, London, Gollancz, 1970

SECTION FIVE INTRODUCTION: PEACE?

W ith the emergence of the peace process, some of the rules of media coverage appeared to change. The chapter included here, by **David Miller and Greg McLaughlin**, examines the extent of those changes. It focuses especially on British network television news coverage of the peace process between September 1993 and May 1994, and examines its role in legitimating changes in government policy.

24.

David Miller and Greg McLaughlin

REPORTING THE PEACE IN IRELAND

(Paper presented to 'Turbulent Europe: Conflict, Identity and Culture', First European Film and Television Studies Conference, London, 19-22 July 1994)

As soon then as pourparlers between the government and Sinn Féin began, the *Sunday Express* published the news exclusively, and strongly supported the action of Ministers... When the conference or successive conferences began to meet, I intensified the propaganda in favour of agreement. I felt it was vital that Ministers should not feel that they had no backing in the country, and that their signatures to a settlement might spell their ruin. This was a somewhat daring policy for a newspaper, most of whose readers were educated to think in different terms. I was told the course I was adopting would ruin the *Daily Express*, and it did unquestionably involve a great breach both with the traditions of the newspaper and with my own past views in politics. The *Daily Express* had been an anti-Home Rule organ; I had sat as a Unionist in the House of Commons. Now we were advocating Home Rule for the South and West of Ireland. And then there was a more formidable difficulty still to face. When ever the *Daily Express* urged a settlement with the Sinn Féinners, it was promptly replied to by the opposing press that this was a condonation of the murders perpetrated by the Irish extremists. The 'shaking hands with murder' outcry was very dangerous. There is no doubt that the policy pursued by the *Daily Express* in this matter, though it has already been justified by the event and is likely to be approved as wisdom by history, was unpopular with its readers. But once the decision that settlement on its merits was right, there was no use hesitating. It was necessary to go through with the advocacy of the policy at any cost... Most of the conservative newspapers simply reiterated the objection to 'shaking hands with murder' without suggesting any alternative plan (Beaverbrook, 1925: 40-41).

Here we have both a historical precedent for contemporary events and an interesting contrast. A precedent in that we might expect, should the peace process advance further, at least one tabloid newspaper to break with its past reporting and endorse a settlement with today's republican movement. Likewise, the problem of overcoming the 'shaking hands with murder' accusation is still with us. The British government has gone to extraordinary lengths to minimise the perceived extent of their contacts with Sinn Féin and to cling to the official position that no 'negotiations' have taken place. Much of the media and especially television has bent over backwards to give the government the benefit of the doubt in their accounts of the peace process. Fair appraisals of the truth of the situation have been indelibly marked by the spectre of giving favour to the enemy.

Beaverbrook's comments are a contrast in that the government's action in initiating talks with the republican movement in 1990 and the revelation of contacts was supported by nearly every British newspaper and the only political party in parliament to complain vigorously about either the contacts or the lying was Ian Paisley's DUP. The British press have in general continued to condemn the IRA and oppose concessions to them until the government is caught in the act of conceding ground.

For all that, the media have been central to the peace process. This paper examines the media politics of the 'peace process' in Ireland, concentrating on the period from the announcement of the Hume-Adams initiative (in September 1993) to the publication of the British government's response to Sinn Féin's request for 'clarification' (in May 1994). We have examined press and television coverage paying particular attention to television news. Our sample of TV news is based on coverage of key events in the peace process from the Hume-Adams statement, 25 September 1993, to the British government's 'clarification' of 20 questions from Sinn Féin, 19 May 1994.[1]

British government policy

The importance of focusing on the media politics of the peace process in Ireland is that in many ways they are quite different from the media politics of the war which preceded it and currently coexists with it. The most important change here is the shift in the position of the British government. For the better part of 25 years the British government has publicly adhered to the position that the conflict in Ireland is caused by 'terrorists', primarily of the republican variety, whose motivations are criminal, material or pathological. In general the government have claimed that their response has been to operate within the law. However, occasionally Ministers have gone further. In 1989 Home Secretary Douglas Hurd stated:

> I believe that, with the Provisional IRA and some of the Middle-Eastern groups, it is really nothing to do with a political cause any more. They are professional killers. That is their occupation and their pleasure and they will go on doing that. No political solution will cope with that. They just have to be extirpated (cited in Rolston, 1991: 170)

Government policy has been that there will be no talks with 'terrorists'. Yet we are now told that the year after this statement was made contact with Sinn Féin was initiated and continued until November 1993. The enormity of the apparent change in government thinking is underlined by a statement from a 'key British source' to the *Observer* which gives a very different analysis to that given by Douglas Hurd. It is extraordinary in that it is a complete reversal of the official analysis of the conflict. Moreover it makes almost all mainstream media reporting over the last 25 years seem seriously threadbare. According to the source:

> the Provisional IRA was imbued with an ideology and a theology. He then added the breathtaking statement that its ideology included an 'ethical dimension' - that members would not continue killing for the sake of it. He went on to argue that the Provisionals did not kill 'for no purpose', and that if that purpose was removed, there was no reason why they should not stop killing (Bevins, 1993: 3).

This is a dramatic departure for a government spokesperson.[2] Even after this statement, however, the mainstream news media, especially the main television news bulletins, continued to act as if government pronouncements could be implicitly trusted.

Mood Swings: The success of impression management

Part of the reason for this is the continued success of the lobby system of mass unattributable briefings (Cockerell et al, 1984; Harris, 1990; Hennessy, 1987). A more fundamental reason is that Northern Ireland is beyond the pale of the routine criticism and commentary which is required for other topics. In the margins of the press or in more open formats, such as editorials (see Miller, 1994), journalists can acknowledge that there is more to the political process than official statements. Displaying an unusual awareness of this, following the revelation of government talks with Sinn Féin, the *Guardian* editorialised:

> The world of political propaganda still says that British governments can never talk to men of violence until they throw in their hand and lay down their arms. In the world of political reality, however, we now have confirmation that life is very different indeed ('The journey is worth the secrecy', *The Guardian*, 29 November 1993).[3]

However, such a recognition did not become part of television news accounts.[4]

On 25 September 1993, John Hume and Gerry Adams revealed that their five months of talks had made 'considerable progress' and that they would forward a report to the Irish government. Television news reporters seemed unsure what to make of it. The BBC's Ireland correspondent, Denis Murray, thought that John Hume's optimism about the talks had to be taken seriously since he 'doesn't say things like that lightly' (BBC1, 22.20, 25 September 1993). Two days later, ITN reported on a bomb in Belfast and concluded that 'this new peace process seems only to have aggravated tension' (ITN, 22.00, 27 September 1993).

In the immediate aftermath of the Shankill Road bombing in October, the news media condemned to death not just the Hume-Adams initiative but the whole 'peace process'. The IRA bomb killed nine people including one of the bombers. ITN reported that the attack cast 'a shadow on the future of talks aimed at bringing peace to the Province', and that the Hume-Adams initiative 'left the sides more polarised than ever' (16.40, 23 October 1993). It later deemed the initiative 'very close to extinction' (20.45. 23 October 1993). On 25 October, ITN's early evening bulletin led with the headlines 'The government made it clear today that it regarded the ... peace initiative ... as buried in the rubble of the Shankill Road bomb'. And in a report from 10 Downing Street, Michael Brunson remarked that 'from today, in Mr Major's view, [the] talks are stone dead' (17.40, 25 October 1993).

The BBC seemed reluctant at first to fall in behind the public outcry. Denis Murray reckoned the bombing was 'an imperative for Mr Hume to try and keep going with his efforts, as he sees them, to get peace' (BBC1, 17.15, 23 October 1993). Jim Dougal said it was 'a serious embarrassment to John Hume', but that Hume-Adams was still alive (BBC1, 21.50, 23 October 1993). The tone hardened the following week when Gerry Adams helped carry the coffin of the IRA bomber, Thomas Begley. Murray reported that the gesture 'makes any chance of success from the Hume-Adams talks very slight indeed' (21.00, 27 October 1993), and later declared the talks were 'finished' (21.00, 28 October 1993). The headline on *Newsnight* asked if the funeral procession might 'trample the Hume-Adams so-called peace process into the ground?' (BBC2, 27 October 1993). *Channel Four News* reported that negative public reaction put the peace process 'beyond recovery' (27 October 1993) and 'destroyed completely any hopes remaining for the Hume-Adams initiative' (28 October 1993). In the event, such prognostications were inaccurate and in May 1994, *Channel Four News* reversed the news judgement, reporting that the Shankill bombing in October 1993 'increased the momentum behind the Downing Street Declaration' (19 May 1994).

Nevertheless, this pattern of reporting continued in the run up to the Anglo-Irish Summit in Dublin on 3 December and the Downing Street

Declaration on 15 December. When British and Irish officials met on 1 December, ahead of the Dublin summit, *BBC News* pointed to 'fundamental differences over the future of Ulster', and referred to 'a definite scaling down of expectations' (21.00). ITN led with the headline, 'Reynolds and Major struggle to agree on Northern Ireland' and reported that 'optimism about the ... peace process was dented ... when the differences between the British and Irish positions began to sink in'. Their political editor, Michael Brunson, betrayed the source of the doom and gloom when he exclaimed, 'No wonder a Downing Street source said tonight, "The further you go down this road, the harder it gets"!' (22.00). The following day, the *News At Ten* gave the very opposite impression of progress. Once again, their report hinged on government briefings. Suddenly, the Foreign Secretary, Douglas Hurd, was hinting at 'the possibility ... of a real breakthrough', while Irish officials were said to be in 'a rather upbeat mood' (2 December 1993). The two leaders ended their summit the next day with talk of progress on remaining differences. The main bulletins followed suit with almost identical headlines: 'Some progress in the talks on Northern Ireland ... the search for peace goes on' (BBC1, 21.00), 'Progress in Dublin - the struggle for peace goes on' (ITN, 22.00). But there was an alternative view of the Summit. Referring to the revelation of secret contacts with the republicans, Nik Gowing talked of 'a bitter whiff of British double-dealing, even of British deceit' (*Channel Four News*, 19.00). And *Newsnight* led with the headline, 'No breakthrough as seven hours of Anglo-Irish talks are overshadowed by bitterness about British contacts with the IRA'. Their reporter suggested that the day was 'a complete disaster in Anglo-Irish terms' (BBC2, 22.30).

The mood swings continued in the run-up to the Downing Street Declaration. One day, news bulletins led with Albert Reynolds' statement from Dublin that the talks were 'firmly on course' (BBC1, 21.55 and ITN, 22.30, 5 December 1993). The next day, the BBC reported that the murder of two Catholics in Belfast 'undermined the hope that is needed for any peace process' (21.00, 6 December 1993). Major and Reynolds met again on 10 December at the European Summit in Brussels. Headlines hailed 'More progress in the talks to find a peace formula' (BBC1, 21.00) and declared that 'the peace process is back on track' (ITN, 22.00). BBC's political editor, Robin Oakley, spoke to 'senior officials from both ... governments' and was asked if it was 'premature to talk of a breakthrough?'. He replied:

> I don't think so ... there's no doubt of the growing feeling on both sides that they can now agree on a political declaration which will bring about a cessation of violence and lead to a political settlement ... And, significantly, the British side has now joined Mr Albert Reynolds in talking of a possible deal before Christmas, something they were reluctant to do before they came here to Brussels (21.00).

Two days later, ITN reported that 'Hopes for peace ... by Christmas were dealt another blow today after two police men were shot dead by the IRA' (ITN, 22.30, 12 December 1993). The next day, the *Nine O'Clock News* reported from the House of Commons where 'The Prime Minister has given his strongest indication yet that his peace initiative ... may end in failure'. However, *News at Ten* declared that, 'The search for peace ... seems firmly back on track tonight ... because officials have been able to make good progress'. By the eve of the Downing Street Declaration (14 December), both news channels were hailing 'an historic deal' (ITN, 17.40) and 'a breakthrough' (BBC1, 21.00). Once again, we have to turn to the minority-viewing programmes to hear journalists ask questions and point up the contradictions and short-cuts in the negotiations. *Channel Four News* questioned the speed with which major differences were resolved and suggested it was possible only because 'some of the most difficult issues ... are unlikely to be included in the declaration' (19.00).

Throughout this whole period lobby journalists rarely showed critical awareness of official mood management. Two days before the Downing Street Declaration, Robin Oakley reported the rise and fall of expectations as matter of fact.

> Officials toiling behind the scenes haven't moved things on yet to the point where it's worth the promised phone call between Mr Major and Albert Reynolds setting up a third meeting. Hopes rose at the weekend when the British talked for the first time of a deal before Christmas. They flopped again with Mr Reynolds hinting the document was too cautious in recognising nationalist aspirations for him to sign. And today Mr Major was at his gloomiest yet about their prospects of reaching agreement. (21.00, 13 December 1993)

Here we are very firmly in the world of political propaganda via the Downing Street briefing. [...]

The Unbelievable Truth: Talking to Sinn Féin

A similar lack of self-awareness was evident in television news coverage of the revelation of talks with Sinn Féin. The story trickled out slowly following leaks rumoured to be from intelligence personnel to unionist politicians. On 1 November John Major said in parliament that talking with Sinn Féin 'would turn my stomach'. On 7 November the Downing Street Press Office said, 'We have made clear on many occasions that we don't speak to those who carry out or advocate or condone violence to further their political aims'. On 11 November the Northern Ireland Office dismissed renewed suggestions, saying: 'No such meetings have taken place'. The Head of Information at the NIO, Andy Wood, scoffed that such reports belonged 'more properly in the fantasy of spy thrillers than in real life' (McKittrick, 1993). But truth in Northern Ireland is stranger than fiction and the story was then confirmed by Sinn Féin on 15 November, but the government continued to deny it.[5] It is difficult to overstate the significance of the revelations about contacts with the republican movement.[6]

Managing the disclosure

According to Moloney (1993) the *Observer* first took the documents it had received from Unionist MP Willie McCrea to the government on Friday 26 November in advance of the publication on Sunday 28 November. This gave the government between 48 and 72 hours to perfect its version of the contacts. According to Moloney the government then briefed James Molyneaux, the leader of the Ulster Unionist Party, and John Hume was contacted by the Permanent Secretary of the NIO, John Chilcott, the central figure in the contacts with Sinn Féin (Moloney 1993).

The government explanation was that they had been approached by Martin McGuinness in February 1993 with the message, 'The conflict is over, but we need your advice on how to bring it to a close'. This was presented as indicating that the IRA sought a unilateral cease-fire: 'The government had a duty to respond' to such a message said Mayhew.[7] Following this there were two 'unauthorised' meetings with Sinn Féin and a number of documents had been exchanged. This had not amounted to 'negotiations'. The crux of Sir Patrick's account was that the government's public and private policies were identical. He said:

> It is clear that [the government] message was consistent with our declared policy: namely that if such people wanted to enter into talks or negotiations with the government they first had genuinely to end violence. Not just temporarily but for good ... That remains our policy (Northern Ireland Information Service, 1993: 7).

Although it was a clear break with previous policy, Sir Patrick presented it as if there had been no real choice, since the process had been initiated by the republicans. As Colin Brown and David McKittrick of the *Independent* put it: 'After years in which ministers denied the existence of such channels, Sir Patrick yesterday presented its existence as a matter almost of common sense' (Brown and McKittrick 1993: 1).

This version of events was rejected by Sinn Féin which claimed that the contacts had been protracted and intensive and that the British had offered delegation meetings in return for a two-to-three week IRA cease-fire at which republicans would be convinced that armed struggle was no longer necessary. On the contrary said Martin McGuinness: 'They were authorised meetings which became unauthorised meetings when they were caught out' (McKittrick, 1993: 6). Whether or not this is true, it is reasonably clear that when the first British government representative retired in 1991, the British government appointed a replacement. When journalists compared the documents released by Sinn Féin with the British versions it became clear that 'vital parts had been altered by one of the parties' (McKittrick, 1993: 6). The key dispute was over the alleged fabrication of the initial 'conflict is over' message. Sinn Féin flatly denied it, describing it as 'bogus'. The key nine-paragraph 19 March British document touched on this. The government version read:

> We note that what is being sought at this stage is advice ... We confirm that if violence had genuinely been brought to an end, whether or not that fact had been announced, then dialogue could take place (Northern Ireland Office, 1993a).

This supported the government contention that it was Sinn Féin who had initiated the contact. However the republican version stated more neutrally:

> What is being sought at this stage is advice ... If violence had genuinely been brought to an end, whether or not that fact had been announced, then *progressive entry into* dialogue could take place (our italics, Sinn Féin, 1994).

In this version it could have been the British seeking advice. But the contradiction between the two versions was resolved when David McKittrick of the *Independent* noticed the seemingly innocuous phrase 'progressive entry into dialogue'. This turned up again in a British version of a subsequent republican message which asked for clarification of the phrase. Since it didn't appear anywhere else, how could the government explain it?

Changing the documents

The NIO were then forced to issue corrections, which they did, 'late on Wednesday night, too late for *News at Ten* or the first editions of the newspapers' (McKittrick, 1993: 5), on 1 December. These discrepancies were described as 'typographical errors' or in the case of the crucial nine-paragraph note setting out the British position, the result of transcription being 'mistakenly made from a late draft' (Northern Ireland Information Service, 1993b: 5). According to Patrick Mayhew, the corrections 'do not change the sense of the messages' (Northern Ireland Information Service, 1993b: 2). It is clear, however, that they make the British version of events substantially less convincing. The British nine-paragraph note, as corrected, was now identical to the Sinn Féin version of the document. However, there are still substantial variations between the documents published by both sides. Most important is the question of whether the British offer of talks was conditional upon a total cessation of republican armed struggle or only a two-to-three week suspension. Sinn Féin says that the phrase 'even though it will be of a short duration' has been removed from the British version of one of their messages dated 10 May. Three weeks later the government says it received an IRA offer of a total cessation. Sinn Féin say this message is a fabrication. However the government's own documents 'tend to support the Sinn Féin version' (McKittrick, 1993: 6). The next

British message on 17 July, which is not disputed by either side contains the sentence, 'The reasons for not talking about a permanent cessation are understood' (Northern Ireland Information Service, 1993: 20; Sinn Féin, 1994: 38). [...] Certainly this was the conclusion of many broadsheet journalists. As David McKittrick put it:

> If even half of what the republicans claim is correct, a truly appalling vista[8] is being revealed: ministers lied to parliament and public about their contacts, are lying still about the real extent and nature of these; passed information on the Irish government to terrorists; and have published concocted documents as part of a continuing cover-up (McKittrick, 1993: 6).

Even those on Conservative papers such as the *Sunday Telegraph* concluded reluctantly that: 'Perhaps the strangest consequence of the process has been that the IRA have now become more believable than the government' ('Comment: Careless talks' *Sunday Telegraph*, 5 December 1993: 29). By contrast, television news was unable to consider that the government had lied and stuck to promoting the version of events given in official briefings and statements.

Reporting the documents

Because of this they were able to approve of the contacts. They accepted the official line that the IRA had offered a cease-fire and the government would have been irresponsible to turn down such an offer.

When Sinn Féin revealed the first details of the contacts, and the government denied it outright, reporters were in no doubt then whom to believe. ITN referred to 'a senior government source ... who denied privately that these meetings took place. He said categorically no, without any question' (22.00, 15 November 1993). *Newsnight* reported that the contacts were 'vigorously and emphatically denied by Downing Street sources ... and indeed the Northern Ireland Office ... has told us that no such meetings have taken place' (15 November 1993). The briefings held good for quite some time after. The next evening, the BBC's political editor said the claim was 'vigorously denied by Downing Street sources' (21.00, 16 November 1993). But [...] Vincent Kearney of the *Belfast Telegraph* spoke with a 'good source' in Sinn Féin and told *Newsnight* that when he 'put it to him that the (NIO) were denying these claims, he says they were perfectly entitled to do so because they probably wouldn't know about them. As far as he was concerned, they had been by-passed. Downing Street ... had actually initiated the discussions' (16 November 1993).

So was the government telling lies? Weasel words abounded as journalists struggled with the unbelievable truth. A BBC reporter thought 'the best interpretation you can put on the government's statement is that they're simply playing with words' (21.55, 27 November 1993). He went further to say that it 'could well be that both sides are convinced they're telling the truth ... the nuances can get changed as things go along so it's possible that neither side actually feels it's telling lies' (BBC1, 13.00, 29 November 1993). ITN could only say that the government was being 'economical with the truth' (18.20, 28 November 1993), that there were 'still question marks' and that 'the whole truth has yet to come out' (22.00, 29 November 1993).

It was only when Sinn Féin hinted they had documentary evidence of contacts that the government owned up. It sought to limit the damage with the claim that it was all in the cause of peace and that it would have been unforgivable to turn the opportunity down. The news media played a key role in helping the effort. They successfully negotiated the awkward fact of John Major's statement that it would 'turn his stomach' to talk to the IRA (1 November 1993). BBC Ireland Correspondent Denis Murray remarked, 'I think the government feels it has a defensible position' (BBC1, 21.55, 27 November 1993), and that 'of course there's been embarrassment but the government's position is that if they hadn't taken up this offer then that really would be a resignation matter' (20.50, 28 November 1993). The government's efforts to turn vice into virtue got a further boost when ITN's Michael Brunson watched their defence in parliament. He reported that, 'By the time Sir Patrick Mayhew got to his feet he was already out of political trouble ... And so (he) was able to set out the record of a serious bid for peace' (ITN, 22.00, 29 November 1993). *Channel Four News* reported from the Anglo-Irish Summit in Dublin that 'British sources said the issue of Britain's contact with the IRA had not been an issue today. "Irrelevant", said one source' (3 December 1993).

Each side produced documents to support their version of the contacts. *Newsnight* 'subjected [them] to a thorough scrutiny' (29 November 1993) and, again, there was little doubt which set of evidence carried most weight. For example, *Channel Four News* thought the government documents 'did seem to bear out the government's claim that at no point had the IRA been offered anything in private it hadn't been offered in public'. Furthermore, said the reporter, it 'showed the extent of the IRA's anxiety for a formula it could sell to its supporters' (29 November 1993). *Newsnight* pointed out that while verbal messages 'may be open to question', they 'must accept the government version' (29 November 1993). Only when it emerged that the government documents were 'riddled with errors' did ITN report that: 'To Whitehall's embarrassment it seems Sinn Féin's published account of what happened may be more accurate' (ITN, 22.00, 2 December 1993). Yet in spite of further revelations about the contacts, reporters continued to attach credence to government denials and to treat Sinn Féin's claims as mere propaganda. For example, on 2 December, the eve of the Dublin Summit, Sinn Féin claimed that the government was on the verge of talks with the IRA in return for a fourteen-day cease-fire. News bulletins reported they had 'stepped up the propaganda war' to 'win some of the pre-summit spotlight' (BBC1, 21.00), and that they were, 'clearly determined to cause the government maximum discomfort' at the Summit (ITN, 22.00). Both channels reported a Downing Street statement refuting the evidence without offering a similar analysis of government motives (BBC1, 21.00 and ITN, 22.00, 2 December 1993). *Newsnight* asked reporter, Mark Urban, 'What are the IRA's motives in giving out these conflicting versions of events over these meetings?' The IRA, he began, were trying to prevent a split in the ranks with

> the big figures in Sinn Féin trying desperately to reassure their own people ... You can see their sensitivity and this is why I think they're denying the really salient points, certainly that the government would argue, and that is that they sought some form of cessation of hostilities ... and so naturally now they're not prepared to admit that they were seeking such a secret unannounced cessation of hostilities (3 December 1993).

This could easily have applied to the government, but that would have been beyond the limits of 'objective' reporting. In all of this, television journalists refrained from asking the hard questions about British government strategy and about contradictions with previous policy.

The media and the negotiations process

The documents themselves make fascinating reading. It is evident from the British record, but more especially from the Sinn Féin record, that the possibility of media interest in the secret contacts was of real concern. The republicans in particular were concerned that the British might leak details to the media or that elements within the British hierarchy might try to sabotage the process by doing so. On 11 May 1993, the day after the crucial Sinn Féin document outlining the basis for entry into dialogue was lodged with the British government representative, Sinn Féin raised the first[9] query in an oral message to the British:

> We are reliably informed that an English reporter in USA has picked up a story about talks between you and us. May be working for the Sunday Times. We are told he was briefed by your people in Washington? (Sinn Féin, 1994: 34).[10]

Two days later the British respond in a semi-coded written message in which the 'Bank' refers to the government and the 'loan business' is the negotiations:

> I was very concerned to hear about the alarming press story you told me. I've checked on this with the Bank's press department who said, 'Oh that old story from Washington? It's all gibberish. We'd heard it was going to be in last Sunday's papers, but we think that the editors must have realised that it didn't make sense'. Please reassure your friends that this is the last thing that we would do or want. We believe that somebody visiting Washington from Stormont who was not privy to the loan business was shooting his mouth off

and a journalist embellished it out of all proportion. If asked, our press people will deny it (emphasis in original, Sinn Féin, 1994: 34).

In July a further message was sent complaining that

we are most displeased at what we read in the popular press. It seems obvious to ourselves that some of [your] colleagues are leaking what we had come to regard as a confidence between ourselves and [you]. The [RUC] are clearly well informed of whatever the situation was and even more clearly are briefing people like [a journalist is named]. As usual we have kept our word and there hasn't been any deviation from our established position of saying nothing (Northern Ireland Office, 1993: 18; Sinn Féin, 1994: 37).[11]

There appears to have been no British response to this, but Sinn Féin sent a further message on 30 August:

We reiterate our concern at the continuing leaks from your side. The *Sunday Times* story of 22nd August 1993[12] was but the latest in a recent series which include a previous *Sunday Times* article and several informed references in public statements by a number of Unionist spokesmen. We are also convinced and concerned that the recent Cook Report[13] is connected to the above revelations (Northern Ireland Office, 1993: 28; Sinn Féin, 1994: 39).

Again the British denied that the leaks were their doing:

Recent media reports and speculation do not result from authorised briefing. Nor do they serve the interests of anybody seeking to bring these exchanges to a successful conclusion. As both sides recognise, that depends on maintaining maximum confidentiality. Recent reports are certainly not being inspired, let alone orchestrated by the government side to which they are most unwelcome. Accordingly the government side will continue to respect the confidentiality of these exchanges (Northern Ireland Office, 1993: 31; Sinn Féin, 1994: 40-41).

It seems reasonably clear that the leaks were coming from official sources. However, it is less clear whether they were deliberate on the part of the government or whether they betray serious division within official circles on the contacts with Sinn Féin. What is clear from these messages is the importance both sides attributed to secrecy. Publication of the contacts is held by both sides to severely compromise the chances of success. Keeping the media away from the negotiations is seen as a precondition for success. This does not mean that both sides maintained a media silence in this period. An air of business as normal is required. However, it was also seen as necessary to do some public preparing of the ground for a potential settlement. Thus from around 1990 successive Northern Ireland Secretaries (Peter Brooke and Patrick Mayhew) had made conciliatory speeches spelling out that Britain no longer had any strategic military or economic interest in remaining in Ireland. Sinn Féin leaders had also softened their position in public speeches. It seems likely that these overtures were directed at the public climate as well as directly at each other. It is now clear that advance copies of these speeches were being communicated between the British and the republicans. This public limbering up was accompanied by other behind the scenes exchanges.

The problem for the British is to sell the idea of talks with a party which they have consistently excoriated. There is some evidence from the documents that the government were anxious to create a climate in the media in favour of talks with Sinn Féin which they would then apparently accede to. In one extraordinary passage (not included in the British government account) the British give Sinn Féin advice on public relations strategy. The republicans are told to emphasise that it is the British government which is holding up the peace process. The message, received on September 6 1993 suggested:

> that Sinn Féin should comment in as major way as possible on the PLO/Rabin deal; that Sinn Féin should be saying 'If they can come to an agreement in Israel, why not here? We are standing at the altar why won't they come and join us'. It is also said that a full frontal publicity offensive from Sinn Féin is expected, pointing out that various contingencies and defensive positions are already in place (Sinn Féin, 1994: 41).

In fact only 12 days later the *Guardian* carried a full page interview with Martin McGuinness of Sinn Féin, headed 'The time to talk is now', in which McGuinness is quoted as saying: 'If the British government was prepared to learn from South Africa and Israel, then we could see a solution within six to 12 months' (Johnson, 1993: 25). We have no evidence that the two are connected, but it is highly interesting that the government should apparently want to give Sinn Féin public relations advice.[14]

Clarification, Commentary, Exposition and Explanation

The main Sinn Féin response to the Downing Street Declaration was to call for 'clarification'. At a press conference on 21 December, Gerry Adams stated: 'We have a document here which in its ambiguity, in its lack of mechanism and in its lack of clear process needs to be clarified' (Grogan, 1993: 4). John Major's response in a one day visit to Belfast was that Adams ought to 'stop the violence' first and then 'the questions Mr Adams wants answered will be answered' ('Major: I won't wait forever', *Newsletter*, 23 December 1993: 1). Over the next five months Ministers repeatedly stated that there was no need for clarification. Yet in off-the-record briefings, ministerial speeches and even in an article by John Major in the Belfast nationalist paper the *Irish News*[15] hints were dropped and threats made about what could be expected if Sinn Féin accepted the Declaration. As we heard night after night that the peace initiative was dead or still on track, it became evident that the government was indeed engaged in clarification and negotiation via a kind of megaphone diplomacy in the media. It has been exceptionally rare for television journalists to acknowledge that the briefings they are given are not a transparent reflection of government thinking but actually part of the negotiation process.

Television and clarification

'It's all come down to a stark problem of language', said Michael Brunson of the peace process (ITN, 22.00, 1 December 1993). This was certainly true of the 'clarification' issue and the way it was reported in the news. The government consistently refused to clarify the Downing Street Declaration for Sinn Féin. It gave some 'explanation' on 19 May 1994, but that did not mean 'clarification'. The language problem is that all along news accounts have accepted that the two words mean completely different things, thus easing the effective government U-turn. ITN thought the government's refusal to clarify the Declaration seemed quite understandable. With no regard to the history of official contacts with Sinn Féin and the IRA, or of the Declaration, Tom Bradby remarked that, 'of course ... the governments don't want to go down a road where they'll actually be talking to Sinn Féin, where they're engaged in dialogue whilst the violence continues' (22.00, 21 December 1993). Thus, the refusals were seen as principled and were reported without question.

In early January 1994, the BBC reported that 'Sinn Féin leaders have again asked for more explanation of the Downing Street Declaration ... though the government has already said that no further clarification will be given' (BBC1, 21.00, 8 January 1994). Later in the month, Gerry Adams wrote to John Major, again asking for clarification. His reply made headline news: 'John Major has told Gerry Adams he won't clarify the Downing Street Declaration - "Take it or leave it!"' (BBC1, 21.00, 21 January 1994), 'The Prime Minister gave a firm "No" ... to Sinn Féin's request for clarification' (ITN, 22.00, 21 January 1994). The government had spoken. The position was clear. But as the month closed, ITN had no problem reporting that 'the Secretary of State's position appeared to have shifted. Clarification might not be possible but explanation could be' (28 January 1994). It was rare to hear reporters point out the glaring contradiction in the official line.

Media management and 'clarification'

When clarification was given, the government continued to stick to its public policy of no negotiation until after a cease-fire. They had suggested all along that clarification equalled negotiation, so responses to Sinn Féin had to be euphemised. When John Major wrote a piece in the *Irish News* the paper described it as 'clarification'. Sir Patrick Mayhew however insisted that it was only 'exposition'. The reply to Sinn Féin's queries in May was also the subject of euphemism. 'Commentary' was one description by British officials. Patrick Mayhew referred to the response as 'explanation' and the 21-page document from the NIO used the term 'elucidation' (Northern Ireland Office, 1994: 2). British Officials also tried to play the response to Sinn Féin down by suggesting that only one question from Sinn Féin genuinely involved 'explanation' of the text of the declaration. BBC television news dutifully played along with this line. Political Correspondent John Pienaar commented:

> The Northern Ireland Secretary had clarified one point only, what he called the obvious fact that any vote on the future of the province would be decided by majority (BBC1 2100, 19 May 1994).

However, the government response, (which includes Sinn Féin's questions) runs to 21 pages and did include departures from previous statements in response to questions derided by the government as not genuine queries. For example, the government stated for the first time that the Government of Ireland Act would be on the table for renegotiation. More importantly, for the first time since Sinn Féin contested elections in 1982, the government explicitly recognised the integrity of Sinn Féin's electoral mandate.[16] This was one of the key Sinn Féin demands emphasised by senior party figures in early April.[17] While British journalists were being briefed that the government had given Sinn Féin short shrift, the Dublin government was briefing the Irish media that the response included the significant departures referred to above.[18]

Discussion

The government and the Northern Ireland Office evidently regard the media as very important in the success of their strategy, hence the efforts to manage media coverage. The republicans too see the media as crucial. On the one hand they are wary of British manipulations and disinformation and on the other they are conscious of the pressures they can exert on the government via the media. The British, the republicans and the Irish government have all used the media to engage in megaphone diplomacy, by flying kites, floating suggestions, giving clarification's or issuing threats.

This raises questions for the still influential concept of 'primary definition' (Hall et al, 1978) in which definitions are assumed to originate in the centres of political power and to be transmitted unaltered by the mass media. Yet how are we to account for the apparent dramatic shift in government thinking outlined above? Are we to say that this has nothing to do with the troubles of the last 25 years and in particular with the armed struggle of the IRA? The government have tried to present their initiatives on peace as being fundamentally different from those put forward in the Hume-Adams agreement. Yet it is clear that at least part of the momentum behind the Downing Street Declaration has been an attempt to regain the public relations initiative from Sinn Féin. Even if the government is able to secure complete dominance in media coverage of the peace process (which, it has not) this would not indicate that the state was the 'primary definer' of mass media coverage (cf. Miller, 1993).

The emergence of the 'peace process' in Ireland has caught journalists on the hop. For 25 years Northern Ireland has been covered from within the 'anti-terrorism' paradigm. 'Terrorism' was the cause of the conflict. It was devoid of political motivation and the only way to bring peace was to defeat the IRA and convince people to live together. Now it seems that the official view has changed. Sinn Féin are now to be regarded as having a legitimate electoral mandate and at some point a place at the negotiating table. The paradigm is plainly in crisis, but by and large television news has contrived not to notice.

The central problem has been a lack of perspective. Slavishly repeating the latest briefings from the government with very little indication that the function of briefings might be to put a particular spin on events is especially hard to defend when the government has been caught misleading the media and the public. Either the government is engaged in an honest attempt to progress the peace process by political propaganda and news management or they are engaged in information management and propaganda to cover up their duplicity. In either case the rationale of an unreflective parroting of government propaganda lines as if they were straightforward insights into government thinking (in phrases such as 'the government believes') is less than adequate for journalists supposedly bound by legislative demands to objectivity. The role of the British media has been to defend the government for its principled or astute action even as the government slips further towards negotiations with the 'terrorists'. As one broadsheet leader writer put it:

> The media tend to declare *sotto voce* that there must be no compromise with the IRA, yet many newspapers are clearly prepared to accept the government shifting its position over negotiations and clarification of the Downing Street Declaration. The media tend to hold the line while allowing it to shift gradually by sleight of hand. Journalists are prepared to accept being lied to even as they castigate the government for lying over other sensitive issues such as arms sales to Iraq (interview with the authors, June 1994).

If the peace process advances any further, there will be other shifts in government positions and the media will hold the line further down the hill. One day soon, with barely a ripple, we might find that British opinion, journalism and political culture has been radically changed. There is a precedent there in the Irish settlement of the early 1920s and in the more recent settlements in South Africa and Palestine. Former Northern Ireland Correspondent for the *Times* and now Middle East Correspondent for the *Independent* Robert Fisk recorded a similar process in the agreement between the PLO and the Israeli government:

> So it is 'Chairman Arafat' now. Just as 'terrorist leader' Kenyatta became 'Mr President'. Just as 'terrorists' Menachem Begin and Yitzhak Shamir both became 'Mr Prime Minister'. From 'terrorist mastermind' to 'statesman' in the length of time it took Yitzhak Rabin to write his name on a piece of paper. How swiftly are we reprogrammed (*Independent*, 12 September 1993).

We await the recasting of Sinn Féin leaders in the event of a peace deal in Ireland.

Endnotes

1. We included all main bulletins from *BBC News* (BBC1 13.00, 18.00, 21.00; and BBC2, *Newsnight*, 22.30) and ITN (12.30, 17.40, 22.00; *Channel Four News*, 19.00) on the following dates:
   1993.
   25-27 September: Hume-Adams send report to Irish government
   7 October: John Hume meets Taoiseach Albert Reynolds, Dublin
   23 October - 2 November: Shankill bomb, Greysteel; Anglo-Irish process geared towards regaining political initiative from Sinn Féin
   15-16 November: Major offers Sinn Féin and IRA part in negotiations in return for cease-fire; Sinn Féin release details of contacts with British government; British government denies contacts
   26-7 December: British government admits contacts; 'document war'; Anglo-Irish summit, Dublin
   10-31 December: Downing Street Declaration; clarification
   1994.
   1 January-28 February: clarification
   19 May: Government answers Sinn Féin's 20 Questions on Downing Street Declaration
2. Although it should be remembered that the statement was made anonymously on lobby terms and is therefore deniable.
3. Even while the *Guardian* is recognising that the British government engages in propaganda, this statement shows that it still regards the British government as the only one which can authoritatively confirm contacts with the republicans. The British government is still the last word on authoritative information.
4. In the 1991 Gulf conflict the sheer quantity of news coverage did mean that on occasion on low audience low status live, unscripted news programmes such sentiments could appear. (Philo and McLaughlin, 1992)
5. On Radio Four's *Today* programme on 16 November Mayhew said: 'Nobody has been authorised to talk or negotiate on behalf of the British Government with Sinn Féin. We have always made it clear that there will be no talking or negotiating with Sinn Féin or any other organisation that justifies violence' (cited in Bevins, 1993: 3).

6. Our reading of these documents and their various inconsistencies was considerably helped by the excellent accounts by David McKittrick in the London *Independent* (McKittrick, 1993) and Ed Moloney in the Dublin *Sunday Tribune* (Moloney, 1993).

7. Mayhew later acknowledged that he had not taken the alleged message as a surrender: 'I don't think I ever thought of it in terms of surrender. I thought of it in terms that they concluded that they were not going to advance their political objective by armed means ... I considered it as a realistic assessment of the political position ('A Mountain to Climb', *Panorama*, BBC1 21 February 1994). The view that there was no military solution to the Northern Ireland conflict had for some years been the public position of Sinn Féin, but it is quite different from the meaning promoted by the government at the time.

8. However a close reading of Mayhew's statement suggests that not all documents have been released by the British. Furthermore, it suggests that the alleged message from the IRA which in PR briefings was said to have triggered the process, was not the first serious communication. Mayhew stated: 'There has for some years been a means of communication by which messages could be conveyed indirectly, between the Government and the IRA leadership ... At the end of February this year a message was received from the IRA leadership ... I have placed in the Library and the vote Office all consequent messages which HMG has received and despatched' (Northern Ireland Information Service, 1993a: 1-2). Mayhew speaks only of a message, with the implication that it is the first. Similarly he talks of all documents consequent instead of subsequent. This suggests that other subsequent but not consequent documents have been retained. It seems likely that the documents released by Sinn Féin will be among these.

9. BBC1, *Panorama*: 'A Mountain To Climb', 21.30, 21 February 1994; reporter, P. Taylor.

10. Lord Lane's phrase when dismissing the Birmingham Six Appeal. The possibility that the entire British judicial system had been corrupted - from police investigation to trial and conviction - was too much for him to accept and therefore, he suggested, the accused were indeed guilty.

11. This is the first query in the published version of the exchanges. However, in his introduction to Sinn Féin's version, Martin McGuinness states that 'During this time [May 1993] there were a number of leaks to the media which hinted at contact between us and the British. We made a number of formal complaints as we had done on previous occasions' (Sinn Féin, 1994: 14). However, none of these previous messages is included in either the British or Sinn Féin accounts of the contacts, suggesting strongly that at least some messages have been withheld.

12. This message and the response to it are missing from the British account.

13. The brackets in this quotation are in both the NIO and Sinn Féin versions.

14. See *Sunday Times*, 22 August 1993: A1/A18

15. This was an edition of the investigative programme which claimed to prove that Martin McGuinness was a leader of the IRA.

16. At a theoretical level, this type of conspiracy between enemies raises problems about defining 'official' source and about the concept of 'primary definition'. Is McGuinness potentially acting as an official source by carrying out British government recommendations? Clearly we need to understand that winning

definitional battles in the media may be entirely irrelevant to the exercise of power or the implementation of particular policy options. In the current case, the problems for the government arise precisely because of their ability to win the definitional battle over 'terrorism' in the media. The problem is that a dramatic change of policy without any preparation in mood management is likely to make it harder for them to win the definitional battle for the new policy.

17. John Major, 'SF cannot argue for peace and frustrate it', *Irish News*, 25 February 1994.

18. The NIO document states: 'The British government accept the validity of all electoral mandates, including that of Sinn Féin; and, being committed to the democratic process, endorses the freedom of voters to choose their elected representatives' (Northern Ireland Office, 1994: 14).

References

Beaverbrook, Lord, *Politicians and the Press*, London, Hutchinson and Co., 1925.

Bevins, Anthony, '"IRA has an ethical dimension"', *Observer*, 28 November 1993: 3.

Brown, Colin and McKittrick, David, 'Leak puts Major on rack', *The Independent*, 29 November 1993: 1.

Cockerell, Michael, Hennessy, Peter and Walker, David, *Sources Close to the Prime Minister*, London, Macmillan 1984.

Grogan, Dick, 'Adams seeks direct talks with governments on declaration', *Irish Times*, 22 December 1993: 4.

Hall, Stuart, Critcher, Chas, Jefferson, Tony, Clarke, John, and Roberts, Brian, *Policing the Crisis: Mugging, the State and Law and Order*, London, Macmillan, 1978.

Harris, Robert, *Good and Faithful Servant: The Unauthorised Biography of Bernard Ingham*, London, Faber 1990.

Hennessy, Peter, 'The Quality of Political Journalism', *Journal of the Royal Society of Arts*, November 1987: 926-934.

Johnson, Paul, 'The time to talk is now', *The Guardian*, 18 September 1993: 25.

McKittrick, David, 'Disbelief in Britain's words', *Independent on Sunday*, 5 December 1993: 6.

Miller, David, 'Official Sources and Primary Definition: The Case of Northern Ireland', *Media, Culture and Society*, 15 No. 3, July 1993: 385-406.

Miller, David, *Don't Mention the War: Northern Ireland, Propaganda and the Media*, London, Pluto, 1994.

Moloney, Ed, 'The battle of the documents', *Sunday Tribune*, 5 December 1993: A12-A13.

Moloney, Ed, 'SF softens stance on declaration', *Sunday Tribune*, 3 April 1994: A1.

Northern Ireland Information Service, 'Parliamentary Statement: Messages between the IRA and the Government', *News Release*, 29 November, London, Northern Ireland Information Service, 1993(a).

Northern Ireland Information Service, 'Messages between the IRA and the Government', *News Release*, 1 December, London, Northern Ireland Information Service, 1993(b).

Northern Ireland Office, *Messages Passed between HMG and the Provisional Movement, February and November 1993*, 29 November, London, NIO, 1993.

Northern Ireland Office, *Statement by the Northern Ireland Office*, 19 May, London, NIO, 1994.

Philo, Greg and McLaughlin, Greg, *The British Media and the Gulf War*, Glasgow, Glasgow University Media Group, 1992.

Rolston, Bill, 'Containment and its Failure: The British State and the Control of Conflict in Northern Ireland', in Alexander George (ed), *Western State Terrorism*, Cambridge, Polity, 1991.

Sinn Féin, *Setting the Record Straight: A record of communications between Sinn Féin and the British government, October 1990-November 1993*, Belfast, Sinn Féin, 1994.

INDEX

Television and radio programmes and feature films listed are in parantheses and italicised. Books and other such publications are italicised, but not in parantheses.